D0203938

A HISTORY OF PSYCHOLOGY

A HISTORY OF PSYCHOLOGY

JOHN G. BENJAFIELD

Brock University

WARNER MEMORIAL LIBRARY
EASTERN UNIVERSITY
ST. DAVIDS, PA 19087-3696

ALLYN AND BACON

Boston London Toronto Sydney Tokyo Singapore

1-30-04

BF 81 .B3 1996
Benjafield, John G.
A history of psychology

Vice President and Publisher, Social Sciences: Susan Badger
Editorial Assistant: Jennifer Normandin
Executive Marketing Manager: Joyce Nilsen
Senior Editorial Production Administrator: Susan McIntyre
Editorial Production Service: Ruttle, Shaw & Wetherill, Inc.
Composition Buyer: Linda Cox
Manufacturing Buyer: Aloka Rathnam
Cover Administrator: Suzanne Harbison

Copyright © 1996 by Allyn & Bacon
A Simon & Schuster Company
Needham Heights, MA 02194

All rights reserved. No part of the material protected by this copyright notice may be reproduced or utilized in any form or by any means, electronic or mechanical, including photocopying, recording, or by any information storage and retrieval system, without written permission from the copyright holder.

Text Credits appear on page xv.

Library of Congress Cataloging-in-Publication Data
Benjafield, John G.
A history of psychology / John G. Benjafield.
p. cm.
Includes bibliographical references and index.
ISBN 0–205–15403–4
1. Psychology—History I. Title
BF81.B3 1996
150′.9—dc20 95-42263
CIP

Printed in the United States of America

10 9 8 7 6 5 4 3 2 1 00 99 98 97 96 95

CONTENTS

PREFACE xiii

CHAPTER 1 TOUCHSTONES: THE ORIGINS OF PSYCHOLOGICAL THOUGHT 1

Pythagoras (570–495 B.C.) 1
Pythagorean Cosmology 3
The Pythagorean Opposites 3
Pythagorean Mathematics 4
Plato (427–347 B.C.) 6
Pythagoras, Plato, and the Problem of the Irrational 6
The Forms 7
Lao-Tsu (6th century B.C.) 11
The Tension between Confucianism and Taoism 11
What Is Tao? 12
The Book of Changes 12
Aristotle (384–323 B.C.) 15
Aristotle's Differences with Plato 15
The Nature of Human Action 17
Memory 18
The Scala Naturae 20
St. Thomas Aquinas and the Medieval View of the Universe 21

CHAPTER 2 TOUCHSTONES: FROM DESCARTES TO DARWIN 23

René Descartes (1596–1650) 23
The Body as a Machine 25
Isaac Newton (1642–1727) 27
The Laws of Motion 27
Can Newton's Laws Be Generalized to Psychology? 28
The Nature of Color 28
The British Empiricists: John Locke (1632–1704), George Berkeley (1685–1753), and David Hume (1711–1776) 30
The British Empiricists 30
John Locke 30
George Berkeley 32
David Hume 33
Mary Wollstonecraft (1759–1797) 35
Universal Education 35
The Importance of Emotion 36
The Utopian Tradition in Psychology 36

Immanuel Kant (1724–1804) 37
Kant's "Second Copernican Revolution" 37
Can Psychology Be a Science Like Other Sciences? 38
Charles Darwin (1809–1882) 40
Darwin and Psychology 44
Studying the History of Psychology 45
Ixion's Wheel or Jacob's Ladder? 45
Person or Zeitgeist? 45
Rediscovering the Past 46

CHAPTER 3 NINETEENTH-CENTURY PIONEERS: OVERVIEW 49
Johann Friedrich Herbart (1776–1841) 49
Herbart's Influence on Educational Psychology 51
Gustav Theodor Fechner (1801–1887) 52
Psychophysics 53
Experimental Aesthetics 56
Hermann von Helmholtz (1821–1894) 56
Helmholtz and the Nature of Perception 57
Ewald Hering (1834–1918) 59
Christine Ladd-Franklin (1847–1930) 60
Francis Galton (1822–1911) 61
Hereditary Genius 61
Eugenics 62
Statistics 62
Memory 64
Herbert Spencer (1820–1903) 64
Social Darwinism 65

CHAPTER 4 WUNDT AND HIS CONTEMPORARIES 69
Wilhelm Wundt (1832–1920) 69
Investigations in the Laboratory 69
Psychophysical Parallelism 73
Cultural Psychology 73
Wundt's Influence 74
Hermann Ebbinghaus (1850–1909) 75
The Experimental Study of Learning and Remembering 75
Mary Whiton Calkins (1863–1930) and the Invention of "Paired Associates" 76
Franz Brentano (1838–1917) 77
The Würzburg School 78

CHAPTER 5 WILLIAM JAMES (1842–1910) 83
The Principles of Psychology 83
Habit 84

The Methods and Snares of Psychology 84
The Stream of Thought 85
The Consciousness of Self 88
Attention 89
The Emotions 89
Will 91
Other Topics 92

CHAPTER 6 FREUD AND JUNG 95

The Unconscious 95
Sigmund Freud (1856–1939) 98
Hysteria 98
The Project for a Scientific Psychology 100
The Interpretation of Dreams 100
The Development of the Personality 102
The Structure of the Personality 103
Religion and Culture 104
Freud's Death 106
Freud and America 106
Freud's Critics within Psychoanalysis 107
Freud and Women 108
Anna Freud (1895–1982) 108
Karen Horney (1885–1952) and the Psychology of Women 109
Carl G. Jung (1875–1961) 110
Jung's Relationship with Freud 110
Analytical Psychology 112
Extraversion and Introversion 112
Archetypes 114
Balancing Opposites 115
The Four Functions 115
The Collective Unconscious and the External World 116
Synchronicity 117

CHAPTER 7 STRUCTURE OR FUNCTION? 121

Edward B. Titchener (1867–1927) 121
Structuralism 123
Titchener's Experimental Psychology 124
Titchener and the Imageless Thought Controversy 125
Titchener and the Dimensions of Consciousness 125
Titchener's Influence 126
Functionalism 127
John Dewey (1859–1952) 127
Critique of the Reflex Arc Concept 127
Dewey's Influence on Educational Practice 128
James R. Angell (1869–1949) 129

Robert S. Woodworth (1869–1962) 130
The S-O-R Framework 131
Intelligence Testing 131
James McKeen Cattell (1860–1944) 132
Alfred Binet (1857–1911) 133
Intelligence Testing in the United States Army 134
What Is "Intelligence," Anyway? 135
Psychology in Business 136
Frederick W. Taylor (1856–1915) 137
Elton Mayo (1880–1949) 138
Comparative Psychology 139
Edward L. Thorndike (1874–1949) 140
Learning as the Formation of Connections 141

CHAPTER 8 BEHAVIORISM 147

Ivan P. Pavlov (1849–1936) 147
Conditioned Reflexes 148
Speech 150
Temperaments and Psychopathology 151
Vivisection and Anti-Vivisectionism 151
Vladimir M. Bekhterev (1857–1827) 152
John B. Watson (1878–1958) 153
Psychology as the Behaviorist Views It 154
Watson's Psychology 155
Emotional, Manual, and Verbal Habits 155
Watson and Rosalie Rayner 157
Watson's Second Career in Advertising 158
Karl S. Lashley (1890–1958) 158
Cortical Localization of Function 158
The Problem of Serial Order in Behavior 161
B. F. Skinner (1904–1990) 162
The Nature of Behaviorism 162
Skinner's Radical Behaviorism 162
The Behavior of Organisms 163
"A Case History of Scientific Method" 164
The "Baby Tender" 165
Teaching Machines 165
Skinner's Utopian and Dystopian Views 166

CHAPTER 9 GESTALT PSYCHOLOGY 171

Max Wertheimer (1880–1943) 172
Phi Phenomenon 172
The Minimum Principle 173
Precursors of Gestalt Psychology 173

The Laws of Perceptual Organization 174
Productive Thinking 176
Gestalt Psychology as a Philosophy 177
Wolfgang Kohler (1887–1967) 179
The Mentality of Apes 179
The Nature of Learning 180
The Concept of Isomorphism 180
Kurt Koffka (1886–1941) 182
Principles of Gestalt Psychology 182
The Growth of the Mind 183
Kurt Lewin (1890–1947) and the Emergence of Social Psychology 184
The Zeigarnik Effect 186
Group Dynamics 187
Fritz Heider (1896–1988) 187
Solomon Asch (1907–) 188
Kurt Goldstein (1878–1965) 190
Organismic Theory 191
The Abstract Attitude 191

CHAPTER 10 RESEARCH METHODS 195

Philosophy of Science 195
Logical Positivism 195
Operationism 197
Where Did Psychologists Stand? 197
Criticisms of Operationism 198
Experimental Methods 198
Statistical Inference 198
Ronald A. Fisher (1890–1962) 198
Fisher's Approach to Designing Experiments 198
The Null Hypothesis 199
Correlational Methods 200
Charles Spearman (1863–1945) 201
Cyril Burt (1883–1971) 202
The Burt Scandal 202
Louis Leon Thurstone (1887–1955) 204
"The Two Disciplines of Scientific Psychology" 204

CHAPTER 11 THEORIES OF LEARNING 209

Ernest R. Hilgard (1904–) 209
Edwin R. Guthrie (1886–1959) 211
Contiguity 211
Repetition 212
Reward 212
One-Trial Learning 212

Clark L. Hull (1884–1952) 213
The Formal Structure of Hullian Theory 214
The Hypothetico-Deductive Method 214
Postulates 214
Kenneth W. Spence (1907–1967) 216
Charles E. Osgood (1916–1991) 217
The Semantic Differential 218
Edward C. Tolman (1886–1959) 219
Purposive Behavior 220
Cognitive Maps 220
The Place versus Response Controversy 221
The Verbal Learning Tradition 222
Functionalism and Verbal Learning 222
Acquisition 225
Serial Learning 226
The Fate of Verbal Learning 226
Donald O. Hebb (1904–1985) 226
The Emergence of Neuroscience 226
The Organization of Behavior 227
Motivation 228
Experiments in Sensory Deprivation 229
Albert Bandura (1925–) 231
Social Learning Theory 231
Behavior Modification 231
Reciprocal Determinism 232

CHAPTER 12 THE DEVELOPMENTAL POINT OF VIEW 235

G. Stanley Hall (1884–1924) 236
The Theory of Recapitulation 236
Hall's Life and Career 236
Hall's Recapitulationism 237
Questionnaires 237
"Adolescence" 238
James Mark Baldwin (1861–1934) 238
Psychology of Mental Development 239
Heinz Werner (1890–1964) 241
The Comparative Psychology of Mental Development 241
Uniformity versus Multiformity 242
Continuity versus Discontinuity 242
Unilinearity versus Multilinearity 242
Fixity versus Mobility 243
Microgenesis 244
Jean Piaget (1896–1980) and Bärbel Inhelder (1913–) 245
Genetic Epistemology 245

The Development of Intelligence 246
Piaget's Clinical Method 246
Stages in the Development of Intelligence 247
Piaget as a Structuralist 250
Wholeness 250
Systems of Transformations 250
Self-Regulation 251
Can Development Ever End? 251
Lev S. Vygotsky (1896–1934) 252
Thought and Language 252
The Zone of Proximal Development 253
Erik H. Erikson (1902–) 254
Life-Span Developmental Psychology 254
Epigenesis 255
The Eight Stages 255
Eleanor J. Gibson (1910–) 257
Perceptual Learning 258
The Visual Cliff 260
Eleanor Gibson on the Future of Psychology 261

CHAPTER 13 HUMANISTIC PSYCHOLOGY 265

Existentialism 265
Søren Kierkegaard (1813–1855) 265
Friedrich Nietzsche (1844–1900) 266
Jean-Paul Sartre (1905–1980) 267
Ludwig Binswanger (1881–1966) 268
The Emergence of Humanistic Psychology 268
Rollo May (1909–1994) 270
Abraham H. Maslow (1908–1970) 271
The Hierarchy of Needs 272
The Self-Actualizing Person 273
Peak Experiences 275
The Psychology of Science 275
Carl R. Rogers (1902–1987) 276
Client-Centered Therapy 277
Eugene T. Gendlin 279
Encounter Groups 280
What Happened to Humanistic Psychology? 281
George A. Kelly (1905–1967) 282
The Psychology of Personal Constructs 283
The Repertory Test 284
Research in Personal Construct Theory 285
Qualitative Research Methods 286

CHAPTER 14 COGNITIVE PSYCHOLOGY 289

The Concept of "Information" 289
Noam Chomsky (1928–) 291
Syntactic Structures *291*
Cartesian Linguistics *292*
George A. Miller (1920–) 293
The Magical Number Seven *294*
Plans and the Structure of Behavior *294*
Subjective Behaviorism *297*
Giving Psychology Away *297*
Jerome S. Bruner (1915–) 298
The "New Look" in Perception *298*
A Study of Thinking *299*
Sir Frederic Bartlett (1887–1969) 300
Ulric Neisser (1928–) 302
Cognitive Psychology *302*
James J. Gibson (1904–1979) *305*
Cognition and Reality *306*
Herbert A. Simon (1916–) 307
Spurious Correlation and the Nature of Causality *307*
Computer Simulation *308*
Criticisms of Computer Simulation *311*

CHAPTER 15 THE FUTURE OF PSYCHOLOGY 315

The New History of Science 315
Does Psychology Have Paradigms? *317*
Contextualism 318
Feminism and the Psychology of Women 320
Is Psychology a Social Construction? 322
Ludwig Wittgenstein (1889–1951) *322*
Psychological Research as a Social Construction *325*
Is Psychology Postmodern? 326
Modernism *326*
Postmodernism *328*
The American Psychological Society *329*
Future Histories 332

BIBLIOGRAPHY 335

INDEX 369

PREFACE

Over the twenty-five years that I have been teaching the history of psychology, I have observed a recurring pattern in the attitudes of students toward such a course. Usually students register for the history of psychology only because it is required. At first, they cannot believe that anyone would be so perverse as to insist that they study such arcane figures as Wollstonecraft and Titchener. However, by the end of the course, students often say that they now realize why such a course is required, because they understand that without a historical perspective it is simply impossible to understand why psychology is the way that it is. The teacher of the history of psychology not only has the task of imparting crucial information about psychology, but also has the task of transforming students' attitudes toward psychology. Let me say something about how I think one should go about accomplishing these goals.

A traditional issue is whether the story of psychology should be told in terms of significant individuals or in terms of the cultural context within which these individuals worked (e.g., Boring, 1950a). As a pedagogical question, the answer seems to me to be straightforward. Understanding psychology as the work of individuals is easier than understanding it as the complex interplay between individuals and the cultural forces acting on them. This suggests that the best approach to teaching the history of psychology is to present the ideas of significant individuals, while gradually making clear to the student the role of cultural context in shaping the ideas that become dominant at a particular time. In the end, the student should be ready—even eager—for a thorough consideration of alternative conceptions of psychology as a historically conditioned discipline. This is the approach I have followed in this book. In the last chapter I have tried to show how contemporary concerns such as feminism, social constructionism, and postmodernism are reshaping the history of psychology.

Instructors will find that this book differs from most other texts in several ways. For example, I have included more material on the role of mathematics in the development of science in general and psychology in particular. I have also changed the order in which topics are usually presented. For example, psychoanalysis is treated relatively early, in keeping with the fact that this viewpoint grows directly out of late nineteenth-century scientific attitudes, and should be seen in that context. I have also tried to show how some historically important concepts (e.g., imagery) are being applied in current practical and research settings. Although this book is largely a history of American psychology, I have tried to indicate some of the ways in which the work of traditions and individuals other than the usual ones (e.g., Mary Wollstonecraft, Taoism) have been important, if neglected, influences on the development of psychology in North America.

Students often take the history of psychology as a capstone course (e.g., Raphelson, 1982). The pedagogical importance of such capstone courses has become clearer through the research of scholars such as Bahrick (1984; Bahrick & Hall, 1991) and others (e.g., Conway, Cohen & Stanhope, 1991) who have studied long-term retention for material taught in school. Bahrick's findings suggest that it is very important to spread courses in a subject over several years, with lots of repetition of central concepts, rather than to take a concentrated, short course of study. A capstone course gives the student the opportunity not only to acquire new perspectives, but also to strengthen previously learned material. It has certainly been my experience that senior students come across material in the history of psychology course with which they were previously acquainted, but that they may only dimly remember. One function of the history course is to provide another chance to strengthen those memory traces. Thus, I have tried to make sure that concepts central to an understanding of psychology (e.g., Boneau, 1990) are repeated here in their appropriate historical context.

ACKNOWLEDGMENTS

Jaroslav Havelka first taught me the history of psychology when I was an undergraduate at Western. His enthusiasm and encyclopedic knowledge sparked my interest in this material. At Brandeis I was fortunate to be able to take a course in the history of psychology from Frank Manuel, a true historian of ideas, that provided a rich context within which to see a discipline like psychology. Subsequently, Solomon Asch's history of psychology seminar at Rutgers provided a model of tolerance for opposing viewpoints. All of these teachers have shaped my own attempts to be a productive teacher of the history of psychology.

Brock University provided me both with the opportunity to teach the history of psychology and with many willing and able students who have made the experience worthwhile. I have also learned a great deal over the years from numerous interactions with my Brock colleagues. My wife, Gail, my daughter, Megan, and my son, Ian, have also provided me with many thoughtful discussions as I have worked on this book. Finally, I have the warmest memories of my old friend, Roly, whose company made the time spent writing this book so much more pleasant than it would otherwise have been.

I thank the reviewers whose comments and criticism made this a better book: Jeffrey Altman, Roberts Wesleyan College; Paul Haerich, Loma Linda University; Matthew Sharps, California State University/Fresno; and Michael Ehlert, Brigham Young University.

CREDITS

McKeon, R. (Ed.). (1941). *The basic works of Aristotle.* Oxford: Oxford University Press. By permission of Oxford University Press.

Locke, J. (1964). *An essay concerning human understanding.* London: Fontana/Collins. By permission of HarperCollins Publishers Limited.

James, W. (1890). *The principles of psychology* (2 vols.). New York: Holt. By permission of Harcourt, Brace & Company.

Excerpts as submitted from *The collected papers,* Volumes 1, 4, and 5 by Sigmund Freud. Authorized translation under the supervision of Joan Riverie. Published by BasicBooks, Inc., by arrangement with the Hogarth Press, Ltd. and the Institute of Psycho-Analysis, London. Reprinted by permission of BasicBooks, a division of HarperCollins Publishers, Inc.

Freud, S. (1950). *An autobiographical study* (J. Strachey, Trans.). By permission of W. W. Norton.

Freud, S. (1964). *New introductory lectures on psychoanalysis* (J. Strachey, Trans.). Copyright 1965, 1964 by James Strachey. By permission of W. W. Norton.

Freud, S. (1977). *Introductory lectures on psychoanalysis* (J. Strachey, Trans.). Copyright 1966 by W. W. Norton. By permission of Liveright Publishing Corporation.

Freud, S. (1968). *Standard edition of the complete psychological works of Sigmund Freud* (Translated and edited by James Stachey). London: Hogarth Press. By permission of Sigmund Freud Copyrights, the Institute of Psychoanalysis, and Hogarth Press.

A HISTORY OF PSYCHOLOGY

CHAPTER 1

TOUCHSTONES: THE ORIGINS OF PSYCHOLOGICAL THOUGHT

PYTHAGORAS (570–495 B.C.)
Pythagorean Cosmology
The Pythagorean Opposites
Pythagorean Mathematics
PLATO (427–347 B.C.)
Pythagoras, Plato, and the Problem of the Irrational
The Forms
LAO-TSU (6TH CENTURY B.C.)
The Tension between Confucianism and Taoism
What Is Tao?
The Book of Changes
ARISTOTLE (384–323 B.C.)
Aristotle's Differences with Plato
The Nature of Human Action
Memory
The Scala naturae
ST. THOMAS AQUINAS AND THE MEDIEVAL VIEW OF THE UNIVERSE

The word *touchstone* originally referred to a stone used to test the quality of gold or silver because of the mark left on the stone from the metal being rubbed against it. Subsequently, *touchstone* came to mean any criterion by which the value of something is measured. In both this chapter and the next, we examine some famous thinkers who have left their mark. Their works are touchstones for evaluating the theories that have descended from them, and their ideas have stood the test of time.

Important ideas in psychology or any other discipline do not come out of nowhere. This generation of psychologists draws on a rich store of ideas from previous generations. Throughout history, the contributions of each generation would have been impossible without the foundation laid by its predecessors. It is a commonplace for the deepest and most profound thinkers to confess their indebtedness to those who have gone before them. A recurring phrase that expresses this indebtedness is that "we stand on the shoulders of giants" (Manuel, 1965, p. 69). In these two chapters we consider the work of several of these giants.

PYTHAGORAS (570–495 B.C.)

Pythagoras is one of the most famous figures in the Western intellectual tradition, who is often characterized as having had a peerless influence on the course of Western thought (e.g., B. Russell, 1945, p. 29). Very little can be said with certainty about Pythagoras's life, and so in dealing with Pythagoras we are dealing as much with a mythic as with a real person (e.g., Gorman, 1979). He was often described as having miraculous powers, and even referred to as the incarnation of Apollo, the Greek god most typically associated with other-worldly wisdom. He was thought to have studied in Egypt, and to have been initiated into the mathematical and religious secrets of the priesthood there. The mythic aura surrounding Pythagoras is annoying because it prevents us from seeing the person clearly. Historically, however, the myth has captured the thought of many real people. It is the *myth* of Pythagoras that has had such a great influence on the way many people in the West think about the world.

One of the central features of the Pythagorean myth is that he founded a semi-secret society in Italy. The members of this society were supposed to have been able to attune themselves to the *harmony* that ordered the universe. The concept of harmony is a central one in Pythagorean thought. It is closely linked to the notion, which has been so influential in the history of science, that the structure of mathematics is the structure of reality. The story has often been told of how Pythagoras first understood that reality has an underlying mathematical order. It is said that on hearing the sounds from a blacksmith's hammers he realized that pitch and the hammer's weight were correlated—high sounds with light hammers, low sounds with heavy hammers. The same sort of correlation exists between the length of plucked strings and the sound they produce. An example of this kind of relationship is shown in Figure 1.1. As one goes up the scale on a piano, the piano strings get progressively shorter. These relations are not arbitrary. Rather, the notes one hears and the lengths of the corresponding strings bear exact relations to one another. There is nothing mythic about the relation between mathematics and music. A provocative contemporary account of this relationship, and its importance for psychology, is given by Leonard Bernstein (1976).

Pythagoras was astounded by his discovery of mathematical relationships in everyday experiences such as listening to music. He felt that he had an insight into the unity of the cosmos. While our experiences are many and varied, they are not chaotic. Rather, the phenomena of our experience are united mathematically.

According to Cornford (1922/1974, 1950/1967), in his classic accounts of Pythagoreanism, the view that phenomena are ordered mathematically is one way of resolving the puzzles with which everyday experience presents us. The Pythagoreans were convinced of the virtue of *unity,* and all that this concept implies. *Unity* implies *wholeness* and *oneness;* a simplicity that is perfect. The opposite of *unity* is undesirable, leading to *chaos.* It is clear to all of us that everyday life is not a series of purely positive experiences. Rather, we can find all manner of opposing tendencies in our experience: *light* and *dark; good* and *evil; strong* and *weak.* Although *unity* and *wholeness* are what we value, our experience can only be described in terms of contradictory tendencies. A problem felt by every person is how to reconcile the discordant state of affairs we normally experience with the one that we value.

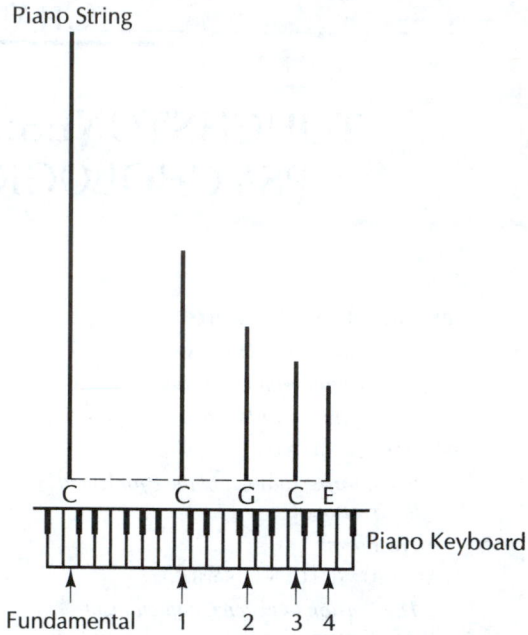

FIGURE 1.1 The relation between different pitches on a piano and the length of the corresponding strings. (Reprinted by permission of the publishers from *The Unanswered Question* [p. 23] by Leonard Bernstein, Cambridge, Mass.: Harvard University Press, Copyright © 1976 by Leonard Bernstein.)

Pythagorean Cosmology

The Pythagoreans responded to this puzzle in a way that is partly distinctive and partly similar to answers given by thinkers in other, very diverse cultures (Cornford, 1922/1974, p. 150). As we shall see, there are surprising similarities across ancient world views, ranging from the Pythagorean cosmology to the Yin/Yang philosophy of Chinese Taoism (Osgood & Richards, 1973). Many see the universe as initially a unity that becomes differentiated into pairs of opposites. These opposites are then reunited, or *harmonized,* so as to generate the various forms of life we witness. This conception of the process of creation—from unity to differentiation to integration—is by no means an ancient relic, with no relevance to modern thought. In contemporary psychology, the process of *ontogeny* (individual development) is sometimes understood in a similar way, as we will discover in Chapter 12 on developmental psychology. While there are, of course, important differences between the ancient and modern conceptions, it is still correct to say that the basic frames of reference are similar. There are, however, several features of the Pythagorean world view that are elaborated in a distinctive way. The most important of these are their ideas concerning: (a) the nature of *opposites;* and (b) the importance of *number* in regulating phenomena.

The Pythagorean Opposites

The Pythagoreans believed that some pairs of opposites were particularly useful to describe our experience (Cornford, 1939, p. 6; Philip, 1966). The most important is *limited* versus *unlimited.* This distinction is regarded as crucially important to the process of creation. Opposites arise out of an original unity. The integration of opposites produces the *limited.* We do not experience things that are *unlimited.* Everything we experience has a *limit.* The union of the unlimited and limited produces the world we experience. While this all sounds mysterious, the phenomena the Pythagoreans had in mind are quite obvious. Consider a mundane phenomenon like snow. I know from my own experience that while I am shoveling it, snow seems to be limitless. However, as *Johann Kepler* (1571–1630) observed, if you carefully examine particles of snow under a magnifying glass, you will see that all snowflakes have "six corners" (1611/1966, p. 7). Each snow crystal demonstrates that snow, while appearing to be an unlimited substance, in fact has a precise mathematical structure. Similarly, if we examine *any* of our experiences, we will see that each one involves something that is potentially unlimited, like snow, being given a precise mathematical structure, or *limit.* Echoes of the Pythagorean view of phenomena may easily be found in contemporary thought. Thus, a book on natural forms by Stevens (1974) is full of examples of the ways in which natural phenomena take on definite configurations.

> *[T]he visual patterns and forms in the natural world . . . are peculiarly restricted . . . the immense variety that nature creates emerges from the working and reworking of only a few formal themes. Those* limitations *on nature bring harmony and beauty to the natural world. (p. 3, emphasis added)*

From the Pythagorean conception that the union of *limit* and *unlimited* produces all sensible phenomena, it is but a short step to the idea that there should be a proper balance between opposites. When the mixture of opposite tendencies is just right, the result is a *harmony.* Central to Pythagorean doctrine is the concept of *proportion.* When opposites are mixed in the right proportion, there is a harmonious outcome, a "union of opposites," which achieves the unity and integrity we value. The *psyche,* or soul, seeks precisely such a harmony. When it is properly "tuned," when the opposing forces within the individual are properly blended, then the soul can resonate to other harmonious structures. Specifically, the soul can resonate to the mythic *music of the spheres* that surrounds us always. We seldom hear this "music," because, as one of Pythagoras's commentators put it, we are like "bronze smiths who become so accustomed to the noise of their forge that they grow oblivious of it." We are able to experience harmonious structures around us only if we are organized ourselves in a way that is sympathetic to them. Ordinarily, however, we overlook the beauty that surrounds us, not having reached the state where we can mimic that which would make us most happy. This doctrine is less arcane than it may sound. We have a saying, "The fish is the last to discover water," which captures the flavor of the Pythagorean notion. Some twentieth-century psychologists (e.g., Kohler, 1940/1960, p. 5) have insisted that the most important phenomena were possessed of a simple, beautiful structure, but, like snowflakes, were often overlooked precisely because they were so simple. Along the same lines, the Russian poet Shklovskij (cited by Chomsky, 1968) said:

> *People living at the seashore grow so accustomed to the murmur of the waves that they never hear it. By the same token, we scarcely ever hear the words that we utter. We look at each other, but we do not see each other any more. Our perception of the world has withered away; what remains is mere recognition. (p. 21)*

Thus, a particularly important task in psychology is to remind ourselves of things that are significant but so commonplace that we may fail to see their significance. From a Pythagorean viewpoint, the things we overlook are those harmonies developing out of the interplay of opposites.

While *limited versus unlimited* was the most important of the Pythagorean opposites, there were also others such as good versus evil, light versus dark, odd versus even, unity versus disunity, and square versus oblong. In each case, the first member represents a "positive" quality, while the second member refers to a "negative" quality. This evaluation must be understood from within the Pythagorean system. While it seems intuitively obvious to us that, for example, *good* is positive and *evil* negative, it is perhaps less obvious that *limited* is positive and *unlimited* negative. However, the Pythagoreans used these terms in a very precise way. *Unlimited* as it is used here does not carry the positive connotations conveyed by such phrases as "unlimited resources." Rather, that which is unlimited is regarded as being out of balance; as lacking proportion. It is only by putting limits on something that it attains its proper balance. Similarly, *light* is positive, and *dark* negative because the former allows us to see things (limited phenomena) which cannot be seen in the limitless dark. The other members of the set of dimensions also are not haphazardly chosen, but are closely related to one another. To illustrate this, let us take the positive terms *odd, unity,* and *square* and contrast them with their negative opposites *even, plurality,* and *oblong.* A consideration of these dimensions not only sheds light on the logic of Pythagoras's system but also serves to introduce us to Pythagorean mathematics.

Pythagorean Mathematics

In ancient times it was customary in mathematical discussions to use pebbles to stand for units, and to draw figures in the sand (Kirk & Raven, 1957, p. 243; Wheelwright, 1966, p. 204). Consider the configuration at left in Figure 1.2 and imagine it as an arrangement of 16 pebbles. At this point it will be useful to introduce the concept of a *gnomon.* Concretely, this word refers to a carpenter's square, but abstractly it means the addition or subtraction of one figure from another figure of the same shape. This may sound confusing, but to see how simple it really is, consider Figure 1.2. Suppose we begin our discussion of the figure by considering the lefthand set of pebbles. The right-angle line above and to the right of the first pebble in the lower left-hand corner is the first gnomon. It is a

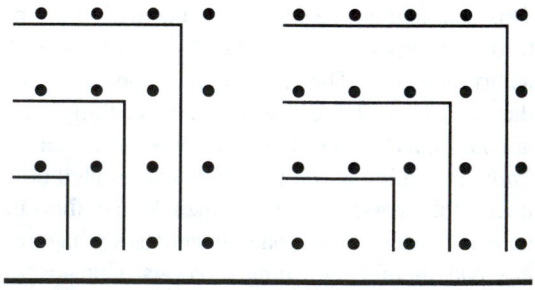

FIGURE 1.2 Pebbles in the sand.

part of the total figure that has the same shape as the whole figure. We can add successive gnomons, as indicated by the lines above and to the right of the next three, five, and seven pebbles, respectively. Notice that as the area enclosed by the gnomons increases in size, it nonetheless retains several invariant features. We begin with *unity* (one pebble), and, as we add successive gnomons, *odd* numbers of pebbles—3, 5, 7, and so on—are enclosed. The figure is always a *square.* By way of contrast, consider the configuration at the right of Figure 1.2. Here we begin not with unity (one pebble), but with two. The successive gnomons enclose *even* numbers—4, 6, 8, and so on—and the figure tends to no definite shape, but rather becomes increasingly *oblong.* The basic contrast between the two figures is that the first has a definite *limit,* and thus the properties of *odd, square,* and *unity,* while the second is *unlimited,* being also *plural, oblong,* and *even.* These examples show that the Pythagorean opposites were intended to refer to specific occurrences. Moreover, they denote mathematically precise relationships, illustrating the Pythagorean belief that everything that occurs can be described in a mathematically exact way.

The Pythagoreans viewed numbers as underlying all the phenomena we experience. Numbers are responsible for uniting the opposites in a harmonious manner. For example, in the sequence of positive integers, *odd* and *even* numbers alternate. This sequence is a *union of opposites,* brought together through number itself. Thus, for the Pythagoreans, number was a property of everything. When we examine things and events, then we discover number *in* them. Cornford (1922/1974) put it this way: "To him [Pythagoras] numbers and their relations were not only invested with a halo of divine and mysterious properties, but were also implicated in the sensible world, serving as the substructure of reality within that world and occupying space" (p. 152). The harmony to which numbers gave rise can most clearly be seen in the proportions that parts of geometrical constructions bear to one another. The famous *theorem of Pythagoras* is a demonstration of invariant proportion. The square on the hypotenuse of a right-angle triangle *always* equals the sum of the squares on the other two sides. Thus, consider a right-angle triangle with sides of lengths 3 and 4 units, and a hypotenuse of 5 units, as shown in Figure 1.3. It turns out that $3^2 + 4^2 = 5^2$.

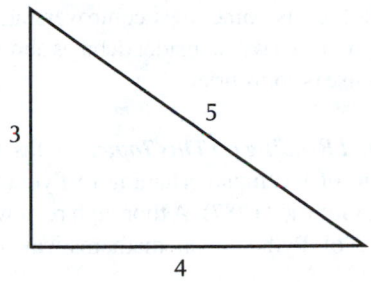

FIGURE 1.3 The theorem of Pythagoras.

More than one young initiate into the truths of geometry has found Pythagoras's theorem, and others like it, both beautiful and profound. For example, H. E. Huntley (1970) wrote a lovely book on geometry in which he described the enthusiasm of one of his teachers, who had drawn a figure on the blackboard to demonstrate an important geometrical relation.

> *Striding rapidly up and down between the class and the blackboard, waving his arms about excitedly, with his tattered gown, green with age, billowing out behind him, he spoke in staccato phrases: "Och, a truly beautiful theorem! Beautiful! . . . Beautiful! Look at it!* Look at it! *What simplicity! What economy!" . . . His voice rises in a crescendo. "What elegance! . . . Its generality is* astonishing.*" Then, muttering to himself "Beautiful! . . . beautiful! . . .," he stopped, slightly embarrassed . . ., and returned to earth. (p. 5)*

If you are fortunate enough to have had such a teacher, then you may have caught an enthusiasm for mathematics yourself. Even if you do not have much of a feeling for mathematics, you should still appreciate how important such a feeling is in the history of all sciences, including psychology. As we will see, the mathematical analysis of phenomena is a central feature of many branches of psychology. However, the application of mathematics in psychology is sometimes controversial, and at several points we will consider debates about when and if its use is appropriate.

Additional Reading on This Topic. A fascinating collection of writings pertaining to Pythagoreanism is in Guthrie (1987). A thorough review of the influence of Pythagorean mathematical ideas is O'Meara (1987).

PLATO (427–347 B.C.)

Pythagoras, Plato, and the Problem of the Irrational

We have already discussed the way that the Pythagorean theorem followed from a mathematical view of reality. Ironically, the Pythagorean theorem itself eventually led to a serious difficulty for the Pythagorean world view. For triangles of the right proportions, such as the 3-4-5 triangle we considered above, the numbers describing the lengths of the sides were *rational.* For others, however, no rational solution was possible, in the sense that no *integers* could be found to express the lengths (Thompson, 1929). For example, consider a right-angle triangle with sides of 1 unit each, as shown in Figure 1.4. In this case, the sum of the squares of the sides is $1^2 + 1^2$, which equals 2. This means that the square on the hypotenuse must equal 2, and that the length of the hypotenuse is the square root of 2, or $\sqrt{2}$. The square root of 2 cannot be expressed as a single number; it is an irrational number. Thus, the Pythagoreans came upon the *irrational* as an unavoidable aspect of reality (Chakerian, 1972). The way the Greeks and subsequent thinkers tried to comprehend things that were irrational is an important part of our story.

The problem of the irrational became a preoccupation for Greek mathematicians. "It was the irrational number . . . which was a constant object of search, whose nature as a number was continually in question, and whose genesis as a number cried aloud for explanation or justification" (Thompson, 1929, p. 44). Following Pythagoras, many attempts were made to solve the problem of the irrational.

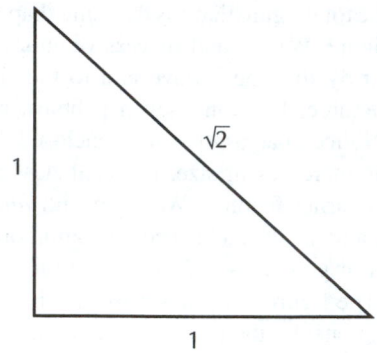

FIGURE 1.4 A root-two right-angle triangle.

Thompson shows how this was done for the *Golden Section,* a famous proportion in the history of Western thought. Rightly or wrongly, it has often been claimed to be a more beautiful proportion than any other, and to be used frequently by artists in their work (Benjafield, 1985). Moreover, the Golden Section has intrigued many of the psychologists we will study later on (e.g., Fechner, 1871; Hilgard, 1987, p. 165; Thorndike, 1917; Witmer, 1894; Woodworth, 1938, pp. 384–391).

The Golden Section can be obtained by dividing a line into two segments such that the smaller is to the larger as the larger is to the whole line. A line divided in its Golden Section is shown in Figure 1.5. In that figure, BC/AB = AB/AC. This means that AB is approximately 0.618 of the entire line AC.

The Golden Section is an irrational proportion. Its value can, however, be approximated by using the following series of numbers. Suppose you begin with the numbers 0 and 1, and then generate additional numbers such that each one is the sum of the two preceding numbers. Thus the series would go:

$$0, 1, 1, 2, 3, 5, 8, 13, 21, 34, 55, 89, \ldots$$

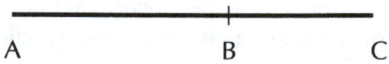

FIGURE 1.5 The Golden Section.

The series is called the *Fibonacci numbers* after the thirteenth-century mathematician who introduced the arabic number system into Europe. According to Thompson (1929, p. 52), the ancient Greeks used the properties of the Fibonacci numbers to understand the nature of the irrational. In order to see how they did this, we need to note the close relationship between the Fibonacci numbers and the Golden Section. As the successive numbers in the Fibonacci series become larger and larger, the ratio of any two successive numbers gets closer and closer to the Golden Section, as shown below.

1/2 = .050	8/13 = 0.615
2/3 = 0.67	13/21 = 0.619
3/5 = 0.60	21/34 = 0.6176
5/8 = 0.625	34/55 = 0.6182

There are two things to note about the preceding list. The first is that the series very rapidly generates good approximations to the Golden Section. The second is that the successive approximations are alternately greater than and less than the value of the Golden Section, which is 0.6180 to four decimal places.

People often read a lot of meaning into simple facts. In this case, Thompson (1929) argued, the Greeks found the relationship between the Fibonacci numbers and the Golden Section full of meaning. The Golden Section is an ideal proportion. A series of numbers that alternately exceeds and falls short of such an ideal value can be used to represent the notion that each particular thing we experience is a more or less imperfect representation of something ideal. No matter how close we may come to our ideals, we always seem to fall a little short, or go a little too far. Thompson (1929) draws the analogy between the way we try to reach ideals, and the process of discovery in science. For example, consider the attempts of biologists to describe a particular species:

> *Just as we study the rational forms of an irrational number, and through their narrowing vista draw nearer and nearer to the ideal thing, but always fail to reach it by the little more or the little less; so we may, as it were, survey the whole motley troop of feathered things, only to find each one of them falling short of perfection, deficient here, redundant there: all with their inevitable earthly faults and flaws. Then beyond them all we begin to see dimly a bird such as never was on sea or land, without blemish, whether of excess or defect: it is the ideal* Bird . . . *(p. 55)*

Thompson is presenting us with the notion that each bird we see will be an imperfect example of some ideal Bird. The same would be true of any creature. Each individual dog or cat, for example, illustrates only imperfectly the perfect specimen that would embody all the ideal features of the species. To generalize further, *any* event is only an imperfect illustration of some ideal event. Think of athletics. Even though judges at the Olympics now occasionally give "perfect 10's" to a gymnast, or a figure skater, or a diver, are not all athletic performances imperfect, if only slightly? Perhaps it is the *judges* whose performance is the most imperfect of all!

The Forms

The distinction between the way things *appear*, and the way things *really are* is a very important distinction, not only in the history of Western thought generally, but in psychology in particular. Plato advanced the notion that there are *perfect forms* on the one hand and *imperfect appearances* on the other. The perfect forms are in an important sense more *real* than the imperfect appearances. Belief in an ideal world of perfect forms can arise as a result of confronting problems such as the nature of the irrational. Such problems can force us to give up seeking answers in the things we experience through our senses, because our senses give us imperfect information. Instead, we can imagine another world that underlies the one we typically experience, and which contains the perfect forms we seek. Our everyday world is flawed and incapable of satisfying us; perhaps there is another world that has what we are actually looking for. Such Platonic ideas have attracted thinkers for ages, and it is to a consideration of them we now turn.

It is commonplace to refer to the history of Western thought as but a footnote to Plato. Box 1.1

BOX 1.1

The Relative Importance of Plato and Other Thinkers

There are many ways to measure the impact in the English-speaking world of the seminal thinkers we are considering in the first two chapters. An imperfect, but interesting, way of measuring their relative importance is to count the number of times they are mentioned in the *Oxford English Dictionary* (*OED*). The *OED* is one of the standard reference works for the English language. The print version of the second edition (1989) is 20 volumes, 22,000 pages, and defines over 500,000 words. The *OED* is one of the great scholarly achievements of the English-speaking world. A useful feature of the *OED* is that it not only provides such information as the part of speech, pronunciation, and etymology of each word, but also includes quotations to illustrate the various senses of a word. Thus, to take an arbitrary example, the word *tufthunter* is defined as someone "who meanly or obsequiously courts the acquaintance of persons of rank and title . . . at the universities." It goes on to give several quotations containing this word, including one dated 1789 from a periodical named *The Loiterer,* stating that tuft-hunting has a long history of occurrence at Oxford. There are nearly 2.5 *million* quotations like this in the *OED.*

Recently, the second edition of the *OED* became available on CD-ROM (1992). *CD-ROM* stands for Compact Disk-Read Only Memory. The entire contents of the *OED* fit on a single CD-ROM disk which, as you probably know, looks exactly like the compact disks used in ordinary CD players. This means that, given a suitably equipped personal computer, anyone can now search the *OED.* This makes it possible to access information that otherwise would be impossible to obtain from the print version. For example, suppose I wanted to find out how often Plato is mentioned in the *OED.* This is obviously not a reasonable task for the user of the print version. It is absurd to read through hundreds of thousands of entries in the print version of the Dictionary, all the while looking for Plato's name. However, in a few seconds this information is available using the CD-ROM version. There are, in fact, over 2918 such mentions, occurring in entries for words ranging from *abraid, abrase,* and *Academian* to *youthful, zero,* and *Zingaro.*

Below is a table giving the frequencies with which the theorists considered in the first two chapters are mentioned in the *OED.* This is only one possible measure of a theorist's impact, and obviously applies only to the English-speaking world. Notice that Plato outranks such native English speakers as Darwin, Newton, and Hume. This is a testament to the centrality of Plato to the history of Western thought.

However, the point has often been made that Western intellectual history can be *ethnocentric.* To be ethnocentric is to regard the values of one's own culture as superior to those of any other culture. Ethnocentrism acts to reduce our ability to appreciate the virtues of different forms of thought in other cultures, as well as the thought of people in our own culture who do not share the typical values of our culture. For example, many of us in the English-speaking world may have emphasized the thought of English-speaking *men,* and not paid enough attention to the thought of English speaking *women,* not to mention the thought of people from non-English speaking cultures. Notice that the *last* three people in the table below include a woman, a Chinese sage, and a French philosopher. In the chapters that follow, we will have to guard against ethnocentric biases, while at the same time giving an accurate account of the development of psychological thought in the English-speaking world.

NAME	FREQUENCY OF MENTION
Plato	2918
Darwin	2408
Newton	1929
Hume	1634
Aristotle	806
Kant	393
Pythagoras	162
Descartes	109
Wollstonecraft	81
Lao-Tsu	7

illustrates the influence of Plato throughout Western history. His philosophy has been the benchmark against which all other subsequent systems of thought have been measured. In large part, his success is the result of his ability to articulate the implications of the thought of his predecessors. Much of Platonic thought was an extension of the Pythagorean doctrines we considered earlier (Sambursky, 1956, p. 43). We have already seen how one possible outcome of the search for the irrational is a belief in perfect "forms" underlying the world of appearances. From a Platonic point of view, it is possible to gain knowledge of these forms, but we are usually not aware of them. The phenomena with which we interact are mere "shadows" of their forms, or essences.

Plato advanced his theories by means of dialogues in which *Socrates* was the protagonist. Socrates (469–399 B.C.) was one of the great figures of ancient Greece. It is difficult to separate Plato's ideas from those originating with Socrates. Much more was written about Socrates than appeared in Plato's dialogues (Ferguson, 1970), but it is through Plato's dialogues that Socrates' fame persists. Following Weimer (1973), we focus on one of Plato's dialogues, the *Meno.*

The *Meno* developed a typical theme that runs throughout all the dialogues. Here is the beginning of the dialogue, spoken by Meno (Hamilton & Cairns, 1961).

> *Can you tell me, Socrates—is virtue something that can be taught? Or does it come by practice? Or is it neither teaching nor practice that gives it to a man but natural aptitude or something else? (p. 354)*

Psychology students will recognize this as a type of question that still arises in practically all areas of psychology. Whether it is the nature of virtue (or morality), or any other psychological concept such as *intelligence* or *personality,* we can always ask whether it is something we learn, or something we have innately. Are people innately virtuous (or immoral)? Is a person's intelligence innately determined, or is it acquired? Is temperament innate, or is it learned?

Socrates makes the point that it is very difficult to define concepts such as *virtue.* Any definition that is proposed includes either too much or too little, is either too narrow or too broad. While Meno is able to give examples of virtuous behavior, he is unable to answer the question "what is virtue?" by specifying what it is that all virtuous behaviors have in common (Hamilton & Cairns, 1961, p. 355). Again, this is a recurrent problem with any psychological concept. As we shall see in Chapter 5, when psychologists in this century became fascinated with the concept of *intelligence,* they were able to come up with many different examples of intelligence, such as the ability to remember strings of numbers (digit span), the ability to give the meanings of words (vocabulary), and so on. Nevertheless, a great debate has raged over precisely what is meant by the term *intelligence,* and whether intelligence, properly so-called, is innate or acquired. It is just this kind of question Plato (through Socrates) was exploring in the *Meno.*

Socrates' resolution of the problem is to suggest that someone cannot "know what a part of virtue is, without knowing the whole" (Hamilton & Cairns, 1961, p. 362). That is, we would not be able to give examples of virtue, unless we knew what virtue itself really was.

> *Thus the soul, since it is immortal and has been born many times, and has seen all things both here and in the other world, has learned everything that is. So we need not be surprised if it can recall the knowledge of virtue or anything else which, as we see, it once possessed. All nature is akin, and the soul has learned everything, so that when a man has recalled a single piece of knowledge*—learned *it in ordinary language—there is no reason why he should not find out all the rest, if he keeps a stout heart and does not grow weary of the search, for seeking and learning are in fact nothing but recollection. (p. 364)*

A famous example of the process of awakening *innate knowledge* is given by Plato in the *Meno,* where he describes Socrates' ability to elicit from a slave boy the solution to Pythagoras's theorem. The point of Socrates' interrogation of the boy is to

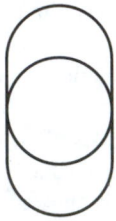

FIGURE 1.6 The altar window problem: Painters are at work, painting and decorating the inner walls of a church. Above the altar there is a circular window. For decoration, the painters have been asked to draw two vertical lines tangent to the circle, and of the same height as the circular window; they were then to add half circles above and below, closing the figure. This area between the lines and the window is to be covered with gold. For every square inch, so and so much gold is needed. How much gold will be needed to cover this space (given the diameter of the circle); or, what is the area between the circle and the lines?
Source: M. Wertheimer. (1959). *Productive thinking.* New York: Harper, p. 266. Reprinted by permission of HarperCollins Publishers, Inc.

demonstrate that the solution is already "known" in the sense of being a deduction from what the boy knows innately. A more recent illustration of the same kind of point comes from the work of the German psychologist Max Wertheimer (1959). Wertheimer was a member of a group of psychologists called *Gestalt psychologists.* We will study them in detail later on. For now all you need to know is that *Gestalt* means "form" or "configuration," and the Gestalt psychologists stressed the importance of innate tendencies toward "good form." Thus, for them, our experience is shaped by our innate tendencies toward "good form." A good example of this Gestalt notion is Wertheimer's (1959) "altar window problem." The problem goes as follows, and is illustrated in Figure 1.6.

> *Imagine that there is a circular altar window, and that it is to be decorated by surrounding it with gold paint. The area to be painted gold is bounded by two parallel, vertical lines tangent to the circle, and equal in length to the diameter of the circle. These lines are joined by semi-circles. How much paint is needed? Or, what is the area inside the lines but outside the window? (p. 266)*

It is easy to find the area of the window itself, since it is just a circle. Similarly, it is easy to find the area of the semicircles at the top and the bottom of the figure. However, that leaves the problem of finding the area of "the four funny remainders."

Wertheimer gave this problem to a child with no mathematical training, whose first reaction to the problem is to say that, of course, he cannot solve it. Immediately thereafter, however, he realizes that the top and bottom semicircles fit inside the window. Thus, the solution to the problem is simply to find the area of the square drawn with its sides tangent to the circle. If you cannot see this solution, ask a friend to help you with it.

Wertheimer's example is congruent with that of Socrates and the slave boy. In both cases, the solution to a problem *emerges* on the basis of what the child already knows. The child is capable of seeing certain necessary relationships, and this (apparently) innate ability is all that is required to enable him to derive the solution. The implication of both Plato's and Wertheimer's analysis is that we are all in possession of all we need to know in order to fully understand our experience. However, we must draw out the implications of what we already know.

From this point of view, then, the difficulties we experience in everyday life stem from an inability to perceive essential relationships. Since, from the Platonic viewpoint, the ability to perceive relationships is given innately, our difficulties are due to our inability to *remember* the basic ideas that allow us to organize our experiences in a meaningful way. Often we act as if we have forgotten what we most need to know, and behave as if we have lost touch with those ideas that could give our experience depth and meaning. "All so-called learning is actually remembering; . . . there is no real "learning" at all. This is the doctrine of *anamnesis* (recollections)" (Weimer, 1973, p. 16). A skilled, "Socratic" teacher is one who can make the student aware of what it is they already know, but do not know that they know.

If our deepest and most important ideas are innate, then what is the origin of these innate ideas? This is one of the most recurrent issues in psychology, and many different reasons for the existence of innate ideas have been given. From the Platonic viewpoint, innate ideas exist because "the human soul is immortal (divine) and is purified through a round of incarnations, from which, when completely purified, it may finally escape" (Cornford, 1935/1960, p. 2). Recall the quote from the *Meno* given earlier. "Thus the soul, since it is immortal and has been born many times, and has seen all things both here and in the other world, has learned everything that is" (Hamilton & Cairns, 1961, p. 362). This is a religious view of the origin of innate knowledge, and it has had several defenders over the millennia. However, we will come across several other interpretations of the nature of innate knowledge as we go along, so keep an eye out for them.

Additional Reading on This Topic. For additional examples of the ways in which Platonic ideas have been used by psychologists, see Bregman (1977). Generally useful books are MacLeod (1975) and Stevenson (1974). Both contain accounts of Plato's psychology, as well as reviews of many of the other figures we consider in this book. More on the implications of the doctrine of the *Golden Section* may be found in Tracy (1969).

LAO-TSU (6TH CENTURY B.C.)

Lao-Tsu is as much of a mythical figure as is Pythagoras, there even being some debate about whether or not he actually existed (Kaltenmark, 1969; Lau, 1963). He was said to have lived a very long life, and one of the meanings of *Lao Tsu* is *old man.* At that time in China old age and wisdom were thought to go together, an insight that we seem to be rediscovering today (e.g., Baltes & Staudinger, 1993). Lao-Tsu is an example of a *sage.* According to the *Oxford English Dictionary* (1989), a *sage* is "a person of profound wisdom; especially one of those persons of ancient history or legend who were traditionally famous as the wisest of mankind." The wisdom of Lao-Tsu is called *Taoism.*

The Tension between Confucianism and Taoism

Many people today are similar to people in ancient China in that they have the same desire for explicit guidelines in dealing with the problems that arise in everyday life. Just as there is no shortage today of advisers to tell us how to live (many of whom are psychologists), so it was in ancient China. We will come to Lao-Tsu's advice presently, but first we should briefly consider the contrasting advice given by another great Chinese sage, *Confucius.* Confucius's advice affirmed the importance of developing one's intelligence through education, and of following traditional values, such as loyalty to one's family and to one's government (Kaltenmark, 1969, p. 9).

Bond and Hwang (1986) summarize the recommendations of Confucianism as follows. People "exist through, and [are] defined by, [their] relationships to others; . . . these relationships are structured hierarchically; . . . social order is ensured through each party's honoring the requirements in the role relationship" (p. 216). Important role relationships, such as being a father, a son, or a friend, provided a framework within which social behavior was regulated.

A famous incident in the story of Lao-Tsu's life was an encounter he had with Confucius. In descriptions of this meeting, it almost appears as if Lao-Tsu is making fun of Confucian traditionalism. Here is a part of what Lao-Tsu is supposed to have said to Confucius (taken from Kaltenmark, 1969).

> *The man who is intelligent and clear-sighted will soon die, for his criticisms of others are just; the man who is learned and discerning risks his life, for he exposes others' faults. The man who is a son no longer belongs to himself; the man who is a subject no longer belongs to himself. (p. 8)*

Although Confucianism and Taoism share much in common, Taoism is typically regarded as less explicit and more mystical. Confucianism emphasized the social and moral order, to the exclusion of an interest in natural phenomena. By contrast, Taoism treated the natural and social orders as continuous (Ronan & Needham, 1978, p. 94). As the great Chinese scholar Joseph Needham (1962) puts it, Confucianism "was masculine and managing: the Taoists condemned it and sought after a feminine and receptive knowledge which could arise only as the fruit of a passive and yielding attitude in the observation of Nature" (p. 33). For the Taoist, both nature and society worked the same way. Everything illustrated the *Tao*.

What Is Tao?

The simplest translation of the word *Tao* is "the Way." *The way* referred to the "way in which the Universe worked; in other words, the order of Nature . . . which brought all things into existence and governs their every action, not so much by force as by . . . controlling the orderly processes of change" (Needham, 1962, p. 36).

The writings attributed to *Lao-Tsu* are called the *Tao-Te Ching*. Here is an oft-quoted passage from the *Tao-Te Ching* that illustrates the Taoist preoccupation with the nature of change (Lau, 1963).

> *Is not the way of heaven like the stretching of a bow?*
> *The high it presses down,*
> *The low it lifts up;*
> *The excessive it takes from,*
> *The deficient it gives to. (p. 139)*

This passage expresses the belief that any situation is always in the process of changing into its opposite. This means that it is fruitless to search for something that does not change. Many scholars (e.g., H. Wilhelm, 1975, p. 15) have compared the Taoist view of change to that of the Greek philosopher *Heraclitus* (c. 540–c. 470 B.C.). Here is a quote from Heraclitus (Wheelwright, 1966) that illustrates this similarity to Taoism:

> *You cannot step into the same river twice, for other waters and yet others go ever flowing on. (p. 71)*

This emphasis on the pervasiveness of change should be contrasted with Plato's views (Lau, 1963, p. 20). While Plato believed that it was possible to discover a permanent world of forms behind the flow of everyday experience, for the Taoist such a hope is illusory. The Tao cannot be "discovered" or "named" (Lau, 1963):

> *The way is forever nameless . . .*
> *Only when it is cut are there names*
> *As soon as there are names*
> *One ought to know that it is time to stop. (p. 91)*

What we can describe are individual phenomena. However, we cannot give a general description of the Tao that "explains" all individual phenomena. The Tao resists description because any name that can be applied to it is misleading: "Dimly visible, it cannot be named" (Lau, 1963, p. 93).

As mentioned above, Taoism emphasizes the virtue of a passive observation of nature (Needham, 1962, p. 57). Such passivity does not impose itself on nature, but is open to observing what is actually there. In a way, this aspect of Taoism anticipates what has become a very important aspect of scientific observation. When properly conducted, science makes no assumptions about what nature *must* be; it is not founded on dogmatic principles. Rather it begins with observations of what *actually* happens, regardless of what anyone's theory says *should* be happening.

The *Book of Changes*

Many of you will have come across the *I Ching*, or *Book of Changes* (1967). As an expression of ancient Chinese culture, it has an affinity with both Confucian and Taoist ideas. The *I Ching* has fascinated many Western scholars, from *Leibniz* (1646–1716) to *Jung* (1875–1961).

At its most superficial level, the *I Ching* is a fortune-telling device. Wanting to predict one's future is a pervasive wish today just as it was in ancient China. In order to make such predictions, one needs a system for codifying possible future outcomes. It is here that the *I Ching* is particularly prescient, because its codification scheme involves what later came to be known as a *binary number system.*

A binary system uses only two values, such as 1 and 0. In the *I Ching,* these two values are labeled *Yang* and *Yin.* Yang and Yin represent the fundamental cosmic forces. Yang may be characterized by opposing pairs of adjectives such as masculine, firm and light, while adjectives appropriate to Yin are feminine, yielding and dark (Osgood & Richards, 1973). In general, Yang and Yin are both equally important, although one or the other may predominate in a particular situation. As it says in the *I Ching* (1967),

> *That which lets now the dark, now the light appear is tao . . . The primal powers never come to a standstill; the cycle of becoming continues uninterruptedly. The reason is that between the two primal powers there arises again and again a state of tension, a potential that keeps the powers in motion and causes them to unite, whereby they are constantly regenerated. Tao brings this about without ever becoming manifest. The power of tao to maintain the world by constant renewal of a state of tension between the polar forces, is designated as good. (pp. 297–298)*

Notice that change is conceptualized as *cyclical.* This sense of "a movement that returns to its starting point . . . may have been derived from the orbits of the heavenly bodies or the course of the seasons. . . . The notion of progress . . . is alien to the ancient concept of change" (H. Wilhelm, 1975, pp. 19–20). The notion that historical change is cyclical is a possibility we will need to take seriously. As we go along we consider further the question of whether the history of psychology involves more repetition than progress.

A simple and easily understood way of representing cyclical change is by means of a circle. In the *I Ching,* this is accomplished by using a circular diagram like that in Figure 1.7. This circular diagram is generated by combining *trigrams,* each of which is composed of three lines. Each line is either solid (Yang) or broken (Yin). There are eight unique trigrams. For example, a trigram of three unbroken (Yang) lines is called *Ch'ien: the Creative,* while its opposite is a trigram of three broken (Yin) lines, called *K'un: the Receptive.* The entire set of trigrams is given in Figure 1.8. Notice that each row of Figure 1.8 contains four Yang and four Yin lines, and that the eight trigrams represent all possible combinations of three solid/broken lines. The 64 *hexagrams* of Figure 1.7 are obtained by combining the eight trigrams in all possible ways. Each hexagram has a different name, and represents a different possible state of affairs. For example, look at the bottom of Figure 1.7, where the hexagram containing all broken lines is located. This hexagram is called *K'un: the Receptive,* and represents "the nature of the earth, strong in devotion; among the seasons it stands for late autumn,

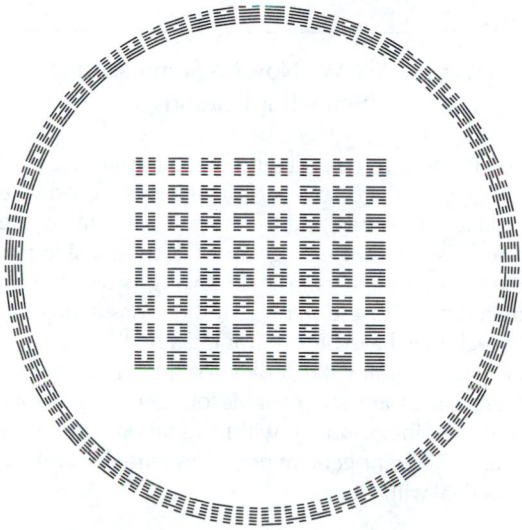

FIGURE 1.7 The circular structure of the *I Ching.*
Source: H. Wilhelm. (1975). *Change* [Cary F. Baynes, Trans.]. London: Routledge & Kegan Paul, p. 84. Reprinted by permission.

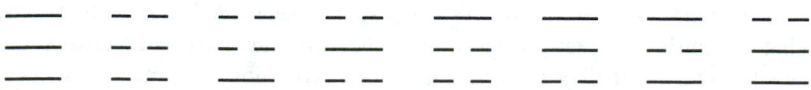

FIGURE 1.8 The eight trigrams underlying the *I Ching.*

Box 1.2

Where Are We Now? A Summary and Some Implications

So far we have considered the contrasting views of Pythagoras, Plato, and Lao-Tsu. Now is a good time to take a breather, and try to spell out some of the major issues that emerge from a consideration of these three thinkers. The following issues can be traced back to the period we are considering, although they have been formulated in different ways at different times. Regardless of how they are put, these issues are still capable of generating debate in psychology, and we will have an opportunity of seeing different generations of psychological theorists deal with them.

1. *Nature versus culture.* Taoism treats human behavior as a part of the natural order, and not as something different from other natural phenomena. An alternative approach would be to regard human behavior as determined by principles unique to it. For example, culture might have so powerful an effect on behavior as to make it impossible to understand as a purely natural phenomenon. The issue here is this: Can human behavior be understood in the same way as we understand natural phenomena, or must it be understood in terms of its own culturally determined rules?
2. *Process versus structure.* Taoism treats change as the fundamental characteristic of experience. Platonism encourages us to seek a perfect world of unchanging forms. This issue can be phrased as follows: Is psychology best seen as the study of *processes* that are in continuous change, or is it best seen as the study of the underlying *structures* that determine behavior? What is the relation between process and structure? As we will see, the great American psychologist William James (1890) compared consciousness to a stream, just as Heraclitus compared life to a stream. If consciousness is like a stream, then nothing recurs in it. If nothing recurs, then can it have any permanent structure?
3. *The individual case versus the general law.* If it turned out to be true that our experience has no underlying structure, then there would appear to be nothing very general that can be said about human behavior. Each person's life will be relatively unique, and it would be pointless to try to see his or her behavior as the result of some general laws. However, if, as Pythagoras believed, everything has a mathematical structure, then everything will be an illustration of an underlying law.
4. *A theoretical observation versus theory-driven observation.* The Taoist approach to observation was to make no assumptions about what we will find in nature. Perhaps observation should be passive, and not determined by theoretical preconceptions. If our observations of behavior are determined by a preconceived theory, then we may not be open to observing what people actually do. However, is it always wise to approach the study of behavior without a theory? Does not a good theory provide direction to one's exploration of nature?

when all the forces of life are at rest" (R. Wilhelm, 1967, p. li). At the top of the circle is *Ch'ien: the Creative,* which has the opposite meaning to *K'un.* "Ch'ien . . . whose symbol is heaven . . . is associated with the Chinese fourth month, approximately our May—that is, the time when growth and flowering is at a peak" (H. Wilhelm, 1975, p. 50).

For our purposes, the fact that the *I Ching* has traditionally been used to tell fortunes is not its most important feature. What has intrigued great scholars such as Leibniz is the fact that the *I Ching* begins with a simple binary arithmetic from which is constructed a model of all possible situations (Mungello, 1977; H. Wilhelm, 1975, pp. 90–92). Moreover, the circular structure enables the representation of the way that phenomena may be transformed over time.

Circular models are common in the history of psychology, although they are typically models of much smaller scope than the *I Ching.* Such models, often called *circumplexes,* have been created for many domains in psychology. In Western psychol-

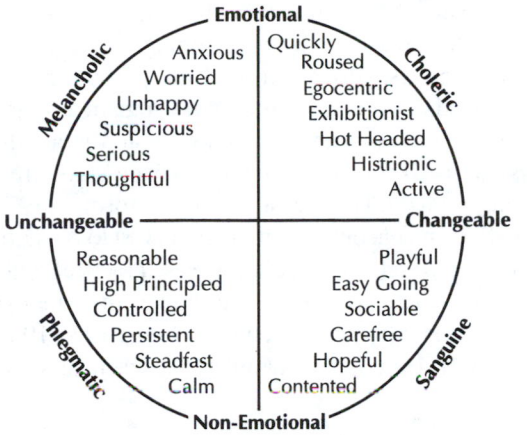

FIGURE 1.9 Galen's circumplex model of temperament.

Source: H. J. Eysenck & M. W. Eysenck. (1985). *Personality and individual differences.* New York: Plenum Press, p. 45. Reprinted by permission.

ogy, the most pervasive circumplex model has been *Galen's* (A.D. 129–c. 199) *typology* of temperaments. Galen identified four temperaments, called *melancholic* (or pessimistic); *sanguine* (or sociable); *choleric* (or proud); and *phlegmatic* (or controlled). These four temperaments can be arranged in a a circle as shown in Figure 1.9. This model has influenced many subsequent psychologists (Martindale & Martindale; 1988; Miller, 1988). Other areas in which circumplex models have been applied in psychology include color (e.g., Goethe, 1840/1970, p. lvii); facial expression (e.g., Schlosberg, 1952); interpersonal characteristics (e.g., Kiesler, 1983); and emotion (e.g., J. A. Russell, 1980). We will examine some of these models later on. Box 1.2 summarizes the major issues with which we have dealt thus far.

Additional Reading on This Topic. Murphy and Murphy (1968) edited a compendium of sources on Asian psychology that is a thorough introduction to this area. An appreciation of Taoism is perhaps best gained through exposure to its art, and a good beginning source is Rawson and Legeza (1973; also Legeza, 1973). Taoism as a contemporary religion is thoroughly considered by Lagerwey (1987).

An investigation of the enormous range of Eastern psychology is beyond the scope of this book. In particular, the teachings of Buddha (566–480 B.C.) have intrigued many psychological thinkers. There are different varieties of Buddhism, and Suzuki (1956) is a good introduction to one strand. A good example of the way Buddhism is influencing contemporary psychology is Varela, Thompson, and Rosch (1991).

ARISTOTLE (384–323 B.C.)

Aristotle's Differences with Plato

As a young man, Aristotle studied with Plato at the Academy in Athens. After Plato's death, Aristotle left Athens, and subsequently became tutor to the young man who was to become Alexander the Great. On returning to Athens, he founded his own school, called the Lyceum. Aristotle's mature philosophy is among the most influential in the history of Western culture. Let us begin a consideration of Aristotle's contributions to psychology by sketching the way in which his views differed from those of Plato.

In the first place, Aristotle rejected Plato's theory of forms. Recall that Plato believed that there was a world of ideal forms existing independently of the world of ordinary experience. Aristotle argued instead that form and matter were intertwined. Matter does not exist without form, nor does form exist without matter. Far from being arcane, Aristotle's point is an expression of what has become common sense in Western culture. In order to see how intuitively obvious Aristotle's point is, let us briefly consider an argument made by the linguist *Benjamin Lee Whorf* (1897–1941). Whorf (1956) suggested that all of us in the Western world unconsciously construct our experience in a particular way, and observed that we commonly "carve up" reality into units which are defined by the general formula *form-plus-substance.* Thus, we say "a *quart* of *milk*" and not just "a milk"; "a *kilogram* of *meat,*" and not "a meat"; a "*snow crystal,*" and not just "a snow." This is close to Aristotle's view: we ordinarily understand all substances as having particular forms, and that forms cannot exist apart from the substances they shape.

Aristotle observed that substances had the *potential* to take on different forms. What a substance *actually* became depended on the form it took. Baumrin (1975) uses the following example to illustrate how the distinction between *potentiality* versus *actuality* worked in the case of living beings.

> *By way of illustration, consider the stillborn fetus. It is a body that is both material and has form but not soul. Its body is the sort of body that could potentially live; moreover it actually had to have been alive for some time to have the form it has at birth. The soul is both the form of a living body in the sense that it is the organization of that body and in the sense that it is the life of that body when it is alive. (p. 487)*

The distinction between a living and a dead body is that the former has a soul. However, different living things have different powers, and Aristotle compared the powers possessed by plants, animals, and human beings. Plants fulfill minimal conditions for being alive in that "they grow up and down, and everything that grows increases its bulk alike in both directions or indeed in all, and continues to live so long as it can absorb nutriment" (McKeon, 1941, p. 557).

At the next level are creatures with "the power of sensation." What distinguishes animals from plants is that the former have senses, such as touch: "The primary form of sense is touch, which belongs to all animals" (McKeon, 1941, p. 557). Aristotle argued that human beings have five senses, including vision; the sense of sound (audition); the sense of smell (olfaction); and the sense of taste in addition to touch. This fivefold classification of the senses became 'common sense', and "has upon it the sanction of the centuries" (Geldard, 1972, p. 258).

In addition to the powers of "self-nutrition" and sensation, human beings also possess the power to think (McKeon, 1941, p. 559). To Aristotle, reasoning seemed like a peculiarly human attribute, and he delineated the forms of reasoning in great detail. Among these forms, Aristotle was particularly interested in the *syllogism.* A syllogism consists of two premises and a conclusion, and in a valid syllogism the conclusion follows necessarily from the premises. There are a great many forms of valid syllogism, but one of particular interest to Aristotle was the *practical syllogism.* We use practical syllogisms when "the conclusion drawn from the two premises becomes an action" (Henle, 1962/1968, p. 103). Here is an example of a practical syllogism.

> *Premise 1:* It is necessary for me to understand psychology as a whole.
> *Premise 2:* The only way to understand psychology as a whole is through the study of the history of psychology.
> *Conclusion:* Therefore, it is necessary for me to study the history of psychology.

You may disagree with the premises, but if you accept them, then the conclusion necessarily follows. Henle (1962/1968) has provided examples showing that the practical syllogism is a very common feature of everyday life. One of her examples is the following: "It is too far to walk to the public library; I must take the subway or bus. The Fifth Avenue bus passes the Public Library. I must take the Fifth Avenue bus" (p. 103). Henle goes on to observe that "it is difficult to see how the individual could cope with the ordinary tasks of life if the practical syllogism embodied techniques which are not . . . the common property of the unsophisticated subject" (p. 103). The practical syllogism is an illustration of the way our behavior is regulated by our reason. Our ability to reason is what most distinguishes human beings from other forms of life.

Aristotle believed certain parts of the soul, particularly the power of reason, were indestructible. This meant that even though bodily functions decline throughout the process of normal aging, reason is left intact. However, it may *seem* as if reason declines, because the body declines, and the body is the only vehicle through which reason can express itself. In the following quotation, the word *impassible* means "to be incapable of suffering pain." Thus, when Aristotle says the mind is impassible he means that it is not prone to the diseases and degeneration that may afflict an aging person.

> *The case of mind is different; it seems to be an independent substance implanted within the soul and to be incapable of being destroyed. If it could be destroyed at all, it would be under the influence of old age. What really happens in respect of mind in old age is, however, exactly parallel to what happens in the case of the sense organs; if the old man could recover the proper kind of eye, he could see just as well as the young man. The incapacity of old age is due to an affection not of the soul but of its vehicle, as occurs in drunkenness or disease. Thus it is that in old age the activity of mind or intellectual apprehension declines only through the decay of some other inward part; mind itself is impassible. (McKeon, 1941, p. 548)*

The issue then is whether reason itself declines, or whether its full expression is prevented because of disease or decay in other parts of the body, such as the brain. Although this is an ancient question, its relevance has not diminished with the passage of time. Consider the famous cases depicted by the neurologist Oliver Sacks (1974). In his book *Awakenings,* which was subsequently made into a film, Sacks described patients with Parkinson's disease. People who have severe cases of Parkinsonism may deteriorate into "a 'frozen' state of rigid immobility and unresponsiveness to external stimuli" (Flowers, 1987, p. 590), that may persist for several years. However, this does not mean that their mental life has irreversibly ceased. Sacks described several cases of people who, as a result of drug therapy, were "awakened" for at least a while, and showed signs of reason and other mental powers where there had appeared to be none before. Aristotle would surely have seen such "awakenings" as illustrations of his point that the mind is impassible, and able to recover with the appropriate therapy to the appropriate parts of the body (in this case, the brain). Although contemporary neurologists would, no doubt, offer other, and vastly more detailed, accounts of such phenomena, the view that people have souls, and that the soul is indestructible, is still very widely held in our culture.

The Nature of Human Action

If we follow Aristotle, and say that human behavior can be regulated by our reason, then we will expect people to be able to give reasons for their actions. These reasons are usually statements of what Aristotle called the *final cause.* Final causes are "the end, i.e., that for the sake of which a thing is, e.g., health is the cause of walking. For 'Why does one walk?' we say 'that one may be healthy'; and in speaking thus we think we have given the cause" (McKeon, 1941, p. 752). Human behavior appears to be *purposive.* We act with certain ends in mind, and those ends may explain our action. Thus, if you meet me when I am out walking, and ask me what I am doing, I may explain myself by saying that I am walking for my health. My health is the goal that determines my behavior.

Hamlyn (1953/1962, p. 63) has shown how Aristotle's conception of human action requires us to distinguish *action* from simple *motion.* Actions can be accomplished in a variety of ways. Thus, suppose I want to mail a letter. I may accomplish this through any number of bodily movements. For example, I may open the letter box with my right hand, or with my left hand. It is impossible to specify the particular movements that are required in order to accomplish an action. It follows that an explanation of bodily movements will not be a complete explanation of action. A complete explanation of actions will involve the actor's *reasons* for behaving in a particular way.

If someone pushes me off the edge of the Grand Canyon, then my fall is aptly described as motion. This motion can be given a completely mechanical explanation—someone applied a force to my back, and then gravity took over. Falling into the Grand Canyon is not something for which I can give an explanation in terms of my goals. However, if I am *walking* down a trail toward the floor of the Grand Canyon, then it is reasonable to expect me to be able to give an explanation of my behavior in terms of my goal. Thus, if I am asked why I am walking down the trail, I might answer that I want to be able to appreciate the canyon from that vantage point.

Psychology is often defined as the study of *behavior.* As Hamlyn (1953/1962, p. 62) observes, the word "behavior" is often used in an ambiguous way. Sometimes "behavior" refers to the movements that organisms make; other times it refers to their actions. The explanation of behavior may require more than an explanation of bodily movements; it may also require an explanation in terms of the person's goals or purposes. Explanations in terms of goals are called *teleological.* The role of teleological explanations of behavior has often been problematic in the history of psychology, and we will return to this issue often as we go along.

Memory

Aristotle defined *memory* as the process whereby a person revives a previous experience. Memory involves the "reinstatement in consciousness of something which was there before but had disappeared" (McKeon, 1941, p. 613). Aristotle is often called the originator of the notion that memory is governed by *associations* (e.g., Mandler & Mandler, 1964, p. 8). For an associationist, one idea will follow another in memory if they were previously experienced in relationship to each other. The doctrine of associationism is very important in the history of psychology, and we will follow its development closely.

According to Aristotle, when we try to remember something, we follow a chain of associated ideas until we succeed in recovering what it is we wanted to recall. We may not find what we want to remember right away. Rather there may be a sequence of ideas that begins with "something either similar, or contrary, to what we seek, or else from that which is contiguous with it" (McKeon, 1941, p. 612). The hypothesis that associations are produced by *similarity, contrast,* and *contiguity* is one of Aristotle's most important contributions.

1. *Association by similarity* means that we tend to be reminded of something to the extent that it resembles what we are currently experiencing. For example, on thinking of Plato we may then think of Aristotle because they share many common properties, such as being not only ancient and Greek, but also philosophers.

2. *Association by contrast* refers to the fact that we are sometimes reminded of something to the extent that it means the opposite of what we are currently experiencing. Thus, if I ask you to say the first thing that comes into your head when I say *black,* you are liable to respond with *white.*

3. *Association by contiguity* occurs whenever we are reminded of something because it had been previously experienced together with whatever we are currently experiencing. For example, if I ask you to say the first thing that comes into your head when I say *salt,* you are liable to respond with *pepper* because salt and pepper shakers tend to be put side by side.

These three can be called the first *laws of association.* Over the years, there has been a great deal of debate over the relationship among these three laws, and which of them is most important. We develop the story of associationism in Chapter 2 when we come to the British Empiricists. However, we should not leave Aristotle's account of memory without noting that it contained more than just the principles of association. For example, Aristotle noted that "recollection is, as it were, a mode of inference. For he who endeavors to recollect *infers* that he formerly saw, or heard, or had some such experience, and the process . . . is, as it were, a sort of investigation" (McKeon, 1941, p. 616). Here Aristotle is suggesting that recollection can be more like imagination than a literal rendition of the past.

Mnemonics. The central role of imagination in memory was well known to the ancients. Imagination played a crucial part in their elaborate *mnemonic techniques.* A mnemonic technique is a way of improving your memory, and we have probably all used mnemonic techniques at one time or another. For example, if I want to remember to buy eggs, cherries, lemons, and margarine at the supermarket, I may take the first letters of each item, rearrange them, and make a name out of them, such as CLEM. Then all I have to do is remember the one word rather than the four items, and properly decode the word when I am in the supermarket.

Such simple mnemonics are feeble attempts when compared to the elaborate mnemonic techniques described by Aristotle and practiced from ancient times throughout the Middle Ages and into the Renaissance.

Ancient memory systems were explored by Frances Yates (1966) in a very influential book. She begins by presenting an outline of mnemonics given in an anonymous document called the *Ad Herennium,* written in the first century B.C. Written for students, it describes an *artificial memory* that would enable someone who was properly trained to accurately recall a great many items. The system is called an "artificial memory" to distinguish it from the memory we have naturally, without training. In order to develop an artificial memory, a student would have to invest a considerable amount of time and effort, as we shall see.

The *artificial memory* has two parts, *places* (*loci*) and *images.* "A *locus* is a place easily grasped by the memory, such as house, an intercolumnar space, a corner, an arch, or the like. Images are forms, marks . . . of what we wish to remember. For example, if we wish to recall the genus of a horse, of a lion, of an eagle, we must place their images on definite *loci*" (Yates, 1966, p. 6). The "art of memory" involves creating a memory that can be read like a book:

> *The art of memory is like an inner writing. Those who know the letters of the alphabet can write down what is dictated to them and read out what they have written. Likewise those who have learned mnemonics can set in places what they have heard and deliver it from memory. For the places are very much like wax tablets or papyrus, the images like the letters, the arrangement and disposition of the images like the script, and the delivery is like the reading. (Yates, 1966, pp. 6–7)*

Learning a set of loci is the would-be mnemonist's first task. It was necessary to learn a great many loci by following these rules:

- The loci must be learned in a particular serial order, and overlearned so that the student could imagine going in either direction from any particular locus. Aristotle was apparently referring to this ability when he described people who "are supposed to recollect sometimes by starting from mnemonic *loci*" (McKeon, 1941, p. 614).
- Loci should be selected from "a deserted and solitary place" such as a building when no one is around (Yates, 1966, p. 7).
- The loci should be as much unlike one another as possible.
- The loci should be a fair distance apart, and bright. The *Ad Herennium* suggests a distance of about 30 feet.
- Every fifth locus should be marked in a distinctive way. For example, one could "mark the fifth locus with a golden hand" (Yates, 1966, p. 7). The hand has five fingers, and so is a good symbol for the fifth locus.

The loci could be reused again and again. Having constructed a series of loci, the student was ready to place the to-be-remembered material in them. This material was encoded in the form of *images,* a single image for each item to be remembered. Each image was stored in a locus. The student could then recall this material by mentally strolling through the loci, collecting the images stored there. The images should be as bizarre and distinctive as possible, "of exceptional beauty or singular ugliness; . . . ornament some of them, as with crowns or purple cloaks . . . or . . . disfigure them, as by introducing one stained with blood or soiled with mud" (Yates, 1966, p. 10).

By using this method, the ancients are reputed to have been able to recall astonishing numbers of items. For example, "the elder Seneca . . . could repeat two thousand names in the order in which they had been given; and when a class of two hundred students or more spoke each in turn a line of

Box 1.3

Ancient Mnemonics and Contemporary Psychology

At first the artificial memory may strike us as bizarre, and as representing a gross deviation from the psychology of 'normal' memory. However, it turns out that this ancient system employs several well-known, twentieth-century principles of learning. For example, overlearning the loci means that they will resist interference from other material (e.g., Saltz, 1971, p. 232). During the acquisition period, the loci would initially be only weakly connected to one another, but with increased practice they would become organized into a single unit that would resist interference from elements outside the system (e.g., Mandler, 1962). An overlearned set of loci would provide a stable setting within which to place the images.

The loci and the images themselves are selected so as to maximize differentiation between them. It has become well-known that the more distinctive an item is, the more likely we are to recall it (e.g., Kohler, 1940/1960, p. 34). Moreover, marking every fifth locus makes good sense from the point of view of cognitive economy. Since we are usually able to keep about five items in mind at one time (e.g., Miller, 1956), marking every fifth locus would allow a speaker to collect a few items and hold them in mind until it was time to go on to the next sequence. Finally, imagery itself has come to be recognized as a powerful aid to memory (e.g., Paivio, 1971; 1986).

The elaborate mnemonic techniques of the ancients faded away with the arrival of printing, which made it easy to store large amounts of information outside of one's memory. However, after Yates (1966) wrote her book, there was renewed interest in mnemonics. A particularly important paper in this revival was written by Bower (1970), who showed that many of the ancient techniques have a sound psychological basis, and are still useful today. A modern adaptation of the *artificial memory* is given in a charming book by Crovitz (1970). If you are interested in learning more about mnemonics, start with Bower's paper. Other useful works on mnemonics include Einstein and McDaniel (1987) and Morris, Jones, and Hampson (1978).

poetry, he could recite all the lines in reverse order, beginning from the last one said and going right back to the first" (Yates, 1966, p. 16).

Aristotle discussed the artificial memory on several occasions. For example, he described people who dream that they are "mentally arranging a given list of subjects according to the mnemonic rule" (McKeon, 1941, p. 619). Yates (1966, p. 31) notes that this is "rather a warning, one would think, against doing too much in artificial memory," but goes on to show that the importance of imagination in Aristotle's theory of memory was consistent with the way that ancient mnemonists approached their task. For example, Aristotle argued that "imagining lies within our own power whenever we wish (e.g., we can call up a picture, as in the practice of mnemonics by the use of mental images)" (McKeon, 1941, p. 587). Not only did Aristotle believe that imagery was an important mnemonic tool, but he also held that thinking was impossible without images. After all, the mind requires something to think about, and what else do we think with other than images? This is a claim that has been controversial throughout the history of psychology, as we shall see. Contemporary explorations of the artificial memory are considered in Box 1.3.

The *Scala Naturae*

Recall that Aristotle had differentiated between forms of life in terms of the powers that they possessed. Thus, plants had only the power of self-nutrition, animals had both self-nutrition and sensation, while humans were also able to think in addition to the first two powers. Notice that this creates a *hierarchy* with humans at the top, followed by animals, and then plants. If all creatures "could be ranked on a unitary, graded, continuous dimension" (Hodos & Campbell, 1969, p. 338), then one would have what has been called a *scala naturae.* Aristotle conceived of this "natural scale" as a measure of the "degree of perfection" of each creature. "It is based on the 'powers of the soul' . . . from the nutritive, to which plants are limited, to the rational, characteristic of man . . . each higher order possessing all the powers of those below it in the scale, and an additional differentiating one of its own" (Lovejoy, 1936/1971, p. 58).

ST. THOMAS AQUINAS AND THE MEDIEVAL VIEW OF THE UNIVERSE

Such a hierarchical order was greatly elaborated over the years following Aristotle, especially during the Middle Ages, or *Medieval period,* which lasted from about A.D. 500 until roughly the fifteenth century. During this period Christianity became the dominant religion in Europe. One of Aristotle's most successful interpreters was the great Catholic theologian, *St. Thomas Aquinas* (1225–1274). Aquinas demonstrated that much of what Aristotle said was consistent with a Christian world view. For example, the idea of a *scala naturae,* or *great chain of being* (Lovejoy, 1936/1971, pp. 73–77) was quite consistent with Catholic theology. According to Aquinas, "the universe is hierarchically arranged" with beings ordered "according to their internal perfection" (Wulf, 1922/1959, p. 62). In this system, "reality mounts step by step from one specific nature to another, following a certain definite order. . . . Things evolve . . . in a certain order, the investigation of which is the work of the particular sciences, and calls for patient observation. If there are any leaps in nature, they are never capricious" (Wulf, 1922/1959, p. 72). The *great chain of being* illustrates God's plan, as described in the following quote from Aquinas (Pegis, 1948):

> *Hence we must say that the distinction and multitude of things is from the intention of the first cause, who is God. For He brought things into being in order that His goodness might be communicated to creatures, and be represented by them. And because His goodness could not be adequately represented by one creature alone, He produced many and diverse creatures, so that what was wanting to one in the representation of the divine goodness might be supplied by another. For goodness, which in God is simple and uniform, in creatures is manifold and divided; and hence the whole universe together participates in the divine goodness more perfectly, and represents it better, than any given single creature. And because the divine wisdom is the cause of the distinction of things, therefore Moses said that things are made distinct by the Word of God, which is the conception of His wisdom; and this is what we read in* Genesis *(1:3, 4):* God said: Be light made. . . . And he divided the light from the darkness. *(pp. 260–261)*

It is impossible to overestimate the importance to Western culture of this religious conception of the evolutionary process. Here is a summary of some of its main features:

> *Creatures are hierarchically ordered, reflecting God's purpose. Nothing in this plan is "capricious" (i.e., occurs merely by chance). Rather, everything and everyone has a place in a purposeful order that culminates in God. This view of nature is consistent with what we are told in the Bible, which is an irrefutable source of knowledge.*

This view of the world as a hierarchically ordered, planful system with God at its apex, and humans as the most God-like creatures remained in place for hundreds of years in Western culture. It was not until Darwin presented his theory of evolution in the nineteenth century that the religious world view faced its most serious challenge. We will review the dispute between traditional theology and Darwinian evolutionary theory later on. However, the stability of the Medieval system was shaken well before the nineteenth century by the coming of the Renaissance, a topic to which we turn in the next chapter.

Additional Reading on This Topic A thorough outline of Aristotle's approach to psychology is found in Robinson (1989). A brief, readable introduction to the psychological implications of Aquinas's philosophy is given by Fitzpatrick (1987), which appears in Gregory's (1987) *Oxford Companion to the Mind.* Generally speaking, this is a very useful reference book.

KEY NAMES AND CONCEPTS

What follows is an index of some of the most important material in this chapter. The list includes the individuals, concepts, and topics you should know. Read through the list, and if anything on it seems unfamiliar, then go back and re-read the appropriate section of the chapter. You should be able to define each concept, briefly discuss each topic, and state the importance of each person on the list. In addition, you should be able to write an account of the work done by each person whose name is printed in boldface.

Ad Herennium, 19
- artificial memory, 19
- loci and images, 19

Aristotle, 15
- action versus motion, 17
- differences with Plato, 15
- final cause, 17
- impassible, 17
- laws of association, 18
- memory, 18
- mnemonic techniques, 18
- potentiality versus actuality, 16
- practical syllogism, 16
- scala naturae, 20
- syllogism, 16
- teleology, 18

Box 1.1—The relative importance of Plato and other thinkers, 8

Box 1.2—Where are we now? 14

Box 1.3—Ancient mnemonics and contemporary psychology, 20

Confucius, 11

Galen's typology, 15

Gestalt, 10

I Ching, 12
- and circumplexes in psychology, 14
- and Leibniz, 14
- as a binary number system, 13
- cyclical change, 13
- trigrams, 13
- Yang and Yin, 13

individual case versus general law, 14

Jung, 12

Kepler, Johann, 3

Lao-Tsu, 11
- similarity of Heraclitus's views, 12
- Tao-Te Ching, 12
- Taoism, 11
- Taoism and Confucianism, 11
- the Tao, 12

Leibniz, 12

Plato, 6
- doctrine of anamnesis, 10
- Forms, 7
- innate knowledge, 9
- *Meno,* 9

Platonism
- Fibonacci numbers, 7
- Golden Section, 6

psyche, 3

Pythagoras, 1
- cosmology, 3
- harmony, 2
- problem of the irrational, 6
- Pythagorean mathematics, 4
- Pythagorean opposites, 3, 5
- union of opposites, 5

Socrates, 9

St. Thomas Aquinas, 21
- great chain of being, 21

Whorf, Benjamin L., 15

CHAPTER 2

TOUCHSTONES: FROM DESCARTES TO DARWIN

RENÉ DESCARTES (1596–1650)
The Body as a Machine
ISAAC NEWTON (1642–1727)
The Laws of Motion
Can Newton's Laws Be Generalized to Psychology?
The Nature of Color
THE BRITISH EMPIRICISTS: JOHN LOCKE (1632–1704), GEORGE BERKELEY (1685–1753), AND DAVID HUME (1711–1776)
The British Empiricists
John Locke
George Berkeley
David Hume
MARY WOLLSTONECRAFT (1759–1797)
Universal Education
The Importance of Emotion
The Utopian Tradition in Psychology
IMMANUEL KANT (1724–1804)
Kant's "Second Copernican Revolution"
Can Psychology Be a Science Like Other Sciences?
CHARLES DARWIN (1809–1882)
Darwin and Psychology
STUDYING THE HISTORY OF PSYCHOLOGY
Ixion's Wheel or Jacob's Ladder?
Person or Zeitgeist?
Rediscovering the Past

Renaissance means "rebirth," and refers to the renewal of interest in classical antiquity that originated in Italy in the fourteenth century and spread throughout Europe in the fifteenth and sixteenth centuries. This renewed interest in classical sources also brought with it a questioning attitude toward the received wisdom of the Medieval period, "a spirit of criticism which first undermined, then finally destroyed the old beliefs, the old conceptions, the traditional truths. . . . Little by little, doubt stirs and awakens. If everything is possible, nothing is true. If nothing is assured, the only certainty is error" (Koyré, 1954). It was in this climate of doubt and uncertainty that René Descartes took it on himself to discover what, if anything, could be known for sure.

RENÉ DESCARTES (1596–1650)

Born in France, Descartes traveled extensively and lived for most of the latter part of his life in Holland. In 1619, while serving in Germany as a soldier, Descartes found himself without the sort of companion with whom he could discuss philosophical issues. This led him to spend time by himself, reflecting on what was worth believing. During one day of isolation, he had a clear vision of what was beyond doubt. To begin with, Descartes saw that our beliefs typically grow in the way that cities grow. "Ancient cities which were originally mere boroughs, and have become large towns in the process of time, are as a rule badly laid out" (Anscombe & Geach, 1954, p. 15) because they were constructed over a very long time by many different people. Similarly, our beliefs are the result of a very long process of development that lacks any clear plan. What is required is for *one person* to begin again. Just as "buildings undertaken and carried out by a single architect are generally more seemly and better arranged than those several hands have sought to adapt," so Descartes felt that the best chance of finding truth was for him to start from the beginning and see what he could discover by himself. "I was . . . forced to become my own guide" (Anscombe & Geach, 1954, pp. 20–21).

In order to carry out this project, Descartes vowed to accept as true "only what presented itself to my mind so clearly and distinctly that I had no occasion to doubt it," and to make inferences using "long chains of perfectly simple and easy reasonings by means of which geometers are accustomed to carry out their most difficult demonstrations" (Anscombe & Geach, 1954, pp. 20–21). Thus, Descartes' way of discovering the truth begins with *clear and distinct ideas* that cannot be doubted. These ideas are treated as premises from which conclusions can be drawn by "simple and easy reasoning." Such a procedure is the hallmark of *rationalism:* Provided our premises are correct, our ability to use reason is sufficient to provide us with the truth.

Notice that rationalism requires us to begin with sound premises, and thus the discovery of a premise that is beyond doubt is of primary importance. Descartes began by deciding to act as if

> *everything that had entered my mind hitherto was no more than the illusions of dreams. But immediately upon this I noticed that while I was trying to think everything false, it must needs be that I, who was thinking this (*qui le pensais*), was something. And observing that this truth 'I am thinking (*je pense*), therefore I exist' was so solid and secure that the most extravagant suppositions of the sceptics could not overthrow it, I judged that I need not scruple to accept it as the first principle . . . I was seeking. (Anscombe & Geach, 1954, pp. 31–32)*

This passage is one of the most important in the history of Western thought. Descartes reasoned that he cannot doubt the fact of his own thought, and therefore there must be a thinker who is thinking those thoughts. The thinker is, of course, Descartes himself, and so the fact of his existence is beyond doubt. In Latin, the passage "I am thinking, therefore I exist" is *Cogito, ergo sum.* This argument is traditionally "known as Descartes' *Cogito,* and the process by which it is reached is called *Cartesian doubt*" (B. Russell, 1945, p. 564).

For Descartes, several significant conclusions follow from the *Cogito.* Clear and distinct ideas must come from God, since Descartes himself was too imperfect to have generated them on his own. Such ideas include the truths derived through mathematical reasoning, such as that "the idea of a sphere includes the equidistance of all parts (of its surface) from the center" (Anscombe & Geach, 1954, p. 35). There are things that people know without having to learn them, and such truths can be called *innate ideas.* As we have already seen, the question of whether people know things innately is a perennial issue in psychology. For Descartes and his followers, the existence of innate knowledge is beyond question.

Descartes went on to argue that the mind is quite separate from the body. Each of us is essentially a *conscious being* who is capable of mental acts such as doubt and imagination. While a mind may interact with the body in which it is housed, each is of a different nature than the other. The notion that mind and body are fundamentally different is called *dualism.* From Descartes' viewpoint, the mind comes from God, and is immortal. By contrast, the body is mechanical, and operates in the same way as a clock, or any other machine. This way of seeing things naturally raises the question of where, exactly, the mind interacts with the body. Descartes suggested that the interaction took place *via* the *pineal gland,* a singular structure at the base of the brain, because

> *[A]ll other parts of the brain are double, and . . . the organs of 'external sense' are also double—two eyes, two ears, and so on. . . . The pineal gland is also termed the* common sense *. . . [and] may be regarded as the central agency which receives sensory impres-*

sions from various organs, coordinates them, and sends out other impressions so as to enable the adaptive functioning of the body. Descartes [regarded] many [of these] . . . coordinations . . . as purely reflexive *or automatic. (Pastore, 1971, pp. 20–21, emphases added)*

Although the hypothesis that the pineal gland is the seat of the soul is no longer taken seriously, Descartes' overall model of mind-body interaction has been enormously influential. In fact, Descartes' model of the mind-body relation, often called *interactionism,* became so widespread as to be almost "common sense" itself. As one famous twentieth-century philosopher observed, Descartes' view is that the mind is in the body as if it was a *ghost in a machine* (Ryle, 1949):

The official doctrine, which hails chiefly from Descartes, is something like this: . . . every human being has both a body and a mind. [B]ody and mind are ordinarily harnessed together, but after the death of the body [the] mind may continue to exist and function. Human bodies are in space and are subject to the mechanical laws which govern all other bodies in space. Bodily processes and states can be inspected by external observers. So a [person's] bodily life is as much a public affair as are the lives of animals. . . . But minds are not in space, nor are their operations subject to mechanical laws. The workings of one mind are not witnessable by other observers; its career is private. Only I can take direct cognisance of the states and processes of my own mind. A person therefore lives through two collateral histories, one consisting of what happens in and to his [or her] body, the other consisting of what happens in or to his [or her] mind. The first is public, the second private. (p. 11)

Because the Cartesian model has been so central to Western psychology, it is important that we be absolutely clear about its most important features. Consider the following list carefully, which is derived from Ryle's (1949) description given above.

- Mind and body are separate.
- While the human body is subject to the same mechanical laws as any other physical body, the mind operates according to its own rules, which come from God.
- We know our own mind directly, through *introspection.* We cannot know other people's minds directly, since we cannot observe them. All we can observe about other people is the state of their bodies.

Introspection means "the act of looking inward, the examination of one's mental experience" followed by "the report of . . . the mental contents of one's consciousness" (Reber, 1985, p. 373). The Cartesian model seems to point toward introspection as a psychological method, and we will examine introspective psychologies later on. For now, all we need to be aware of is that Descartes leaves us with a picture of the mind as a private place in which thoughts and other mental events occur (Ryle, 1949, p. 27).

The Body as a Machine

Not only was Descartes' model of the mind influential, but so was his conception of the body as a machine. By comparing the body to a machine, Descartes was illustrating a well-known scientific strategy. Gigerenzer (1991) has pointed out that the history of science is replete with examples of machines that have been treated as models of human nature. Consider this quote from the British philosopher *Thomas Hobbes* (1588–1679, as cited by Mischel, 1967, p. 5): "What is the heart but a spring, the nerves strings, the joints wheels giving motion to the whole body?" Hobbes was using tools such as springs and wheels, to provide models for the way that the body works. Although the heart is not really a spring, Hobbes found it useful to think about it that way. Although Hobbes and Descartes disagreed about many things, they both found such *mechanical models* to be extremely useful.

Another good example of the use of mechanical models may be found in the work of the eighteenth-century inventor Jacques de Vaucanson (Fryer & Marshall, 1979) who not only built a statue that played the flute, but also a duck that "stretches out its neck to take corn out of your hand, it swallows it, and discharges it digested by the usual passage" (Fryer & Marshall, 1979, p. 267). These models

BOX 2.1

The Concept of Perspective

One can learn a lot about the history of psychology by examining the history of art. Renaissance artists revived the classical use of *perspective* whereby a scene is depicted from a single *point of view* (Edgerton (1975). The use of perspective relies on the notion that a picture is like a window. To see what this means, examine Figure 2.1, which illustrates the *projective model of vision* (Sedgwick, 1980).

The projective model represents the eye as being located at the apex of a *visual pyramid.* What the artist represents on the *picture plane* is a *projection* of the surface of an object. The result is that objects depicted in a picture appear to lie behind the picture plane. The picture plane is like a window through which you are looking at objects in the distance. Notice that the eye can only be at one place when the picture is constructed. That position is called the *station point* (Sedgwick, 1980, p. 40). The station point gives the spectator a *point of view.* Changing the station point changes what will be represented in the picture, just as moving in relation to a window changes what you see through it. "As we approach a window we see more of the scene; as we move to the left, a portion of the scene on the left side becomes hidden by the window frame while more is revealed on the right, etc." (Sedgwick, 1980, p. 41).

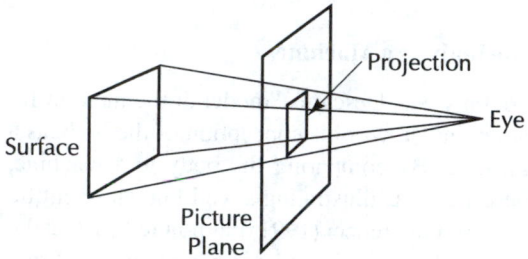

FIGURE 2.1 The visual pyramid and the picture plane.

Source: H. A. Sedgwick. (1980). The geometry of spatial layout in pictorial representation. In M. A. Hagen (Ed.), *The perception of pictures* (p. 36). New York: Academic Press. Reprinted with permission.

A great deal of research and theory in the psychology of perception is based on the projective model, and we will explore it further as we go along. However, for now we only note one other consequence of the projective model, which is discussed by Edgerton (1975, chap. 11) and by Kubovy (1986, chaps. 9 & 10). Over time the projective model has become generalized far beyond its original context of painting. We now talk about individuals having different "points of view" on a situation, and mean more than just that they have different station points. We use the concept of a "point of view" to indicate that there are many different possible "perspectives" on a situation. A great scientist, like a great artist, gives us a perspective that we might never have thought of taking ourselves. However, in most cases, no one person's viewpoint is more privileged than anyone else's, and each person's viewpoint is worth taking seriously.

were not merely entertainments, although they did intrigue the French aristocracy, but a part of a serious attempt to construct machines that were capable of imitating organisms. If an organism is like a machine, then one should be able to build a machine which is indistinguishable from that organism. For generations, scientists have been so impressed with the similarity between people and machines that they often try to build machines to simulate people, believing that if they are successful, they will have shown that they really understand something important about people. This is an idea that many people in our era have had about computers, believing that computers will ultimately be able to mimic everything that people do.

Descartes himself did not believe that the attempt to mimic *human* behavior by means of a machine could succeed. However, he did believe that "if there were machines with the organs and appearance of a monkey, or some other irrational animal, we should have no means of telling that they were not altogether of the same nature as those animals" (Anscombe & Geach, 1954, p. 41). People, however, differ from both animals and machines in being much more flexible in response to changing circumstances. For example, we are able to speak in ways that are spontaneous and novel, something Descartes believed no animal or machine could be trained or made to do. It is the fact that humans possess minds that enables them to adjust so smoothly to changing situations.

While Descartes made a sharp distinction between people and animals, he made none whatsoever between animals and machines. Animals did not possess souls, and so were indistinguishable from machines. Descartes' attitude toward animals is one that many people may find offensive today. "Animals were . . . not conscious, not really living—machines without will or purpose or any feeling whatever. [Descartes] dissected them alive (anesthetics were far off in the nineteenth century) amused at their cries and yelps since these were nothing but the hydraulic hisses and vibrations of machines" (Jaynes, 1973, p. 170). In the years since Descartes, animal research has become common practice. The proper treatment of animals used in research has been a persistent issue ever since.

Our discussion in this section of Descartes' views concerning the body has led to three controversial issues to which we will return later on. These issues are as follows:

1. Can a machine be built that will simulate human behavior in a way that makes it indistinguishable from human behavior?
2. Are there qualitative differences between humans and other organisms?
3. Should we be able to do whatever we want with animals in our research?

Among the areas to which Descartes made strong contributions was the study of *visual perception* (Pastore, 1971). The study of the laws of visual perception was an area of intense activity during the Renaissance, and some of the discoveries of Renaissance artists and scientists have shaped psychological theories ever since. An illustration of this fact is given in Box 2.1.

Additional Reading on This Topic. For a description of an approach to psychology that relies heavily on Descartes, see Stillings et al. (1987).

ISAAC NEWTON (1642–1727)

Sir Isaac Newton has been called "the greatest scientific genius the English-speaking peoples have produced" (Randall, 1953, p. ix). As J. M. Keynes (1956) put it,

> *He was the last of the magicians, the last of the Babylonians and Sumerians, the last great mind which looked out on the visible and intellectual world with the same eyes as those who began to build our intellectual heritage rather less than 10,000 years ago. Isaac Newton, a posthumous child born with no father on Christmas Day, 1642, was the last wonder-child to whom the Magi could do sincere and appropriate homage. (p. 277)*

No less an authority than Albert Einstein (1952) said of Newton that "Nature to him was an open book, whose letters he could read without effort" (p. lix). Newton's interests were extraordinarily broad, including covering everything from *alchemy* (a mystical precursor to chemistry) to history. However, his fame rests largely on a work known as the *Principia* which was published in 1687, when Newton was 45. While the *Principia* forms the foundation for classical physics, it also has important implications for psychology.

The Laws of Motion

A *law* is a basic rule or truth. Sciences that are older and simpler than psychology often lay claim to certain laws. Typical, and famous, examples are Newton's *laws of motion.* Here is Newton's *First Law of Motion:*

> *Every body continues in a state of rest, or of uniform motion in a straight line, unless it is compelled to change that state by forces impressed upon it. (Sears & Zemansky, 1970, p. 15)*

We are also interested in Newton's *Second Law of Motion.* This law deals with *acceleration,* or the rate of change in velocity:

> *Acceleration . . . is . . . the resultant of all the external forces exerted. (Sears & Zemansky, 1970, p. 13)*

In other words, the extent to which a body will move faster or slower depends on how many forces are acting on it, and how intense those forces are.

Newton was able to express these laws in precise mathematical terms. His achievement can be seen as a triumph of the attempt, which began with Pythagoras, to give nature a precise mathematical description.

Can Newton's Laws Be Generalized to Psychology?

Consider the title of a paper by Kimble (1990): "Mother Nature's Bag of Tricks Is Small." This title suggests that the same laws will hold in all areas of inquiry, whether in the natural sciences, such as physics, or social sciences such as psychology. Thus, Kimble is suggesting that Newton's laws apply in psychology just as they do in physics. This is an argument that has been made in many forms over the years. Many psychologists have been impressed by the success of the physical sciences in explaining inanimate matter, and wish to import concepts from the physical sciences in general, and physics in particular, in order to explain psychological events. Thus, instead of seeing psychology as having a unique subject matter, it is possible to see organisms as physical systems operating according to the same laws that regulate other physical systems. We can attempt to take physics and apply it to mental life, and try to explain the mind in the same way as we would any other physical system. This endeavor has several important consequences for psychological research.

One consequence of taking physics as a model for psychology is that the *subject matter* of psychology is seen as essentially the same as that of physics. For example, in Newtonian physics, the basic subject matter is the *motion* of objects. In physics, scientists try to discover the laws that regulate motion—how much force is required to move an object, how fast things move if a force is applied to them, and so on. Kimble argues that *motion* is also the subject matter of psychology, but it is the motion of organisms—*behavior*—rather than the motion of inanimate objects that the psychologist tries to understand.

As we saw above, Newtonian physics tells us that an object will remain at rest unless some force is applied to it. If we transfer that idea to psychology, it means that the organism will not move unless some force is applied to it. However, the organism will not move if *just any* force is applied. That is the point of Newton's second law—the forces acting on the organism must be above a certain level before the organism will act. You can see this for inanimate objects easily enough. If you push lightly on a coffee cup, or other small object, it does not move because of its *inertia.* Only if you apply enough force does it begin to slide across the table. Then, only if you increase or decrease the force you are applying will the speed of the object change. Similarly, the organism will remain at rest until the forces acting on it are sufficient to make it move. Once the organism begins to move, then it will only change its behavior if the forces acting on it change. Box 2.2 gives some examples of the relationship between behavior and the forces controlling it.

Many psychologists have searched for very abstract relationships, such as those proposed by Newton, that may also apply in psychology. As we observed earlier, perhaps it is possible to understand human behavior in the same way as we understand other natural phenomena. Many psychologists have tried to use concepts that have been imported from outside of psychology, particularly from physics (Marks, 1984). This illustrates the persistent attempt to find "underlying unity amidst apparent variety" (Arnheim, 1974).

The Nature of Color

Newton (1730/1952) not only proposed laws of potentially great generality, but he also did experimental work on concrete phenomena such as *color.*

BOX 2.2

The Concept of a Threshold

When the forces acting on the organism are not strong enough to manifest themselves in behavior, then we say that they are *below* threshold. The concept of a threshold, or *limen,* has a very distinguished history in psychology. It is an especially important notion in *psychophysics,* which we will consider in a later chapter. Kimble (1990) has shown that the threshold concept is very powerful. Examine Figure 2.2. It shows how a threshold model can be applied to a wide variety of situations. In the figure, *potential* refers to the readiness of a system to respond and *instigation* refers to the amount of a stimulus that is applied to the system. The threshold curve shows that the greater the potential, the lower the instigation required in order to elicit a response from the system.

Kimble (1990, p. 37) gives several examples that illustrate this relationship:

- The more sensitive the observer, the more easily a signal can be picked up.
- If someone is racially biased, then they pick up even the slightest evidence as proof of their prejudice.
- If someone is prepared to learn, then you only have to suggest a direction for inquiry, and the student does the rest on his or her own.
- Some people can only take a small quantity of a drug before showing its effects; others seem to have a much higher tolerance.
- In certain situations, some people show the effects of stress before others. Everyone can tolerate a certain amount of stress, but as it accumulates, even those who are relatively invulnerable to it will show its effects.

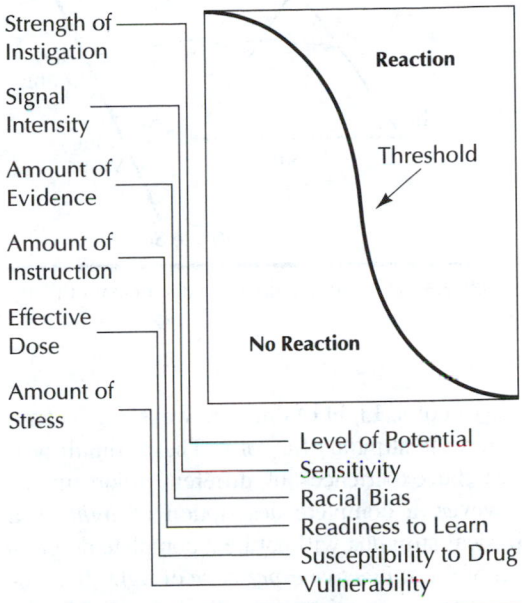

FIGURE 2.2 Kimble's threshold model.

Source: G. A. Kimble (1990). Mother Nature's bag of tricks is small. *Psychological Science, 1,* 36–41. Reprinted with permission.

In fact, Newton's work on color had far-reaching consequences for psychology.

One of Newton's best known experimental procedures is illustrated in Figure 2.3 on page 30. By passing white light through a prism, Newton discovered that it was decomposed into the colors of the spectrum. It appeared that white light yielded a mixture of the other colors. Newton was able to further demonstrate color mixture by passing the colors of the spectrum through another prism. This procedure yielded white light.

Newton's experiment might appear to mean that there are some elementary colors (such as red, yellow, green, and blue) that can be combined to give other colors (such as white). However, Newton did not believe that light rays themselves were colored. "Indeed, rays, properly expressed, are not colored. There is nothing else in them but a certain power or disposition . . . [to] produce in us the sensation of this or that color" (Newton, 1730/ 1952, cited by Judd, 1970, p. ix). Newton distinguished between the *stimulus* for color, and the *subjective experi-*

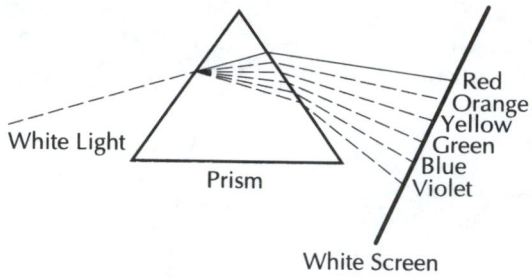

FIGURE 2.3 The use of a prism to disperse white light.

ence of color. Light of different wavelengths constitutes the stimulus for color. These stimuli produce the experiences of different colors in us. However, a complete description of *light* as a physical stimulus will not be a complete description of the *subjective experience* of light. In addition to the description of the physical stimuli, one would also need a description of the resulting experiences.

This last point was taken up with great enthusiasm by the German poet and naturalist Johann Wolfgang von *Goethe* (1840/1970). Goethe failed to give Newton credit for the subtlety of his understanding of color phenomena, and misinterpreted him as meaning that color itself could be understood as a physical property of light. Although Goethe misinterpreted Newton, he did make many peerless descriptions of color as a subjective experience. Here is an example (Goethe, 1840/1970):

> *Let a small piece of bright-colored paper . . . be held before a moderately lighted white surface; let the observer look steadfastly on the small colored object, and let it be taken away after a time while his eyes remain unmoved; the spectrum of another color will then be visible on the white plane. (pp. 20–21)*

Goethe is describing the phenomenon known as *afterimages*. For example, if you stare at a red patch displayed against a white background for about 2 minutes, and then gaze at a blank white background, you will see a green patch (e.g., Coren, Porac & Ward, 1984, p. 204). Afterimages are of great theoretical interest and historical importance, as we will see later on. However, for now it is only necessary to observe that, although he completely misunderstood Newton, Goethe was still capable of making interesting psychological observations. Descriptions of value to psychology need not be (and sometimes are not) accompanied by any very good explanation of *why* the phenomena are as they are.

Additional Reading on This Topic. The historian Frank Manuel (1968, 1974) has written about Newton with great psychological insight. Smith (1987) describes one of the ways in which Newton's ideas were imported into the psychology of *David Hartley* (1705–1757), who belonged to the school of British associationists we consider next.

THE BRITISH EMPIRICISTS: JOHN LOCKE (1632–1704), GEORGE BERKELEY (1685–1753), AND DAVID HUME (1711–1776)

The British Empiricists

Perhaps no group has influenced the subsequent development of Western psychology as much as the one that we are about to consider. The British Empiricists Locke, Berkeley, and Hume invented concepts of far-reaching import for psychology. *Empiricism* is to be contrasted with the sort of *rationalism* that was characteristic of Descartes' approach. Rather than rely on reason to provide us with the truth, the empiricist trusts only the evidence provided by our senses.

John Locke

Born in England, Locke became a physician and a political activist. His political activities brought him into disfavor with King Charles II (Alexander, 1987). As a result, he fled to Holland in 1683, where he wrote much of what was to become his most influential work, *An Essay Concerning Human Understanding,* which was published on his return to England (Locke, 1690/1964).

In his *Essay,* Locke began by arguing that "there are no innate principles in the mind," thus taking a position contradictory to Descartes. Locke's argument is partly that even if there were ideas in which everyone believed, that would not show them to be innate, since people could have arrived at this unanimity in some other way. In any case, one can always find people, such as "children and idiots" (Locke, 1690/1964, p. 68), who do not possess any idea you care to name.

By an *idea,* Locke meant "whatsoever is the *object* of the understanding" when someone thinks (Locke, 1690/1964, p. 66). The following are examples of ideas: "*whiteness, hardness, sweetness, thinking, motion, man, elephant, army, drunkenness*" (Locke, 1690/1964, p. 89). Locke suggested that we get ideas from two different sources. The first is *sensory experience,* which furnishes us with the experiences we need in order to have ideas such as "*yellow, white, heat, cold, soft, hard, bitter, sweet* and all those we call sensible qualities" (Locke, 1690/1964, p. 90). The second source of our ideas is *reflection,* by which Locke meant the "perception of the operations of our own mind within us" (Locke, 1690/1964, p. 90). We can observe ourselves engaged in such operations as "*perception, thinking, doubting, believing, reasoning, knowing, willing*" (Locke, 1690/1964, p. 90), and thus come to have some idea of these activities. If we follow Locke, then self-observation will be the most important source of information about psychological concepts.

For Locke, and for the British Empiricists generally, our understanding is primarily the product of our experience, and not of our reason. In fact, that is what it means to be an empiricist. "Light and colors are busy at hand everywhere, when the eye is but open; . . . it will be easily granted that, if a child were to be kept in a place where he never saw any other but black and white till he were a man, he would have no more ideas of scarlet or green than he that from his childhood never tasted an oyster, or a pine-apple, has of those particular relishes" (Locke, 1690/1964, p. 92). Locke is here suggesting that even basic concepts, such as those of color, must be acquired, along with less common experiences, such as the taste of an oyster.

Simple and Complex Ideas. *Simple ideas,* as the name suggests, cannot be reduced to anything more elementary, such as "the coldness and hardness" felt "in a piece of ice being as distinct ideas in the mind as the smell and whiteness of a lily" (Locke, 1690/1964, p. 99). *Complex ideas* are compounded out of simple ones, and by this process of combination we may arrive at very abstract ideas such as *army, constellation* and, ultimately, *universe* (Locke, 1690/1964, p. 199).

The existence of complex ideas points to the importance of the *association of ideas,* a process we considered earlier when we were discussing Aristotle. While people have many ideas in common, each of us may also have ideas that may strike others as unusual, because each of us have had some idiosyncratic experiences. Moreover, each of us may have particular *sequences* of ideas that "always keep in company, and the one no sooner at any time comes into the understanding but its associate appears with it; and if there are more than two which are thus united, the whole gang, always inseparable, show themselves together" (Locke, 1690/1964, p. 251). An example Locke uses is the way a familiar tune will run itself off after the listener hears only a few notes. Another example comes from education (Locke, 1690/1964):

> *Many children, imputing the pain they endured at school to their books they were corrected for, so join those ideas together that a book becomes their aversion, and they are never reconciled to the study and use of them all their lives after; and thus reading becomes a torment to them, which otherwise possibly they might have made the great pleasure of their lives. (p. 254)*

Locke's (1690/1964, p. 251) view is "custom settles habits of thinking." The beliefs and attitudes we express are the result of the way in which our ideas have become *associated.* As we shall see, many psychologists have regarded the process of association as *the* basic psychological process.

Primary and Secondary Qualities. Objects have *qualities,* by which Locke meant "the power to produce any idea in our mind . . . . Thus a snowball [has] the power to produce in us the ideas of white, cold and round" (Locke, 1690/1964, p. 112). A *primary quality* is one that is in the object itself. For example, the fact that an object is *moving* is a primary quality, because motion is a property of the object itself. When we perceive motion, we are perceiving a primary quality. Other primary qualities include *size* and *number* (how many or how few objects there are). However, objects also have the power to produce experiences in us that are not the same as any property of the object. Locke (1690/1964, p. 112) names "*colors, sounds* and *taste*" as examples. Recall our discussion of Newton's color theory, in which we noted the importance of the distinction between the *stimulus* for color, and the *experience* of color. Locke is making a similar point, by drawing our attention to *secondary qualities* which, unlike primary qualities, do not correspond to the experience to which they give rise. A feather can tickle you, but the tickle is not in the feather, it is only in you.

George Berkeley

Born in Ireland, Berkeley was a precocious intellect who wrote his most important work before he was 30 years old (Warnock, 1987). In his first book, *A New Theory of Vision* (Berkeley, 1709/1910), he argued that there were no unambiguous visual cues to the spatial location of objects. Although Berkeley's argument is both complex and subtle, some inkling of his major point can be gained from an examination of Figure 2.4. Figure 2.4 uses the same concepts as Figure 2.1, but introduces the possibility that surfaces at different distances could look as if they were at the same distance from the observer. As an observer, how could you tell which object was closest to you, since they all yield the same projected surface? It seems as if the information available on your retina would not be enough to enable you to locate objects precisely.

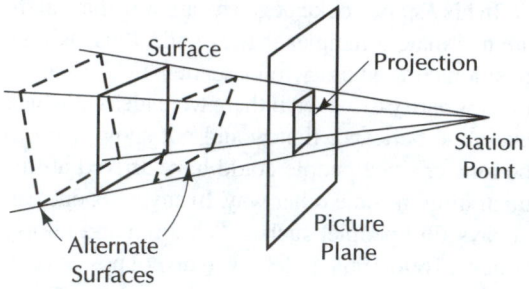

FIGURE 2.4 Three surfaces at three different distances from the eye that might look as if they were the same distance away.

Source: H. A. Sedgwick (1980). The geometry of spatial layout in pictorial representation. In M. A. Hagen (Ed.). *The perception of pictures* (p. 48). New York: Academic Press. Reprinted with permission.

Berkeley (1709/1910) resolved this problem by suggesting that the *sense of touch* provided the observer with an important source of information that supplemented the visual information available.

> *Having of a long time experienced certain ideas, perceivable by touch . . . to have been connected with certain ideas of sight, I do upon perceiving these ideas of sight, forthwith conclude what tangible ideas are . . . like to follow. Looking at an object, I perceive a certain visible figure and color . . . which from what I have formerly observed, determine me to think that if I advanced so many paces or miles, I shall be affected with such and such ideas of touch: so that in truth and strictness of speech, I neither see distance itself nor anything that I take to be at a distance. (pp. 32–33)*

In order to better understand what Berkeley is talking about, consider why it is that you do not see an object as actually getting smaller as it recedes from you. After all, as an object (e.g., a car) gets farther and farther away, it will make a smaller and smaller image on the surface of your retina. However, rather than see the car as shrinking, we see it as staying the same size but getting farther away. This phenomenon is called *size constancy.* Berkeley's explanation is that we remember how far we would have to travel in order to reach an object that yielded a visual image of the size we are currently experiencing. The visual image of an object is *associated* with a previous experience of moving a certain distance in order to touch the object. Perceiving distance is really a form of remembering, and is thus something we must learn. From an empiricist viewpoint like Berkeley's, very young children would not have size constancy, since they lack the requisite experiences.

Here is a concrete illustration from my own experience of the sort of phenomenon dear to the hearts of empiricists. I once wore a set of goggles fitted with a pair of *displacing prisms.* The use of such prismatic lenses has a long tradition in psychology, beginning with *George Stratton* (1897/1964), who wore lenses that made the world appear to be upside down. The goggles I wore had a less spectacular effect—they made everything appear to be displaced to the right. This meant, for example, that if you threw darts at a dartboard, then you would systematically throw the darts too far to the right. However, if you continued to throw darts at the dartboard for a few minutes, you would become more and more accurate. Your visual perception of the dartboard would be brought into line with feedback you were getting from your throwing of the darts. Your action corrects your vision. This illustrates one of Berkeley's points: the perceived location of objects is determined by what you do in relation to them.

If a Tree Falls in the Forest, Does Anybody Hear? This question is the title of a song by Bruce Cockburn (1988). Although Cockburn intends the song to be an environmentalist's lament for our apparent inability to preserve our forests, the title is also reminiscent of one of Berkeley's most famous doctrines. Berkeley (1709/1910, p. 114), argued that "unthinking things" could not "have any existence, out of the minds or thinking things which perceive them." Berkeley's position is often put in terms of the following slogan: *To be is to be perceived.* Nothing exists apart from our experience of it.

Berkeley's doctrine is often treated as being so arcane as to not be worth taking seriously. However, there is an important psychological point behind it. If a tree falls in the forest, and no one is there to hear it, then it is not psychologically real for anyone. An event must be in at least one person's experience in order to be capable of having an effect on anyone's behavior. What is real for us is only what we experience.

David Hume

Hume (1748/1951) was a Scot whose ideas had a profound effect on many subsequent thinkers, including Kant, whom we consider later in the chapter. Hume made incisive observations about such fundamental concepts as *causality* and the *self.*

Causality. Hume (1748/1951, p. 199) observed that "it is a general maxim in philosophy that *whatever begins to exist, must have a cause of existence.*" The category of *causality* is a fundamentally important one. We use it to understand why things are the way that they are. Causality is an idea we can hardly do without. And yet, what does causality actually amount to? If we examine our experience, what do we find that corresponds to our idea of *causality?*

Let us examine a possible cause–effect relationship, adapted from a paper by the Nobel Prize winning psychologist *Herbert Simon* (1954), whom we encounter in a later chapter. Suppose we do a study of employee absenteeism in a particular company. We discover that the average number of absences per week per employee is highly correlated with the average number of children per employee. We would then probably conclude that children make demands of one sort or another on parents' time, which in turn increases absenteeism. That is, we would believe that having children *causes* absenteeism, at least in part. However, notice that what we actually have is a *correlation* between number of children and absenteeism, and nothing more than a correlation. In fact, in any case we can imagine, our notion of causality always boils down to mere correlation.

Hume (1748/1951, p. 71) argued that if we look closely at any cause-effect relationship, then we will "immediately perceive that, even in the most familiar events, . . . we only learn by experience the frequent *conjunction* of objects, without ever being able to comprehend anything like *connexion* between them." There is nothing in our experience corresponding to a 'cause,' if by a cause we mean some 'necessary connection' between two events (Pears, 1990, p. 75). When one billiard ball hits another, there is only the experience of one ball moving followed by the other ball moving. "And experience only teaches us how one event constantly follows another; without instructing us in the secret connexion which binds them together, and renders them inseparable" (Hume, 1748/1951, p. 67).

We do not perceive causality. The experience of causality is the result of an association built up between one event and another. After repeatedly experiencing one event (e.g., having many children) followed by another (e.g., absenteeism), we find it natural to think of the latter as the effect of the former. Thus Hume's (1748/1951, p. 78) definition of cause as "*an object followed by another, and whose appearance always conveys the thought to that other.*"

If correct, Hume's conclusion places sharp limits on what it is that we can ever hope to understand. We can never have a deep insight into the inner workings of nature. Our knowledge can never amount to more than a set of beliefs based only on our experience of what goes with what.

Hume is usually regarded as a *skeptic,* or someone who finds it difficult to believe that certain knowledge is possible. Hume's skeptical attitude is well expressed by the following quotation (Hume, 1757/1927):

> *The whole is a riddle, an enigma, an inexplicable mystery. Doubt, uncertainty, suspense of judgment appear the only result of our most accurate scrutiny, concerning this subject. (p. 283)*

The Self. Recall that Descartes had begun his inquiries by being certain of only one thing: that he existed. Indeed, it has seemed obvious to many people that "we are every moment intimately conscious of what we call our *self;* that we feel its existence and its continuance in existence; and are certain, beyond the evidence of a demonstration, both of its perfect identity and simplicity" (Hume, 1757/1927, p. 226). Hume, however, was not convinced that the self is so easily grasped. In order to see why Hume thought that it was not at all obvious that the self existed, we first need to introduce his distinction between *impressions* and *ideas.* By an *impression,* Hume (1757/1927, p. 16) meant "all our more lively perceptions, when we hear, or see, or feel, or love, or hate, or desire, or will. And impressions are distinguished from ideas, which are the less lively perceptions, of which we are conscious, when we reflect on any of those sensations or movements above mentioned." All of our ideas are derived from impressions. We have an idea of ourselves, but, Hume (1757/1927, p. 227) wondered, "from what impression could this idea be derived?"

> *For my part, when I enter most intimately into what I call* myself, *I always stumble on some particular perception or other, of heat or cold, light or shade, love or hatred, pain or pleasure. I can never catch* myself *at any time without a perception, and can never observe anything but the perception. (p. 227)*

Since the *self* would appear to be a central concept in psychology, its status its particularly important. Hume is suggesting that there is nothing that uniquely corresponds to the concept of a self. Our belief that we possess a self is an illusion. If we honestly examine our experience, then we will discover that all we really possess is a series of impressions of one sort or another. Of course, many people have resisted Hume's stark conclusion, and later on we will see how they have tried to keep the self alive.

Additional Reading on This Topic. An excellent review of the British Empiricists is in Bennett

(1971). Much of contemporary neuropsychology has an associationist flavor, and this is well captured by Buckingham (1984). The close relationship between the Newtonian world view and associationism is discussed by Smith (1987).

MARY WOLLSTONECRAFT (1759–1797)

You will have noticed that we have, until now, only been discussing the work of men, and mainly of European men at that. Until recently, there has been a tendency for history to be only the story of Dead White European Males, or DWEMs (e.g., Knox, 1993). This is particularly unfortunate in psychology, in which most of the students are women.

It is generally believed that women have a lower status in contemporary North American and European society than do men. One reason for this conclusion is the fact that women typically find employment in occupations of a relatively low status (Archer & Lloyd, 1982, chap. 8). During the prehistoric era, women may have enjoyed a higher status relative to men than they do now (Tanner, 1983), but masculine roles appear to have had a higher status than feminine ones throughout most of our recorded history (Hartmann, 1976). Generally speaking, this has been true for disciplines such as psychology, in which the high status roles have traditionally tended to be filled by men, with the rest being left for women. Furomoto (1987) has shown that

> *historically women have been relegated to the bottom of the professional hierarchy, to "the 'dirtiest' areas of professional service . . . those involving the most human contact with all its attendant complexities" (Brunberg & Tomes, 1982, pp. 287–288). More specifically, during the nineteenth century women assumed primary care of such problematic clienteles as the young, the poor, the immigrant, the intemperate and the sick. The best employment opportunities for women thus came to be found in the so-called helping professions, such as social work and public health. . . . The high status branch of the field, academic psychology, abstract and isolated within its ivory tower, was never welcoming to women, and few were able to find a place there. (p. 109)*

Problems similar to those described by Furomoto (1987) were perceived with extraordinary clarity by Mary Wollstonecraft in the late eighteenth century. Wollstonecraft may already be familiar to you as the mother of Mary Shelley, the author of *Frankenstein* (1818/1963). However, our interest is in Wollstonecraft's book *A Vindication of the Rights of Women* (1792/1988).

Universal Education

Wollstonecraft (1792/1988) argued that women had the right to education, which they had previously been largely denied. She spoke out against those who believed that "woman would be unsexed by acquiring strength of body and mind, and that beauty, soft bewitching beauty would no longer adorn the daughters of men. I am of a very different opinion, for I think that, on the contrary, we should then see dignified beauty, and true grace, . . ." and went on to argue that "were boys and girls permitted to pursue the same studies together, those graceful decencies might early be inculcated which produce modesty without those sexual distinctions that taint the mind." (p. 165)

Although Wollstonecraft believed, as did empiricists such as Locke, that there were no innate ideas, and that the mind is a blank slate or "*tabula rasa* on which experience must write," she also believed that the properly educated mind could discover things for itself (Sapiro, 1992, pp. 53–55). This ability to draw out the implications of what one had learned should be a principal goal of education. The capacity to think independently could only be fostered by an educational system that encouraged this form of behavior, and did not require children to merely imitate their teachers and blindly obey their instructions (Sapiro, 1992, p. 113).

To attain these goals, Wollstonecraft (1792/1988, p. 167) proposed a system of education in which "boys and girls might be educated together, absolutely free and open to all classes," at least for the younger children. Treating women equally in the educational system would undermine the tradition whereby women were "shut out from all political and civil employments; for by thus narrowing their minds they are rendered unfit to fulfill the peculiar duties which nature has assigned them" (Wollstonecraft, 1792/1988, p. 169).

Although Wollstonecraft wanted women to break with some aspects of their traditional roles, she did not argue that they should abandon these roles altogether. "The conclusion I wish to draw is obvious; make women rational creatures, and free citizens, and they will quickly become good wives, and mothers; that is—if men do not neglect the duties of husbands and fathers" (Wollstonecraft, 1792/1988, p. 178).

The Importance of Emotion

As Burns (1979) observed, Wollstonecraft had (for her time) a very sophisticated view of the relation between *emotion* and *reason.* Emotion has often been thought of as entirely a bodily process, less abstract and "psychological" than reason. For example, the *Oxford English Dictionary* (1989) gives these two early meanings of the word *emotion:* "a moving stirring perturbation (in physical sense)" and "agitation or disturbance of mind, feeling, passion; any vehement or excited mental state." Often there is a stereotype of women that they are more *emotional* and less *rational* than men. If emotional people are conceived of as susceptible to "disturbances of mind," then this stereotype is very unflattering to women. Without accepting the stereotype, Wollstonecraft nonetheless accepted the notion that women were more influenced by their feelings than were men. However, she also introduced the idea that emotions were not merely bodily 'agitations.' She suggested that feeling could also provide a point of view on a situation that supplemented the point of view given to us by reason alone. Wollstonecraft used the word *sensibility* to refer to this aspect of emotion. "Sensibility is not a cold calculation of what is right; it is a spontaneous warmth of virtuous emotion. To use literary conventions, reason is the proper work of the head, sensibility is the proper work of the heart" (Sapiro, 1992, p. 65).

Nowadays we are more comfortable with the notion that emotion can provide information about ourselves and others that is obtainable in no other way. We have phrases such as "being in touch with our feelings" that convey this sentiment. However, before the efforts of Wollstonecraft and others that we study later on, emotion did not have the same dignity as did other psychological processes such as *reason* and *choice.* Throughout the nineteenth century, interest in emotion as a psychological process continued to grow, and in the twentieth century the psychology of emotion has become a central part of the discipline.

The Utopian Tradition in Psychology

Wollstonecraft belongs to a somewhat neglected aspect of the history of psychology that historians such as Manuel (1966) and Morawski (1982) have identified as *the Utopian tradition* in psychology. Like Wollstonecraft, many psychologists actively seek to improve the well-being of themselves and others through changing the nature of the society in which they live. Such social activism is characteristic of many twentieth-century psychologists whom we examine in subsequent chapters.

Additional Reading on This Topic. Over the years, Wollstonecraft has served as a beacon for many social scientists, including the famous American anthropologist Ruth Benedict (1959).

> *In the National Portrait Gallery hangs a picture of Mary Wollstonecraft, a picture of her as she was a scant few months before her death. I remember the child I was when I saw it first, haunted by the terror of youth before experience. I wanted so desperately to know how other women had saved their souls alive. And the woman in the little frame arrested me, this woman with the auburn hair, and the sad steady brown eyes and the gallant poise of the head. She* had *saved her soul alive; it looked out from her eyes unafraid. (p. 519)*

John Stuart Mill (1806–1873) was an important nineteenth-century British Empiricist, whose book *The Subjection of Women* (1861/1986) is a famous argument against "the legal subordination of one sex to the other" and in favor of the "principle of perfect equality, admitting no power or privilege on the one side, nor disability on the other" (p. 7).

IMMANUEL KANT (1724–1804)

Kant conforms to one persistent stereotype of an intellectual, that of a person who is "strongly influenced by ideas, though his ideas have their origin not in objective data but in his subjective foundation. He will follow his ideas . . . inwards and not outwards. . . . His judgment appears cold, inflexible, arbitrary and ruthless, because it relates far less to the object than to the subject . . . it always bypasses the object and leaves one with a feeling of the subject's superiority" (Jung, 1921/1976). As we will see, Kant tried to demonstrate that Hume's skepticism was wrong, and that one could reach definite conclusions through the use of reason. One of these conclusions was that we could arrive at certain necessary truths about our subjective experience, although nothing could be known about the world external to ourselves.

Kant was born and raised in Konigsberg (Germany), and reportedly never left it, becoming a professor in 1770. "Kant led an uneventful life: no change, no travel, no reaching out for the unusual, not much interest outside his study room and university classroom. Kant's life was a life of thought. . . . Rain or shine, peace or war, revolution or counter-revolution had less effect on his life than a new book he read, and certainly counted less than a new idea that grew in his own mind. Kant's thoughts were to him the center of the universe, even more so than Descartes' *Cogito* was to Descartes" (Wolman, 1968, p. 229).

Kant's philosophy is often understood in contrast to Hume's skepticism, and, indeed, Kant credited Hume with making him think deeply about fundamental issues. We saw earlier how Hume had shown that some concepts that we take for granted are actually quite empty. For example, Hume appeared to show that there really was no *self* and nothing corresponding to our concept of *causality* than mere correlation. In order to meet Hume's challenge, Kant had to show that such concepts were meaningful even though they were "neither logically necessary, nor derived from experience" (Beck, 1950, p. x).

Kant's "Second Copernican Revolution"

In order to discover the nature of our ideas, Kant recommended that we take an approach similar to that taken by *Copernicus* (1473–1543) in his attempt to understand planetary motion. As you may remember, Copernicus's revolutionary way of understanding the solar system was to insist that the earth was not at its center. "Failing of satisfactory progress in explaining the movements of the heavenly bodies on the supposition that they all revolved around the spectator, he tried whether he might not have better success if he made the spectator to revolve and the stars remain at rest" (Kant, 1787/1965, p. 22). In other words, Copernicus completely changed the frame of reference within which planetary motion was explained. Similarly, Kant attempted to completely change the frame of reference within which the origin of our concepts was understood. Kant changed the frame of reference used by empiricists such as Hume. They believed that our concepts were derived from events in the external world. Kant argued that it was a mistake to assume that a concept such as *causality* referred to something outside ourselves, and insisted that our experience was actually shaped by our concepts, rather than the other way around. In order to discover the nature of our concepts we need look no further than ourselves.

Kant's *second Copernican revolution* involves denying that our experience is completely determined by events outside ourselves. On the contrary, the person ultimately constructs his or her own experience.

> *Instead of measuring the content, meaning and truth . . . [of our concepts] by something extraneous which is supposed to be reproduced in them, we must find in*

> *. . . [our concepts] themselves the measure and criterion for truth and intrinsic meaning. [Our concepts] are not imitations, but organs of reality, since it is solely by their agency that anything becomes an object . . . [and] is made visible to us. (Cassirer, 1946, p. 8)*

Without our concepts, we would not have experience. Our concepts make our experience possible.

This may sound mysterious, but the phenomena Kant has in mind are actually quite simple and obvious. Kant observed that everyone (not just scientists) tends to organize their experiences in terms of causes and effects. We impose cause and effect relationships *on* the world, rather than observing them *in* the world. Perhaps you have had an experience of the sort that Kant had in mind. For example, "when a gust of wind blows a door shut, and at the same time an electric light happens to go on at the other end of a corridor, the impression of a causal relation is forced upon us" (Michotte, 1963, p. 16). Whenever we observe two events occurring close together in space and time there is a tendency for us to experience one as causing the other. Our minds spontaneously and inevitably organize our experiences, using concepts such as causality. Another example that illustrates the tendency for us to impose our own organization on our experience is given in Box 2.3.

Kant (1783/1950) was not suggesting that everyone organizes every aspect of their experience in the same way. Individual experiences may be unique. "When we say, 'The room is warm, sugar sweet, and wormwood bitter,' we have only subjectively valid judgments. I do not at all expect that I or any other person shall always find it as I now do" (Kant, 1783/1950, p. 47). However, in addition to having our own unique experiences, we can and do make judgments that are much more general. (Kant, 1783/1950) gives the example of someone saying

> *"When the sun shines on the stone, it grows warm." This judgment, however often I and others may have perceived it, is a mere judgment of perception and contains no necessity; perceptions are only usually conjoined in this manner. But if I say, "The sun warms the stone," I add to the perception a concept of the understanding, namely, that of cause, which necessarily connects with the concept of sunshine that of heat. . . . (p. 49)*

My conclusion that one thing (the sun) has caused another thing (the rock) to become warm is more than just a sequence of perceptions; it is a result of applying the concept of causality *to* my perceptions. For Kant, this is not an isolated example, but an illustration of the way that concepts shape our experience. As the example in Box 2.3 shows, our judgment is determined by the concepts we use to think about a situation, not simply by our "impression" of the situation.

Can Psychology Be a Science Like Other Sciences?

Like other intellectuals of his day, Kant took Newtonian physics to be the model for any true science (Friedman, 1990). Kant was enormously impressed by Newton's ability to give his laws a mathematical expression, and claimed "that in any particular theory of nature we can find only so much of real science as we can find mathematics . . . hence any theory of nature will contain only so much of real science as it permits the application of mathematics" (as cited by Cassirer, 1945/1963, p. 62). We have already seen how intimately the history of mathematics and science are interwoven. In Kant's case, the identification of science with mathematics means that psychology is necessarily excluded from the sciences, properly so-called (Mischel, 1967).

In order to see why Kant believed that psychology could never achieve the status of a true science, we must explore his distinction between the *external sense* and the *internal sense.* Our experience of what goes on outside of us is given to us through our external senses, such as vision. Our visual experience is organized spatially in relation to ourselves, such that things are near or far, high or low, left or right (Kant, 1768/1968; Bryant, Tversky & Franklin, 1992). Insofar as we can understand what goes on in this spatially extended world outside of

BOX 2.3

Finding the Area of a Rectangle

Look at Figure 2.5. Imagine that the figure labeled A is an inelastic string stretched tight around four small posts so that it takes the form of a square that is 2 inches by 2 inches. You know how to calculate the area of the square. You multiply 2 by 2 and get 4 square inches. Now look at the figure marked B. In this figure the same string has been stretched tight around the same four posts, but the posts have been moved so that we now have a rectangle that is narrower and longer than figure A. Now, quickly, answer the following question: Is the area of figure B equal to, larger than, or smaller than the area of figure A? If you are like most adults (including me when I was first shown this problem by A. Jonckheere), you will conclude that figure B has the *same* area as figure A. The reason you will give is that although the second figure is narrower than the first, it is also longer, and these changes compensate for each other. Therefore, the two areas must remain the same. Furthermore, if you are like most adults, you will persist in this conclusion as you are shown figure C and figure D, although you may begin to doubt yourself when you see figure E.

As it turns out, we are mistaken if we conclude that these figures all have the same area. We saw that figure A had an area of 4 square inches. Suppose that figure B is .5 inch longer, and therefore .5 inch narrower. That would make it 2.5 inches long and 1.5 inches wide. Multiply 1.5 by 2.5 and you will get 3.8 inches, which is less than the 4 square inches of the original figure. Similarly, suppose that figure C is another .5 inch longer and .5 inch narrower than figure B. That makes it 3 inches long and 1 inch wide, for an area of 3 square inches, or less than either of the previous figures. As a matter of fact, the figures get progressively smaller in area, as you can work out for yourself in the remaining cases.

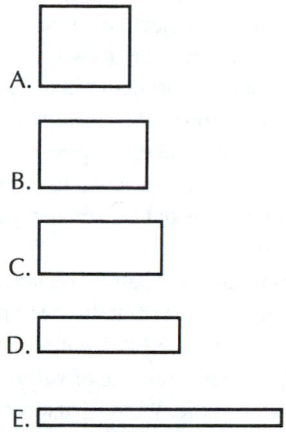

FIGURE 2.5 Which figure has the largest area?

Why do we make this mistake? A Kantian would give something like the following explanation. We do not rely on our perception of each individual rectangle to make a judgment about its area. Rather, we understand the area of *any* rectangular figure as being determined by multiplying the height and width of the figure. We apply this way of thinking to our perception of the figure. In general, it is *not* the things themselves, but the way that we think about them that determines the judgments we make.

The preceding problem is discussed by Kline (1985, p. 33), whose book contains a good introduction to Kant's view of mathematics. For another example of the way our perception and our reason can lead to opposite conclusions, see Benjafield (1969a).

us, this understanding is provided by disciplines like physics. The data of physics are given by our external senses, and Newton showed that mathematics can describe what is given by our external senses. However, our experience of what goes on *inside* ourselves is not organized spatially, but temporally. Our subjective experience is organized in terms of *time*. We have a sense of things happening before and after this moment. Kant believed that psychology has as its subject matter the data of this internal sense, and he argued that these data cannot be organized mathematically. Therefore, the data of psychology cannot rest firmly on a mathematical foundation, and psychology can never be a true science. "Since there can be no pure, mathematical science of mind for objects of inner sense, whose only form is time, we have no way of understanding why inner states must occur in the way they do" (Mischel, 1967, p. 603). Psychology can only provide a crudely empirical description of our subjective states, and cannot provide us with any deep understanding of why our personal experiences are the way that they are.

The notion that there can be no scientific study of our inner life is a recurrent theme in psychology. In what follows, we will see some psychologists attempt to show that a science of *subjective experience* really is possible. We will also see other psychologists attempt to show that psychology is actually *not* about inner experience at all, but about *behavior,* which is something we experience through our external senses. Perhaps a science of behavior is the answer, although Kant would not have thought so (Mischel, 1967, p. 605). There are still other psychologists who are less concerned that psychology be a true science, and more concerned that it faithfully represent the nature of our subjective experience. It is this last group that most closely approximates the kind of psychology that Kant thought was possible. It is up to you to decide which of these alternatives, if any, adequately comes to grips with the problems Kant raised.

Additional Reading on This Topic. For a taste of the kind of empirical psychology that followed Kant in the nineteenth century, see Hilgard (1980). Some of Kant's own writings are quite "psychological," particularly his little book *Observations on the Beautiful and the Sublime* (Kant, 1763/1960).

CHARLES DARWIN (1809–1882)

Like Kant, Darwin thought deeply about the relation between people and the world in which they live. Unlike Kant, Darwin was much more interested in exploring the external world (Jung, 1921/1976, p. 383). By thinking about what he found on these explorations, Darwin reached conclusions that helped bring about a revolutionary change in the way that many people think about themselves.

Observing the behavior of Charles Darwin as an undergraduate student, it would have been hard to predict his future eminence as a great scientist. Although he came from a family with a rich intellectual tradition (see Box 2.4), he did not regard his own formal education as much of a preparation for the creative work he was to do later in his life (Gruber, 1981, p. 73). About his years attending Cambridge University (1828–1831), Darwin (1892/1958) later wrote:

> *[M]y time was sadly wasted there, and worse than wasted. From my passion for shooting and for hunting, and, when this failed, for riding across the country, I got into a sporting set, including some dissipated low-minded young men. We used often to dine together in the evening, though these dinners often included men of a higher stamp, and we sometimes drank too much, with jolly singing and playing at cards afterwards. I know that I ought to feel ashamed of days and evenings thus spent but as some of my friends were very pleasant, and we were all in the highest spirits, I cannot help looking back to these times with much pleasure. (pp. 19–20)*

Thus described, Darwin's undergraduate experience sounds not very different from that of a great many undergraduates, both then and now. However, Darwin, in common with many other former undergraduates, appeared to exaggerate "the Bacchanalian nature of these parties" (F. Darwin, 1892/1958, p. 20), and his time at Cambridge may actually have given him a useful framework for his future work (Gruber, 1981, p. 82).

In some important ways Darwin's background resembles that of many highly innovative people. Simonton (1984, 1988) has demonstrated that people who make creative contributions to our culture often have the following characteristics:

- They suffer the loss of a parent when young.
- They receive neither too much nor too little formal education.

Darwin lost his mother in 1817, when he was 8 years old (Darwin, 1892/1958, p. 5), and his formal education stopped when he received his B.A. from

Box 2.4

The Evolution of "Evolution"

Evolution was not a word invented by Darwin. The history of this very important word is given by the *Oxford English Dictionary* (*OED*), and may be summarized as follows:

- One of the oldest uses of the word is to denote the process of *unfolding,* or opening out, as when a bud flowers.
- Darwin's grandfather, *Erasmus Darwin* (1731–1802) was apparently the first to use *evolution* to refer to the process whereby an organism develops from immaturity to maturity.
- The phrase *theory of evolution* appears to have originated with the Swiss naturalist *Charles Bonnet* (1720–1793), who was one of the foremost advocates of the *theory of preformation.* According to this theory "embryonic features of a given species unfolded simultaneously; all limbs separated themselves at the same time and grew at exactly the same rate; none came before or after the other. Growth [was] nothing more than a swelling up of parts already present" (Grinder, 1967, p. 2).
- It was not until the nineteenth century that *evolution* came to mean the process whereby different species originate from earlier forms of life. The *OED* credits Darwin's friends, the geologist *Charles Lyell* (1797–1875) and the botanist *Joseph Hooker* (1817–1911), with helping to introduce this meaning of the word. It is interesting that Darwin (1859/1964) himself never used the word *evolution* in the first edition of his classic work, *The Origin of Species* (Toulmin, 1972, p. 331). In its place, Darwin used the phrase *descent with modification* (R. O'Hara, personal communication, September, 1993).
- It is generally agreed that *Herbert Spencer* (1820–1903) did the most to make *evolution* a household word. We will thoroughly explore Spencer's ideas in Chapter 3.

Cambridge in 1831. Simonton (1984, 1988) speculates that the early loss of a parent forces children to think and do things for themselves, rather than simply take over their parents' ideas and habits. Of course, one needs a basic education in order to be acquainted with fundamental facts in a discipline, but too much education may lead to rigid habits of thought that stultify creativity. Darwin did not have this problem. Of course by no means everyone who loses a parent or who attains a moderate level of education will become a successful innovator! Darwin also had other advantages, such as his family's intellectual tradition. Moreover, it was not so much Darwin's background as what he proceeded to do with it that brought about the theory of evolution.

***The Voyage of the* Beagle.** In his autobiography, Darwin (1892/1958, p. 6) observed that his "taste for natural history, and more especially for collecting was well developed" even as a schoolboy. Thus, it is not entirely surprising to find Darwin serving as a naturalist aboard the *Beagle,* which was in the charge of a Captain Fitz-Roy. The *Beagle* left Plymouth (England) on December 27, 1831, bound for South America, and did not return to England until October 2, 1836. Darwin's job was to record the geological formations and collect specimens of the animals found in the various places the *Beagle* visited.

> *During the first two years my old passion for shooting survived in nearly full force, and I shot myself all the birds and animals for my collection; but gradually I gave up my gun more and more, and finally altogether, to my servant, as shooting interfered with my work. . . . I discovered, though unconsciously and insensibly, that the pleasure of observing and reasoning was a much higher one than that of skill and sport. (Darwin, 1892/1958, pp. 29–30)*

Darwin took a copy of Charles Lyell's (1830–1833/1969) *Principles of Geology* with him on his voyage. Lyell had argued that the earth was of a very great age, and that all the changes that had taken place since its beginning could be explained in terms of purely natural forces (Eiseley, 1956/1987, pp. 67–68). This provided Darwin with a *historical* framework within which to think about the ways in which the population of organisms in an area changes. "According to Lyell, change in fauna and flora could largely be explained in terms of organisms having moved from place to place, limited by barriers and ecological influences. The aim of biogeography, as Darwin was developing it, was to trace species to their places of origin in the light of their capacity for dispersal and the history of geological change" (Ghiselin, 1983, p. 65).

Darwin began to go beyond this simple historical framework as a result of observations he made as the voyage progressed. The most famous of these observations took place in 1835 in the Galapagos Islands, which are located off the west coast of South America. Darwin discovered some finches. "The finches are of special interest, for although obviously closely related they have become separated off into at least 13 distinct species showing extraordinary modifications of the beak in accordance with different modes of life" (Hindle, 1983, p. 67). This, together with other, similar observations, suggested that all species had not been created by God at the beginning of time, and remained invariant thereafter. Rather it began to seem possible that new species could emerge as descendants of other species.

The Development of the Theory of Evolution. When Darwin returned to England, he began to ruminate about his findings. He first considered the emergence of different species in terms of the theory originally developed by *Jean Baptiste Lamarck* (1744–1829). Lamarck (1809/1914) promoted the *law of the inheritance of acquired characteristics.* This law held that animals can acquire characteristics in their lifetime that they can pass along to their immediate descendants. Useful habits acquired by an animal in one generation may not only be passed along to offspring, but the structure of the animal may change as a consequence. The most famous example used by Lamarck is the giraffe. The giraffe typically lives in regions devoid of grass, in which the only food source comes from trees. As a result of habitually reaching for leaves high up in trees, the giraffe has acquired both long legs and a long neck. Lyell (1853/1979, pp. 12–13) noted that Lamarck had also speculated on the possibility that humans had evolved from orangutans, through a very slow process. As a result of "the habit of climbing trees, and of hanging on by grasping the boughs with their feet as with hands," the forelimbs changed from being used as feet to being used as hands, and walking upright became necessary. Lamarckianism had a powerful influence during the nineteenth century, although, as we shall see, it was supplanted by Darwin's own theory.

More important than Lamarck in shaping Darwin's thinking was *Thomas Malthus* (1766–1834). Darwin read Malthus's (1798/1956) *Essay on the Principle of Population As It Affects the Future Improvement of Society* in 1838. Malthus (1798/1956, p. 1193) had argued that "the population has a constant tendency to increase beyond the means of subsistence." According to Malthus's calculations, the food supply increases arithmetically, while the population increases geometrically. What this means is illustrated in Figure 2.6, which is based on the same numbers used by Malthus. Suppose we start with a population that requires only as much food as is available. Over a period of 200 years, the population would increase to over

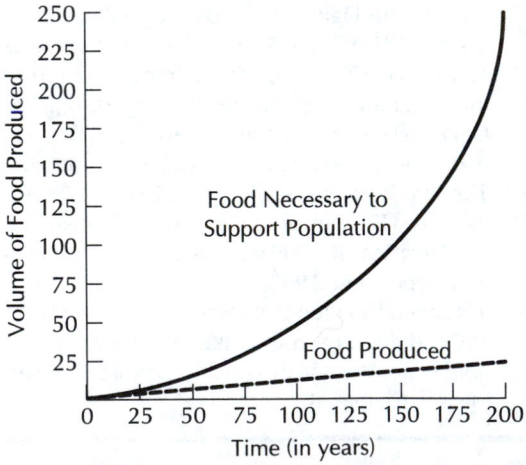

FIGURE 2.6 Malthus's calculation of the relationship between food produced and food necessary to support the population.

250 times what it was initially, while the food supply would only increase to a level 9 times what it was initially. The necessary result is too many people competing for too little food. Some people will be losers, and die as a result.

While Malthus's precise calculations may have been faulty, they still provided Darwin with the idea that it was necessary for individuals to compete for resources in order to survive (Ghiselin, 1983, p. 66). "Malthus dichotomized nature into humankind on the one hand, and its food supply on the other. . . . Darwin was interested in describing all of nature, including humankind, in the same terms. Struggle is not only for food but against all the conditions of life" (Keegan & Gruber, 1983, p. 19). As a result of this struggle, some species become extinct, but others adapt and survive.

Darwin went on to progressively refine his views, and eventually published the theory for which he became justly famous. The theory was based on *natural selection,* or *the survival of the fittest.*

> *Let it also be borne in mind how infinitely complex and close-fitting are the mutual relations of all organic beings to each other and to their physical conditions of life; and consequently what infinitely varied diversities of structure might be of use to each being under changing conditions of life. Can it, then, be thought improbable, seeing that variations useful to man have undoubtedly occurred, that other variations useful in some way to each being in the great and complex battle of life, should occur in the course of many successive generations? If such do occur, can we doubt (remembering that many more individuals are born than can possibly survive) that individuals having any advantage, however slight, over others, would have the best chance of surviving and of procreating their kind? On the other hand, we may feel sure that any variation in the least degree injurious would be rigidly destroyed. This preservation of favourable individual differences and variations, and the destruction of those which are injurious, I have called Natural Selection, or the Survival of the Fittest. (Darwin, 1859/1964, pp. 63–64)*

The preceding quotation is from *The Origin of Species,* which Darwin did not publish until 1859, 23 years after the return of the *Beagle* to England. There has been a lot of speculation about why it took Darwin so long to announce his theory (Richards, 1983). Some have argued that Darwin was afraid of the social consequences of presenting a view that apparently contradicts traditionally religious conceptions of the origins of human beings. Others have suggested that Darwin's theory emerged only slowly, and required many years to become fully developed. Whatever the reasons, Darwin had the shock of his life when on June 18, 1858 he received an essay from *Alfred Russel Wallace* (1823–1913). Wallace wanted Darwin's opinion of the essay, in which Wallace demonstrated that he understood the process of evolution in very much the same way that Darwin did. Darwin had previously confided some of his views on evolution to friends such as the geologist Lyell, and they had warned him that if he did not publish his theory, someone else would beat him to it. "Darwin at once wrote to Charles Lyell: 'Your words have come true with a vengeance—that I should be forestalled—I never saw a more striking coincidence. . . . So all my originality, whatever it may amount to, will be smashed, though my book, if it will ever have any value, will not be deteriorated, as all the labour consists in the application of the theory'" (Hindle, 1983, p. 67). Darwin was prepared to let Wallace get the credit, but it was arranged that the theory should be announced in a joint paper given to the Linnean Society on July 1, 1858 ("On the Tendency of Species to Form Varieties; And on the Perpetuation of Varieties and Species by Natural Means of Selection," by C. Darwin and A. Wallace). Darwin then wrote and published the *Origin of Species* in a little over a year.

It is important to be clear about the difference between *natural selection* as Darwin described it, and the Lamarckian principle of *the inheritance of acquired characteristics.* Lamarck's view was that organisms attempt to adapt to their environments, and adaptations acquired during their lifetime can be passed along to their offspring. By contrast, Darwin proposed that the chief mechanism of evolution was what has come to be called *blind variation and selective retention* (Campbell, 1960).

Within each generation "variation in nature is so inexhaustible that there are never two individuals that are completely identical and equally well adapted" to the environment in which they happen to find themselves (Mayr, 1991, p. 123). These variations are *blind,* in the sense that they occur by chance, and without any foresight on the part of the organism as to their adaptive consequences. Those variations that happen to be adaptive tend to be *retained,* in that they "have the greatest probability to survive, to reproduce, and to transmit their attributes to the next generation" (Mayr, 1991, p. 123). Although Darwin allowed Lamarckianism a place in his theory, it is now discredited as a theory of evolution (e.g., Dawkins, 1983, 1988), in favor of the principle of natural selection.

To see how the theory of evolution conflicted with established religious accounts of the origins of human beings, note the difference between the principle of natural selection and the world view of St. Thomas Aquinas we considered earlier (see Chapter 1). The conflict between 'Darwinism' and traditional theology has never been resolved, and a great many people continue to believe that human beings were created by God. In the *Origin of Species,* Darwin left the door slightly open to creationism by admitting "the possibility that the whole lawful system of material nature might have had a supernatural Creator, a First Cause, who then left all else to 'secondary causes'" (Gruber, 1981, p. 210). However, Darwin never suggested that God directly intervened in the process of evolution once it had begun, and Darwin's views were persistently under attack by conventionally religious people throughout his lifetime. Nevertheless, Darwin was buried in Westminster Abbey, near to Isaac Newton (Stone, 1983), a tribute to the immense impact of his work.

Darwin and Psychology

The influence of evolutionary theory on psychology has been very great indeed. As Heidbreder (1933, p. 106) observed, Darwinian theory implied that psychologists had to study people in terms of their "development both genetic and phylogenetic, [their] position in the array of animal species, and the means by which [they] adapt themselves to [the] environment." Each of these implications became an area of study in psychology. We will examine these areas in great detail in subsequent chapters, and only briefly mention them here.

- *Comparative psychology.* Darwinism led to the idea that there are important similarities between people and other animals. This suggests that a great deal can be learned about people by comparing them with other species. Thus, the study of animals should be part of psychology (e.g., Bitterman, 1967).
- *Individual differences.* Another Darwinian idea that profoundly influenced psychology was *variation* between members of the same species (Herrnstein & Boring, 1966, p. 407). Individual members of a species differed from each other, and these *individual differences* determined how well or how poorly individuals adapted to the environment. The measurement of individual differences has been the focus of a great deal of work in psychology (e.g., Anastasi, 1965).
- Many other topics of study in psychology also received a Darwinian stamp. For example, Darwin's (1872/1955) *The Expression of the Emotions in Man and Animals* deeply influenced the psychology of *emotion.* Darwin (1859/1964) also discussed the role *instincts* play in human behavior, and the instinct concept has been used in many areas of psychology from ethology to social psychology (Beer, 1983). The subtitle of Darwin's (1871/1964) *The Descent of Man* is *Selection in Relation to Sex,* and the study of *sexuality* was a central feature of Darwin's work (e.g., Ghiselin, 1966, chap. 9). It is not surprising that sexuality subsequently became a preoccupation of many psychological theories, of which Freud's is the most obvious example. Finally, although *child psychology* began before Darwin, he still contributed a framework that has informed the work of many developmental psychologists (Vidal, Buscaglia & Voneche, 1983). However, Darwin's influence on

developmental psychology was not as great as has sometimes been supposed (Charlesworth, 1992).

Additional Reading on This Topic. A wonderful compilation of Darwiniana is available on a multimedia CD-ROM created by Goldie (1992). This disk contains the text of several of Darwin's major works, as well as a Darwin bibliography and many intriguing images and sounds relevant to the study of evolutionary theory.

STUDYING THE HISTORY OF PSYCHOLOGY

Ixion's Wheel or Jacob's Ladder?

We have examined several famous thinkers who have left their mark on subsequent theories. Now we can look back over this history, and see if there are any patterns in it, in addition to those we have already considered in Box 1.2 (page 14). Anytime that one takes an overview of the history of thought, there will be two contrasting patterns that can be perceived. The distinguished historian Frank Manuel (1965, p. 4) called these the *progressive* and the *cyclical:* "On the one hand the historical world seen as movement either to a fixed end, or to an indefinite end that defines itself in the course of the progression, history as novelty creating and always variant; on the other hand circularity, eternal recurrence, return to the beginning of things, sheer reiteration or similar recapitulation." Manuel (1965) used Ixion and Jacob as personifications of this polarity. Ixion is a figure from ancient Greek mythology, who was condemned to rotate forever on a wheel of fire. In the Bible (Genesis 28:12), Jacob "dreamed that there was a ladder set up on the earth and the top of it reached to heaven." Manuel (1965, pp. 5–6) asked us to consider whether history is "like Ixion in Hades tied to a perpetually revolving wheel" or like "Jacob dreaming of the ladder that reaches up to the heavens?"

Progress in any discipline, including psychology, cannot be taken for granted. Psychology may not always get better and better. Sometimes psychology is cyclical. An idea may go out of fashion for a while, then get forgotten, and finally come back again as a "new" idea. Berlyne (1975) put it this way:

> *That many disputes now dividing psychologists are essentially rehashes of debates that have gone on for centuries, or for some cases for millennia, is hardly an original observation. In psychology, as in clothing, there is a limited number of possibilities. Nether garments must be based on the trousers principle, the skirt principle, or the loin cloth principle, and in each case, there is a finite number of discriminable gradations between floor length and zero. There is continuous oscillation among the possible alternatives, but there has to be some passage of time before what was once grotesquely frumpish can reappear as the refreshingly unconventional. (p. 79)*

Knowledge of the history of psychology should put us in the position of being able to detect those parts of the current psychological scene that are genuinely novel, and those parts that are recapitulations of previous ideas.

Of course, it is entirely possible that psychology *both* progresses *and* is cyclical. Ideas may keep being "rediscovered," but understood in progressively more sophisticated ways. A *spiral* may be a useful symbol of such a process (e.g., Piaget, 1970, pp. 124–125), in which ideas recur, but at higher and higher levels. The ideas of the people we have already considered will be harked back to again and again by the people we will now go on to consider. Modern thinkers "have the advantage of time and can choose prototypes from a greater array of models. Moderns can learn from many more sources than could ancients, and though nature is no more prolific in genius . . . in one generation than in its predecessor, sheer accumulation of examples itself becomes an advantage" (Manuel, 1969, pp. 66–67).

Person or *Zeitgeist*?

The ideas of psychologists do not come only from the past. Individual creativity also plays its part. In addition, it is impossible to neglect the role that "prevailing ideologies and/or the socioeconomic situation of the period" play in shaping ideas (Mayr, 1991, p. 123). In addition to the contribution that an original thinker makes, it is necessary to understand each person's work in terms of the cultural context within which it takes place. This cultural context is called the *Zeitgeist,* or "spirit of the times." There is often a lot of controversy about whether an important idea is the result of one person's originality, or the inevitable outcome of forces acting within the culture at that time (e.g., Boring, 1950a). For example, is the theory of evolution the product of Darwin's genius, or would someone else (like Wallace) have produced it anyway, given the way ideas were developing in nineteenth-century European culture? We will need to be attentive to this kind of question, and give due credit to the *person* where it is due, as well as acknowledging the role of the *Zeitgeist.*

Rediscovering the Past

When we study the history of psychology, we try to rediscover what each psychologist was attempting to accomplish. The history of psychology, like history generally, is not important simply because it lays the groundwork for what we have now. We should not regard all previous thinkers as obsolete, and we should guard against the danger of being too critical of the past. If we dwell on the weaknesses and failings of previous thinkers, then we may fail to understand them, and if we do not understand them, then we will lose an important part of our heritage. The great psychologists are like important works of art—by appreciating them we enrich ourselves. Earlier psychologists are still relevant, although it is up to us to connect what they had to say to our present concerns. To do this we must put aside our prejudices about what psychology should be, and approach each theorist as sympathetically as we can. "This means rethinking the thought" (Collingwood, 1946, p. 283) of the psychologists we are studying and trying to understand each theory on its own terms before we are critical of it.

There is much more to say about the relation between the history of ideas and psychology. However, now we will go on to review some of the major approaches to psychology in the late nineteenth and twentieth centuries. As we go along, we will introduce some additional ideas about the nature of history as it applies to psychology. Then finally in Chapter 15, we return to the topic of the way in which the study of psychology's history illuminates the nature of psychology itself.

KEY NAMES AND CONCEPTS

What follows is an index of some of the most important material in this chapter. The list includes the individuals, concepts, and topics you should know. Read through the list, and if anything on it seems unfamiliar, then go back and re-read the appropriate section of the chapter. You should be able to define each concept, briefly discuss each topic, and state the importance of each person on the list. In addition, you should be able to write an account of the work done by each person whose name is printed in boldface.

Berkeley, George, 32
New Theory of Vision, 32
size constancy, 32
To be is to be perceived, 33
Box 2.1—The concept of perspective, 26
Box 2.2—The concept of a threshold, 29
Box 2.3—Area of a rectangle, 39
Box 2.4—Evolution of "evolution," 41
British Empiricists, 25
Conceptions of history, 45
Ixion's wheel, 45
Jacob's ladder, 45
Copernicus, 37
Darwin, Charles, 40

and traditional theology, 44
blind variation and selective retention, 43
Galapagos Islands, 42
influence of evolutionary theory on psychology, 44
influence of Lamarck, 42
influence of Malthus, 42
natural selection, 43
survival of the fittest, 43
Voyage of the *Beagle,* 41
Descartes, René, 23
Cartesian doubt, 24
clear and distinct ideas, 24
Cogito, ergo sum, 24
dualism, 24
ghost in the machine, 25
innate ideas, 24
interactionism, 25
introspection, 25
mechanical models, 25
pineal gland, 24
rationalism, 24
reflex, 25
empiricism, 25
Goethe, Johann Wolfgang von, 30
after images, 30
theory of color, 25
Hartley, David, 25
Hobbes, Thomas, 25
Hume, David, 33
causality, 33
impressions and ideas, 34
the self, 34
Kant, Immanuel, 37
external sense, 38
internal sense, 38
nature of causality, 38
nature of psychology, 38
second Copernican revolution, 37
Lamarck, Jean-Baptiste, 42
law of the inheritance of acquired characteristics, 42
Locke, John, 25
association of ideas, 31
primary and secondary qualities, 32
reflection, 31
simple and complex ideas, 31
Lyell, Charles, 41
Malthus, Thomas, 42
Mill, John Stuart, 37
Newton, Sir Isaac, 27
alchemy, 27
laws of motion, 27
theory of color, 28
Renaissance, 23
Simonton, D. K., 40
characteristics of creative people, 40
Stratton and prismatic lenses, 33
Utopian tradition, 36
Wallace, Alfred Russel, 43
Wollstonecraft, Mary, 35
sensibility, 36
views on education, 35
Women and psychology, 35
Zeitgeist, 45

CHAPTER 3

NINETEENTH-CENTURY PIONEERS: OVERVIEW

JOHANN FRIEDRICH HERBART (1776–1841)
Herbart's Influence on Educational Psychology
GUSTAV THEODOR FECHNER (1801–1887)
Psychophysics
Experimental Aesthetics
HERMANN VON HELMHOLTZ (1821–1894)
Helmholtz and the Nature of Perception
Ewald Hering (1834–1918)
Christine Ladd-Franklin (1847–1930)
FRANCIS GALTON (1822–1911)
Hereditary Genius
Eugenics
Statistics
Memory
HERBERT SPENCER (1820–1903)
Social Darwinism

JOHANN FRIEDRICH HERBART (1776–1841)

Recall that Kant did not believe that psychology could be a science, properly so-called, because it could not be mathematical. Although Herbart succeeded to Kant's position at the University of Königsberg, he differed from Kant by believing that mathematics was applicable to psychological events. Because of this belief, Herbart is often regarded as one of the earliest, if not the first, mathematical psychologist (Leary, 1980; Miller, 1964, p. 13).

In the last chapter we reviewed the many ways in which the *threshold* concept has been used in psychology. Herbart is usually credited with making this concept central to psychology by embedding it in a rich theory of mental life. Herbart was not only interested in what went on *above* the threshold of consciousness, but also in what went on *below* the threshold of consciousness. Events below the threshold of consciousness were *unconscious,* and, under the right circumstances, could become conscious. Herbart tried to show mathematically that these relationships were true.

Herbart's (1891/1966) psychology rests on the assumption that all mental life is the "result of the action and interaction of elementary ideas" (Ward, 1910). By elementary ideas, Herbart meant "entirely simple concepts or sensations—e.g., red, blue, sour, sweet, etc." (Herbart, 1891/1966, p. 395). In some respects, Herbart is similar to the associationists such as Hume whom we considered earlier (Hoffding, 1900/1955). However, Herbart went beyond the simple laws of association advocated by his predecessors. He suggested that ideas may be opposed to one another, and act like forces upon each other. Such inconsistent ideas will tend to reduce the *intensity* with which each one is experienced. For example, as I am writing this, all my thoughts tend to be connected to Herbart's psychology. Any other thoughts, such as whether the Boston Red Sox will ever win a World Series again, tend to be suppressed by my preoccupation with Herbart. In general, ideas vary in intensity, or clearness.

As the preceding example shows, some ideas *facilitate* each other, whereas other ideas *inhibit* each other. The process of inhibition can be put into mathematical terms. (The following example is similar to that used by Ward, 1910, p. 337, and by Boring, 1950b, p. 259). Consider two ideas A and B, of which A is the stronger. Suppose that the two ideas are inconsistent with one another, and therefore inhibit each other. Obviously, A will inhibit B more than B will inhibit A because A is the stronger of the two. This means that A is experienced with a greater intensity than B, and another assumption of Herbart's psychology is that intensity can be quantified. This is very important, because, if it is true, then a mathematical treatment of mental life becomes possible.

Let us now see if we can work out exactly how much B is inhibited by its competition with A. The greater the difference in strength between A and B, the more A will inhibit B. If both ideas are roughly equal, then B will be less inhibited than if A is much stronger than B. In any case, B will be inhibited by some amount. At this point, let us introduce a new variable called I. I is the amount by which each idea is weakened as a result of its competition with the other. To put it a different way, A will cause B to become less intense by a quantity equal to I. The more intense A is relative to B, the greater I will be. Herbart cast this relationship in the form of the following equation:

$$\frac{A}{(A+B)} = \frac{I}{B}$$

The greater A is relative to the sum of A and B, then the greater I is relative to B. If we multiply both sides of the equation by B, then we get this result:

$$\frac{(A \times B)}{(A+B)} = I$$

In order to see how much B will be inhibited by A, we must subtract I from B:

$$B - \frac{(A \times B)}{(A+B)} = B - I$$

This simplifies to:

$$\frac{B^2}{(A+B)} = B - I$$

This equation is significant because it shows that no matter how much B is inhibited by A, it will never be less than zero. A and B began as positive quantities, and the ratio of $B^2/(A + B)$ must be a positive quantity as well. This means that $B - I$ must also be positive, meaning that no matter how much B is inhibited by I, it must always be greater than zero. Herbart interpreted this to mean that one idea can never push another completely out of awareness, and ideas above the threshold of awareness never reach a state of complete balance, or *equilibrium* (Ward, 1910, p. 337). However, there are usually a great many ideas active at the same time, and Herbart's mathematical analysis suggested that two or more ideas acting together could drive another idea below the threshold of consciousness. Thus, consciousness would tend to consist of those ideas that mutually facilitate each other, while inconsistent ideas would tend to be below threshold. Any one idea may be kept outside of awareness if "the field of consciousness is occupied by a long-formed and well-consolidated 'mass' of presentations—as, e.g., one's business or garden, the theater, &c—which properly inhibit the isolated presentation if incongruent, and unite it to themselves if not" (Ward, 1910, p. 337). Herbart used the term *apperceptive mass* to refer to that set of ideas that *assimilates* ideas consistent with it, and rejects ideas inconsistent with it.

Herbart (1891/1966, p. 397) believed that "all concepts strive against suppression, and certainly submit to no more of it than is absolutely necessary." This striving for expression in consciousness is the source of the emotions. "So far as it represents or conceives, the soul is called *mind;* so far as it feels and desires, it is called the heart. . . . *The disposition of the heart, however, has its source in the mind*" (Herbart, 1891/1966, p. 408). An unpleasant feeling will result if an idea is pressing to enter consciousness, but is resisted. If, however, an idea pressing for expression finds several allied ideas, and consequently a welcome in consciousness, then this process is experienced as pleasant. "Here is the source of the cheerful disposition, especially of joy in successful activity. Here belong various movements, instigated from without, which . . . favor one another as in the case of dancing and music. . . . [S]uch too is the insight based on understanding several reasons which confirm one another" (Herbart, 1891/1966, p. 411). As you can see, Herbart's psychology is very dynamic, with the contents of consciousness in constant flux, and ideas passing back and forth across the threshold of consciousness.

The process of *apperception* was central to Herbart's psychology, as well as to the thought of many of the other psychologists we examine later on. The concept of apperception originated with *Leibniz* (1646–1716), who used it to refer to the process whereby the mind becomes fully aware of ideas. The *Oxford English Dictionary* (1989) gives the following as one definition of apperception: "any act or process by which the mind unites and assimilates a particular idea (especially one newly presented) to a larger set or mass of ideas (already possessed), so as to comprehend it as part of the whole." No idea is meaningful by itself, but is understood in relation to the other ideas that make up the apperceptive mass.

Since the apperceptive mass is capable of considerable variation over time, it is always possible for an idea to be incomprehensible at first, but to become understandable later on. Thus it is that children come to understand better the precepts of their parents when they themselves become parents. Only when one assimilates experiences as a parent do parental ideas truly make sense. The same point can be made for anyone's point of view: understanding it requires the observer to have the equivalent apperceptive mass.

Herbart's Influence on Educational Psychology

Herbart believed that "education's primary mission is to instill in the young the values held dear by the custodians of established social order, to believe, in short, in all things that law-abiding citizens of Christendom believe in, from truth and justice to service, duty, good works, and a healthy body and mind. Not knowledge, but character and social morality, should be the end of education" (Meyer, 1975, pp. 236–237). These goals of education could be achieved through the application of Herbart's psychological theory to the pedagogical process. Herbart (as cited by Bantock, 1984, p. 153) put it like this: "Pedagogics as a science is based on ethics and psychology. The former points out the goal of education; the latter the way, the means, and the obstacles."

Herbart's educational psychology implied that instruction should proceed through four steps (Dunkel, 1970, p. 165). These were later extended to what are called *the five ways* (Meyer, 1975, p. 238), a list of which follows:

- *Preparation.* Given the centrality of apperception in Herbart's psychology, it is obviously necessary for the appropriate apperceptive mass to be engaged before any new material can be properly assimilated. One does not begin a class assuming that students are already thinking about previously learned information that is relevant to the new information that the teacher wishes to impart. One contemporary mechanism for preparing students is the "advance organizer" (Ausubel, 1968; Mayer, 1983, p. 80), which is an outline summary of the topics to be covered in the lesson, and by which the teacher primes the student for the new material. Herbart felt that it was important at the outset to make sure that the student was not distracted from the learning process, but focused clearly on the material at hand (Dunkel, 1970, p. 163).

The importance of the first stage of preparation has been recognized not only in education but in other areas as well. For example, its centrality was acknowledged in a famous description of the creative process introduced by Wallas (1926). There is no substitute for gathering as much relevant information as you can before embarking on any attempt to understand a topic or discover something new.

- *Presentation.* Given that the stage is set, then the lesson can be sensibly introduced. Of course, Herbart and his generation did not have the educational tools available to them that we have today. Not only were there no computers, but there were no overhead projectors, either! Still, with Herbart's emphasis on maintaining student *interest,* he would have quickly seen the importance of employing whatever technology is available to engage the student when material is presented. "Interest characterizes . . . the kind of mental activity which education ought to arouse, since it cannot be satisfied with mere knowledge. . . . He who holds his knowledge firmly seeks to extend it, has *interest* for it" (Herbert, as cited by Bantock, 1984, p. 153).

• *Association.* After the student has taken in the point of the lesson, the teacher should connect the new material with other relevant material. Recall that Herbart adopted much of the associationist psychology that we considered earlier. The educator could take advantage of these laws to embed new material in the context of what the student already knows. From Aristotle onward, *similarity* and *contrast* were regarded as fundamental principles of association. Thus, it was natural for Herbart to encourage teachers to point out similarities and differences between the current and earlier lessons (Meyer, 1975, p. 238).

• *Generalization.* It is not enough for the student to simply have a set of associations, but they must also be well organized. Much of what is taught in school is systematic, as in the "grammar of a foreign language, the parts and sub-divisions of a science" (Dunkel, 1970, p. 166). Notice that systematization comes only after the student has acquired a set of ideas capable of being organized.

• *Application.* Once the student understands something, then there should be some way in which that knowledge can be applied. Knowledge should be imparted to some purpose, and Herbart advocated putting ideas into practice. In fact, Herbart's educational psychology is itself an example of putting Herbart's own system into practice in the field of education. Herbart claimed that "pedagogy has never been for me anything but the application of philosophy" (as cited by Dunkel, 1970, p. 195).

Herbart is important to the history of psychology in several ways. One obvious contribution is the emphasis he placed on the notion that ideas can move back and forth across a threshold of consciousness. This is an idea we will meet again in several different guises. A second contribution is his attempt to apply mathematics to psychology. While his particular mathematization of psychology has not endured, others have subsequently followed his example and used mathematics to formulate important psychological principles and theories. Finally, Herbart's educational psychology was by no means the last attempt to apply psychological ideas to education. There has long been an intimate association between education and psychology, and we will see that many of the people we examine have profoundly influenced educational theory and practice.

Additional Reading on This Topic. If you wish to explore Herbart's educational ideas more thoroughly, see Dunkel (1969).

GUSTAV THEODOR FECHNER (1801–1887)

As much as anyone, Gustav Theodor Fechner is responsible for creating an approach to psychology that was seen as truly scientific. Of course, at this time, there were no psychology departments, and to the extent that psychology was studied at all, it was advanced by people trained in other fields. Fechner studied medicine in Leipzig (Germany), but found that he had lost confidence in the field of medicine: "In part I did not feel that I had any practical talents in the field. I moved consequently into the literary field, which detracted me gradually from the medical profession" (Bringmann, DePace & Balance, 1992, p. 2). His writing paid enough to allow him to study physics, and he eventually became a professor of physics at Leipzig University.

In his autobiography, Fechner describes a "mysterious illness" that came upon him in 1839. "I soon hurt my eyes, however, through experiments on subjective color phenomena, which required me to look for long periods of time directly into the sun through colored glasses. Eventually, I had to resign my position, because my condition developed into a complete aversion to light and resulted, together with my earlier mental exertions, in a disease of my head" (Bringmann, DePace & Balance, 1992, p. 3). Fechner's condition did not improve until 1843, at which time he began a "new career" in which he lectured "no longer in the field of physics, but [on] the greatest good, the relationships between body and soul, the field of psychophysics, esthetics, and the philosophy of nature" (Bringmann, DePace & Balance, 1992, p. 3).

Psychophysics

Fechner was a person of many talents and idiosyncrasies. He had a mystical side to his character. Fechner's mysticism influenced his choice of topics to study, and the way he interpreted what he found. One expression of his mysticism was his doctrine of *panpsychism.* This is the notion that mind permeates everything in the universe. Fechner's position was nicely summed up by Hoffding (1900/1955):

> *I only have experience of my own soul; I can only infer the existence of other souls by way of analogy. What is to hinder me then from extending the analogy from men and animals to plants and heavenly bodies? . . . The transition from the animal to the plant world is so continuous that there is no justification for assuming so great an opposition between the two kingdoms as is connoted by animate and inanimate. The consciousness of plants may be as far below that of animals as the latter is below that of men. And why should not the heavenly bodies be animated? Men and animals are bound up with the earth, and the earth-soul may be related to the individual souls of men and animals as the earth-body is to their bodies. . . . Lastly, all souls are part of the highest, all-embracing soul, whose life and reality is manifested in the causal law; and the causal law is the principle of all particular natural laws, of all interconnection and all order in the universe. (p. 527)*

Some readers may find this passage reminiscent of contemporary ecological formulations that stress the mutual interdependence of all events (e.g., Lovelock, 1987). Indeed, Arnheim (1986, p. 40) describes Fechner's view that "everything organic and inorganic in the universe possesses a soul, including the earth itself and other planets," and refers to him as a "deeply religious pantheist to whom we owe the most poetical ecology ever written." This organic approach to the universe led Fechner to believe that "the companionship of body and mind pervades the entire universe so that nothing mental is without its physical substratum while, conversely, a good deal of what happens physically is reflected in a corresponding mental experience" (Arnheim, 1986, pp. 40–41).

Fechner's interest in the relation between physical and mental events should be seen against this religious background. Fechner assumed that there was an intimate relationship between consciousness (the mental) and events in the nervous system (the physical). He assumed that this relationship was one of *psychophysical parallelism:* "A strict parallelism exists between soul and body in such a way that from one, properly understood, the other can be constructed" (Marshall, 1990, p. 46). The study of the relationship between mind and brain came to be a part of what Fechner calls *inner psychophysics* (Murray, 1993, pp. 117–118). However, Fechner became most famous in psychology for his elaboration of *outer psychophysics.* Outer psychophysics investigated the relationship between events in the external world and the experiences to which they give rise. Concretely, this involved the study of the connection between stimulus magnitudes and the intensity of the resulting sensations.

Fechner believed that the relationships between the brain and experience and between experience and events in the external world could be expressed mathematically. In this respect Fechner stands in the long line of scientists, many of whom we have already considered, who believed that scientific knowledge is properly expressed by mathematical formulations. Fechner was particularly insistent on the notion that mathematics could be applied not only to inorganic systems, but equally well to living systems (Marshall, 1990, p. 47). Fechner saw no contradiction between the application of mathematics to human experience and the possibility of individual freedom. Mathematical laws only set the limits within which the individual acts. A good example is "a flag fluttering in the wind [which] shows a multitude of forms and movements and is thus capable of a certain incalculable freedom or uncertainty; . . . yet limits are set on the possibilities by the dimensions, the texture, and the fastening of the flag" (Marshall, 1990, p. 48). Similarly, each one of us acts as an individual in particular ways that are unpredictable, but still constrained by very general laws.

What would such a general law look like? On October 22, 1850, in a moment of insight famous in the history of psychology, Fechner saw a way of expressing the relation between physical energy and mental activity. Suppose there is a change in some stimulus, such as a light in a room becoming brighter. To what degree will our experience mirror the change in the light stimulus? Fechner saw that the change in our experience would depend on the original magnitude of the stimulus, and not just on the magnitude of the change. Thus, if I have 10 candles in a room, and add one, that will make a bigger difference to my experience of the brightness of the room than if I have 1000 candles in a room, and add one candle. In the latter case, I may not notice the difference at all (Heidbreder, 1933, p. 81). Fechner intended this relationship to extend beyond simple physical stimuli, such as the intensity of light. The following quotation illustrates the potential range of the relationship that intrigued Fechner (1860/1966):

> *Our physical possessions . . . have no value or meaning for us as inert material, but constitute only a means for arousing within us a sum of psychic values. In this respect they take the place of stimuli. A dollar has, in this connection, much less value to a rich man than to a poor man. It can make a beggar happy for a whole day, but it is not even noticed when added to the fortune of a millionaire. (p. 197)*

Drawing on earlier work by *Ernst H. Weber* (1795–1878), Fechner (1860/1966, p. 112) formulated the relationship between stimulus magnitudes and the resultant experience as follows: "A difference between two stimuli . . . is always perceived as equal . . . if its ratio to the . . . stimulus to which it is added remains the same, regardless of how the absolute size changes. For example an addition of 1 unit to a stimulus expressed as having a magnitude of 100 units is perceived the same as an addition of 2 to a stimulus of 200 units, of 3 to 300 units, and so on." Fechner (1860/1966, p. 112) called this relationship *Weber's law* and characterized it as "a main foundation for psychological measurement." Weber's law expresses the relation between a stimulus magnitude and the amount by which that magnitude must be changed in order for the subject to perceive a *just noticeable difference,* or *jnd.* The law is usually written as follows:

$$\frac{\Delta I}{I} = K$$

This equation should be read as: Delta I over I equals K for the *jnd.* ΔI, or Delta I, represents the amount by which a stimulus magnitude must be changed; I represents the original stimulus magnitude; and K is a constant. Thus, to return to our earlier example, if someone has \$10, then giving that person \$1 might very well make a difference to him or her. However, if the person already has \$100, then adding \$1 to his or her wealth may not constitute a just noticeable difference. It may take \$10 before this person feels noticeably enriched. To continue the series further, the lucky person who begins with \$1000 may not notice an increase in personal wealth until he or she has gained an additional \$100. This example reduces to the following equalities:

$$\frac{1}{10} = \frac{10}{100} = \frac{100}{1000} = \frac{\Delta I}{I} = K$$

Of course, Weber's law is merely a conjecture unless empirical methods can be used to verify it. Fechner developed three such methods which were to become staples of the emerging discipline of experimental psychology. These methods are described in Box 3.1.

BOX 3.1

Fechner's Psychophysical Methods

In his *Elements of Psychophysics,* Fechner (1860/1966, chap. 8) outlined three methods for making psychophysical measurements.

Method of Just Noticeable Differences

Also known as the *method of limits,* this procedure can be used to measure both the absolute threshold and the differential threshold. In its simplest form the method involves increasing or decreasing the magnitude of a stimulus until the subject reports a change. Thus, for example, we could use a device that emitted a tone, the volume of which could be continuously varied (e.g., Woodworth & Schlosberg, 1954, p. 196). We could begin with the volume control completely off, and then gradually increase the volume until a listener reported being able to hear the tone. We would then record the volume at which the listener began to report being able to hear the tone. Alternatively, we could begin with the volume control set quite high, and then gradually decrease the volume until the listener reports not being able to hear the tone. Once again, we would record the volume at which the listener stopped being able to hear the tone. After repeating these ascending and descending series several times, we can calculate the average volume at which the listener goes from being able to hear the tone to not being able to do so, or vice versa. This value is called the *absolute threshold:* the point above which the observer reports being able to perceive a stimulus, but below which the observer reports not being able to perceive it.

A more complex version of this method requires the observer to compare two stimuli. Thus, we could use two tones, one of which is clearly audible, while the other is noticeably lower in volume. We would then increase the volume of the second tone until the observer reports them as equal in volume, and then continue increasing the volume of the second tone until the observer reports it as louder than the first. The first tone does not vary in volume. This procedure would be repeated, but with the second tone starting louder than the first. By averaging the results of ascending and descending series, you can determine the *difference threshold,* or the amount by which one stimulus must differ from another in order to be reported as greater or less in magnitude. The difference threshold corresponds to the just noticeable difference.

Method of Right and Wrong Cases

This procedure is also called the *method of constant stimuli,* because it relies on a set of preselected stimuli that vary in magnitude. These stimuli are presented to the observer in a random order, and it is the observer's task to say whether or not each one is perceptible. The absolute threshold corresponds to that value of the stimulus that the observer reports being able to perceive 50 percent of the time.

Method of Average Error

The method of average error is similar to the method of limits, in that it involves one stimulus that does not vary, and another stimulus that does. However, in this case the variable stimulus is under the control of the observer, and is not varied by the experimenter. For example, the observer could be shown a line of a given length, and asked to adjust a variable line so that the two appear equal. This is called the *point of subjective equality.* There will almost inevitably be some error in the subject's judgments, the average of which constitutes the difference threshold.

The psychophysical methods are not mere historical curiosities, but the foundation of measurement in experimental psychology. Many of the most important experiments that we review in subsequent chapters utilize methods that can be traced back to Fechner's psychophysical methods. We have already seen several times how fundamental the concept of a threshold is to psychology, and Fechner provided psychologists with methods to begin the measurement of thresholds.

Notice that Weber's law makes sense if and only if we can regard our basic experiences, or sensations, as *quantifiable.* If sensations do not vary in magnitude, then the entire enterprise of outer psychophysics is based on a misconception. In the nineteenth century many of Fechner's critics argued that "mind was not possessed of magnitude and that mental measurement was an impossibility.

. . . Introspection . . . does not show that a sensation of great magnitude ever contains other sensations of lesser magnitude in the way that a heavy weight may [supposedly] be made up of a number of smaller weights" (Boring, 1921/1963d, p. 258). Such a refusal to go along with the fundamental assumption of psychophysics is called the *quantity objection* to psychophysics. The quantity objection has some points of similarity to Goethe's objection to Newton that we considered in Chapter 2. Basically, the objection is that "mental magnitudes are artificially constructed and resulted from a confusion between sensation and stimulus" (Hornstein, 1985, p. 5). Although stimuli may vary in magnitude, there is no introspective evidence that the resultant sensations vary in magnitude. Sensations may vary in quality, but not in magnitude. The great American psychologist William James (cited by Hornstein, 1985, p. 4) put it this way: "Our feeling of pink is surely not a portion of our feeling of scarlet; nor does the light of an electric arc seem to contain that of a tallow candle in itself." As we have already seen, whether or not experience can be quantified has been a recurrent issue in psychology, although the quantity objection did not carry the day in the nineteenth century. Indeed, Fechner's methods were widely adopted and practiced, and, as we shall see later in the text, formed the basis of the development of an entire range of techniques for mental measurement.

Experimental Aesthetics

The experience of beauty is a fundamental feature of human life, although psychology has perhaps not attended to it as much as it warrants (Hilgard, 1987, p. 164). Be that as it may, the psychology of the arts is one of the oldest areas in psychology, in which many outstanding psychologists have done research (Kreitler & Kreitler, 1972). Fechner (1876) played a central role in founding a psychology of beauty, or what came to be called *experimental aesthetics.* To begin with, Fechner distinguished between an *aesthetics from above* and an *aesthetics from below.* Aesthetics from above refers to the traditional approaches to aesthetics taken by philosophers and art critics. They approach art "from above" by attempting to evaluate art according to standards derived from some theory of what art should be. By contrast, an aesthetics from below is empirical: it depends on observation of a spectator's responses to art in order to try to understand the effects that art has on people (Gilbert & Kuhn, 1953/1972, p. 525). "Unlike philosophers who speculated about the nature of the beautiful, . . . Fechner hoped to furnish the missing factual base of aesthetics by determining what people in fact find beautiful" (Winner, 1982, p. 56). Fechner's most famous investigation in this area concerned the *Golden Section,* which we discussed in Chapter 1. Fechner's research persuaded him that objects displaying this proportion were more pleasing than objects displaying other proportions.

The distinction between aesthetics from above and aesthetics from below reflects a general trend in the development of experimental psychology in the latter part of the nineteenth century. The new breed of experimental psychologists thought of themselves as replacing speculation with observation. Experimental psychologists intended to replace windy philosophical treatises with factual investigations conducted under controlled experimental conditions. Their attempts to do so will be a central part of our story in future chapters.

Additional Reading on This Topic. A classic discussion of Fechner is in Boring (1961/1963b, pp. 126–131). A solid overview of the development of psychophysics is given by Murray (1993).

HERMANN VON HELMHOLTZ (1821–1894)

Now we arrive at a figure who is one of the greatest scientists of the nineteenth century. Helmholtz's career was marked by "enormous learning in physiology, physics and mathematics and his ability to bring all three fields to bear on any one subject" (Kline, 1962, p. vii). Helmholtz "belong[s] to a dying age in which a full synthetic view of nature was still possible, in which one [person] could not only unify the practice and teaching of medicine, physiology, anatomy and physics, but also relate these sciences significantly and lastingly to the fine arts" (Margenau, 1954, p. i).

Helmholtz (1881/1962) embodied the spirit of confidence in scientific progress that was so characteristic of the nineteenth-century scientist. This belief that scientific inquiry would lead to great benefits for humankind is well expressed in the following quotation, from an essay that Helmholtz wrote criticizing Goethe's attempts to understand color:

> *But we cannot triumph over the machinery of matter by ignoring it; we can triumph over it only by subordinating it to the aims of our moral intelligence. We must familiarize ourselves with its levers and pulleys, fatal though it be to poetic contemplation, in order to be able to govern them after own will, and therein lies the complete justification of physical investigation, and its vast importance for the advance of human civilization. (p. 21)*

Notice some important themes running through this quotation. Nature is described using mechanistic terms such as "machinery," "levers," and "pulleys." The scientific understanding of nature is "fatal" to "poetic contemplation." Nature is something to be dominated, "subordinated" and "governed." This view of the relation between science and nature has been very widespread in many disciplines, including psychology. We will see many examples of psychologists who describe their goal in terms that are similar to those used by Helmholtz. However, this picture of the nature of scientific understanding has not gone unchallenged over the years, and we will also see examples of more "contemplative" psychologies as well.

Helmholtz and the Nature of Perception

Helmholtz's theorizing (1881/1962, p. 118) did not take place in a vacuum, and among those whose contributions he acknowledged was *Johannes Müller* (1801–1858). Müller was one of Helmholtz's teachers, and advanced a theory called the *specific energy of nerves.* Müller's doctrine (1838/1964, p. 38) was designed to explain the apparent fact that the same stimulus "gives rise to different sensations in each sense." Thus, for example, when I touch the back of my hand, I experience one kind of sensation that is quite different than the sensation I experience if I shut my eyes and press on my eyelid. In the latter case, I may experience "a luminous circle; by more gentle pressure the appearance of colors may be produced, and one color may be made to change to another" (Müller, 1838/1964, p. 38). A tactile stimulus yields a visual experience when applied to the visual sense because each sense gives rise to its own characteristic kind of experience, regardless of how it is stimulated.

From Müller's doctrine it follows that we do not experience the external world directly, but that "what, therefore, we directly apprehend is not the immediate action of the external exciting cause upon the ends of our nerves, but only the changed condition of the nervous fibers which we call the state of *excitation* or functional activity" (Helmholtz, 1881/1962, p. 119). Helmholtz did not believe that these different experiences arose because the nerves of different senses had different properties. Rather, he argued that all nerves operate in the same way, and transmit impulses at the same speed, which he estimated to be 100 ft/sec. Different experiences arise when nerves connect different sense organs to different places in the brain. Helmholtz (1881/1962, p. 120) compared nerves to telegraph wires. All wires are the same, but each is capable of transmitting entirely different messages from sender to receiver.

In the case of vision, the optic nerve is connected to the retina. The retina contains receptors called rods and cones, so named because of their shape. Rods and cones are specialized to respond to light. Light varies in terms of wavelength, and these receptors in the retina are capable of picking up some of these wavelengths. The cones are the basis of color vision, with the rods involved in the experience of light and dark. The "cones allow us to distinguish colors by day and the rods enable us to see shapes by night" (Rossotti, 1983, p. 120). There are three types of cone, each one sensitive to a different range of the *visual spectrum,* or the range of wavelengths of light that are visible.

Now examine Figure 3.1, which is similar to one drawn by Helmholtz (1909/1961, p. 13). Helmholtz's figure, like this one, was not based on real data, but on hypothetical data of the sort that Helmholtz believed should be true. The horizontal axis represents the visual spectrum. Of course, as we saw in our earlier discussion of Newton (see Chapter 2), light is not itself colored, but gives rise to the experience of color. Thus, along the horizontal axis are given the various colors to which the spectrum gives rise. The three types of cone are represented by the letters A, B, and C. The vertical axis gives the relative degree to which the cones respond to different parts of the spectrum, with the maximal response arbitrarily set at 100. First of all, notice that each cone is capable of responding to some degree over a large part of the spectrum, and that cones differ in the extent to which they are generally sensitive to the entire spectrum. However, notice also that cones labeled A have their most sensitive region at the blue end of the visual spectrum; cones labeled B have their most sensitive region in the green part of the spectrum, and cones labeled C have their most sensitive region at the red end of the spectrum.

Helmholtz (1909/1961, p. 14) argued that the degree to which each cone was stimulated determined the color we see. "Pure red light stimulates the red-sensitive fibers strongly and the other two kinds of fibers feebly; giving the sensation red. . . . Pure yellow light stimulates the red-sensitive and green sensitive fibers moderately and the violet-sensitive fibers feebly; giving the sensation yellow," and so on. Notice that, according to this theory, colors such as yellow have no specific receptor, but derive from mixtures of the other receptors. As we will see later on, this is a controversial aspect of Helmholtz's theory. Helmholtz credited *Thomas Young* (1773–1829) with being the originator of this theory, and so it is usually called the *Young-Helmholtz theory of color perception.* The theory is also called the *trichromatic theory of color perception* because it holds that three colors—red, green and blue—are the most fundamental, and that our perception of other colors is formed by blending these three in different proportions.

Helmholtz (1885/1954) used similar principles to construct a theory of the perception of different tones. Sound waves vary in frequency. The higher the frequency, the higher the pitch of the sound that is perceived. How are we able to perceive different

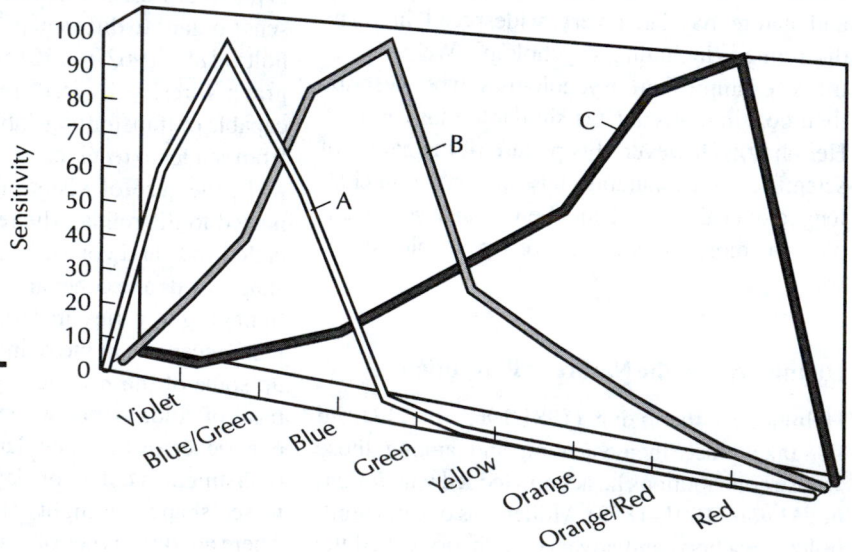

FIGURE 3.1 The relation between the visual spectrum and relative sensitivity in three types of cone, according to Helmholtz's theory.

pitches, such as different musical notes, for example? Helmholtz (1881/1962, p. 135) suggested that the notes of a musical scale are analogous to colors, and argued that "in the cochlea of the internal ear the ends of the nerve fibers lie regularly spread out side by side, and provided with minute elastic appendages (the rods of Corti) arranged like the keys and hammers of a piano. . . .[E]ach separate nerve fiber is constructed to take cognizance of a definite note." Helmholtz's theory is called a *place theory* because it assumes that nerves located at different places in the cochlea are responsible for the perception of different pitches. Although no longer believed to be entirely correct, aspects of Helmholtz's place theory are still incorporated in contemporary theories of pitch perception (e.g., Dowling & Harwood, 1986, p. 33).

Unconscious Inference. Helmholtz is also famous for his theory of the way in which we perceive objects in the external world. At this point it would be useful for you to recall the *projective model of vision* and our discussion of the perception of pictures in Chapter 2. Helmholtz (1881/1962, p. 158) noted, as had *Leonardo da Vinci* (1452–1519) before him, that each eye receives a slightly different picture of the external world. The two images painted on each retina represent slightly different points of view. Nevertheless, we perceive a single three-dimensional scene. Helmholtz demonstrated that we can integrate two different pictures of the world by looking through the *stereoscope,* an invention of *Charles Wheatstone* (1802–1875). The stereoscope is a device that presents two different views of a scene that can be fused when examined through special lenses, and many of you will have used one, or something like it. Another simple demonstration recommended by Helmholtz is to hold your finger up and look at it with your left eye closed. Then look with only your left eye open. Notice how the scene behind your finger shifts as you view it with now one eye and then the other.

Any theory of perception needs to explain how we are able to integrate the two different retinal images so as to yield our experience of a world in three dimensions. Notice that this problem is similar to the one posed by Berkeley, which we considered in Chapter 2, and Helmholtz's solution is also similar to that proposed by Berkeley (Pastore, 1971, p. 161). "We always believe that we see such objects as would, under conditions of normal vision, produce the retinal image of which we are actually conscious" (Helmholtz, 1881/1962, p. 177). We infer, on the basis of previous experience, that particular objects in the external world have given rise to the images on our retinas. The result of this inferential process is the three-dimensional world we experience. Notice that we are not aware of the inferences we make, a fact that leads this process to be called *unconscious inference.* The concept of unconscious inference has had a long life in perceptual theory, still making its appearance in many contemporary theories (e.g., Gregory, 1970, p. 30; Rock, 1983).

Helmholtz's explanation (1881/1962, p. 179) of perception leads to a very useful distinction between two kinds of knowledge. On the one hand, there is knowledge that enables us to do things, such as ride a bicycle, or play a violin. It is very difficult to *say* precisely how one executes skills like this. We may not be able to put this kind of knowledge into words, and so it is, in a sense, "unconscious." This kind of knowledge is to be contrasted with knowledge that can be put into words, and of which we are fully aware, such as knowing that Helmholtz's first name is "Hermann." This particular distinction between conscious and unconscious knowledge is one we will have occasion to examine further later on in the text.

Ewald Hering (1834–1918)

Hering (1878/1961) is famous for formulating a competing theory to Helmholtz's theory of color perception. Recall that, for Helmholtz, yellow was not a primary color, but was derived through the blending of other colors. However, Hering, along with many others, noted that yellow was not experienced as a blend of other colors, but seemed to be as much a primary color as did red, green, and blue.

Hering also wanted a theory that would capture the distinction between *achromatic* and *chromatic* colors. Achromatic colors cover the range between black through gray to white. Chromatic colors have hue, and are embodied by colors such as red, green, yellow, and blue. Hering invented what came to be called an *opponent process theory of color vision* (Hurvich & Jameson, 1957). Hering imagined that the visual system was based on three pairs of antagonistic processes. The pairs are yellow-blue, red-green, and white-black, the last being responsible for achromatic colors. In the absence of stimulation, all pairs give rise to the experience of gray, which represents a state of balance between opponent processes. Light acts on each pair so as to yield one of its component colors, but inhibit the other. Thus, we cannot experience a "reddish green" because red and green form an antagonistic pair. However, one can experience a "greenish yellow" or a "reddish blue," because these colors can both be activated at the same time (Hurvich & Jameson, 1957, p 400). The Hering theory was quite successful at explaining a number of important color phenomena such as *negative afterimages.* If you stare at a colored patch (e.g., green) for about 30 seconds and then transfer your gaze to a white background, you are likely to see the opposite color (i.e., red) projected onto the white surface. From the viewpoint of Hering's theory, the afterimage occurs as balance is restored after excitation of the green component and inhibition of the red component. Of course, the process could work in the reverse manner, by staring at red and subsequently experiencing an afterimage of green.

Christine Ladd-Franklin (1847–1930)

Ladd-Franklin is a particularly interesting figure because she became an eminent scientist at a time when women were rigorously excluded from the academic and scientific communities. Furomoto (1992) has documented the many professional barriers and difficulties with which Ladd-Franklin had to deal. For example, she did all the work for a Ph.D. in logic and mathematics at Johns Hopkins University, but was not awarded the degree because she was a woman (Furomoto, 1992, p. 180). Regular university positions were closed to her because for most of her career she was a married woman, and the place of married women was supposed to be in the home. However, as Furomoto (1992) observes, Ladd-Franklin had the strength of purpose to become a very influential scientist partly because she came from a family that had a history of promoting the rights of women, and partly because her husband supported her efforts. Those who remember her (e.g., Hilgard, 1987, p. 124) report her to have been a particularly strong-willed advocate of her own work.

Ladd-Franklin (1929) became famous for her theory of color perception, which was somewhat more sophisticated than either Helmholtz's or Hering's theory. The theory was an evolutionary one, which is best understood in relation to Figure 3.2. Initially, vision would have been sensitive only to achromatic colors ranging from white to black. The rods are thus representative of the earliest stage of the evolutionary development of vision. The next stage consists of the emergence of cones sensitive to yellow and blue. Some of the cones sensitive to yellow undergo a further specialization to become cones sensitive to red and green.

Evidence in favor of the Ladd-Franklin theory comes from the study of *color blindness,* a common form of which is the inability to see red and green, but the ability to see yellow and blue. To explain this fact, Ladd-Franklin invoked a widely used principle to the effect that the last system to evolve is the first to show the effects of degeneration. This is a sort of "last in, first out" principle that

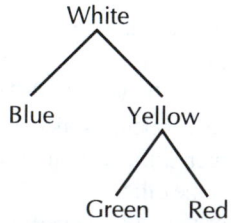

FIGURE 3.2 Ladd-Franklin's evolutionary theory of color perception.

Brown (1958, p. 297) has called the *law of progressions and pathologies.* According to this principle, since the red/green system is the last to evolve, it should be the first to show the effects of pathology, leaving behind only the more primitive yellow/blue system. We will see that other theorists make use of the law of progressions and pathologies to explain very diverse sets of phenomena.

Additional Reading on This Topic. A recent review that deals with many of the topics considered important by Helmholtz, Hering, and Ladd-Franklin is that of Livingstone (1988). This paper deals with the perception of form, color, and depth and relates these perceptual processes to some intriguing visual effects in art.

FRANCIS GALTON (1822–1911)

Galton was born in England, a cousin of Charles Darwin, and one of the most versatile and prolific scholars in the history of psychology. His contributions are many and varied, and some of his opinions are still controversial. In what follows we will sample some of his work in areas as diverse as memory and individual differences.

Hereditary Genius

Reading Darwin's *Origin of Species* (1859/1964) was a very important event in Galton's life (McClearn, 1991). Another important influence was his travels in other countries, which led to his curiosity about "the mental peculiarities of different races" (Galton, 1869/1965, p. 239). Galton (1869/1965) developed the hypothesis that "ability seemed to go by descent" and that "genius was hereditary" (p. 239). Galton (1869/1965) stated his theory as follows:

> *I propose to show . . . that a man's natural abilities are derived by inheritance, under exactly the same limitations as are the form and physical features of the whole organic world. . . . The arguments by which I endeavor to prove that genius is hereditary, consist in showing how large is the number of instances in which men who are more or less illustrious have eminent kinsfolk. (p. 240)*

Galton believed that appropriate evidence in support of his theory would be to show that there is a link between a person's *reputation* and the family to which he or she belongs, with people of outstanding reputation tending to run in families. A person's reputation is supposed to be an index of his or her "natural ability," and by "reputation" Galton (1869/1965, p. 242) meant "the opinion of contemporaries, revised by posterity—the favorable result of a critical analysis of each man's character." In order to assemble a group of worthwhile candidates in such diverse categories as judges, commanders and poets, Galton took "as an index of natural ability the appearance in such handbooks of eminence as *Dictionary of Men of the Time.* From these biographical encyclopedias Galton drew a sample . . . spanning two centuries" (Kevles, 1985, p. 3). For each category, Galton found to his satisfaction that eminent people tend to be related to other eminent people.

Galton remarked on the fact that an interesting feature of his data was that eminent fathers tend to have eminent sons to a greater extent than eminent grandfathers have eminent grandsons. This was presumably due what came to be known as *Galton's law,* which is defined by the *Oxford English Dictionary* (1989) as "a formula proposed by him to account for ancestral heredity, by which the parents each contribute a quarter of the characters to their offspring, the grandparents each contribute an eighth of the characters, and so on." Thus, the eminent grandparents inevitably contribute less "natural ability" to their grandchildren than to their children, all other things being equal.

Before exploring some of the social implications that Galton drew from his studies, it should be noted that Galton's conclusions do not necessarily follow from his data. It is not obvious that "reputation" and "natural ability" must go together (Kevles, 1985, p. 4). After all, one's "reputation" may be the result of a great many factors, including the possibility that being born into the upper classes provides one with a "head start" that is not inherited so much as it is purely social. One's social class may be a very important determinant of how well one does in life. However, Galton did not see it that way. To him, all abilities clustered together, and were innately determined. Thus, Galton believed that people of genius were also physically superior as well. "A collection of living magnates in various branches of intellectual achievement is always a feast to my eyes; being as they are, such massive, vigorous, capable looking animals" (Galton, 1869/1965, p. 248).

Eugenics

To Galton, the clear implication of his studies was that society should encourage selective breeding of humans. The process whereby the human race was to be improved through the production of superior offspring was called *eugenics,* a term Galton coined in 1883. By "eugenics," Galton (1883/1973, p. 17) meant "the study of the agencies under social control that may improve or impair the racial qualities of future generations, either physically or mentally." The theory of evolution provided Galton with a context within which to justify a eugenic approach to social planning. Whereas formerly people had been misguided by religion, now society could take its future into its own hands (Kevles, 1985, p. 12).

The eugenics movement that Galton founded became extraordinarily influential in the early part of this century. "In America, thousands of people filled out their "Record of Family Traits" and mailed it to Charles B. Davenport's Eugenics Record Office, at Cold Spring Harbor, Long Island" (Kevles, 1985, p. 58). In Canada, "few scientists or doctors . . . were not drawn to the notion that the breeding of humans followed the same . . . laws and was as predictive in nature as that of other sexually reproducing organisms" (McLaren, 1990, p. 23). In general, eugenicists were opposed to the emerging feminist movement. Galton himself was an ardent antifeminist, and an opponent of birth control. "The greatest anti-social act committed by the better type of woman was the avoidance of pregnancy . . . the finer females, in restricting family size, were snuffing out the strains of hereditary intelligence . . . the better sort of woman was shirking her maternal duty" (McLaren, 1990, p. 23).

In his work on "hereditary genius" Galton spawned a number of issues that continue to resonate in psychology. One of them is the recurrent question of the nature of *intelligence,* which Galton identified with "natural ability," and believed to be innate. Precisely what "intelligence" is and how it is transmitted from one generation to another have been hotly debated ever since Galton.

Statistics

The Normal Distribution. Galton helped to introduce statistical analysis as an important aspect of many forms of psychological inquiry. One idea that is central to many forms of statistical analysis is the *normal distribution.* In order to get a sense of what a normal distribution is, look at Figure 3.3, which is a drawing of a device similar to one used by Galton (Stigler, 1986, p. 276). A metal pellet is dropped in the opening at the top. Below this opening are several rows of pins. The pellet will hit a pin in each row, being deflected to the left or right

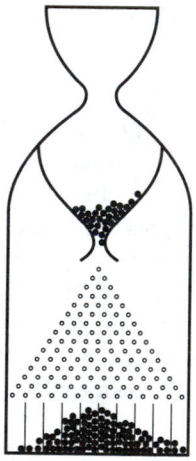

FIGURE 3.3 Galton's device for demonstrating the normal distribution.

Source: Stephen M. Stigler. *The history of statistics: The measurement of uncertainty before 1900.* Cambridge, MA: Harvard University Press, Copyright © 1986 by the President and Fellows of Harvard College. Reprinted by permission of the publishers.

each time it hits a pin. Eventually, the pellet ends up in some position at the bottom of the apparatus. Suppose we drop several pellets in this manner. The pellets will tend to pile up at the bottom as shown in Figure 3.3. Most of the pellets end up more or less in the middle of the device, fewer fall a bit farther away, and fewer still fall at the extreme ends of the instrument. There is an exact mathematical description of this kind of distribution, but for our purposes we need only observe that this *normal distribution* characterizes the way in which events are often distributed in the real world. Notice that this distribution is *symmetrical,* with equal numbers of events occurring on the left and right. Measurements, such as height and weight, may turn out to be distributed in this fashion.

Galton himself made a great many measurements of such things as *keenness of eyesight, breath capacity, strength of hand squeeze, height, arm span,* and *weight* (Johnson, MacClearn, Yuen, Nagoshi, Ahern & Cole, 1985). He was interested in discovering a way of calculating the degree to which such measurements were *correlated.*

Regression toward the Mean. According to the *Oxford English Dictionary* (*OED;* 1989) "regression" means "the action of returning to a place or point of departure." The *OED* notes that the word has the following technical sense in genetics: regression occurs when children "slip back toward the average of the population from which the parents were chosen." To understand what this means, take a look at Figure 3.4. The line labeled *M* represents the average, or *mean,* height of parents of a set of parents sampled from the British population in the nineteenth century. The left vertical axis repre-

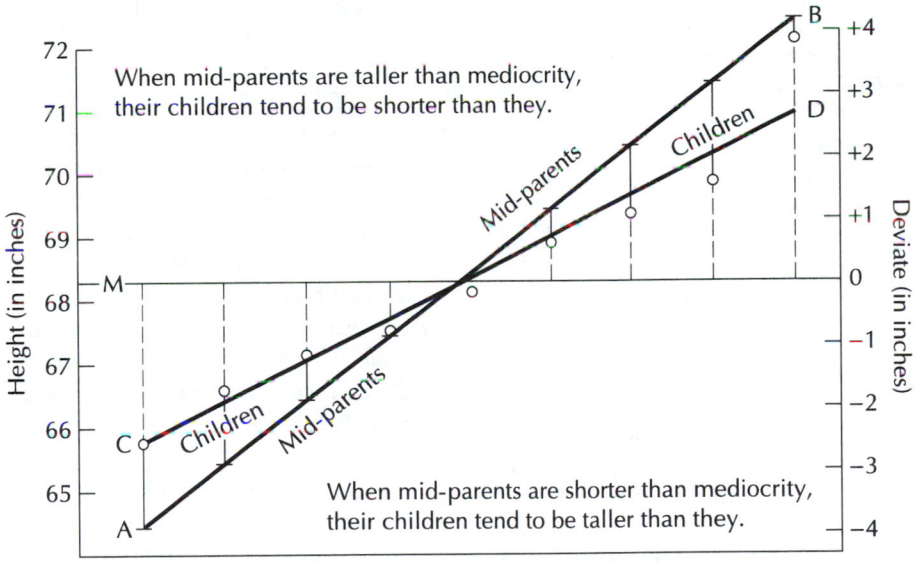

The circles give the average heights for groups of children whose mid-parental heights can be read from the line AB. The difference between the line CD (drawn by eye to approximate the circles) and AB represents regression toward mediocrity.

FIGURE 3.4 Rate of regression in hereditary stature. The deviates of the children are those of their mid-parent as 2 to 3.

Source: F. Galton. (1886). Regression toward mediocrity in hereditary stature. *Journal of the Anthropological Institute, 15,* 253. Copyright 1886 by the Royal Anthropological Institute. Reprinted by permission.

sents the parents' height. You can read the graph by first noting the parents' height. Thus, at the point labeled *A* the parents' height is less than 65 inches. Observe that the children's height at the corresponding point *C* is closer to the mean value, *M*. Now look at the opposite end of the distribution, at point *B*, where the parents' height is close to 72 inches. Note that the children's height (point *D*) is closer to the mean. You should be able to verify for yourself that for all values of parents' height, the children's height is closer to the mean. In general, the children tend to *regress toward the mean.*

Regression toward the mean occurs as a mathematical necessity whenever two variables are not perfectly correlated (Cohen & Cohen, 1983, p. 45). Galton (1889, as cited in Senders, 1958), described it as follows:

> *The law of Regression tells heavily against the full hereditary transmission of any gift. Only a few out of many children would be likely to differ as widely as the more exceptional of the two parents. The more bountifully the Parent is gifted by nature, the more rare will be his good fortune if he begets a son who is endowed yet more largely. But the law is even-handed: it levies an equal succession-tax on the transmission of badness as of goodness. If it discourages the extravagant hopes of a gifted parent that his children will inherit all his powers; it no less discountenances extravagant fears that they will inherit all his weakness and disease. (p. 106)*

Memory

Galton (1883/1973) undertook to examine his own memory in great detail, using techniques that have developed into widely used experimental procedures. Galton was surprised at how many of his memories consisted of "childish recollections, testifying to the permanent effect of many of the results of early education" (p. 131). One of the techniques Galton (1879/1970) used to generate memories was to take walks "during which time I scrutinized with attention every successive object that caught my eyes, and allowed my attention to rest on it until one or two thoughts had arisen through direct association with that object; then I took very brief mental note of them, and passed on to the next object" (p. 27). As a result of these observations, Galton (1879/1970) found that

> *samples of my whole life had passed before me, and that bygone incidents, which I never suspected to have formed part of my stock of thoughts, had been glanced at as objects too familiar to awaken the attention. I saw at once that the brain was vastly more active than I had previously believed it to be, and I was perfectly amazed at the unexpected width of the field of its everyday operations. (p. 26)*

Galton discovered that individual events could serve as the cues for *autobiographical memories,* or memories for events in one's life. A variant of Galton's technique for eliciting autobiographical memories is still widely used (e.g., Crovitz & Schiffman 1974; Crovitz, Schiffman & Apter, 1991), and I would encourage you to experiment with it yourself, in order to experience some of the phenomena that intrigued Galton.

As a result of his experiments, Galton (1879/1970) ended up being impressed by the "multifariousness of the work done by the mind in a state of half-unconsciousness, and the valid reason [these phenomena] afford for believing in the existence of still deeper strata of mental operations sunk wholly below the level of consciousness, which may account for such mental phenomena as cannot otherwise be explained" (p. 35). There is a similarity between some of Galton's views and those of such subsequent thinkers as Sigmund Freud (Roth, 1962), and we will explore this connection more thoroughly later on.

Additional Reading on This Topic. A good account of the relation between Galton's life history and his orientation to psychology is in Fancher (1983), who has also written about a fascinating attempt by Galton to use civil service examinations as a measure of intelligence (Fancher, 1989).

HERBERT SPENCER (1820–1903)

Spencer was one of the most influential thinkers in the world during the latter part of the nineteenth century. Although the phrase *survival of the fittest* was used by Darwin, and is typically associated with him, Spencer actually first coined the phrase in 1852. His most influential work was *First Principles* (1862/1880, p. v), in which Spencer laid out a grand theoretical scheme intended to be true "not of one class of phenomena but of *all* classes of phenomena." Spencer (1862/1880) made it clear that his ideas predated Darwin's, although they were often mistakenly attributed to Darwin.

> *As the first edition of 'Origin of Species' did not make its appearance until October, 1859, it is manifest that the theory set forth in this work and its successors had an origin independent of, and prior to, that which is commonly assumed to have initiated it. (p. vi)*

Spencer's theory was an evolutionary theory in the broadest sense, intended to apply to the inorganic, organic and "super-organic." By "super-organic," Spencer (1862/1880, p. 273) meant societies. Indeed, Spencer's application of evolutionary concepts to society played an important part in the emergence of sociology.

Much of *First Principles* was concerned with articulating what Spencer called *the law of evolution.* Spencer (1862/1880, p. 329) believed that evolution was a process whereby a system moved from "an indefinite, incoherent homogeneity, to a definite coherent heterogeneity." While this may at first strike you as gobbledygook, in fact Spencer had specific phenomena in mind when he proposed this principle. Whether we are discussing the evolution of the solar system, of a person, or of a culture there is an initial state in which the system is simple and undifferentiated. The system initially lacks definite parts, and is a homogeneous whole. As evolution proceeds, the system develops into parts, and these parts become increasingly interdependent.

Spencer gave a large number of examples of this process. Our solar system has passed from being initially an undifferentiated whole to consisting of a number of different bodies (planets, their satellites, and the sun) that are all in balance with one another. The child begins as a relatively simple creature, initially capable of only the most concrete forms of thought, and evolves into the more complex adult, increasingly capable of abstract thought that coordinates a wide range of actions. Primitive societies are much simpler in their organization than are modern industrial societies, which are regulated by "governmental, administrative, military, ecclesiastical, legal, etc.," classes that would be inconceivable to a "barbarous" society (Spencer, 1862/1880, p. 275).

Spencer's (1855/1968) way of thinking about the evolution of mind is well illustrated in the following quotation. Read it carefully, because it sounds many themes that will be taken up by successive generations of psychologists:

> *If the doctrine of evolution is true, the inevitable implication is that Mind can be understood only by observing how Mind is evolved. If creatures of the most elevated kinds have reached those highly integrated, very definite, and extremely heterogeneous organizations they possess, through modifications upon modifications accumulated during an immeasurable past—if the developed nervous systems of such creatures have gained their complex structures and functions little by little; then, necessarily, the involved forms of consciousness which are the correlatives of these complex structures and functions must have arisen by degrees. And it is impossible truly to comprehend the organization of the body in general, or of the nervous system in particular without tracing its successive stages of complication; so it must be impossible to comprehend mental organization without similarly tracing its stages. (pp. 181–182)*

In particular, note that Spencer argues that no aspect of a creature can be understood without an evolutionary perspective. By an evolutionary perspective, Spencer means "tracing its successive stages." As we will see, the tracing of stages of development became an important aspect of both comparative and developmental psychology.

Social Darwinism

Social evolution and progress amounted to the same thing for Spencer. Since evolution was inevitable, so progress was inevitable. *Equilibration* was the process whereby societies regulated themselves by balancing opposing forces. The relation between supply and demand is an example of one such balancing process. Eventually, a society will evolve in which there is an "equilibrium between man's nature and the conditions of his existence" (Spencer, 1862/1880, p. 442). In such an equilibrated society, "the individual has no desires but those which may be satisfied without exceeding his proper sphere of action, while society maintains no restraints but those which the individual voluntarily respects. The progressive extension of the liberty of citizens and the reciprocal removal of political restrictions are the steps by which we advance toward this state" (Spencer, 1862/1880, p. 444). So long as the evolutionary process is left to work itself out naturally, without interference, there will eventually be established a society "of the greatest perfection and complete happiness" (Spencer, 1862/1880, p. 448).

As the preceding quotations from Spencer demonstrate, he argued that the state should not interfere with the evolutionary process. This position came to be known as *social darwinism,* the meaning of which is essentially that individuals should be left to their own devices. Those who win the struggle for survival should do so because of their own strengths. Those who were losing the struggle for survival should not be prevented from dying out. Systems, such as state welfare programs, for keeping the losers afloat would be an artificial imposition on a natural process. However, as Hofstadter (1955/1979, p. 393) observes, Spencer "was not opposed to voluntary private charity to the unfit, since it had an elevating effect on the character of the donors and hastened the development of altruism."

Successful American businesspeople, such as *John D. Rockefeller* and *Andrew Carnegie,* took up social darwinism with enthusiasm (Hofstadter, 1955/1979, p. 397). Carnegie's espousal (1900/1979) of "the gospel of wealth" is a particularly important expression of this ideology:

> *The Socialist or Anarchist who seeks to overturn present conditions is to be regarded as attacking the foundation upon which civilization itself rests, for civilization took its start from the day when the capable, industrious workman said to his incompetent and lazy fellow, "If thou dost not sow, thou shalt not reap," and thus ended primitive Communism by separating the drones from the bees. (pp. 399–400)*

The "rugged individualism" characteristic of Andrew Carnegie and late nineteenth-century America provided a social context within which a peculiarly American psychology emerged. That psychology was called *functionalism,* and we will see how it developed in a later chapter.

Additional Reading on This Topic. Spencer (1897) is his classic work in psychology.

KEY NAMES AND CONCEPTS

What follows is an index of some of the most important material in this chapter. The list includes individuals, concepts, and topics you should know. Read through the list, and if anything on it seems unfamiliar, then go back and re-read the appropriate section of the chapter. You should be able to define each concept, briefly discuss each topic, and state the importance of each person on the list. In addition, you should be able to write an account of the work done by each person whose name is printed in boldface.

Box 3.1—Fechner's psychophysical methods, 55
Carnegie, Andrew, 66
gospel of wealth, 66
color
chromatic versus achromatic, 60
color blindness, 60
Fechner, 52

experimental aesthetics, 56
inner psychophysics, 53
just noticeable difference, 54
method of average error, 55
method of just noticeable differences (method of limits), 55
method of right and wrong cases (method of constant stimuli), 55
outer psychophysics, 53
panpsychism, 53
point of subjective equality, 55
psychophysical parallelism, 53
psychophysics, 53
quantity objection, 56
threshold, absolute, 55
threshold, difference, 55
Weber's law, 54
functionalism, 66
Galton, Francis, 61
autobiographical memories, 64
eugenics, 62
Galton's law, 61
hereditary genius, 61
intelligence, 62
normal distribution, 62
regression toward the mean, 63
Helmholtz, Hermann von, 56
place theory of pitch perception, 59
trichromatic theory of color perception, 58
unconscious inference, 59
Young-Helmholtz theory of color perception, 58
Herbart, Johann Friedrich, 49
apperception, 51
apperceptive mass, 50
assimilation, 50
educational psychology, 51
equilibrium, 50
five ways, 51
inhibition, 50
interest, 52
mathematics, 49
threshold, 49
unconscious, 49
Hering, Ewald, 59
opponent process theory of color vision, 60
Ladd-Franklin, Christine, 60
law of progressions and pathologies, 61
Leibniz, Gottfried Wilhelm, 51
apperception, 51
Leonardo da Vinci, 59
Müller, Johannes, 57
specific energy of nerves, 57
negative afterimages, 60
Spencer, Herbert, 64
law of evolution, 65
equilibration, 65–66
social darwinism, 65
survival of the fittest, 66
stereoscope, 59
visual spectrum, 58
Weber, Ernst H., 54
Wheatstone, Charles, 59
Young, Thomas, 58

CHAPTER 4

WUNDT AND HIS CONTEMPORARIES

WILHELM WUNDT (1832–1920)
Investigations in the Laboratory
Psychophysical Parallelism
Cultural Psychology
Wundt's Influence
HERMANN EBBINGHAUS (1850–1909)
The Experimental Study of Learning and Remembering
Mary Whiton Calkins (1863–1930) and the Invention of "Paired Associates"
FRANZ BRENTANO (1838–1917)
The Würzburg School

WILHELM WUNDT (1832–1920)

Wundt is a pivotal figure in the history of psychology. Born in Germany, Wundt studied with both Johannes Müller and Helmholtz before becoming a professor at Leipzig in 1875. For many years, Wundt's fame in American psychology rested on two facts. The first is that he founded what is often called the *first laboratory in experimental psychology* at Leipzig in 1879. The second is that his laboratory attracted a great many young scholars, often Americans, who then went on to develop psychology elsewhere (Benjamin, Durkin, Link, Vestal & Acord, 1992). The influence Wundt had on other scholars guaranteed him a place of eminence in any history of psychology. In fact, a recent survey of historians of psychology (Korn, Davis & Davis, 1991) placed Wundt first in a ranking of the most eminent psychologists of all time. A comparison of Wundt's ranking with other well-known psychologists is given in Box 4.1 on page 70.

Wundt's (1912/1973, p. 151f) approach to psychology extended well beyond the laboratory. As far as he was concerned, laboratory research was only appropriate for relatively simple psychological processes, an example of which is considered below. More complex psychological processes, such as our ability to use language, could not be understood using only experimental methods. Rather they required observations of the products of language and thought as they occurred naturally (Blumenthal, 1975). Thus, in the beginning, Wundt established the precedent that there are at least two kinds of method that are necessary in psychology. One kind of method is laboratory-based experimentation, and is suited to the investigation of simple psychological phenomena. The other kind of method involves naturalistic observation, and is suited to the exploration of psychological processes as these are influenced by social and cultural factors (Danziger, 1983).

Investigations in the Laboratory

Wundt's laboratory procedures involved *introspection.* It may seem intuitively obvious that introspection should be a useful psychological method, but, beginning with Wundt, a large part of the history of psychology is concerned with at-

BOX 4.1

Can Eminence Be Measured?

Korn, Davis, and Davis (1991) surveyed prominent historians of psychology. A part of the survey asked these historians to list those psychologists they considered to be the 10 most important of all time, in rank order. After averaging the scores, the resulting ranking was as follows: Wilhelm Wundt, William James, Sigmund Freud, John B. Watson, Ivan Pavlov, Hermann Ebbinghaus, Jean Piaget, B. F. Skinner, Alfred Binet, and Gustav T. Fechner. We have already considered one of these "top 10" figures in Chapter 3 (Fechner). In addition to Wundt, we consider Ebbinghaus and Binet in this chapter. The others are considered in subsequent chapters. At the very least, this ranking indicates that we should take Wundt's work very seriously indeed.

Asking psychologists to rank-order the eminence of other psychologists is a tradition in psychology, going back to the work of *James McKeen Cattell* (1903). Cattell was an American student of Wundt, who obtained rankings of leading *American* psychologists in 1903. Cattell's original "top 10" were: William James, J. McKeen Cattell, Hugo Münsterberg, G. Stanley Hall, J. Mark Baldwin, Edward B. Titchener, Josiah Royce, George T. Ladd, John Dewey, and Joseph Jastrow. We consider several of these psychologists in later chapters, but you should note that of this list, only William James makes the current "all time" list. This shows how ephemeral such rankings can be.

Korn, Davis, and Davis (1991) make the further point that there was a lot of variability in the rankings that they obtained. This means that the historians often disagreed about which psychologists should be ranked where. Thus, the average ranks conceal quite a bit of individual uncertainty concerning the true eminence of the various psychologists.

Some of Korn, Davis, and Davis's respondents (1991) expressed misgivings about attempting to rank-order psychologists at all. Such procedures may tend to reinforce existing biases, and overlook important, but not widely known psychologists. Thus, Korn, Davis, and Davis (1991) argue that the following should be *included on any "top 10" list: Cecil Sumner* was "the first black man to receive the doctorate of philosophy degree in psychology, a feat accomplished in spite of innumerable social and physical factors mitigating against such achievements by black people in America" (Guthrie, 1976, p. 177). *Margaret Floy Washburn* was the author of *The Animal Mind* and the first woman to earn a Ph.D. in psychology. She also overcame innumerable social barriers. *Kenneth B. Clark* and *Mamie Phipps Clark* carried out an impressive series of studies of race, one of which influenced a major Supreme Court decision on desegregation (p. 792).

tempting to develop a scientifically respectable introspective method. Wundt himself was acutely aware of the problems associated with any introspective method. To begin with, he made a distinction between two forms of introspection: self-observation and inner perception (Danziger, 1980, p. 244). *Self-observation* of the sort casually engaged in by everyone cannot be the basis of a scientific psychology because it is open to personal bias. *Inner perception* comes closer to the required method, because it involves deliberately observing one's own mental processes. However, such observations would still be too subjective to be trustworthy unless they were made under strictly controlled conditions. This is why the experimental method was so important to Wundt. By doing experiments, one can present a subject with a simple, objective stimulus condition, and have the subject report on the experiences that result. It is obviously important that these experiments be kept as simple as possible, so that the experiment can be easily repeated, and the subject's observations checked by other observers (Mischel, 1969, p. 23).

Let us examine Wundt's experimental method by replicating one of his experiments ourselves. Wundt's experiments often required the use of apparatus, and one piece of apparatus that Wundt (1912/1973, p. 2f) discussed at length was the *metronome.* As you know if you have ever taken music lessons, a metronome is a device that can be set to emit a sound, or *beat,* at a regular interval. The beat can be made faster or slower, and the musician can use these beats to guide his or her playing. Nowadays, most metronomes are electronic, but in Wundt's day metronomes looked like the one shown in Figure 4.1. A clockwork metronome consisted of "an upright standing pendulum, on which a sliding weight is attached. . . . If the weight is fixed at the upper end of the pendulum, the beats follow each other at an interval of two seconds; if at the lower end, the interval is shortened to about a third of a second" (Wundt, 1912/1973, p. 2). If you have access to a metronome, go and get it now. Either a clockwork or an electronic metronome will do. In fact, an electronic metronome has certain advantages, as we shall see.

Try the following exercise with a partner, with each of you taking turns being the "subject" and the "experimenter." Set the metronome so that the beats occur about once a second. If you are the subject, you should begin by realizing that you are not to listen to the metronome in the way that you would if you were using it under normal circumstances (e.g., while playing the piano). Rather, as the subject your task is to carefully attend to the experiences that the metronome gives rise to in you. When the experimenter says "ready," then close your eyes and prepare yourself to attend to these experiences. What are your experiences as the metronome beats? Try to say what these experiences are.

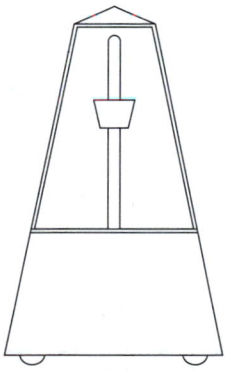

FIGURE 4.1 A metronome.

Source: John G. Benjafield. (1994). *Thinking critically about research methods.* Boston: Allyn & Bacon, p. 7. Reprinted by permission.

I have often used this exercise in my classes, and I know that at first this task yields a very wide range of reactions. One common reaction is questioning the task's purpose—what it is that the task is designed to elicit. That is one of the reasons why Wundt used *trained subjects.* Subjects need to be informed about what they are supposed to be experiencing before they can do this kind of task properly. So, here is a hint: try to experience the beats *without* emphasizing every second beat, in the way that we hear a clock go "tic-toc," with the emphasis on the "toc."

With an electronic metronome, the successive beats have exactly the same *physical* characteristics. However, the successive beats do not have the same *psychological* characteristics. "For we notice in this experiment that it is really extraordinarily difficult to hear the beats in absolutely the same intensity, or, to put it in other words, to hear unrhythmically. Again and again we recur to the ascending or descending beat. We can express this phenomenon in this sentence: Our consciousness is rhythmically disposed" (Wundt, 1912/1973, p. 5).

Why is rhythm such a central feature of our experience? Wundt observed that a great many aspects of our lives are rhythmically organized, from breathing to our heartbeat, from walking to running. These activities provide a background against which the metronome beat is experienced. This context shapes our experience of the beats. The rhythmic way we experience the beats illustrates the process of *apperception.* Apperception is the process whereby we organize and make sense out of our experience. Our experience is not simply a sum of the individual impressions (such as individual beats) to which we attend, but is a *creative synthesis* of those impressions. Creative synthesis refers to the fact that, through apperception, our experience becomes a unified whole and not just a series of elementary sensations. As noted in Chapter 3, in the discussion of Herbart, apperception is a concept that has been very widely used in psychology to explain the way in which our experience is integrated.

As a result of our metronome experiment, we can see that the flow of experience can be described as a sequence of stages or levels (e.g., Blumenthal, 1977, p. 16). We begin with individual beats, which we *apprehend.* By *apprehension,* Wundt (1912/1973, p. 35) meant the process whereby individual impressions enter consciousness. The *span of apprehension* referred to how many impressions we could be aware of at one time, and Wundt (1912/1973, p. 31) thought that this number was about six. For example, we could be aware of about six beats at any one time. Investigations into the span of apprehension have been a central part of experimental psychological research ever since (e.g., Miller, 1956), and we will come across this topic again later on. Apperception follows apprehension, as we attend to those events we have apprehended. These two processes are by no means the whole story. From Wundt's perspective, *emotion* was also a central feature of mental life. In fact, we can demonstrate this by following our metronome experiment a little further.

The Tridimensional Theory of Feeling. Suppose we set the metronome at the slow speed that Wundt mentioned: about one beat every 2 seconds. What do you experience when the metronome is beating out that particular rhythm? Of course, you can hear the beats, one after the other, but is there anything else in your experience in addition to your perception of the beats? Wundt (1912/1973, p. 53) observed that immediately after you hear one beat, you begin to anticipate the occurrence of the next one. You experience increased *tension* until the next beat occurs. However, this tension disappears once you hear the next beat, at which point you experience *relief.* In addition, this slow rhythm tends to make you feel a bit sad, or *depressed.* By contrast, what do you experience if we speed the metronome up, to two or three beats a second? Now the rhythm is no longer depressed, rather it gives rise to a feeling of *excitement.*

Wundt found that by manipulating the speed of the metronome, you can discover a set of basic feelings. So far we have found two dimensions along which feelings can vary: *tension-relief* and *excitement-depression.* Wundt also noted that some rhythms strike us as *pleasant,* and others strike us as *unpleasant.* This results in Wundt's famous *tridimensional theory of feeling.* It is illustrated in Figure 4.2. Any feeling can be thought of as being located within three-dimensional space. Wundt believed that this model was completely general. "We find everywhere the same pairs of feelings that we produced by means of the metronome" (Wundt, 1912/1973, p. 59). In fact, variants of Wundt's three-dimensional model have been supported and extended by numerous other investigators (Blumenthal, 1977, p. 108).

Wundt did not believe that feelings were incidental accompaniments to other psychological processes. Rather, he believed that emotion was a central aspect of all psychological processes. "According to classical Wundtian theory, emotion is the primary source of all experience and is the primordial form of consciousness, both in the life of the individual and in the historical evolution of living organisms. This view finds some support in

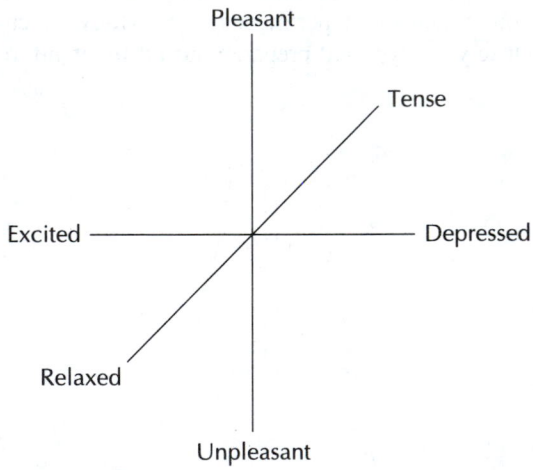

FIGURE 4.2 Wundt's tridimensional theory of feeling.

Source: John G. Benjafield. (1994). *Thinking critically about research methods.* Boston: Allyn & Bacon, p. 9. Reprinted by permission.

the observation that the parts of the nervous system that are associated primarily with emotional reactions are, in the evolutionary sense, the oldest parts, and among the earliest structures to develop in the fetus" (Blumenthal, 1977, p. 103).

In Wundtian psychology, there was a close relationship between emotion and *volition,* or acts of the will. Wundt (1912/1973, p. 63) argued that the will was, in fact, an emotional process: "There is no act of volition in which feelings of greater or less intensity . . . are not present." Whether a process was best described as simply emotional or as also involving an act of the will depended on how the emotion was expressed. An example used by Wundt is that of a person who displays an emotion such as anger in the way that he or she looks, but who does not act on the basis of the anger. This emotional reaction is to be distinguished from that of a person who hits another person out of anger with that person. In this instance there is a simple motive behind the action, and then "we call the volitional process an *impulsive act*" (Wundt, 1912/ 1973, p. 65). However, when there are conflicting emotions, then acts of the will develop more slowly, and are called *voluntary acts.* We all experience this sort of thing when we are uncertain about what to do, and mull over different alternatives until we reach a decision. "We look upon the will as our most private possession, the one that is most identical with our inner nature itself; . . . at bottom our will coincides with our 'ego'" (Wundt, 1912/1973, p. 68).

Psychophysical Parallelism

Wundt believed in a form of psychophysical parallelism that differed somewhat from the rigid doctrine proposed by Fechner, which we considered in Chapter 3. Wundt (1912/1973) agreed that "there is no psychical process, from the simplest sensation and affective elements to the most complex thought-processes, which does not run parallel with a physical process" (p. 186). However, there was not a point-for-point correspondence between every mental event and every event in the nervous system. Mental structures had to be understood in terms of their own laws of combination, and so mental events could not be entirely explained by physical events. Psychological explanation was complementary to physiological explanation. Both psychology and physiology study the person, but from two sharply different points of view. Physiology treats the person as an object, to be understood in the way that other physical objects are understood. Psychology, by contrast, deals with the experiencing subject, and has a "universal importance, since all mental values and their development arise from immediately experienced processes of consciousness, and therefore can alone be understood by means of these processes" (Wundt, 1912/1973, pp. 197–198).

Cultural Psychology

Wundt was quite clear about the fact that experimental investigations, of the sort we have just considered, "cannot be sufficient to account for the special characteristics and phenomena of the development of thought. To do this we must turn our attention to this development itself, as it is shown in the documents of the spoken expression of thought at different stages of consciousness" (Wundt, 1912/1973, p. 151). Now we are dealing with Wundt's *Volkerpsychologie,* a word that is sometimes translated as "folk psychology," but is perhaps better translated as "cultural psychology." Wundt (as cited by Farr, 1983, p. 294) characterized cultural psychology as the study of "those mental products which are created by a community of human life, and are, therefore inexplicable in terms merely of individual consciousness, since they presuppose the reciprocal action of many."

Wundt explicitly rejected the possibility of studying the development of thought by studying the development of children's thinking. Such a developmental approach is pointless, because a child develops within a particular culture, and cultures vary widely from the primitive to the advanced. Child development is not invariant across cultures, but is a product of the culture within which development takes place. Thus, in order to understand complex mental phenomena, we must study the artifacts of particular cultures. Language is one such cultural artifact that is a particularly important index of the mental life of a culture.

Wundt's aim in creating a cultural psychology was to "trace the evolution of mind in man" (Farr, 1983, p. 295). To do so, one needed to adopt in psychology the same approach that Darwin had adopted in biology. "The variety of species which were still extant was sufficiently rich to provide Darwin with the raw materials he needed to develop his theories. Wundt took as his raw material the varieties of human nature around the world as these were reflected in the anthropological accounts available to him" (Farr, 1983, p. 295). It was Wundt's hope that the conclusions of cultural psychology "would converge with the findings that had been obtained through studying individuals in the laboratory" (Danziger, 1983, p. 309).

In addition to theorizing about the cultural development of language, Wundt also had a fairly sophisticated theory of the way individuals produce and understand their language that anticipates many later theories (Blumenthal, 1970, p. 17). This theory made use of the concept of apperception that we considered earlier in the chapter. Remember that apperception involves understanding something as a whole. When we speak, we begin with some such general idea. This idea is then divided into its component parts. This process is illustrated in Figure 4.3, in which a general impression is partitioned into a subject and a predicate. Here is an example. Imagine that you are listening to music with your roommate. You think the music is too loud, and you want to tell her so. You initially have an overall impression of what it is you wish to say, without having any particular words in mind. This overall impression, or "simultaneous cognition" as Wundt (1912/1970, p. 22) called it, may be all that we are ever aware of at the time. Without our awareness, the process of creating a sentence takes this overall impression and transforms it into a more differentiated representation to which words can be attached to form a sentence. This process may generate a simple sentence containing just a subject ("The music") and predicate ("is too loud"), or something more complex. In order to understand a sentence we reverse the process and synthesize an idea out of the parts of the sentence. Thus, speaking and understanding language involves a hierarchical process that moves back and forth between general ideas and particular words.

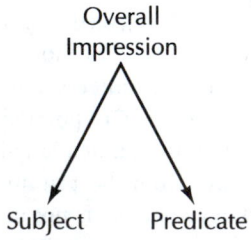

FIGURE 4.3 A tree diagram of a general idea divided into its component parts.

Wundt's Influence

To a large extent, Wundt was a figure against whom many subsequent psychologists reacted negatively (Danziger, 1990). As we shall see, even those who professed to be faithful to his ideas often actually distorted them (Blumenthal, 1975; Brock, 1993). However, due to recent reappraisals, Wundt's cultural psychology in particular is being appreciated again for its recognition that the human mind is inevitably a product of social and historical forces, and cannot be accurately studied in isolation from the social context within which it develops (Farr, 1983, p. 296).

Wundt's cultural psychology involved the comparative study of different cultures, and this kind of work has occasionally been linked to racism. Certainly, there were forces in Germany during the Nazi period after 1933 that attempted to establish a racial psychology that characterized some cultures as inferior to other cultures. However, this does not appear to be at all true of Wundt's cultural psychology, and so it cannot be regarded as a precursor to Nazi doctrines. Wundt's cultural psychology "had no room at all for studies of 'national character.' . . . Wundt was interested in psychological processes which he took to be universal . . . [and] was at pains to point out that he did not consider the intelligence of 'primitive man' to be inferior to that of 'civilized man'. . . . [In Wundt's work one finds] a great deal of discussion about 'humanity' and 'human nature' but nothing at all about racial or biological differences" (Brock, 1992, p. 210).

Additional Reading on This Topic. Lyons (1983, 1986) is a very good overview not only of Wundtian approaches, but also those approaches we will consider as we develop the topic of introspection further. Wundt's work on emotion was developed further by his successor at Leipzig, *Felix Krueger* (Blumenthal, 1979, p. 2).

HERMANN EBBINGHAUS (1850–1909)

Ebbinghaus was educated at the University of Bonn, and subsequently traveled extensively in England and France. By chance, he came across a used copy of Fechner's *Elements of Psychophysics* at a bookseller's in Paris. As a result of reading Fechner, Ebbinghaus was impressed by the potential for applying objective methods to the study of psychological processes. He subsequently conducted an intensive series of investigations of learning and memory that have continued to attract the interest of psychologists ever since (Gorfein & Hoffman, 1987).

The Experimental Study of Learning and Remembering

Ebbinghaus (1885/1964) pioneered the use of *nonsense syllables,* which consist of a consonant followed by a vowel followed by a consonant, such as PIB or WOL. He argued that there were good reasons not to study the way in which meaningful material, such as poetry or prose, is learned. Such material has a wide variety of characteristics that may influence the learning process in unpredictable ways: "The content is now narrative in style, now descriptive, or now reflective; it contains now a phrase that is pathetic, now one that is humorous; its metaphors are sometimes beautiful, sometimes harsh; its rhythm is sometimes smooth and sometimes rough" (Ebbinghaus, 1885/1964, p. 23). Nonsense syllables are relatively meaningless, and so are relatively uninfluenced by previous learning. Any one nonsense syllable is no more or less difficult to learn than any other. Studying the ways in which people learn nonsense syllables appeared to Ebbinghaus to provide a window on the way that learning and memory occur in their simplest and most basic forms. By using nonsense syllables, Ebbinghaus hoped to discover fundamental laws of learning. Moreover, the use of nonsense syllables provided a quantifiable measure of learning and memory in terms of such variables as the number of syllables remembered and the number of trials required to learn a list of a given length.

In his experimental work, Ebbinghaus acted as his own subject. Nowadays we might regard this as inevitably leading to bias, but Ebbinghaus was so fastidious in his methods that his findings have proved to be remarkably resilient over the years. Many other investigators have repeated his experiments and obtained essentially the same results. Ebbinghaus's experiments involved constructing lists from a pool of 2300 nonsense syllables, and all 2300 were used before any were repeated. The experiments took place between 1879–1880 and 1883–1884. In learning a list of nonsense syllables, Ebbinghaus would go through the list from beginning to end, reading the syllables at a rate governed by a metronome at 150 beats per minute.

Ebbinghaus's work on *forgetting* has been enormously influential (Slamecka, 1985). In one of his experiments, he read and re-read lists of 13 nonsense syllables until he could recite each list perfectly twice from memory. After various intervals, he then determined how long it took him to relearn a list. Naturally, the longer the time since the original learning, the longer it took to relearn a list. From these experiments, he was able to estimate how much had been forgotten after different periods of time. In general, forgetting was greatest immediately after learning, followed by a more gradual decline. Ebbinghaus's results have often been replicated by other experimenters, and can be summarized in the famous *forgetting curve,* an example of which is shown in Figure 4.4 on page 76.

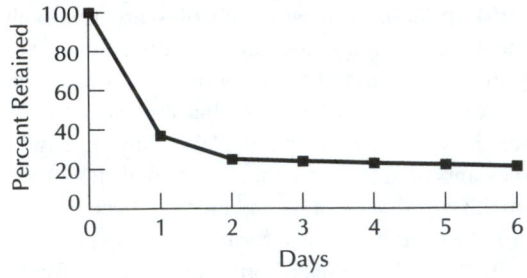

FIGURE 4.4 The Ebbinghaus forgetting curve.

Ebbinghaus believed that when he learned a list of items, associations appeared to be formed not only between adjacent items, but also between all items in the list. This appeared to confirm Herbart's hypothesis that all the members of a series of items were associated with each other. "The strongest connections bound adjacent ideas and those that linked nonadjacent ideas were called remote associations" (Slamecka, 1985, p. 416). The concept of *remote associations* has been very influential over the years. It is consistent with a conception of the mind as a vast network of connections of varying strength. The ability to utilize remote associations has been linked to creativity (e.g., Mednick, 1962), the hypothesis being that the ability to recover remote associations will allow the person to experience ideas that do not occur very often to people, but are potentially valuable.

Ebbinghaus's lasting reputation derives from the fact that he applied the experimental method to the study of the formation of associations. We have already seen that many theorists from Aristotle to Hume have written about the importance of associations. No one prior to Ebbinghaus had provided experimental evidence bearing on the associative process, and "the significance of Ebbinghaus' work was recognized as soon as it appeared" (Hilgard, 1964).

Mary Whiton Calkins (1863–1930) and the Invention of "Paired Associates"

Calkins is another pioneer in the experimental study of the formation of associations. Although she has never received the same degree of recognition as Ebbinghaus, the technique she invented became a standard method in the study of human learning. She also "reported many experimental effects that were rediscovered and recognized as fundamental much later" (Madigan & O'Hara, 1992, p. 170).

An example of Calkins's technique is given in Table 4.1. Instead of simply learning a list of individual items, Calkins had her subjects learn *pairs* of items. This technique came to be called the *paired associates method,* although Calkins herself never used the phrase. By means of this method, it was possible for Calkins to attempt to experimentally determine which factors were the most important determinants of learning. In a typical paired associates experiment, the subject is first shown a list of pairs of items, after which the subject is given one of the members of the pair, and asked to give the first response that comes to mind. For example, in the paired-associates list in Table 4.1,

TABLE 4.1 Example of Calkins's (1896) Experimental Materials: Paired Associate List to Test Frequency Effects

SERIAL POSITION	STUDY SERIES		TEST SERIES
	Color	*Number*	*Color*
1	Green	47	Blue
2	Brown	73	Light grey
3	Violet	26	Strawberry
4	Light grey	58	Green
5	Violet	61	Violet
6	Orange	84	Orange
7	Blue	12	Brown
8	Violet	61	Medium grey
9	Medium grey	39	Light grey
10	Violet	61	
11	Light green	78	
12	Strawberry	52	

Source: S. Madigan, & R. O'Hara. (1992). Short-term memory at the turn of the century: Mary Whiton Calkins's memory research. *American Psychologist, 2,* 170–174. Copyright © 1992 by the American Psychological Association. Reprinted by permission.

different colors are paired with different numbers. However, the color violet is paired with the number 26 once, but with the number 61 three times. The test series requires the subject to say the first number that comes to mind after seeing each color, and gives a measure of the importance of *frequency* in determining the subject's response. Frequency, or repetition, has long been considered an important determinant of the strength of associations, and Calkins's technique introduced a way of investigating variables such as frequency experimentally.

Calkins's interest in the role of frequency in learning was not merely academic. She believed that this kind of work could eventually lead to practical applications. "The prominence of frequency is of course of grave importance, for it means the possibility of exercising some control over the life of the imagination and of definitely combating harmful or troublesome associations" (Calkins, 1896/1966, p. 534). Here we see an anticipation of what became a major justification for experimental psychology: that it would ultimately enable us to control a person's learning history so that "harmful or troublesome associations" could be eliminated, and socially beneficial associations acquired instead. We will see how other experimental psychologists developed this theme later on in the text.

Calkins did not continue working in the experimental psychology of learning for her entire career. Rather, she became interested in the concept of the *self.* Calkins saw the self as "first of all a 'totality, a one of many characters,' secondly, 'a unique being in the sense that I am I and you are you,' thirdly 'an identical being (I the adult self and my ten year old self are in a real sense the same self),' and yet also 'a changing being (I the adult self different from that ten year old)'" (Furomoto, 1991, pp. 62–63). By regarding psychology as the study of the self, Calkins anticipated many later developments in the psychological study of personality.

Like Ladd-Franklin, whom we considered in Chapter 3, Calkins's task was made more difficult because of prevailing attitudes toward women. While she did all the work for a Ph.D. at Harvard, she was denied it because she was a woman. Nevertheless, she went on to become the first woman president of the American Psychological Association in 1905. Her career did not have a lasting impact on psychology, and "in slightly more than ten years after her death, psychology had essentially forgotten Mary Calkins. . . . She did not teach at a major university, but rather at a small women's college, she did not direct a single Ph.D. study, since Wellesley did not have a doctoral program. That is why Mary Calkins never founded a dynasty. This is why Mary Calkins was forgotten" (Stevens & Gardner, 1982, p. 88).

Additional Reading on This Topic. Roediger (1985) edited a volume of the *Journal of Experimental Psychology: Learning, Memory and Cognition* that reviews and updates Ebbinghaus's contribution. Calkins wrote many books in philosophy, and her introduction to a selection of Berkeley's writings (Calkins, 1929) is particularly interesting because her attitude toward Berkeley is clearly that of a kindred spirit, who, like her, had a "conception of the universe as personal" (p. li).

FRANZ BRENTANO (1838–1917)

Brentano (1874/1973) became a Catholic priest in 1864 and began working at the University of Würzburg. After struggling with religious questions for many years, he left the priesthood in 1873. He was appointed as a professor to the University of Vienna in 1874, where he lectured for 20 years. In 1880, he chose to marry a prominent Viennese woman. The marriage was awkward because of a law stating that former priests could not marry. In order to facilitate the union, Brentano resigned his professorship. He never regained the status of professor in Vienna, although he continued to live and work there until 1895 (Kraus, 1926/1976). Then he moved to Florence, where he continued to write on psychology virtually until his death. One of Brentano's most productive students was *Carl Stumpf,* who went on to do important work in the psychology of music and himself influenced many important figures in psychology, as we shall see.

Brentano defined the subject matter of psychology by distinguishing mental phenomena from physical phenomena. Every mental phenomenon involves a *mental act,* of which "hearing a sound, seeing a colored object, sensing warm or cold" are examples (Brentano, 1874/1968, p. 480). By contrast, physical phenomena are "a color, a shape, a landscape, which I see; a musical chord, which I hear; heat, cold, odor, which I sense; as well as comparable images, which appear to me in my imagination" (Brentano (1874/1968, p. 480).

Brentano's distinction between mental and physical phenomena may not strike you as particularly obvious at first, and so, to clarify it, let us go back to the metronome experiment with which we began this chapter. When we were introspecting in a Wundtian manner, we were careful to attend to our own experiences. Thus, we focused on the experiences that the metronome gives rise to in us. Brentano, however, would ask us to do something different. We should try to understand the *act* of listening that takes place. When we *listen* to the metronome, the *act* of listening should be our focus of interest, rather than that to which we are listening. This focus on mental acts meant that Brentano's approach was called (not surprisingly) *act psychology.*

Mental acts "can properly be named only by an active verb. They fall into three fundamental classes; those, namely, of Ideating (I see, I hear, I imagine), of Judging (I acknowledge, I reject . . .), and of Loving-Hating (I feel, I wish . . . I desire). . . . [W]e must always bear in mind that the psychical phenomenon is active, as a sensing or a doubting or a recalling or a willing" (Titchener, 1921/1968, pp. 84–85). Every mental act involves "reference to a content . . . [and] includes something as object; . . . in judgment something is affirmed or denied, in love [something is] loved, in hate [something] hated, in desire [something] desired" (Brentano, 1874/1968, p. 483). The technical term for this feature of mental acts—that they are always pointing toward some content—is that mental acts are *intentional.*

Brentano believed that psychology could adopt an empirical approach toward the study of mental acts, by observing them as they occurred. By insisting that the most basic feature of mental life is that it is intentional, Brentano laid the groundwork for what came to be known as *phenomenological psychology.* As developed by Brentano's student Stumpf, and later by *Edmund Husserl* (1910/1965), the phenomenological method is an attempt to describe consciousness as it presents itself to us, without any presuppositions as to its nature or purpose. Husserl developed Brentano's concept of *intentionality,* and argued that, by comparing a number of similar experiences, we can intuitively grasp their essential nature (Klein & Westcott, 1994, p. 136). A phenomenological study of consciousness shows that we always have "directedness—that is, our consciousness is always as if there were an object" even when that object does not exist, as when we imagine Count Dracula (Føllesdall, 1982, p. 36). To the extent that our experience is intentional, then it makes sense to characterize people as goal-oriented, purposive creatures who have expectations about what sorts of things they will experience. Such a characterization of people is in sharp contrast to many of the associationist psychologies we have already examined, and phenomenological psychology tends to regard persons as quite distinct from physical objects to which we do not ascribe consciousness. Phenomenological approaches tend not to be experimental, but to rely on an intuitive description of experience. Such approaches have been quite common throughout the twentieth century, and we will examine some of them in later chapters.

Additional Reading on This Topic. Rancurello (1968) provides a thorough overview of Brentano's influence.

The Würzburg School

During the first decade of this century, a group of psychologists at the University of Würzburg began studying complex mental processes by means of introspection. Remember that Wundt did not believe that anything but elementary mental processes could be studied by the experimental method, and so what the Würzburg group was attempting flew in the face of Wundt's conception of psychology, properly so-called (Humphrey, 1951, p. 31).

The mentor of the group was *Oswald Külpe,* but the ones who did the actual experiments included *A. Meyer & J. Orth* (1901/1964); *Narciss Ach* (1905/1951); and *Karl Bühler* (1907/1951). The method they developed came to be called *systematic experimental introspection.* This method was described by Külpe (1912/1964, p. 214) as follows: "Observation itself is a particular act, a committed activity of the ego. No other activity can be executed next to it at the same time. Our mental efficiency is limited, our personality is a unitary whole. But observation can take place after the completion of a function and can make it the object of self perception." The method Külpe described came to be called *retrospection* because subjects (who were usually the Würzburgers themselves) looked back on their experiences after they occurred, and then described them.

In order to get some idea of the sort of thing that the Würzburg group was doing, here is a version of one of their experiments. In order to do this little experiment, you will need a partner, who should write a number between 1 and 9 down on a piece of paper, but not let you see what it is. After your partner has done this, think of a number between 1 and 10 yourself. Pick any number. Once you have chosen the number, think about adding the number your partner has written down to the number you have chosen. Once you have this task clearly in mind, ask your partner to show you the number he or she wrote down, add it to your number, and report the result. Repeat this exercise several times. Sometimes try to add the numbers, sometimes subtract them, and sometimes multiply them. After each trial, retrospectively examine your experience, and see if you can describe what you experienced as you added (or subtracted, or multiplied) the two numbers.

What the Würzburgers discovered was that the mental operations corresponding to activities such as addition or subtraction were not easy to put into words. Moreover, there did not seem to be any images that consistently corresponded to such activities. Thus, in the previous exercise, you can easily imagine a number (e.g., 5), the task (add 3), and the solution (8), but it is not easy to say what comes in between the task and the solution. The Würzburgers were surprised by this result, and called such experiences *imageless thoughts.*

The notion that thought could occur unaccompanied by imagery called some previous theories of mind into question. Had not Aristotle himself believed that all thought was accompanied by images? In fact, many psychologists were (and still are) convinced of the primacy of imagery, and the fact that imagery seemed to be irrelevant to important mental activities was a controversial result. It is worth noting that *Alfred Binet* (1903/1969), who was later to become famous for his work developing intelligence tests, independently reached conclusions similar to those of the Würzburgers. After doing experiments on the experiences aroused by listening to a sentence, he remarked on "the contrast between richness of thought and poverty of imagery . . . [and] the image is only a small part of the complex phenomenon to which we give the name thought" (Binet, 1903/1969, pp. 213, 218).

However, there was more to the Würzburgers' psychology than imageless thought. These investigators were beginning to realize, as had Binet (1903/1969, p. 221), that, to a large extent, "thought is an unconscious act of the mind." This is clearly shown by the work of Ach (1905/1951) on *determining tendencies.* To understand what a determining tendency is, let us briefly reconsider our arithmetic experiment. Suppose you are thinking about the number 7, and your task is to *add* the next number. If the next number is 6, then you get 13 as the result. Now suppose the first number is 7, but your task is to *subtract* the next number. If the next number is 6, then you get 1 as the result. The task (adding or subtracting) *determines* what you do with the two numbers. Determining tendencies give thinking a direction, and in this case correspond to the idea we have of the goal we are trying to achieve (e.g., "add two numbers"). Notice that determining tendencies can operate independently of the content of thought. Operations such as adding and subtracting can be applied to any numbers.

Ach (1905/1951) attempted to demonstrate that determining tendencies can operate unconsciously in an experiment on *posthypnotic suggestion.*

> *The following suggestion was given to subject G. in deep hypnosis: "Later on I will show you two cards with two numbers on each. To the first card you will react with the sum, to the second with the difference of the numbers. When the card appears you will immediately, and of your own will, say the correct number, without thinking of what I have now told you." . . . Thereupon G. was awakened from hypnosis; . . . after a few minutes of indifferent conversation I showed G. a card with the numbers 6/2. G. immediately said "8." To the second card, 4/2, he immediately said "2." I asked G.—showing him the first card—"Why did you say 8"? "Just happened to say it" . . . "How about this one?" (showing the second card). "It was just accidental that I said 2" . . . "Didn't you think that 4 – 2 = 2?" "No." (pp. 17–18)*

The work of the Würzburg group introduced several complications into psychology at the turn of the century. Introspection could no longer be regarded as a simple procedure investigating simple phenomena. At least some important mental processes appeared to be inaccessible to introspection because they were unconscious. These complications would have far-reaching consequences for psychology, as we shall see.

Additional Reading on This Topic. An interesting development of the Würzburg approach concerned the exploration of religious experience using introspective techniques (Wulff, 1985).

KEY NAMES AND CONCEPTS

What follows is an index of some of the most important material in this chapter. The list includes Individuals, concepts, and topics you should know. Read through the list, and if anything on it seems unfamiliar, then go back and re-read the appropriate section of the chapter. You should be able to define each concept, briefly discuss each topic, and state the importance of each person on the list. In addition, you should be able to write an account of the work done by each person whose name is printed in boldface.

Binet, Alfred, 79
Box 4.1—Can eminence be measured? 70
Brentano, Franz, 77
act psychology, 78
intentionality, 78
mental act, 78
Calkins, Mary Whiton, 76
frequency and associative learning, 77
paired associates method, 76
self, 77
Cattell, James McKeen, 70
Clark, Kenneth B., 70
Clark, Mamie Phipps, 70
Ebbinghaus, Hermann, 75
forgetting, 75
forgetting curve, 75
nonsense syllables, 75
remote associations, 76
Husserl, Edmund, 78
intentionality, 78
Krueger, Felix, 75
phenomenological psychology, 78
Stumpf, Carl, 77
Sumner, Cecil, 70
Washburn, Margaret F., 70
Wundt, Wilhelm, 69
apperception, 71
creative synthesis, 71
cultural psychology, 73
first laboratory, 69
impulsive versus voluntary acts, 73
influence, 74
inner perception, 70
introspection, 69

language, 74
psychophysical parallelism, 73
span of apprehension, 72
trained subjects, 71
tridimensional theory of feeling, 72
volition, 73
Würzburg school, 78
Ach, Narciss, 79
Bühler, Karl, 79
determining tendencies, 79
imageless thoughts, 79
Külpe, Oswald, 79
Meyer, A., 79
Orth, J., 79
retrospection, 79
systematic experimental introspection, 79

CHAPTER 5

WILLIAM JAMES (1842–1910)

THE PRINCIPLES OF PSYCHOLOGY
Habit
The Methods and Snares of Psychology
The Stream of Thought
The Consciousness of Self
Attention
The Emotions
Will
Other Topics

William James published his *Principles of Psychology* in 1890. It has been called "a classic . . . probably the best general review of the subject that has yet been written" (Ayer, 1968), and it continues to influence contemporary psychological thought, 100 years later (Estes, 1990). You may recall from our discussion of "eminence" in Chapter 4, that James was rated the most eminent American psychologist in 1903, and was second on the "all time" list after Wundt. Thus, James has been traditionally regarded as a figure of considerable importance, particularly in American psychology.

James was born in New York City to a wealthy family of liberal, democratic values with intense and wide-ranging interests (Ross, 1992). His brother Henry (1843–1916) went on to become a famous novelist. From early childhood, the family visited Europe often, and James received a very thorough education. As a young adult, James felt depressed and aimless, a condition that often recurred and that we explore later in the chapter. In 1861, James began studying at Harvard, first in chemistry and finally in medicine; he graduated in 1869. He began to teach physiology at Harvard in 1872. He was 30 years old, and it was his first job. James proved to be "a great success in the classroom. Having been included in intellectual discussions from an early age in his liberal household, James was at ease with students and they with him. His varied background and his attempts to relate class material to life situations were appealing to students. The breadth of his experiences and reading, his ability to communicate, and his engaging style added to his popularity" (Ross, 1992, p. 18).

James began writing the *Principles* in 1878. It took him 12 years to finish it. When it was finally published, it proved to be a great success, and James's reputation as the most outstanding American psychologist of the time (or possibly any time) was secure. Partly because the *Principles* is such a central work in the history of psychology, and partly because it is so beautifully written, I would encourage you to read all of it. Each of its two volumes is almost 700 pages long (cf. Lindsley, 1969), and you might want to wait until a vacation to read it. It would, however, be worth the effort and the wait. All we can do here is to indicate some of the reasons why this book has been so important to psychology.

THE PRINCIPLES OF PSYCHOLOGY

Although each of the chapters of the *Principles* is worth reading, in what follows we dwell on those chapters that have been, and continue to be, widely cited by others in subsequent work in psychology.

Habit

James observed that people are largely creatures of habit, and that the formation of habits depends on *plasticity.* Plasticity is an extremely useful word in psychology and refers to the ability of an organism to alter its behavior as circumstances change. James made the point that habits come about as organisms adapt to their surroundings, and remain relatively constant as long as conditions do not change in any important way. In this formulation you can see James's darwinian approach. Habits, like other psychological phenomena, can often be understood in terms of their role in the adaptive life of the organism. One function of a habit is to make our behavior more efficient. Once an action has become habitual, then we no longer need to pay as much attention to it (James, 1890/1950, Vol. I, p. 114).

James (1890/1950, p. 121) regarded habit as a socially conservative force, and said that it was "the great flywheel of society." Without ingrained habits, society would be anarchic. To a large extent, James believed, our habits are crystallized early on in life. "Habit . . . dooms us all to fight out the battle of life upon the lines of our nurture or our early choice. . . . [Habit is something] from which a man can by-and-by no more escape than his coat sleeve can suddenly fall into a new set of folds; . . . in most of us, by the age of thirty, the character has set like plaster, and will never soften again" (James, 1890/1950, Vol. I, p. 121).

James's book was not just an academic exercise, but also contained practical suggestions throughout. In the case of habits, James observed that it was crucially important to "make automatic and habitual, as early as possible, as many useful actions as we can" (James, 1890/1950, Vol. I, p. 122). Not only does this enable us to focus on more serious matters, but it also liberates us from having to decide every minute detail of our lives. When we are first acquiring a habit, it is important to be consistent, and not allow ourselves to sway from the path we have chosen. We should also get in the habit of forming useful habits, and this is facilitated by doing "a little gratuitous exercise every day" (James, 1890/1950, Vol. I, p. 126). While this advice may sound gratuitous, James's point is that such an activity is like money in the bank. When you need to draw on reserves of self-discipline, they will be there.

The Methods and Snares of Psychology

James's approach to psychology was to consider every issue in as open-minded a fashion as he could. "It was his opinion that nothing that presented itself as a possibility should be dismissed without a hearing" (Heidbreder, 1933, p. 157). Thus, the *Principles* not only considers topics that one would expect to find in any introductory psychology textbook, but also sympathetically reviews material concerned with such topics as freedom of the will that were often missing in subsequent treatments of psychology.

Introspection—"the looking into our own minds and reporting what we there discover"—seemed to James (1890/1950, Vol. I, p. 185) to be the most natural and obvious psychological method. He did not doubt that introspection presented difficulties to the observer, and readily admitted that it was prone to error. However, he also argued that it was like any other form of observation in this respect. No method is perfect, but introspection was an indispensable source of data in psychology.

Many historians see James as a precursor to *phenomenology* (e.g., MacLeod, 1969). As you may recall, phenomenology is the method we considered in Chapter 4 that follows from the work of Brentano and Husserl. James anticipated that method by not "imposing a set of prior categories on experience" but "by observing experience itself and letting experience dictate the categories" (MacLeod, 1969, p. v). James may be said to differ from later phenomenologists by presenting his psychology "in simple English instead of in an obscure jargon" (MacLeod, 1969, p. vi). James said that the *psychologist's fallacy* was to confuse "his own standpoint with that of the mental fact about which he is making his report" (p. 196). No theory should stand between the psychologist and the observations being made. Insofar as possible, we should let the facts speak for themselves. "For James . . . the data of experience were intrinsically interesting. His great gift was [that] he could observe, describe, and render recognizable the nuances of experience that all of us have had" (MacLeod, 1969, p. ix).

However, James is much more than a phenomenologist. He argued that psychology was a natural science, and that the minds the psychologist studies were objects in the natural world just like any other kind of object. Remember that James was trained as a physiologist, and the *Principles* are full of physiological explanations of mental processes. James (1890/1950, Vol. I) assumed a correspondence between "the succession of states of consciousness and the succession of total brain processes," but precisely how mind and brain "hang indubitably together . . . no mortal may ever know" (p. 182). In this, as in all other matters, James did not state unequivocal and final opinions, but always tentative, provisional formulations.

James was not much of an experimentalist. Although he acknowledged the importance of the *experimental method,* he never took much interest in it himself. James also acknowledged the *comparative method,* by which we gather data on different species and different cultures in the hope that the data from one will throw light on the others. Even in James's day there was a great deal of comparative data gathered by means of surveys and questionnaires. James was obviously skeptical of such an atheoretical, data-driven approach. There is no guarantee that gathering a mountain of data will by itself yield greater understanding. "Comparative observations, to be definite, must usually be made to test some pre-existing hypothesis; and the only thing then is to use as much sagacity as you possess, and to be as candid as you can" (James, 1890/1950, Vol. I, p. 194).

One of the most characteristic features of James's method is the astute use of *metaphor.* As Gentner and Grudin (1985) observed, metaphor is not just a literary device. Metaphors have been widely used in psychology, notably at the time in which James was writing, which was the period during which psychology was emerging as a discipline. One function of such metaphors "is to convey an overall sense of complexity or potential richness without necessarily specifying precise" relations between the phenomena under discussion (Gentner and Grudin, 1985, p. 189). In support of this notion, Gentner and Grudin (1985) cite James (1890/1950) to the effect that "at a certain stage of the development of every science a degree of vagueness is what best consists with fertility" (p. 6). A good example of James's vague but fertile metaphors is the one with which we now deal: the stream of thought.

The Stream of Thought

By the phrase "stream of thought," James did not mean to describe only intellectual events. The word "thought" should be taken to refer very broadly to all of our experiences. James (1892/1962) published a shorter version of the *Principles* in which the chapter on the stream of thought was renamed "the stream of *consciousness,*" and that is perhaps a better title. James (1890/1950, Vol. I, p. 225) listed five characteristics of the stream of consciousness, and we consider each of them in turn.

1. "Every thought tends to be part of a personal consciousness" (p. 225). "No thought ever comes into direct *sight* of a thought in another personal consciousness than its own" (James, 1890/1950, Vol. I, p. 226). James's point is that every thought is *my* thought, and I never have someone else's thought. This may at first seem unquestionably true, but after a moment's reflection you may wonder what James would say about multiple personalities? James (1890/1950, Vol. I) considered these to be "secondary personal selves" which "still form conscious unities, have continuous memories, speak, write, invent distinct names for themselves" (p. 227). Thus, any thought is always someone's thought, and there is no thought apart from the personal self who has it, even if one person may have many selves.

2. "Within each personal consciousness thought is always changing" (p. 225). The stream of thought metaphor allows James to make a point that goes back to Heraclitus, whom we considered in Chapter 1. Heraclitus said that "you cannot step into the same river twice, for other waters and yet others go ever flowing on" (Wheelwright, 1966, p. 71). Similarly, James (1890/1950, Vol. I) said that "no state once gone can recur and be identical with what it was before" (p. 230). Just as a stream is never the same twice, so consciousness is never the same twice. We can be conscious of the same thing on more than one occasion, but our experience of that thing is never the same on two different occasions. "For an identical sensation to recur it would have to occur the second time in an unmodified brain" (James, 1890/1950, p. 232), and that is an impossibility. Consequently, it is foolish to look for elementary, recurrent units of consciousness, such as the "ideas" about which psychologists such as Herbart theorized. "A permanently existing "idea" . . . which makes its appearance before the footlights of consciousness at periodic intervals, is as mythological an entity as the Jack of Spades" (James, 1890/1950, Vol. I, p. 236).

3. "Within each personal consciousness thought is sensibly continuous" (p. 225). From the stream of consciousness metaphor, it also follows that consciousness occurs "without breach, crack or division" (James, 1890/1950, Vol. I, p. 237), because streams flow continuously. Of course, James then has to deal with the apparent fact that consciousness is interrupted by periods of unconsciousness, such as sleep. James argues that there is still a feeling of continuity that arches over such interruptions:

> *When Peter and Paul wake up in the same bed, and recognize that they have been asleep, each one of them mentally reaches back and makes connection with but one of the two streams of thought which were broken by the sleeping hours. As the current of an electrode buried in the ground unerringly finds its way to its own similarly buried mate, across no matter how much intervening earth; so Peter's present instantly finds out Peter's past, and never by mistake knits itself onto that of Paul (p. 238)*

James (1890/1950, p. 239) intentionally used the stream of thought metaphor, because of his belief in its superiority to other metaphors that had been used previously. Consciousness is not adequately described as a *train of thought,* or a *chain of thought,* because these metaphors imply that consciousness can be broken up into separate "links" connected together. Whether or not you think James was right in this, you should realize, as did James, the importance of the metaphor you choose on the way you will subsequently think about a phenomenon (Gentner and Gentner, 1983).

Here is another metaphor. Consciousness is "like a bird's life" because "it seems to be made of an alternation of flights and perchings" (James, 1890/1950, p. 243). What James means is that there are places where the stream of consciousness flows at different rates. If a river is wide it flows slowly; where it is narrow it speeds up. James called the places where the stream flows slowly *substantive* parts, and the places where it flows quickly *transitive* parts of consciousness. In order to see what James means, imagine being in Los Angeles. Now imagine being in New York. The thoughts you have of situations like Los Angeles and New York are likely to be substantive states, in that you imagine particular states of affairs that you could easily describe. However, the transition from imagining Los Angeles *to* imagining Boston is less easy to describe, and corresponds to what James meant by a transitive state. It is "very difficult, introspectively to see the transitive parts for what they really are" (James, 1890/1950, Vol. I, p. 243), and they tend not to have names. Our language is well-suited to describing substantive parts, but poor at providing us a way of describing transitive parts.

The stream of consciousness does not have a well-defined edge, and it is difficult to say where consciousness ends and unconsciousness begins. James (1890/1950, Vol. I, p. 258) spoke about events of which we are dimly aware lying beyond the *fringe of consciousness.* A good example of something beyond the fringe occurs when we attempt to remember someone's name, but just cannot quite come up with it. This has been called the *tip-of-the-tongue phenomenon* (Brown & McNeill, 1966), and James (1890/1950, Vol. I) described it as follows:

> *Suppose we try to remember a forgotten name. The state of our knowledge is peculiar. There is a gap therein; but no mere gap. It is a gap that is intensely active. A sort of wraith of the name is in it, beckoning us in a given direction, making us at moments tingle with the sense of our closeness, and then letting us sink back without the longed for term. If the wrong names are proposed to us, this singularly definite gap acts immediately so as to negate them. They do not fit into its mould. And the gap of one word does not feel like the gap of another, all empty of content as both might seem necessarily to be when described as gaps. When I try vainly to recall the name of Spalding, my consciousness is far removed from what it is when I vainly try to recall the name of Bowles. (p. 251)*

Over the years, there have been several different experimental techniques used to elicit the tip-of-the-tongue state. If you want to experience it yourself, try naming the Seven Dwarfs (Meyer & Hilterbrand, 1984).

4. "Consciousness always appears to deal with objects independent of itself" (p. 225). Consciousness "is cognitive, or possesses the function of knowing" (James, 1890/1950, p. 271). This point is closely related to the point made by Brentano, which we considered in Chapter 4, that consciousness is intentional. James insisted that the object of our thought was experienced as an "undivided state of consciousness" and rejected the associationist claim that thought can be analyzed into components. To see what James means, examine Figure 5.1. It is a representation of the thought that occurs as you say "I am the same I, that I was yesterday. Each of the numbers 1 through 9 stands for a particular instant in the process. If we make a solid wooden frame with the sentence written on its front, and the time-scale on one of its sides, if we spread flatly a sheet of India rubber over its top, on which rectangular co-ordinates are painted, and

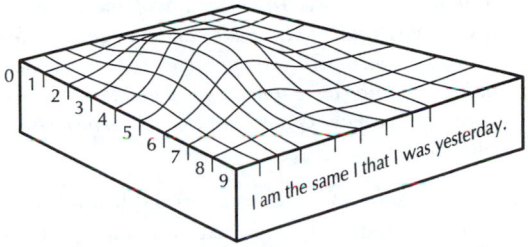

FIGURE 5.1 James's illustration of the unity of consciousness.

Source: William James, (1890/1950). *Principles of psychology.* New York: Holt, p. 283. Reprinted by permission of Harcourt Brace & Company.

slide a smooth ball under the rubber in the direction from 0 to 'yesterday,' the bulging of the membrane along this diagonal at successive moments will symbolize the changing of the thought's content. . . . Or, to express it in cerebral terms, it will show the relative intensities, at successive moments, of the several nerve processes to which the various parts of the thought object correspond" (James, 1890/1950, Vol. I, p. 283). Although you only have one thought in mind from the beginning to end of the utterance, the various parts of the utterance pass smoothly from one to the other supported by a continuously flowing brain process. Such holistic neurological models have a strikingly contemporary flavor (Schull, 1992).

5. "It is interested in some parts of these objects to the exclusion of others, and welcomes or rejects—*chooses* from among them, in a word—all the while" (p. 225). James (1890/1950, Vol. I) observed that many things go on around us of which we could be aware, but which we appear not to notice. The world around us contains an enormous amount of information, and we attend to only a tiny fraction of it:

> *Let four men make a tour of Europe. One will bring home only picturesque impressions—costumes and colors, parks and views and works of architecture, pictures and statues. To another all this will be non-existent; and distances and prices, populations and drainage arrangements, door and window fastenings, and other useful statistics will take their place.*

> *A third will give a rich account of the theaters, restaurants and public balls, and naught beside; whilst the fourth will perhaps have been so wrapped in his own subjective broodings as to tell little more than a few names of places through which he passed. (p. 286)*

The fact of *selectivity* raises several questions that have been extensively explored ever since James's time. For example, what determines the selections we make? James (1890/1950, Vol. I) suggested that one crucial determinant was what we considered to be ours. We are interested in something to the extent that we feel it to be close to ourselves. "The altogether unique kind of interest which each human mind feels in those parts of creation which it can call 'me' or 'mine' may be a moral riddle, but it is a fundamental psychological fact" (p. 289).

The Consciousness of Self

In *Psychology: Briefer Course,* James (1892/1962) observed that "whatever I may be thinking of, I am always at the same time more or less aware of myself, of my personal existence. At the same time, it is *I* who am aware; so that the total self of me . . . [is] partly known and partly knower, partly object and partly subject" (p. 189). The self has two parts. One part knows things, including oneself. James called that part the "I." The other part is what I know about myself, and James called that part the "me." The part called "me" was characterized by James as the *empirical self,* while the part called "I" was the *pure ego.*

James divided the empirical self into three parts: the material self, the social self, and the spiritual self.

The Material Self. The material self consists of all those *things* you would call yours. Some parts of the material self feel closer to you than do others. Your body is the most intimate part of your material self, then come possessions such as your clothes. Also included in your material self are people you regard as yours, such as your mother, your father, your brother or sister. There will be wide variations between people in terms of what constitutes their material self, and how important each part is to them. For example, at one time in a young person's life, a collection of hockey cards might become a central feature of their material self, and if it was lost or stolen, then the person might feel that they had lost a part of themselves.

The Social Self. Our social self is tied to those occasions when other people recognize us. Although each of us can imagine cases in which we would prefer to be incognito, we usually want to be recognized, and "no more fiendish punishment could be devised, were such a thing physically possible, than that one should be turned loose in society and remain absolutely unnoticed by all the members thereof" (James, 1890/1950, Vol. I, p. 293). James made a shrewd observation when he noted that "we have as many social selves as there are people who know us" (p. 294), implying that each of us shows different sides of ourselves depending on the company we keep. The opinions of others shape your opinion of yourself, and since the opinions of others are not always consistent, so our social self need not be terribly consistent but may contain many incongruent roles.

The Spiritual Self. The spiritual self refers to a person's "inner or subjective being" (James, 1890/1950, p. 296). It does not refer to the "soul," but to all of the conscious experiences that we own as ours. Of all these experiences, our feelings seem to come closer to this private self than do our thoughts. James discussed one feeling in particular, self-esteem, or the degree to which we feel positively about ourselves. He noted that self-esteem can be calculated by the following formula:

$$\text{Self-esteem} = \frac{\text{Success}}{\text{Pretensions}}$$

"Such a fraction may be increased as well by diminishing the denominator as by increasing the numerator. To give up pretensions is as blessed a relief as to get them gratified" and we tend to give up our pretensions whenever "disappointment is incessant and the struggle unending" (James, 1890/1950, pp. 310–311). Many a dieter, or smoker, will know exactly what James means!

The Pure Ego. You should recall from our discussion of Hume in Chapter 2 that he denied the existence of personal identity. Rather, all we had was our experiences, our "spiritual self" as James called it. James also struggled with the question of whether or not one can say anything about a self that exists over and above our experiences. He noted that our "sense of personal identity" is based on the resemblance of experiences to one another in a "fundamental respect" (James, 1890/1950, Vol. I, p. 334). We feel that these experiences are similar and belong to each of us alone. But what "pure ego" lies behind these experiences, and is responsible for the continuity we experience? James concludes that there is nothing of the pure ego that we can observe. So the pure ego cannot be a part of a psychology that is based on empirical observation. The pure ego, if it exists, cannot turn around on itself and observe itself (James, 1890/1950, Vol. I, p. 343). The empirical self is the only one about which we have any direct knowledge.

Attention

James's descriptions of attention are still cited by contemporary theorists (e.g., LaBerge, 1990). One of the passages most frequently cited is the following (James, 1890/1950):

> *Everyone knows what attention is. It is the taking possession by the mind, in clear and vivid form, of one out of what seem several simultaneously possible objects or trains of thought. . . . It implies withdrawal from some things in order to deal effectively with others, and is a condition which has a real opposite in the confused, dazed, scatter-brained state which . . . is called* distraction. *(p. 403)*

James appreciated the complexity of attention. For example, he realized that *inattention,* or the process whereby we *do not* pay attention to what we are doing, was extremely common, and described how some

> *very absent-minded persons in going to their bedroom to dress for dinner have been known to take off one garment after another and finally get into bed, merely because that was the habitual issue of the first few movements when performed at a later hour. (James, 1890/1950, Vol. 1, p. 115)*

The execution of habitual, or *automatic,* acts when our behavior is not under attentional control has been the subject of extensive research over the years. One aspect of this topic in which James was keenly interested was *automatic writing.* In its simplest form, automatic writing involves not paying attention to what you are writing. Box 5.1 on page 90, outlines the reasons why this activity is interesting, and gives a brief review of some of the research devoted to it.

The Emotions

Perhaps no part of James's psychology has been more misunderstood that his theory of the emotions (Ellsworth, 1994). This theory is often called the *James-Lange theory* because a similar viewpoint was independently advanced by the Danish philosopher *Carl G. Lange* (1834–1900). The theory appears to have been systematically misinterpreted for decades. So, when you read the following passage from the *Principles* (James, 1890/1950, Vol. II) read it carefully, and try to formulate for yourself exactly what the theory is. In what follows, the phrase "the coarser emotions" refers to "big" emotions such as *grief, fear, rage,* and *love.*

> *Our natural way of thinking about these coarser emotions is that the mental perception of some fact excites the mental affection called the emotion, and that this latter state of mind gives rise to the bodily expression. My theory, on the contrary, is that* the bodily changes follow directly the perception of the exciting fact, and that our feeling of the same changes as they occur *is* the emotion. *Common-sense says, we lose our fortune, are sorry and weep; we met a bear, are frightened and run; we are insulted by a rival, are angry and strike. The hypothesis here to be defended says that this order of sequence is incorrect, that the one mental state is not immediately induced by the other, that the bodily manifestations must first be interposed between. (pp. 449–450).*

James's theory has typically been interpreted to mean that "emotions are *nothing but* our sensation

BOX 5.1

Automatic Writing

Automatic writing refers "either to instances where writing occurs while the writer is preoccupied with something else . . . or to situations in which, although the individual is aware of the writing, he does not feel he is its author" (Koutstaal, 1992, p. 6). James studied automatic writing in the 1880s, but one of the most famous explorations of automatic writing was made by *Gertrude Stein* and L. M. Solomons at Harvard in the 1890s (Hirst, Neisser & Spelke, 1978). Stein is a particularly noteworthy investigator, because of her subsequent impact on twentieth-century culture. She presided over a salon in Paris in which she knew many of the people who were to become the most important artistic figures of the time. Stein also wrote in a manner that was influenced by the study of automatic writing.

Stein's automatic writing experiments, like many others, involved the use of a planchette, similar to that used in a ouija board. In one variant of these experiments, subjects would be given a task, such as reading a novel, while the writing hand rested on the planchette. "Solomons and Stein found that . . . writing movements rapidly became automatic and did not interfere with the subject's giving his full attention to his reading" (Koutstaal, 1992, p. 14). They also explored situations in which subjects had to take dictation while reading a story. After much practice, subjects could take dictation automatically (i.e., without being aware of the fact that they were doing so) for brief periods.

Automatic writing is problematic because it goes against the intuition that we can only pay attention to one thing at a time, and that if we are required to do two complex tasks, then we must switch our attention back and forth between the two. James (1890/1950, p. 299) believed that automatic writing implied "that the processes in one system give rise to one consciousness, and those of another system to another simultaneously existing consciousness." If something like this is true, then we would have a state of affairs called *divided attention*.

Decades after Gertrude Stein's work, divided attention was again explored by Spelke, Hirst & Neisser (1976), who replicated one of the Solomon and Stein studies by training two subjects to read short stories and copy dictated words. This task was extremely demanding at first, but subjects who kept at it for several weeks were found to have a performance level when they did both tasks simultaneously that was as good as their performance when doing only one of the tasks. Further studies confirmed and elaborated these findings (e.g., Hirst, Spelke, Reaves, Caharack & Neisser, 1980). The conclusion—that people appear to be able to learn to divide their attention between multiple complex tasks—should not be too surprising. One real-world example of such a feat is the simultaneous translator, who listens to one language while simultaneously translating it into another language (Hirst, Neisser & Spelke, 1978, p. 61). Can you think of any other examples?

---

of bodily changes" (Ellsworth, 1994, p. 222). James's point (1890/1950) was actually more subtle, and he put it thus: "*If we fancy some strong emotion, and then try to abstract from our consciousness of it all the feelings of its bodily symptoms, we find we have nothing left behind*" (p. 451). James recognized that many people would be unable to understand his point, which was that an emotion without bodily sensations is not an emotion worthy of the name.

What about the "finer" emotions, such as aesthetic experiences, or what Martindale (1984) has called the "small emotions." These might include experiences such as "the pleasure induced by a sunset, a painting, an elegant mathematical proof, or a piece of music" (Martindale & Moore, 1988, p. 661). While James (1890/1950, Vol. II) did recognize that some people *might* have aesthetic experiences that would be dependent only on cortical events, he hesitated to call them emotions: "cerebral processes are almost feelingless, so far as we can judge, until they summon help from parts below" (p. 472).

Another common misinterpretation of James's theory of emotion is that the bodily sensations occur directly as a response to a stimulus, and are not mediated by the person's interpretation of the situation (Ellsworth, 1994, p. 223). However, if you read the quotation from James that begins this section, you will see that the bodily changes are contingent upon *perception* of the emotion-provoking stimulus. For James, perception involved apprehending the meaning of the situation. Perceiving a bear is different from perceiving a baby, and the different meanings entailed by these perceptions necessarily lead to different bodily responses, and thus to different emotional experiences. James's position is not inconsistent with those contemporary theorists who stress the primary role of appraisal in determining emotional experience (e.g., Lazarus, 1984).

Nevertheless, the reaction to the James-Lange theory focused on the role of the body in determining emotion. The most famous criticisms were proposed by *Walter B. Cannon* (1871–1945), who did several studies showing that changes in the state of the viscera (internal organs) were not necessary in order for emotion to occur. However, "James is falsely credited with saying that feeling is defined by the perception of differing *visceral* patterns" (Mandler, 1975, p. 97). In fact, James included bodily reactions of all sorts, including voluntary movements, as determinants of feeling (Izard, 1977, p. 55). Nevertheless, Cannon's work was generally taken to be very damaging for the James-Lange theory.

Will

You may recall that James was prone to depression, and it was during one such period—in 1870—that he resolved to lift himself out of it, partly by choosing to believe in free will. James did not believe that we could freely choose to do anything whatsoever. Rather, our will can make a difference when we are in a conflict situation. Here is an example of his idea of will (James, 1890/1950, Vol. II):

> *We know what it is to get out of bed on a freezing morning in a room without a fire, and how the very vital principle within us protests against the ordeal. Probably most persons have lain on certain mornings for an hour at a time unable to brace themselves to the resolve. We think how late we shall be, how the duties of the day will suffer; we say "I* must *get up, this is ignominious," etc.; but still the warm couch feels too delicious, the cold outside too cruel, and the resolution faints away and postpones itself again and again just as it seemed on the verge of bursting the resistance and passing over into the decisive act. Now how do we* ever *get up under such circumstances? If I may generalize from my own experience, we more often than not get up without any struggle or decision at all. We suddenly find we* have *got up. (p. 524)*

I have often read this passage to undergraduate students, and have found them to have a very good grasp of this phenomenon. James believed that this example illustrated in miniature the nature of the will. The exercise of the will "requires the absence of conflict. . . . [James] was taking his stand against Victorian willpower, the exercise of a separate faculty called "will power" that must have failed him dismally in his own life and led him into the paralysis which expressed itself in his depressions" (May, 1969a, p. 77).

James's post–Victorian preoccupation with "will power" is well-illustrated by his support of the self-help movements that flourished as the twentieth century began. The notion that one could help oneself by following simple principles was enormously attractive to many people, including James, who wanted to believe "that everyone was capable of personal change and self-control" (L. Simon, 1992, p. 34). Consider the example of *Horace Fletcher,* an advocate of the practice of chewing each mouthful of food 32 times. This regimen enabled Fletcher to lose 60 pounds within 5 months, and he was an enthusiastic proselytizer, so much so that the ritual came to be known as *fletcherizing*. Many people took up the habit, and James said of Fletcher's practices that "it is impossible to overestimate their revolutionary import" (L. Simon, 1992, p. 38). "The 'revolutionary import' to which James referred was a new perception of the human body. . . . Portliness, in James's time, reflected wealth and power. Now Fletcher was [saying] that a slim, muscular body reflected true power—will-power, which was the quintessence of power" (L. Simon, 1992, p. 38). In the attitude of William James toward Horace Fletcher we see the beginnings of the modern American perspective on willpower and self-control as learnable skills rather than inherited faculties.

Other Topics

As we observed earlier, in both the *Principles* and other works, James showed a deep interest in topics that later were not considered part of mainstream American psychology. These topics included *parapsychology* and *religious experience* (e.g., James, 1902/1958). Spiritualism flourished in the late nineteenth century and James was convinced that at least some of the spiritualistic phenomena were worth investigating. These included trances and communication with spirits of the dead (e.g., James, 1890/1950, Vol. I, p. 396). James, who had been an early supporter of the American Society for Psychical Research, took the attitude that psychologists "should simply study phenomena presented to them—which included telepathy and spiritualistic phenomena—and describe the functional relationships among them" (Coon, 1992, p. 147).

Most of James's colleagues in psychology, both then and now, would have preferred it if such topics were not considered a legitimate part of the discipline. However, issues such as parapsychology appear to be subjects that simply will not go away (e.g., Bem & Honorton, 1994; Schmeidler, 1992), and so perhaps it is better to face them squarely, as James did, than to insist that such areas of investigation are off-limits to a scientific psychology.

James (1908/1968) believed that a fundamental distinction between people was *tough-mindedness* versus *tender-mindedness*. The tough-minded person tends to place great store in facts; to be materialistic, pessimistic, and skeptical. The tender-minded person tends to believe in principles; to be idealistic, optimistic, and religious. People who are clearly one or the other may have an easy time understanding their experience. However, these opposites can be blended in the same person, as they appear to have been in James: "The interesting fact is that James himself cuts sharply across this classification. In some ways he is markedly tough-minded; an extreme empiricist . . . a materialist . . . a skeptic. On the other hand, he is temperamentally optimistic, religious, a believer in free-will. . . . What he wanted therefore was to make the best of both worlds . . . [and] reconcile idealism and materialism" (Ayer, 1968, pp. 191–192).

James met Sigmund Freud when the latter visited America in 1909. About this meeting, Freud said that it "made a lasting impression on me. . . . I shall never forget one little scene that occurred as we were on a walk together. He stopped suddenly, handed me a bag he was carrying and asked me to walk on, saying that he would catch me up as soon as he had got through an attack of angina pectoris which was just coming on. He died of that disease a year later; and I have always wished that I might be as fearless as he was in the face of approaching death" (Jones, 1963, pp. 260–261). One member of Freud's entourage recalls James as being "very friendly to us and I shall never forget his parting words . . .: "The future of psychology belongs to your work" (Jones, 1963, p. 261). Whether or not James's judgment was correct in this instance is the subject of the next chapter.

Additional Reading on This Topic. The following papers bring some of James's concepts up to date: Markus (1990) on the self; Hilgard (1969) and Kihlstrom and McConkey (1990) on consciousness; and Mandler (1990) on emotion. A good review of contemporary approaches to free will is Sappington (1990). Adler (1992) compares James's philosophy with that of Fechner, and shows some surprising similarities.

KEY NAMES AND CONCEPTS

What follows is an index of some of the most important material in this chapter. The list includes individuals, concepts, and topics you should know. Read through the list, and if anything on it seems unfamiliar, then go back and re-read the appropriate section of the chapter. You should be able to define each concept, briefly discuss each topic, and state the importance of each person on the list. In addition, you should be able to write an account of the work done by each person whose name is printed in boldface.

Box 5.1—automatic writing, 90
Cannon, Walter B., 91
Fletcher, Horace, 91
fletcherizing, 91
James, William, 83
as a phenomenologist, 84
attention, 89
comparative method, 85
consciousness as changing, 86
consciousness as continuous, 86
consciousness as personal, 85
consciousness as selective, 87
consciousness deals with objects, 87
emotions, 89
empirical self, 88
experimental method, 85
fringe of consciousness, 86
habit, 84
introspection, 84
James-Lange theory, 89
material self, 88
metaphor, 85
methods, 84
parapsychology, 92
plasticity, 84
Principles of Psychology, 83
psychologist's fallacy, 84
pure ego, 89
self, 88
social self, 88
spiritual self, 88
stream of thought, 85
substantive versus transitive parts, 86
tip-of-the-tongue phenomenon, 87
tough-minded versus tender-minded, 92
will, 91
Lange, Carl G., 89
Stein, Gertrude, 90

CHAPTER 6

FREUD AND JUNG

THE UNCONSCIOUS
SIGMUND FREUD (1856–1939)
Hysteria
The Project for a Scientific Psychology
The Interpretation of Dreams
The Development of the Personality
The Structure of the Personality
Religion and Culture
Freud's Death
Freud and America
Freud's Critics within Psychoanalysis
Freud and Women
Anna Freud (1895–1982)
Karen Horney (1885–1952) and the Psychology of Women
CARL G. JUNG (1875–1961)
Jung's Relationship with Freud
Analytical Psychology
Extraversion and Introversion
Archetypes
Balancing Opposites
The Four Functions
The Collective Unconscious and the External World
Synchronicity

THE UNCONSCIOUS

In this chapter we will be dealing with a group of psychologists who made the *unconscious* a household word in the twentieth century. However, as we have already seen, there were many other theorists prior to the twentieth century who also theorized about the unconscious, and many alternative meanings attach to this word today. Because it is such a central concept in psychology (Ellenberger, 1970), we would do well to be as clear as we can about the various possible meanings of the word "unconscious" before we explore the intricacies of psychoanalytic and related theories.

There is no single definition of the word "unconscious" because it has meant so many different things at different times. In what follows, we examine the recent history of the meaning of "unconscious" in the way that Natsoulas (1978) analyzed the concept of "consciousness." Natsoulas used the *Oxford English Dictionary* (1989) as a guide to the various meanings of "consciousness," and we also use the *OED* to provide an outline of the various meanings of "unconscious." The *OED* is organized historically, with each entry tracing the historical development of the various senses of a word. In the entry for "unconscious" the *OED* provides four basic senses of the word:

1. "Not conscious or knowing within oneself; unaware, regardless, heedless."
2. "Not characterized by, or endowed with, the faculty or presence of consciousness."
3. "Not realized or known as existing in oneself."
4. "Not attended by, or present to, consciousness; performed . . . without conscious action."

At first these various senses of the word may seem similar, and indeed they do shade into one another. However, the various ways in which the word "unconscious" has been used involve very different psychological assumptions that have far-reaching consequences for both theory and practice.

> Meaning no. 1: Not conscious or knowing within oneself; unaware, regardless, heedless.

The simplest use of "unconscious" is to refer to those beings that lack consciousness entirely. Thus, it might be supposed that inanimate matter is totally devoid of consciousness, although as we saw earlier Fechner would not have agreed. Besides, drawing the line between those things that are conscious and those things that are not conscious (i.e., "unconscious") has never been easy. Are animals truly unconscious, as Descartes believed?

A more interesting way of using the word "unconscious" is to refer to beings that are capable of consciousness, but who are not conscious of some particular event or class of events. A good example of this sense of the word is the quotation, given by the *OED,* describing an "unconscious model, i.e., one taken unawares with a detective camera." Another illustration from the *OED* is the case of animals who "never having been disturbed, . . . were unconscious of danger." This meaning of "unconscious," while covering a great many cases, has not been of interest to psychologists because it refers to events that leave no psychological trace in the person.

> Meaning no. 2: Not characterized by, or endowed with, the faculty or presence of consciousness.

This sense of "unconscious" is more complex, and closer to the way in which some psychologists have used the word. The *OED* quotes William James (1890/1950, Vol. I, p. 199) from the *Principles of Psychology,* where he refers to "sleep, fainting, coma, epilepsy, and other 'unconscious conditions.'" "Temporarily devoid of consciousness" is an important variant of this sense of the word. According to this reading of the word's meaning, we may be unconscious for a while, but return to consciousness later, as in one of James's examples we considered in Chapter 5. However, this particular sense of the word has never excited the curiosity of psychologists as much as the following, which the *OED* lists as another variant of the second sense of the word. However, this meaning is so important to psychologists as to almost merit a category of its own.

> Meaning no. 2a: Applied to mental or psychic processes of which a person is not aware but which have a powerful effect on his [or her] attitudes and behaviour . . . processes activated by desires, fears, or memories which are unacceptable to the conscious mind and so repressed; also designating that part of the mind or psyche in which such processes operate.

The *OED* labels this meaning as peculiarly psychological, and associates it specifically with "Freud's psychoanalytic theory." To illustrate this meaning of the word, the *OED* cites Freud (1912/1959, p. 25): "The term unconscious, which was used in the purely descriptive sense before, now comes to imply something more. It designates not only latent ideas in general, but especially ideas with a certain dynamic character, ideas keeping apart from consciousness in spite of their intensity and activity." This quotation is from a paper Freud wrote in English for the Society for Psychical Research. In that paper, Freud introduces this particular meaning of "unconscious" partly because it seems to him to be required by the phenomena of hypnosis, in particular *posthypnotic suggestion.* Freud described one case as follows:

> *While he was in a hypnotic state, under the influence of a physician, he was ordered to execute a certain action at a certain fixed moment after his awakening, say half an hour later. He awakes, and seems fully conscious and in his ordinary condition; he has no recollection of his hypnotic state, and yet at the pre-arranged moment there rushes into his mind the impulse to do such and such a thing, and he does it consciously, though not knowing why. (Freud, 1912/1959, p. 23)*

In fact, there is an intimate relationship between Freud's meaning of "unconscious" and the concept of hypnosis, which itself developed out of the work of *Anton Mesmer* (1734–1815). Mesmer attributed hypnotic effects to a force called *animal magnetism:*

> *A widely held oversimplification of the history of hypnotism has been that of the concept of "animal magnetism"; a quasi-electrical fluid responsible for certain interesting phenomena, was displaced in the second half of the nineteenth century by the concept of "hypnosis," which was in turn closely linked to newly emerging notions about the unconscious mind. But in fact ideas about the unconscious mind, or dissociated or relatively independent streams of consciousness, initially emerged in the context of animal magnetism . . . and were well advanced long before hypnotists took them over. (Gauld, 1992, p. 159)*

The preceding paragraph treats the *unconscious mind* and *dissociated streams of consciousness* as equivalent, but Freud (1912/1959, pp. 25–26) was clear about the fact that this is not what he meant by the term. He argued that "we have no right to extend the meaning of this word so as to make it include a consciousness of which its owner is himself not aware," and ridiculed the idea of an "unconscious conscious," presumably because it was an oxymoron. Nevertheless, it has not always been easy to disentangle "hidden streams of consciousness" (Gauld, 1992, p. 395) from what is meant by the "unconscious."

Freud was also at pains to distance himself from conceptions of the unconscious such as Herbart's. Freud (1912/1959, p. 25) said that his conception of the unconscious differed from the notion that "every latent idea was so because it was weak and that it grew conscious as soon as it became strong." Latent ideas that present themselves to consciousness as they gain strength were to be called *preconscious* to distinguish them from truly unconscious ideas.

Meaning no. 3: Not realized or known as existing in oneself.

Here we have a different approach to the nature of "unconsciousness," which blends together some of the former meanings of the word. Unlike the first sense of the term, this sense suggests that what is unconscious is psychologically real. However, unlike the second sense, this sense suggests that what is now unconscious may never have been conscious. Thus, the unconscious contains what has yet to become conscious. This includes unrealized potentialities of both a positive and a negative character. This sense of the unconscious sounds most like what Jung (1933) meant by the term:

> *The unconscious is not a demonic monster but a thing of nature that is perfectly neutral as far as moral sense, aesthetic taste, and intellectual judgment go. It is dangerous only when our conscious attitude towards it becomes hopelessly false. And this danger grows in the measure that we practice repressions. (p. 19)*

Meaning no. 4: Not attended by, or present to, consciousness; performed, employed, etc., without conscious action.

This meaning of "unconscious" was perhaps best captured by James R. Angell (1907/1978) in his famous Presidential address to the American Psychological Association. In that address, he defined conscious as "accommodatory activity" (p. 87), and argued that "consciousness [is] substantially synonymous with adaptive reactions to novel situations" (p. 89), and "no real organic accommodation to the novel ever occurs, save in the form that involves consciousness" (pp. 89–90). This makes of consciousness the "primary accommodative process" (p. 101). This way of conceiving of consciousness leads directly to a conception of unconscious processes as responsible for regulating our behavior in familiar situations: "consciousness is constantly at work building up habits out of coordinations imperfectly under control; . . . as speedily as control is gained the mental direction tends to subside and give way to a condition approximating physiological automatism" (p. 89). Although not usually associated with Angell, his distinction between *controlled* (conscious) and *automatic* (unconscious) processes has become a staple of much contemporary psychology (e.g., Shiffrin & Schneider, 1977). We will return to Angell in the next chapter when we explore American functional psychology.

When we look back over the variety of possible meanings of "unconscious," it is clear that it is a complex but rich concept. We must keep this complexity in mind as we now turn to explore the thought of those who have made such extensive use of this concept.

SIGMUND FREUD (1856–1939)

Freud (1935/1950) believed that his Jewish ancestors had lived for many years at Cologne, but "as a result of a persecution of the Jews during the fourteenth or fifteenth century, they fled eastwards, and that, in the course of the nineteenth century, they migrated back from Lithuania . . . into German Austria. When I was a child of four I came to Vienna, and I went through the whole of my education there. At the 'Gymnasium' I was at the top of my class for seven years; I enjoyed special privileges there, and was required to pass scarcely any examinations" (p. 13). Freud (1935/1950, p. 14) mentioned that as a young person "the theories of Darwin . . . strongly attracted me." At university, he experienced anti-Semitism: "I found I was expected to feel myself inferior and an alien because I was a Jew" (Freud, 1935/1950, p. 14), an experience that toughened him for the role of independent thinker that he was later to play. Freud graduated as a Doctor of Medicine in 1881, after entering university in 1873. In 1886, Freud felt well enough established that he could marry *Martha Bernays,* "the girl who had been waiting for me . . . for more than four years" (Freud, 1935/1950, p. 23).

Among Freud's most influential teachers was *Ernst Brücke,* who taught Freud neurology. Brücke was himself a student of Johannes Müller, and an associate of Helmholtz. Brücke believed that "no other forces than the common physical-chemical ones are active in the organism" and that these are "reducible to the forces of attraction and repulsion" (Amacher, 1965, p. 10). This was a theme that often expressed itself in Freud's work, as we shall see.

In 1885 Freud went to Paris to study with *Jean-Martin Charcot* (1825–1893), one of the great neuropsychological figures of the age. Charcot worked at the *Salpêtriére,* an institution that was first made famous in the history of psychiatry by *Philippe Pinel* (1745–1826), who had freed the inmates from their chains. Charcot's clinical work had continued to expand the reputation of the Salpêtriére. Charcot specialized in studying *hysteria,* a condition that had also been investigated by *Joseph Breuer* (1942–1925), whom Freud had met while working in Brücke's laboratory. Hysteria was long believed to be exclusively a woman's disease. Primitive theories of hysteria attributed symptoms to a "wandering womb" that moved about in a woman's body. Before Charcot, few medical professionals took it seriously.

Hysteria

Although hysteria has been described in many and various ways, the most interesting form of it, for our purposes, is called *conversion hysteria.* In such cases, the patient has a physical symptom, such as paralysis or lack of feeling in a part of the body. One such symptom is called a *glove anesthesia,* in which the patient has no sensation in the hand below the wrist. Suppose that this symptom cannot be explained neurologically, because not only is there no observable neural damage, but, in any case, no possible pattern of injured nerves that could conceivably account for the symptom (Freud, 1893/1959, p. 54). Such cases were often thought to be malingerers, and to simply be consciously inventing the symptom to avoid work. Notice two alternative explanations of the symptom: either it is due to a neural disorder, or the patient is making it up. There is, however, a third possibility (MacIntyre, 1958, p. 9). Perhaps the patient is not consciously playing the part of someone with a symptom, but rather the symptom is determined by forces of which the patient is unconscious. If we accept this line of reasoning, then we are forced to ask, "what must the unconscious be like in order to produce symptoms like this?"

One famous case in the history of psychoanalysis was a woman given the pseudonym *Anna O.* who was treated by Breuer beginning in 1880, and whose real name was *Bertha Pappenheim* (Freeman, 1980). The first symptom Breuer found Pappenheim to be displaying was paralysis of both legs and right arm. Breuer diagnosed hysteria, since there were no apparent physiological reasons for the symptoms. Many physicians, including Breuer and Charcot, used hypnosis to treat hysteria, and Breuer hypnotized Anna O. He discovered, and subsequently told Freud, that her symptoms disappeared if she was encouraged to talk about them while hypnotized. Freud himself began to adopt this procedure with his hysterical patients, and published an account of this *cathartic method* with Breuer (Breuer & Freud, 1893/1959). *Catharsis* is a concept that originated with Aristotle, who used it to refer to the purging experience that occurs in the spectator who witnesses a strong emotion being acted in a play. In psychotherapy, the term came to mean the process whereby the expression of an emotion removes its pathological effect. Notice that the implication of this formulation is that a "pent-up affect" (Breuer & Freud, 1893/1959, p. 41) can have pathological consequences, by being converted into symptoms (as in *conversion hysteria*). Few ideas have been more influential in the twentieth century than this one!

Freud went on to develop his own therapeutic procedures. He gave up on hypnosis, partly because it occasionally led to awkward situations. One patient, for example, "as she woke up on one occasion, threw her arms round my neck," and, while Freud (1935/1950, p. 48) "was modest enough not to attribute the event to my own irresistible personal attraction," he realized that it was necessary for patients to be as aware as he was of what was happening in the therapeutic situation. "So I abandoned hypnotism, only retaining my practice of requiring the patient to lie upon a sofa while I sat behind him, seeing him, but not seen myself" (Freud, 1935/1950, p. 49).

The new method led Freud to develop a new way of understanding hysteria. He began to see hysterical symptoms as the result of sexual trauma that had occurred in early childhood. "These *infantile* experiences are . . . *sexual* in content"; they are "sexual experiences undergone by the patient personally, of sexual intercourse (in a wide sense)" (Freud, 1896/1959, p. 197). It is important to realize that at this point Freud believed in the "reality of the infantile sexual scenes" and that patients' recovered memories referred to events they "must actually have experienced" (Freud, 1896/1959, p. 200). At the time, Freud based this conclusion on a sample of 18 cases, 6 men and 12 women. One of Freud's innovations was to regard hysteria as potentially a male as well as a female disorder.

Freud argued that the symptoms of the hysteria sufferer were the result of *repression.* Repression is a process whereby the person actively forgets something he or she has experienced, because it would be too painful to recall. However, a memory trace of the event still exists, although it has become unconscious. The unconscious memory is the source of the person's symptom. Under the right conditions, the person can re-experience the repressed material, and relieve the symptom. As we have seen, Freud originally believed that these repressed memories were of episodes of infantile sexual abuse that had actually taken place. However, Freud later decided that he had been too credulous, and that the descriptions of sexual abuse provided by his patients were actually fantasies. These fantasies represented infantile wishes on the part of the patients. For example, a male child might fantasize about having sexual relations with his mother, a condition Freud termed the *Oedipus complex,* after the mythological Greek king who killed his father and married his mother. Such fantasies, rather than actual seductions, were the true source of the person's neurotic symptomatology according to Freud.

There has been a great deal of controversy over whether or not Freud's patients had actually experienced sexual abuse, or were recalling imaginary incidents. Some (e.g., Fraser, 1994; Masson, 1984) have argued that Freud "covered up" the incidence of sexual abuse by depicting it as imaginary, and that the true incidence of sexual abuse of children was then and is now much higher than is usually acknowledged. Others have pointed to the difficulty of establishing retrospectively whether or not such incidents have taken place (e.g., Loftus & Loftus, 1980). Perhaps no issue has been as emotionally charged in recent years as has this one.

The *Project for a Scientific Psychology*

Freud was not only a clinician. During his university student days, he was torn between becoming a researcher or a practicing physician. Later on, his clinical work provided him with material that he used to construct psychoanalytic theory. One of his first theoretical efforts was the *Project for a Scientific Psychology,* written in 1895, and published posthumously in 1950.

The *Project* was written in neurological language, and one of its goals is to explain the nature of consciousness in neurological terms (Pribram & Gill, 1976, p. 19). Freud believed that the principle of inertia could be applied to the nervous system. In this context, you should recall our discussion of Newton's laws in Chapter 2, one of which said that things tend to remain at rest unless some force makes them move. If you apply this law to the nervous system, then the nervous system tends to remain at rest unless something forces it to act. It is the *primary process* of the nervous system to discharge energy as it accumulates, and return to a state of relative inertia.

As energy accumulates in the organism, the person wishes for objects that would reduce the level of tension in the nervous system, and primary processes can result in the person hallucinating such an object. Of course, imagining an object is not as gratifying as actually having it, and the person must develop *secondary processes,* which are ways of getting what one wants in the real (as opposed to the imagined) world. Secondary processes involve inhibiting primary processes, and using some energy to develop reliable means for gratifying wishes in accordance with the demands of reality. Thus, while primary processes follow only the *pleasure principle,* secondary processes follow the *reality principle.*

Things do not always go as they should, however. A traumatic experience, such as sexual assault, can precipitate the use of energy to maintain repressed memories. This means that energy cannot be discharged in the usual way. As energy accumulates in the system, without being appropriately discharged, then the person is at risk for displaying symptoms such as those found in hysteria. Hysterical symptoms are a way of defending oneself against the memory of a traumatic experience, and it is the goal of psychoanalytic psychotherapy to overcome the patient's *resistance* to remembering such an experience (Knight, 1984).

Cathexis is the name for the process whereby we become attached to activities that will gratify wishes. The process whereby a person gives up such attachments came to be called *countercathexis.* When the wish for something is repressed, then it is countercathected. Countercathexis amounts to forgetting that one wants a particular thing. We will discuss these processes further below.

The *Project for a Scientific Psychology* served as a kind of draft of Freud's preliminary ideas. Although the *Project* was not published in Freud's lifetime, it did contain many concepts that were to be developed and elaborated in his subsequent work.

The Interpretation of Dreams

In many ways, it is in *The Interpretation of Dreams* (1900/1965) that Freud set out his theory most clearly. The first part of the book presented a selective review of previous work on dreams and dreaming (Lavie & Hobson, 1986). In Chapter 7, Freud presented his own theory that "certain memories actually cause dreams," a view that later came to be "so widely accepted that it constitutes a major article of belief in American popular and literary culture, not to mention its pervasive influence within clinical psychiatry" (McCarley & Hobson, 1977).

Freud's theory of the dream process is best understood with reference to Figure 6.1, a representation of what is called Freud's *dynamic model.* The triangle represents different types of mental

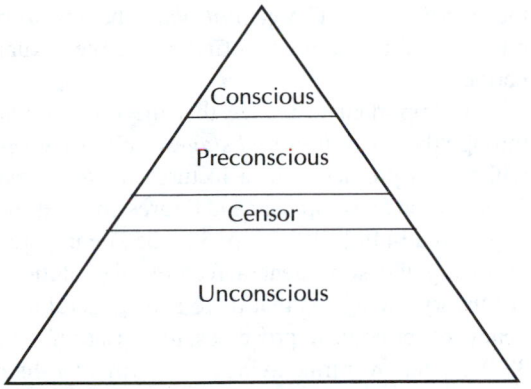

FIGURE 6.1 A representation of Freud's dynamic model.

event. At the top is the *conscious system* (Cs), containing all those things of which we are aware. The *preconscious system* (Pcs) contains all thos things of which we are not now aware, but of which we could become aware. Here might be located memory traces of such things as one's telephone number, for example. The *unconscious system* (Ucs) contains those things of which one is not aware, and cannot directly become aware. Notice that the preconscious system intervenes between the unconscious system and the conscious system, and nothing can become conscious without first passing through the preconscious system. The unconscious does not have direct access to the conscious system (e.g., Kubie, 1961). Moreover, the unconscious system is inhibited, or *censored,* such that repressed material cannot normally gain access to consciousness through the preconscious.

Figure 6.1 represents the relationship between these systems for an adult. However, the state of affairs for a newborn is different. In that case, the censor has no influence, and unconscious material gains free access to consciousness. Freud argued that when an adult dreams, then *regression* occurs. Regression means "returning," or "going back to." Dreams are the outcome of a regressed state, in which unconscious wishes are relatively more able to avoid censorship. However, they must still pass through the preconscious, and the dream as we experience it is an amalgam of unconscious wishes and preconscious material. Disguised by preconscious material, the dream does not transparently express an unconscious wish. That is why a dream must be interpreted if it is to divulge the unconscious wish it represents.

What we experience when we dream is called the *manifest content.* What we discover by analyzing a dream is called the *latent content.* In psychoanalysis, dreams may be interpreted through the technique of *free association,* a procedure whereby the patient begins by thinking about a dream, and then saying whatever comes to mind, without censoring anything. With the help of the analyst, and honest hard work on the part of the patient, the meaning of the dream may gradually become clear. It is important to realize that Freud did not advocate a mechanical approach to the analysis of dreams. He pointed out that a dream is not like a rebus. A rebus is a puzzle consisting of a series of pictures. By translating each picture, you arrive at the meaning of the puzzle. For example, if there is a picture of a baseball, a team, and an oar, then you can put all three parts together and get ball-team-oar, or "Baltimore." By saying that dream analysis was *not* like this, Freud was insisting that a particular dream had to be interpreted in the context of the rest of the patient's life, and a symbol that meant one thing in one patient's dream might mean something quite different in another patient's dream.

While it is natural to emphasize the contribution that the unconscious makes to the dream, it is also important to appreciate the contribution of the preconscious. Freud compared the unconscious to a capitalist, who has lots of money but does not know what to do with it. The preconscious is like an entrepreneur, who has lots of good ideas, but no money. They both need each other to accomplish their own ends, and so they join forces to produce a dream. In this analogy, money = energy. By coming together in a dream, the unconscious and preconscious dissipate some energy. Freud often used economic analogies like this.

Evidence for the role of preconscious material in dreams was provided by *Otto Pötzl* (1917/1960), who used a technique that subsequently proved to be very influential in the study of preconscious and unconscious processes. Pötzl's procedure involved showing a subject pictures (e.g., temple ruins at Thebes) *tachistoscopically.* A tachistoscope is a device that allows a visual stimulus to be presented so briefly (e.g., 1/100 second) that a subject may have difficulty saying what it is he or she has been shown. Pötzl believed that such briefly exposed scenes subsequently influenced the content of his subject's dreams. This was in line with Freud's (1900/ 1965, p. 197) speculation that things that happened to us during the day but to which we pay little attention—the so-called *day residue*—end up in the preconscious available for further processing in a dream.

The use of briefly exposed stimuli to study unconscious processes has been extremely common throughout the twentieth century (e.g., Kihlstrom, 1987). Among the topics that have been elaborated in this way is *subliminal perception,* the process whereby subthreshold stimuli are supposed to have subsequent effects on behavior (e.g., Greenwald, Spangenberg, Pratkanis & Eskanazi, 1991). Although such explorations have not always been conducted within the theoretical framework of psychoanalytic theory, they do follow historically from the ideas provided in *The Interpretation of Dreams.*

The Development of the Personality

As his theory matured, Freud came to believe that *sexual instincts* dominated a person's development from the very beginning of life. *Libido,* or sexual energy, does not have sexual intercourse as its only object, but in early life is diffuse. The first object in which libido is invested is the person's own body. There are *erogenous zones,* such as the mouth, which provide the child's original sources of pleasure. Sucking on the mother's breast, for example, may be the first form of gratification. The child cathects the mother's breast and other parts of her body during this *oral stage.* The *anal stage* begins when the child gains control of the anal sphincter, and derives pleasure from this function also. Subsequently, the genitals become the child's focus in the *phallic stage.* The *genital phase* begins with puberty and the attempt to find a suitable sexual partner.

It is important to realize that the progression through these *psychosexual stages* is almost never without its problems. In a lecture called "Some Thoughts on Development and Regression-Aetiology," Freud (1920/1977, pp. 339–357) compares his theory with some general features of evolutionary theory. He agrees that there is a "general tendency of biological processes to variation" (p. 339), so that over time living forms will alter their modes of adaptation. Each of the stages of development is an attempt at adaptation, but not all of them work equally well. Some of the person's early attempts to adapt are not entirely successful, and so the person will not completely pass through the developmental stages. Freud suggests that parts of these adaptations "will be permanently held back" (p. 339) and as a result the person will become more or less *fixated* at that stage.

In order to clarify the developmental process, Freud makes use of the analogy of what happens "when, as often happened in early periods of human history, a whole people left" one area and migrated to another (p. 339). He points out that it is overwhelmingly likely that not everyone who started out on the journey will arrive at the final destination of the group. Some individuals choose to remain at various "stopping places" along the route. Similarly, individual development is like a migration with various stopping places along the route. These stopping places are times when the person becomes attached to something or someone. When that attachment is given up (i.e., countercathected), then a part of the person is left behind, so to speak. As we are forced to move on, we leave a part of ourselves still connected to our earlier, childish attachments.

A central implication of Freud's analysis is that we do not give up an attachment unless we must do so (Toman, 1960). To revert to the analogy of migration, it is likely that people usually immigrate from one country to another because they have to, not because they freely choose to. So far as we know, everyone in America, including native people, is either an immigrant or descended from people who migrated from somewhere else in the world. Since recorded history, we have a continuous record of people coming here to escape the conditions they faced in their mother country. If they had remained where they were, they might have starved, or faced political persecution, or worse. Thus, it was necessary for them to give up their attachments in the mother country and form new attachments here. But notice that the old attachments seldom wither away completely. People tend to keep alive the customs of the mother country, at least for a generation or so, and perhaps even return to the homeland under certain conditions. Similarly, when a child develops and must give up his or her original attachments for new ones, it still retains some affection for the old ways. The old attachments must have been somewhat gratifying, even if they were in some deeper sense truly awful. If a child survives to adulthood, then there must have been *some* wishes gratified in childhood, otherwise the child would have died (Toman, 1960, p. 16). Under the right conditions, the adult may return to these childhood sources of gratification, just as an immigrant may return to his or her homeland for a visit, no matter how deprived his or her life may have been there. Thus, *fixation* at early stages of development is almost a necessity of development. Later on in life the person may *regress* to these earlier stages. Regression is particularly likely when the person meets powerful "external obstacles" (Freud, 1920/1977, p. 341). For example, the death of a spouse might trigger regressive behavior. Fixation and regression are complementary processes. If a person is strongly attached to a particular object, then he or she is likely to regress to that attachment if other gratifications are lost. As Freud (1920/1977) put it, continuing the analogy with migration, "if a people which is in movement has left strong detachments behind at the stopping places on its migration, it is likely to retreat to these stopping places if they have been defeated or have come up against a superior enemy. But they will also be in the greater danger of being defeated the more of their number they have left behind on their migration" (p. 341). Thus, successful development depends on being able to form new attachments, and not remain too attached to childish things.

The fact that we all remain somewhat attached to childish things illustrates a phenomenon Freud (1920/1957) called *repetition compulsion.* We are always trying to replicate the original conditions under which our wishes were gratified. The members of our families are usually, in this culture, our original sources of gratification, no matter how awful they may have been to us in other ways. If we survive to adulthood, then we must have had at least some minimal gratifications from them. As a result, we inevitably strive to form relationships that duplicate our original family relationships (Toman, 1971). This is why people sometimes make the same mistakes over and over again, and seem not to be able to learn from experience.

The Structure of the Personality

Now examine Figure 6.2, which is similar to one presented by Freud (1933/1964, p. 78). Notice that it contains the unconscious, preconscious, and conscious systems that were represented in Figure 6.1. However, blended in with these systems are the structural aspects of the personality—*id, ego,* and *superego.* The id is "the dark, inaccessible part of our personality . . . a chaos, a cauldron full of

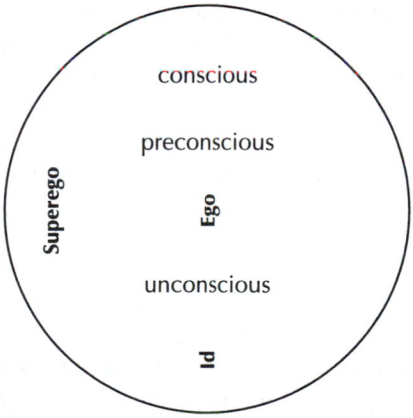

FIGURE 6.2 Freud's structural model.

seething excitations. . . . It is filled with energy reaching it from the instincts, but it has no organization . . . only a striving to bring about the satisfaction of the instinctual needs" (Freud, 1933/1964, p. 73). The superego represents the standards that other people have imposed on the person, and which the person has made his or her own, or *introjected.* A convenient way of thinking about the superego is that it does not contain your own wishes, but rather the wishes that other people have for you (Toman, 1960, p. 89). Freud (1933/1964, p. 77) sympathetically described the "poor ego" that "serves three severe masters and does what it can to bring their claims and demands into harmony with one another. No wonder that the ego so often fails in its task. Its three tyrannical masters are the external world, the superego, and the id." Corresponding to these three masters are three forms of anxiety: "If the ego is obliged to admit its weakness, it breaks out in anxiety—*realistic anxiety* regarding the external world, *moral anxiety* regarding the super-ego and *neurotic anxiety* regarding the strength of the passions in the id" (Freud, 1933/1964, p. 77).

Notice that in Figure 6.2 there are not sharp demarcations between the various parts of the personality, and that id, ego, and superego do not correspond to unconscious, preconscious, and conscious. For example, parts of the ego are unconscious. Think of acts such as walking, which you carry out more or less automatically, but which are still regulated by the ego as you move about in the external world. Thus, the unconscious contains more than repressed wishes. Notice also that part of the superego is unconscious. We are usually unaware of the many ways in which we have taken our values from other people, and the subtle ways in which these values unconsciously regulate our behavior.

As Arnheim (1986, p. 141) has observed, Freud's way of representing the structure of the personality, as shown in Figure 6.2, illustrates a common feature of theoretical thinking, not just in psychology but in any area of inquiry. Freud represented the structure of the personality in terms of a visual image that could be drawn. As the saying goes, "A picture is worth a thousand words." The "mental model" (Gentner & Stevens, 1983) in Figure 6.2 served to guide Freud's thinking. Of course, the number of possible models of the mind is innumerable—Freud's is by no means the only one possible. Indeed, as we go along, you should watch out for other mental models that have served other theorists in the way that Freud's model served him.

Religion and Culture

In his theorizing about religious practices, Freud (1913/1946) often used examples drawn from the work of others, notably Wundt's cultural psychology and the cultural anthropology of *Sir James Frazer* (1854–1941). One of Frazer's most influential ideas is discussed in Box 6.1. Of course, Freud gave a distinctive twist to his explanations of widely observed cultural practices such as the *incest taboo.* The word "taboo" originated in Polynesia, and entered the English language as a result of the voyage of Captain Cook in 1777. It was used to refer to sacred practices or prohibitions, of which incest is an example. In explaining why there is a universal taboo against incest, Freud elaborated a suggestion of Darwin to the effect that primordial humans lived in small groups, each dominated by the strongest male. In such a *primal horde,* the dominant male might drive out the other males, who would then have to seek mates elsewhere. Freud added the speculation that the weaker males might join together and kill the leader. This band of brothers would then be faced with the fact that none of them individually could replace the person they had killed. Partly out of a sense of guilt, and partly in order to survive as a group, they would all have to give up any interest in their female kin. Not only would the incest taboo be the result of the primal murder, but so too it would be the beginnings of a religious attitude in which an imaginary father substitutes for the now dead one, and becomes not only the source of hope and protection, but also of fear, awe, and dread. Given enough time, more universal religious maxims, such as "Thou shalt not covet thy neighbor's wife," eventually develop out of the primitive conditions of the primal horde.

BOX 6.1

Magical Thinking: The Influence of Sir James Frazer (1854–1941)

Sir James Frazer's social anthropology (1959/1911) had a profound influence not only on social science but also the arts in the twentieth century. Among those who have confessed their intellectual debt to him are Sigmund Freud and T. S. Eliot (Vickery, 1973). Frazer provided detailed examples of superstitious ways of behaving that exemplified what came to be called *magical thinking.*

Someone who thinks magically acts as if events in the world are regulated by two laws: the *law of similarity* and the *law of contagion.* The first of these laws leads the magical thinker to believe that causes are similar to the effects that they produce. The law of similarity leads "the magician to infer that he can produce any effect he desires merely by imitating it in advance" (Frazer, 1911/1959, p. 5). The law of similarity is not only a source of magical power, as in the "consumption of lion flesh by Hottentots to induce courage and strength," but also leads to numerous fears, such as "the ancient Greek belief that eating the flesh of the wakeful nightingale would prevent a man from sleeping; . . . avoidance of hedgehog by adult males in Madagascar, so that they will not become shy and retiring; . . . avoidance of deer by Dyak males so as not to become timid" (Rozin, 1990, p. 101).

The law of contagion leads the magical thinker to believe that things which have once been in contact continue ever afterward to act on each other (Frazer, 1911/1959, p. 5). "Perhaps the last relic of such superstitions which lingered about our English kings was the notion that they could heal scrofula by their touch. The disease was accordingly known as the King's Evil; and . . . we may perhaps conjecture that the skin disease of scrofula was originally supposed to be caused as well as cured by the king's touch. . . . Dr. Johnson was touched in his childhood for scrofula by Queen Anne" (Frazer, 1909, p. 15).

Frazer (1909, p. 2) believed that magical thinking often had a beneficial effect, in that it promoted respect for the monarchy, private property, marriage, and human life generally. However one evaluates such superstitious behavior, there is little doubt that it is not a relic of so-called "primitive" cultures, but is still a feature of everyday life. The work of Paul Rozin (Rozin, Fallon & Augostoni-Ziskind, 1985; Rozin, Millman & Nemeroff, 1986; Rozin & Fallon, 1987) demonstrates the continuing prevalence of such thinking.

Because Freud emphasized the role that sexuality plays in determining our actions, many people have assumed that he took a *laissez-faire* attitude toward sexual behavior and was in favor of loosening whatever restrictions there may be against the direct expression of such instincts. If anything, however, Freud (1927/1953; 1930/1961) took the opposite position, stressing the importance of providing culturally sanctioned outlets for the instincts. Nowhere is this position clearer than in a letter written to *Albert Einstein* in 1932 (Freud, 1932/1959), in response to a letter from Einstein written as a part of series of exchanges sponsored by the League of Nations.

Freud began by outlining what he took to be the primordial way in which people settle disputes—by the use of violence. As we have evolved, we have confirmed that "the superior strength of a single individual could be rivalled by the union of several weak ones" (Freud, 1932/1959, p. 275). The rule of law at this stage of evolution is made possible by the fact that the group can exact revenge on any individual who "gets out of line." However, in order to be effective the group must maintain itself over time by means of "emotional ties . . . feelings of unity which are the true source of its strength" (Freud, 1932/1959, p. 276). Nevertheless, there will inevitably be situations that lead to violence as a result of conflicts within the group, or between rival groups.

In his letter to Freud, Einstein had wondered why it appeared to be so easy to arouse the wish to go to war, and Freud responded with his own belief that people's lives are ultimately ruled by two instincts, the *life instinct* (Eros) and the *death instinct* (Thanatos). The former is a constructive tendency to build things up, while the latter is a destructive tendency to tear things down. Freud regarded this formulation as "no more than a theoretical clarification of the universally familiar opposition between Love and Hate which may perhaps have some fundamental relation to the polarity of attraction and repulsion that plays a part" in physics (Freud, 1932/1959, p. 281). Here we should pause to recall that Freud began his career as a scientist who subscribed to the belief, held by Helmholtz, Brücke and others, that all phenomena could ultimately be understood in terms of the fundamental forces of attraction and repulsion. Freud's postulation of a death instinct can be seen as the culmination of his attempt to remain true to this vision (Shakow, 1969, p. 94).

Few of Freud's own followers, and even fewer nonpsychoanalysts, ever accepted the hypothesis of a death instinct. However, Freud himself saw it as a necessity in order to explain the awesome carnage witnessed in an event such as World War I, for example. He also believed that the goal of the life and death instincts were, at bottom, the same. Just as the erotic tendencies operate so as to reduce tension, so its opposite tends to return us to our "original condition of inanimate matter" (Freud, 1932/1959, p. 282). Such a state would be, of course, completely tension free.

Regardless of how seriously one takes the notion of a death instinct, one might nonetheless agree with Freud that some mechanism is required in order to deal with aggressive tendencies, and that the best safeguard is the development of emotional attachments between people. In this connection Freud quoted the Bible: "Thou shalt love thy neighbor as thyself," but observed that such a state of affairs can only be brought about through indirect means, if at all. Even though culture causes us problems by inhibiting the expression of instinctual urges, it is still our best guard against the irrationality of war. Culture provides "a strengthening of the intellect, which is beginning to govern instinctual life," and so "whatever fosters the growth of culture works at the same time against war" (Freud, 1932/1959, p. 287).

Freud's Death

The analogy Freud made between development and migration applies in a particularly concrete way to the end of Freud's own life. When the Nazis came to power in Germany, psychoanalysis was not viewed with great favor, particularly since it had been invented by a Jew. The Nazis annexed Austria in 1938, and it became more and more dangerous for Freud to remain in Vienna. Many of Freud's followers were concerned that he leave for a safer place, but Freud stubbornly held fast. The necessity for leaving did not become obvious to Freud until his daughter, *Anna,* to whom he was very attached, was interrogated by the Gestapo. Soon after that episode the Freuds left Vienna for England. Freud's sojourn there was brief. He had suffered from cancer of the palate since at least 1923, and had previously arranged with his personal physician *Max Schur* to assist him in dying when the time came. Freud's suffering was intense, and he finally decided that there was no point in going on. He died after a dose of morphine on September 23, 1939.

Freud and America

In 1909, Freud lectured on psychoanalysis at Clark University in Worcester, Massachusetts, and by 1915 the psychoanalytic approach had become reasonably well-known in America (Hornstein, 1992). Many psychologists were impressed, and historians of psychology in the first half of the twentieth century (e.g., Heidbreder, 1933; Boring, 1950b) counted Freud's theory among the most important of psychological theories (Shakow & Rapaport, 1964, p. 73). However, there was considerable resistance to Freud's approach, particularly from academic psychologists. This resistance had two sources. One arose from the fact that academic psychologists were accustomed to laboratory evidence being used to support a theory, and there was a relative absence of experimental evidence in support of psychoanalytic theory. "To the analyst, science had nothing to do with method, with controlling variables or counting things. What made something scientific was that it was true . . . The efforts of [experimental] psychologists, with their bulky equipment and piles of charts and graphs, seemed superficial and largely irrelevant [to the psychoanalyst]" (Hornstein, 1992, pp. 254–255). Added to this incommensurability of method was the attitude, so clearly stated by Freud (1933/1964), that in order to understand psychoanalysis, you had to be psychoanalyzed yourself.

> *It is in general so hard to give anyone who is not himself a psychoanalyst an insight into psychoanalysis. You can believe me when I tell you that we do not enjoy giving an impression of being members of a secret society and of practising a mystical science. Yet we have been obliged to recognize and express as our conviction that no-one has a right to join in a discussion of psychoanalysis who has not had particular experiences which can only be obtained by being analyzed oneself. (Freud, 1933/1964, p. 69)*

This is a particularly pernicious argument, because it places the psychoanalyst in a win/win situation in relation to critics of the theory. If you approve of the theory, then you are an insightful person. If you disapprove of the theory, then you are just resisting the truth and are in need of analysis yourself! Many academic psychologists found this attitude reprehensible, and, as we see in later chapters, demanded more objective standards for the validation of psychoanalysis or, for that matter, any other theory.

Although psychoanalytic *theory* was not easily assimilated by academic psychology departments, many prominent psychologists availed themselves of psychoanalytic *therapy.* Some of them published accounts of their analysis in a symposium in the *American Journal of Psychology* (American Psychological Association, 1940/1953). "By its very nature the symposium could not provide systematic data. It did, however, offer a forum for the presentation by psychologists of a wide variety of material, ranging from views about the psychoanalytic process itself, through reports of actual experiments on psychoanalytic themes, to suggestions for revision of psychoanalytic theory. Even the most impersonal of the reports were sufficiently detailed to give some indication of the effects of the analytic process on the participants. The symposium leaves one with the distinct impression of important contributions to psychology from psychoanalysis" (Shakow & Rapaport, 1964, pp. 77–78).

If discussions of psychoanalytic therapy helped embed psychoanalysis in psychology, so did the fact that psychoanalytic concepts began to appear in introductory textbooks, although they were often presented without much discussion of psychoanalytic theory itself (Hornstein, 1992, p. 259). However, what is taught in an introductory course in psychology is an important index of the extent to which particular ideas occupy a central place in a discipline (e.g., Morawski, 1992), and psychoanalytic concepts became a core part of the discipline in the sense that students were expected to know something about them.

As Hornstein (1992, p. 261) observed, "American psychology has always been distinguished by an uncanny ability to adapt itself to cultural trends as quickly as they emerge. Once it became clear that the public found psychoanalysis irresistible, psychologists found ways of accommodating to it. Instead of concentrating all their efforts on criticism, they identified those parts of the theory that were potentially useful to their own ends and incorporated them." In future chapters, we will see examples of how psychologists incorporated psychoanalytic concepts into their own theories.

Freud's Critics within Psychoanalysis

Consider what the following quotation reveals about Freud's proprietary attitude toward psychoanalysis:

> *For psychoanalysis is my creation; I was for ten years the only person who concerned himself with it . . . no-one can know better than I what psychoanalysis is, how it differs from other ways of investigating the life of the mind, and precisely what should be called psychoanalysis and what should be described by some other name. (Freud, 1914/1959, p. 287)*

After reading that quotation, it should not surprise you to learn that Freud did not tolerate dissent within the psychoanalytic movement. One of the chief dissenters, *Carl G. Jung,* founded his own version of psychoanalysis that we will consider later in the chapter. Others also created distinctive versions of the theory. Among the most prominent was *Alfred Adler* (1870–1937). Like many of the dissidents, Adler was uncomfortable with the notion that sexuality was the be-all and end-all of human existence, and instead chose to emphasize the role that *feelings of inferiority* play in human development.

Adler's emphasis on inferiority draws attention to the dimension of dominance-submission as a particularly important aspect of human affairs. Rather than regard erotic urges as the prime mover of human behavior, Adler focused on the centrality of power. Adler spoke of "the absolute primacy of the *will to power* . . . which asserts itself more forcibly . . . the stronger the inferiority feeling of the child" (Ansbacher & Ansbacher, 1964, p. 111).

Among the forces that influence feelings of inferiority, Adler believed that *birth order* was particularly important. He pointed out that "it is a common fallacy to imagine that children of the same family are formed in the same environment," and that because of "the order of their succession" each child was born into a different situation (Ans- bacher & Ansbacher, 1964, p. 376). Based on his clinical experience, Adler gave thumbnail sketches of the typical personality to be found in each sibling position, and these make entertaining reading (Ansbacher & Ansbacher, 1964, pp. 377–382). However one evaluates these characterizations, there can be no doubt that birth order subsequently became a very intensively investigated variable (e.g., Schachter, 1959; Toman, 1971).

Freud and Women

One of the persistent criticisms of Freud is that he was a misogynist. Certainly, many women have felt compelled to distance themselves from what Freud himself acknowledged was largely a male-centered psychology. In fact, Freud did not directly address differences between men and women until 1923, which is relatively late in his theoretical development (Appignanesi & Forrester, 1992, p. 399). Freud then advanced the infamous hypothesis concerning *penis envy:* women want to have a penis, and feel incomplete without one. Many women have subsequently found this suggestion either preposterous or hilarious, or perhaps both (e.g., Steinem, 1994).

While women often disavowed psychoanalysis (including Breuer's patient Anna O.—Bertha Pappenheim—who eventually became a prominent feminist), there were also many women who managed to develop their own ideas within a modified form of psychoanalysis (Sayers, 1991). Among these was Freud's daughter, *Anna Freud.*

Anna Freud (1895–1982)

Much has been written about the closeness of the relationship between the founder of psychoanalysis and his daughter. She has been described as "her father's secretary, nurse, and main exponent of his ideas. But she also went beyond them" (Sayers, 1991, p. 145). The ideas for which she became best known concerned the *defense mechanisms* (A. Freud, 1936/1946), those procedures that protect the ego from the disruptive influences of unconscious wishes. As we have already seen, repression is the basic mechanism for keeping id impulses under control. However, the ego must often resort to other devices in order to successfully maintain control. Among the best known of these are *displacement, projection, rationalization,* and *reaction formation.*

- *Displacement* is a way of redirecting an impulse toward a safer target. The classic example of displacement is the person who wishes to murder his or her boss, but is afraid to express this anger directly for fear of losing his or her job. Therefore, the anger is vented on the family pet, or worse yet, children and other vulnerable people who are less able to retaliate.

• *Projection* involves attributing one's own unacknowledged wishes to someone else. If you cannot face the fact that you wish to have sex with someone, then you may find yourself thinking that the other person wants to have sex with you. If you unconsciously want to murder someone, then you may find yourself worried that the other person wants to murder you. Of course, in cases such as these, you may feel the need to take precautions against what you believe to be the evil impulses of the other person, and this may lead to some very strange behavior, as you can easily imagine.

• *Rationalization* is a way of making excuses for oneself when one behaves in a way that is inconsistent with the ego's conception of itself. Imagine a teacher who thinks of himself or herself as a brilliant pedagogue, but who always fails more students in his class than any other teacher. The truth may be that the teacher actually hates his or her students, and expresses this by giving them undeservedly low marks. The students may perceive this fact themselves, and curse the day that fate landed them in this teacher's class. The teacher, however, may be reluctant to face the truth about himself or herself, and instead complain about *his* or *her* bad luck in always being given such bad students to teach. Alternatively, the teacher may claim that he or she is the only teacher in the school with proper standards, and is just trying to keep the traditional academic integrity of the school from eroding. If you think about this example for a moment, you will see how difficult it may be to tell the difference between someone who is rationalizing, and someone who is telling the truth. Both people sincerely believe what they say, but the rationalizer is deceiving both himself or herself and his or her audience.

• *Reaction formation* allows the ego to recruit additional energy in the service of repressing a wish. The ego does this by vigorously expressing the opposite behavior to that which would occur if the unconscious wish were given free rein. Suppose you truly love (or hate) someone, but cannot face this about yourself, let alone express it. One way of dealing with such a state of affairs is to express the opposite of what you really (i.e., unconsciously) feel. Typically, reaction formation is said to lead to exaggerated forms of behavior. Perhaps you have experienced the attentions of someone who appears to think you are an absolutely wonderful person, so much so that you begin to wonder if their feelings can possibly be genuine.

The defense mechanisms are good examples of the sort of behavior that interested not only Anna Freud, but psychoanalysts generally. The defense mechanisms beautifully illustrate the psychoanalytic premise that behavior is not always what it seems to be. Like a dream, the meaning of behavior is never transparent. That is why behavior, like the dream, requires *interpretation,* because its true meaning may be the opposite of what it at first appears to be. Moreover, you are not in a good position to interpret your own behavior, because you are probably deceiving yourself. Only an objective outsider—psychoanalyst, for example—will be able to interpret your behavior properly (MacIntyre, 1958). The prevalence of interpreting other people's behavior may be seen as largely due to the influence of psychoanalysis on twentieth-century culture (Trilling, 1972, pp. 140–157). Men and women alike grew accustomed to interpreting each other's behavior, often, without realizing it, along psychoanalytic lines. Finally, psychoanalytic interpretation became so commonplace that it no longer captured the popular imagination in the latter half of the twentieth century, as even Anna Freud (1969) was forced to conclude. However, as the twentieth century progressed, new popular psychotherapies emerged that provided ordinary people with alternative frameworks within which to interpret behavior (Rosen, 1977), and we will examine some of them in Chapter 13.

Karen Horney (1885–1952) and the Psychology of Women

Karen Horney was born and educated in Germany, where she became a medical doctor in 1913. Although she started out as a more or less orthodox psychoanalyst, she gradually developed her own unique theory. In 1932, she moved to the United

States. Horney has been described as one of "the most important women in the history of psychology. A towering intellect, the courage of her convictions, creative imagination, and a genuinely rebellious spirit led to her dramatic secession from orthodox psychoanalysis. She became the first woman to found an independent psychoanalytic society, the American Institute for Psychoanalysis. She contributed brilliant, integrative, and original theories: a theory of neurosis, theories related to personality development, and a radical theory of the psychology of women" (Stevens & Gardner, 1982). There has been renewed interest in Horney recently, with the publication of important books about her and her work (e.g., Quinn, 1987; Westcott, 1986).

Horney argued that the typical male analyst did not see women accurately, but in a distorted, juvenile way (Appignanesi & Forrester, 1992, p. 437). If a woman envied a man, it would not be so much because of his penis, but because of the superior status society accorded the masculine role (Greenglass, 1982, p. 51). Moreover, men may also envy women, a condition Horney called *womb envy.* By this Horney meant concretely that men may envy women for their ability to have children, and, more abstractly, that men may envy women for their creativity. "This 'womb envy' is expressed by men in the form of disparagement of women's natural achievements and glorification of the practical achievements of men" (Greenglass, 1982, p. 248).

Horney (1950, p. 366) "discarded Freud's theory of instincts," and regarded neurosis as the outcome of the child's response to *basic anxiety,* which was defined as a "feeling of being isolated and helpless toward a world potentially hostile." The child, and later the adult, tries to deal with this anxiety in three ways. The first way is *moving toward people,* a pattern of behavior in which the person behaves in a self-effacing, compliant manner toward others; the second way is *moving away from people,* in which the person attempts to live in isolation and maintain an attitude of indifference to what goes on; and the third way is *moving against people,* in which the person maintains an attitude of hostile vindictiveness against others. It is normal for all of us to engage in these forms of behavior, which only become neurotic when the person is no longer able to be flexible, but maintains a rigid adherence to only one pattern of behavior, and engages in it in an exaggerated fashion. Notice that each of these *neurotic types* involves a way of relating to people, and thus Horney's (1950) theory places great emphasis on the importance of interpersonal relationships:

> *Self-realization does not exclusively, or even primarily, aim at developing one's special gifts. The center of the process is the evolution of one's potentialities as a human being; hence it involves—in a central place—the development of one's capacities for good human relations. (p. 308)*

Horney (1950, pp. 370–371) believed that her psychology was different from Freud's in three ways. First, Freud underestimated the importance of social factors in determining personality. Second, Freud generally overestimated the role of sexuality. Third, Freud overemphasized the role of early childhood experiences. By suggesting that there are constructive forces in people that enable them to change neurotic patterns and live authentically as their real selves, Horney believed she had created a more optimistic alternative to Freudianism.

Additional Reading on This Topic. Useful overviews of Freud's life and influence are given by Gay (1988) and Sulloway (1979). Young-Bruehl (1988) is a very useful biography of Anna Freud.

Although psychoanalysis has historically played a central role in the treatment of mental illness, it is also interesting to explore those attempts to deal with this problem before psychoanalysis came on the scene. For a review of nineteenth-century practices in a North American context, see Krasnick (1982) and Shortt (1986).

CARL G. JUNG (1875–1961)

Jung's Relationship with Freud

Jung was trained as a physician, and in the early phase of his career practiced psychiatry at the Burgholzli clinic in Zurich (Switzerland). The chief of

Box 6.2

Sabina Spielrein (1885–1941)

Spielrein is a very good example of a woman who does collaborative work with men, but who fails to receive appropriate credit. "A passionate idealist, a woman of immense strength of character and resilience, Spielrein was the first woman psychoanalyst of significance, and she was until very recently almost entirely forgotten" (Appignanesi & Forrester, 1992, p. 205). Appignanesi and Forrester (1992, pp. 204–226) and Carotenuto (1982) have reminded us of some of the remarkable facts of her life.

- Born in Russia, she began to study medicine in Zurich in 1904. As a result of some sort of problem, she was admitted to the Burgholzli, where she was treated by Jung. After being discharged, she began working with Jung on his word association experiments. Spielrein and Jung became erotically involved, and Jung wrote to Freud, apparently in an attempt to elicit Freud's help in extricating himself from the relationship. The resulting correspondence between the three makes fascinating reading, and is contained in Carotenuto (1982).
- Spielrein became a psychoanalyst, and wrote papers that contained ideas that were later developed by Freud in his theorizing about a death instinct. Her work also influenced Jung's theorizing about the bipolar nature of the mind.
- Spielrein's contributions went well beyond the psychoanalytic arena. Not only did she work on the development of language, but after moving to Geneva, became *Jean Piaget's* analyst. Piaget is, of course, one of the most famous twentieth-century developmental psychologists, and we will consider his work in detail in Chapter 13.
- After returning to Russia, Spielrein met *Alexander R. Luria* and *Lev S. Vygotsky,* two of the giants of Russian psychology. It is entirely possible that she influenced these men as well.

"In 1924 she moved back to her home town of Rostov and taught at the local university. . . . When Rostov was captured by the invading German army in November, 1941, all the Jews of the city, including Spielrein and her two daughters, were taken to the synagogue and shot" (Appignanesi & Forrester, 1992, p. 226).

---

staff at the Burgholzli was *Eugen Bleuler* (1857–1939), who coined the term *schizophrenia* to describe that terrifying condition in which the person seems totally cut off from normal reality. The Burgholzli was a prestigious facility, and it has been suggested that Freud was initially receptive to Jung because of Freud's wish to recruit members of prestigious institutions to the psychoanalytic cause (Zaretsky, 1994).

Jung discovered Freud's psychoanalytic theory by reading *The Interpretation of Dreams,* and began writing to Freud (McGuire, 1974). One of his first letters concerned *Sabina Spielrein,* who, among other things, was a patient and co-worker of Jung. Spielrein was also much more, and her fascinating story is briefly summarized in Box 6.2. Jung visited Freud in Vienna in 1907, and the two men became close friends. Freud began to see Jung as his successor and leader of the psychoanalytic movement. In 1909, Jung accompanied Freud to America, where both gave lectures at Clark University in Worcester, Massachusetts. Jung's lecture concerned the technique of *word association* he had developed as a diagnostic technique (e.g., Jung, 1904/1974). Jung's association experiments involved measuring the reaction time to a series of stimulus words. Words that required a long time to give an association were clues to the person's areas of difficulty.

During the period that Freud and Jung were getting along with each other, they wrote often. In those days, it was very common for people to exchange letters on a regular basis. The postal system was reliable and swift, and a letter from Jung in Zurich could be answered by Freud in Vienna in a few days. Let us examine two letters written toward the end of their friendship. On November 11, 1912, Jung wrote Freud on returning from another visit to America. In the following extract from the letter, the symbol **ΨA** refers to "psychoanalysis," a common abbreviation in both Freud and Jung's correspondence.

> *I gave 9 lectures at the Jesuit (!) University of Fordham, New York—a critical account of the development of the theory of* **ΨA**. . . . *Naturally, I also made room for those of my views which deviate in places from the hitherto existing conceptions, particularly in regard to the libido theory.* I found that my version of **ΨA** won over many people who until now had been put off by the problem of sexuality in neurosis. *(p. 515; emphasis added)*

On November 14, 1912, Freud replied as follows:

> *Dear Dr. Jung,*
> *I greet you on your return from America, no longer as affectionately as on the last occasion in Nuremburg—you have successfully broke me of that habit—but still with considerable sympathy, interest and satisfaction at your personal success.* . . . You have reduced a good deal of resistance with your modifications, but I shouldn't advise you to enter this in the credit column because, as you know, the farther you remove yourself from what is new in **ΨA,** the more certain you will be of applause and the less resistance you will meet. *(p. 517; emphasis added)*

Notice that Jung is proposing a fundamental change in the libido concept (which we will discuss in the next section), and that Freud, as usual, is not receptive to any alterations in what he regards as *his* theory. Notice further that Freud believes that Jung is disowning the essential parts of psychoanalysis, and is offering the public a sugar-coated version that is easier to swallow. As we now move on to discuss Jung's theory, keep Freud's attitude in mind, and see to what extent you think it fits Jung's revision.

The Difference between Freud and Jung. Recall that Freud had advanced the idea that the basic motivating force in human life is libido, which Freud regarded as sexual energy. Jung wanted to desexualize the concept of the libido. Freud felt that such a change would rob psychoanalysis of one of its most basic insights. The two could not reach an accommodation, and communication between them eventually broke down completely. The change in the libido concept that Jung proposed was to equate it with *psychic energy,* which was the total "life force" in the person. Although it might be expressed sexually, it was not solely, or even basically, sexual. Thus, Jung's concept of libido is much broader than Freud's. This "life force" could be a source of inspiration and growth, not just a drive for pleasure.

Analytical Psychology

Jung left the psychoanalytic movement and founded his own theoretical school, called *analytical psychology,* or, as it is more commonly called nowadays, *archetypal psychology* (e.g., Hillman, 1972).

Extraversion and Introversion

After his break with Freud, Jung spent many years working on his book *Psychological Types,* which was published in 1921. In it, Jung (1921/1971) formulated the distinction between *introversion* and *extraversion* which has since become so well-known. These opposing tendencies are examples of what was, for Jung, a general feature of mental life: Bipolar distinctions always underlie psychological processes, and every process is capable of moving in opposing directions (Dallett, 1973).

The introvert-extravert distinction refers to the way in which different people relate to the world. Jung (1921/1971) described the typical extravert as someone who is obviously interested in what goes on in the environment. "Extraversion is an outward-turning of the libido . . . a transfer of interest from subject to object" (p. 427). By contrast, "introversion means a turning inward of libido. . . . Interest does not move towards the object but withdraws from it into the subject" (p. 453). Jung's student, Jolande Jacobi (1968), summarized the relation between introversion and extraversion as follows:

> *Extraversion is characterized by a positive relation to the object, introversion by a negative one. In his*

[or her] adjustment and reaction pattern, the extravert orients himself [or herself] predominantly by the outward, collective norms, the spirit of the times, etc. The attitudes of the introvert, on the other hand are determined mainly by subjective factors. Often he [or she] is poorly adjusted to [the] environment. The extravert thinks, feels, and acts in relation to the object; . . . displaces . . . interest from subject to object and orients [herself or] himself primarily by the world outside. . . . For the introvert the subject is the basis of orientation, while the object plays at most a secondary, indirect role. (pp. 18–19)

We could say that the introvert is more "subjective" than the extravert, who is more "objective." Suppose an introvert and an extravert are in the same situation. The introvert regards the subjective experience of the situation as more important than the situation itself. By contrast, the extravert experiences a situation directly, as of value in its own right (Shapiro & Alexander, 1975). The introvert can be characterized as moving away from the world. This movement is not simply negative, because the introvert is simultaneously moving toward what Jung called the *collective unconscious.* In the collective unconscious are characteristics possessed by the species as a whole. It is indifferent to the individual ego, but rather expresses the most general tendencies there are; it corresponds to what we all have in common. "We have to distinguish between a *personal unconscious* and an impersonal or transpersonal unconscious. We speak of the latter also as the *collective unconscious,* because it is detached from anything personal and is entirely universal, and because its contents can be found everywhere" (Jung, 1943/1956, p. 76).

The personal unconscious is analogous to what Freud meant by "the unconscious," and "contains lost memories, painful ideas that are repressed, . . . subliminal perceptions, . . . contents that are not yet ripe for consciousness," while the collective unconscious "is the object which the libido chooses when it is freed. . . . It follows its own gradient down into the depths of the unconscious, and there activates what has lain slumbering from the beginning. It has discovered the hidden treasure upon which mankind ever and anon has drawn, and from which it has raised up its gods and demons" (Jung, 1943/1956, pp. 76–77).

We can begin to grasp the limitless nature of what Jung meant by the collective unconscious by examining Figure 6.3. About that diagram, Jung (1969, p. 21) said:

If you suppose AA[1] to be the threshold of consciousness, then you would have in D an area of consciousness referring to the ectopsychic [i.e., external] world B . . . But on the other side, in C, is the shadow-world. *There the ego is somewhat dark, we do not see into it, we are an enigma to ourselves. We only know the ego in D, we do not know it in C. Therefore we are always discovering something new about ourselves. Almost every year something new turns up which we did not know before. We always think we are now at the end of our discoveries. We never are. We go on discovering that we are this, that, and other things, and sometimes we have astounding experiences.*

As Rycroft (1969) has pointed out, it is instructive to compare Jung's diagram with Freud's structural model given in Figure 6.2. Both Freud and

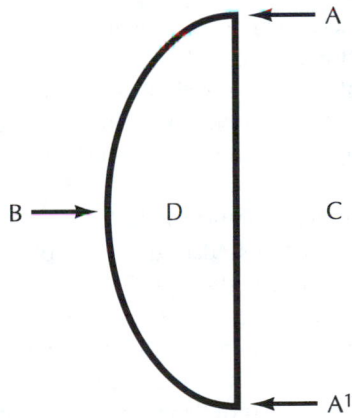

FIGURE 6.3 Jung's representation of the relation between consciousness, the external world, and the inner world.

Source: C. G. Jung. (1977). The symbolic life. Princeton, NJ: Princeton University Press, p. 21. Copyright © 1977 by Princeton University Press. Reproduced by permission of Princeton University Press.

Jung conceive of the mind using spatial metaphors. As we observed earlier, the use of such metaphors can be a great aid to the theorist's thinking. They should not be taken literally, but rather as metaphorical models of the mind.

Archetypes

It is through exploration of the collective unconscious that one becomes aware of the existence of *archetypes.* According to the *Oxford English Dictionary,* the word "archetype" originally meant "the pattern or model from which copies are made; a prototype." There is a similarity between the concept of archetypes and Platonic ideas, although unlike Platonic ideas, archetypes have not only a cognitive function but also an emotional aspect (Jacobi, 1971, p. 49). On the one hand, archetypes give rise to characteristic emotions, while at the same time generating typical images or ways of representing events. From Jung's viewpoint, the mind is not a blank slate at birth, but meets life with archetypal predispositions to perceive, feel, and act in particular ways. Archetypes do not give rise to specific mental contents or images. Their action is more general, in that they organize our experience without determining its content. They are innate organizational tendencies that are dynamic and emotional, carrying with them general feeling qualities. We never encounter archetypes directly, but rather particular images that have been shaped by them.

Here is an example of the way in which an archetype functions, adapted from Jacobi (1968, p. 44) and Campbell (1964, pp. 73–74). We all have an image of what a hero is. Close your eyes and imagine the person who, of all your personal acquaintances, best exemplifies a hero. The image you have is the sort of thing we are now interested in. These images are obviously different for different people, and different for one individual at different times. But they are all related to one another, in that they all express the archetype of "the hero." In addition to people of your own acquaintance, you could have images of heroes whom you may never have encountered. These might include famous warriors (like George Washington), or people who battled for the rights of others (like Susan B. Anthony or Martin Luther King). You could also have images of heroes you may have discovered as a child through the media, such as Batman or Catwoman, as well as mythical heroes such as Hercules. The contribution the archetype makes to each image is greatest the more it is removed from actual people and situations. However, to a greater or less extent, the archetype will shape every image, even those we have of real people. No image is simply a copy of what is given by the external world. Images vary from those which are relatively "extraverted" (i.e., largely conform to an external reality) to those which are relatively "introverted" (i.e., largely conform to an inner reality). Neither is more "accurate" than the other. Each reflects its own reality. The extraverted image is faithful to the outer reality, while the introverted image is faithful to the inner reality.

It is difficult to say how many archetypes there are, although Jungians typically argue that the number is finite, and corresponds to our most "fundamental experiences incurred . . . since primordial times. . . . They are the same in all cultures. We find them recurring in all mythologies, fairy tales, religious traditions, and mysteries" (Jacobi, 1968, p. 47). Among the archetypes most frequently discussed in the Jungian literature are the *anima* and the *animus.* The anima is the masculine image of femininity, while the animus is the feminine image of masculinity. Each of us has a mask, or *persona,* that constitutes our public self. To the extent that we identify with this mask, we will be cut off from those parts of ourselves that are inconsistent with it. Someone whose persona is excessively masculine may be totally unaware of their feminine side, represented by the *anima,* while someone whose persona is excessively feminine may be totally unaware of their masculine side, represented by the *animus.* These unacknowledged parts of the person exist in the "shadow world" represented in Figure 6.3. It is a major part of a person's lifework to integrate these opposing parts of the personality into a coherent whole.

Balancing Opposites

In many psychological theories, the goal of the organism is said to be tension reduction. As we saw earlier, in the standard psychoanalytic theory of motivation, our basic motive is to eliminate the unpleasure that occurs as libido accumulates, and in order to do this we seek objects that will reduce tension. No doubt there is some truth to this notion, but Jung thought that the true situation was somewhat more complex. He believed that the overriding goal of the person was to balance the opposing tendencies contained within. The integration of these opposites was the person's major task. By proposing the *union of opposites* as a basic process, Jung is echoing a theme that, as we saw in Chapter 1, has been sounded for a long time. Indeed, Jung was a formidable scholar, and not only drew on Western sources, but also from Eastern traditions such as Taoism (e.g., Jung, 1950).

We can illustrate how this balancing process might work using the extraversion-introversion distinction. Jung argues that it is most common for the person to be extraverted at first, but somewhere around midlife to begin to turn inward and become more introverted. The shift from extraversion to introversion is not only a shift in the orientation to the external world, but also a shift in orientation to the inner world. This means increased attention to the collective unconscious. If this process works well, it does not involve simply an oscillation from objective observation to the cultivation of an "inner vision." Rather it involves an integration into a unified whole of both orientations, a union of opposites.

Jung's concept of a union of opposites was drawn in part from medieval *alchemy.* Alchemy was primitive chemistry, and involved the search for a way of turning lead into gold. One part of alchemy became modern chemistry. However, alchemy itself is still relevant because of its symbolic value. Jung believed that the alchemical search for gold symbolically represented the search for a union of the opposing parts of ourselves. The process whereby this union is achieved is symbolically represented not only in alchemy, but also in countless myths and legends, such as the search for the Holy Grail. The process of Jungian psychotherapy was intended to facilitate this quest for wholeness. To have the person produce art can be an important part of this process. Among the most interesting forms of art are *mandalas,* or balanced structures expressing the person's unified *self.*

The Four Functions

As you might expect, Jung's description of psychological processes was organized along bipolar dimensions. We have already noted one such distinction, extraversion-introversion. For Jungians, another important distinction is that between *perception* and *judgment.* There are two perceptual functions, *sensation* and *intuition,* as well as two judgmental functions, *thinking* and *feeling.* Figure 6.4 illustrates the way in which these pairs stand in opposition to one another. Typically, the person specializes in one of these functions, in which case the opposite function remains relatively primitive. Thus, someone might favor thinking as a way of making judgments, which would mean that he or she evaluates something in terms of whether it is true or false. In that case, their feeling function, which evaluates things in terms of good versus bad, might be underdeveloped. Alternatively, someone might specialize in intuition, the process that grasps situations as whole. In that case, their sensation function, which deals with particular facts, might be underdeveloped.

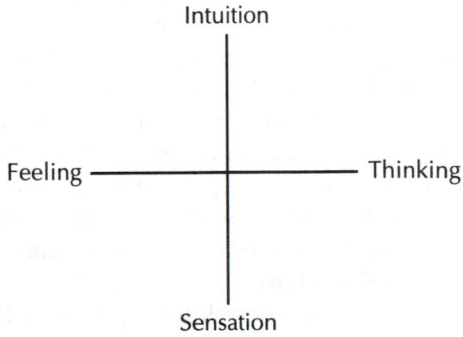

FIGURE 6.4 The four functions.

Since a function can be either extraverted (looking outward) or introverted (looking inward), you can see that a great many possible combinations exist. Jung's typology (e.g., Briggs & Myers, 1976) has become extremely popular in business and in education as a way of representing individual differences (e.g., Benfari, 1991), although academic psychologists have long had serious doubts about it (e.g., Stricker & Ross, 1964).

The Collective Unconscious and the External World

At first glance it appears that nothing could be more unlike the external world than the collective unconscious. The external world seems to be "objective," while the collective unconscious is "subjective." However, Jung sometimes called the collective unconscious the *objective unconscious,* because, like the external world, it is relatively neutral with respect to the individual ego. At bottom, the external world and the collective unconscious are both aspects of the same underlying reality. Jung believed that the collective unconscious can be a rich source of inspiration.

Here is an example of the creative process of the sort that Jungians liked, although you should realize that a Jungian explanation of this example is by no means the only one. "The German chemist *Friedrich A. Kekulé* said that many of his early insights into the nature of chemical bonds and of molecular structure arose out of idle reveries in which he spontaneously experienced kinetic visual images of the dancing atoms hooked up to form chainlike molecules. Kekulé's cultivation of this visionary practice culminated in his celebrated dream in which one of these snakelike, writhing chains suddenly twisted into a closed loop as if seizing its own tail; thus was the startled Kekulé provided with his long-sought answer to the problem of the structure of benzene—a structure fundamental to all of modern organic chemistry" (Shepard, 1978, p.126).

Jungians might approach this example as follows. Dreams and fantasy often reveal the effects of the collective unconscious. When we stop consciously attending to a problem, then ideas fall below the threshold of awareness and can make contact with archetypal material in the collective unconscious. One such archetypal image is the *uroboros,* the snake eating its tail, of which the art historian Ernst Gombrich (1965, p. 46) said: "This image which stands for time can tell us in a flash what discursive argument can only enumerate, such as the proposition that time is swift, that time in its turning somehow joins the beginning to the end, that it teaches wisdom, and brings and removes things." The uroboros is an ancient symbol that manifests itself in diverse cultures. In Kekulé's dream it organizes his real-world problem, giving it the structure necessary for him to see the solution. In general, archetypal material that emerges in dreams or fantasy can restructure mundane thinking, which can then be mapped back onto the world in a productive way. Introverted images can help us understand the extraverted reality. From Jung's viewpoint, the fact that archetypal structuring of our thinking can help us in our dealings with the external world should not surprise us. Because the collective unconscious and the external world are part of Nature, they share the same reality. Jung referred to this commonality as reflecting the ultimately *psychoid* nature of reality, meaning that Nature is neither mental nor physical, neither inner or outer, but everything at once.

Many people in the arts, sciences, and religion were drawn to Jung's ideas. One example is the physicist *Wolfgang Pauli* (1955). He pointed out that we cannot take so introverted an attitude that we are ignorant of the external world. However, if we want a unified world view, then we must accept that introverted experience plays a significant role in the genesis of scientific ideas. Scientific creativity requires a relatively more introverted attitude than has customarily been advocated in most modern science. The extraverted attitude, says Pauli, enables us to fit our ideas to reality, while the introverted attitude accesses the archetypal images that inform scientific ideas to begin with. Pauli argues that great scientists such as Kepler have understood the importance of balancing both sides of the equation.

As we saw when we reviewed Pythagorean ideas in Chapter 1, one of the most salient aspects of scientific thought in the West has been the application of mathematical ideas to the external world. Jungians, such as *Marie-Louise von Franz* (1974, pp. 18–19) argued, as had Pauli, that basic mathematical ideas "should be included in Jung's concept of archetypal ideas. . . . If we accept Pauli's contention that certain mathematical structures rest on an archetypal basis, then their isomorphism with certain outerworld phenomena is not so surprising. For we know that archetypes engender images and ideas . . . which lie at the basis of [our] grasp of the outer world, and that they serve to release generally adequate adaptation reactions (comparable to the patterns of behavior in animals) that are probably not dependent on anything radically different from the basic structure of the physical world itself." Thus, exploration of the collective unconscious may bring to light mathematical structures that not only regulate mental events, but also physical and biological ones as well.

Synchronicity

You will have gathered by now that Jung and Jungians generally are prepared to explore topics that other psychologists regard as far removed from their usual concerns. One of these areas of inquiry is *synchronicity.* Few of Jung's ideas are more obscure yet at the same time more influential than this one. Simply stated, synchronicity refers to *meaningful coincidences.* These are cases in which events seem to be connected to one another although they are not causally related. Almost everyone can report experiences of this sort, and most people resist explaining them as merely due to chance (Falk, 1989). Here is an example from Jung (1960/1973):

> *A young woman I was treating has, at a critical moment, a dream in which she was given a golden scarab. While she was telling me this dream I sat with my back to the closed window. Suddenly I heard a noise behind me, like a gentle tapping. I turned round and saw a flying insect knocking against the windowpane from outside. I opened the window and caught the creature in the air as it flew in. It was the nearest analogy to a golden scarab that one finds in our latitudes, a scarabaeid beetle the common rose-chafer* (Cetonia aurata) *which contrary to its usual habits had evidently felt an urge to get into a dark room at this particular moment. I must admit that nothing like it ever happened to me before or since, and that the dream of the patient has remained unique in my experience. (p. 22)*

One could treat such an incident as merely a coincidence, and not read very much into it. However, Jung (who was interested in parapsychology throughout his life) insisted on the meaningfulness of such coincidences. He suggested that events may be meaningfully connected in a noncausal manner, through the collective unconscious. Mysterious as such a formulation sounds, it attracted many adherents (e.g., Koestler, 1974).

Additional Reading on This Topic. A good introduction to Jung is his autobiography, *Memories, Dreams and Reflections* (Jung, 1965).

KEY NAMES AND CONCEPTS

What follows is an index of some of the most important material in this chapter. The list includes individuals, concepts, and topics you should know. Read through the list, and if anything on it seems unfamiliar, then go back and re-read the appropriate section of the chapter. You should be able to define each concept, briefly discuss each topic, and state the importance of each person on the list. In addition, you should be able to write an account of the work done by each person whose name is printed in boldface.

Adler, Alfred, 108
birth order, 108
feelings of inferiority, 108
will to power, 108

Anna O., 99
Bertha Pappenheim, 99
Bernays, Martha, 98
Bleuler, Eugen
schizophrenia, 11
Box 6.1—Magical thinking, 105
Box 6.2—Sabina Spielrein, 111
Breuer, J., 98
Brücke, Ernst, 98
catharsis, 99
Charcot, Jean-Martin, 98
conversion hysteria, 98
Einstein, Albert, 105
Freud, Anna
defense mechanisms, 108
Freud, Sigmund
cathexis and countercathexis, 100
censor, 101
conscious, preconscious, and unconscious, 101
day residue, 102
dynamic model, 100
erogenous zones, 102
fixation, 102
free association, 101
hysteria, 98
id, ego, and superego, 103
incest taboo, 104
infantile sexuality, 99
interpretation of dreams, 100
introjection, 104
latent and manifest content, 101
libido, 102
life and death instincts, 105
Oedipus complex, 99
oral, anal, phallic, and genital stages, 102
penis envy, 108
pleasure principle, 100
primal horde, 104
primary process, 100
Project for a Scientific Psychology, 100
psychosexual stages, 102
realistic, moral, and neurotic anxiety, 104
reality principle, 100
regression, 101
repetition compulsion, 103
repression, 99
resistance, 100
secondary process, 100
sexual instincts, 102
glove anesthesia, 98
Horney, Karen, 109
American Institute for Psychoanalysis, 110
basic anxiety, 110
neurotic types, 110
womb envy, 110
Jung, Carl G., 108, 110
alchemy, 115
analytical psychology, 112
anima and animus, 114
archetypal psychology, 112
archetypes, 114
collective unconscious, 113
introversion and extraversion, 112
objective unconscious, 116
persona, 114
personal unconscious, 113
psychic energy, 112
psychoid, 116
self, 115
shadow, 113
synchronicity, 117
union of opposites, 115
word association, 111

Kekulé, Friedrich, 116
Luria, Alexander R., 111
Mesmer, Anton, 97
  animal magnetism, 97
Piaget, Jean, 111
Pinel, Philippe, 98
Pötzl, Otto, 101
Salpêtriére, 98
Schur, Max, 106
subliminal perception, 102
tachistoscope, 102
unconscious, 95
  Angell's meaning, 97
  controlled versus automatic, 97
  Freud's meaning, 96
  Jung's meaning, 97
Franz, Marie-Louise von, 117
Vygotsky, Lev S., 111

CHAPTER 7

STRUCTURE OR FUNCTION?

EDWARD B. TITCHENER (1867–1927)
- *Structuralism*
- *Titchener's* Experimental Psychology
- *Titchener and the Imageless Thought Controversy*
- *Titchener and the Dimensions of Consciousness*
- *Titchener's Influence*

FUNCTIONALISM

JOHN DEWEY (1859–1952)
- *Critique of the Reflex Arc Concept*
- *Dewey's Influence on Educational Practice*
- *James R. Angell (1869–1949)*
- *Robert S. Woodworth (1869–1962)*
- *The S-O-R Framework*

INTELLIGENCE TESTING
- *James McKeen Cattell (1860–1944)*
- *Alfred Binet (1857–1911)*
- *Intelligence Testing in the United States Army*
- *What is "Intelligence," Anyway?*

PSYCHOLOGY IN BUSINESS
- *Frederick W. Taylor (1856–1915)*
- *Elton Mayo (1880–1949)*

COMPARATIVE PSYCHOLOGY
- *Edward L. Thorndike (1874–1949)*
- *Learning as the Formation of Connections*

EDWARD B. TITCHENER (1867–1927)

In the meantime, there was Edward B. Titchener (cf., Heidbreder, 1933, p. 152). Born in England, Titchener graduated from Oxford before going to Leipzig to study with Wundt from 1890 to 1892. He then went to Cornell, in Ithaca, New York, where he established a psychological laboratory. Titchener's work was similar to Wundt's experimental psychology in many ways. However, the complexity of Wundt's approach to psychology was lost in Titchener's much simpler approach. Moreover, like many academic psychologists, Titchener was unsympathetic to psychological explanations that invoked concepts such as "the unconscious," which he believed to be an explanatory fiction. The result is a psychology that has very few points of contact with the psychologies we considered in the previous chapter. Indeed, by considering Titchener at this point you will be able to realize just how broad is the range of possible psychologies.

Like Wundt, Titchener (1910/1966) distinguished psychology from other disciplines such as physics in terms of the different *point of view* taken by psychologists. What Titchener meant can best be grasped by using one of his own examples, the Muller-Lyer illusion shown in Figure 7.1. The horizontal line on the left is actually the same length as the horizontal line on the right. If you doubt this, get a ruler and measure each line. Measuring the line with a ruler is what a physical scientist would

FIGURE 7.1 The Muller-Lyer illusion.

do in order to determine the true length of a line. However, from the point of view of an ordinary person simply reporting how long the two lines appear to be, then the line on the left is obviously longer than the line on the right. The physicist gives us a description of "experience as altogether independent of any particular person; we will assume that it goes on whether or not anyone is there to have it," while the psychologist gives us a description of experience "as altogether dependent upon the particular person" (Titchener, 1910/1966, p. 601). This means that the proper method for psychology will be *introspection,* the process whereby individuals describe their experience.

This way of defining the subject matter of psychology leads to the definition of *mind* as "the sum-total of human experience considered as dependent upon a nervous system" (Titchener, 1910/1966, p. 602). Human experience is embodied in the sense that it cannot exist apart from someone's nervous system. However, Titchener did not reduce human experience to events in the nervous system. Rather, events in the nervous system run parallel to those in human experience, but should not be seen as causing them. The analogy Titchener used was that the nervous system bears the same relation to our mental processes as a map does to our experience of a journey. Consider what your experience is like when you take a trip by car from one city to another. Perhaps you will take a map along, particularly if you have not made the trip before. Without reference to the map, all you have are your particular experiences as you travel along. By looking at the map, you can get a deeper understanding of where you are, where you have been, and where you are going. Notice that the map improves your understanding of the journey you are taking, but is not a cause of your journey. Similarly, by referring to events in the nervous system we may be able to explain mental processes without regarding those events in the nervous system as causing mental processes. This is what Titchener meant by *psychophysical parallelism.*

The truly academic nature of Titchener's approach to psychology can be seen by considering what he believed to be the proper scope of the discipline. Titchener believed psychology to be, first and foremost, the study of the "generalized human mind" by means of experimental introspection (Heidbreder, 1933, p. 125). Let us take the various parts of this statement and examine them in turn.

- By "generalized," Titchener meant that psychology should develop principles that were true of *all* minds, not just some minds. Notice that this rules out the study of the peculiarities of individual minds, and, as we shall see, Titchener's attitude toward the study of *individual differences* was a source of considerable controversy, partly because the study of deviant minds is left out as well. Although Titchener acknowledged that many interesting cases of unusual mental processes occur, these were not to be used to form the basis of psychology. Thus, Titchener begins in a very different place than did Freud, for example, for whom the study of so-called *abnormal psychology* was a central part of psychological inquiry.
- Psychology is essentially the study of adult, human minds, and this means that it is only peripherally concerned with the study of children or animals. Interestingly, Titchener did not believe that only humans have minds. Rather he argued that "the range of mind . . . appears to be as wide as the range of animal life" (Titchener, 1910/1966). One of his students, *Margaret Floy Washburn* (1871–1939), wrote a very influential book on the psychology of animals, and Titchener "himself sought information on bird song in an effort to differentiate rival theories of its evolution" (Dewsbury, 1992a, p. 210). However, animal psychology was not, from Titchener's viewpoint, a central feature of the discipline.
- By saying that psychology was the study of "mind," Titchener was taking a position that may have seemed obvious at the time, but that became increasingly problematic. *Mind* began to seem to other psychologists to be a very slippery category, and, as we shall see in Chapter 8, they began to redefine the discipline in ways that took the mind out of it.
- Is psychology only an "experimental" discipline? Remember that Wundt had argued that experimentation could only carry psychology so far,

and that other forms of observation were equally important. However, by insisting on the necessity of *experimentation,* Titchener was taking a position that a great many academic psychologists subsequently espoused, but that was nonetheless the focus of continuous controversy.

- What about "introspection"? Is introspection the only legitimate method in psychology? Many psychologists began to question introspection as a method, even if it was practiced under rigorously controlled conditions. If *introspection* is to be rejected as the primary psychological method, what is to take its place?

Thus, all parts of Titchener's approach to psychology appear controversial. In many ways, this is Titchener's major contribution to American academic psychology. By defining his position and that of his opponents with extraordinary clarity, Titchener provided other psychologists with a benchmark against which they could measure their own orientation (e.g., Heidbreder, 1933, pp. 150–151). Let us now briefly examine the content of Titchener's psychology, and see why so many psychologists subsequently defined their psychology in opposition to it.

Structuralism

Titchener's psychology was often called *structuralism,* because it aimed to uncover the elementary structure of mind. However, since Titchener's day, there has been another intellectual movement called "structuralism," which included such figures as the great Swiss developmental psychologist, Jean Piaget. It is important for you to realize that Titchener's structuralism and Piaget's structuralism have virtually nothing to do with one another.

Tweney (1987) has divided Titchener's career into four phases. In the first phase during the 1890s, Titchener established the basic characteristics of his introspectionist approach. The second phase lasted for most of the first decade of this century; Titchener was then preoccupied with methodological issues. The subsequent period until 1915 (the third phase) was taken up with defending himself against various critics. Finally, in the fourth phase, he made some radical changes to his previous beliefs. Thus, Titchener, like most people, went through several changes throughout his professional career.

During his *first phase,* Titchener (1898/1966) tried to differentiate between a *structural* and a *functional* psychology. He approached this topic by means of an analogy with biology, which is given schematically in Figure 7.2. Among other things, biology has both a structural and a functional component. The structural approach to biology is anatomy, in which "we may inquire into the structure of an organism, without regard to function" (Titchener, 1898/1966, p. 35). For example, we may attempt to understand the anatomical structure of the eye without worrying about what function the eye serves. After understanding anatomy, we may then turn to physiology for an understanding of the function of organs such as the eye. Anatomy logically precedes physiology. Similarly, in psychology one can take a structural or functional approach. The subject matter of psychology is consciousness, and it may be understood in terms of what it is (its underlying structure), or in terms of what it does (its function). Naturally, we should know what consciousness *is* before we try to say what it is for. We can discover the structure of consciousness through introspective experimentation. A functional psychology should be postponed until we have a solid structural basis for psychology.

We ordinarily experience perceptions, ideas, and emotions. By means of introspection, these "were reduced to their characteristic elements by means of analysis, just as the chemist breaks down

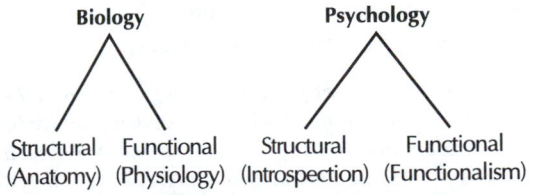

FIGURE 7.2 Titchener's distinction between structure and function.

complex substances into further unanalyzable substances" (Evans, 1973, p. 84). When it comes to saying what this underlying structure of consciousness is, Titchener (1898/1966, p. 41) argued that "everyone admits that *sensations* are elementary mental processes," and underlie our perceptions. *Images* also figured large in Titchener's system. Ideas were believed to always be accompanied by images. In this context you should recall that the British Empiricists regarded mental life as being compounded out of elementary units like sensations, and that Titchener had been trained in that tradition at Oxford. Titchener's psychology is a variant of the British associationist psychology.

In addition to sensations and images, Titchener (1898/1966) believed that *affection* was the elementary process underlying emotion. Recall that Wundt had an elaborate tridimensional theory of feeling. Titchener, however, eventually simplified the number of affective dimensions into just one, *pleasant-unpleasant.*

Titchener's *Experimental Psychology*

During his *second phase,* Titchener (1902/1971; 1905/1971) produced his *Experimental Psychology: A Manual of Laboratory Practice.* This is a remarkable set of volumes for a contemporary student to read, and if your library has them, I would strongly encourage you not only to have a look at them, but also to compare them with whatever texts are currently being used in experimental psychology. Titchener lays out in great detail how a beginning student in experimental psychology is to acquire the fundamental skills of the discipline. "A psychological experiment consists of *an introspection or a series of introspections made under standard conditions*" (Titchener, 1902/1971, p. xiii). Of course, in order to introspect properly, the student must learn the appropriate vocabulary:

> *The importance of good terminology can, from the point of view of the teacher and student, hardly be overestimated. A rose by any other name would smell as sweet; but we do not teach botany by smell. The teacher of psychology is required, in a very limited time, to bring . . . pupils within the circle of science; to start them psychologizing, to train them in method, to give them facts and uniformities. How much of his success must depend upon his choice of words, and how completely is the beginner at the mercy of his phrasing! (Titchener, 1905/1971, p. cl)*

Titchener is here attempting to confront a problem that was to bedevil introspectionism. The problem arises when students are to be taught the language to use when describing their experience (Mischel, 1969). What words should be used? Titchener (1905/1971, pp. cli–clii) said that "a good terminology should be absolutely transparent, letting the facts be seen through the words," and suggested "the terms chosen must neither be familiar terms which bring with them misleading associations, nor terms so unfamiliar that their assimilation would itself be difficult."

Students must be taught a new language if they are to introspect properly because ordinary language typically describes events in the external world, and not our experience of those events (Boring, 1921/1963d, p. 256). When we pick up two objects, for example, we do not say "this complex of cutaneous and organic sensations is more intensive than that one, but that this box or package is heavier than this other" (Titchener, 1905/1971, p. xxvi). Describing the object rather than one's experience of the object was called the *stimulus error,* and students had to be trained to avoid it. However, critics of introspectionism argued that it was never really clear precisely how the person learning to introspect was to choose one word as opposed to another, and that the language of experimental introspection was imprecise and potentially unreliable.

The content of Titchener's experimental psychology was divided into two parts: *qualitative* and *quantitative.* The former is the sort of experiment most frequently associated with introspectionism, and includes the study of sensation, affection, attention, perception, and the association of ideas. As we have already seen, sensation and affection were regarded as elementary processes. Attention was "a state of consciousness" in which "events attended-to are the clearest and most distinct," while "events attended-from are unclear and indistinct, relegated, as it were, to the background of consciousness" (Titchener, 1905/1971, p. 109).

Perception "is an aggregate, or group of sensations" (Titchener, 1905/1971, p. 127). The study of the association of ideas allowed students to examine experimentally the formation of associations according to traditional associationist laws such as frequency and recency. Finally, the quantitative part of Titchener's experimental psychology consisted largely of the psychophysical methods associated with Fechner, which we reviewed in Chapter 3.

Titchener and the Imageless Thought Controversy

During his *third phase* Titchener defended himself against such critics as the Wurzburgers. You should recall from Chapter 4 that this group of psychologists reported that introspection often yielded nothing more clear and distinct than *imageless thoughts.* The concept of an imageless thought was inconsistent with Titchener's way of analyzing mental processes, since he had maintained that ideas were always accompanied by images. The Würzburgers' analysis implied that some important mental processes may be "unconscious" and therefore inaccessible to introspection. Workers in Titchener's laboratory, however, were able to find that so-called imageless thoughts were not really imageless at all. Titchener argued that sensitive introspection disclosed kinesthetic sensations, perhaps arising from the speech musculature as the person spoke silently to themselves while introspecting (Humphrey, 1951, p. 121).

The imageless thought controversy tended to bring experimental introspection into disrepute, since there were different introspectionist laboratories apparently coming up with entirely different results. However, the results of Titchener's work in this area were not entirely negative. As Tweney (1987, p. 47) has observed, Titchener's work on imageless thought "had a direct influence on the later work by Jacobson on the progressive relaxation technique." Jacobson's work is of considerable intrinsic as well as historical interest, and is reviewed in Box 7.1 on page 126.

Titchener and the Dimensions of Consciousness

During his *fourth phase,* Titchener developed an abstract approach to the study of consciousness. Rather than conceive of the structure of consciousness in terms of elements such as sensations, Titchener began to stress the analysis of consciousness in terms of *dimensions.* Titchener was concerned with "the number and nature of the dimensions of the psychological world, just precisely as the physicist is concerned with mass and time and space as the dimensions of his physical world" (Evans, 1973, p. 87).

Titchener never settled the question of precisely what and how many dimensions there were, and died before producing the great work on the subject that many of his students expected. Some hint of what that work might have been like is given in a posthumous publication (Titchener, 1929/1972). Fortunately, one of his most famous students, Edwin G. Boring (1886–1968), published an account (1933/1963a, chap. 2) of what he took to be some of Titchener's central views, in which he singled out four dimensions for discussion: *quality, intensity, extensity,* and *protensity.* These dimensions all refer to sensory experience. Quality refers to variation in basic experiences, such as different colors or tastes. Intensity refers to the strength of an experience, such as how strong an odor is. Extensity is best seen in relation to senses such as touch (Boring, 1933/1963a, p. 28), in which an experience can vary across a wide area. Protensity refers to the duration of a sensory experience in time.

Boring noted the *phenomenological* nature of the dimensional approach to experience, and many other commentators have also suggested that before his death Titchener had been moving away from elementarism toward phenomenology. "The transition . . . to the doctrine of dimensions is so easy that one is apt to lose sight of the fact that [it] combines the freedom of phenomenology with the systematic organization of abandoned elementarism. The description of consciousness now resembles the description of a picture. With a picture one simply describes the qualitative-intensive-exten-

BOX 7.1

Edmund Jacobson and Progressive Relaxation

Edmund Jacobson's book, *You Must Relax* (1977) is a relatively recent popularization of his book, *Progressive Relaxation,* which was originally published in 1929. As mentioned in the text, Jacobson's investigations were strongly influenced by working in Titchener's laboratory at Cornell. Historically, Jacobson's work is interesting not only because of its association with Titchenerian introspectionism, but also because it was continued at the University of Chicago with the support of the functional psychologist *Harvey Carr* (Jacobson, 1925).

As did Titchener, Jacobson (1938) emphasized the importance of using subjects who are "accomplished in the method of observing . . . sensory and imaginal experiences," and that properly trained individuals will find that "thought-processes and other intellectual activities always involve experiences of sensation and images, including sensations from muscles" (p. 193). Jacobson (1938, p. 195) argued that "the activity of thinking, . . . to the best of our present knowledge consists physiologically (chiefly or entirely) of a series of sensations, images and neuromuscular . . . tensions."

Jacobson observed that stress and tension were a central feature of modern life, and made use of introspective techniques to attempt to reduce tension. In order to uncover and eliminate muscular tension, Jacobson (1938, p. 196) pointed out the importance of avoiding what Titchener had called the *stimulus error.* People who want to reduce tension must focus on muscular *sensations,* and not imagine what the muscle itself is doing. The subject "should report first the processes experienced and second what he is thinking about. If the latter alone is reported, he fails to distinguish the process of tenseness and therefore does not know what and where to relax" (Jacobson, 1938, p. 196).

In order for people to be able to relax, they must first stop paying attention to their thoughts, and attend instead to the sensations that underlie them. Jacobson argued that by first discovering muscular tensions, and then progressively relaxing them, the person will find that disturbing thoughts diminish. Tension is not to be reduced by thinking about one's problems. Rather, relaxation will lead to less thinking about one's problems! While Jacobson recognized the similarity of some of his views to Eastern meditative techniques, he believed that his practices were not borrowed from them, but rooted in experimental science.

sive pattern. For consciousness one adds the protensive dimension and extends the qualitative account over the various sense-departments" (Boring, 1933/1963a, p. 30).

Titchener's Influence

Boring's *Physical Dimensions of Consciousness* (1933/1963a) proceeded to develop Titchener's doctrine of conscious dimensions along more physicalistic lines. "We are not yet ready to give up the conscious dimensions. We need them now, but I think we are already seeing how it can come about that we shall eventually be able to do without them" (Boring, 1933/1963a, p. xii). Thus, in the end there was little left of the content of Titchener's system to influence subsequent generations of psychologists. Moreover, as we shall see later on in the book, Titchener's method of introspection received less and less support as other psychologists proposed other methods. However, Titchener's proposition that psychology was first and foremost an *experimental* discipline continued to receive widespread support in American academic psychology. Here again, his student E. G. Boring (1929, 1950b) was influential. His *History of Experimental Psychology* has been a very widely used text for many years, and presents psychology as a fundamentally experimental discipline.

Additional Reading on This Topic. Titchener often became embroiled in colorful disputes with those who did not share his views. Krantz (1969) provides a good example of this.

FUNCTIONALISM

It did not take long for opposition to Titchener's structuralism to make itself felt. *Functionalism* is the name of one of the forms this opposition took. Functionalism is usually characterized as one of the *schools of psychology.* A "school" is a "group of scholars or researchers whose approach to a field of study is . . . structured around a particular point of view" (Reber, 1985, p. 669). Titchener's structuralism is one example of a school, and Freud's psychoanalysis is another example. Typically the members of one school are more or less intolerant of the members of another school. As we shall see later in the chapter, functionalism is not as pure an example of a school as is structuralism or psychoanalysis, because it was much more open to alternative viewpoints and less well organized than other schools (Heidbreder, 1969). In spite of its ill-defined nature, there are still some characteristic attributes of a functional psychology.

- Functionalism is a distinctively American psychology. To the extent that it has a birthplace, it is at the University of Chicago. If there is a grandparent of functionalism, it is William James whose open-minded attitude toward psychology was widely shared by functionalists.
- Functionalism deliberately sets out to violate the strictures that Titchener tried to place on psychology. It is open to alternative methods to introspection, and in fact is *eclectic.* Eclecticism is the attempt to select the method of solution to fit the particular problem with which you are confronted. Eclectics are not bound by any one approach, but borrow methods as the need arises.
- As the name implies, functionalists are particularly interested in what function psychological processes serve. Heavily influenced by Darwin, functionalists focus on the way in which organisms adapt to their environment (Heidbreder, 1969, p. 39).
- Functionalism attempts to be practical as well as scholarly. This means that functionalists are often actively interested in topics such as education and in applied psychology generally.

With these broad, orienting attitudes in mind, let us now examine the work of some of the major functionalists.

JOHN DEWEY (1859–1952)

Dewey did his undergraduate work at the University of Vermont, where physiology was the subject that attracted his greatest interest. He then earned a Ph.D. in philosophy at Johns Hopkins, graduating in 1884. In 1894, Dewey joined the University of Chicago, where he remained for 10 years. At Chicago he was chair of the department of philosophy, psychology, and education. From 1904 until 1930 Dewey was at Teachers College, Columbia University, New York.

Critique of the Reflex Arc Concept

Dewey's paper, "The Reflex Arc Concept in Psychology" (1896/1963) presents the basic ideas that were to inform his subsequent approach to psychology and education. As you should recall from Chapter 2, the reflex concept goes back at least to Descartes. Dewey's paper not only contains a criticism of the reflex concept as elementaristic and mechanistic, but also provides a positive statement of a more organic approach to psychological phenomena.

Dewey argued that the reflex was inappropriately understood as a stimulus followed by a central process followed by a response. The true fact of the matter was that "sensory stimulus, central connections and motor responses [should] be viewed, not as separate and complete entities in themselves, but as divisions of labor, functioning factors, within the single concrete whole" (Dewey, 1896/1963, p. 253). In order to illustrate what he meant,

Dewey made use of James's (1890/1950, Vol. I, p. 25) example of a baby who "sees a candle-flame for the first time, and . . . extends his hand to grasp it, so that his fingers get burned." One might identify two stimuli and two responses in this situation. First, the candle-flame is a stimulus that elicits the grasping as a response. Then the intense heat of the flame is another stimulus that reflexively causes the response of suddenly withdrawing the hand. Such an analysis seems intuitively obvious, and yet it is precisely this sort of analysis that Dewey believed to be wrong.

Dewey suggested that a stimulus does not elicit a response, but rather a stimulus is created by the organism through the act of paying attention to something. The candle does not exist as a stimulus until the organism sees it. "Now if this act, the seeing, stimulates another act, the reaching, it is because both of these acts fall within a larger coordination; because seeing and grasping have often been so bound together to reinforce each other, to help each other out, that each may be considered practically a subordinate member of a larger coordination" (Dewey, 1896/1963, p. 254). The reflex arc conception is false insofar as it regards stimulus and response as distinct elements in a chain of events, when in fact they mutually influence one another to the extent that "the arc . . . is virtually a circuit" (Dewey, 1896/1963, p. 255).

Figure 7.3 illustrates these two contrasting conceptions of the relation between stimulus and response. The standard conception is given in Figure 7.3A. Notice that the stimulus (*S*) elicits the response (*R*) directly through the central connection (symbolized by an arrow). What Dewey proposed is represented in Figure 7.3B. Notice that in this case the stimulus and response determine each other. What constitutes a stimulus depends on what you are doing at the time. "The fact is that stimulus and response are . . . teleological distinctions, that is distinctions of *function,* or part played with reference to reaching, or maintaining an end" (Dewey, 1896/1963, p. 260, italics added). The relation between stimulus and response cannot be seen in isolation from the other activities of the organism of which it is a part, but must be understood in

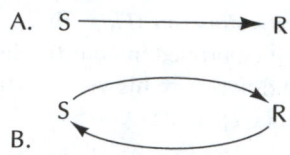

FIGURE 7.3 Two different conceptions of the reflex.

terms of its function in enabling the organism to achieve its goals. How I respond to a candle depends on what I am doing at that moment. If I am trying to shed additional light on the situation, then I will do one thing; if I am trying to warm my hands, then I will do something quite different.

Although Dewey's paper was written in 1896, it anticipates later twentieth-century developments that we consider in later chapters. As has often been pointed out (e.g., Dennis, 1948, p. 355), Dewey not only articulated a functional approach to the analysis of psychological phenomena, but also anticipated one of the criticisms of behaviorism. Moreover, his emphasis on the necessity of seeing individual responses in relation to the goals of the organism as whole is similar to one of the tenets of Gestalt psychology. So, keep Dewey in mind when we consider behaviorism in Chapter 8, and Gestalt psychology in Chapter 9.

Dewey's Influence on Educational Practice

Dewey's Presidential address to the American Psychological Association (1900/1978) laid down the foundations of what was to become his very influential approach to psychology and education. Dewey pointed out that teachers are strongly influenced by whatever psychological assumptions they make about children and the educational process, and singled out two issues that he believed to be particularly important for teachers to understand:

- In the first place, children and adults are different, in that the adult is already in possession of cognitive abilities that the child is only in the process of developing. Children are not like adults, only smaller. Children should be "busy in the formation of a flexible variety of habits whose sole immediate criterion is their relation to full growth, rather than in acquiring certain skills whose value is measured by their reference to specialized technical accomplishments" (Dewey, 1900/1978, p. 67). It is difficult to overemphasize the influence on twentieth-century educational practice of Dewey's contention. Dewey argued *against* teaching the "3 R's" as "technical acquisitions which are to be needed in the specialized life of the adult," and argued *for* curriculum reform in which the goal is "the facilitation of full normal growth, trusting to the result in growth to provide the instrumentalities for later specialized adaptation" (Dewey, 1900/1978, p. 67). Thus, Dewey (1900/1978, p. 67) challenged "the ideal of *formal discipline,*" which advocated that children master a discipline such as mathematics in the form in which it would be useful to them as adults. Such a curriculum is marked by "the excessive use of logical analytical methods" and assumes that children possess "ready-made faculties of observation, memory, attention, etc." (Dewey, 1900/1978, p. 67)

- Although children are different from adults in terms of the abilities they bring to the educational situation, they are similar to adults in that they achieve "power and control . . . through realization of personal ends and problems, through personal selection of means and materials which are relevant, and through personal adaptation and application of what is thus selected" (Dewey, 1900/1978, p. 68). The problems on which the child works in school should not be rigidly set by others; they should at least in part be selected by the child. Children differ from one another in terms of what is relevant to them at any particular time, and the curriculum will have to allow attention to be paid to the particular context within which individual children live.

Dewey became identified with the movement known as *progressive education.* Advocates of progressive education developed a reputation for schools that imposed no discipline on pupils and allowed children to study whatever they wanted. This is not what Dewey (1938/1970) had actually advocated. Far from believing that teachers had no responsibilities, Dewey (1938/1970) believed that teachers had a greater responsibility for providing their pupils with

> *experiences that are worthwhile. Traditional education did not have to face this problem; it could systematically dodge this responsibility. The school environment of desks, blackboards, a small school yard was supposed to suffice. There was no demand that the teacher should become intimately acquainted with the conditions of the local community, physical, historical, economic, occupational, etc., in order to use them as educational resources. A system of education based upon the necessary connection of education with experience must, on the contrary, if faithful to its principle, take these things constantly into account. This tax upon the educator is another reason why progressive education is more difficult to carry on than was ever the traditional system. (p. 234)*

Additional Reading on This Topic. Dewey was an extremely prolific writer. One book that captures the flavor of his ideas in a popular format is *Individualism Old and New* (1930), which is an extension of articles he originally wrote for *The New Republic.*

James R. Angell (1869–1949)

Angell studied with both Dewey and James, and became Professor of Psychology at Chicago in 1894. Angell was known as one of the chief proselytizers for a functional psychology. Indeed, there are few clearer or more famous statements of the functionalist orientation than Angell's Presidential address (1907/1978) to the American Psychological Association.

Angell observed that functionalism possessed the "peculiar vigor which commonly attaches to Protestantism of any sort," meaning that functionalism was a protest movement. Of course, the orthodoxy against which it was protesting was Titchener's structuralism. However, Angell realized that functionalism was not merely a protest movement, but had historically important ancestors, including Aristotle, Spencer, and Darwin. Aristotle is mentioned because of his belief that human behavior was purposeful and could only be understood in relation to the goals the person was trying to achieve. Spencer and Darwin provide an evolutionary/biological context within which to understand the purpose, or function, of psychological processes.

Angell (1907/1978) argued that the "mental contents" of which Titchener spoke were "evanescent," and an insecure foundation on which to construct psychology. Psychological functions are far more obvious and durable. Consciousness is not to be searched for its contents, but appreciated for its function. Consciousness is an *accommodatory process,* a feature we considered briefly in our discussion of the unconscious in Chapter 6. Saying that consciousness is the primary accommodative process means that consciousness controls our adaptation to novel situations. Psychology studies the ways in which mental processes facilitate adjustment to the environment as it changes.

When it comes to method, Angell did not believe in restricting psychology to laboratory investigation. Psychology has a lot to learn from comparative psychology, genetic (developmental) psychology, and the study of pathology. In all these areas, it is desirable to adopt a functional approach. This is particularly true in genetic psychology, where the adoption of longitudinal as opposed to cross-sectional studies means that one can begin to understand how psychological functions develop over time. (We will consider the rich history of developmental psychology in Chapter 12.)

Angell (1907/1978) did not lay down any dogmatic classification of psychological functions, but suggested that the old division of the mind into cognition, emotion, and the will was an "intrinsically biological" division with "the first reporting to us the outer world, the second our general organic tone and the third supplying experiences of our motor activity by means of which voluntary control is developed." In the end, however, Angell acknowledged that different psychologists might find it necessary to use different classificatory systems depending on their particular interests. By saying this Angell demonstrated the eclectic and pragmatic nature of functional psychology. Functionalism "means today a broad and flexible and organic point of view in psychology" (Angell, 1907/1978, p. 103).

Robert S. Woodworth (1869–1962)

Woodworth had a strong background in both mathematics and physiology before beginning to teach psychology at Columbia in 1903. Even after his retirement in 1942, he continued to be extremely productive. Woodworth's career exemplifies the maturation of functional psychology from a protest movement into an established form of psychological inquiry. Functional analysis ceased to be anything special, and "the general orientation . . . became firmly established in American psychology, not as the special concerns of any one group or school, but as obviously having a place in the pursuits proper to psychology. Before long they were simply taken for granted" (Heidbreder, 1969, pp. 48–49).

Woodworth wrote an introductory text, called *Psychology,* that sold over 400,000 copies between 1922 and 1939, "thereby assuring Woodworth's financial well-being during this period" (Winston, 1989, p. 102). A more significant contribution from a historical viewpoint was Woodworth's *Experimental Psychology* (1938), which was a thorough review of the literature on topics ranging from psychophysics to the psychology of thinking. "Between 1938 and 1954, nearly 44,000 copies of *Experimental Psychology* were sold in the U.S. and Canada. . . . The revised edition (Woodworth & Schlosberg, 1954) sold over 23,000 copies between 1954 and 1959. Assuming conservatively that half of the books were reused by other students, nearly 100,000 North American psychology majors and graduate students probably used Woodworth as their guide for experimental research. . . . The textbook *Experimental Psychology* thus served as a major element of socialization for new recruits to the discipline" (Winston, 1989, p. 102).

The S-O-R Framework

Woodworth proposed that experiments were concerned with the relationship between stimulus (S), response (R), and the subject or organism (O). The experimenter manipulates a stimulus, and observes O's response to it. In Titchener's *Experimental Psychology, O* did not stand for "organism," but for "observer." However, as introspection declined as a method, the subject in an experiment was no longer treated as an observer who reported on his or her mental processes, but as an "organism" that responded to stimuli, and this was the meaning of *O* that came to be adopted (e.g., Woodworth & Schlosberg, 1954, p. 2). The task of the experimenter is to discover what goes on between S and R.

The S-O-R formula seems to contradict Dewey's recommendation that R be seen as interacting with S, and not simply as determined by S. However, Woodworth took into account the interactive nature of the organism's relations with the environment by means of another formula: W-O-W. In this formula, *O* stands for organism as before and *W* stands for world or environment. "The environment does things to the individual, and the individual does things to the environment. . . . This interaction goes on continually . . . Since the interaction works both ways, we could just as well transpose the formula and write O-W-O" (Woodworth, 1940, p. 23).

Another important concept in Woodworth's system was *set.* "Set" is similar in meaning to the "determining tendency" of the Würzburgers. "An individual often prepares to act before beginning the overt effective action," as when sprinters take their mark on the starting line (Woodworth, 1940, p. 29). There are many different kinds of set. For example, there are preparatory sets, as illustrated by the sprinters, executive sets that guide the organism through a sequence of responses as when you drive a car; and goal sets that represent what the organism aims to achieve. Woodworth regarded sets as temporary organizations in the brain that act "by facilitating some responses, while preventing or inhibiting others. . . . While looking eagerly for a lost object you do not notice sounds that at other times would surely attract your attention. Readiness for one act is at the same time unreadiness for other acts" (Woodworth, 1940, p. 33).

Woodworth used the idea of "sets" to combine the S-O-R formula and the W-O-W formula. This "combined formula" was:

$$W - S - Ow - R - W$$

The "small w attached to O symbolizes the individual's adjustment to the environment, [or] set" (Woodworth, 1940, p. 36). By means of this formula, Woodworth was able to represent the notion that the S-O-R relationship is nested within the W-O-W relationship. The world is full of stimuli, but only those for which the organism is set will be important in determining responses. These responses in turn change the world, creating a new environment with new stimuli. This process goes on continuously.

Woodworth nicely illustrates both the strengths and weaknesses of a functional psychology. On the one hand, it was an extremely broad orientation, welcoming a variety of methods and topics. On the other hand, its theoretical formulations were criticized for being vague and imprecise (e.g., Henle, 1957/1986). For example, E. J. Gibson (1941) explicitly targeted the concept of "set" as being too vague to be of much explanatory value.

Additional Reading on This Topic. Woodworth (1931) also wrote a text on the history of psychology that went through many editions. In it he demonstrated his tolerant, middle-of-the-road approach to controversial issues.

INTELLIGENCE TESTING

Functionalism created a climate in America within which applied psychology could flourish. One of the best examples of the application of psychological methods to practical problems is the emergence of the *intelligence test* as a prominent feature of

American life. You should recall that Galton had already begun the study of intelligence in the United Kingdom. The study of intelligence in Britain was carried forward by *Charles Spearman* (1863–1945) and *Cyril Burt* (1883–1971), and we will consider their efforts in Chapter 10. However, our concern now is to trace the development of intelligence testing in the United States.

James McKeen Cattell (1860–1944)

Cattell trained with Wundt at Leipzig, and subsequently became acquainted with Galton's methods for studying individual differences during a year spent at Cambridge in England. Galton's influence on Cattell was decisive, and he devoted much of his career at Columbia University to the further development of measures of individual differences. Cattell's tests were similar to those that Galton had originally pioneered, and Cattell was the first to introduce the term *mental test* in 1890.

A partial list of Cattell's tests (1890/1948) is given in Table 7.1. Notice that these are by and large measures associated with psychophysics and quantitative experimental psychology. Few of these items will strike you as familiar from intelligence tests that you may have taken yourself. In fact, Cattell's measures did not relate very closely to academic performance, which is something that a valid measure of intelligence might be expected to do (Von Mayrhauser, 1992, p. 248). A *valid* measure is one that measures what it purports to measure, and Cattell's measures seemed to be of questionable validity. Consequently, Cattell's measures did not end up forming the backbone of intelligence tests as these were subsequently developed.

In any case, Cattell's mental tests were not his most significant achievements. In addition to being able to lay claim to being the first person appointed a professor of *psychology* (as opposed to philosophy or physiology), he was responsible for awarding the Ph.D. to many students who subsequently became important figures, including two of the persons we are considering in this chapter, Woodworth and Thorndike. Moreover, "he became a psychological statesman. He was the first psychologist elected to the National Academy of Science, he became the editor and owner of *Science,* the leading general scientific publication, and he organized and published *American Men of Science,* still [as *American Men and Women of Science*] the leading

TABLE 7.1 Examples of Cattell's Mental Tests

TEST	DESCRIPTION
Dynamometer pressure	Strength of hand squeeze
Rate of movement	How quickly the hand can be moved a distince of 50 cm
Sensation areas	Two-point threshold: How far apart on the skin must two stimuli be in order to be detected as two, and not just one
Pressure causing pain	Amount of pressure applied to the forehead at which the subject reports pain
Least noticeable difference in weight	Psychophysical procedure using two weights, one in each hand
Reaction time for sound	Time required to respond to a sound
Time for naming colors	Time required to name different colored papers (red, green, yellow, blue)
Bisection of a line	The accuracy with which a 50-cm line can be divided into two equal parts
Judgment of time	The accuracy with which a 10-second interval can be estimated
Letter span	The number of letters that can be repeated after hearing a series

directory in the field" (Watson, 1979, p. 215). Cattell was also one of the movers and shakers who helped organize the American Psychological Association in 1892, and became its President in 1895 (Clifford, 1968/1973, p. 236). Finally, Cattell specialized in the "order of merit" procedure, whereby items are ranked in terms of their worth. We have already encountered one of his rankings in Chapter 4, Box 4.1.

Alfred Binet (1857–1911)

Not only did Binet contribute to the experimental psychology of thinking, as we saw in Chapter 4, but he also invented the most influential form of intelligence test. This test was developed in Paris, in collaboration with *Theophile Simon*. "In October, 1904, the Minister of Public Instruction named a Commission which was charged with the study of measures to be taken for insuring the benefits of instruction to defective children. . . . They decided that no child suspected of retardation should be eliminated from the ordinary school and admitted to a special class without first being subjected to a pedagogical and medical examination from which it could be verified that because of the state of his intelligence, he was unable to profit . . . from the instruction given in the ordinary schools" (Binet & Simon, 1905b/1965, p. 30). Binet was a member of the Commission, and, in order to comply with its directive, Binet and Simon created a test that was designed to discriminate between normal and subnormally intelligent children. Binet and Simon (1905b/1965) defined intelligence as

> *a fundamental faculty the alteration or lack of which is of the utmost importance for practical life. This faculty is judgment, otherwise called good sense, practical sense, initiative, the faculty of adapting oneself to circumstances. To judge well, to comprehend well, to reason well, these are the essential activities of intelligence. (p. 38)*

Notice the *functional* nature of the definition—intelligence is "practical sense," "the faculty of adapting oneself to circumstances," and consists of "activities" such as reasoning and comprehension.

TABLE 7.2 Examples of Binet and Simon's Items

AGE	ITEM
3	Give family name
4	Repeat three numbers
5	Compare two weights
6	Distinguish morning and afternoon
7	Describe a picture
8	Give day and date
9	Name months of the year in order
10	Criticize absurd statements
12	Define abstract words
15	Give three rhymes for a word in one minute
Adult	Give three differences between a president and a king

Some items from the Binet and Simon (1911/1915) test are given in Table 7.2. These items are a far cry from the more "structural" items used by Cattell. Binet and Simon were careful to base their scale on a substantial body of empirical research. Their items are "arranged in a real order of increasing difficulty" (Binet & Simon, 1908/1965), in the sense that children tend not to fail items at a lower level and then pass items at a higher level. Moreover, of "203 children studied individually . . . 103 pupils . . . have exactly the mental level that we attribute to their age; 44 are advanced; 56 are below their age level" (Binet & Simon, 1908/1965, p. 44). The Binet-Simon scale allows children to be compared in terms of their *mental age*, which is determined by the age level of the items a child can pass.

The Binet-Simon scale seemed to many people in the United States to be just the sort of thing they were looking for. *Lewis M. Terman* (1877/1956) developed the most successful adaptation of the scale for the American context. Terman did this work at Stanford University, and so this version of the Binet test was called the *Stanford-Binet*. One of Terman's most durable innovations (1916/1948) was the intelligence quotient, or *IQ*. The IQ was itself an adaptation of a suggestion by the German psychologist *William Stern* (1871–1938; Staeuble, 1983) that a useful measure of intelligence could be obtained by dividing the person's mental age (MA) by their chronological age (CA). Terman made use of Stern's idea (1912/1966, p. 453) in his equation for IQ:

$$IQ = \frac{MA}{CA} \times 100$$

The formula means that "normal" children will have IQ's of 100. Terman (1916/1948, p. 489) obtained Stanford-Binet IQ scores for 905 children between the ages of 9 and 14, and reported that they were approximately normally distributed. Moreover, there was a significant relationship between IQ and such variables as teachers' estimates of childrens' intelligence, suggesting that the test had some validity. Partly because of these properties, the Stanford-Binet test became a very widely accepted test of intelligence.

Intelligence Testing in the United States Army

As the saying goes, "It is an ill wind that blows nobody good," and while World War I (1914–1918) was a disaster for the world as a whole, it was a boon for the emerging profession of psychology in the United States. The United States declared war on Germany in April 1917. Also in April 1917, *Robert M. Yerkes* (1876–1956) was appointed chair of a committee to investigate ways in which psychology could contribute to the war effort.

> *As mobilization for World War I approached, Yerkes got one of those 'big ideas' that propel the history of science: could psychologists possibly persuade the army to test all its recruits? If so, the philosopher's stone of psychology might be constructed: the copious, useful, and uniform body of numbers that would fuel a transition from dubious art to respected science. Yerkes proselytized within his own profession and within government circles, and he won his point. As Colonel Yerkes, he presided over the administration of mental tests to 1.75 million recruits during World War I. Afterward he proclaimed that mental testing helped win the war (Gould, 1981).*

The tests that Yerkes and his group developed were derived from many sources, including the Binet tests. If a soldier could read and write, then he would be given the *Army Alpha.* Among the items on this form of the test were analogies like "Washington is to Adams as first is to . . ." "Nearly one third of the men examined were unable to read or write, or else did so poorly to be classed as illiterate, and to these was given a special examination prepared for illiterates" (Garrett, 1948, p. 31). This second test was called *Beta,* and contained such items as pictures with something left out that the examinee would have to complete (e.g., a profile with a nose missing). Alpha and Beta could be administered in groups, but if a soldier managed to fail Beta, then he would be given an individually administered Binet-like test. Gould (1982) observes that at least some items on all these tests can be seen as culturally biased. For example, the analogy given above requires some knowledge of United States history. Another item singled out by Gould (1982, p. 349) is the following multiple choice question: "Christy Mathewson is famous as a: writer, artist, baseball player, comedian," which also requires some familiarity with the culture of the United States.

The question of cultural bias is important because of the interpretations that were sometimes made when the data were analyzed and reported after World War I (Yerkes, 1948/1921; Brigham, 1923). One controversial finding concerned *national differences in intelligence.* For example, men who were originally from such countries as England, Scotland, Holland, and Germany scored higher than men originally from such countries as Greece, Russia, Italy, and Poland. One interpretation of these results follows from the fact that immigrants from the former group tended to have been in the United States for a longer time. Perhaps "foreign-born men, long exposed to American customs, language, and ways of life are enabled thereby to make higher scores" (Garrett, 1948, pp. 51–52). There were, however, those who preferred an alternative interpretation, which is that these results reflected innate differences in intelligence between racial groups. Gould (1982) argued that this hereditarian interpretation was widely influential, and was one of the reasons for the passage of the Immigration Act of 1924, which discriminated against some groups in favor of others by "imposing quotas on immigration based on the percentage of immigrants from each country as of the census of 1890. Using the 1890 census effectively excluded many immigrants from southern and eastern Europe, which had sent most of its refugees to America after 1890, in favor of those from northern and western Europe" (Snyderman & Herrnstein, 1983, p. 991). However, Snyderman and Herrnstein (1983) were unable to find very much documentary evidence that intelligence test results were an important part of the decision-making process that led Congress to pass this act, and they concluded that racism in the testing movement and the Immigration Act "do not appear to be causally related to each other" (p. 994), but that both reflect attitudes that may have been prevalent in the United States at that time.

Another widely interpreted result from the Army data was that, generally speaking, black soldiers had lower intelligence test scores than whites. One interpretation of this difference is that the black recruits were educationally disadvantaged. However, many observers chose to give this finding a hereditarian interpretation, arguing that blacks were innately less intelligent than whites. The hereditarian interpretation was challenged by the black scholar *Horace Mann Bond* (Urban, 1989, p. 325), who showed, among other things, that blacks "from some northern states, namely Illinois, New York, Ohio, and Pennsylvania, scored higher than did whites from the southern states of Mississippi, Kentucky, Arkansas, and Georgia." This finding is not easily interpreted along strictly hereditarian lines.

What Is "Intelligence," Anyway?

Controversy over the degree to which intelligence is innate or acquired has been, and continues to be a fixture of debate in psychology. Gould (1982, p. 151) observed that Binet never regarded "intelligence" as a single, scalable entity, but rather as a collection of different skills. However, it is easy to believe that because we have one word, "intelligence," then there must be one thing to which it refers. The question of whether or not intelligence is one thing or many things is not easy to answer, and we will examine some of the difficulties inherent in this question in Chapter 10. For now, we deal only with answers to this question that emerged in the aftermath of World War I. During this time one of the most influential answers was proposed by the ubiquitous E. G. Boring (1923/1969), who had been one of the members of Yerkes' team. Boring's paper was originally published in *The New Republic,* and was intended to educate the general public concerning the meaning of "intelligence." He argued "that intelligence as a measurable capacity must at the start be defined as the capacity to do well in an intelligence test. Intelligence is what the tests test" (Boring, 1923/1969, p. 26). Even though the correlation between the tests and performance in real-world situations is not perfect, that only means that each real-world situation requires special skills other than intelligence. Intelligence is one thing: what intelligence tests measure. Notice that this formulation places great emphasis on the importance of the tests themselves. The tests *define* intelligence.

After World War I, the intelligence test became progressively embedded in American culture. In its various forms, such as the *Scholastic Aptitude Test,* it has exercised enormous influence over the lives of countless people. One of the best known of contemporary researchers on intelligence, *Robert J. Sternberg* (1992, p. 134), has suggested that "the intelligence test of today is quite similar to that of Alfred Binet." That is, in spite of variations in form and content, intelligence tests tend to be similar to the one originally invented by Binet. Intelligence may not be only one thing, but intelligence tests do tend to be only one thing!

Sternberg (1992, p. 134) points out that "testing is today, and has been for many years, a market driven industry. Testing companies are no different

BOX 7.2

What Intelligence Test Consumers Want

- Predicting achievement. The main use of intelligence tests [is] prediction of school achievement.
- Reliability. Test scores are relatively stable over time. No one can afford the time or money to give the same test again and again.
- Standardization. Administrators are very concerned about how . . . their school compares with . . . other schools. Thus, they need accurate . . . norms.
- High correlation with other, similar tests. When . . . a decision is made to switch tests one year, . . . the administration wants to know that the tests used in the past will provide scores that are at least roughly comparable to the tests of the present.
- Ease of administration. [G]roup tests need to be administered by teachers with little or no training in psychological testing.
- Ease of interpretation. The interpreters of the test scores [may] have little or no knowledge about psychological testing.
- Objectivity of scoring. Administrators do not want to get into arguments with parents . . . over "right answers" . . .
- Perceived fairness. The tests should be perceived to be fair and hence not biased in favor of . . . one group over another.
- Cost effectiveness. [T]he . . . tests should be as cheap as possible and yield information worth at least what they cost.
- Legal defensibility. [T]he tests should be legally defensible should their use be brought to court.

Source: Adapted from R. J. Sternberg. (1992). Ability tests, measurements, and markets. *Journal of Educational Psychology 84:* 135.

than any other business in their desire to maximize" both sales and profits. This means that a central issue for companies that produce tests is, "what do consumers of intelligence tests want?" Sternberg accounts for the remarkable durability and popularity of intelligence tests by the way in which they have been sensitive to what the market for such tests requires. Sternberg identifies ten market forces that have shaped the nature of intelligence tests. These are given in Box 7.2. It is important to realize that the intelligence test has not only been shaped but is also maintained by the kind of market forces Sternberg has identified. The intelligence test is not a purely intellectual exercise designed entirely to provide scientific data. Perhaps we can generalize on the basis of this example. As Sternberg (1992, p. 135) has pointed out, it is possible to regard psychology generally as being at least partly responsive to market forces. Although market forces may determine some aspects of psychology more than others, you should ask yourself as we go along what the market forces are [or were] for each aspect of psychology we encounter.

Additional Reading. Fancher (1985) provides a thorough review of the issues and persons involved in the measurement of IQ.

PSYCHOLOGY IN BUSINESS

At the same time as the mental testing industry was beginning to develop, the application of psychology to problems of interest to business was also emerging as a discipline in its own right. Two names often associated with this aspect of applied psychology in the United States are *Hugo Munsterberg* (1863–1916) and *Walter Dill Scott* (1869–1955).

Munsterberg was trained by Wundt, and came to Harvard in 1892. Although originally expected to be primarily a laboratory worker, Munsterberg later demonstrated that he had wide- ranging interests. He published popular books on topics as diverse as psychology and the law and psychology in industry. Scott was also a student of Wundt, and had the same sort of protean career as did Munsterberg. He was particularly interested in developing mental tests that were suited to the business environment (Von Mayrhauser, 1989), and founded the *Scott Corporation,* which was devoted to providing psychological services to business.

While Munsterberg and Scott are undoubtedly important figures in this area, it is instructive to compare the work of *Frederick W. Taylor* with that of *Elton Mayo.* Together they define the range of services that psychology was able to offer the business community.

Frederick W. Taylor (1856–1915)

Taylor displayed an interest in the efficiency of human movement early in life. The story goes (Brown, 1954, p. 12) that as a college student he changed the game of baseball by introducing overhand as opposed to underhand pitching. Overhand pitching was a much more efficient and effective way of doing the job, and showing people how to do things more efficiently and effectively became Taylor's lifework. While working as an engineer, he became distressed with the amount of inefficiency he observed in the way that manual laborers performed their tasks, and set about to eliminate "awkward, inefficient, or ill-directed movements" (Taylor, 1911/1967, p. 5). Taylor argued that the interests of worker and employer were identical, not antagonistic. If workers were trained to produce goods in the most efficient manner possible, and given raises as their output increased, then workers would get more money and employers would reap higher profits.

One of the most famous examples of Taylor's method took place at the Bethlehem Steel Company. There were 80,000 tons of pig iron that had been sold and needed to be loaded onto railway cars. Workers typically loaded 12.5 tons a day, a number Taylor believed could be increased to 47.5 by using efficient methods. Taylor began by selecting a workman, whom he called *Schmidt,* "who had been observed to trot home for a mile or so after his work in the evening about as fresh as he was in the morning. . . . He also had the reputation of . . . placing a very high value on a dollar" (Taylor, 1911/1967, p. 44). Thus Schmidt was a well-conditioned, highly motivated individual, and selecting the best workers is an essential part of Taylor's system. Schmidt had been earning $1.15 a day, and was asked if he would like to earn $1.85 a day for loading pig iron. After answering in the affirmative, he was told to "do exactly as this man tells you to-morrow, from morning till night. When he tells you to pick up a pig and walk, you pick it up and you walk, and when he tells you to sit down and rest, you sit down. You do that straight through the day" (Taylor, 1911/1967, p. 46). Taylor had already figured out what the most efficient blend of work and rest would be, and Schmidt "was told by the man who stood over him with a watch, 'Now pick up a pig and walk. Now sit down and rest. Now walk—now rest, etc.'" (Taylor, 1911/1967, p. 47). This regime produced 47.5 tons loaded at day's end. Taylor proceeded to induct additional workers, and eventually "was able to decrease the number of workers needed to load wagons at the steel company from 500 to 140, increase daily earnings by 60%, and save the firm about $75,000 a year" (Brown, 1954, p. 15).

Taylor (1911/1967) called his system *scientific management,* and characterized its most important feature as follows. "The work of every workman is fully planned out at least one day in advance, and each man receives in most cases complete written instructions, describing in detail the task which he is to accomplish, as well as the means to do the work" (p. 39). Workers did not always take kindly to having someone stand over them with a watch, particularly since the goal of Taylor's method (1911/1967, p. 95) was not only to increase the output of individual workers, but also to reduce the total number of workers required, as occurred in one project involving "girls inspecting bicycle balls" in which "thirty-five girls did the work formerly done by one hundred and twenty." Thus, one assumption of Taylor's technique (1911/1967, p. 95) is that "personal ambition always has been and will remain a more powerful incentive to exertion than a desire for the general welfare."

Taylor's methods were developed further by the husband and wife team of *Frank and Lillian Gilbreth.* Frank Gilbreth first made his mark in 1909 by analyzing the motions of bricklayers, and reducing them from a languid 18 to a crisp 5. This type of analysis, whereby "needless motions can be entirely eliminated and quicker types of movements substituted for slow movements" has been called *time and motion study* (Taylor, 1911/1967, p. 80). The life of the Gilbreths was made the subject of a 1950 movie called *Cheaper by the Dozen* starring Clifton Webb as Frank, and Myrna Loy as Lillian, Gilbreth.

Elton Mayo (1880–1949)

Mayo (1933/1960) became famous because of some work he did not himself begin. In 1926, the National Research Council had made a curious discovery in its investigation of the effect of changing levels of illumination upon worker output in the Western Electric plant in Hawthorne, Illinois. The particular workers studied made telephone relays, and so the measure of output is simply the number of relays produced per week. One part of the study, described later by Mayo (1933/1960, pp. 53–54), involved two rooms of workers, in one of which the level of illumination was systematically varied, while in the other illumination remained constant. One would expect no change in output for the group for which the lighting stayed the same. However, one might expect the group being subjected to variation in illumination to show changes in performance as a result of this manipulation of an important environmental variable. However, both groups showed roughly the same level of output regardless of illumination. In a certain sense, the experiment was a failure because it did not show any effect of changing illumination on performance. "Somehow or other that complex of mutually dependent factors, the human organism, shifted its equilibrium and unintentionally defeated the purpose of the experiment" (Mayo, 1933/1960, p. 54).

Mayo, who was at Harvard in the Department of Industrial Research from 1926 until 1947, became part of a group called in to investigate further. This time "no attempt was made to test for the effect of single variables. Where human beings are concerned one cannot change one condition without inadvertently changing others—so much the illumination experiment had shown" (Mayo, 1933/1960, p. 54). Briefly stated, Mayo's researches seemed to show that no matter what one did to change working conditions, output went up. For example, more rest pauses, reduced rest pauses, going home early, even returning to the original work conditions all resulted in increased output when introduced (Brown, 1954, pp. 71–72). This phenomenon came to be known as the *Hawthorne effect:* any change in work conditions increases output.

While there has been considerable debate about the generality and limitations of the Hawthorne effect, Mayo's explanation of it was influential. The investigators were paying attention to the workers in the Hawthorne plant, and this act of paying attention was important to the workers themselves. For example, workers were interviewed using a technique Mayo (1933/1960, pp. 93–94) compared to that used by *Jean Piaget,* the great Swiss developmental psychologist whose own work we examine in Chapter 12. One aspect of Piaget's technique was to be open and attentive to the interviewees' concerns, and not simply work through a list of prepared questions. Merely listening to workers' concerns in this unstructured way seemed to have a beneficial effect. As his studies progressed, Mayo began to realize that work is an inherently *social* activity, regulated by the group to which the worker belongs. The workers in the Hawthorne study appeared to have developed a feeling of pride in the accomplishments of their group as a whole. This suggested that business needs to work with such groups in order to ensure worker cooperation in attaining corporate goals.

The contrast between Taylor and Mayo represents in part a difference in philosophical assumptions concerning human nature. Taylor assumed that the individual was motivated by self-interest, while Mayo saw the individual as motivated by the concerns of the group to which the person belonged. Taylor's focus was on individual behavior seen as a collection of bodily movements, while Mayo's focus was on behavior as determined by the quality of one's interpersonal relationships. These differences are not peculiar to industrial psychology, but represent fundamental differences in orientation that reveal themselves again and again in the work of the various psychologists that we examine in subsequent chapters.

Additional Reading on This Topic. Barnes (1968) provides a compendium of the techniques that have evolved from Taylor's original line of work. A review of the influence of the Hawthorne study is given by Landsberger (1958).

COMPARATIVE PSYCHOLOGY

Comparative psychology is that branch of the discipline that attempts to understand the evolution of behavior through the comparison of different species. The end of Chapter 2 noted that comparative psychology was a logical outgrowth of Darwinism, and so it is not surprising to discover that functional psychology was open to the comparative point of view.

George John Romanes (1848–1894) is often considered to be the founder of a comparative approach to psychology. Although born in Canada, Romanes became famous for work done in Britain. Romanes (1883/1977) wrote about his procedure for studying animals as follows:

> *What is the kind of activities that may be regarded as indicative of mind? I certainly do not so regard the flowing of a river or the blowing of the wind. Why? First, because the objects are too remote in kind from my own organism to admit of drawing any reasonable analogy between them and it; . . . they afford no evidence of feeling or purpose. In other words, two conditions require to be satisfied before we even begin to imagine that observable activities are indicative of mind: first, the activities must be displayed by a living organism; and secondly they must be of a kind to suggest the presence of two elements which we recognize as the distinctive characteristics of mind as such—consciousness and choice. (p. 2)*

Notice that Romanes regarded "mind" as the subject matter of comparative psychology, and drawing analogies between human and animal mental processes as the proper method. Romanes (1883/1977, p. 10) himself described his psychology as *anthropomorphic,* meaning that it involved projecting human characteristics onto animals. "The mental states of an insect may be widely different than those of a man, and yet most probably the nearest conception that we can form of their true nature is that which we form by assimilating them to the only mental states with which we are acquainted" (p. 10).

Romanes believed that it was reasonable to apply this method because there "must be a psychological, no less than a physiological, continuity extending throughout the length and breadth of the animal kingdom" (Romanes, 1883/1977, p. 10). The hypothesis of *continuity* is very important, because it implies that there are no qualitative differences between humans and other species. We can find in other species characteristics similar to ourselves, although other creatures may very well display a more primitive form of these characteristics.

Romanes' psychology was criticized for being *anecdotal* in that it consisted largely of stories about animals, "often provided in the form of letters and even rumors regarding the feats of members of this or that species . . . there is no instance of experimentation" (Robinson, 1977, p. xxii). Romanes' great competitor in late nineteenth-century comparative psychology was *C. Lloyd Morgan* (1852–1936), another British naturalist, who adopted a more experimental approach to the study of animal behavior. While Morgan acknowledged that one could interpret animal behavior in terms of the observer's own subjective experience, he also stressed the importance of the objective observation of behavior. He saw each as complementing the other.

One oft-cited example of Morgan's approach is his analysis of the behavior of his dog, *Tony,* who, "when he wanted to go out into the road, used to put his head under the latch of the gate, lift it, and wait for the gate to swing open" (Morgan, 1894/1979, p. 184). The observer of such behavior should not interpret it as meaning that the dog "perceived how the end in view was to be gained, and the most effective means for effecting his purpose" (Morgan, 1894/1979, p. 184). By carefully observing the way in which the dog learned how to get out of the yard, Morgan found that Tony had hit upon the correct response more or less by chance, after sticking his head between the bars of the fence until the latch was accidentally lifted. On subsequent occasions, the dog did not go immediately and open the latch, but only gradually perfected this habit, and eliminated incorrect responses. "It was nearly three weeks . . . before he went at once and without hesitation to the right place and put his head without any ineffectual fumbling beneath the latch" (Morgan, 1894/1979, p. 184). Thus, it makes no sense to interpret the dog's action as the outcome of "reasoning." A much simpler explanation is possible, namely that the dog gradually acquired the correct response through a process we could call trial and error.

Morgan's greatest claim to fame is his *canon.* A "canon" is a rule that regulates the way one is supposed to investigate something. Lloyd Morgan's (1894/1968) canon is intended to guide the way in which investigators interpret observations of behavior:

> *In no case may we interpret an action as the outcome of the exercise of a higher psychical faculty if it can be fairly interpreted as the outcome of the exercise of one which stands lower on the psychological scale. (p. 468)*

Lloyd Morgan's *canon* has usually been interpreted as a principle of parsimony. Such principles, which go back at least to *William of Ockham* (c. 1285–1349), assert that our explanations of any phenomenon should be kept as simple (parsimonious) as possible. In the case of the explanation of animal behavior, we should not invoke complex human mental processes such as "reasoning" when simpler explanations such as "trial and error" will do. However, as Costall (1993, p. 117) has pointed out, Morgan's canon did not rule out "the interpretation of a particular activity in terms of the higher processes, if we already have independent evidence of the occurrence of these higher processes in the animal under consideration." Morgan's canon was not intended to prohibit anthropomorphic explanations, but only to limit them to cases in which they appeared to be necessary.

Additional Reading on This Topic. A classic introduction to the history of the psychology of animals is Warden, Jenkins, and Warner (1934).

Edward L. Thorndike (1874–1949)

Thorndike was the son of a clergyman in Lowell, Massachusetts. This fact is relevant because Thorndike was not only an American pioneer in comparative psychology, he was also a typical late nineteenth-century American scientist in that "among Americans born around 1870 . . . the striking fact is that a clergyman's household, combined with a New England setting, was the best predictor of a future career in science" (Clifford, 1968/1973, p. 233). This is partly because at the time "organized religion was losing stature in the nation's social and intellectual life . . . [and] science was usurping its place in academic disputations and attracting college graduates away from ministerial careers" (Clifford, 1968/1973, p. 234). Thorndike's career exemplified that of the zealous scientist for whom science was an all-consuming passion. "In 1934 Thorndike was chosen President of the AAAS [American Association for the Advancement of Science]; except for economist W. C. Mitchell in 1928, no other social scientist headed this professional organization of the whole body of scientists since Thorndike's tenure until . . . 1966" (Clifford, 1968/1973, p. 237).

In an autobiographical sketch, Thorndike (1936/1949) described the beginning of his research as a graduate student at Harvard when he

> *suggested experiments with the instinctive and intelligent behavior of chickens as a topic, and this was accepted. I kept these animals and conducted the experiments in my room until the landlady's protests became imperative. [William] James tried to get a few square feet required for me in the Laboratory, and then the Agassiz Museum. He was refused, and with his habitual kindness and devotion to underdogs and eccentric aspects of science, he harbored my*

chickens in the cellar of his own home for the rest of the year. The nuisance to Mrs. James was, I hope, somewhat mitigated by the entertainment of the two youngest children. (pp. 2–3)

Thorndike subsequently completed his doctoral work on *animal intelligence* at Columbia under Cattell. "The motive for my first investigations of animal intelligence was chiefly to satisfy requirements for courses and degrees. Any other topic would probably have served me as well. I certainly had no special interest in animals . . ." (Thorndike, 1936/1949, pp. 3–4). The fact that Thorndike had no passionate interest in working with animals, and yet did work that became central to psychology, is a lesson that many students would do well to heed! You do not need to work on a topic that you regard as crucial to your being in order to make a significant contribution.

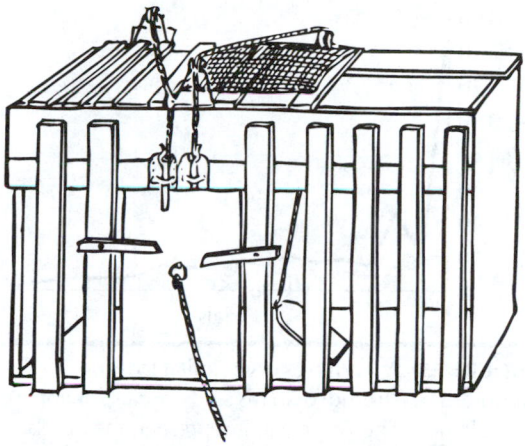

FIGURE 7.4 One of Thorndike's puzzle boxes.
Source: E. L. Thorndike. (1898). *Animal Intelligence.* Psychological Review Monograph Supplements, 2(Serial No. 8), p. 8.

Learning as the Formation of Connections

Thorndike's (1898/1948) work on animal intelligence used equipment that became both famous and controversial. These pieces of apparatus were the *puzzle boxes,* contraptions Thorndike assembled out of wooden crates and assorted odds and ends (Burnham, 1972). Remember that this was before the time when researchers might expect to have grants to support their efforts, and many, like Thorndike, built all their apparatus themselves. One of the boxes is illustrated in Figure 7.4. A cat would be placed in the box, with food outside. If the cat pulled on a loop or other device, then the door would open and the animal would be freed. Thorndike (1898/1979) described the cat's behavior as follows:

When put into the box the cat would show evident signs of discomfort and of an impulse to escape from confinement. It tries to squeeze through any opening; it claws and bites at the bars or wire; it thrusts its paws out through any opening and claws at everything it reaches; it continues its efforts when it strikes anything loose and shaky; it may claw at things within the box. It does not pay very much attention to the food outside, but seems simply to strive instinctively to escape from confinement. . . . The cat does not look over the situation, much less think *it over, and then decide what to do. It bursts out at once into the activities which instinct and experience have settled on as suitable reactions to the situation "confinement when hungry with food outside." The one impulse, out of many accidental ones, which leads to pleasure, becomes strengthened and stamped in thereby, and more and more firmly associated with the sense-impression of that box's interior. (pp. 255–256)*

Notice that Thorndike acknowledges that the animal has an instinct to escape from confinement. By "instinct," Thorndike meant anything the animal does in a situation that is experienced for the first time. In the puzzle box, instinct is not enough to provide the cat with the means to escape. However, the animal does not reason its way out of its predicament, but accidentally does the right thing. Thorndike studied several cats, and plotted the time it took for them to escape from the puzzle box on successive trials. Such learning curves tended to look like Figure 7.5 on page 142. Thorndike observed that these learning curves did not suddenly improve, but rather the amount of time the animal spent in the box gradually and irregularly got to be less and less. This suggested that the animal did not

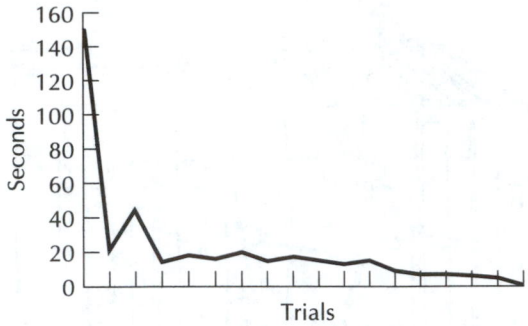

FIGURE 7.5 A learning curve similar to those reported by Thorndike in his study of cats solving a puzzle box. The vertical axis represents the number of seconds the cat spends in the box before escaping.

suddenly realize what it had to do in order to free itself, but that the connection between the animal's situation and the response that freed it was gradually stamped in. What Thorndike's data demonstrated to him was "the wearing smooth of a path in the brain, not the decision of a rational consciousness" (Thorndike, 1898/1979, p. 256).

For Thorndike, learning involved the formation of connections in the brain between situations and actions, and he invented the *law of effect* to explain the formation of these connections. Over the course of Thorndike's career, the law of effect took different forms, with a late form being "that the immediate consequence of a mental connection (in particular, a satisfying state of affairs following a connection and belonging to it) can work back upon it to strengthen it" (Thorndike, 1933/1949, p. 13). By a "satisfying state of affairs," Thorndike (1933/1949, p. 14) meant "one which the animal does nothing to avoid, often doing things to maintain or renew it." The influence of a satisfier on a connection was presumed to be direct, and did not require the subject to realize that a particular connection had been rewarded. "It is, on the contrary, as natural in its action as a falling stone, a ray of light, a line of force, a discharge of buckshot, a stream of water, or a hormone in the blood" (Thorndike, 1933/1949, p. 15).

Thorndike took the cat's behavior in a puzzle box to be paradigmatic of what happens when any animal (including human animals) learns anything. All learning involved the formation of connections, and connections were strengthened according to the law of effect. With Thorndike's work, learning began to come to the forefront in American psychology as the most important psychological process.

> *Man's power to change himself, that is, to learn, is perhaps the most impressive thing about him. . . . Civilization is, indeed, the chief product of human learning. Homes and tools, language and art, customs and laws, science and religion are all created by changes in the minds of men. Their maintenance and use also depend on human modifiability—the ability of man to learn. If that were reduced by half. . . most of human civilization would be unusable by the next generation and would soon vanish off the face of the earth. (Thorndike, 1931/1966, p. 3)*

For Thorndike, a person's capacity to learn was limited by their general level of intelligence, as measured by an intelligence test. Intelligence is the ability to form connections, and humans are the most evolved animal because they are, in general, able to form more connections than any other animal. However, there are great individual differences in "general intelligence," which Thorndike believed to be innately determined. This view made Thorndike (1931/1966, pp. 199–200) sympathetic to eugenics, since we should "provide the intellect of man with higher and purer sources than the muddy streams of the past. If it is our duty to improve the quality of what is learned and the means of learning it, it is doubly our duty to improve the original inborn ability of man to learn."

Thorndike stands in the tradition of associationist psychology, one of his innovations being the study of the formation of associations in animals under experimental conditions. Thorndike's theory is often called *connectionism,* a model of the nervous system as a telephone switchboard with a vast network of connections between inputs and outputs (Pribram, 1981). One might have expected

Morgan to have approved of the simplicity of Thorndike's system, but in fact he was critical of the evidence on which Thorndike built his theory, in particular the original experiments with cats in puzzle boxes. Morgan (as cited by Costall, 1993, p. 120) wrote that "the conditions of his experiments were perhaps not the most conducive to the discovery of rationality in animals if it exists. The sturdy and unconvinceable advocate of reasoning (properly so-called) in animals may say that to place a starving kitten in a cramped confinement of one of Mr. Thorndike's box-cages, would be more likely to make a cat swear than to lead it to act rationally." Similar criticisms were voiced by other animal psychologists (e.g., Maier & Schneirla, 1935/1964, pp. 358–363). Thorndike's reputation, however, did not depend solely on his animal work. Over the span of his career he published extensively on topics in human learning that generally supported his original conclusions.

The implications of Thorndike's work for education were considerable. A famous study done with Woodworth (Thorndike & Woodworth, 1901/1948) investigated the degree to which learning would transfer from one situation to another. For example, if subjects were trained to pick out "words containing certain combinations of letters (e.g., s and e)" (Thorndike & Woodworth, 1901/1948, p. 391) would such training generalize to words containing other letter combinations? In general, the results did not show very much *transfer of training* from one situation to another. The educational implications of such a result were that students should not be taught the principles that applied to one situation in the hope that they will be generalized to novel situations. Rather, the specific components of each skill need to be taught separately. For example, when a child is taught arithmetic, then the teacher should "analyze arithmetical learning into the unitary abilities which compose it, showing just what, in detail, the mind has to do in order to be able to pass a thorough test on the whole of arithmetic" (Thorndike, 1922/1949, p. 165). Although Thorndike's psychology was quite different from Dewey's, they both helped undermine the traditional curriculum that emphasized learning subjects such as Latin in the hope that the acquisition of general principles would provide the student with rules that could be applied to situations the pupil would encounter in everyday life as an adult (Ellis, 1965/1979, pp. 72–73).

In many ways, Thorndike exemplified the functional psychologist by having an evolutionary viewpoint, being interested in individual differences, and attempting to apply his findings. In other ways, however, Thorndike's work anticipated the movement we examine in the next chapter. By demonstrating the important role of animals in experimental research, and emphasizing the importance of learning while de-emphasizing the importance of "higher mental processes," Thorndike helped lay the groundwork for behaviorism.

Additional Reading on This Topic. Thorndike (1949, p. 11) was particularly interested in "the science and teaching of language," and began "with the humble task of counting the frequency of occurrence of English words, publishing the facts for a ten-million count in 1921 and an extension of it in 1931. Dr. Irving Lorge and I brought out a greatly extended and improved count in 1944." The Thorndike and Lorge (1944) word count has been cited countless times by psychologists interested in language, and is worth perusing if only to see how much labor went into this project, illustrating Thorndike's remarkable capacity for hard work.

KEY NAMES AND CONCEPTS

What follows is an index of some of the most important material in this chapter. The list includes individuals, concepts, and topics you should know. Read through the list, and if anything on it seems unfamiliar, then go back and re-read the appropriate section of the chapter. You should be able to define each concept, briefly discuss each topic, and state the importance of each person on the list. In addition, you should be able to write an account of the work done by each person or topic printed in boldface.

Angell, James, 129
consciousness as an accommodatory process, 130
Army intelligence tests, 134
national differences in intelligence, 134
Binet, Alfred, 133
definition of intelligence, 133
mental age, 133
Bond, Horace M., 135
Box 7.1—Progressive relaxation, 126
Box 7.2—Market forces determining intelligence tests, 136
Burt, Cyril, 132
Carr, Harvey, 126
Cattell, James McKeen, 132
mental test, 132
Comparative psychology, 139
continuity, 139
Dewey, John, 127
attitude toward formal discipline, 129
critique of the reflex arc concept, 127
progressive education, 129
views on education, 128
Functionalism, 127
attributes of a functional psychology, 127
eclecticism, 127
Gilbreth, Frank and Lillian
time and motion study, 138
Intelligence testing, 131
validity, 134
Mayo, Elton B., 138
Hawthorne effect, 138
Morgan, C. Lloyd, 139
canon, 140
Tony, his dog, 139
Muller-Lyer illusion, 121
Munsterberg, Hugo, 136
Ockham, William of, 140
Psychology in business, 136
Romanes, George J., 139
anecdotal, 139
anthropomorphism, 139
Scholastic Aptitude Test, 135
schools of psychology, 127
Scott, Walter D., 136
Scott Corporation, 137
Simon, Theophile, 133
Spearman, Charles, 132
Stern, William, 133
Sternberg, Robert J., 135
Taylor, Frederick W., 137
Schmidt, 137
scientific management, 137
Terman, Lewis M., 133
IQ, 133
Stanford-Binet test, 133
Thorndike, Edward L., 140
animal intelligence, 141
connectionism, 142
law of effect, 142
puzzle box, 141
transfer of training, 143
Titchener, Edward B., 121
affections, 124
dimensions, 125
first phase, 123
fourth phase, 125
images, 124
introspection, 122
mind, 122

phenomenology, 125
point of view, 121
psychophysical parallelism, 122
qualitative and quantitative methods, 124
quality, intensity, extensity, protensity, 122
scope of psychology, 122
second phase, 124
sensations, 124
stimulus error, 124
structuralism, 123
structure versus function, 123
third phase, 125
Washburn, Margaret Floy, 122
Woodworth, Robert Sessions, 130
Experimental Psychology, 130
set, 131
S-O-R formula, 131
W-O-W formula, 131
Yerkes, Robert M., 134

CHAPTER 8

BEHAVIORISM

IVAN P. PAVLOV (1849–1936)
Conditioned Reflexes
Speech
Temperaments and Psychopathology
Vivisection and Anti-Vivisectionism
Vladimir M. Bekhterev (1857–1927)
JOHN B. WATSON (1878–1958)
Psychology as the Behaviorist Views It
Watson's Psychology
Emotional, Manual, and Verbal Habits
Watson and Rosalie Rayner
Watson's Second Career in Advertising
KARL S. LASHLEY (1890–1958)
Cortical Localization of Function
The Problem of Serial Order in Behavior
B. F. SKINNER (1904–1990)
The Nature of Behaviorism
Skinner's Radical Behaviorism
The Behavior of Organisms
"A Case History of Scientific Method"
The "Baby Tender"
Teaching Machines
Skinner's Utopian and Dystopian Views

Thorndike had done much to create a climate in which comparative psychology could flourish. It is an obvious but nonetheless important point to realize that animals cannot be asked to introspect, and so comparative psychology implicitly called introspection as a psychological method into question. Animals cannot be asked to explain their own behavior, as people can. Animal behavior is something that the psychologist can only observe, and comparative psychology implicitly promoted the objective observation of behavior (e.g., Krech, 1962, p. 41). Thorndike himself, however, never entirely moved away from describing behavior as having a subjective aspect. That is why he should be seen as a transitional figure, occupying a middle ground between those functionalists who were untroubled by including introspection as a proper psychological method, and those investigators we will explore in this chapter who called for the total abandonment of subjectivity in favor of an entirely objective description of behavior. This movement, usually called *behaviorism,* "originated independently in America and in pre-Revolutionary Russia. In both countries one of the sources was animal research. In Russia this source was Pavlov's work on conditioned reflexes" (Bauer, 1952, p. 53).

IVAN P. PAVLOV (1849–1936)

Like Thorndike, Pavlov was born the son of a clergyman. He originally set out to become a priest like his father, but abandoned this pursuit to enter the University of St. Petersburg. He there developed a keen interest in physiology, and in 1883 became a medical doctor. However, his great passion was scientific research, which he carried out with such skill and ingenuity that he was awarded the Nobel prize in 1904 for his work on the physiology of the digestive system. He subsequently became famous for his work on *conditioned reflexes,* which we discuss in detail below.

When Pavlov was a student, he lived with his brother, who apparently took care of all of Pavlov's daily requirements, including buying Pavlov's clothes. Pavlov married Serafima Karchevskaya in 1880, and thereafter was as dependent on her as he had formerly been on his brother (Gantt, 1928, pp. 14–15). In this respect, Pavlov was extremely fortunate to have other people around him whose efforts on his behalf freed him to devote himself to research.

Like Thorndike, when Pavlov began his work with animals he would often take them home with him because of a lack of facilities at the university. However, as his career progressed he was able to command more resources, and eventually had an *Institute of Experimental Medicine* constructed for him in 1891 (Gantt, 1928, p. 16). Pavlov's devotion to his research made a strong impression on those who worked for him. Gantt (1928, p. 25) quotes the following story from one of Pavlov's assistants, which describes an incident that occurred during the Communist revolution in 1917.

> *During the revolution it was very difficult to get to the laboratory at all, because besides other things there was often shooting and fighting in the streets. However, Pavlov was generally present, even though nobody else was. One of those days when I was about ten minutes late for an experiment, I found Pavlov already there punctually, though no one else had come. Seeing that I was not on time, he immediately lit into me with his customary vivaciousness. "Why are you late, Sir?" I asked him if he did not know that there was a revolution going on outside. "What difference does a revolution make when you have work in the laboratory to do!"*

Pavlov's international fame as a scientist meant that he was relatively immune to persecution after the Communist takeover in Russia. Moreover, Pavlov's work on the physiology of the central nervous system using the procedure he called *conditioned reflexes* seemed to fit in with the temper of the times. "Pavlov's work captured the fancy of many prominent persons and . . . *Pravda,* the central organ of the [Communist] Party, said that the doctrine of conditioned reflexes was one of the foundations of *materialism* in biology, and *Izvestia,* the government organ devoted a special laudatory article to Pavlov's work" (Bauer, 1952, pp. 54–5). Materialism is the doctrine that physical events constitute the only reality. Pavlov himself never subscribed to a simpleminded materialism, saying instead that "we are now coming to think of the mind, the soul and matter as all one, and with this view there will be no necessity for a choice between them" (cited by Gantt, 1928, p. 25).

Conditioned Reflexes

It is important to realize at the outset that for most of his career Pavlov thought of himself as a physiologist, and not a psychologist. He regarded his chief inspiration to have come from the work of the Russian physiologist *Ivan M. Sechenov* (1829–1905), who published a book called *Cerebral Reflexes* in 1863. Sechenov had proposed that mental life should be understood entirely in physiological terms, and that the reflex was the appropriate unit of explanation. Pavlov (1927/1960, p. 3) dissociated himself from the psychology of the time, observing that psychologists as prominent as William James and Wundt did not claim that psychology was even close to being a science. Physiology clearly *was* a science and the physiologist had no need for psychology.

Interestingly, Pavlov (1928, pp. 39–40) did acknowledge that "some years after the beginning of the work with our new method I learned that somewhat similar experiments on animals had been performed in America, and indeed not by physiologists but by psychologists . . . and now I must acknowledge that the honor of having made the first steps along the path belongs to E. L. Thorndike. By two or three years his experiments preceded ours . . ." However, Pavlov believed that his work was completely different in orientation than Thorndike's, which he characterized as focusing on behavior to the exclusion of exploring the causes of behavior in the central nervous system. By contrast Pavlov regarded his approach as a more balanced blend of both the study of behavior and physiology. He believed that it was best to approach psychological questions through physiology, rather than to do psychology first and then try to find physiological explanations.

The experiments that made Pavlov a household word developed as a result of something Pavlov noticed while observing the action of salivary glands. Saliva would be secreted not only in the presence of food, but also by "the dish in which it is presented, the furniture upon which it is placed, the room, the person accustomed to bring it, and the noises produced by him" (Pavlov, 1928, p. 52). The connection between food and salivation seems natural and inevitable, but how should one account for the power of stimuli such as furniture to elicit a response such as salivation with which furniture has no necessary connection?

In order to understand such phenomena, Pavlov made a distinction between *unconditioned reflexes* and *conditioned reflexes.* A reflex is unconditioned if the same response always occurs in the presence of the same stimulus. Food is an *unconditioned stimulus* and salivation is an *unconditioned response* to the food. Thus, "unconditioned" means that the connection is *unconditional:*

> *Our starting point has been Descartes' idea of the nervous reflex. This is a genuine scientific conception, since it implies necessity. It may be summed up as follows: An external or internal stimulus falls on some one or other nervous receptor and gives rise to a nervous impulse; this nervous impulse is transmitted along nerve fibres to the central nervous system, and here, on account of existing nervous connections, it gives rise to a fresh impulse which passes along outgoing nerve fibres to the active organ. . . . Thus a stimulus appears to be connected of necessity with a definite response, as cause with effect. (Pavlov, 1927/1960, p. 7)*

The unconditioned reflexes corresponded to the instincts of the animal. Pavlov preferred the term "unconditioned reflex" because it was less vague and more directly descriptive of the nervous system. There were a large number of unconditioned connections. In addition to the obvious ones we will consider below, Pavlov listed such reflexes as defense, freedom, and purpose. Each of these is intended to refer to specific behaviors. For example, the reflex of defense is the animal's spontaneous reaction to anything that threatens it; the reflex of freedom occurs when the animal is confined and attempts to escape; the reflex of purpose is observed when the animal attempts to attain something of value to it.

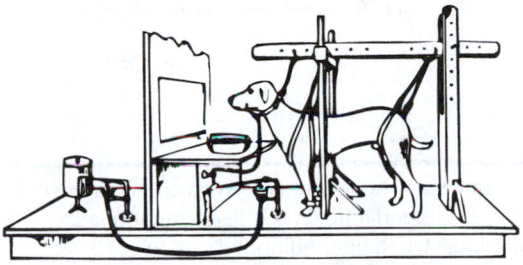

FIGURE 8.1 Pavlov's experimental apparatus.
Source: R. M. Yerkes & S. Morgulis. (1909). The method of Pavlov in animal psychology. *Psychological Bulletin, 6,* 264.

Conditioned reflexes are *conditional* in the sense that they only occur under certain conditions. The best way to see the relationship between conditioned and unconditioned reflexes is with reference to Figure 8.1. This figure represents the famous experimental situation in which a dog is fitted with a harness, and a surgically implanted device is used to collect salivary output. A typical experimental procedure consisted of sounding a tone, followed by the presentation of food to a hungry animal. After repeated pairing of the tone with the food, the tone by itself will come to elicit salivation. The tone has become a *conditioned stimulus,* and the saliva it elicits is a *conditioned response.* The experimental procedure allows for the formation of a *conditioned reflex.* The relation between conditioned and unconditioned connections is represented in Figure 8.2 on page 150.

Here are three key facts about conditioning:

- A conditioned response is typically smaller in magnitude than an unconditioned one. In the experimental situation described above, the amount of saliva elicited by the tone is usually less than the amount of saliva elicited by food (Kimble, 1961, p. 53).

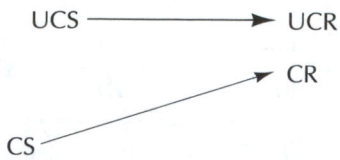

FIGURE 8.2 The relation between conditioned and unconditioned reflexes. UCS, unconditioned stimulus; UCR, unconditioned response; CS, conditioned stimulus; CR, conditioned response.

- If a conditioned reflex has been formed, and then the conditioned stimulus is repeatedly presented by itself, in the absence of the unconditioned stimulus, then the conditioned response will eventually cease. This phenomenon is called the *extinction* of a conditioned response (Pavlov, 1927/1960, p. 297).
- Suppose that a conditioned response has been extinguished, and the animal has been returned to its home cage. If the animal is then brought back to the experimental situation after a rest, the previously extinguished conditioned response may return. The phenomenon whereby a previously extinguished conditioned response returns after an interval during which it has not been tested is called *spontaneous recovery* (Kimble, 1961, pp. 82–83).

These facts about conditioning were not mere curiosities, relevant only to the laboratory situation. The power of Pavlov's experiments lay in the way that his findings could apparently be generalized from the laboratory to situations outside the laboratory. The experiments formed the basis for Pavlov's speculations about the adaptive nature of the conditioning process in the real world. Unconditioned reflexes are not by themselves sufficient to ensure the survival of the organism. For example, the animal must not only eat food when it is presented, but also be able to find food for itself. Consider an animal hunting for prey. It must follow signs that lead it to its quarry. This is exactly the function of conditioned stimuli: They are *signals* that guide the animal to an unconditioned stimulus. As long as these signals are reliable, then the animal continues to respond to them. However, the environment is always changing. The essence of adaptability is the ability to be flexible, and change one's responses as the environment changes. Thus, when conditioned stimuli fail to lead to unconditioned stimuli, then extinction occurs. The key thing about conditioned stimuli is that they form *temporary* connections that are *inhibited* when they become unreliable signals (Pavlov, 1928, p. 123). However, just as a reliable signal may become unreliable, so an unreliable signal may once again become reliable as the environment fluctuates. Spontaneous recovery provides the organism with an opportunity to "check out" a signal that may have become reliable again. Although conditioning is often portrayed as a rigid, mechanical process, it is important to see that Pavlov's view was that conditioning enables the organism to form an adaptive, flexible relationship with its environment.

Pavlov (1928, pp. 24–25; 1927/1960, p. 123) used the analogy of a central telephone switchboard to explain the way that cortical connections functioned in the conditioning process. It is obviously inefficient to have connections between each phone and every other phone. Far better is to have phones connected through a central switchboard as required. Similarly, while there are some inborn connections in the nervous system (the unconditioned reflexes), there are new connections continuously being formed through the cerebral hemispheres.

Speech

Higher order conditioning occurs when a second conditioned stimulus is paired with a conditioned stimulus that has already been established (Pavlov, 1927/1960, p. 33). This process is represented diagrammatically in Figure 8.3. This procedure leads to two levels of signals. The *primary signaling system* consists largely of sensory stimuli, such as the tone we described above. In humans, the *secondary signaling system* plays a crucial role, because it consists largely of *words*. Words name primary signals. A single word can stand for an entire class of signals, and thus greatly extend the range of sti-

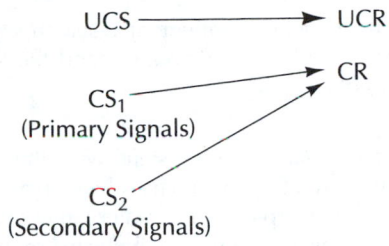

FIGURE 8.3 Higher order conditioning.

muli to which a person can respond. For example, the word "pencil" is not just a label for a particular pencil, but a label for all pencils, and having learned to write with one pencil, you can generalize to any other pencil you come across. It is speech that most differentiates humans from other animals, and gives them their greater flexibility and power over the environment.

> *Obviously for man speech provides conditioned stimuli which are just as real as any other stimuli. At the same time speech provides stimuli which exceed in richness and many-sidedness any of the others, allowing comparison neither qualitatively nor quantitatively with any conditioned stimuli which are possible in animals. Speech, on account of the whole preceding life of the adult, is connected up with all the internal and external stimuli which can reach the cortex, signaling all of them and replacing all of them, and therefore it can call forth all those reactions of the organism which are normally determined by the actual stimuli themselves. (Pavlov, 1927/1960, p. 407)*

Temperaments and Psychopathology

Pavlov believed that the fundamental cortical processes were *excitation* and *inhibition*. In order to be properly adjusted to the environment, it is necessary to inhibit all but those responses that are appropriate to the current situation. "[T]his is of the greatest importance in our life as well as in the life of animals; . . . that under any given circumstance and at any moment a certain activity must be manifested, but in another situation, inhibited. Upon this principle is founded the highest orientations of life. In such a way, a continual and proper balancing of these two processes lays the basis of a normal life for both man and animal. These two opposite processes . . . [are] coexistent and are equally important in nervous activity" (Pavlov, 1928, p. 373).

Pavlov observed great individual differences between animals in terms of the ease with which they formed conditioned reflexes. At one extreme was an *excitatory* group, which is easily conditioned, while at the other extreme is an *inhibitory* group, which is difficult to condition. Pavlov (1928, p. 376) believed that this dimension characterized differences between people also. In attempting to characterize such individual differences in human terms, Pavlov (1928, p. 376) drew on the work of *Hippocrates* (c. 460 B.C.–377 B.C.), who had classified people into four *temperaments:* choleric, sanguine, phlegmatic and melancholic. Pavlov regarded the four temperaments as arranged on a scale from extremely excitatory (choleric) to extremely inhibitory (melancholic), with the sanguine and phlegmatic in between. The excitatory/inhibitory imbalance of the extreme temperaments is associated with pathology, by contrast with the relative equilibrium of the middle temperaments. Pavlov (1928, p. 377) described the choleric temperament as "pugnacious, passionate and easily and quickly irritated," while the melancholic "believes in nothing, hopes for nothing, in everything he sees only the dark side, and from everything he expects only grievances." The sanguine and phlegmatic types stand "in the golden middle . . . well-equilibrated and therefore healthy [and] stable" (Pavlov, 1928, p. 377).

Vivisection and Anti-Vivisectionism

Pavlov often performed surgery on his animals to prepare them for his experiments, and was acutely aware of the fact that many people found such experimental work on live animals to be objectionable. The dissection of live animals is called *vivisection* and the movement against the use of live animals in research was called *anti-vivisectionism.* Pavlov (1928, p. 21) justified such procedures, which occasionally did result in "painful and vio-

BOX 8.1

Animal Rights?

A persistent issue in psychological research is the proper treatment of animals. Experimentation on animals goes back a long way. We noted in Chapter 2 that in the seventeenth century Descartes treated animals merely as machines with no feelings. This is an attitude that many people would find offensive today.

Experimental work on live animals has often been seen by members of the general public as giving researchers an opportunity to use techniques that would be unacceptable if performed on humans. For decades, some people have feared that what is done to research animals today will be done to people tomorrow, particularly to people who are not in a position to object to maltreatment. Thus, over the years there has been a concern in some quarters that researchers who use animal subjects may be abusive to animals, and ultimately to people. An excellent review of the early period of this controversy is by Lederer (1985).

Recently, the controversy over animal experimentation has entered a new phase. The nature of the current debate is well illustrated by the reaction to a recent article by Johnson (1990). Johnson argued that there are currently two contrasting views of what constitutes ethical treatment of research animals. The first he calls *animal welfare,* and the second *animal rights.*

- *Animal welfare* is consistent with the Judeo-Christian tradition, which has always maintained that, while people are of greater value than animals, people have a responsibility to promote the welfare of animals. However, from this viewpoint, it is ethical to use animals in research that will benefit people. Without animal subjects, we are forced to abandon research "that would have saved lives or eased the pain" of people who may be suffering from one disorder or another (Johnson, 1990, p. 214). Of course, the use of animals in research should be as humane as possible, with no unnecessary suffering. This would be the position that researchers like Pavlov adopted.
- The *animal rights* activists adopt a different value system. People are not necessarily superior to other life forms. For example, both people and animals are capable of experiencing pain. Pain is a great leveler. It is immoral to inflict pain on any animal, human or otherwise. Application of this principle eliminates research with animals that would not be ethical if done with humans.

What do you think?

lent deaths of animals," by saying that there was no other way to understand how the nervous system worked. It was necessary to sacrifice some animals in order to benefit mankind. Pavlov also noted that animal experimentation was a small source of pain compared to the consequences of recreational hunting and the slaughter of animals for food. Further discussion of this issue is in Box 8.1.

Vladimir M. Bekhterev (1857–1827)

In addition to Pavlov, the objective approach in Russia was also carried forward by Bekhterev's *reflexology.* Bekhterev argued that reflexology "must not be confused with physiology, 'which is the science of the functions and regulation of the organs of the human body, including the brain' . . . Reflexology, particularly human reflexology, is a scientific discipline which sets for itself the problem of studying the responsive reaction to external and internal stimuli" (Bauer, 1952, p. 55). Reflexology was also not to be confused with psychology, which reflexology was intended to replace.

Bekhterev developed a technique for studying *associated motor reflexes* in both dogs and humans. The technique involved applying electrical shock to, for example, a person's finger resting on a metal surface. The response was withdrawal of the finger on being shocked. This response could come to be elicited by a signal that had preceded the shock, and Bekhterev called this the *association reflex.* "An attitude of avoidance, shown by the movement of the finger develops. But it is very difficult to know whether this is *really* conditioning or voluntary behavior. Moreover, if the subject feels that the experimenter is testing him, he can decide (courageously as he thinks) to keep his finger on the electrode. Pavlov himself severely criticized this method" (Le Ny, 1964, p. 23). Nevertheless, Bekhterev's procedure was extensively used by Watson, whose American form of behaviorism we examine next.

Additional Reading on This Topic. Windholz (1990) describes the work of the group of researchers surrounding Pavlov from 1896 to 1936. Sokolov (1969) provides an account of some important Russian work on language in the period after Pavlov. Gantt, Pickenhain, and Zwingmann (1970) give a review of Pavlov's work in relation to pathology.

JOHN B. WATSON (1878–1958)

Watson is one of the most colorful figures in the history of twentieth-century psychology in the United States. He was born in South Carolina, the son of a boisterous father who was more often away from than at home, and a mother who, as a devout Baptist, hoped that young John B. Watson would become a preacher. As we shall see, Watson did indeed become a preacher of sorts, although his message went against received wisdom.

Watson attended Furman University, graduating in 1899. He was ambitious, and in spite of a mediocre record managed to get accepted as a graduate student at the University of Chicago. As we saw in the last chapter, Chicago was the home of functional psychology, and Watson worked with J. R. Angell, among others. However, the ideas of *Jacques Loeb* (1859–1924) also made quite an impression on him (Buckley, 1989, pp. 40–41). Loeb was particularly interested in *tropisms,* which are movements that are under the direct control of a stimulus. An example would be a tendency for an animal to turn toward light. A tropism in an animal is conceived of as "a forced response, in the sense that the organism is governed by the . . . stimulus in a mechanical way, just as pressing a switch in an electrical circuit turns on an appropriate light bulb" (Tavolga, 1969, p. 77). Loeb was a materialist, and believed that mechanisms similar to tropisms governed all behavior.

Watson's doctoral dissertation was in animal psychology. He used *white rats* as subjects, a practice that was relatively novel at the time, but which became very widespread later on (Wertz, 1994). Among other things, Watson investigated the behavior of rats in mazes, another method that was not invented by Watson, but which also became extremely common in psychology. Watson received his Ph.D. in 1903.

> *He was the youngest to have earned that degree from the University of Chicago. Yet he felt what he called his "first deep-seated inferiority," which grew into years of jealousy, when he was told by Dewey and Angell that his doctoral exam was inferior to that of* Helen Thompson Wooley, *who had graduated two years before. Watson was often a willing mentor to his female students, but he was extremely uncomfortable with women as professional peers (Buckley, 1989, pp. 45–46).*

After receiving his degree, Watson stayed on at Chicago. He married a student there named *Mary Ickes* in 1903, and they had a daughter in 1905. Watson was never happy with the level of support for his research that he received from the university administration, and moved to Johns Hopkins University in 1908, where he was appointed as a full professor at age 29.

The head of Watson's department at Hopkins was *James Mark Baldwin,* whose work we will consider in Chapter 12 on developmental psychology. For now, however, Baldwin is relevant only insofar as he played a part in Watson's career. Watson's animal work had been attracting much favorable attention, and Baldwin was enthusiastic about adding Watson to his department. Baldwin also had other enthusiasms. "In the summer of 1908, Baldwin had been caught in a police raid on a 'colored house' of prostitution. He gave a false name to the police and the charge was eventually dropped" (Pauly, 1979, p. 38). Baldwin would have been out of the woods, except that the mayor of Baltimore nominated him for the school board, apparently not aware of Baldwin's escapade. At that point, somebody blew the whistle, and Baldwin's indiscretion became widely known. The upshot was that the Trustees of Johns Hopkins asked Baldwin to resign, and he left the country.

As we have observed before, "It is an ill wind that blows nobody any good," and Baldwin's misfortune was Watson's great chance. He became head of the department, which provided him with the platform he needed to achieve his ambitious goals. He began to do the work that would transform psychology in the United States.

Psychology as the Behaviorist Views It

In 1913, Watson (1913/1966) published a paper that challenged psychologists to change virtually every aspect of their discipline as it was then being practiced. Watson (1913/1966, p. 70) began the paper by saying that "psychology as the behaviorist views it is a purely objective experimental branch of natural science." The rest of the paper laid out the consequences of taking this proposition with utter seriousness.

The first consequence is that psychology is not in any way the study of consciousness. The comparative psychologist studies behavior without any reference to consciousness, and in so doing is leading the way for psychologists who study humans. Human behavior can and should be studied in the same way as animal behavior. A part of Watson's message (1913/1966, p. 74) was that it is time to finally replace the unreliable method of introspection with the reliable, objective observation of behavior: "The time seems to have come when psychology must discard all reference to consciousness; when it need no longer delude itself into thinking that it is making mental states the object of observation."

Functional psychology was also to go by the boards. It was a vague grab bag of topics and methods, ill-suited to a scientific psychology. By including a discussion of "mind," it simply muddies the waters. Questions about the relation between mind and body are relics of "philosophical speculation" and "need trouble the student of behavior as little as they trouble the student of physics. . . . I can state my position here no better than by saying that I should like to bring my students up in the same ignorance of such hypotheses as one finds among the students of branches of science" (Watson, 1913/1966, p. 76). Evidently there would be no courses in the history of psychology for Watson's students!

Watson's psychology (1913/1966, p. 76) would begin with "the observable fact that organisms, man and animal alike, do adjust themselves to their environment by means of hereditary and habit equipments." These adjustments are responses to particular stimuli, and the prediction of behavior is a realistic possibility given an understanding of *stimulus-response relationships*. Psychology concerns itself with the *prediction and control of behavior*. This makes of psychology not just an experimental discipline, but also a truly applied discipline. Psychology is able to provide "the educator, the physician, the jurist and businessman" with information that will be useful in their professions (Watson, 1913/1966, p. 78).

At the end of his paper, Watson (1913/1966, p. 83) made a statement that is undoubtedly true. "If you grant the behaviorist the right to use consciousness in the same way that other natural scientists employ it—that is, without making consciousness a special object of observation—you have granted all that my thesis requires." Watsonian behaviorism comes down to this: A real science uses consciousness to make observations; it does not observe consciousness itself. Watson never denied the existence of consciousness, or that observers were conscious. He only denied that observers in psychology should act differently than observers in any other science. A scientific psychology would have as its subject matter the behavior of organisms, no more and no less.

Watson's message had a profound impact on other psychologists, many of whom felt that it was a breath of fresh air. In place of the interminable quarrels about what psychology was and how it should go about its business, Watson promised a clear and simple solution. Just study behavior; forget about the rest, and all will be well.

Watson' s 1913 paper is the first in a series of what might be called his *promissory notes* (Soyland, 1994, pp. 230–231). In the context of the history of science, a promissory note is a claim that if a certain research direction is followed, then the results will be worthwhile. Promissory notes are quite common in the history of science, and certainly in the history of psychology. Throughout his career, Watson issued several promissory notes, and here is an example of the rhetoric he (1930/1962, p. 104) used to try to persuade people to accept the promise of behaviorism:

> *I should like to go one step further now and say, "Give me a dozen healthy infants, well-formed, and my own specified world to bring them up in and I'll guarantee to take any one at random and train him to become any type of specialist I might select—doctor, lawyer, artist, merchant-chief and, yes, even beggar-man and thief, regardless of his talents, penchants, tendencies, abilities, vocations, and race of his ancestors." I am going beyond my facts and I admit it, but so have advocates of the contrary and they have been doing it for many thousands of years. Please note that when this experiment is made I am to be allowed to specify the way the children are to be brought up and the type of world they have to live in.*

Although some people had reservations about his radical *environmentalism,* many were quite happy to accept Watson's promissory note. Of course, such a promissory note must pay off at some point with real research findings. What was the content of the psychology Watson actually proposed, and did it live up to its promise?

Watson's Psychology

Conditioning. In 1916, Watson (1916/1970, p. 35) wrote a paper in which he reflected on his earlier criticisms of introspection, and said that it was now necessary to "suggest some method which we might *begin* to use in place of introspection. I have found, as you easily might have predicted, that it is one thing to condemn a long-established method, but quite another thing to suggest something in its place." However, he had not only been reading about the work of Pavlov and Bekhterev, but also beginning to use their methods in his own laboratory. At that point, Watson (1916/1970, p. 44) had gathered data on "eleven human subjects, one dog and seven chickens." Although he was concerned about the validity of using conditioning methods with humans who might "get the drift of what is expected of them as the experiment proceeds" (Watson, 1913/1970, p. 44, 46), he felt confident that conditioning would be useful with a variety of types of subjects and topics in psychology. Gradually, Watson became more and more closely identified with conditioning.

> *Not only was Pavlovian conditioning a practical, objective, and deterministic framework in which to cast as much of psychology as one's imagination encompassed, but it was built upon the reflex itself, Watson's first love in psychological analysis. The marriage was a natural, and there were no impediments to it.*
>
> *Watson's conversion to the conditioned reflex went hand in hand with a change in the scope of his behaviorism. Instead of a mere faction within an academic discipline, it became a program for social control and improvement. During the 1920's, Watson's books became more and concerned with practical questions . . . [and] were usually compilations . . . of articles that had appeared in various popular magazines . . . [such as] "The behaviorist looks at instincts" (*Harper's, *1927); "Feed me with facts" (*Saturday Review of Literature, *1928); "The weakness of women" (*The Nation, *1928); "Can we make our children behave?" (*Forum, *1929); "It's your own fault" (*Collier's, *1928); "The heart or the intellect?" (*Harper's, *1928); "Are parents necessary?" (*New York Times, *1930). (Herrnstein, 1967, pp. xxvi–xxvii)*

Emotional, Manual, and Verbal Habits

In his book *Behaviorism,* Watson (1930/1962, p. 197) argued that humans are unique in the animal kingdom because of the variety of useful habits they can form through conditioning. These habits are of three kinds. First, there are *visceral* or *emotional* habits; second there are *manual* habits; and third there are *laryngeal* or *verbal* habits. Let us consider each of these in turn.

Emotional Habits. Watson (1930/1962, p. 141) was contemptuous of James's theory of emotion because it relied on introspective evidence gathered from adults. The only way to study emotion is to examine very young children and see what emotional responses are elicited by what stimuli. Watson (1930/1962, pp. 152–154) came to the conclusion that humans come equipped with three emotional responses that are tied to particular stimuli. These are *fear, rage,* and *love.* Obviously, by these three words Watson did not mean any kind of subjective experience. They referred to unlearned responses. Fear was a baby's reaction in the presence of a sudden, loud sound, or when it suddenly loses support: "there is a catching of breath, clutching with the hands and crying" (Watson, 1930/1962, p. 153). Watson's example of rage is the behavior elicited when the body is restrained, and involves "stiffening of the whole body . . . and holding of breath" (Watson, 1930/1962, p. 154). Love responses occur in the baby through the stimulation of "erogenous zones, such as the nipples, the lips and the sex organs" that results in behaviors such as "gurgling and cooing" (Watson, 1930/1962, p. 155).

Little Albert. These primitive emotional responses constitute the platform on which a much more complicated variety of emotional responses is built. Watson and *Rosalie Rayner* (1920/1979) described a procedure for producing conditioned emotional reactions. The subject on their experiment is one of the most famous in the history of American psychology, Albert B., or *Little Albert,* as he came to be called, an 11-month-old infant who was "the son of one of the wet nurses in the Harriet Lane Hospital. He had lived his whole life in the hospital" (Watson, 1930/1962, p. 159). At first, the child was quite happy to touch any object brought near to him. However, "a fear reaction could be called out . . . by striking a hammer upon a suspended steel bar" behind the child (Watson & Rayner, 1920/1979, p. 280). By pairing this sound with the sight of a white rat, Albert could be made to show a fear reaction to the rat as well. Watson and Rayner reported that this fear reaction subsequently transferred to other white, furry things such as a rabbit and a Santa Claus mask. Watson (1930/1962, pp. 163–164) called these generalizations "undifferentiated emotional reactions," and believed that they were particularly characteristic of "most of us in infancy, . . . many adults, especially women . . . [and] all primitive peoples." However, he also believed that with proper training people could be taught to differentiate between the original fear-producing stimulus, and those that had become fear producing accidentally. It is, of course, one of the goals of psychotherapy to attempt to rid a client of unnecessary fears. As we see in Chapter 11, Watson and Rayner's study has often been cited as a classic precursor of psychotherapeutic procedures deriving from theories of conditioning.

Manual Habits. By "manual habits," Watson (1930/1962, p. 197) meant the entire range of muscular responses including those in the "trunk, legs, arms and feet." Stimuli are forever eliciting manual responses of one sort or another. The act of responding to one stimulus, places the person in a new stimulus situation which elicits another response, and so on. Through repetition, manual habits form that allow for a smooth transition from one situation to another. Watson (1930/1962, p. 212) advocated the "formation of early work habits in youth," believing this to be the "most reasonable explanation we have today not only for success in any line, but even for genius." When it came to the acquisition of a skill, Watson advocated *distributed practice,* as opposed to continuous, or *massed practice.* Practice is distributed if the number of trials is spread out, with intertrial intervals in which no work is done on the task. For many skills, it appears that distributed practice leads to better results.

Verbal Habits. Watson loved to make exaggerated claims, and then retract them just a little bit. One such claim is "thought is nothing but talking to ourselves" (Watson, 1930/1962, p. 238). This claim was often taken to mean that thinking is nothing but movements in the larynx, but Watson (1930/1962, p. 238) denied that this is what he actually meant, although he admitted to having said it "for pedagogical purposes." What he actually meant was that thought and internal speech are one and the same. Internal speech can be generated by any number of muscular activities, including movements in the larynx. For example, people who know sign language may speak to themselves using minute movements of their fingers. The point was not that thought took place in the larynx, but that verbal habits, however realized, constituted thinking, properly so-called. In support of this contention, Watson pointed out that young children talk out loud, even when alone. Under the pressure of socialization, this speech becomes silent, and although still present it is hard to notice. Thinking is this subvocal speech, and involves running off verbal habits that enable us to accomplish things that range from recalling the words of a song to planning our day.

Speech is an example of a chain of responses, sentences consisting of one word after another. As such, speech is but one example of a very large class of *serially ordered behaviors.* We are constantly performing complex tasks that require us to generate responses in the proper sequence. Driving a car and playing the piano are only two examples. Watson believed that the process whereby such habits are formed worked in the way that is illustrated in Figure 8.4. First there is a sequence of stimuli, each of which elicits a response in the manner depicted in part I of the figure. With repetition, the first stimulus by itself is capable of setting off the entire chain. Each response in the chain serves as the stimulus for the next response, as shown in part II of Figure 8.4. Watson's example (1930/1962, p. 257) of this process was playing the piano. At first, every note on the page elicits a key press, but with practice you can look at the first note, and then play the entire piece without looking at the music.

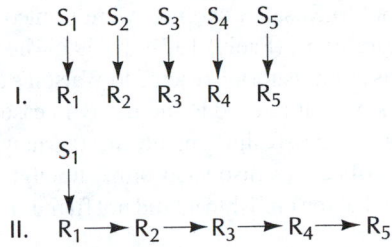

FIGURE 8.4 Watson's model of serially ordered behavior.

Watson believed that it was an important function of internal speech to guide these serially ordered acts. For example, as you drive a car you might be able to catch yourself as you say things that serve as stimuli for your actions. However, there are some things we do that are not under verbal control. Watson had a special role for behaviors for which we have no verbal label, which he called the *unverbalized.* There are any number of infantile responses to which a verbal label never becomes attached. For example, "What child has ever verbalized its incestuous attachments?" (Watson, 1930/ 1962, p. 263). For Watson, the unverbalized was what Freud had called the "unconscious" (Watson, 1930/1962, p. 262). The "unconscious" occurred of necessity because early childhood experience took place before the child could verbally label any of its experiences.

Watson and Rosalie Rayner

Rosalie Rayner, the graduate student with whom Watson had done the Albert study, was not only his co-worker. Rayner was "the daughter of a prominent Baltimorean who some years earlier had donated $10,000 to the University, and niece of a former US senator. Watson left his wife in April 1920; he and Rosalie were seen together so much that many thought they were married. . . . When Mrs. Watson sued for divorce she submitted as evidence a number of letters Watson wrote 'breathing affection' to Rosalie; excerpts were printed in the Baltimore *Sun*" (Pauly, 1979, p. 39). The Johns Hopkins administration reacted to Watson's case in the same way it reacted to the Baldwin case. Watson was asked to resign, and he did so. Many of his former colleagues disowned him, although a few thought that the punishment did not fit the crime.

Watson's Second Career in Advertising

Watson and Rayner were married on New Year's Eve, 1920 (Buckley, 1989, p. 132), and moved to New York. There he worked first for the J. Walter Thompson advertising agency, and then for William Esty & Co. until he retired in 1946 (Herrnstein, 1967). The step from academia to advertising was not so great for Watson as it might have been for other professors. As we have already seen, Watson was keenly interested in developing a psychology that could be of use in the real world, and what could be more of an applied psychology than advertising? Advertisers wanted to be able to provide "a controlled and predictable body of consumers," and who better to provide this than Watson "who claimed to have the techniques that could be used to predict and control human behavior" (Buckley, 1982, p. 211).

Watson recommended to his colleagues that they take advantage of conditioned responses. "To insure the appropriate reaction from the consumer, tell him something that will tie up with fear, something that will stir up a mild rage, that will call out an affectionate or love response, or strike at a deep psychological or habit need" (Buckley, 1982, p. 212). In order to accomplish this goal, Watson relied on several techniques that have by now become well-known. In general, these techniques did not sell a product on the basis of its intrinsic virtues, but rather attempted to associate positive features with the product. For example, Watson employed experts and celebrities who would recommend the product in advertisements, and himself played this role in advertisements for coffee and toothpaste (Buckley, 1982, pp. 215–216). One might wonder whether merely repeating a commercial that paired a positive figure with a commodity would be sufficient to establish an association, but there is a great deal of subsequent research that "mere exposure" to a stimulus is enough to cause it to become positively evaluated (Bornstein, 1989). At any rate, Watson was a great success in his second career, widely respected by his colleagues in the business world.

As time went on, the attitudes of Watson's former associates in academia softened. Finally, in 1957, Watson was given a citation by the American Psychological Association, which read as follows:

> *To Dr. John B. Watson, whose work has been one of the vital determinants of the form and substance of modern psychology. He initiated a revolution in psychological thought, and his writings have been the point of departure for continuing lines of fruitful research. (Watson, 1930/1962, p. Iii)*

Additional Reading on This Topic. James B. Watson has recounted his experiences as Watson and Rayner's son (Hannush, 1987).

KARL S. LASHLEY (1890–1958)

Lashley had a background in biological science, receiving his undergraduate training at the University of West Virginia, and then doing his Ph.D. with the geneticist *Herbert S. Jennings* at Johns Hopkins. Lashley then did postdoctoral studies with John B. Watson. The two became great friends, and a part of their subsequent correspondence is discussed in Box 8.2. Throughout his entire career, Lashley considered himself to be a behaviorist (Hebb, 1980b), even though, as we shall see, his interests diverged considerably from Watson's.

Cortical Localization of Function

Watson and Lashley "developed different interests in conditioning research. . . . Lashley's interest was in finding out how conditioned reflexes are represented in the nervous system" while Watson was never very interested in the physiology of the nervous system (Bruce, 1991, p. 311). Lashley initially thought that it might be possible to "understand the

Box 8.2

Watson and Lashley: The Boys of Summer, or Something Else?

John B. Watson destroyed most of his correspondence, but some letters written in the 1950s to and from Karl Lashley survived (Dewsbury, 1992b). In these letters Watson and Lashley freely express their personal views on a variety of issues, including women and race. They probably never thought about the possibility that their letters would be made available to a wider audience. Nowadays their views would be called "politically incorrect." For example, Lashley concludes some of his letters with the phrase "Heil Hitler and Apartheit."

The purpose of this box is not to provoke prurient curiosity, but to echo a question that Weidman (1994b) has raised with respect to these letters, and by extension to all the personal views held by psychologists. Dewsbury (1992b, p. 4) saw the letters in the context of the time in which they were written, and regarded them as only helping to "flesh out our understanding of these two significant psychologists as the ends of their lives approached." Weidman saw the letters as having a broader explanatory potential, and wondered if we can separate the private and public views of psychologists. Can we explain the theoretical orientation of a psychologist as an extension of his or her personal life, or is scientific activity a purely objective matter? The standard answer is that the personal beliefs of scientists have nothing to do with their scientific work. "Yet we must be aware that there is nothing natural about removing science in this way from its social and political context. We will not necessarily understand it better by doing so, and we must acknowledge that in so choosing to remove it, we are ourselves making a political choice" (Weidman, 1994b, p. 7).

What do you think?

physiological processes underlying the establishment of conditioned reflexes and to trace such reflexes through the brain" (Bruce, 1986, p. 34). Lashley's endeavor should be seen in the context of a long-standing controversy in psychology, called the *localization of function controversy.* Lashley was by no means the first person to wonder where particular psychological functions were located in the nervous system. As Krech (1962) observed, the attempt to discover which parts of the brain are specialized for which tasks goes back at least to *Franz Joseph Gall* (1758–1828) and his student *J. G. Spurzheim* (1776–1832). Gall and Spurzheim promoted *phrenology.* You have probably seen phrenological charts like the one in Figure 8.5 on page 160. They purport to represent the locations of various psychological functions. Although Gall and Spurzheim's charts are not taken seriously any longer, their underlying premises still deserve consideration (Krech, 1962).

> *Their argument reduced to three basic principles: (1) The brain is the sole organ of the mind. (2) The basic character and intellectual traits of man are innately determined. (3) Since there are differences in character and intellectual traits among individuals as well as differences in various intellectual capacities within a single individual, there must exist differentially developed areas in the brain, responsible for these differences! Where there is variation in* function *there must be variation in the controlling* structures. *(p. 33)*

Gall and Spurzheim's method for locating functions in the brain was highly speculative. They believed that the more highly developed a function, the larger it would be. Furthermore, the larger a function, the more it would manifest itself as a protrusion on the skull. Thus, one could divine a person's strengths and weaknesses by examining the shape of the skull. In spite of the obvious weakness of this method, the underlying hypothesis that specific functions are localized in specific parts of the brain has many adherents today (e.g., Gardner, 1983).

Lashley began his studies of localization in 1916 with *Shepherd Ivery Franz* (1874–1933). Franz was an expert in the technique of *ablation,* whereby parts of the cortex are destroyed, and the results observed. If functions were localized in the

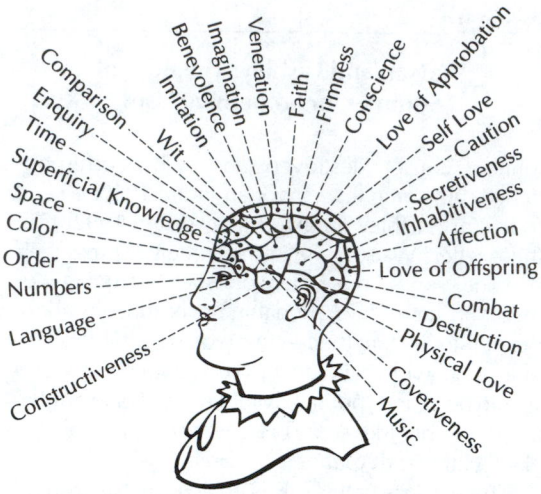

FIGURE 8.5 A phrenological chart.
Source: D. Krech & R. S. Crutchfield. (1958). *Elements of psychology* (p. 481). New York: Knopf. Copyright © 1958 by David Krech & Richard S. Crutchfield. Copyright © 1969 by Alfred A. Knopf, Inc. Reprinted by permission of Hilda Krech.

cortex, then the effect of ablation of cortical tissue should depend on the area destroyed. However, on the basis of his observations, Franz (1912) believed that "mental processes are not due to the independent activities of individual parts of the brain, but to the activities of the brain as a whole" and that "it would appear best and most scientific that we should not adhere to any of the phrenological systems" (p. 328).

Lashley and Franz studied the effects of ablation of the frontal lobes in rats. Their technique was to make "small holes in the animal's skull rather than opening up the skull, and determine by later histology precisely where the lesions had occurred" (Bruce, 1986, p. 38), and determine the effect of such lesions on the retention of a simple learned maze habit. Their results persuaded them that as long as sufficient tissue remained after the operation, then the location of the tissue was irrelevant.

In 1917, Lashley moved to the University of Minnesota. Largely as a result of work at Minnesota and elsewhere, he published a classic in the area of localization of function, called *Brain Mechanisms and Intelligence* (1929). This research developed further the procedures he had learned from Franz. Lashley lesioned the cortex of rats in different places and to different degrees. He reasoned that "if there were reflex paths transversing the cortex . . . then surgery would destroy them" (Weidman, 1994a, p. 166). Lashley (1929, p. 74) observed the ability of rats to learn or remember such tasks as finding their ways through mazes of different levels of difficulty, and found that performance in simple mazes was not greatly affected by brain damage. Rather, performance declined as the difficulty of the task increased, and/or the amount of brain damage increased. Lashley (1930/1978) summarized the implications of his results:

> *What is the evidence that the cortex itself contains the definite specialized synapses which are demanded by the reflex theory? Small lesions either produce no symptoms or very transient ones, so that it is clear that the mechanisms for habits are not closely grouped within small areas. When larger areas are involved, there are usually amnesias for many activities. . . . After injuries to the brain, the rate of formation of some habits is directly proportional to the extent of the injury and independent of the position within any part of the cortex. (p. 271)*

There was no evidence for specialized connections developed as a result of learning in the brain. Rather, neither learning nor memory are "dependent upon the properties of individual cells," but rather are functions of "the total mass of tissue"

(Lashley, 1930/1978, p. 271). These results came to be formulated as the *law of mass action* (learning and memory depend on the total mass of brain tissue remaining) and the *law of equipotentiality* (even though some areas of the cortex may become specialized for certain tasks, within limits any part of an area can do the job of any other part of that area). Lashley (1930/1978, p. 271) used the metaphor of an electric sign as a model to explain his findings. The "functional organization plays over" cortical cells "just as the pattern of letters plays over the bank of lamps in an electric sign." A single bank of bulbs in an electronic sign can be used to display any number of messages, and similarly the cortex can be organized in any number of ways depending on circumstances.

While Pavlov had attempted to approach psychological problems through physiology, Lashley (1930/1978, p. 282) attempted to do the reverse. He argued that

> *psychology is today a more fundamental science than neurophysiology. By this I mean that the latter offers few principles from which we may predict or define the normal organization of behavior, whereas the study of psychological processes furnishes a mass of factual material to which the laws of nervous action in behavior must conform. . . . For immediate progress it is not very important that we should have a correct theory of brain activity, but it is essential that we shall not be handicapped by a false one.*

Needless to say, Pavlov was not pleased with the direction in which Lashley's work had taken him. In his talk to the International Congress of Psychology in 1929, Lashley (1930/1978) had advanced a "vigorous attack on Pavlovian reflex theory. . . . Afterwards, Pavlov denounced Lashley's lecture so vehemently that his interpreter, trying to keep up with the 20-minute tirade, finally gave up and said simply at the end of it, 'Professor Pavlov said: No!' . . . [For Pavlov] to have had one of the foremost behaviorists of the time reject his ideas so thoroughly must have been a bitter disappointment" (Bruce, 1991, p. 314).

The Problem of Serial Order in Behavior

The importance of Lashley's work on the localization of function problem would have ensured his place in the history of psychology. However, Lashley went on to do other work that may in the long run turn out to be his most important (e.g., Bruce, 1994a,b). The best expression of this work was in a paper which Lashley presented in 1948, and which was published in 1951.

Recall that Watson had proposed that a chain of responses, such as a sentence consisting of one word after another, consisted of a sequence of responses cued by an initial stimulus. Watson's theory was that in such a chain each response was cued by the preceding response. It was just such an *associative chain theory* that Lashley criticized.

Organisms are almost always engaging in serially ordered acts such as speaking, writing, playing the piano, or running through a maze, and any adequate explanation of behavior must explain the way sequences of behavior become organized. Lashley pointed out that any associative chain theory has difficulty explaining phenomena such as *priming* of responses. A response sometimes occurs earlier in a sequence than it would if it was elicited by the immediately preceding stimulus. One of Lashley's examples (1951, p. 119) was typing "wrapid writing" rather than "rapid writing." The *w* in *writing* had been *primed,* or activated, before the word *rapid* had been typed. "Not infrequently words are introduced which should occur much later in the sentence, often five or six words in advance" (Lashley, 1951, p. 119). Lashley also discussed *spoonerisms,* which are errors named after an Oxford professor (William Archibald Spooner, 1844–1930) about whom many stories were told. He was supposed to have said such things as "You have tasted your worm" to a student who had wasted his term, and to have discussed "the weight of rages" when he meant to speak about the rate of wages (Augarde, 1991, p. 206). In the first example, the *t* in *term* was primed before the sentence was uttered, and intruded earlier in the sequence. "In these contaminations, it is as if the aggregate of words were in a state of partial excitation, held in check by the requirements of grammatical structure, but ready to activate the final common path" (Lashley, 1951, p. 119). Some central organization of such sequences is required that is different from the peripheral stimulus-response process postulated by Watson's theory.

Lashley's ideas were ahead of his time. Citations of his serial order paper have continued to increase ever since it was published in 1951 (Bruce, 1994a, p. 94). Lashley's ideas about the necessity of central control of behavior anticipated developments that were to take place later on when cognitive psychology challenged behaviorism for control of psychology. These developments will form an important part of our story in subsequent chapters.

Additional Reading on This Topic. Donald O. Hebb, late of McGill University, was one of Lashley's most influential students. His book *The Organization of Behavior* (1949) has influenced generations of neuropsychologists, particularly in Canada. Hebb originally wanted Lashley to collaborate with him on this book, but Lashley refused (Hebb, 1980, p. 296).

B. F. SKINNER (1904–1990)

The Nature of Behaviorism

The three theorists we have considered in detail thus far demonstrate that the orientation to psychology called "behaviorism" was able to accommodate a variety of approaches. Both Lashley and Pavlov considered physiological explanations of behavior to be a necessity, but Watson thought that the study of behavior was sufficient in its own right. Lashley and Pavlov differed from each other with respect to the primacy of physiology, with Pavlov regarding psychology as dependent on physiology and Lashley seeing it the other way around. Although behaviorists differ in some ways, what they all have in common is just what their name suggests: they all regard behavior as the only subject matter and reject subjective experience as a legitimate topic in psychology. We now come to B. F. Skinner, who many regard as the foremost behaviorist of all time. As we shall see, Skinner shared more with Watson than with either Pavlov or Lashley.

Skinner's Radical Behaviorism

B. F. Skinner was not only a behaviorist, but also one of most famous American psychologists of any persuasion in this century. Terms associated with Skinner have become a part of the English language. Herrnstein (1977) pointed out that *skinner box* was an entry in *Webster's Third New International Dictionary.* More recently, *The Oxford English Dictionary* (1992) has entries for *Skinner* ("The name of the American psychologist . . . used to indicate the theories or methods concerned with conditioning human or animal behavior associated with him; esp[ecially] as *Skinner box,* a box in which an animal is isolated, equipped essentially with a bar or other device that it learns to use either to obtain a reward or to escape punishment"), *Skinnerian,* and *Skinnerism.* Herrnstein (1977, p. 593) also remarked on a survey conducted by a popular magazine "to determine the 100 most important people who ever lived: Jesus Christ was first, and Skinner was about 40th, not far from Luther and Calvin."

In a paper marking the fiftieth anniversary of Watson's paper "Psychology as the Behaviorist Views It," (1913/1966) Skinner (1954, p. 81) paid homage to "John B. Watson who made the first clear, if rather noisy, proposal that psychology should be regarded simply as a science of behavior." It is proper to see Skinner as the true inheritor of Watsonian behaviorism. For both of them, the most important thing a psychologist needs to understand is that mental events do not explain behavior. For Skinner (1954, p. 81), the "central argument" was "that behavior which seemed to be the product of mental activity could be explained in other ways."

Skinner (1954) believed that consciousness was a form *of* behavior, and not a mysterious process responsible *for* behavior. It is unscientific to conceive of people as having minds that control their behavior. The notion that people have minds is rooted in the *animism* of primitive people. Animism is the belief that all objects, including plants and animals, have souls. Animism arose in primitive societies as a way of explaining such phenomena as dreams. Dreams seemed to simpleminded folk to be the result of the soul leaving the body and wandering through other worlds. Eventually, people began to believe in a soul, and even brilliant philosophers like Descartes defended the notion. People took it for granted that there was "a little person in the head," or *homunculus,* that controlled our behavior. From Skinner's viewpoint, this is only a primitive explanation of behavior. To believe that a soul controls our behavior simply postpones an explanation of behavior. After all, once you say that the soul controls behavior, then you are left with the problem of answering the question, "What controls the soul?" All mentalistic explanations have the same problem: They never reach a full understanding of the causes of behavior. If we believe that behavior is a product of mental activity, then we are the victim of old-fashioned beliefs.

We need to realize that all events are in principle public events. Even events "within the skin" (Skinner, 1954, p. 84) would be open to public observation if we had sophisticated enough measuring devices. Behaviors inside the skin are still behaviors. There need be no "private" events, known to the person alone. We may falsely believe that behaviors are "private" if we are not aware of the stimuli that are controlling them, but our feelings of privacy and self-control are illusory.

The Behavior of Organisms

Skinner first came to widespread attention when he published *The Behavior of Organisms* in 1938. In that book he made a distinction between *respondent* and *operant* behavior. Respondent behavior is the kind of behavior Pavlov studied. It is behavior that is elicited by a known stimulus. By contrast, operant behavior has no known eliciting stimulus. Operant behavior may be studied by means of the apparatus known as a Skinner box, which is a sophisticated version of one of Thorndike's puzzle boxes. A white rat is placed in the box, which has a lever protruding from one side. At some point the rat will press the lever. The stimulus that elicits lever pressing is unknown. However, the experimenter has arranged things such that when the rat presses the lever, then a food pellet will be dispensed into the food tray. The food pellet is a *reinforcing stimulus* for pressing the lever. Reinforcing a response will increase the probability of its future occurrence. "A reinforcing stimulus is defined as such by its power to produce the resulting change. There is no circularity about this; some stimuli are found to produce the change, others not, and they are classified as reinforcing and non-reinforcing accordingly" (Skinner, 1938, p. 62). Skinner's studies of the *reinforcement* of lever pressing were extensions of Thorndike's studies of cats in a puzzle box. In general, Skinner's investigations of the role of reinforcement in regulating human behavior have been extremely influential.

According to Skinner, behavior is regulated by *three-term contingencies* (Mazur, 1990, p. 121): the environment provides a *stimulus* situation, which elicits a *response,* which is followed by a *reinforcing stimulus.* Reinforcing stimuli may be either rewards or punishments. In general, rewards are environmental consequences which make the behavior more probable, and punishments make behavior less probable. While the presence of a reward is *positively reinforcing,* its removal constitutes a form of "negative punishment." While the presence of a punishment depresses behavior, its absence constitutes what Skinner called *negative reinforcement:* whatever behavior caused the removal of the punishment is reinforced. Kimble (1993) has pointed out that this terminology can be confusing for students, and it is important to realize that negative reinforcement and punishment are not the same thing. "Punishment" occurs when an aversive stimulus occurs as a consequence of a response. "Negative reinforcement" occurs when a response gets the organism out of a noxious situation. Kimble's example is being told that "if you do well enough on the earlier exam, then you don't have to take the final" (Kimble, 1993, p. 254).

Skinner (1984) considered learning to involve the natural selection of behaviors in a manner analogous to the evolutionary process. "What we call behavior evolved as a set of functions furthering the interchange between the organism and environment. In a fairly stable world [behavior] could be as much as part of the genetic endowment of a species as digestion, respiration, or any other biological function" (p. 477). However, two processes evolved in order to deal with novel environments. "Through respondent (Pavlovian) conditioning, responses prepared in advance by natural selection could come under the control of new stimuli. Through operant conditioning, new responses could be strengthened ('reinforced') by events which immediately followed them" (p. 477).

Notice that it is the events which *immediately* follow behavior that have the greatest impact, while events that occur later on will have far less effect. In education, for example, children will be shaped by the immediate consequences of their actions in the classroom more than by the grades they get at the end of the year. "Immediate reinforcement singles out some particular recent behavior, while long-run reinforcement is ambiguous, not indicating which of thousands of previous behaviors is responsible for it" (Platt, 1973, p. 643).

"A Case History of Scientific Method"

When Skinner (1956) discussed the ways in which he made his discoveries, he applied the principles of his own psychology to his own creativity. He offered the following list of "unformalized principles of scientific practice." While at first these principles may sound frivolous, they are actually serious points about how psychologists actually do research, as opposed to how psychologists are taught that they should do research.

- "When you run into something interesting, drop everything else and study it" (Skinner, 1956, p. 223). In the course of doing research on one topic, Skinner accidentally discovered something intriguing. He put aside his original research question to take up this new one. Notice how Skinner's behavior as a scientist was being regulated by its immediate consequences. Scientists learn in the same way that everyone else learns.
- "Some ways of doing research are easier than others" (Skinner, 1956, p. 224). Skinner recounts how he invented a precursor to the Skinner box because he did not want the trouble of constantly handling the animals in his experiments. So he built a piece of apparatus that fed the animal and kept track of its responses without his intervention. By keeping things simple, Skinner had also managed to create an apparatus that gathered very useful data.
- "Some people are lucky" (Skinner, 1956, p. 225). An accidental feature of the apparatus Skinner built was that it allowed him to keep track of the cumulative frequency with which the animal responded. These cumulative frequency curves showed how the animal's rate of responding was a function of different *schedules of reinforcement.* A schedule of reinforcement is "a specification of the way in which reinforcers occur in time. Some simple schedules include *fixed ratio* (the last of a certain number of responses is reinforced), *variable ratio* (the required number varies from one reinforcer to the next), fixed interval (the first response after a certain period of time has elapsed is reinforced), and variable interval (the interval varies from one reinforcer to the next) (Skinner, 1980, p. 361). One of Skinner's most important contributions has been the extensive exploration of schedules of reinforcement as they influence behavior not only in the Skinner box, but also in everyday life. For example, "hunting and fishing are on a variable-ratio schedule. Incentive wages contain ratio elements. The craftsman or private contractor is essentially on piecework" (Skinner, 1980, p. 195).
- "Apparatuses sometimes break down" (Skinner, 1956, p. 225). As Epstein (1991) noted, Skinner's approach to creativity emphasized *generativity:* behavior is inevitably and spontaneously novel, and thus we are continuously being presented

with new opportunities to explore. When something goes wrong, it is an opportunity to learn something new.

- All of Skinner's principles of research (1956) can be summarized by one word: *serendipity,* or "the art of finding one thing while looking for something else" (p. 227). Serendipity is defined by the *Oxford English Dictionary* (1989) as "the faculty of making happy discoveries by accident." The *OED* notes, as does Skinner (1956, p. 227), that the word was coined by Horace Walpole, an eighteenth-century British politician. Walpole used it to refer to people who "were always making discoveries, by accident and *sagacity,* of things they were not in quest of" (italics added). In this statement Walpole is drawing attention to a feature of serendipity that is not always brought out, namely that it not only involves luck, but also requires sagacity. "Sagacity" is defined by the *OED* (1989) as the "aptitude for investigation or discovery; keenness and soundness of judgment in the estimation of persons and conditions, and in the adaptation of means to ends." Thus, Skinner's discoveries are not due to chance alone. Someone less sagacious than Skinner would never have realized what he or she had discovered.

The "Baby Tender"

Like Watson, Skinner always explored the practical implications of his psychology. Many of his innovations and recommendations have been controversial, although the controversy surrounding some of his projects was not always of his own making. For example, consider his use of an *aircrib* or "baby tender" that he built for his second daughter, Debbie (Skinner, 1945b). "Air entered through filters at the bottom and, after being warmed and moistened, moved upward through and around the edges of a tightly stretched canvas, which served as a mattress. A strip of sheeting ten yards long passed over the canvas, a clean section of which could be yanked into place in a few seconds" (Skinner, 1979, p. 275). Skinner built the baby tender in response to his wife Yvonne's concern that caring for a child during its first year was very onerous. Anyone who has parented a child during its first year will share Yvonne's concerns! "When Debbie came home, she went directly into this comfortable space and began to enjoy its advantages. She wore only a diaper. Completely free to move about, she was soon pushing up, rolling over, and crawling. She breathed warm, moist filtered air, and her skin was never waterlogged with sweat or urine. Loud noises were muffled (though we could hear her from any part of the house), and a curtain pulled over the window shielded her from bright light when she was sleeping" (Skinner, 1979, p. 276).

Like Watson before him, Skinner wrote about his innovative approach to child rearing in the popular press, in particular the *Ladies Home Journal* (Skinner, 1945b). On doing so, Skinner discovered a fact that many popular writers also discover when their work is published, namely that it is often highly edited (and therefore potentially misleading), and its impact may not be what you intend. For example, the title of the article was "Baby in a box," a title which was chosen by the editor, not by Skinner. There were newspaper, radio, and film reports of the Skinners' home life, some of which led to "the impression that we used a baby-tender to keep Debbie out of the way as a trouble-maker. . . . As people began to hear of the baby-tender by word of mouth, misunderstanding spread. Details of Debbie's actual life and the care we gave her were lost in the retelling. . . . It was natural to suppose that we were experimenting on our daughter as if she were a rat or a pigeon" (Skinner, 1979, pp. 304–305). The rumors about Deborah Skinner's fate persisted for many years, and may even exist today. However, Deborah Skinner herself never attributed any negative consequences to her experience with the aircrib, and there is no evidence that it harmed her in any way (Bjork, 1993, p. 133).

Teaching Machines

Skinner's belief in the power of positive reinforcement was nowhere more evident than in his advocacy of what came to be called *teaching machines.* He argued that "the most serious criticism of the current classroom is the relative infrequency of reinforcement" (Skinner, 1954/1962, p. 25), pointing out that a single teacher cannot possibly reward a classroom of students often enough so that a complex subject such as mathematics is properly learned. The usual classroom situation is reinforcing only when the child does the work required in order to avoid punishment of one kind or another, and this situation is far from ideal. "In this welter of aversive consequences, getting the right answer is in itself an insignificant event, any effect of which is lost amid the anxieties, the boredom, and the aggressions which are the inevitable by products of aversive control (Skinner, 1954/1962, p. 25). He suggested that a curriculum needs to be properly programmed such that the correct responses that constituted a discipline like mathematics could be developed systematically. Students should be reinforced for each response in a sequence that gradually builds up a discipline.

In order to provide such *programmed learning,* Skinner and his students built on ideas that had been advanced much earlier by *Sidney Pressey* (1926), who had described "devices . . . which at once inform a student about the correctness of his answer to a question, and then lead him to the right answer" (Pressey, 1950/1962, p. 113). J. G. Holland (1959/1962), one of Skinner's associates, described how such a program was implemented at one university:

> *At Harvard there is a self-instruction room with ten booths, each containing a machine. The student gets one set of material from the attendant and places it in the machines. He closes the machine and begins his studies.*
>
> *This machine presents one item of material at a time. The subject reads the statement which has one or more words missing and he completes the statement by writing in the answer space. He then raises the lever and a small shutter opens revealing the correct answer, and simultaneously his answer is moved under glass where it can be read and compared with the new-exposed correct answer. After comparing his answer with the correct answer the student indicates to the machine, with an appropriate movement of the lever, whether his answer was correct or incorrect and the next item appears in the window. All items answered wrong are repeated after he completes the set of items. Correctly answered items are not repeated.*
>
> *A critical feature of this machine is that it provides immediate reinforcement for correct answers. Being correct is known to be a reinforcer for humans. . . . In machine teaching reinforcement is immediate. (pp. 35–36)*

This approach was criticized, as Skinner foresaw, by those who regarded it as treating children mechanically, and not leading to "understanding," but only rote learning. Skinner saw these criticisms as misguided, since the machines were designed precisely to directly influence behavior, and not deal with ephemeral matters such as "understanding." After all, from a behaviorist standpoint, "understanding" was nothing but the appropriate behaviors. In any case, much of what teaching machines were designed to do was later taken over by computer aided instruction, which involved techniques adopted from cognitive psychology, an approach quite different than Skinner's, and which we will consider in detail in Chapter 14.

Skinner's Utopian and Dystopian Views

In his utopian novel, *Walden Two,* Skinner (1948) envisioned a community regulated entirely by positive reinforcement. The original "Walden" had, of course, been described by Henry David Thoreau, in 1854. Thoreau's Walden evoked "the theme of the sage who makes a voluntary break with society in order to discover his genuine self in a context of solitude and nature" (Frye, 1966, p. 46). Skinner's version of utopia also involves a break with conventional society, but there is nothing solitary about it. Skinner's utopia "is an environment in which people just naturally do the things they need to do to maintain themselves (with something to spare for the future) and treat each other well, and then just naturally do a hundred other things they enjoy doing because they do not *have* to do them. And when I say natural, . . . I simply mean positively reinforced. The labor we save in Walden Two is the unnecessary labor forced upon people by a badly designed environment" (Skinner, 1987, p. 41). To the charge that behavior controlled by positive reinforcement is not voluntary, Skinner replied that concepts like "freedom" and "dignity" are no more than feelings. One of his characters says that "in Walden Two we behave under relatively undemanding contingencies of reinforcement, and we feel free" (Skinner, 1987, p. 39).

Skinner's utopian novel received mixed reviews, but has continued to be widely read, over 40 years after its publication. Skinner wrote it in one summer, and some critics have suggested that it is not entirely serious (Frye, 1966, p. 32). However, the subsequent course of Skinner's career demonstrated his very serious concern about the drift of modern society. Platt (1973, p. 652) has pointed out that Skinnerian theory is very good at describing some well-known situations in which people get "started in some direction . . . that later proves to be unpleasant or lethal, and that they see no easy way to back out of or avoid." One example is the "tragedy of the commons" (Hardin, 1968). Suppose that people are allowed to freely graze their cattle on public land. The more cows you graze, the more rewarding it is monetarily. However, the number of cows soon exceeds the number that can be supported. The consequence is that everyone ends up on the short end of the stick. As Platt points out, the fact that one's actions are controlled by their immediate positive consequences can lead to a future which no one wants. You will undoubtedly be familiar with many examples of this scenario. Platt defined a behavioral trap as occurring when "there is an opposition between the highly motivating short-run reward or punishment . . . and the long-run consequences" (p. 643). Smoking and overeating are possible examples of such traps.

A description of a society which is the opposite of a utopia is called a *dystopia* (e.g., Mumford, 1966), and toward the end of his life Skinner (e.g., 1986) began increasingly to characterize the dystopian features of modern life in the West:

> *Many of those who live in the Western democracies enjoy a reasonable degree of affluence, freedom, and security. . . . In spite of their privileges, many of them are bored, listless or depressed. They are not enjoying their lives. They do not like what they are doing; they are not doing what they like to do. In a word, they are unhappy (p. 568)*

Skinner never swerved from his commitment to positive reinforcement as the best agent for social control, but regarded contemporary Western societies as having created problems for themselves by moving away from important behavioral principles. Skinner argued that primitive people lived like other primates, hunting, gathering and building shelters. However, "a unique evolutionary step" occurred with the emergence of language because "people could then tell as well as show each other what to do [Skinner, 1957]. Extraordinarily complex social environments or cultures evolved [and these cultures] eroded the close relationships between organisms and the environment" (Skinner, 1986, p. 568). Culture comes to intervene between the organism and its environment, and the consequences, from Skinner's viewpoint, are not all good.

In order to understand why the development of our culture has had maladaptive consequences, Skinner (1986, p. 569) believed that we needed to distinguish between the *pleasing* effects of reinforcement and the *strengthening* effects of reinforcement. Something can be pleasing, but not strengthen any particular behavior. Skinner argued that our cultural environment provides us with things that please us, but which do not strengthen adaptive behavior. What Skinner had in mind is straightforward, and an example is the contemporary wage system. It is pleasant to get a paycheck, or an allowance if you are a child, at the end of some time period, such as once a month or once a week. However pleasing such a monetary reward is, it does not strengthen any particular behavior, because it is not linked to any particular behavior (Skinner, 1986, p. 570).

Skinner was particularly concerned about the ease of access to rewarding activities such as television, movies, and a veritable cornucopia of food.

All these things could be enjoyed without having to actually do anything to achieve them, and that is just the problem. We seem to have reached a state in which we can be rewarded for doing nothing at all. "How much richer would the whole world be if the reinforcers in daily life were more effectively contingent on productive work" (Skinner, 1986, p. 573). Precisely how one is to effect the changes Skinner saw as necessary is not clear, but perhaps it would be a worthwhile exercise for you to think through the ways in which social policy would change if Skinner's views were taken seriously. What would happen to child rearing practices? Education? Communications? The family?

Additional Reading on This Topic. Benjamin (1988) gives a useful summary of the history of teaching machines and Keller (1991) wrote an obituary for B. F. Skinner.

KEY NAMES AND CONCEPTS

What follows is an index of some of the most important material in this chapter. The list includes individuals, concepts, and topics you should know. Read through the list, and if anything on it seems unfamiliar, then go back and re-read the appropriate section of the chapter. You should be able to define each concept, briefly discuss each topic, and state the importance of each person on the list. In addition, you should be able to write an account of the work done by each person or topic printed in boldface.

animism, 163
anti-vivisectionism, 151
Baldwin, James M., 153
Bekhterev, Vladimir, 152
associated motor reflex, 152
association reflex, 152
reflexology, 152
Box 8.1—Animal rights? 152
Box 8.2—Watson and Lashley, 159
dystopia, 167
Franz, Shepherd I., 159
ablation, 159
Gall and Spurzheim, 159
phrenology, 159
Hebb, Donald O., 162
Hippocrates
temperaments, 151
homunculus, 163
Ickes, Mary, 153
Jennings, Herbert S., 158
Lashley, Karl S., 158
Brain Mechanisms and Intelligence, 160
laws of mass action and equipotentiality, 161
the problem of serial order in behavior, 161
localization of function, 158
Loeb, Jacques
tropisms, 153
Pavlov, Ivan P., 147
conditioned connections as temporary, 150
conditioned reflexes as conditional, 149
conditioned stimuli and responses, 149
conditioned stimuli as signals, 150
excitation and inhibition, 151
extinction, 150
inhibition, 150
Institute of Experimental Medicine, 148
materialism, 148
primary and secondary signaling systems, 150
psychopathology, 151

speech, 150
spontaneous recovery, 150
unconditioned reflexes, 149
unconditioned response, 149
unconditioned stimulus, 149
Pressey, Sidney, 166
Rayner, Rosalie, 156
Sechenov, Ivan M., 148
Skinner, B. F., 162
baby tender, 165
generativity, 164
negative reinforcement, 163
operant behavior, 163
positive reinforcement, 163
principles of scientific practice, 164
punishment, 163
reinforcement, 163
respondent behavior, 163
sagacity, 165
schedules of reinforcement, 164
Skinner box, 162, 163
teaching machines, 165
three-term contingency, 163
Walden Two, 166
Spooner, William A.
spoonerism, 161
Watson, John B., 153
career in advertising, 158
distributed versus massed practice, 156
emotional habits, 156
environmentalism, 155
fear, rage and love, 156
Little Albert, 156
manual habits, 156
prediction and control, 154
resignation from Hopkins, 154
serially ordered behavior, 157
stimulus-response relationships, 154
unverbalized, 157
verbal habits, 157
white rats, 153
Wooley, Helen T., 153

CHAPTER 9

GESTALT PSYCHOLOGY

MAX WERTHEIMER (1880–1943)
Phi Phenomenon
The Minimum Principle
Precursors of Gestalt Psychology
The Laws of Perceptual Organization
Productive Thinking
Gestalt Psychology as a Philosophy
WOLFGANG KOHLER (1887–1967)
The Mentality of Apes
The Nature of Learning
The Concept of Isomorphism
KURT KOFFKA (1886–1941)
Principles of Gestalt Psychology
The Growth of the Mind
KURT LEWIN (1890–1947) AND THE EMERGENCE OF SOCIAL PSYCHOLOGY
The Zeigarnik Effect
Group Dynamics
Fritz Heider (1896–1988)
Solomon Asch (b. 1907)
KURT GOLDSTEIN (1878–1965)
Organismic Theory
The Abstract Attitude

When we turn to Gestalt psychology we encounter something radically different than either the introspectionism of Titchener or the behaviorism of Watson. In fact, Gestalt psychologists regarded both introspectionism and behaviorism as varieties of the same mistaken orientation to psychology. The differences between introspectionism and behaviorism, while important to their practitioners, were trivial compared with the fact that both exemplified a "science intent upon a systematic collection of data, yet often excluding through that very activity precisely *that* which is most vivid and real in the living phenomena it studies. Somehow the thing that matters has eluded us" (Wertheimer, 1925/1967, p. 1). The "thing that matters," which was missing from other approaches to psychology, was an appreciation of the fact that a psychological phenomenon is a *Gestalt:* an integrated whole that could not be understood solely in terms of the parts that made it up. Our experience of a melody, for example, is more than the sum of the individual notes. The melody is a whole, a unity, a Gestalt. Since there was no adequate translation of the German word "Gestalt," it has entered the English language as a term referring to unified wholes. The plural of "Gestalt" is "Gestalten."

Approaches such as introspectionism and behaviorism take things apart and analyze them in order to try to understand them from the bottom up, in terms of elements such as sensations or stimuli. Gestalt psychologists believed that such an approach is doomed to failure. "There are wholes, the behavior of which is not determined by that of their individual elements, but where the part[s] are themselves determined by the intrinsic nature of the whole" (Wertheimer, 1925/1967, p. 2). Nowadays we are familiar with an ecological approach to phenomena, and we are accustomed to hearing that things are interconnected and mutually influence each other within a larger whole. But the Gestalt psychologists emerged at a time in the early part of this century before the ecological movement was conceived. To them, at least, their holistic ideas were revolutionary.

Gestalt psychology has many precursors, and we will consider some of them later in this chapter. However, it would be just as well to begin by considering a specific phenomenon, apparent motion, that marks the beginning of Gestalt psychology as a distinctive movement. The theoretical importance of this phenomenon was first appreciated by Max Wertheimer, who is usually considered to be the founder of Gestalt psychology.

MAX WERTHEIMER (1880–1943)

Wertheimer's career did not begin with the invention of Gestalt psychology. Born in Prague, he did his doctoral dissertation in 1904 at the University of Würzburg. His dissertation topic concerned the use of the *word association method* for the detection of complexes, a topic that was central to the development of Jung's career, as you should recall. Wertheimer and Jung squabbled about just who was the inventor of the method. Current opinion favors Wertheimer (Michael Wertheimer, King, Peckler, Raney, & Schaef, 1992). However, Wertheimer's research interests subsequently moved in the direction that was to lead to the founding of Gestalt psychology. In particular, Wertheimer's studies, done at the University of Frankfurt, of a form of apparent motion called *phi phenomenon* attracted great attention.

Phi Phenomenon

Wertheimer was very skillful at using *demonstrations* to illustrate the Gestalt psychologists' contention that when we perceive things we tend to do so holistically. A demonstration is a simple, easily observed phenomenon, usually requiring only minimal apparatus, and that has the same effect for almost everyone. Figure 9.1 illustrates the famous Gestalt demonstration, called *phi phenomenon.* The two lights can be alternately turned on by means of the switch. Each light casts a different shadow on the screen. However, at the right rate of alternation,

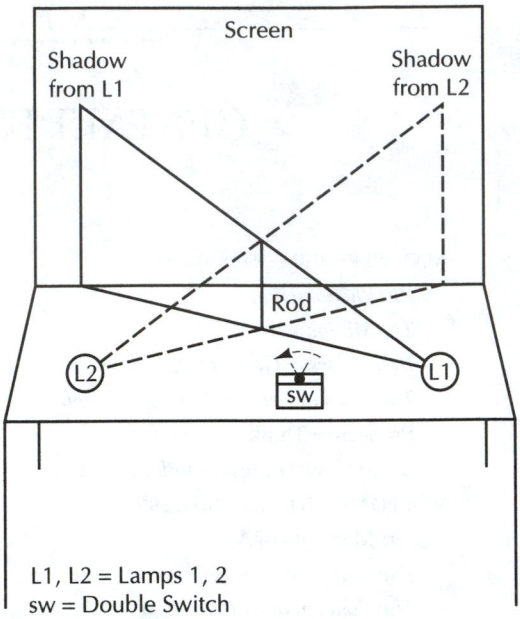

FIGURE 9.1 Apparatus to demonstrate apparent motion.

Source: W. Kohler. (1969). *The task of Gestalt psychology* (p. 36). Princeton: Princeton University Press. Copyright © 1969 by Princeton University Press. Reprinted by permission of Princeton University Press.

a subject does not see *two* shadows, but *one* shadow moving back and forth. "So what?" you might think, and psychologists before Wertheimer did not think that apparent motion was a very interesting topic. They tended to give it an explanation like this: "I regard this second object as identical with the first and conclude that the first has simply moved from the one place to the other" (Kohler, 1967/1969, p. 70). This explanation holds that apparent motion occurs as a result of an inference. However, Wertheimer insisted that the experience of apparent motion did not include any inferences. Rather, if one took the experience seriously, as it presented itself and without any theoretical bias, then you discovered a *perception* of motion, even though no stimulus moved. Wertheimer argued that there was a lot to be learned from phenomena like these.

For one thing, demonstrations such as the phi phenomenon constituted evidence that our perception was not just a copy of the stimulus. Rather our experience tended to be as simple as possible. Thus, when conditions allow, we perceive one thing moving, rather than two things flashing on and off.

The Minimum Principle

The phi phenomenon demonstrated to the Gestalt psychologists that experience could be simpler and more unified than the stimulus conditions giving rise to the experience. Instead of seeing two separate events, you see only one moving event. This illustrated a very general law, called the *minimum principle* (Kohler, 1920/1967), that not only applied to perception, but to the organization of other systems as well.

The Gestalt psychologists pointed out that the minimum principle means that we do not perceive what is actually in the external world so much as we tend to organize our experience so that it is as simple as possible. This tendency toward simplicity is well illustrated in Figure 9.2. Leeuwenberg and Boselie (1988) observed that we could see Figure 9.2A as either one rather strange animal, or as two horses, and we tend to see two horses. Since we have seen horses before, then we should be ready to see horses now, and so the fact that we see horses is not surprising. Notice further, however, that our perception is following the minimum principle because seeing two animals that overlap is a less complex alternative than seeing one animal with two heads and extra legs. Thus, sometimes the simplest perception is also the most realistic one. However, in Figure 9.2B and C, we tend to see the simplest alternative rather than the most realistic one. We see one animal with two heads, or one animal with no heads, even though we are not likely to ever have encountered such creatures in the world. This illustrates the Gestalt contention that simplicity is a principle that guides our perception and may even override the effects of previous experience (e.g., Gottschaldt, 1926/1967).

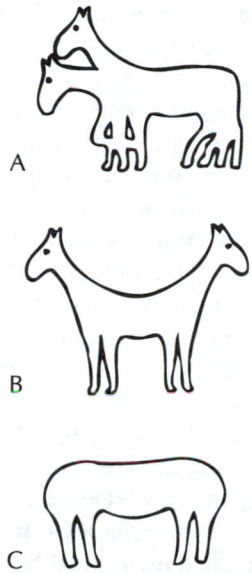

FIGURE 9.2 Simplicity versus likelihood.

Source: E. Leeuwenberg & F. Boselie. (1988). Against the likelihood principle in visual form perception. *Psychological Review, 95,* 485–491. Copyright © 1988 by the American Psychological Association. Reprinted by permission.

The minimum principle has now been investigated for a long time (Beck, 1982), and is one of the Gestalt ideas that still receives support. Experience may tend toward the simplest possible state for the same reason that any system tends toward simplicity (Hatfield & Epstein, 1987). The laws that govern processes in the nervous system, are after all, the same laws that govern what happens in any other realm. From a Gestalt viewpoint, simplicity and coherence in experience emerge for the same sort of reason that they emerge in other structures. In an organism, simplicity in experience is the necessary outcome of basic processes in the brain. We will consider additional implications of this idea later in this chapter.

Precursors of Gestalt Psychology

Wertheimer's ideas had to some extent been anticipated by *Christian von Ehrenfels* (1859–1932), who suggested that experiences, such as that of a melody, should be understood as composed of individual sensations, such as those corresponding to the individual notes, *plus* a *Gestalt quality* that provided the form of the experience, such as the melody as a whole. Wertheimer rejected the existence of Gestalt qualities superimposed on sensations. In fact, Wertheimer rejected the existence of sensations as such. One could not understand experience by beginning with elementary units, such as sensations, because "in psychology . . . the possibility of advance requires a procedure 'from above', *not* 'from below upward.' Thus the comprehension of whole properties and whole-conditions *must* precede consideration of the real significance of 'parts'" (Wertheimer, 1925/1967, p. 15). One had to begin with a Gestalt, and understand how parts are determined by the whole of which they are a part. This was not only true in psychology, but in other areas as well, such as physiology. "The cells of an organism are *parts* of the whole and excitations occurring in them are thus to be viewed as part-processes functionally related to whole-processes of the entire organism" (Wertheimer, 1925/1967, p. 15). What was true of the individual organism was also true of the relations between people. "When a group of people work together it rarely occurs . . . that they constitute a mere sum of independent Egos. Instead the common enterprise often becomes their mutual concern and each works *as* a meaningfully functioning part of the whole" (Wertheimer, 1925/1967, p. 6).

One of the true ancestors of Gestalt psychology is *Immanuel Kant,* whom we considered in Chapter 2. Recall that Kant argued against the associationist notion that our experience was derived from events in the external world. Kant argued that our experience was a construction, and not a mirror of external events. Recall Kant's view that we impose cause and effect relationships *on* the world, rather than observing them *in* the world. Whenever we observe two events occurring close together in space and time there is a tendency for us to experience one as causing the other. Notice how similar Kant's view of causality is to the way in which we experience apparent motion. We spontaneously and inevitably see one thing moving when there are in fact two stationary objects. The phi phenomenon is an example of the tendency for us to impose an organization on our experience. Just as Kant opposed the associationist psychologies of the British Empiricists, so the Gestalt psychologists opposed neoassociationist psychologies such as those espoused by structuralists and behaviorists.

Another movement with which Gestalt psychology had much in common is *phenomenology.* As we saw in Chapter 4, *Edmund Husserl* (1910/1965) developed phenomenology as a philosophical method designed to describe consciousness as it presents itself to us, without any presuppositions as to its nature or purpose. It was this type of description of direct experience that Gestalt psychologists practiced, rather than the type of description carried out by trained introspectionists. "We call this kind of observation 'phenomenology,' a word that has several other meanings that must not be confused with ours. For us phenomenology means as naive and full a description of direct experience as possible" (Koffka, 1935, p. 73). The Gestalt psychologists made a sharp distinction between their phenomenological methods and introspection, which "became unpopular in America because American psychologists saw its barrenness. But in their justified criticism they threw out the baby with the bath . . . tending to leave out phenomenology altogether" (Koffka, 1935, p. 73). Thus, the Gestalt psychologists refused to go along with behaviorists like Watson, and ban the study of experience altogether. Rather they saw phenomenology as different from trained introspection because it was less biased and very useful as a starting point in psychological investigation. We will see further along in the chapter precisely how the Gestalt psychologists utilized the phenomenological method.

The Laws of Perceptual Organization

Now examine the configurations in Figure 9.3. They illustrate the *Gestalt laws of organization.* These laws, presented by Wertheimer (1923/1958),

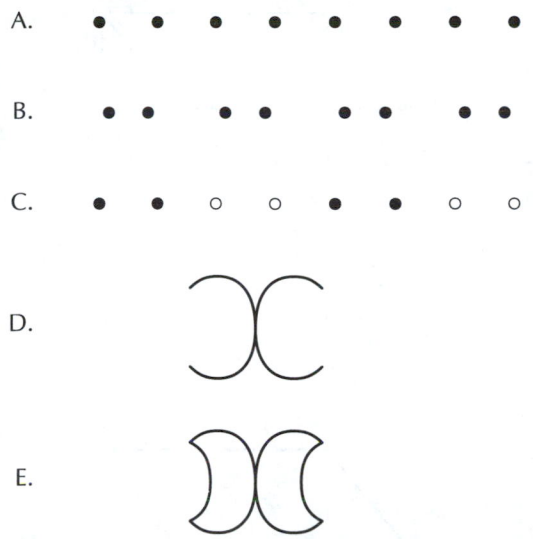

FIGURE 9.3 Examples of the Gestalt laws of organization.

Source: S. E. Palmer. (1992). Common region: A new principle of perceptual grouping. *Cognitive Psychology, 24,* 437. Copyright © 1992 by Academic Press. Reprinted by permission.

were intended to describe the basic ways in which we organize our experience as simply and coherently as possible. "When we are presented with a number of stimuli, we do not as a rule experience 'a number' of individual things. . . . Instead larger wholes . . . are given in experience; their arrangement and division are concrete and definite" (Wertheimer, 1923/1967, p. 72). For example, compare rows A and B in Figure 9.3. Notice that in line B there is a tendency to group the dots in pairs, but that there is no such tendency in A. This example illustrates the Gestalt law of *proximity:* we tend to group things together that are close together in space. In Figure 9.3C, however, even though the dots are equidistant, we see them in pairs because of the law of *similarity.* In Figure 9.3D, we see two lines crossing. We do not see "two angles meeting at a point" (Palmer, 1992, p. 438). The principle operating here is called *good continuation.* However, in Figure 9.3E we *do* see two forms meeting at a point. This is because of the principle of *closure,* a very important Gestalt principle stating that we tend to make our experience as complete as possible. To summarize: the Gestalt psychologists believed that *proximity, similarity, good continuation,* and *closure* are examples of principles that govern the way in which our experience is organized (e.g., Coren & Girgus, 1980).

Figure and Ground. Another basic principle of perceptual organization is the distinction between figure and ground. In order for perception to occur it must be organized into something that stands out and to which we pay attention (the figure) displayed against a background to which we tend not to pay attention. The importance of the distinction between figure and ground was discovered by *Edgar Rubin* (1915/1958). What is figural at any one time depends on many factors. Consider the configuration shown in Figure 9.4A. It is probably easiest to see a black cross as figure against a white background, but it is also possible to see a white

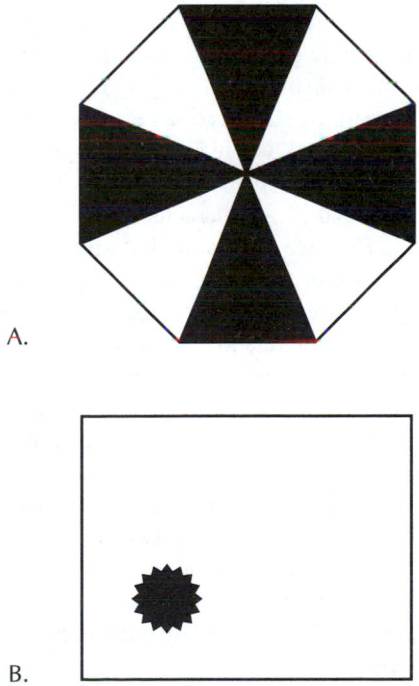

FIGURE 9.4 Which area is figural?

cross against a black background. The black cross is smaller in area, and it is usually the smallest area that is figural. The background appears to pass beneath the figure. This feature of figure–ground organization can be seen in Figure 9.4B. At first one might see a black seal displayed against a white background. However, it is also possible to see the black area as a cutout of the white foreground revealing the black surface underneath.

Productive Thinking

Among Wertheimer's most influential works was his book *Productive Thinking* (1959). We considered one of the examples from that book in Chapter 1, Figure 1.6. You may want to go back and review that problem now. Wertheimer liked to point out that improper teaching methods lead to a rote memorization of solutions that does not transfer well to new situations, while good teaching methods lead to a deep understanding of the structure of a problem. Such understanding involved grasping the Gestalt of a problem—the way in which the parts of a problem were related to each other. Another Gestalt psychologist, *George Katona* (1940/1967) phrased this distinction thusly: "There are two kinds of learning. Connections established by the conditioned-reflex technique or by repeating the same contents or responses over and over again, as in all forms of drill, are characteristic of one kind of learning. Then we draw a thick dividing line. On the other side of the barrier we find processes of learning that are described by such expressions as 'apprehension of relations,' 'understanding of a procedure,' 'insight into a situation.'... 'Senseless' may be written on one side of the line where there is the depository of connections, and 'meaningful' on the other side, where the achievement brought about by learning may be called understanding" (pp. 5–6). The difference between "structurally blind" teaching methods and those that teach students principles that can be generalized to new situations is well illustrated by the problem shown in Figure 9.5.

Students can be shown the parallelogram in Figure 9.5A, and taught how to find its area by dropping a line from the upper left corner and a line from the upper right corner, and then connecting the base line to meet the second perpendicular. The area of the parallelogram is found by multiplying the height by the width of the new figure. Wertheimer (1959, pp. 14–16) shows that students can learn this procedure by rote, without understanding. In such a case, students will have a hard time generalizing the solution to a parallelogram such as that in Figure 9.5B. They can drop a line from the left-hand corner, but since it falls outside the figure they do not know what to do. These "structurally blind" students do not understand the nature of the solution. In order to teach the solution in a holistic manner, Wertheimer had students cut out the figure of a parallelogram from a piece of paper, and then tape together the two diagonal ends of the parallelogram to form a tube. When the tube is cut, the result is a rectangle, as shown in Figure 9.5C. Students can then understand that the parallelo-

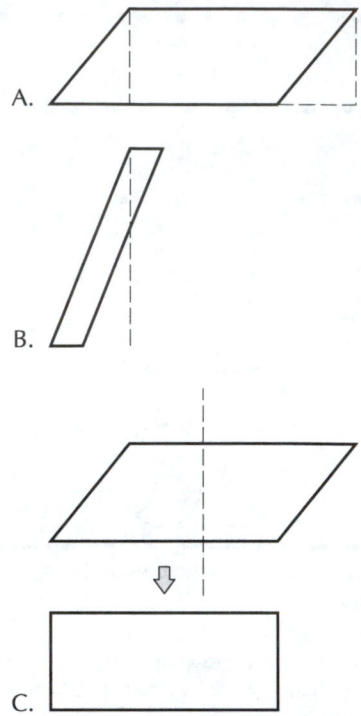

FIGURE 9.5 Finding the area of a parallelogram.

gram and the rectangle are equivalent, and thus grasp the reason for multiplying the height by the width to get the area. Such structural understanding will generalize to any parallelogram. "If we ask whether these features are learned, are acquired in accordance with the traditional associationist conception of past experience, this seems improbable indeed in the light of experiments concerning gestalt laws, etc. They center in laws of organization and reasonable structure; they are an outcome of the structural way of working of our mind and brain rather than of blind associations" (Wertheimer, 1959, p. 63).

Gestalt Psychology as a Philosophy

The Gestalt approach was not limited to psychology, but was also a theory of knowledge as well as a theory of ethics (e.g., Wertheimer, 1934/1961; 1935/1961). "Science is the will to truth. With the will to truth it stands or falls. Lower the standard even slightly and science becomes diseased at the core. Not only science, but [people]. The will to truth, pure and unadulterated, is among the essential conditions of [our] existence; if the standard is compromised [we] easily become a kind of tragic caricature of [ourselves]" (Wertheimer, 1934/1961, p. 19).

Wertheimer contrasted the Gestalt theory of truth with the *correspondence theory of truth,* according to which a statement is true if it corresponds to the facts, and false if it does not. For example, consider a statement such as "Linda assaulted Lisa." The statement is true if Linda did indeed assault Lisa, and false if she did not. However, such a simple theory of truth cannot be the whole story. Suppose Linda did not commit the act of assault herself, but hired someone else to do the dirty work. Is Linda guilty of assault, or not? Usually we would regard Linda as guilty even though she did not physically perform the act. If Linda said "I did not assault Lisa," she would be telling the truth according to the correspondence theory. However, she would be lying according to the Gestalt theory.

		Gestalt	
		T	F
Correspondence	t	Tt	Ft
	f	Tf	Ff

FIGURE 9.6 The Gestalt part–whole theory of truth compared to the correspondence theory of truth.

The difference between the two theories can be illustrated by means of Figure 9.6. There is a fundamental difference between *pieces* and *parts* (Krecz, 1986). In general, parts are related to a whole, while pieces are arbitrary fragments. The heart is a part of your body, but a splinter is just a piece of wood. Something can be understood piecemeal, or as a part of a larger whole. "Let us indicate piecemeal truth and falsity by t and f; and by T and F what we have called the real truth, in which the statement and its object are considered as parts in their related wholes" (Wertheimer, 1934/1961, p. 21). In the preceding example, to say Linda did not assault Lisa is to speak the truth in a piecemeal way (t). To say that Linda did not assault Lisa is to speak falsely in a deeper sense (F). Thus, in Figure 9.6, something can be true when considered merely as a piece (t), but false as a part (F). Something can also be false as a piece (f), but true as a part (T): "for example an excellent caricature. It may be wrong in practically every detail and yet be a truer representation of its object than a photograph which is accurate in every detail" (Wertheimer, 1934/1961, p. 23). Similarly, to say that Linda assaulted Lisa is false as a piece (f), but true as a part (T).

An interesting consequence of the Gestalt theory of truth is that a fact can change its meaning depending on the context within which it is seen. To return to the Lisa/Linda example, we might at

Box 9.1

Gestalt Psychologists Migrate to the United States of America

Other scholars joined Wertheimer, most notably Wolfgang Kohler, who had been trained in physics, Kurt Koffka, who wrote a classic text in Gestalt psychology, and Kurt Lewin, whose work was to profoundly influence social psychology. We consider their individual contributions in later sections of this chapter. "Kohler, in 1920, became acting director, and soon afterward director, of the Psychological Institute of the University of Berlin. Wertheimer was already there, as was Kurt Lewin, whose work bears a significant relationship to Gestalt psychology. From that time until the coming of the Nazis to power, Gestalt psychology flourished. Graduate students were coming to the institute from a number of countries; the *Psychologische Forschung,* the journal of the Gestalt psychologists, was founded, and work was progressing in many directions" (Henle, 1977/1986, p. 119). The first to move to the United States was Koffka, who went to Smith College, in Massachusetts. Subsequently, Wertheimer went to the New School for Social Research in New York City, and Kohler to Swarthmore in Pennsylvania.

Many people associated with the Gestalt movement left Germany because they found life under the Nazis intolerable. A good example is Kohler. Because he was not a Jew, he was not dismissed from his university position. "On November 3, 1933, the government decreed that professors must open their lectures with the Nazi salute. Kohler flipped his hand in a caricature of the salute and said:

"Ladies and gentlemen, I have just saluted you in a manner that the government has decreed. I could not see how to avoid it.

"Still, I must say something about it. I am a professor of philosophy in this university, and this circumstance obligates me to be candid with you, my students. A professor who wished to disguise his views by word or by action would have no place here. You could no longer respect him; he could no longer have anything to say to you about philosophy or important human affairs.

"Therefore I say: the form of my salute was until recently the sign of very particular ideas in politics and elsewhere. If I want to be honest, and if I am to be respected by you, I must explain that, although I am prepared to give that salute, I do not share the ideology which it usually signifies" (Henle, 1978/1986, p. 229).

Eventually, Kohler resigned from the Psychological Institute. A Nazi director was appointed, and the Gestalt-trained students and assistants went elsewhere. Many of them ended up in settings very different from a university laboratory. Far from functioning as a unified whole, the Gestalt psychologists ended up being scattered throughout America and other parts of the world. You can imagine what an enormous adjustment the Gestalt psychologists had to make. Although deeply appreciative of their welcome in the United States, they were also faced with learning the ways of a new culture at a time when their research should have been at its peak. Moreover, at that time in the United States, behaviorism was rampant, and behaviorism was not congenial to Gestalt ideas (Sokal, 1984). It was difficult under these circumstances to begin to train the next generation of Gestalt psychologists, and to a large extent there never was a next generation. However, Gestalt ideas percolated through American psychology as we shall see, and not only had but continue to have an effect on psychological thinking.

first believe that Linda did not assault Lisa if we were with Linda at the time, and know that she was nowhere near the site of the assault. However, as our horizon expands we may become aware of new facts that change our original belief about Linda. As we see her behavior as part of a larger whole, then our perception of her may change. At first we may understand things piecemeal, and then have our understanding radically changed as we see the part–whole relationships that actually determine a situation.

While Wertheimer was technically the founder of Gestalt psychology, the movement was essentially a group effort. Some facts about the members of the group, and their migration from Germany, are given in Box 9.1.

WOLFGANG KOHLER (1887–1967)

We have already considered some of the facts of Kohler's life in Box 9.1, but one additional fact is extremely important: During World War I Kohler was marooned on Tenerife, in the Canary Islands. He had been appointed Director of the Anthropoid Station there in 1913, and "with the outbreak of World War I, he was effectively confined there, a circumstance that left him isolated but did not interfere with his scientific activities. Indeed this was an extraordinary productive period" (Asch, 1968a, pp. 110–111). It was while on Tenerife that Kohler did the work that was to result in one of his most influential publications, *The Mentality of Apes* (Kohler, 1925/1956).

The Mentality of Apes

Kohler described his work as concerned with testing "the intelligence of the higher apes . . . whether they do not behave with intelligence and insight under conditions which require such behavior" (Kohler, 1925/1956, p. 3). Chimpanzees were useful subjects because they could be placed in an experimental situation and required to solve a problem that they may never have faced before. Kohler described the behavior of one of his chimpanzees, Sultan, who was in a cage with fruit outside beyond his reach. There was a small stick *in* the cage, and a longer stick just *outside* the bars. The longer stick "cannot be grasped with the hand. But it can be pulled within reach by means of the small stick. Sultan tries to reach the fruit with the smaller of the two sticks. Not succeeding, he tears at a piece of wire that projects from the netting of his cage, but that, too, is in vain. Then he gazes about him; (there are always in the course of these tests some long pauses, during which the animals scrutinize the whole visible area). He suddenly picks up the little stick once more, goes up to the bars directly opposite to the long stick, scratches it towards him with the [small stick], seizes it, and goes with it to the point opposite to the objective, which he secures. From the moment his eyes fall upon the long stick, his procedure forms one consecutive whole . . . [and] follows, quite suddenly on an interval of hesitation and doubt" (Kohler, 1925/1956, pp. 155–156).

To Kohler, the behavior Sultan displayed was insightful. Kohler provided examples of insight in different problem situations using different animals. By *insight,* Kohler meant the ability to understand the way in which the parts of a situation are related to one another. Insight occurred spontaneously and suddenly, and involved a perceptual restructuring of the situation. The animal suddenly saw how to solve the problem. Insightful problem solving was all-or-none: the animal saw the solution or it did not.

Kohler's chimpanzee experiments should be compared to Thorndike's puzzle box experiments, which we considered in Chapter 7. You should recall that Thorndike's cats appeared to him to show no signs of anything you could call insight, and learned to escape by trial-and-error. Why is there such a difference between Kohler's and Thorndike's results? The Gestalt psychologists argued that Thorndike's cats had been placed in a situation in which there was nothing to be understood. How can a cat possibly understand the relation between pulling on a string and escaping from a box, since it is an entirely arbitrary relationship created by the experimenter. All the cat can do is respond by trial-and-error, and that is what it falls back on.

Some observers believed that Kohler's studies were persuasive. "Taken as a whole, the behavior of the chimpanzee in solving these problems excludes interpretation in terms of accident or previous learning. . . . When all of the evidence is considered, one becomes convinced that the ape behaved intelligently or had what Kohler called *insight* into the situation" (Maier & Schneirla, 1935/1964, p. 469). However, other critics, particularly in America, felt that Kohler's experiments lacked the quantitative rigor of Thorndike's, and that his definition of insight was too vague to make of it a scientific concept. In spite of these reservations, the concept of insight has continued to be a focus of research (e.g., Metcalfe & Wiebe, 1987), although a controversial one (e.g., Weisberg & Alba, 1981).

The Nature of Learning

In a paper charmingly entitled "Simple Structural Functions in the Chimpanzee and the Chicken," Kohler (1918/1967) considered a form of learning that was to prove problematic for associationist psychologists. The logic of Kohler's experiments is illustrated in Figure 9.7. Suppose chickens are presented with two shades of gray, labeled A and B as shown in the top of Figure 9.7. Suppose further that the chickens are trained to peck at A (by placing corn on A, for example, but not on B). What has the chicken learned? From an associationist viewpoint, there has been a learned connection formed between the response of pecking and the stimulus A. Now look at the pair labeled A and C marked "Test" in the top half of Figure 9.6. If, after training, the chicken is presented with these two stimuli, neither of which has corn on them, which will it choose to peck at? (Of course, in such an experiment the position of the two stimuli relative to each other must be systematically varied.) Since it learned to peck at A in the training phase of the experiment, should it not peck at A in the test phase? Actually, the chicken tends to peck at C.

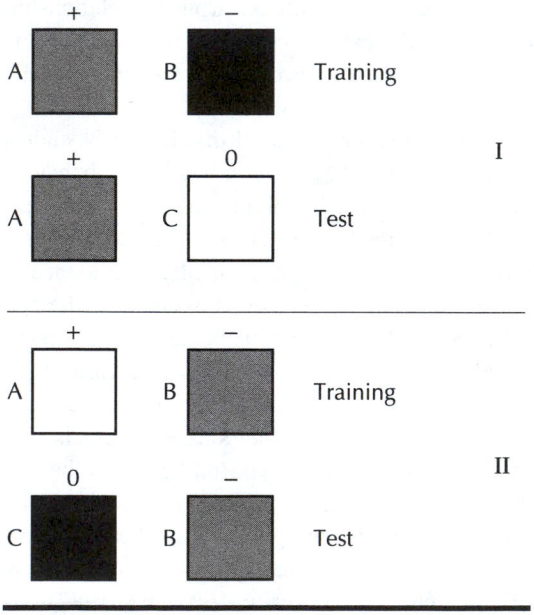

FIGURE 9.7 Kohler's transposition experiment.

This is surprising from an associationist viewpoint, because the animal has not been reinforced for pecking at C, and so it should be a neutral stimulus (symbolized by 0).

Now consider the situation in the lower half of Figure 9.7. Once again the animal is trained to peck at the stimulus labeled A, but in the "test" phase the stimulus to which the animal learned *not* to respond is paired with a previously neutral stimulus. In this case the animal does not respond to the neutral stimulus, but to the stimulus to which it had learned not to respond.

From a Gestalt viewpoint, these results are not at all surprising. This is because the animals are responding to the *relationships* between stimuli, and not to the stimuli themselves. Thus, in the situation in the top half of Figure 9.7, the animal learns to respond to the *lighter* of two stimuli. Consequently, when faced with a choice between A and C, it chooses C because it is the lighter of the two. Similarly in the bottom portion of Figure 9.7, the animal learns to respond to the lighter of two stimuli, and so chooses B in the "test" phase. Of course, we could have done the experiment by training animals to choose the darker of two stimuli, in which case they would have chosen the darker stimuli on the test. It is only when one considers the relations between the parts of the situation—the Gestalt—that the animals' behavior becomes comprehensible.

The ability to take a relationship acquired in one situation, and apply it in another situation is called *transposition.* Transposition is a very important phenomenon as far as the Gestalt psychologists are concerned. Transposition of relationships is what enables someone to transfer what they have learned in one situation to another situation, as in the "area of a parallelogram" problem we considered earlier. Kohler thought that his experiments showed that Gestalt principles applied not only to humans, but also applied in comparative psychology.

The Concept of Isomorphism

Before becoming a psychologist, Kohler had been trained as a physicist, and developed definite ideas concerning the way in which theoretical physics and psychology should inform each other. Kohler (1920/1967) believed that there were parallels between the phenomena of psychology and those of physics. Kohler (e.g., 1969, pp. 60–62) liked to quote eminent physicists such as *Clerk Maxwell* and *Max Planck* to the effect that modern physics begins with whole systems, and then proceeds to understand parts of those systems. For example, "an electric circuit is a system precisely because the conditions prevailing at any given point are determined by those obtaining in all the other parts" (Kohler, 1920/1967, p. 19). Kohler (1967/1969, p. 77) argued that the Gestalt approach "agreed with perfectly clear procedures and facts in natural science. In a sense, Gestalt psychology has . . . become a kind of application of field physics to essential parts of psychology and brain physiology."

Kohler used the term "field physics" to refer to the study of those regions, such as magnetic fields, that exert their influence over an entire area, and that cannot be understood simply as a sum of local effects. From a Gestalt viewpoint, the brain was such a region, in which fields of electric current determined our experience.

> *By this we mean that the neural functions and processes with which the perceptual facts are associated in each case are located in a continuous medium; and that the events in one part of this medium influence the events in other regions in a way that depends directly on the properties of both in their relation to each other. This is the conception with which all physicists work. The field theory of perception applies this simple scheme to the brain correlates of perceptual facts. (Kohler, 1940/1960, p. 55)*

Field theory required a novel approach to the relation between experience and the brain, which Kohler named *isomorphism.* Isomorphism is a variant of psychophysical parallelism, the doctrine of the mind-brain relation held by many previous psychologists, including Titchener. Isomorphism goes beyond simple parallelism by claiming that there is not a simple point-for-point correspondence between events in the brain and events in experience. Rather the correspondence between brain and mind was *structural:* brain processes and experience shared the same Gestalt.

If isomorphism is correct, then changes in the structure of brain processes should yield corresponding changes in the structure of experience. Kohler (1965/1971; Kohler & Wallach, 1944) did some controversial experiments in an attempt to demonstrate this relationship. The general spirit of these investigations can be gathered by examining the configuration in Figure 9.8. This is a famous figure called a *Necker cube,* named after a geologist, *Louis Albert Necker* (1832/1964), who was the first to remark on its psychologically interesting properties. When you focus on the cube face labeled ABCD, then that face seems to be in the foreground. Eventually, however, the figure will reverse itself, and the face labeled EFGH will come to the foreground. Kohler's idea was that such alterations were produced as a result of prolonged inspection of a figure. The cortical representation of the figure becomes *satiated* (fatigued), or only weakly capable of supporting electrical fields, and so another part of the cortex then begins to represent the figure. As the cortical representation changes, so too does one's perception of it.

Kohler's satiation theory was roundly attacked by prominent psychologists, including *Karl Lashley* (Lashley, Chow & Semmes, 1951) and *Roger Sperry* (Sperry & Milner, 1955). Using different procedures, Lashley and Sperry attempted "to dis-

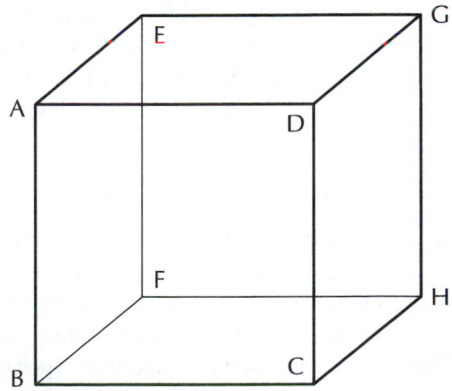

FIGURE 9.8 A Necker cube.

turb the flow of visual currents in monkeys and cats, and then gave these animals tests with visual patterns, between which they had learned to choose before those measures were taken" (Kohler, 1965/1971, p. 280). The fact that the animals could still make the discriminations between patterns in spite of the supposed disruption of brain currents was taken as evidence against Kohler's theory. "Although Kohler subsequently argued that serious objections could be raised against these experiments, they were generally accepted as decisive by the psychological community, thus sounding the death knell for his theory of brain interaction through electrical fields" (Palmer, 1990, p. 291).

Although the specifics of Kohler's brain theory are no longer taken seriously, the general orientation is apparently still viable. "Even though Gestalt ideas about electrical fields were erroneous, the more general proposal that the brain is a dynamic system . . .—physical *Gestalten* in Kohler's terminology—may turn out to be correct" (Rock & Palmer, 1990, p. 90). There is currently a great deal of interest in *neural networks,* systems of neurons that function in a way analogous to the way Kohler described physical Gestalten. The dynamics of such systems appear to be able to explain such Gestalt phenomena as unstable figures, of which the Necker cube is an illustration (Palmer, 1990). Thus it is possible that some of Kohler's ideas may find a new life, after having been totally written off. This would be a good example of the way in which ideas get recycled in psychology. A few years ago no one would have predicted the resurrection of these particular ideas, and so this case also demonstrates the difficulty of predicting which ideas are good candidates for recycling.

KURT KOFFKA (1886–1941)

Koffka attended the University of Berlin, but before going there "he spent a year at the University of Edinburgh, where he came under the influence of several outstanding British scientists and scholars. This student year abroad, in addition to perfecting his use of the language, brought him in close touch with English-speaking people and laid the foundation for the international scientific recognition that was to be his" (Harrower, 1983, p. 253). This international recognition largely stemmed from a book Koffka wrote in 1935, *Principles of Gestalt Psychology,* that became known as the "Bible" of Gestalt psychology, and a classic in the history of psychology (Henle, 1987).

Principles of Gestalt Psychology

Koffka's book (1935) introduced several important concepts. One of these was the distinction between the *geographical* and the *behavioral environment.* Koffka (1935, pp. 27–28) presented an anecdote in order to clarify this distinction. Apparently a man had crossed a snow-covered plain, and, on reaching the other side met another man. The second man expressed amazement that the first man had been foolhardy enough to cross a newly frozen lake. At which point the first man, realizing that he had crossed a lake rather than a plain, had a heart attack and died. The man's behavior had been determined by his understanding of what his environment was. His behavior was not determined by what the environment actually was.

The geographical environment is the environment as it "actually is." It is the environment that geographers tell us about, and it is the environment in which physical stimuli exist. The behavioral environment is the environment that actually determines our behavior, and it can be quite different from the geographical environment. In the example of the man crossing the lake, the behavioral environment was different from the geographical one. It was only when the geographical environment entered the man's behavioral environment that it affected him (i.e., he had a heart attack). The behavioral environment contained the person's *phenomenal world* of lived experience. While the word "phenomenal" has as one of its meanings "extraordinary," in this context it refers to things as they are experienced.

My behavior can be an item in my behavioral environment, or it can be an item in someone else's behavioral environment. That is, I may understand my behavior one way, and someone else may understand my behavior in another way (Koffka, 1935, p. 40). As psychologists we must be careful to understand someone else's behavior in terms of *their* behavioral environment, and not interpret it in terms of our own.

Why Do Things Look as They Do? This was the fundamental psychological question as far as Koffka was concerned. Things do not appear to us as they "really are," as items in the geographical environment. In fact, it is necessary to distinguish *distal stimuli,* which are things as they exist in the geographical environment, from *proximal stimuli,* which are the effects that distal stimuli have on the surface of a receptor organ. For example, we must distinguish between the actual, rectangular shape of a table top (a distal stimulus) from the shape it projects onto the surface of our retina (a proximal stimulus). The proximal stimulus may not be at all rectangular in form, and will change as we move about in the geographical environment. (We considered this problem briefly in Chapter 2, Box 2.1, and you may wish to review that material now.)

Proximal stimuli are our only source of information about events in the "real world," since we are not in direct contact with distal stimuli. Since proximal stimuli are almost always changing, how do we manage to experience a stable, coherent world? This question is particularly interesting in relation to the *perceptual constancies,* which refer to the fact that our *perception* of the properties of objects remains the same even though the proximal stimulus may change. For example, *shape constancy* refers to the fact that the perceived shape of an object (e.g., a table top) remains the same regardless of our viewing angle. *Size constancy* refers to the fact that the size of an object appears the same regardless of its distance from us (a problem addressed by Berkeley, and that we also considered in Chapter 2). We do not perceive a car as getting smaller as it retreats down the road, but only as getting farther away. How are such phenomena possible? The Gestalt answer, as presented by Koffka, is that the parts of the perceptual field remain in the same relationships to one another as the proximal stimulus changes. Thus, a car that is close to us can be compared in size with trees close to us. As we move away from that car, its size relative to the trees around it remains the same. It is invariant relationships of this sort that make the constancies possible.

The Growth of the Mind

The Gestalt psychologists are often said to be "nativists." However, this is actually not true: "The Gestalt psychologists are not nativists. They do not accept the nativism-empircism dichotomy; there is a third class of factors, invariant dynamics, that applies to all of nature. In Kohler's words, 'An enormous part of the business of living can never, as such, have been affected by the changes introduced during evolution' (1969, p. 87). He continues: 'Why so much talk about inheritance, and so much about learning—but hardly ever a word about invariant dynamics? It is this invariant dynamics . . . which keeps organisms and their nervous systems going' (1969, p. 90)" (Henle, 1977/1986, p. 123).

The charge of nativism has been leveled at the Gestalt psychologists because such principles as the Gestalt laws of organization *seem* to be "innately determined," and not the result of learning. However, the Gestalt psychologists did not conceive of such principles as the Gestalt laws of organization as being "innately determined" in the sense of being the result of genetic programming. Rather, the Gestalt laws of organization were the necessary consequence of the operation of physical laws. Just as soap bubbles tend toward a spherical shape because of the operation of the minimum principle, so too does our perception tend toward *pragnanz* (good form) because of the operation of the minimum principle. The minimum principle is a physical law, and it would be a mistake to use either "innate" or "learned" to refer to such laws.

In *The Growth of the Mind,* Koffka (1928/1959) presented a Gestalt approach to child psychology. In it he reviewed the competing approaches to the study of children, such as behaviorism, and presented the Gestalt alternative. He argued that the earliest experiences of children are figure/ground relationships, such as a "luminous point set off from a uniform background; something cold at a place upon the skin set off from the usual temperature of the rest of the skin; the too cold or too warm milk in contrast with the temperature level of the mouth-cavity" (p. 146). Thus, Koffka rejected the associationist view that the earliest experiences were simple sensations. Moreover, Koffka claimed that infants did not have to learn the emotional meaning of their perceptions. Percepts have expressive qualities, or *physiognomic properties,* that are understood even by very young children. "In the middle of the first year the reaction to a 'friendly' face is quite different from the reaction to an 'angry' face. Furthermore, this difference is of a kind which obliges us to conclude that 'friendly' and 'angry' faces are phenomenal facts to the infant, and not mere distributions of light and shade. It seems quite impossible to explain this behavior by experience, upon the assumption that these phenomena arise from an original chaos of sensations in which single visual sensations combine with one another, together with pleasant or unpleasant consequences" (Koffka, 1928/1959, pp. 148–149).

There is a demonstration of Kohler's (1947/1959, pp. 133–134) that is often used to make the point that percepts have intrinsic emotional meanings. Kohler showed subjects shapes like those in Figure 9.9, and asked them which one was the "maluma" and which one was the "takete" (pronounced takaytay). Generally speaking, subjects have no difficulty assigning the "maluma" label to figures like that on the left, and the "takete" label to figures like that on the right. Both the figure and the label seem to go together naturally, even though one may never have experienced them together before. The naturalness of the pairing of label and figure follows from the fact that both have the same expressive quality: soft and round for the "maluma" sound and shape, and sharp and jagged for the "takete" sound and shape. From a Gestalt viewpoint, physiognomic properties are intrinsic features of percepts, and do not need to be learned.

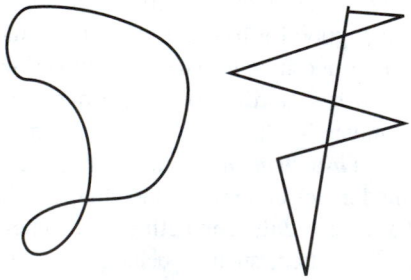

FIGURE 9.9 Which is the maluma and which is the takete?

Subsequent investigations of infant perception (e.g., Kellman & Spelke, 1983) suggest that infants are capable of perceiving configurations at a very young age. However, at the present time there appears to be scant evidence that infants' perception tends to follow the Gestalt laws of organization. Even though infant perception does appear to be well organized, principles other than those proposed by the Gestalt psychologists may be necessary to explain it.

KURT LEWIN (1890–1947) AND THE EMERGENCE OF SOCIAL PSYCHOLOGY

Lewin began to study at the University of Berlin in 1910. He did his Ph.D. dissertation at the Psychological Institute under the relaxed supervision of *Carl Stumpf.* "Stumpf gave his students an unusual degree of freedom, though to some it might seem more accurate to say 'lack of attention.' The thesis topic Lewin had selected was presented to Stumpf by an assistant, while Lewin himself waited in another room to learn if it would be acceptable. Lewin could not remember having ever discussed the matter with Stumpf between the time the assistant relayed word that his subject was approved and the day of his final examination four years later" (Marrow, 1969, p. 8). However, at the Psychological Institute, Lewin was influenced by the emerging group of Gestalt psychologists. Decades later he openly disagreed with some aspects of Gestalt theory, such as its emphasis on physiological explanations of psychological events. Nevertheless, although he developed his own unique approach, his theory always bore the mark of the Gestalt influence. Lewin was also profoundly influenced by the neo-Kantian philosopher, *Ernst Cassirer,* whose work we considered briefly when we discussed Kant in Chapter 2. Cassirer believed that people represent their experience by means of diverse *symbolic forms,* such as art, language, and mathematics (Gardner, 1982). Each symbolic form is a different way of representing reality. Symbolic forms create the world we live in, in the sense that we do not experience the world except through them. Symbolic forms are not immutable, but develop throughout history and in the life of the individual. Cassirer's ideas were fundamental to Lewin's subsequent theory construction.

Before Lewin eventually migrated to the United States he had already developed an international reputation. In the United States, Lewin worked first at Cornell from 1933 to 1935, and then at the University of Iowa from 1935 to 1944. In 1944 he became the Director of the Research Center for Group Dynamics at M.I.T. The German pronunciation of "Lewin" sounds like "Laveen." After being in the United States for some time, Lewin began using an Americanized pronunciation of his name, which sounds like "Loo-in" (Marrow, 1969, p. 177).

Lewin's aim was to create a psychology that was practical and that took into account social influences on individual behavior. One of his earliest interests was in humanizing Taylorism, the approach to work efficiency we considered in Chapter 7. Lewin argued that job satisfaction was an indispensable component of job performance. If a job was psychologically satisfying, then work was likely to be done efficiently. Here we can see an enduring theme in Lewin's work, which is an emphasis on understanding a person's behavior as a function of their goals. Lewin's theory of motivation is one of his major achievements.

As befits a theory with a Gestalt orientation, Lewin (e.g., 1951) called his approach a *field theory.* By a "field" Lewin meant all the forces acting on an individual at a particular time. In psychology, the field in which we are interested is the person's *life space.* A life space consists of the "totality of facts which determine the behavior (B) of an individual at a certain moment. The life space (L) represents the totality of possible events. The life space includes the person (P) and the environment (E)" (Lewin, 1936, p. 216). This leads to the following formula.

$$B = f(P, E)$$

This formula may be read as follows "Behavior is a function of the person and the environment." Remember that the person and the environment are both understood as part of the life space. If an event is not a part of the life space, then it cannot influence behavior. Thus, Lewin's concept of a life space is similar to Koffka's concept of a behavioral environment. There are differences between the two conceptions, however. In Lewin's formulation, the person did not have to be aware of an event in order for it to be a part of the life space. "Although Lewin held that phenomenal properties must be included in the psychological environment and although he favored use of subjects' accounts of the world as they experience it, he did not *equate* the psychological environment with the phenomenal world. His basic criterion was whether any given fact had an effect on behavior, not whether it appeared in conscious awareness. He explicitly asserted that the life space should include within it 'unconscious' determinants of behavior" (Cartwright, 1959, p. 68).

Lewin's psychology is concerned with describing the parts of the life space, and the way in which these parts interact to produce behavior. In order to describe the life space, Lewin made use of a version of *topology,* that branch of geometry concerned with the relations between parts of a space. This approach allowed Lewin to go beyond a verbal description of a life space, and to represent life spaces by means of figures such as that in Figure 9.10, which is similar to one of Lewin's (1936, p. 48) examples. This figure represents some of the parts, or *regions,* of the life space of a person who wants to become a clinical psychologist. The person is a part of the life space, located in a particular region. The person, whom we will suppose is a junior, can imagine the tasks that lie ahead. These tasks represent *barriers* to the achievement of the final goal of becoming a clinical psychologist. Thus, the person must satisfy the requirements of entering senior year, at which time the person will be in a new region (sy). Getting into graduate

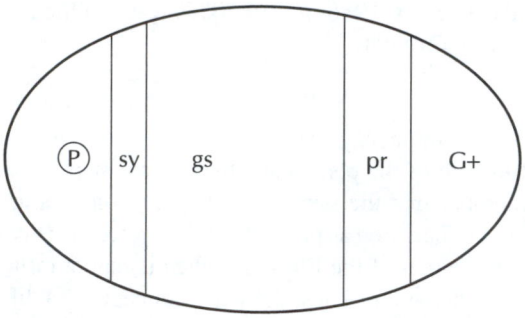

FIGURE 9.10 A life space. P, person; sy, senior year; gs, graduate school; pr, practice; G+, goal with positive valence.

school (gs) is the next barrier, and setting up a practice (pr) after graduating is the final barrier. The goal (G) provides a positive *valence* throughout the entire process. Valences may be positive or negative, and act as forces on the person in the life space.

Notice that in this example some of the regions of the life space are imaginary situations in the future. Events in the life space may, but need not be, representations of events in the "real world." Events in the real world belong to what Lewin called the *foreign hull* that surrounds the life space. The life space itself has a membrane that is more or less *permeable* to events in the foreign hull. Some life spaces are highly permeable, while others are relatively impermeable. In the latter case, the person may seem to others to live in a world apart. Remember, only events in the life space at the current time can influence behavior.

In Figure 9.10, the person is represented inside a simple circle. However, one could represent the person in more detail. It was one of Lewin's principles of development that people tend to become more *differentiated* over time. Thus children have a relatively simple, undifferentiated structure, while adults have a more differentiated structure. There may be regions of the person that are relatively inaccessible, corresponding to what other theorists term the "unconscious." Although there is a tendency toward *equilibrium* between regions, at any one time energy may not be distributed evenly throughout the person. Needs create *tension,* and consequently disequilibrium. The person acts to reduce this tension, but a particularly interesting situation for Lewin was the *barrier problem,* in which a person must initially move away from an object with positive valence. For example, imagine a child who sees a desirable toy in another room through a plate glass window. The child cannot move directly toward the object, because the window is an impermeable barrier. Rather, the child must turn away from the toy, exit the current room, and then enter the room with the toy. Turning away from an object with positive valence creates tension in the person. However, by doing so the child is able in the end to reduce tension by achieving the desirable object. Being able to tolerate increased tension in the short run in order to relieve tension in the long run is an important developmental achievement.

The Zeigarnik Effect

The way tension influences psychological processes was masterfully delineated by one of Lewin's students, *Bluma Zeigarnik* (1927/1967, p. 300), who asked the question, "What is the relation between the status in memory of an activity which has been interrupted before it could be completed and of one which has not been interrupted?" Zeigarnik gave subjects a series of tasks, half of which were interrupted before the person could complete them. After the experiment, subjects were asked to recall the tasks they had been given. Generally speaking, subjects remembered the interrupted tasks best.

> *When the subject sets out to perform the operations required by one of these tasks there develops within him a quasi-need for completion of that task. This is like the occurrence of a tension system which tends towards resolution. Completing the task means resolving the tension system, or discharging the quasi-need. If a task is not completed, a state of tension remains and the quasi-need is unstilled. The memorial advantage enjoyed by interrupted tasks must be due to this continuation of the quasi-need. (pp. 305–306)*

The *Zeigarnik effect* is interesting in part because it shows that it is not necessarily the most rewarding experiences that we tend to remember best. The Zeigarnik effect suggests instead that tension created within a region of the person will tend to persist, and cause us to remember unfinished business. You might want to see if this is true of your own experience. After an examination, which questions do you tend to recall first? The ones you know you answered correctly, or the ones you may have not answered correctly, or not had time to finish?

Group Dynamics

As Lewin's career progressed, he became increasingly interested in exploring applied, social issues. This led to the advocacy of *action research,* which refers to a program of research designed not only to gather data, but also to lead directly to social change. Lewin (e.g., 1946; Lewin & Grabbe, 1945) recognized that new methods were required to overcome barriers to social change. It was not enough to attempt to change individuals, but rather the group within which the individual functioned had to undergo a transformation. The person is to the group as a part is to the whole, and a change in the dynamics of the group will also change the way the individual perceives and acts. The study of *group dynamics* became a central focus for Lewin and his group of researchers.

The interest in group dynamics spawned a very consequential experiment in what came to be called *sensitivity training,* or *T-groups,* where the "T" stands for training. The spark for these groups came from the Connecticut State Inter-Racial Commission, who asked Lewin to assist in "training leaders and conducting research on the most effective means for combating racial and religious prejudice in communities" (Marrow, 1969, p. 210). A group was assembled consisting of people who would be responsible for attempting to effect the desired changes. The most dramatic discovery of the resulting workshops was the effect on group members of feedback on their behavior. As successive group experiments were conducted at what became the *National Training Laboratories* in Bethel, Maine, it began to appear as if the T-groups might be powerful agents of change (Benne, 1964). Being given the opportunity of "seeing yourself as others see you" provided group participants with a valuable source of information about the effects of their behavior on others. This in turn appeared to make participants more tolerant and accepting of both themselves and others. The T-group was subsequently taken up with enthusiasm by humanistic psychologists, whom we will consider in Chapter 13.

Fritz Heider (1896–1988)

Gestalt psychology shaped the thinking of some of the most influential social psychologists of the century, including *Fritz Heider* and *Solomon Asch* (Fiske & Taylor, 1991). We will discuss Asch in the next section. Heider had worked at the University of Berlin when the Gestalt movement was in its prime. Heider (1958, p. 4) acknowledged Lewin as a major influence on his thinking. He subsequently migrated to the United States, and, after a period working at Smith College with Koffka, spent many years at the University of Kansas.

Heider's psychology of interpersonal relations (1958, p. 5) begins with an analysis of *common-sense psychology:* "In everyday life we form ideas about other people and about social situations. We interpret other people's actions and we predict what they will do under certain circumstances. Though these ideas are usually not formulated, they often function adequately." An inspection of common-sense psychology shows that there are several concepts that are at the heart of the way people usually understand interpersonal relations. These include *giving versus taking; benefits versus harms;* and *liking versus disliking.* While this list is far from exhaustive, you can see that such concepts constitute dimensions along which our interpersonal experience can vary. One pole of this dimension tends to be psychologically positive, while the other is psychologically negative (Osgood & Richards, 1973).

Heider was particularly interested in the process whereby people tend to achieve *balanced states* in their relations with others. "By a balanced state (or situation) is meant a harmonious state, one in which the entities comprising the situation and the feelings about them fit together without stress" (Heider, 1958, p. 180). A balanced state is a good Gestalt, while an unbalanced state may "leave us with a feeling of disturbance that becomes relieved only when change within the situation takes place in such a way that a state of balance is achieved" (Heider, 1958, p. 180). Balanced and unbalanced states are easily represented by means of *triads,* which represent the relations between a person (p), another person (o), and a thing (x). A series of such p-o-x triads is given in Figure 9.11. The triad at the top left represents a situation in which there are positive relations between all three components of the triad. For example, suppose you (p) like your roommate (o), and you both like to eat a vegetarian diet (x). This is a balanced state, and there is no need to change it. The triad at the top right is more problematic. Suppose that in this case you (p) like your roommate (o) as before, and your roommate is still a vegetarian, and so likes a meatless diet (x). You, however, have become tired of not eating any meat, and so your relation to the meatless diet (x) is negative. This is an unbalanced situation, and will set in motion processes designed to change the situation. In general, an unbalanced situation is one in which the product of the three relations is negative. Thus, in this triad a negative times a positive times a negative is negative. Notice that there are several things you could do to restore balance. For example, you could decide that you were mistaken about your roommate, and that you do not really like her after all. This would change the sign of the p-o relation to negative, and now a negative times a negative times a negative is positive. The situation is now balanced.

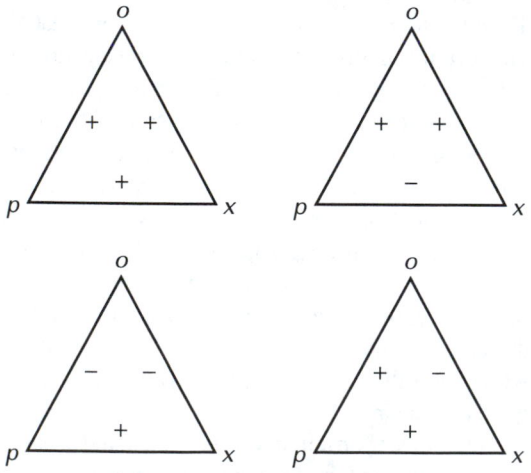

FIGURE 9.11 Examples of Heider's p-o-x triad.

The triad at the lower left in Figure 9.11 is also balanced. In such a situation you (p) have a negative relation with another person (o), but a positive relation with something (x). This is balanced by the negative relation the other person has with something (x). For example, suppose you dislike your roommate, and your roommate dislikes vegetables, while you are a vegetarian. The final triad (lower right) is unbalanced, however, because you (p) bear positive relations to both o and x, while o and x bear a negative relation to each other. Suppose that you like your roommate and you are a vegetarian, but she hates vegetables. In this situation, there will be pressure to change one or more of these relationships. Perhaps you could persuade her to become a vegetarian.

Notice that the stress that produces change is generated by the structural relations between the parts of a triad. It is the Gestalt tendency toward pragnanz, or "good form" that regulates interpersonal processes, just as it regulates most processes from a Gestalt viewpoint (Asch, 1968b, p. 166).

Solomon Asch (1907–)

Asch was born in Warsaw in 1907, but moved to New York City in 1920. He did his graduate work at Columbia, where he studied under Woodworth. As a graduate student he learned a bit about Gestalt psychology and was drawn to it. He subsequently met and was influenced by Wertheimer, and then went to Swarthmore College, which had become an unofficial "headquarters" of Gestalt psychology, mostly because Kohler had settled there. After leaving Swarthmore, Asch was the founding director of the Institute for Cognitive Studies at Rutgers (Ceraso, Gruber, & Rock, 1990).

In addition to being the author of a standard text (Asch, 1952), Asch became well-known for two lines of research in social psychology: forming impressions of personality and conformity. We consider both of these in turn.

Forming Impressions of Personality. Asch's studies of social cognition (1946; Asch & Zukier,1984) are consistent with a basic premise of Gestalt psychology, which is that we tend to experience events as coherent and related to one another. In the social sphere, the corresponding premise is that we experience people as psychological units. Concretely, this means that the individual attributes of people are treated as parts of an overall Gestalt. We do not perceive others as being merely the sum of their pieces. To illustrate this point, consider one of Asch's experiments (1946). Subjects were presented with one of two lists of traits. One group of subjects heard a person described as "intelligent, skillful, industrious, *warm,* determined, practical and cautious," while the other group of subjects heard a person described as "intelligent, skillful, industrious, *cold,* determined, practical and cautious." Notice that the difference between the two lists lies in only one word, *warm* in the first list, and *cold* in the second list. Although the two lists differed by only one feature, the impressions formed by the two groups of subjects were strikingly different. The group given the *warm* list formed an impression of the target person as someone who was "wise, humorous, popular and imaginative," while the subjects given the *cold* list formed an impression of the target person as not possessing these qualities. Thus, "a change in one quality produces a fundamental change in the entire impression" (Asch, 1952, p. 210). People do not form an impression by simply adding up pieces of information about others. If that was the way we form impressions, then changing only one attribute would have only a small effect, and not alter the entire impression. Rather, we appear to relate personal qualities to each other as parts to a whole.

Conformity. Asch (1952, p. 257) characterized the relation between a person and a group as a "part-whole relation that depends on the recapitulation of the structure of the whole in the part." This means that a group exerts its influence on an individual to the extent that the individual takes on the viewpoint of the group as a whole. Asch was particularly interested in situations in which a group member adopts the opinion of a group, even when this group opinion is clearly erroneous.

In a famous series of experiments, Asch (1955, 1956) presented groups of subjects with a series of line judgment tasks. The groups consisted of 7 to 9 men each, and all but one of the group members were confederates of the experimenter. The confederates made incorrect judgments on some of their line judgments. For example, examine Figure 9.12, which shows the standard and comparison lines for the trials on which the confederates deliberately chose the wrong line. Thus, the confederates would say that a 3¾-inch standard line was equal to a 3-inch comparison line, when it is obviously equal to the 3-inch comparison line. What about the one group member—the critical subject—who was not in on the deception? This per-

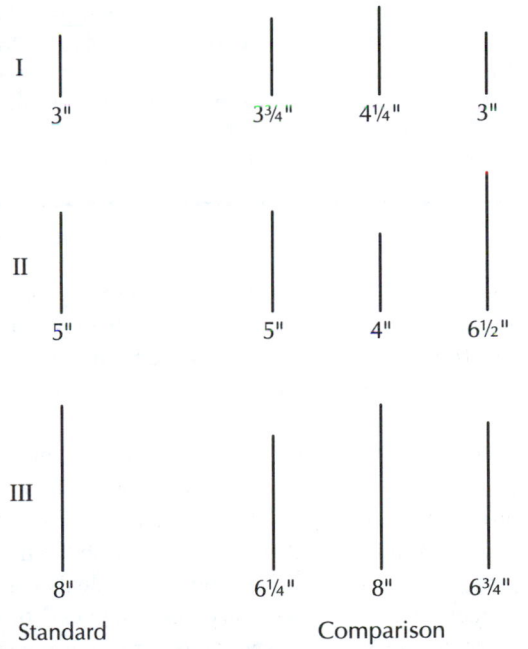

FIGURE 9.12 Standard and comparison lines.
Source: S. E. Asch. (1956). *Studies of independence and conformity: I. A minority of one against a unanimous majority.* Psychological Monographs, no. 70, p. 7.

BOX 9.2

Frame of Reference

In 1992, the *Journal of Experimental Psychology: General* reprinted a series of "classic articles" "as part of the centennial celebration of the American Psychological Association" (Hunt, 1992, p. 403). One article so honored was by Asch and Witkin (1948/1992), which refined some observations that had originally been made by Wertheimer (1912). The problem that Asch and Witkin explored involved the Gestalt notion of *frame of reference*. We perceive the orientation of objects in relation to a particular context. What counts as a vertical or as a horizontal direction is not determined absolutely, but depends on the frame of reference within which directions are understood. This frame of reference is not determined solely by the orientation of our bodies in relation to gravity. For example, as Asch and Witkin (1948/1992) observe, "In [a] plane, disorientation may be so severe that the person can be upside down and perceive himself and the plane as upright, or suddenly see the sky where he believes the earth should be, and so on" (p. 325). To demonstrate the power of frame of reference, Asch and Witkin (1948/1992) asked subjects to set a line to the vertical or horizontal orientation. Ordinarily this is a task that can be accomplished with great precision. However, in Asch's and Witkin's (1948/1992) experiment, the line is set with a rectangular frame, and the frame is tilted by 22 degrees. In one condition, the line is moved off the horizontal and gradually moved by the experimenter. The subject's task is to say when the line is oriented horizontally, that is, in line with the floor of the room in which the subject is standing. It turns out that the frame of reference tends to influence subjects' judgments, so that they deviate from the "true" horizontal, and are more consistent with the frame provided. Thus, even as fundamental a feature of experience as vertical and horizontal directions are influenced by the context of which they are a part.

The concept of a frame of reference has been applied to many more situations in addition to space perception (Rock, 1992). One significant direction of research was to study individual differences in susceptibility to frame effects (e.g., Witkin, Lewis, Hertzman, Machover, Meissner, & Wapner, 1954). Those who were strongly affected by the frame of reference were termed *field dependent,* while those who were less influenced by the frame were termed *field independent.* This difference was extensively explored in relation to other personality characteristics, such as the tendency to be independent, have control of one's impulses, and have high self-esteem. The guiding idea of such research is that all aspects of the person, from perception to personality, are interrelated and influence each other.

son is "in the position of a *minority of one* against a *wrong and unanimous* majority. Perhaps for the first time this person found a massed majority contradicting the clear evidence of his senses" (Asch, 1956, p. 3).

The results showed that the critical subjects conformed to the majority's erroneous judgment on approximately 37 percent of the trials. About 25 percent of the subjects never agreed with the majority on any trials, while some individuals conformed at every opportunity. Asch reported that individual differences were quite consistent across trials. The compliant subjects appeared to be less self-confident, while the independent subjects trusted their own experience. Asch (1955, p. 34) concluded that while "life in society requires consensus," that "consensus, in order to be productive, requires that each individual contribute independently out of his experience and insight." The high rate of conformity "raises questions about our ways of education and about the values that guide our conduct." Would Asch's results be the same today?

Asch also did groundbreaking research in areas that did not utilize techniques peculiar to social psychology. One of these studies is reviewed in Box 9.2.

KURT GOLDSTEIN (1878–1965)

Goldstein was one of the founding editors of *Psychologische Forschung,* which was the Gestalt psychologists' journal, and shared many of the

Gestalt psychologists' orienting attitudes. A physician, Goldstein had wide-ranging interests, and collaborated with and influenced both psychologists and philosophers. "Upon Hitler's assumption of power in 1933, Goldstein was briefly jailed, then released on condition he leave the country" (Simmel, 1968, p. 7) He lived in Amsterdam for a while, and then moved to New York City where he was in private practice and affiliated with Columbia University. Subsequently he moved to the Boston area, where he became a close friend of Karl Lashley (Simmel, 1968, p. 9).

Organismic Theory

Goldstein developed his distinctive approach partly through his attempts to rehabilitate thousands of brain damaged soldiers who were casualties of the First World War. He believed that associationistic psychology was a barrier to understanding the brain damaged person (Goldstein, 1967, p. 151). For example, the organism should not be conceived of as consisting of a set of separate mechanisms such as the reflex. In fact, reflexes did not operate independently of other organismic activity, but needed to be understood in relation to the activity of the whole organism. "Practically nowhere can a simple stimulus response relationship, corresponding to the strict reflex concept, be directly observed" (Goldstein, 1939/1963, p. 79).

Rather than take an associationistic approach, "it is of the utmost importance that one evaluate any aspect of the human organism in relation to the condition of the organism in its totality. On this understanding is based what I have called *self-realization.* The trend toward self-realization is not merely a stimulus but a driving force that puts the organism into action" (Goldstein, 1967, p. 151). Goldstein believed that self-realization, which he also called *self-actualization,* was the only drive that regulated the organism's behavior. As we shall see in Chapter 13, the concept of self-actualization was taken up and developed by humanistic psychologists such as Abraham Maslow.

> *Under various conditions, various actions come into the foreground; and while they thereby seem to be directed toward different goals, they give the impression of independently existing drives. In reality, however, these various actions occur in accordance with the various capacities which belong to the nature of the organism, and occur in accordance with those instrumental processes which are then necessary prerequisites of the self-actualization of the organism. (Goldstein, 1939/1963, pp. 197–198)*

The organismic approach meant that the investigator should not evaluate behavior mechanically, according to a set formula. For example, it made no sense to give a standardized test to a brain damaged patient, and simply count the right and wrong answers. One needed to observe all the behaviors that the person presented "giving no preference in the description to any special one" (Goldstein, 1967, p. 151). Description should be as full and painstakingly complete as possible. Although Goldstein invented tests to be used with brain damaged patients (e.g., Goldstein & Scheerer, 1941), these were intended to provide the investigator with a sample of the range of a patient's behavior, which was then to be interpreted holistically.

The Abstract Attitude

Goldstein (1940/1963) made a distinction between abstract and concrete performance.

> *In 'concrete' performances a reaction is determined directly by a stimulus, is awakened by all that the individual perceives. The individual's procedure is somewhat passive, as if it were not he who had the initiative. In 'abstract' performances an action is not determined directly and immediately by a stimulus configuration but by the account of the situation which the individual gives to himself. The performance is thus more a primary action than a mere reaction, and it is a totally different way of coming to terms with the outside world. The individual has to consider the situation from various aspects, pick out the aspect which is essential, and act in a way appropriate to the whole situation (pp. 59–60).*

Pathology, in forms as disparate as brain damage and schizophrenia, undermines the abstract attitude. Such patients can respond only to the concrete properties of their current situation, they cannot imagine alternative possibilities. Goldstein (1940/1963, pp. 54–55) described a patient who was asked to repeat the sentence "The snow is black." This the patient was unable to do as asked without hesitating before the word "black," or changing it to "white." Snow, after all, is not actually black. It requires an abstract attitude to imagine the possibility that snow *could* be black. The absence of an abstract attitude undermines the person's ability to come to terms with the world. The person lacking such an attitude is particularly susceptible to *anxiety,* which is an experience of dread. Anxiety differs from fear in that anxiety has no object, while fear is always fear of something. People may experience anxiety if they cannot adequately deal with the environment in which they find themselves. By behaving only concretely, damaged individuals can protect themselves from the catastrophic reaction that would result if they confronted the myriad possibilities that the world affords, and with which the abstract attitude enables healthy individuals to deal.

Additional Reading on This Topic. Seaman (1984) provides historical background to research on apparent motion. Gestalt psychology is often confused with Gestalt *therapy,* a technique with which it shares little more than a name. As Henle (1978) showed, Gestalt therapy borrowed some of the concepts of Gestalt psychology, but applied them, along with other ideas from psychoanalysis, in a much looser way than was intended by the Gestalt psychologists themselves.

Gestalt psychology has had a profound influence on the psychology of art. A classic work in this area is Arnheim (1974). Van Elteren (1992) provides a fascinating account of the films that Lewin made in Berlin to illustrate various psychological issues, particularly the world of childhood. Heider's (1983) autobiography is well worth reading.

KEY NAMES AND CONCEPTS

What follows is an index of some of the most important material in this chapter. The list includes individuals, concepts, and topics you should know. Read through the list, and if anything on it seems unfamiliar, then go back and re-read the appropriate section of the chapter. You should be able to define each concept, briefly discuss each topic, and state the importance of each person on the list. In addition, you should be able to write an account of the work done by each person or topic printed in boldface.

Asch, Solomon, 188
conformity, 189
forming impressions of personality, 189
frame of reference, 190
Box 9.1—Gestalt psychologists migrate to the United States, 178
Box 9.2—Frame of reference, 190
Cassirer, Ernst, 184
symbolic forms, 185
correspondence theory of truth, 177
demonstrations, 172
figure and ground, 175
Gestalt
meaning of, 171
Gestalt laws of organization, 174
Goldstein, Kurt, 190
abstract attitude, 191
anxiety, 192
coming to terms with the world, 191
organismic theory, 191
self-actualization, 191
self-realization, 191
Heider, Fritz, 187
balanced states, 187
common-sense psychology, 187
triads, 188
Husserl, Edmund, 174
Kant, Immanuel, 174

Katona, George, 176
Koffka, Kurt, 182
distal and proximal stimuli, 183
geographical and behavioral environment, 182
perceptual constancies, 183
phenomenal world, 182
Principles of Gestalt Psychology, 182
Kohler, Wolfgang, 179
insight, 179
isomorphism, 180
The Mentality of Apes, 179
physiognomic properties, 184
satiation, 181
transposition, 180
Lashley, Karl, 181
Lewin, Kurt, 184
action research, 187
barriers in the life space, 185
equilibrium, 186
field theory, 185
foreign hull, 186
group dynamics, 187
life space, 185
National Training Laboratories, 187
permeability, 186
regions of the life space, 185
sensitivity training, 187
T-groups, 187
topology, 185
valences, 186
Maxwell, Clerk, 181
minimum principle, 173
Necker, Louis Albert
Necker cube, 181
neural networks, 182
parts versus pieces, 177
phenomenology, 174
phi phenomenon, 172
Planck, Max, 181
Rubin, Edgar, 175
Sperry, Roger, 181
Stumpf, Carl, 184
von Ehrenfels, Christian, 173
Gestalt quality, 174
Wertheimer, Max, 172
Productive Thinking, 176
word association method, 172
Witkin, H.
field dependent versus field independent, 190
Zeigarnik, Bluma, 186
Zeigarnik effect, 187

CHAPTER 10

RESEARCH METHODS

PHILOSOPHY OF SCIENCE
Logical Positivism
Operationism
Where Did Psychologists Stand?
Criticisms of Operationism
EXPERIMENTAL METHODS
Statistical Inference
RONALD A. FISHER (1890–1962)
Fisher's Approach to Designing Experiments
The Null Hypothesis
CORRELATIONAL METHODS
CHARLES SPEARMAN (1863–1945)
CYRIL BURT (1883–1971)
The Burt Scandal
LOUIS LEON THURSTONE (1887–1955)
"THE TWO DISCIPLINES OF SCIENTIFIC PSYCHOLOGY"

Virtually all students who major in psychology must take a course in research methods. These methods have not existed since the beginning of time, but have a definite history. Psychology depends on particular *investigative practices,* which generate "products that count as scientific knowledge" (Danziger, 1987, p. 14). We have already met several of these investigative practices as we considered specific psychological practitioners. For example, Titchener was known for the investigative practice called introspection, while Watson was known for the investigative practice called methodological behaviorism. Each particular investigative practice must be justified in terms of prevailing standards at the time it is introduced. The research methods employed by one generation of psychologists may strike later generations as either obsolete or flawed. In this chapter we consider some of the ways in which investigative practices developed in the first half of this century.

PHILOSOPHY OF SCIENCE

Logical Positivism

In the 1920s a philosophy appeared that had a profound influence on psychology. This philosophy goes under various names, one of which is *logical positivism,* a philosophy that began with a group of physicists, logicians, and mathematicians working in Vienna (Austria). They were called the *Vienna Circle,* and they tried to formulate general principles for gathering knowledge, taking these rules from successful knowledge gathering disciplines, such as physics and chemistry.

A very good example of the application of logical positivism to psychology is a paper by *Rudolf Carnap* (1935/1959). Carnap, like other logical positivists, emphasized that knowledge is embodied in language. Thus, any science is at bottom a set of statements referring to observations. The truth of these statements must lie in their correspondence with these factual observations. How can we check to see if the statements we make are in correspondence with the facts? There must be a procedure that is open to public scrutiny for verifying statements. The truth or falsehood of statements must be objectively (i.e., publicly) decidable. This kind of thinking led to the *verification principle,* which stated that the meaning of a statement is its method of verification (Schlick, 1938/1962). "Thus, whenever we ask about a sentence, 'What does it mean?', what we expect is instruction as to the circumstances in which the sentence is to be used; we want a description of the conditions under which the sentence will form a true proposition, and of those which will make it false" (Schlick, 1938/1962, p. 30). From this viewpoint, unless we can describe a procedure for verifying our statements, then they are of no value; they are meaningless.

According to Carnap (1935/1959), when we do experiments, then our observations should be described by *protocol sentences,* which refer to publicly observable events. A meaningful statement is a statement that can be translated into these protocol sentences. If you are unable to translate a statement into protocol sentences, then it is not a meaningful statement. Moreover, once you have translated a statement into protocol sentences, then the protocol sentences *are* the meaning of the statement. There is no *surplus meaning,* in that statements never mean more than the protocol sentences to which they refer.

To illustrate the procedure that Carnap is recommending, let us reconsider Wundt's experiment with metronomes that we considered in Chapter 4. Suppose that, as the experimenter, I play the metronome at a very slow speed (one beat every 2 seconds). Suppose further that I say "This metronome speed makes the subject feel sad." How can a statement like that be meaningful, since I cannot observe the subject's emotional experience? However, if you think about it for a minute, you can see what appears to be a way out of this problem. How do you usually find out that someone is sad? Is it not by observing what the person says and does? If someone says he or she feels sad, and if the facial expression is downcast, and if the posture is slumped, then you might feel justified in saying "that person feels sad." Notice that all of your observations would have been objective: what the person says, the person's facial expression and posture. In Carnap's terms, your descriptions (of what the person said, of the facial expression, and of the posture) would be *protocol sentences.* These descriptions give meaning to your statement "that person is sad." Similarly, in Wundt's experiment, the experimenter can say "the subject feels sad" and mean by it that the subject says "that beat makes me feel sad." What the subject *says* is publicly observable. From Carnap's viewpoint, Wundt was mistaken in believing that the data of psychology consisted of private experiences. In fact, the data of psychology consist of publicly observable occurrences in the form of *behavior,* which includes verbal behavior such as saying "I feel sad." Carnap's argument was consistent with the views of behaviorists such as Watson, who had argued that while introspection was inadmissible as an investigative practice, *verbal reports* could be studied simply as behavior and not as referring to "mental" phenomena.

Carnap went further and argued that psychology involved what he called *dispositional concepts.* Dispositional concepts are descriptions of lawful relationships between independent and dependent variables. Such statements have the following form: *If X then Y,* where X is a stimulus and Y is some behavior. Thus, the following is a dispositional concept: *IF the metronome is played at one beat every 2 seconds, THEN the subject will say "That beat makes me feel sad."*

Dispositional concepts are capable of being *falsified.* As a result of the influence of philosophers such as *Karl Popper* (1965), *falsifiability* came to be regarded as an important characteristic of scientific concepts. As long as your observations are consistent with a dispositional concept, then it can be retained as a law. However, should observations be inconsistent with a dispositional concept, then it must be replaced with a more likely alternative. This alternative can then be tested against publicly observable data until it is falsified. In this way, it was believed that dispositional concepts progressively become more accurate.

Operationism

Psychologists were also influenced by another viewpoint which is quite similar to Carnap's recommendation that all psychological concepts ultimately refer to publicly observable occurrences. That viewpoint is usually associated with the physicist *Percy Bridgman* (1927) and is called *operationism* (Boring, 1945/1963c). Operationism requires the investigator to specify the way in which a concept is to be measured. Such specifications are called *operational definitions*. For any psychological concept whatsoever, a researcher should be able to give an operational definition of it. Thus, an operational definition of a concept such as *intelligence* might be the score a person obtains on an intelligence test (e.g., Boring, 1923/1969). Operational definitions were regarded as a way of making sure that psychological concepts refer to publicly observable events.

Where Did Psychologists Stand?

Logical positivism and operationism were welcomed most warmly by psychologists of a behaviorist persuasion. Indeed we will see in the next chapter how a group of psychologists called *neobehaviorists* explicitly developed theories in accordance with the tenets of logical positivism and operationism. Of the psychologists we have already considered, B. F. Skinner embraced operationism the most warmly (Green, 1992; Rogers, 1989). Skinner (1945a, p. 271) argued that behaviorism was "nothing more than a thoroughgoing operational analysis of traditional mentalistic concepts." Skinner's point was that by defining concepts such as "reward" in a completely objective, publicly observable way, behaviorists had rendered psychological concepts in a scientific manner.

Gestalt psychologists appeared to be damaged by the new philosophy of science. This was because of their preoccupation with the world as it is experienced, a subjectivity that cannot be expressed directly within a logical positivist framework. Gestalt concepts, such as "life space," evidently had surplus meaning, since no operational analysis of them could rid them of their reference to lived experience. By and large, the Gestalt psychologists resisted logical positivism and operationism as being *complete* philosophies of science, and argued for the continued inclusion of subjective experience as a legitimate part of psychology. The fact that operationism became widely accepted, particularly in America, was another reason why Gestalt psychology was relatively unacceptable for many psychologists.

Psychoanalysis was another movement that was roundly criticized by adherents of logical positivism and/or operationism. For example, Skinner (1953/1961, p. 121) said that "Freud appears never to have considered the possibility of bringing the concepts and theories of a psychological science into contact with the rest of physical and biological science by the simple expedient of an operational analysis of terms." Thus, psychoanalysis was out there on its own, speaking a language that had little or no scientific meaning because its concepts were not given scientific definitions. Many philosophers of science were just as critical. "The theory is stated in language so vague and metaphorical that almost anything appears to be compatible with it" (Nagel, 1960, p. 41). This is to say that psychoanalytic theory is untestable. No matter what happens, the theory can be made to explain it. The process of deriving hypotheses that can be falsified is not possible in principle because the theory is too imprecise. Apologists for psychoanalysis agreed that the theory was in need of "data obtained in controlled experiments," but argued that the theory was extremely complex, and could not easily be given an operational analysis without oversimplifying it (e.g., Rapaport, 1959a, pp. 159–163). However, as we noted in our earlier discussion of psychoanalysis in Chapter 6, academic psychologists were largely unsympathetic to the psychoanalysts' call for patience, believing instead that the theory was simply unscientific.

In general, the rise of logical positivism as well as operationism coincided with the dominance of behaviorism in America. Methodological behaviorism met the requirements of scientific method as prescribed by operationists, and until the end of the 1950s methodological behaviorism seemed to most academic psychologists to be common sense.

Criticisms of Operationism

Critics of operationism, such as *Sigmund Koch* (1992) have claimed that some psychologists, including the ones we will examine in Chapter 11, went overboard in their enthusiasm for operational definitions. Koch (1992, p. 265) observed that Bridgman himself was less of a doctrinaire operationist than were many psychologists. "From an early point on, Bridgman repeatedly indicated that operations are necessary conditions for meanings, not *sufficient* ones. More he *stressed*—constantly and emphatically—that he was not advocating a theory or method of *definition,* . . . but only a method for analyzing, perhaps sharpening, the meanings of concepts *already in place.* He did not advocate 'operational *definition*' but rather 'operational analysis', or 'operational method.'" On this account, operationism was not a way of creating psychological concepts, but one way among many of analyzing their meaning. The meaning of a psychological concept would not be reduced to its operational definition, but could mean more than the operations used to investigate it. Koch cites the following paragraph from Bridgman (1940, p. 36) to convey this point:

> *The process that I want to call scientific is a process that involves the continual apprehension of meaning, the constant appraisal of significance, accompanied by a running act of checking to be sure that I am doing what I want to do, and of judging correctness or incorrectness. This checking and judging and accepting, that together constitute understanding, are done by me and can be done by no one else. They are as private as my toothache, and without them science is dead.*

This contrast between the personal, subjective and the impersonal, objective sides of scientific inquiry was echoed in the distinction between the *context of discovery* versus the *context of justification* (Gigerenzer, 1991; Reichenbach, 1938). The thinking that leads to the *discovery* of a method for investigating a problem may be quite different from the thinking that goes into presenting a completed study for consumption by the rest of the scientific community. The latter involves *justifying* the investigative procedure that was used, rather than explaining how the investigator came up with it in the first place. Operationism in psychology placed great emphasis on the context of justification, and as we shall see in later chapters, many psychologists began to feel that too much of the subjective side of psychological inquiry had been sacrificed in the process.

EXPERIMENTAL METHODS

Statistical Inference

As Gigerenzer and Murray (1987, p. 18) point out, experiments done in Wundt's day consisted largely of exhaustive descriptions of individual cases, with no explicit rules for making generalizations. Such experiments proved not to be very convincing to most twentieth-century academic psychologists, partly because, as we saw in Chapter 4, Wundt's experiments appeared to rely on subjective interpretation that seemed to many to be unscientific. Experimental psychologists felt that they had found a better way of thinking about experiments in the work of Sir Ronald A. Fisher (1925/1991), who is generally acknowledged to be one of the most important methodologists of all time (Rao, 1992).

RONALD A. FISHER (1890–1962)

Fisher's Approach to Designing Experiments

Fisher was an English gentleman who made his major contributions in the 1920s, and so the research that amused him might not appeal to everyone today. For example, one experiment he considered involved evaluating the claim made by "a lady [who] declares that by tasting a cup of tea she can discriminate whether the milk or the tea . . . was first added to the cup" (Fisher, 1925/1991, p. 11). This must have been a person of some refinement and gentility, since few people would claim to be able to tell whether the milk or the tea had been added first! It is useful to consider how one would put such claims to an experimental test.

In designing an experiment to test tea tasting ability, Fisher proposed to give the subject 8 cups of tea, 4 with milk added to tea, and 4 with tea added to milk. In Fisher's experiment, the subject knows that there will be 4 cups of each kind, but the order in which the cups are given to the subject is *random.* A random order is not "determined arbitrarily by human choice" (Fisher, 1925/1991, p. 11), but determined by a purely chance procedure such as rolling dice. Why did Fisher insist on a random order? One reason is that a random order of presentation makes it possible to determine how likely the subject is to make the correct choices by chance alone. It turns out that there are 70 different orders in which the cups can be presented, and so the subject has 1 chance in 70 of making the correct choices. The odds are heavily against the subject accomplishing this task by chance alone. Thus, should the subject make the correct choices, then we would feel fairly secure in believing that the subject did not make the correct choices by chance.

Fisher notes that we could make the task even more difficult to accomplish by chance alone by increasing the number of cups. Alternatively, we could make the task easier to accomplish by chance alone by decreasing the number of cups. What degree of chance are we willing to accept? Fisher proposed that researchers adopt a criterion of 1 chance in 20, or 5 percent. To illustrate what this means, consider a tea tasting experiment in which there are 6 cups. As Fisher points out, there are 20 different ways in which the 6 cups can be presented. Therefore, if a subject gets the order right, there is only a 1 in 20, or 5 percent, likelihood that the subject did it just by luck.

The Null Hypothesis

According to Fisher (1925/1991, p. 16), when we do an experiment we typically assume that any difference(s) between the experimental conditions are due only to chance; that is we establish a null hypothesis. In this case, *null* means "no difference." In the tea tasting experiment, the null hypothesis is that the order in which milk and tea are mixed makes no difference. Should the subject guess the sequence of cups correctly, then we may reject the null hypothesis, which "is never proved or established, but is possibly disproved, in the course of experimentation. Every experiment may be said to exist only in order to give the facts a chance of disproving the null hypothesis" (Fisher, 1925/1991, p. 16).

There has been much controversy surrounding the concept of the null hypothesis (Gigerenzer & Murray, 1987). However, over the years, many psychologists have tended to accept the notion that one can only reject, but not accept, the null hypothesis. One can only falsify the null hypothesis. By so doing, one does not confirm an alternative, *research hypothesis.* This point is worth re-emphasizing. If the data allow psychologists to reject the null hypothesis, then that does not mean that any particular alternative hypothesis is correct. It only means that the null hypothesis is apparently false. Thus, Fisher's concept of a null hypothesis is consistent with the logical positivists' emphasis on falsifiability. Psychological hypotheses can only be falsified, they cannot be proved. A hypothesis that is not falsified is provisionally retained, and subject to future testing.

From a statistical viewpoint, Fisher realized that the decision to reject the null hypothesis is not a completely straightforward matter. As we saw above, Fisher recommended that we tolerate a 5 percent chance of making the wrong decision. In the tea tasting example, a subject who guessed all six cups correctly would enable the investigator to reject the null hypothesis, because there would be only a 5 percent chance that the investigator was making a mistake. However, Fisher believed that doing the experiment only once is not as persuasive as *replicating the results.* If the subject could guess all six cups correctly over and over again, then that would be more persuasive than simply getting the order right once. However, the experimenter would

Box 10.1

The "Clever Hans" Phenomenon

The story of *Clever Hans* is one of the most famous in the history of psychology, and has played an important role in challenging psychologists' methodological practices (Suls & Rosnow,1988). Hans was a horse who could answer questions by tapping his hoof. For example, if asked the sum of 3 plus 2, the horse would tap 5 times. Hans could also answer questions of much greater complexity, and was a truly mysterious phenomenon in his day. By the use of careful observation and experimental procedure, a psychologist named *Oscar Pfungst* (1911) showed how Hans did it. For one thing, Pfungst discovered that the kind of spectators made a difference. If the spectators knew the right answer to the question Hans was asked, then Hans would also get the right answer. However, if the spectators did not know the right answer, then Hans did not know either. It turned out that Hans was picking up information from the spectators' behavior. They would make subtle head movements when Hans reached the right answer. Hans was apparently being influenced by the spectators' behavior, not arriving at answers on his own.

The importance of the "Clever Hans" phenomenon to psychological research was emphasized in a series of articles by *Robert Rosenthal* (1966, 1967), who pointed out that experimental subjects may play the role of "Clever Hans," picking up subtle cues from the experimenter that tell the subject what the experimenter expects the subject to do. The *experimenter* may unwittingly *bias* the outcome of the experiment. There may be subtle interactions between experimenter and subject such that each one influences the other's behavior in ways that may escape notice. By the 1960s experimental psychologists began to realize that elaborate precautions may be necessary to eliminate the Clever Hans phenomenon, such as double blind procedures which ensure that neither the experimenter nor the subject knows into what experimental condition the subject has been placed.

still need to be mindful of the kind of bias reviewed in Box 10.1.

Although Fisher realized that the *5 percent level of significance* was completely arbitrary, many psychologists adopted it as an article of faith. By the end of the 1950s, the achievement of "statistically significant" results was an established goal of psychological research, and to a large extent "the quality of research [was] measured by the level of significance" because of a belief that "the level of significance reflects the degree of confidence that the result is *repeatable* and that it specifies the *magnitude* of the effect. However both assertions are incorrect" (Gigerenzer & Murray, 1987, pp. 23–24). Statistical significance, as Fisher understood, is no substitute for repeatability. Gradually, criticisms of the reliance on significance testing began to appear (e.g., Bakan, 1966), but many psychologists continued to rely on the practice nonetheless (e.g., Rosnow & Rosenthal, 1989, p. 1277).

CORRELATIONAL METHODS

By no means all academic psychologists adopted experimental methods. Many psychologists made use of *correlational methods.* Although strictly speaking, correlational methods have the same underlying principles as do experimental designs (Cohen, 1968), they are a sufficiently different tradition so as to merit separate treatment (e.g., Cronbach, 1957/1978; Hilgard, 1987, chap. 20). In a typical correlational study, the investigator obtains a number of different measures on a set of subjects. Correlational methods are usually traced back to Galton. For example, in a study we referred to in Chapter 3, Galton obtained measures for several hundred English subjects in the nineteenth century (Johnson, MacClearn, Yuen, Nagoshi, Ahern, & Cole, 1985, p. 887). His measures included, among other things, social class, and physical measures such as height. For Galton's data, social class can be measured by different occupations, ranging from professional (e.g., physicians) to unskilled workers. There was a very close relationship between social class and the physical measures, with upper class subjects being larger, leading to hypotheses about the possible causes of such differences (e.g., better diet for upper class subjects).

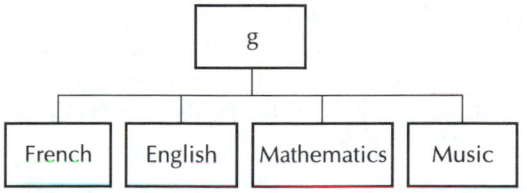

FIGURE 10.1 Spearman's two-factor theory of intelligence.

CHARLES SPEARMAN (1863–1945)

One of the central figures in the development of correlational methods was *Charles Spearman,* who did most of his work at the University of London. Together with *Cyril Burt,* he laid the groundwork for what became *factor analysis* (Lovie & Lovie, 1993). Factor analysis begins with a set of correlations between a number of measures, such as different mental tests. Factor analysis consists of statistical procedures for deriving a number of underlying factors to describe the structure of the set of correlation coefficients. As a result of his analysis of the pattern of correlations between different tests of mental abilities, Spearman (1904) proposed what came to be called a *two-factor theory of intelligence.* This theory held that

> *every individual measurement of every ability . . . can be divided into two independent parts. . . . The one part has been called the 'general factor' and denoted by the letter* g; *it is so named because, although varying freely from individual to individual, it remains the same for any one individual. . . . The second part has been called the 'specific factor' and denoted by the letter* s. *It not only varies from individual to individual, but even for any one individual from each ability to another. (Spearman, 1932/1970, p. 75)*

The two-factor theory is illustrated in Figure 10.1. As you can see, it is a hierarchical model, in which general intelligence, or *g,* underlies a set of specific abilities. In Figure 10.1, the specific factors are represented by the abilities to do well in different school subjects, such as French, English, mathematics, and music. Spearman found that these specific abilities were all correlated with each other, such that people who tend to do well in one specific ability tend to do well in the others, and vice versa. However, the intercorrelations between specific abilities are not perfect. Each specific ability was seen as determined in part by *g* and in part by circumstances specific to that ability. Thus, someone could have a high level of *g,* but varying specific abilities. Spearman was able to formulate a statistical criterion that enabled him to estimate the amount of *g* that contributed to each specific ability.

Spearman said that *g* represented the amount of *mental energy* available to an individual. This was a general, unspecific energy that could be directed toward the specific abilities. The specific abilities were regarded as engines that were driven by *g.* Spearman argued that the overall level of *g* was innately determined. After reviewing a wide range of sources, including the Army Alpha data we considered in Chapter 7, he concluded:

> *On the whole, there has been found a large body of evidence that races do differ from one another, at any rate in respect of* g. *And there have been some indications—as yet hardly decisive—that such differences persist even when the members of the respective races are living in the same environment, educational and otherwise; to this extent, then, the cause would appear fairly traceable to inheritance. Nevertheless such racial differences, even if truly existing, are indubitably very small as compared with those that exist between individuals belonging to one and the same race. (Spearman, 1932/1970, p. 380)*

Spearman exercised considerable influence on the way succeeding generations of psychologists have regarded intelligence. Many subsequent commentators argued that "when the term intelligence is used it should refer to *g,* the factor common to all tests of complex problem solving" (Jensen, 1972,

p. 77). When it came to estimating the effects of education on intelligence, Spearman concluded that heredity was more important than education in determining *g*, but that the specific factors could be shaped by schooling.

CYRIL BURT (1883–1971)

We noted above that *Cyril Burt* was Spearman's co-worker. Burt apparently invented some of the basic statistical techniques underlying factor analysis (Loehlin, 1992, p. 21), although his precise role is controversial (Lovie & Lovie, 1993), as are so many things about him. It was the use of factor analysis that allowed Spearman to claim that *g* was a general factor underlying all specific measures of intelligence. Although Burt believed in a somewhat more complex theory of intelligence than did Spearman, he nonetheless endorsed the hypothesis that *g* was the most important factor in intelligence.

Throughout its history, *g* has been a controversial concept. Burt believed that tests of *g* could be used to identify the educational setting for which the child was best suited. If *g* was believed to be inherited, such a practice would mean that schools would be stratified on the basis of inherited ability. An additional consequence of believing that *g* is inherited is that it would appear to be foolish to try to improve *g* by means of educational interventions, such as providing remedial programs for those whose test scores are low. Thus, there are serious social policy consequences of the belief that intelligence is inherited. Burt was clearly on the side of those who believed in streaming education so as to put those who tested high on intelligence tests in different streams than those who tested low on such tests.

Burt retired from his position at the University of London in 1950. However, after his retirement he continued to publish papers containing data purporting to demonstrate that *g* was largely inherited. His most provocative data came from studies of identical (monozygotic) twins reared apart. Such twins are genetically the same, and are traditionally a much sought-after source of information concerning the degree to which genes determine behavior (Loehlin, 1989). Burt reported that for monozygotic twins reared together, there is a very high correlation between intelligence test scores, and that this correlation is only slightly lower for monozygotic twins reared apart. "The correlations of identical twins with their elder or younger sibs usually averaged about .40–.50; the correlations between identical twins themselves often rose to .70 or over, even when they had been reared apart" (Burt, 1972, p. 179). Data like these reinforced the notion that changing the environment will produce relatively little change in intelligence, and that genetic determinants are the most important.

In a paper written on the occasion of receiving an award from the American Psychological Association, but published one year after his death, Burt (1972) reviewed his accomplishments over a career that had spanned the first six decades of this century. He repeated his argument that differences in *g* reflected differences in the potential of the individual's brain, and, as such, were similar to other biological capacities that were inherited. Burt (1972, p. 188) concluded that "each individual's innate capacity sets a fixed upper limit to what in actual practice he is likely to achieve," but qualified this conclusion by saying that "a given genetic endowment is compatible with a whole range of developmental reactions and consequently of acquired attainments. All a knowledge of a child's genetic endowment permits us to infer are the limits of the range."

The Burt Scandal

One of the key assumptions underlying research methods is that they will be practiced honestly. The consumer of the research literature should be able to assume that the data were not only gathered in a competent way, but that the data are being honestly reported. Intentional falsification of the data strikes at the heart of the scientific enterprise. It is precisely such fraud that Burt has been accused of perpetrating, in one of the most consuming scandals of twentieth century psychology. The following account of the history of the Burt scandal draws heavily on the scholarship of *Franz Samelson* (1992, 1993).

Precisely when Burt's reputation began to unravel is a matter of debate, but an important event was *Leon Kamin's* claim (1974) that Burt's published data were not credible. Kamin began reviewing Burt's work in 1972 (Kamin, 1977), and discovered, as did others, that "a correlation would have the same value in different articles, but the number of cases would differ" (Green, 1992, p. 328). Incidents like this suggested that the data might have been invented. The possibility that Burt may have been less than honest was made more credible when a British journalist, *Oliver Gillie,* was unable to verify that several people whom Burt had listed as having gathered data for him either never existed or never gathered such data. Gillie (1977) called for the establishment of a committee of the British Psychological Society "to consider the problem of how better to facilitate the exposure of fraud in science and how to maintain the highest standards of scientific work and teaching" (p. 257). Shortly thereafter the final nail in Burt's coffin appeared to have been driven by *Leslie Hearnshaw* (1979), whose biography of Burt charged that he had published fraudulent results favorable to his case under a pseudonym, and had published work with a co-author who apparently did not exist. Moreover, Hearnshaw alleged that Burt had painted a false picture of his role in the invention of factor analysis by aggrandizing his contribution, and denigrating Spearman's. At that point, the evidence against Burt seemed to many to be conclusive. The prevailing attitude was exemplified by a statement published in the British Psychological Society's *Bulletin* (1980), flatly stating that "Burt was guilty of deception," including "falsification of the early history of factor analysis" and "production of spurious data on monozygotic twins" (p. 71).

The Burt case was, however, not yet closed. Other investigators, such as *Robert B. Joynson* (1989) and *Ronald Fletcher* (1991), argued that the charges against Burt were exaggerated in some cases and not proven in others. For example, many other psychologists have portrayed themselves in a more favorable light than the facts may have warranted (Green, 1992, p. 329), and psychologists are not alone in this failing. Publishing under a pseudonym is also something that many other psychologists and nonpsychologists have done. There remained some uncertainty about whether or not Burt's co-author actually existed, but many commentators eventually came to believe, with Green (1992, p. 331), that "the charge of deliberately falsifying data can neither be established nor disproved with certitude."

In the end, the question of whether or not Burt's data were falsified has little bearing on the question of whether or not *g* is inherited. To a large extent those who believed that *g* was inherited before the scandal, such as *Arthur Jensen* (1972), continued to believe it afterward, arguing that Burt's data could be discarded and there would still be ample other findings that made the same case. Other psychologists, such as the great American factor analyst *Raymond B. Cattell* (1978), lamented the whole affair because it would "take psychology as a science some time to live down. . . . Journalism has often treated psychology as the comic science" (p. 19).

From the perspective of the history of psychology, the Burt affair is important because of the lessons it has to teach us about what happens when someone's reputation is called into question. One such lesson is that such controversies are often conducted in a very emotional atmosphere, and are not always resolved by discovering the "true facts." Rather, the disputants take definite points of view, and point to facts that they believe are consistent with their point of view (Wisdom, 1957, p. 155). Once a point of view on a controversial issue has been publicly taken, it is difficult for the combatants to back down. Moreover, as Audley (1980) and Samelson (1992, 1993) have observed, arriving at a judgment about a person's reputation is a quasi-judicial process which invokes a host of legalistic concepts, including the right of the accused to be judged innocent until proven guilty beyond a reasonable doubt. Each participant's judgment is inevitably driven by social factors, such as whether or not one was acquainted with the accused. Presumably those who actually knew or worked with Burt would be more likely to defend him than those who never knew him, or who held different beliefs. Such social factors can be very important not only in cases such as Burt's, but also in determining whether or not any viewpoint in psychology will be accepted or rejected. We will return to issues of this kind in Chapter 15 when we discuss the future of psychology.

LOUIS LEON THURSTONE (1887–1955)

Factor analytic techniques were developed in the United States by *L. L. Thurstone* (1938), of the University of Chicago. Thurstone's approach differed markedly from that of Spearman and Burt, in that he wanted to uncover a set of mental abilities that were relatively independent of each other, rather than to measure *g*. He searched for tests that would measure a particular mental ability, but that would be unrelated to other mental abilities. The result of his efforts was a set of six *primary mental abilities:* Verbal (e.g., vocabulary), Number (e.g., arithmetic), Spatial (e.g., identifying a design), Word fluency (e.g., thinking of words of a particular type), Memory (e.g., remembering a series of digits), and Reasoning (e.g., following a rule) (Cronbach, 1960, pp. 256–257).

Thurstone's approach de-emphasized the importance of *g*. Rather than treating *g* as the most important form of intelligence, Thurstone regarded his list of six abilities as more useful than *g*. In understanding an individual's mental abilities it was more important to examine his or her *profile* of abilities than to try to summarize the individual's intelligence in a single number.

> *Mental profiles have been determined for over half a million high school children in Chicago and it has been found that all possible combinations occur in the profiles. The records show many hundreds of interesting case histories. A boy who was a poor reader was considered a dunce by his teachers. His mental profile showed that he had the highest score on Space and Reasoning, and high scores in all other factors except the verbal factor V. His teachers changed their attitudes when they saw that his handicap was quite specific. . . . It requires often considerable insight of the examiner to relate the mental profile to the circumstances of each case, but there is no question but that the profile is more helpful than the IQ in the interpretation of educational and behavior problems. (Thurstone, 1948/1965, p. 64)*

Thurstone (1934/1978, 1944), along with other factor analysts, did not employ the ability profile technique only on tests of mental abilities. In principle, factor analytic procedures can be applied to any set of correlations between different measures. Thus, factor analysis was seen as able to address "the old problem of classifying the temperaments and personality types" (Thurstone, 1934/1978, p. 285). One approach to this problem was to make lists of "the many hundreds of adjectives that are in current use for describing personalities and temperaments" (p. 289). An example of such a list is shown in Table 10.1. Subjects were asked to think of "a person they knew well, and underline every adjective that s/he might use in a conversational description of that person" (p. 293). Averaged over many subjects, such data give some idea of the degree to which different words are used together. Factor analysis showed that five factors apparently explained the structure of these correlations. Thus, for example, *friendly* and *congenial* go together, as do *patient* and *calm, persevering* and *hard-working, self-reliant* and *courageous,* and *self-important* and *sarcastic.* The five factors may be taken as representing the underlying structure of the way our understanding of other people is organized. Factor analytic studies such as Thurstone's have generated a remarkable amount of research that continues to this day (e.g., McCrae, Costa, & Piedmont, 1993).

"THE TWO DISCIPLINES OF SCIENTIFIC PSYCHOLOGY"

Lee J. Cronbach (1957/1978), in his Presidential address to The American Psychological Association, reviewed the development of research methods in psychology through mid-century. He saw psychology not as a unified discipline, but as consisting of two distinct methodological ap-

TABLE 10.1 List of Adjectives Used in Thurstone's Study

persevering	impetuous	suspicious	tactful
crafty	fickle	courageous	careless
awkward	domineering	stern	tidy
self-important	frank	headstrong	precise
determined	pessimistic	jealous	systematic
friendly	spiteful	generous	cheerful
patient	quiet	dependable	conscientious
sarcastic	disagreeable	faithful	grasping
congenial	reserved	reserved	satisfied
hard-working	refined	solemn	cynical
stubborn	unnatural	earnest	courteous
capable	bashful	talented	unconventional
tolerant	self-reliant	frivolous	quick-tempered
calm	broad-minded	eccentric	
peevish	haughty	ingenious	
religious	submissive	accommodating	

Source: L. L. Thurstone (1934). The vectors of mind. *Psychological Review, 41,* 13.

proaches. He called them *experimental psychology* and *correlational psychology.* Cronbach traced this division back to Wundt's distinction between experimental psychology and cultural psychology, with the former adopting laboratory methods and the latter examining correlations as they exist in the "real world." As this distinction evolved, it came to be represented by one science that attempted to "discover the general laws of mind or behavior," and another science "concerned with individual minds" (Cronbach, 1957/1978, p. 440). As we have already seen, experimental psychology came to rely on the analysis of experimental data using statistical approaches advocated by Fisher. Correlational psychology devised measures of individual differences, such as tests of intelligence, that could be administered in applied settings, such as schools, and then analyzed using techniques such as factor analysis.

In order to represent the methodological distinctions present in psychology around mid-century, Cronbach presented a model of the distinctions that separate psychologists. The model is shown in Figure 10.2 on page 206, based on data originally gathered by Thorndike (1954) of psychologists' assessments of those psychologists who have made the greatest contributions. Cronbach's factor analysis of Thorndike's data revealed two factors. The most important factor in the present context is the vertical one, *laboratory data* versus *field data.* As you can see from the diagram, laboratory experiments are the most characteristic of the former, while the study of individual differences (differential studies) are most characteristic of the latter. The wide separation of these two in terms of this factor demonstrates how differently psychologists regarded workers in these two areas. The second factor in Cronbach's model is *quantitative* versus *verbal,* which distinguishes most clearly between those psychologists who rely on numbers (e.g., statistical methods) as opposed to those whose medium is language, such as psychologists who write about theories. Other groups of psychologists, such as those who employ group tests of individual differences, are not so much pure instances of one or another factor, as they are blends of both. Ideally, one could locate the preferences of any psychologist within this two-dimensional space. Where do you see yourself belonging?

Cronbach (1957/1978, p. 439) pointed out that these methodological preferences of psychologists had resulted in stable groups consisting of "person-

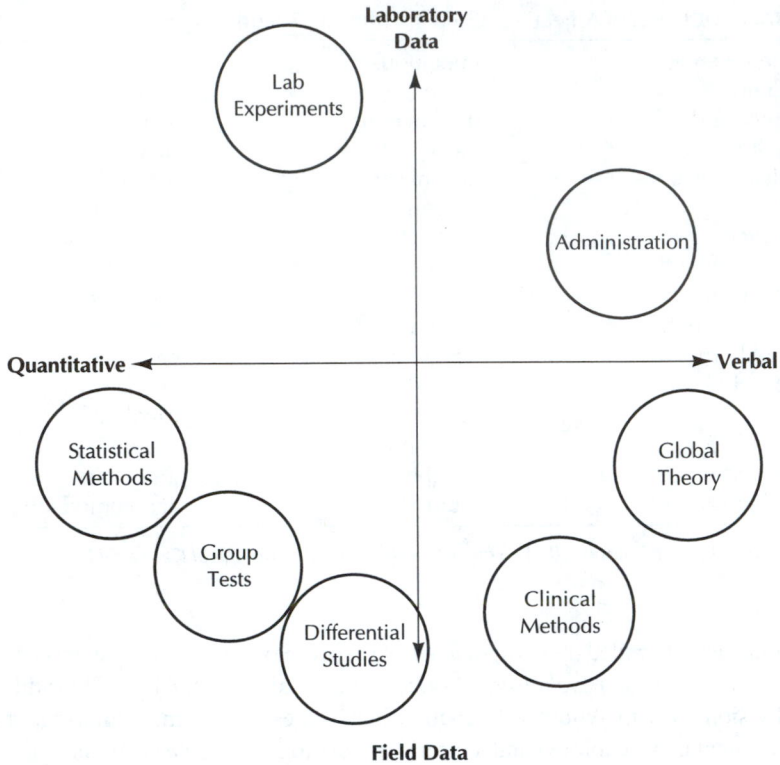

FIGURE 10.2 Factors accounting for the esteem of leaders in psychology by American psychologists.
Source: L. J. Cronbach (1957). The two disciplines of scientific psychology. *American Psychologist, 12,* 672.

ality, social, and child psychologists" on the one hand and "perception and learning psychologists" on the other. Moreover, each group tended to take a dim view of the activities of the members of the other group. "Individual differences have been an annoyance rather than a challenge to the experimenter. His goal is to control behavior . . . [and] individual variation is cast into that outer darkness known as 'error variance'. . . . The correlational psychologist is in love with just those variables the experimenter left home to forget" (Cronbach, 1957/1978, p. 441).

The experimenter is concerned with the effects of particular experimental treatments on behavior. To the extent that all subjects do not respond in the same way to the treatments, the experimenter may feel that he or she has not got proper control over all the relevant variables. However, the correlational psychologist is interested precisely in understanding the fact that all subjects do not respond in the same way to the same treatment. This is particularly clear in applied psychology. "The job of applied psychology is to improve decisions about people. The greatest social benefit will come from applied psychology if we can find for each individual the treatment to which he can most easily adapt. This calls for the joint application of experimental and correlational methods" (Cronbach, 1957/1978, p. 449).

The idea that individuals with different aptitudes may respond differently to different treatments came to be called *aptitude treatment interaction.* In order to investigate such interactions, Cronbach proposed the model shown in Figure 10.3. In this model, the treatments used by experimenters can be of two types: control of past situations that the organism has experienced, and control of the present situation in which the organism is placed. Psychometric information refers to measures of individual differences that enable the

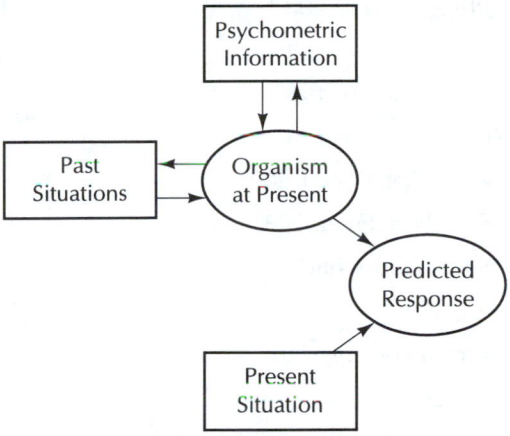

FIGURE 10.3 Theoretical network to be developed by a unified discipline.

Source: L. J. Cronbach (1957). The two disciplines of scientific psychology. *American Psychologist, 12,* 685.

investigator to make much more refined predictions about the responses an organism will make to past and present treatments. Notice the arrows leading both to and from "Past situations" and "Psychometric information." This represents the fact that the effect of past situations and/or variables being measured by psychometric information depends on the current state of the organism, and vice versa.

Cronbach's call for a unified discipline was only partially successful, and in succeeding chapters we will see some psychologists championing one side of the discipline or the other. When Cronbach wrote his paper, psychology consisted of "two solitudes" (a phrase used in another context by MacLennan, 1945), and to some extent it still does. In the next chapter we will examine the history of learning theorists whose exemplification of the experimental approach was extraordinarily influential, and who Cronbach argued had been too narrow. Then in Chapters 12 and 13 we will turn to the history of developmental and humanistic psychology, each of which has tended to involve the study of the individual case.

Additional Reading on This Topic. More information about the history of research methods and their relation to current practice may be found in Benjafield (1994). A very good history of the role of statistical reasoning in modern life is Gigerenzer, Swijtink, Porter, Daston, Beatty, and Kruger (1989).

KEY NAMES AND CONCEPTS

What follows is an index of some of the most important material in this chapter. The list includes individuals, concepts, and topics you should know. Read through the list, and if anything on it seems unfamiliar, then go back and re-read the appropriate section of the chapter. You should be able to define each concept, briefly discuss each topic, and state the importance of each person on the list. In addition, you should be able to write an account of the work done by each person or topic printed in boldface.

Box 10.1—The "Clever Hans" phenomenon, 200
Bridgman, Percy
operationism, 197
Burt, Cyril, 202
Carnap, Rudolf, 196
dispositional concepts, 196
protocol sentences, 196
surplus meaning, 196
Cattell, Raymond B., 203
Clever Hans, 200
Correlational methods, 200
Cronbach, Lee J., 204
aptitude treatment interaction, 206
the two disciplines of psychology, 205

Danziger, Kurt
investigative practices, 195
factor analysis, 201
Fisher, Ronald A., 198
5 percent level of significance, 200
null hypothesis, 199
replication, 200
Fletcher, Ronald, 203
Gillie, Oliver, 203
Hearnshaw, Leslie, 203
Jensen, Arthur, 203
Joynson, Robert B., 203
Kamin, Leon, 203
Koch, Sigmund, 198
logical positivism, 195
neobehaviorists, 197
operational definitions, 197
Pfungst, Oscar, 200
Popper, Karl
falsifiability, 196
research hypothesis, 199
Rosenthal, Robert, 200
Samelson, Franz, 203
Spearman, Charles, 201
g, 201
mental energy, 201
s, 201
two-factor theory, 201
Thurstone, Louis Leon, 204
primary mental abilities, 204
verbal reports, 196
verification principle, 196
Vienna Circle, 195

CHAPTER 11

THEORIES OF LEARNING

ERNEST R. HILGARD (1904–)
EDWIN R. GUTHRIE (1886–1959)
Contiguity
Repetition
Reward
One-Trial Learning
CLARK L. HULL (1884–1952)
The Formal Structure of Hullian Theory
The Hypothetico-Deductive Method
Postulates
Kenneth W. Spence (1907–1967)
Charles E. Osgood (1916–1991)
The Semantic Differential
EDWARD C. TOLMAN (1886–1959)
Purposive Behavior
Cognitive Maps
The Place versus Response Controversy
THE VERBAL LEARNING TRADITION
Functionalism and Verbal Learning
Acquisition
Serial Learning
The Fate of Verbal Learning
DONALD O. HEBB (1904–1985)
The Emergence of Neuroscience
The Organization of Behavior
Motivation
Experiments in Sensory Deprivation
ALBERT BANDURA (1925–)
Social Learning Theory
Behavior Modification
Reciprocal Determinism

ERNEST R. HILGARD (1904–)

Hilgard has been a very important researcher in a number of areas in psychology, as well as a prolific textbook writer. Textbook writers can be extremely important to a pluralistic discipline such as psychology because they articulate for both students and teachers the different strands that make up an emerging discipline, and point the way toward future developments. Of all the psychology textbook writers, E. R. Hilgard is arguably the most important. Not only did Hilgard write an introductory text (Hilgard, 1953) that was rated in the 1970s as "the most successful academic textbook in sales" (Laberge, 1994, p. 184), as well as a history of American psychology (Hilgard, 1987) that "served as both a chronicle of our discipline and a graduate-level introductory textbook" (Kihlstrom, 1994, p. 179), but he also wrote a series of textbooks on learning that "substantially organize[d] and structured an entire research discipline for generations to come" (Bower, 1994, p. 181). It is Hilgard's books *Conditioning and Learning* (Hilgard & Marquis, 1948; Kimble, 1961) as well as the successive editions of his review of *Theories of Learning* (Hilgard, 1948, 1956; Hilgard & Bower, 1966, 1975; Bower & Hilgard, 1981) that defined the era—sometimes called the Age of Learning Theories—that we consider in this chapter. The last three editions of *Theories of Learning* were written with *Gordon H. Bower,* who has become a renowned theorist in his own right.

Hilgard's *Theories of Learning* "became the defining survey textbook for hundreds of teachers who organized their lectures around it. It also

TABLE 11.1 Topics of the Various Editions of *Theories of Learning*

FIRST (1948)	SECOND (1956)	THIRD (1966)	FOURTH (1975)	FIFTH (1981)
Thorndike	Thorndike	Thorndike	Thorndike	Thorndike
Guthrie	Guthrie	Guthrie	Guthrie	Guthrie
Hull	Hull	Hull	Hull	Hull
Tolman	Tolman	Tolman	Tolman	Tolman
Skinner	Skinner	Skinner	Skinner	Skinner
Gestalt	Gestalt	Gestalt	Gestalt	Gestalt
Functionalism	Functionalism	Functionalism	Functionalism	Functionalism
Lewin	Lewin			
Wheeler's organismic theory/Field theories				
	Freud	Freud	Freud	
	Mathematical models	Mathematical learning theory	Mathematical learning theory	Mathematical learning theory (Estes)
		Pavlov	Pavlov	Pavlov
		Information processing models	Information processing theories	Information processing theories
		Neurophysiology of learning	Neurophysiology of learning	Neurophysiology of learning
		Learning and instructional technology	Theory of instruction	Applications to education
			Piaget	

served as a prototype for later survey textbooks and courses in social, personality, and developmental psychology" (Bower, 1994, p. 181). When Hilgard wrote the first edition of *Theories of Learning* in 1948, he included those theorists listed in the first column of Table 11.1. In that list are several approaches that we have already considered, such as Thorndike, Skinner, Gestalt psychology, and functionalism. While we do not consider Thorndike, Skinner and Gestalt further, we elaborate on functionalist as well as other approaches to learning in this chapter, because there are important details about them that we need to understand. However, we spend much of our time dealing with those approaches that recur in all of the editions of *Theories of Learning,* and that may thus be thought of as being of particular historical significance. These core theories include the work of Guthrie, Hull, and Tolman.

Before beginning our discussion of Guthrie, Hull and Tolman, we should explore a bit further the structure of the topics in Table 11.1. The following points are particularly notable:

- Kurt Lewin as well as organismic/field theories are the only topics in the first edition of *Theories of Learning* to subsequently be dropped. To some extent, this material was incorporated into other chapters in subsequent editions, but much of it simply disappeared because it was seen as no longer relevant to the learning theories of the day (Hilgard, 1956, p. v; Hilgard & Bower, 1966, p. v).

• Freud made his appearance in the second edition, because he "so influenced psychological thinking that a summary of theoretical viewpoints, even in a specialized field such as the psychology of learning, is incomplete without reference to him" (Hilgard, 1956, p. 290). Hilgard is known as a "generous skeptic" in relation to psychoanalysis, "one who holds the discipline of psychoanalysis to the canons of scientific methods, but who preserves a respectful interest in the mysterious and the unknown" (Holzman, 1994, p. 191).

• Pavlov does not have a chapter devoted to him until the third edition. His inclusion there is due to "a resurgence of interest in his views, particularly as represented in current developments from the USSR, with recognition given to the significance in human learning of the 'second signaling system' (language)" (Hilgard & Bower, 1966, p. v). It is indeed true that the 1960s saw a resurgence of interest in Soviet psychology as well as in topics such as language, and we will explore the emergence of the psychology of language in Chapter 14.

• In the second edition, mathematical approaches to the construction of learning theories are introduced, and coverage of them continues in subsequent editions. By the fifth edition the major practitioner of mathematical learning theory, *William K. Estes* (1919–), has a chapter of his own.

• Topics such as information processing and neurophysiological theories as well as applications to education are introduced in the third edition and continue to grow thereafter. We review one major contributor to the neurophysiological approach, *Donald O. Hebb* (1904–1985), in this chapter. Information processing theories are considered in Chapter 14 on cognitive psychology.

• Jean Piaget (1896–1980) figures in the fourth edition because his theory "provides, as does Freud, a larger context in which to view the acquisition of knowledge and competence as a consequence of growth and interaction with the physical and social environment" (Hilgard & Bower, 1975, p. 318). Although Piaget's theory had been around for decades it was not really until the 1960s that it began to take hold in the United States. We consider Piaget's theory in detail in Chapter 12 on developmental psychology. Both Freud and Piaget were dropped from the fifth edition, "regrettably . . . because a survey of teachers using the text indicated that those chapters were not being used in the typical course in learning theory" (Bower & Hilgard, 1981, p. vi).

EDWIN R. GUTHRIE (1886–1959)

Guthrie (1959, p. 161) was trained in logic and the philosophy of science, an experience which led him to conclude that "the laws of logic are conventions and not laws of thought." This conclusion made him "impatient with the notion that there can be any completely rigorous deduction, or ultimate validity in an argument. This skepticism colors my notions of the nature of scientific facts and scientific theory." As a result, Guthrie's theory of learning is presented in a relatively informal way. Moreover, early in his career Guthrie's "chief interest lay in undergraduate teaching, a fact that probably accounts for a strong bent toward simplification which, with some justification, has been described as oversimplification" (p. 161). The result is a straightforward theory of learning that has one principle at its core, that of *contiguity*.

Contiguity

Guthrie (1930/1961) wondered if there was "a single formula which can be made to include all or most of the established generalizations concerning the nature of learning? If there is such a formula it will in all probability be some form of the ancient principle of association by contiguity in time, which has been a part of all theories of memory and learning since before Aristotle, and has retained its essential character in spite of a variety of names, such as 'conditioning,' [and] 'associative memory'" (pp. 19–20). Guthrie (1952/1960) then goes on to state this principle as follows: "A combination of stimuli which has accompanied a movement will on its recurrence tend to be followed by that movement" (p. 23). Notice that Guthrie's basic principle proposes that "combinations of stimuli," rather than stimuli singly, act on the organism to produce movements. Many stimulus patterns may have the potential to produce movement, but only some of them are actually effective. The latter are termed *cues* or *signals.*

Guthrie observes that movements are different from acts, a point that goes back to Aristotle, and that we considered in Chapter 1.

> *Playing a tune on the piano is an act. The act is accomplished by movements but it can be accomplished by a wide variety of movements. The naming of the act does not specify the movements. An armless man can learn to play skillfully with his feet. On different occasions a tune can be given a radically different fingering by a player using his hands . . . The difference between act and movement is of vital importance in learning theory because our accepted notion of the mechanism of response is that nerve impulses actuate muscular contraction, and if association or conditioning is to be related to changes in the nervous system it is specific movement patterns which must be dealt with (Guthrie, 1952/1960, pp. 27–28).*

Repetition

By saying that conditioning involves the formation of associations between stimulus patterns and movements, Guthrie places his account of learning well within the traditional associationist principles stretching from Aristotle to Pavlov. However, Guthrie did not agree with the traditional associationist view of the effect of repetition on learning. The typical view is that repetition acts to strengthen the connection between stimulus and response. Guthrie argued instead that repetition provides the opportunity for additional stimuli to become associated with a response. "The habit of smoking is in reality made up of thousands of habits. The sight of tobacco, the smell of it, the mention of it, finishing a meal, finishing an office task, looking at the clock, and innumerable other situations have all become signals for smoking" (Guthrie, 1952/1960, pp. 27–28). Once a habit has been associated with a large number of different stimuli, it is, of course, that much harder to change it.

Reward

Guthrie proposed a unique way of explaining the effect that rewards or reinforcements have on behavior. He does not question the fact that rewards influence behavior, but does not agree with the notion that reinforcement acts to strengthen the connection between stimulus and response. Rather, reward acts to prevent the animal from unlearning the association formed just prior to the reward. For example, in the sequence signal → response → reward, the reward terminates the signal, and allows it to be the only signal connected to the response. Consider Thorndike's puzzle box here (see Chapter 7). The behavior that allows the cat to escape is the last response to be performed before reward. The response does not have the opportunity to become connected to some other signal. "When a signal has been followed by a response that prevents the signal from recurring, there is no opportunity . . . for the attachment of that signal to other responses. If an association is established, it is secure . . . until the [signal] is again present and a different [response] is introduced. The association is protected from unlearning. . . . This makes specific the nature of a reward or reinforcement. Both are defined in terms of straight association by contiguity. They protect learning that has occurred by making unlearning impossible" (Guthrie, 1959, p. 171).

One-Trial Learning

Bower and Hilgard (1981, p. 87) observed that "it was part of the charm of Guthrie's writing that it was closely in touch with everyday life and provided amusing but cogent suggestions for meeting the problems of animal training, child rearing, and pedagogy." In particular, Guthrie proposed ingenious methods for *breaking undesirable habits.* Guthrie's basic approach (1952/1960) was characteristically simple: "The simplest rule for breaking a habit is to find the cues that initiate the action and

BOX 11.1

Changing Undesirable Habits

Here is another example of the practical nature of Guthrie's style of thinking. It is adapted from Guthrie (1952/1960, p. 18), and was also discussed by Bower and Hilgard (1981, pp. 87–88). Imagine a school-age child who has developed the following sequence of habits. Whenever the child comes through the door and enters the house, she throws her coat on the floor and then goes downstairs and watches television. The parent of this child tries everything to get the child to hang her coat up before she does anything else. Thus, the parent makes the child come back upstairs and hang the coat up before she can continue watching television. However, this fails to change the coat-throwing habit. The parent threatens additional punishments, or even rewards such as a favorite food if only the child will hang her coat up before she watches television. Nothing works. From a Guthrian viewpoint, trying to solve this or other problems through rewards and punishments is wrongheaded. What is needed is a careful analysis of the cues that are leading to the undesirable behavior. In fact, we can represent the undesirable sequence of cues and responses as follows.

Enter the house → Throw coat on floor → Go downstairs

The problem is to make another response—"Hang coat up"—the first response after "Enter the house." This can be achieved, Guthrie says, by having the child come back upstairs, put her coat back on, go outside the house, come back in the house, and hang up her coat. This means that hanging up her coat is now the first response made on entering. Notice how Guthrie's proposal, like his other advice, is based on a meticulous attention to the details of the cues and responses in the problem situation.

to practice another response to these cues" (p. 115). Crafts, Schneirla, Robinson, and Gilbert (1950, p. 320) provided examples consistent with Guthrie's principles, such as the old advertising slogan, "Reach for a Lucky instead of a sweet." This slogan appeared at a time when eating candy was a more undesirable habit than smoking, and now the advice might be "Reach for a carrot stick instead of a smoke." In either case, the principle remains the same: a different response must be connected to the same cues. Another practical example is given in Box 11.1.

Additional Reading on This Topic. A good summary of Guthrie's approach may be found in his book, *The Psychology of Human Conflict* (1938).

CLARK L. HULL (1884–1952)

Like so many other psychologists, Hull entered the discipline as a consequence of reading William James, and received his Ph.D. from the University of Wisconsin in 1918. After working in a variety of areas in psychology, Hull's characteristic approach began to crystallize in 1929 when he began working at the Institute of Human Relations at Yale University. By then, Hull had become a proponent of the principles of conditioning, and opposed to the Gestalt approach (Mills, 1988). However, he realized that conditioning could only be the mechanism responsible for the process of learning. In addition, a learning theory needed to provide an understanding of the organism's motives if it was to be credible. The process of conditioning provided an explanation of the way in which learning occurred, while the process of motivation allowed us to understand why learning occurred when it did.

Hull's motivational theory was based on the concept of *drive*. He defined "any persistent and intense stimulus, external or internal, as a drive, that is, a motivation" (Shakow & Rapaport, 1964). The way the drive concept worked in Hull's system will be explored in detail below, but many observers have remarked on the similarity between Hull's drive concept and basic psychoanalytic hypotheses about motivation (e.g., Toman, 1960). However, it is of historical interest to note that while he was developing his theory between 1936 and 1942, Hull held a series of seminars concerned with integrating his behaviorist approach to learning with *Freudian psychoanalytic theory.* Hull was critical of psychoanalytic theory for not being sufficiently rigorous, but encouraged the attempt to "formulate for ourselves various sharply defined alternative hypotheses which are consistent with current psychoanalytic views" (Shakow & Rapaport, 1964, p. 139). Among the members of these seminars were *John Dollard* and *Neal Miller,* who later wrote *Personality and Psychotherapy* (1950), a book that attempted to provide an integration of learning theory and psychoanalysis.

The Formal Structure of Hullian Theory

It is difficult to imagine a more stark contrast than that between Guthrie's and Hull's theories of learning. Whereas Guthrie's approach was almost folksy with its use of simple, practical ideas, Hull's theory of learning (1943; 1952) was abstract and technical. Whereas the relation between theory and data in Guthrie's approach was largely informal, the relation between theory and data in Hull's approach was intended to be quite precise. Hull tried to mimic what he took to be the form of theory construction and testing that had been successful in other sciences. Thus, Hullian theory illustrates very well the kind of procedures recommended by logical positivists, which we considered in Chapter 10 (Bergman & Spence, 1941; Spence, 1944).

The Hypothetico-Deductive Method

Hull attempted to create a mathematical theory from which could be deduced the facts of learning. The theory consisted of *postulates* that are intended to describe the basic laws of behavior. The postulates contain descriptions of *intervening variables.* These variables represent hypothetical processes that go on inside the organism and that are supposed to govern behavior. From the postulates, one can deduce *theorems,* which are experimentally testable hypotheses about behavior. This may all sound obscure, but the way it worked in practice was straightforward. If experimental data are consistent with the theorem, then the postulates are retained unchanged. However, if a theorem is falsified, then the postulates must be changed. New theorems can be derived and tested from the new set of postulates. This process goes on and on, with the postulates being improved as a result of experimentation. Of course, the postulates must also be consistent with one another. This procedure is called the *hypothetico-deductive method,* because the theorems that are *deduced* from the postulates are *hypotheses* that can be tested experimentally.

Postulates

Hull believed that organisms were born with unlearned stimulus-response connections, much like Pavlov's unconditioned connections. The unlearned connections are able to satisfy some of the organism's needs, but must be supplemented by learned connections. New connections are formed as a result of reinforcement. Hull's theory of reinforcement was an elaboration of Thorndike's law of effect. A *primary reinforcer* is any stimulus that results in a reduction in drive. For example, food reduces hunger, and is thus a primary reinforcer. A *secondary reinforcer* is a stimulus that initially has no reinforcing properties, but acquires them through association with a reinforcing stimulus. Money is an example of a secondary reinforcer. By itself it is only a piece of paper or metal that causes no reduction in drive. However, because money allows us to acquire primary reinforcers, such as food, it becomes a reinforcing stimulus itself.

In order to see how the concepts in Hull's theory were related to each other, we first need to list the major intervening variables in the theory.

- *Drive* (D). This is the major motivational concept in Hull's theory. Drive tends to increase as a function of the amount of time that has elapsed since the last reinforcement. Hunger is the paradigmatic example. After being fed, the level of drive drops. The level of drive then increases until the animal is fed again. Of course, drive does not continue to increase forever. After a certain period, if the animal has not been fed then drive tends to drop off. For example, if an animal is starved for a long period, it will begin to wither away.

- *Habit strength* ($_SH_R$). The definition of habit strength illustrates very nicely the attempt at precision in Hull's system. Habits are learned connections between stimuli and responses. In line with the law of effect, habits are formed as a result of reinforcement. However, Hull did not leave it at that, but formulated a precise mathematical definition of habit strength as a function of the number of reinforcements. This definition may be stated in the form of an equation (Hull, 1952, p. 8):

$$_SH_R = 1 - 10^{-aN}$$

This equation should be read as follows: "habit strength ($_SH_R$) is equal to 1 minus 10 to the minus *aN*, where *N* is the number of times a response to a stimulus has been reinforced, and *a* has a constant value of about .03." So defined, habit strength varies between zero and 1. Other intervening variables in Hull's system were given precise definitions like this, but they will not be presented here. The mathematical definition of habit strength is enough to give you the general idea of the ambitious nature of Hull's theory.

- *Stimulus-intensity dynamism* (V). This intervening variable refers to the amount of energy possessed by a stimulus that impinges on the organism.

- *Incentive motivation* (K). Incentive motivation is defined in terms of the amount of reward (such as food or money) that follows a response.

The foregoing intervening variables combine to yield *reaction potential* ($_SE_R$), which is the amount of energy available for a response. The way in which these variables combine is defined precisely. They are assumed to multiply together to give reaction potential, as follows:

$$_SE_R = {}_SH_R \times D \times V \times K$$

While variables such as D, V, K and $_SH_R$ act so as to energize the organism, there are other variables that inhibit responding. These variables are listed below.

- *Reactive inhibition* (I_R). Everyone is familiar with the fact that as we behave we become fatigued. The more the organism responds, the more fatigued it will get, and the greater will reactive inhibition be. Reactive inhibition acts as a negative drive that is reduced by not responding.

- *Conditioned inhibition* ($_SI_R$). By resting, or doing nothing, the organism reduces reactive inhibition. The reduction in reactive inhibition, or fatigue, is reinforcing. Doing nothing is rewarding. The organism develops a negative habit, or conditioned inhibition, that tends to make it less likely to respond.

These last two intervening variables combine with the first set to yield a more complete equation for reaction potential. This equation may be stated as follows (Logan, 1959, p. 323):

$$_SE_R = {}_SH_R \times D \times V \times K - {}_SI_R - I_R$$

There are other intervening variables that make the equation even more complicated, but this version of it is sufficient for our purposes. The first four intervening variables on the right-hand side of the equation ($_SH_R \times D \times V \times K$) contribute to the vigor with which the organism responds, while the last two intervening variables ($_SI_R - I_R$) detract from the vigor with which the animal responds. The first four intervening variables may be thought of as excitatory, while the last two are inhibitory.

One may wonder whether or not equations like Hull's could actually be used to make very precise predictions about behavior. In fact, only relatively crude predictions were made in practice. Some of these predictions were actually quite interesting. For example, imagine a situation in which the organism has a well-developed habit and is in a heightened drive state. Surely this means that the organism will respond no matter what the values of the other variables. Not so. Notice that the value of reaction potential ($_SE_R$) cannot be positive if any one of the first four variables is zero. Thus if incentive is zero, the animal will not respond no matter what the value of the other variables. Intuitively, this makes sense. Thinking of it in anthropomorphic terms, no matter how hungry you were, you would be unlikely to work for someone else if you were not going to get paid for it. We will explore this example further when we contrast Hull's theory with that of Tolman.

Kenneth W. Spence (1907–1967)

Spence (1956, 1960) worked so closely with Hull on the development of the learning theory that it was sometimes called the Hull-Spence approach. One of his earliest and most significant contributions to the Hullian way of thinking was his attempt to explain Kohler's transposition experiments (Spence, 1937). You should recall from Chapter 9 on Gestalt psychology that Kohler (1918/1967) did experiments that appeared to show that animals learned *relationships between* stimuli, and did not learn responses *to* particular stimuli. These experiments involved training animals to respond to one of two stimuli in a series. Thus, an animal might be rewarded for responding to the larger of two stimuli. Subsequently, the animal was presented with another choice between two stimuli, one of which was the stimulus for which it had been rewarded, and the other a stimulus that was still larger than the first. The animal responded to the new stimulus even though it had never been rewarded for doing so, and ignored the stimulus for which it had previously been rewarded.

Spence realized that Kohler's Gestalt explanation of transposition was a threat to an associationist form of explanation such as Hull's. If you examine Figure 11.1, you can begin to appreciate Spence's simple yet powerful alternative to Kohler's explanation. As we noted earlier, in Hullian theory an animal's tendency to respond to a stimulus is the outcome of two opposing tendencies, one excitatory and one inhibitory. Figure 11.1 represents an experiment in which an animal is initially rewarded for choosing the larger (256 cm^2) as opposed to the smaller (160 cm^2) of two stimuli. From an associationist viewpoint, the animal will learn an association between the response and the 256 cm^2 stimulus. In Hullian terms, the animal will form a habit of some strength between the 256 cm^2 stimulus and the response. This habit will generalize to other stimuli that are similar to the one that is rewarded. Thus, the excitatory tendency will be strongest to the stimulus for which the animal is rewarded, and gradually diminish as the difference between the original stimulus and other stimuli increases. This *generalization gradient* is the topmost curve in Figure 11.1. The animal will also learn to inhibit its response to the stimulus for which it is not rewarded. This inhibitory tendency will be strongest at the 160 cm^2 stimulus, and gradually diminish as stimuli become less similar to that stimulus. This gradient of inhibition is the lower curve in Figure 11.1.

While the generalization curves are theoretically derived, they permit some precise predictions. The difference between the excitatory and inhibitory gradients for any particular stimulus represents the net reaction potential for that stimulus. Compare this difference for the 409 cm^2 stimu-

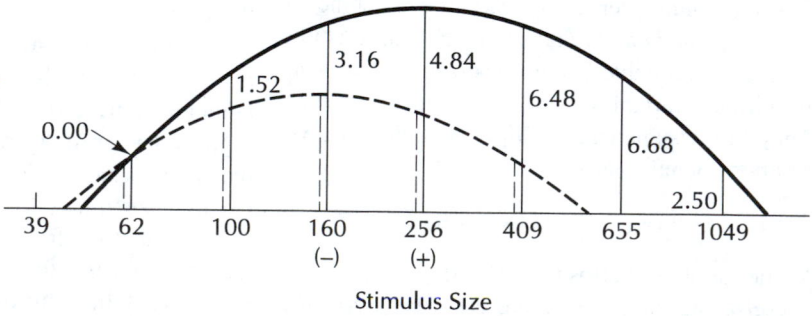

FIGURE 11.1 Curves of excitation and inhibition.
Source: K. W. Spence (1937). The differential response in animals to stimuli varying within a single dimension. *Psychological Review, 44,* 433.

lus and the 256 cm^2 stimulus. Notice that it is greater for the 409 cm^2 stimulus than for the 256 cm^2 stimulus. Thus, given a choice between these two stimuli the animal should choose the 409 cm^2 stimulus. This result is what Kohler found, and on which he based his antiassociationist theory of transposition. However, Spence provided a neoassociationist framework within which to explain Kohler's finding that animals will sometimes respond to stimuli for which they have not been rewarded, and ignore stimuli for which they have been rewarded. Such an analysis provided support for those who believed that theories of learning based on conditioning principles were best able to explain the data.

Spence's analysis of transposition was by no means his only contribution. The study does illustrate, however, the way in which a Hullian form of theory appeared in the beginning to be able to elegantly explain interesting experimental data. One can easily see why so many young psychologists were attracted to it at the time.

Charles E. Osgood (1916–1991)

Osgood (1980) did his graduate work at Yale, beginning in 1940 when he "got swept up, just like everyone else, into the monumental edifice of learning theory that Clark L. Hull was building" (p. 342). However, Osgood extended the Hullian approach in a highly original direction. Hull had postulated the existence of what Osgood (1952) called *mediational processes* that intervened between stimulus and response. Mediational processes guided the organism's reactions. Osgood saw in these mediating processes a way of explaining the way in which stimuli acquired meaning for an organism. The formation of mediational processes was hypothesized to occur in the manner illustrated in Figure 11.2.

The notation used by Osgood in Figure 11.2 is as follows. The letter S with a dot on top represents some stimulus object to which the organism responds (R_T). Osgood's example is a spider, which elicits a complex, and perhaps highly emotional, reaction. The letter S surrounded by a box represents a *sign,* which can come to evoke the same kind of reactions as the stimulus with which it is paired. Thus, in Figure 11.2, the sign might be the word "spider." When paired with an actual spider, as when a child learns the name of a spider, the word will come to evoke a fraction of the reaction evoked by the original stimulus itself. In this way words come to be meaningful, not only by denoting stimulus objects, but also by evoking the internal responses elicited by those objects. These inter-

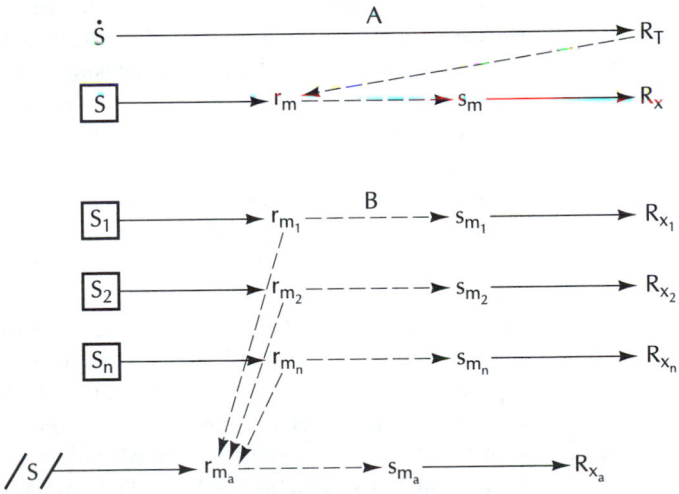

FIGURE 11.2 The development of a mediational process.

Source: C. E. Osgood (1952). The nature and measurement of meaning. *Psychological Bulletin, 49,* 205.

nal responses constitute the first part of a mediating process, labeled $r_m \rightarrow s_m$ in the figure. The internal response (r_m) is itself a stimulus (s_m) that guides the organism's future behavior. In this case, mention of the word "spider" can lead to a mediating process of disgust and/or fear that in turn leads to withdrawal (R_X).

The Semantic Differential

As the preceding example shows, mediating processes in humans are often associated with words. From Osgood's perspective, these mediators carry the meanings of words, particularly their emotional, or affective, meanings. It was Osgood's great contribution to provide a way of measuring this aspect of meaning. This was the *semantic differential* technique (Osgood, Suci, & Tannenbaum, 1957). In its usual form, the semantic differential asks you to rate a person, thing, or event on a set of 7-point bipolar scales such as those given in Figure 11.3.

The task requires you to make a series of judgments about how something (in this case, "spider") is best described. If "spider" in your judgment, was best described as "extremely unpleasant," then you would mark the interval closest to the unpleasant end of the scale. If you thought it was only "quite unpleasant," or "slightly unpleasant," or "neither pleasant nor unpleasant" then you would mark intervals increasingly close to the center of the scale. After you fill out a number of such scales, the result is a profile of the way in which these dimensions go together for you to define this concept ("spider"). Of course, a particular concept will be rated differently by different people, and so we can get a measure of individual differences in the affective meaning of particular concepts. However, suppose we obtain, as did Osgood, a large number of ratings of different concepts by different people on different scales in different cultures. It turns out that ratings tend to be correlated across scales.

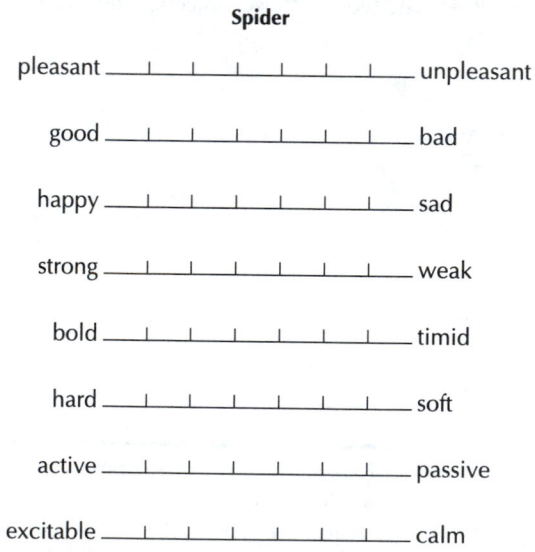

FIGURE 11.3 Semantic differential scales.

At this point you should recall our discussion of factor analysis in Chapter 10. Factor analysis begins with a set of correlations between a number of measures, in this case ratings of concepts. Using factor analysis, one can derive a number of underlying factors that describe the structure of this set of correlation coefficients. In fact, Osgood found that there are three important clusters of dimensions (e.g., Osgood, May, & Miron, 1975). Within each cluster, the dimensions go with one another more than they do with dimensions from the other sets. The first, and largest, set consists of dimensions such as *pleasant-unpleasant, good-bad* and *happy-sad.* Osgood called these the *Evaluative* (E) set of dimensions. The second set contains dimensions such as *strong-weak, bold-timid* and *hard-soft,* and are termed the *Potency* (P) set of dimensions. The third set has dimensions in it such as *active-passive* and *excitable-calm,* and represent an *Activity* (A) set of dimensions.

Osgood, Suci, and Tannenbaum (1957, pp. 72–73) speculated about why Evaluation, Potency and Activity, and not some other factors, emerge as the important aspects of affective meaning. They pointed out the importance of these three factors in our experience. Evaluation is "based on the bedrock of rewards and punishments both achieved and anticipated"; Potency "is concerned with power and the things associated with, size, weight toughness, and the like"; while Activity is "concerned with quickness, excitement, . . . agitation and the like." These three dimensions represent answers to questions such as "How much pleasure or pain is it likely to give us" (Evaluation); "How strong is it relative to us?" (Potency); and "What do we have to do to deal with it?" (Activity). "Survival, then and now, depends upon the answers" (Osgood, May, & Miron, 1975, p. 395).

As Osgood, May, and Miron (1975, p. 394) observe, there is a close similarity between their three factors and Wundt's tridimensional theory of feeling, which we considered in Chapter 4. Evaluation corresponds to Wundt's pleasantness-unpleasantness dimension, Potency corresponds to tension-relaxation, and Activity to excitement-depression. Wundt and Osgood used strikingly different methods, and Osgood did not set out to replicate Wundt's findings. The correspondence between the two is, thus, all the more striking.

Osgood's semantic differential technique generated an enormous amount of research. By 1969, there were at least 1500 studies related to it (Osgood, 1980, p. 354). Semantic differential studies uncovered intriguing similarities in affective meaning across cultures, as reported by Osgood, May, and Miron (1975). For example, *courage* and *success* are consistently rated as positive on all three of Evaluation, Potency and Activity; while *tree* and *knowledge* are positive on Evaluation and Potency, but negative on Activity. For a majority of cultures, concepts such as *freedom, girl,* and *love* are positive on the Evaluation set, but hunger, *snake,* and *thief* are negative on Evaluation. In terms of Potency, *progress* and *sun* are positive while *bird* and *egg* are negative. *Fire,* and *game* are positive in terms of Activity while *sleep* and *stone* are negative.

Osgood (1980) believed that his crosscultural research was relevant to issues of "meaning and survival of the human species in the nuclear age," and saw himself as "trying to bring a strategy for reducing international tensions, based on psychological principles, into the awareness of the public at large and people in government in particular" (p. 360). The fact that many concepts elicited the same subjective reaction cross-culturally was evidence for a widely shared set of meanings. In spite of important individual and cultural differences, it appeared that people had a great deal in common in terms of the way they feel about many basic events. It was Osgood's hope that research such as his would facilitate successful communication between people and cultures, and thus reduce international tensions.

Additional Reading on This Topic. Another important psychologist in the Hullian tradition was *Daniel E. Berlyne* of the University of Toronto. His book *Structure and Direction in Thinking* (1965) is a scholarly tour de force that combines the Hullian approach with European approaches.

EDWARD C. TOLMAN (1886–1959)

Tolman became converted to behaviorism in 1914 while a graduate student at Harvard. However, the behaviorism he developed was quite different from that of Watson. His theory was a "common-sense mentalistic psychology—or what the gestalt psychologists have called phenomenology—in operational behavioristic terms. Kohler has called me a cryptophenomenologist. He is probably right. What I wanted was a behavioristic psychology which would be able to deal with real organisms in terms of their inner psychological dynamics" (Tolman, 1959, p. 94). Tolman's psychology is primarily a blend of methodological behaviorism and Gestalt psychology, with other influences, such as psychoanalysis, also a part of the mix.

In general, Tolman adopted a much looser and more speculative formulation than did Hull. Tolman's attitude toward the relation between research and theory in psychology can be gleaned from the following quotation from a paper written toward the end of his career (Tolman, 1959):

> *The system may not stand up to any final rules of scientific procedure. But I do not much care. I have liked to think about psychology in ways that have proved congenial to me. Since all the sciences, and especially psychology, are still immersed in such tremendous realms of the uncertain and the unknown, the best that any individual scientist, espe-*

cially any psychologist, can do seems to be to follow his own gleam and his own bent, however inadequate they may be. In fact, I suppose that actually this is what we all do. In the end, the only sure criterion is to have fun. And I have had fun.

In spite of the apparently whimsical nature of this remark, Tolman was a very serious investigator whose influence lasted well beyond his lifetime. However, it is important to note that Tolman's description of the way in which he *actually did* research contrasts sharply with the way in which philosophers of science such as the logical positivists said that we *should* do research. As we observed in Chapter 10, there is a difference between the *context of discovery* and the *context of justification* (Reichenbach, 1938; Gigerenzer, 1991). The thinking that leads to the *discovery* of a method for investigating a research problem may be quite different from the thinking that goes into presenting a completed study for consumption by the rest of the scientific community. Tolman's statement nicely illustrates this difference. With that in mind, let us explore some of Tolman's major concepts.

Purposive Behavior

The subject matter of Tolman's (1932/1967; 1951) behaviorism is behavior described with reference to the goal that the animal is seeking. Tolman made an important distinction between *molar* and *molecular* descriptions of behavior. A molecular description of behavior is in terms of specific muscular and glandular reactions, while a molar description is in terms of what the behavior is intended to accomplish. This distinction is quite similar to Aristotle's distinction, considered in Chapter 1 and discussed earlier in relation to Guthrie, between *movements* and *actions*. Descriptions of movements are at the molecular level, while descriptions of actions are at the molar level. Examples of behavior described at the molar level are "a rat running a maze; a cat getting out of a puzzle box; a man driving home to dinner; a child hiding from a stranger; . . . my friend and I telling one another our thoughts and feelings—*these are behaviors* (qua *molar*). And it must be noted that in mentioning no one of them have we referred to, or, we blush to confess it, for the most part even known, what were the exact muscles and glands, sensory nerves, and motor nerves involved. For these responses had other sufficiently identifying properties of their own" (Tolman, 1932/1967, p. 8). Because Tolman attempted to explain molar behavior, his approach is called *purposive behaviorism.*

Cognitive Maps

As far as Tolman was concerned, the explanation of purposive behavior required an understanding of the way that an animal represented its environment. "We believe that in the course of learning, something like a field map of the environment gets established in the rat's brain. . . . Secondly, we assert that the central office itself is far more like a map control room than it is like an old-fashioned telephone exchange . . . [S]timuli . . . are not connected by just simple one-to-one switches to the outgoing responses. Rather, the incoming impulses are usually worked over and elaborated in the central control room into a tentative, cognitivelike map of the environment. And it is this tentative map, indicating routes and paths and environmental relationships, which finally determines what responses, if any, the animal will finally release" (Tolman, 1951, p. 245).

Cognitive maps contain *expectancies,* which are representations of what the animal is likely to find by following the different routes represented in the map. Expectancies are integrated into *sign Gestalts,* which are representations of the way one event leads to other events in the cognitive map. One of Tolman's examples (1951) of sign Gestalts concerns the way in which the perception of an object leads on to the representation of different possibilities: "'This chair if sat on will lead to rest' . . .; or 'that chair, if placed against the wall, can be stood upon like a stepladder to reach this picture'; or 'yonder chair, if placed over there, if placed near such and such other furniture, will form an aesthetically pleasing whole'; or 'this chair, if kicked out of the way, will conduce to the catching of yonder escaped white rat'; and the like" (p. 80). Thus, one important class of sign Gestalt relationships concerns the representation of the uses to which objects can be put, or *means-end expectations.*

The Place versus Response Controversy

A very good illustration of the way in which cognitive maps function is given in an experiment by Tolman, Ritchie, and Kalish (1946/1992). This experiment was selected by the editors of the *Journal of Experimental Psychology* as a classic article and reprinted as part of the centennial celebration of the American Psychological Association. The experiment bears on a controversial issue that was called the *place versus response* controversy (Amundson, 1985). From Tolman's viewpoint, the issue concerned what it is that an animal learns. Does learning consist of the formation of stimulus-response connections, or does it consist of the formation of expectations, as Tolman believed? If learning means the acquisition of stimulus-response connections, then animals would learn specific responses to specific stimuli. If learning means the acquisition of expectations, then animals would learn a cognitive map that contained representations of the *place,* or location, of themselves in relation to different objects in the environment. In order to try to settle this question, Tolman, Ritchie, and Kalish did a study of maze learning in rats that began with the simple maze shown in Figure 11.4.

Approximately 50 rats were trained to follow the path from A through C, D, E, and F to the goal box G, where they were fed. H is a small light. The maze in Figure 11.4 was then replaced with the one shown in Figure 11.5. Notice that the path the animals had learned to run before was now blocked. Where did the rats go instead? It turned out that "36 percent chose path No. 6 which ended at a point four in. to the left of the place where the food box entrance had been during the [training] trials. This path No. 6 was, of all the paths offered, the most direct path to the former goal location"

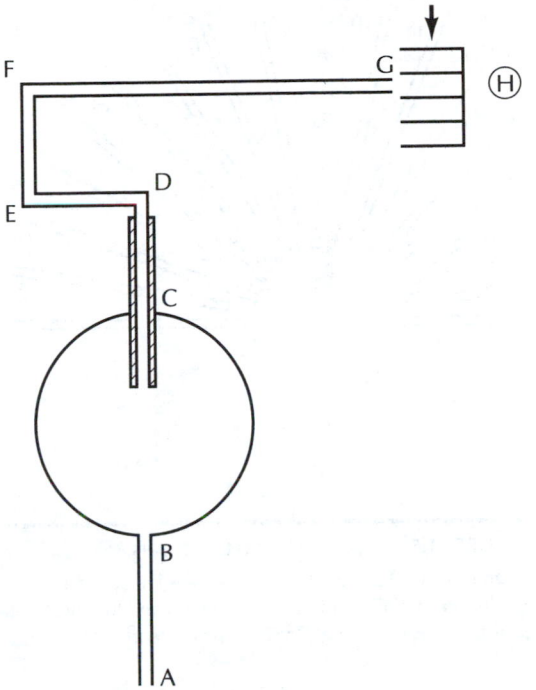

FIGURE 11.4 Apparatus used to train rats.
Source: E. C. Tolman, B. F. Ritchie, & D. Kalish (1992). Studies in spatial learning: I. Orientation and the short-cut. *Journal of Experimental Psychology: General, 121,* 430.

(Tolman, Ritchie, & Kalish, 1946/1992, p. 431). No other path was chosen by anything like this number of rats. "One should note the frequencies on paths No. 9 and 10. These two paths are the ones that are most similar, or spatially closest to, the original path on which the rats were practiced during the . . . training. The *combined* frequencies of these two paths is only nine percent" (Tolman, Ritchie, & Kalish, 1946/1992, pp. 431–432). Thus, the rats did not try to execute the *response* they had learned so much as they tried to find the *location* where they expected to find food. One could say that the animals had formed a cognitive map that enabled them to navigate through the new terrain in which they found themselves.

The *place versus response* controversy was one of a number of contentious issues in the Age of Learning Theories. Another instructive example—

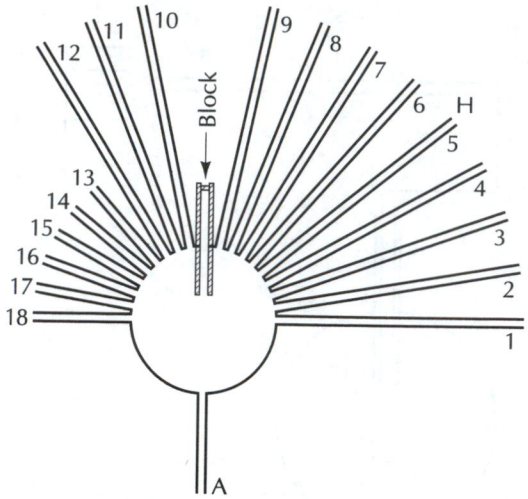

FIGURE 11.5 Apparatus used to test rats.
Source: E. C. Tolman, B. F. Ritchie, & D. Kalish (1992). Studies in spatial learning: I. Orientation and the short-cut. *Journal of Experimental Psychology: General, 121,* 431.

the latent learning controversy—is reviewed in Box 11.2 on pages 223–224.

Like so many controversies in psychology, the place-response and latent learning controversies were never really decided. In this respect, these controversies illustrate a more general feature of theoretical dispute in the Age of Learning Theories. There were many controversial issues, including the transposition controversy we considered earlier, that were collected and analyzed by Goldstein, Krantz, and Rains (1965). By 1965, most of these issues were "considered 'dead,' but it becomes clear in re-examining them that many of them are by no means settled. Research in these fields seems to have petered out without actually clearly resolving the issues" (p. vi). Goldstein, Krantz, and Rains (1965) point out that these controversies illustrate the fact that psychology does not progress simply as a result of the steady accumulation of knowledge. There is a certain amount of trial-and-error involved in psychology, and some 'blind alleys' are simply abandoned after they have been explored. This seems to have happened with much of the research conducted during the Age of Learning Theories. In Chapter 15 we will explore in more detail the extent to which this may be a more general feature of the history of psychology.

Additional Reading on This Topic. An intriguing account of the way that Tolman has been interpreted over the years is given by Ciancia (1988). One of Tolman's most productive and influential associates was Isidore Krechevsky, who subsequently changed his name to *David Krech.* An appreciation of Krech's contributions is given in Petrinovich and McGaugh (1976).

THE VERBAL LEARNING TRADITION

Functionalism and Verbal Learning

The first four editions of *Theories of Learning* (Hilgard, 1948, 1956; Hilgard & Bower, 1966, 1975) included a chapter on *functionalism.* This chapter typically provided a brief history of the functionalist school at Chicago, and a discussion of Woodworth's contributions. Functionalism was characterized as experimental and associationist in orientation. In the fifth edition (Bower & Hilgard, 1981), the chapter on functionalism was replaced with a chapter called Human Associative Memory, and the authors observe that "the verbal learning tradition [is] the strongest modern issue from Functionalism" (p. vi).

Of course, the verbal learning tradition goes back to Ebbinghaus and his studies using nonsense syllables. Variants of these studies continued more or less continuously after Ebbinghaus, as we observed in Chapter 4. Many of these studies used the method of paired associates that had been invented by Mary Calkins, and that we also considered in chapter 3. Studies of verbal learning were concerned with uncovering the basic laws of the formation of associations in humans. *Edward S. Robinson* (1932/1964) wrote an influential account of basic associationist principles, and suggested that

> *the general law [of association] should be written as follows:*
>
> $$A = f(x, y, z \ldots)$$

BOX 11.2

Latent Learning: A Case History in Psychological Explanation

Tolman and Hull were great competitors in the psychology of learning. They offered different explanations for well-known phenomena. Their battles are highly representative of the age of learning theories. One of the best known concerns the nature and explanation of *latent learning.*

As we considered earlier, *habit strength* was an intervening variable in Hull's system. Habit strength referred to the connection between a stimulus and a response, and was postulated to increase gradually whenever an animal was rewarded for responding to a stimulus. For example, suppose that a food-deprived animal, such as a hungry white rat, is placed in the start box of a maze similar to the one in Figure 11.6. Eventually the animal reaches the end of the maze and is fed. From Hull's perspective, this means that there will be an increase in the strength of the habits that connect the stimuli from the maze to the correct responses that enable the animal to reach the food. Thus, turning left, right, right, left, left, right, for example, are the responses that the animal needs to learn. Hull would predict that the time it takes the animal to go from start box to goal box would decline gradually as a function of trials. This hypothesis was deduced from Hull's theory, and can be tested experimentally. In fact, experiments in which animals were rewarded on each trial showed the kind of continuous improvement that Hull's theory predicted. The data seem to support the notion that habit strength increases continuously as a function of trials on which the animal is rewarded. However, these data are not the whole story.

As we have already seen, Tolman's view of the nature of learning was radically different from Hull's. Tolman argued that learning involved the formation of *expectations,* rather than the formation of habits, and these expectations could be learned in the absence of reward. Thus, simply by exploring the maze in Figure 11.6, an animal could learn what to expect at each point in the maze. The animal might not demonstrate that it had learned anything until it became important for it to do so. What are the consequences of the difference between Tolman and Hull? Look at Figure 11.7, which contains data from an experiment by Tolman and Honzik (1930). This graph shows data from three groups of rats, each of which was allowed to run once a day through a maze similar to the one shown in Figure 11.6. One group, called HR for "hungry-reward," was fed every time it reached the food box. Notice that the group behaves just as Hull would have predicted. They go through the maze faster and faster on successive days until they have apparently learned the maze thoroughly, and there is no further improvement. Another group, called HNR for "hungry–no reward," also behaves

(continued)

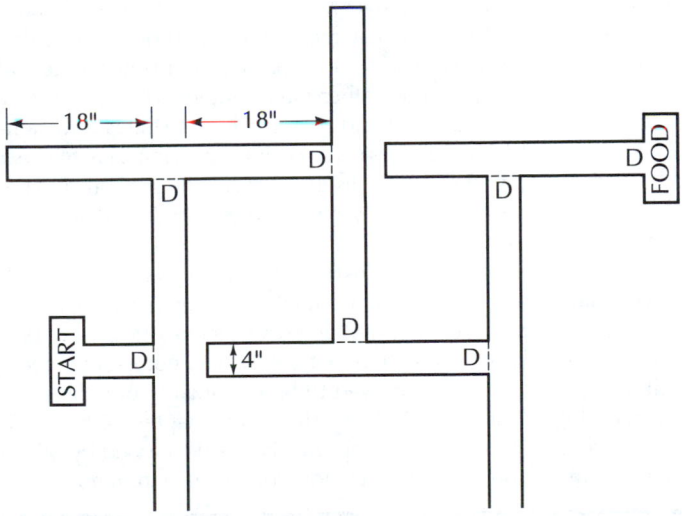

FIGURE 11.6 Six unit alley T-maze.
Source: H. C. Blodgett (1929). The effect of the introduction of reward upon the maze performance of rats. *University of California Publications in Psychology, 4,* 117.

BOX 11.2 continued

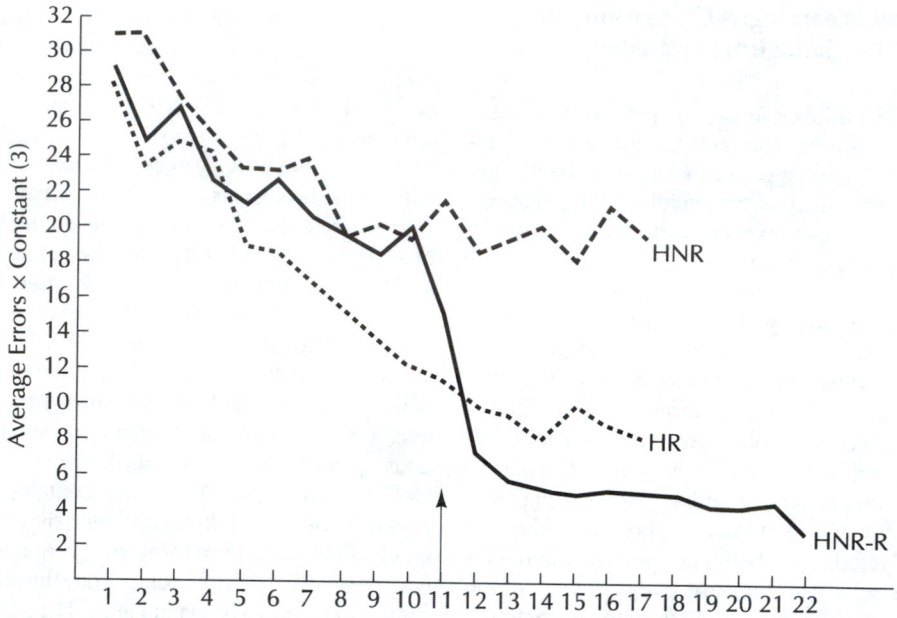

FIGURE 11.7 Data from Tolman and Honzik's "latent learning" experiment.
Source: E. C. Tolman (1948). Cognitive maps in rats and men. *Psychological Review, 55,* 195.

just as Hull would have predicted. This group receives no reward when they reach the end of the maze, and they show no improvement as the days pass, indicating that they may not have learned anything. But wait a minute. Look at the curve for the group labeled HNR-R, for "hungry no reward–reward." This group is not rewarded for the first 10 days. These rats behave just like the no-reward group during this period. According to Hull's theory, they should not have learned anything, because they have not been rewarded. However, when the rats are rewarded on the eleventh and subsequent days, then they very rapidly begin to perform as well as the rats who have been rewarded all along. It is as if these rats learned the maze without reward, but did not display their learning until they were rewarded for doing so. This phenomenon was called *latent learning.* Results such as these led Tolman to make a distinction between *learning,* which could occur without reward, and *performance,* which was influenced by reward. Perhaps you can discover instances of latent learning in your own experience. Can you not learn something without anyone else knowing that you have learned it, like the rats in the HNR-R group. And, again like the rats in that group, do you usually show what you have learned only when it is important for you to do so?

The controversy over latent learning demonstrates how an experiment can provide data that allow a researcher to argue in favor of one theoretical interpretation rather than another. The controversy between Hull and Tolman also illustrates how nonhuman subjects can be used to provide data that bear on a theoretical dispute that is quite general, and not restricted to only one species. Hull's and Tolman's theories were intended to apply to any species whatsoever, and not just to rats or just to people. Although Tolman's theory was challenged on many occasions, and eventually replaced by other theories, the underlying assumption that behavior is guided by expectancies has proved to be remarkably popular (e.g., Olton, 1992). We will see in Chapter 14 how Tolman's cognitive approach was developed by others and emerged in the form of cognitive psychology.

where A is associative strength, x, y, z, etc. are such factors as time-interval, frequency of repetition, the state of other existing connections, sensory intensity, affective intensity, and other factors demonstrably related to associative strength.

Thus, associative strength is a function of some combination of these factors. (p. 129)

Robinson's formulation illustrates the meaning of the word "function" in the context of verbal learning. It refers to the study of the formation of associations "as a function" of different variables such as the ones on Robinson's list. There have been innumerable studies in the verbal learning tradition since Ebbinghaus, and in this section we can only indicate with one or two examples some of the directions that were taken by this line of research.

Acquisition

Recall our earlier discussion of Guthrie, in which we considered his view that repetition provides the opportunity for a learner to acquire a connection, but does not strengthen a connection already formed. A series of experiments conducted by *Irvin Rock* (1957; Rock & Heimer, 1959; Steinfeld & Rock, 1968) explored the hypothesis of *one-trial learning* in a particularly provocative way, although Rock's work was not undertaken from within a Guthrian perspective. Rock's experiments are now somewhat out of date, but they are still regarded as classics in many quarters (e.g., Hilgard, 1987, p. 213).

Rock's experiments call into question an intuition that many of us have about the nature of learning. This intuition can be summarized in terms of the following proverb: "Practice makes perfect." We often believe that repeating something we wish to learn over and over will gradually lead to our being able to remember it. This intuition seems to imply that if we were given a list of unfamiliar items to learn, then we might learn a little bit the first time we read through the list, a little bit more the next time we read through the list, and so on, until finally we would have learned the entire list after a suitable number of repetitions. This view of learning implies that it is a *gradual* process, and that connections are gradually strengthened.

In light of the foregoing, imagine the following experiment (Rock, 1957). First, make up a set of 50 items, consisting of letter-number pairs, such as L-12, or double-letter-number pairs, such as JJ-48. Then, suppose we have two groups of subjects, a control group and an experimental group. The control group is given a list of 12 letter-number pairs to learn. The list is a random sample from the 50 original letter-number pairs. Each of the letter-number pairs is presented on a separate card. After the subject has seen the entire list, he or she is shown each letter, and asked to recall the appropriate number. This procedure is repeated until the subject either recalls all the numbers correctly, or does so badly that the experiment must be terminated before the subject reaches this criterion.

Now let us consider how the experimental group is treated. On the first trial, they receive the same set of letter-number pairs as did the control group. After trial 1, however, the pairs that the subject did not get correct are removed, and new pairs substituted for them. Thus, suppose the subject got 5 correct after trial 1. Then the remaining pairs are deleted, and the subject given a new list of 12 items containing the 5 pairs he or she got right, plus 7 new pairs. This procedure is repeated, with incorrect items being substituted for on each trial, until the subject gets all the numbers correct, or until the experimenter runs out of new items.

In Rock's original experiment, it turned out that, on average, subjects in both groups take virtually the same number of trials to learn the list (about 4.5). This result is surprising because the experimental group is not given the chance to practice on incorrect items until they are correct. Rather, they are always having to learn some new items until they get all the items right. The results were taken by Rock (1957, p. 193) as suggesting that "repetition plays no role in the formation . . . of associations, other than that of providing the occasion for new ones to be formed, each on a single trial."

There were several arguments directed against Rock's experimental procedure (e.g., Postman, 1962; Underwood, Rehula & Keppel, 1962). As was the case in other areas of the psychology of learning, it was difficult to tell whether or not a particular position carried the day. However, Rock's work focused attention on a methodological problem, and helped explore the limits of a particular type of experimental procedure. The question of whether learning is all-or-none or continuous began to be seen as a much more complex issue as a result of Rock's work. In a general way, this was the lesson learned from much of the work in human associative memory from this period.

Serial Learning

> *How does a person manage to learn a succession of responses in a fixed order? The pianist who must play the proper series of notes, or the experimental subject who must master the appropriate sequence of verbal items, is faced with much the same task. What are the processes which underlie the accomplishment of such tasks? This is the problem of serial learning, and it has been studied with human subjects mainly through the presentation of lists of nonsense syllables or unconnected words. (Slamecka, 1967, p. 61)*

When subjects are asked to learn lists of nonsense syllables, "it is found that the syllables in the middle of the list are learned more slowly than are those at the two ends, and in general the initial syllables are learned more rapidly than are the final ones" (McCrary & Hunter, 1953, p. 151). This is a very stable, reliable result, found for just about any kind of material learned under a wide variety of conditions. The reason for the existence of such *serial position curves* was very intensively investigated for many years.

While the serial position curve might seem to be a very esoteric topic, it does turn up in some 'real world' contexts. For example, Roediger & Crowder (1976/1982) showed that when subjects are asked to recall as many of the Presidents of the United States as they can, then the result is a serial position curve, with subjects tending to recall both early and recent Presidents more frequently than those in the middle of U.S. history. The exception to this rule is the heightened tendency to recall Lincoln, presumably because of his prominence in U.S. history. However, Roediger & Crowder note that even this apparent exception can be explained by a principle from verbal learning called the *von Restorff effect* (von Restorff, 1933; Hunt, 1995), which holds that an item that has unique properties will be more likely to be recalled.

The Fate of Verbal Learning

In spite of attempts to apply principles discovered through the study of verbal learning, many observers began to grow impatient with the area. One of the most active and influential students of verbal learning, *Benton J. Underwood* (1964) observed that by the 1960's the area of verbal learning had acquired the reputation of being "dull, narrow, sterile and, in a manner of speaking, deals with a form of learning that is almost intellectually demeaning" (pp. 51–52). While Underwood believed that such an opinion was unjustified, it was clear by that time that the area of verbal learning was not enjoying the prestige that once attached to it. A symposium on "Verbal behavior and general behavior theory" (Dixon & Horton, 1968) brought together several well-known students of verbal learning as well as several critics of the area. The upshot of the conference was that the adequacy of an associationist approach to the study of learning—verbal or otherwise—was called into question. The convenors of the conference, in reviewing the contributions made by the participants, concluded that "a revolution is certainly in the making" (Horton & Dixon, 1968). That revolution was the so-called 'cognitive revolution' which we will review in a later chapter.

Additional Reading on This Topic. Another famous study of one-trial learning is by Estes (1960). Good reviews of verbal learning research are found in Postman and Keppel (1969) and Slamecka (1967).

DONALD O. HEBB (1904–1985)

The Emergence of Neuroscience

Hebb was a Canadian whose career was largely spent at McGill University in Montreal, and who was the first foreign president of the American Psychological Association (Hebb, 1960). As a young man Hebb (1980b) wanted to be a novelist, and supported himself through teaching. It was not until the age of 30 that he went to Chicago to study psychology with Karl Lashley. In 1935, Lashley moved to Harvard, and Hebb went along as his student, graduating with a Ph.D. in 1936. About Lashley's influence, Hebb (1980b, p. 287) said, "Lashley was my model—Lashley the biological scientist interested in the mind." Years later, when Hebb wanted to write a general neuropsychological theory, he asked Lashley to collaborate on it (Bruce, 1994b), "but Lashley was entirely uninterested and remained skeptical of the whole thing" (Hebb, 1980b, p. 296). Hebb (1949) went on to write *The Organization of Behavior* by himself. Although a separate chapter was never devoted to Hebb in any of the editions of *Theories of Learning,* Hilgard (1993) selected Hebb as one of those psychologists who made lasting contributions to psychological theory in the second half of the twentieth century, and singled out *The Organization of Behavior* as having "revitalized physiological psychology, which had been in the doldrums for years" (p. 72).

The Organization of Behavior

Hebb's theory was a *neuropsychology,* in that it combined aspects of psychology, such as learning theory and Gestalt psychology, with neurophysiology (Hochberg, 1988, p. 64). Hebb (1959) described the essence of his theory as follows:

> *The key conception is that of a* cell assembly, *a brain process which corresponds to a particular sensory event, or a common aspect of a number of sensory events. This assembly is a closed system in which activity can "reverberate" and thus continue after the sensory event which started it has ceased. Also, one assembly will form connections with others, and it may therefore be made active by one of them in the total absence of the adequate stimulus. In short, the assembly activity is the simplest case of an* image *or an* idea: *a representative process. The formation of connections between assemblies is the mechanism of association. (p. 628)*

Cell assemblies constitute physiological mediating processes, and are responsible for representing stimulation. They consist of neurons that have become associated as a result of being active simultaneously. Hebb postulated that the mechanism of association occurred through growth at the synapse, or junction between two neurons. "The fundamental physiological assumption of learning is that whenever an impulse crosses a synapse it becomes easier for later impulses to do so. More precisely: when a neuron *A* fires, or takes part in firing, another neuron *B,* some change occurs in *A* or *B* or both which increases *A*'s capacity to fire *B* in the future. The change might be an enlargement of a synaptic knob; or it might be some chemical change" (Hebb, 1958, p. 103). This hypothesis has become known as the *Hebb rule* (e.g., McClelland, Rumelhart, & Hinton, 1986, p. 36), even though "this postulate is one of the few aspects of the theory he did not consider completely original. Something like it had been proposed by many psychologists, including Freud in his early years as a neurobiologist" (Milner, 1993, p. 127).

Cell assemblies represent the basic units of experience that themselves become connected into *phase sequences.* A phase sequence "amounts to one current in the stream of thought" (Hebb, 1959, p. 629). Different phase sequences will occur depending on the circumstances. Thus, cell assemblies represent particular events, while phase sequences constitute the way in which these events are organized in a particular situation. "The sight of a stimulus object may arouse many different trains of thought; which one it does arouse is determined by the already existing central processes which (so to speak) select among these possibilities. . . . [T]he course of thought can have some continuity and directedness, since at each moment the processes now going on tend to pick out, from among the many perceptions of the environment that are possible, only those that are relevant to the activities that have gone before" (Hebb, 1958, p. 106).

Hebb (1960, 1968) believed that the way that cell assemblies represent our experience is well illustrated by the phenomenon of *phantom limbs.* A phantom limb occurs in an adult whenever an active body part, such as an arm or leg, is amputated. The person will still experience the missing body part as "being there," even though they know perfectly well that it is missing. *Marianne L. Simmel* (1956) had shown that the probability of the occurrence of a phantom limb following amputation increases steadily with age, until it reaches nearly 100% in adults. In Hebb's terms (1960), phantom limbs occur as a result of a process whereby each of us develops over time a *body image* that constitutes our representation of our bodies. This body image is the result of cell assemblies that are responsible for representing the typical state of various parts of our body. These cell assemblies will become associated with each other over time, and eventually form a stable system, or *body schema.* Any part of the system can cause other parts to fire. Thus, even in the absence of direct stimulation from a missing limb, the person can still experience that limb because the cell assemblies responsible for representing it can still become active. "No excitation can originate in the missing hand, but the same excitation can in principle arise higher in the pathway by spontaneous firing of the neurons at level *X* in [Figure 11.8]. If [the subject] *S* now reports pain in his imaginary hand we are not dealing with any different mechanism, in brain function, than when a normal *S* reports pain. Report of 'sensation' from a phantom limb is not introspective report" any more than "a dog's yelp when his tail is trod on" is introspective report (Hebb, 1968, p. 467). Such *vocal responses* are objective, behavioral occurrences under the control of physiological processes.

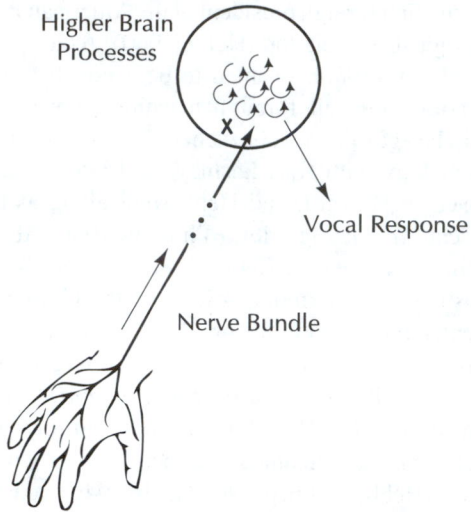

FIGURE 11.8 The relation between normal sensation and the phantom limb.

Source: D. O. Hebb (1968). Concerning imagery. *Psychological Review, 75,* 467. Copyright © 1968 by the American Psychological Association. Reprinted by permission.

Motivation

Hebb (1955) was particularly interested in understanding how the cognitive neuropsychological processes we have already considered are related to motivational processes. He emphasized the importance of the *arousal system,* "the nonspecific or diffuse projection system of the brain stem, which was shown by Moruzzi & Magoun (1949) to be an *arousal* system whose activity in effect makes organized cortical activity possible" (p. 248). Arousal functions in a manner analogous to drive, it "is an energizer, but not a guide; an engine, but not a steering gear" (p. 250). While stimuli have a *cue function* that serves to guide behavior, their effectiveness is determined by the organism's arousal level at the time of their occurrence. This relationship is illustrated in Figure 11.9.

Hebb's diagram proposes that performance will be optimal when arousal is moderate. Low levels of arousal mean the organism takes too little interest in its environment; too much arousal and the organism is paralyzed by competing response tendencies. Hebb, in common with many other psychologists (e.g., Berlyne, 1960), argued that the organism will try to maintain an optimal level of arousal, that is neither too high nor too low. This may require seeking out arousal producing situations when arousal is too low, as well as satisfying needs that may produce states of high arousal. Hebb's hypothesis (1958) that it is important to the organism to avoid "a too-easy or monotonous environment" (p. 176) led to one of his most famous lines of research, involving *sensory deprivation.*

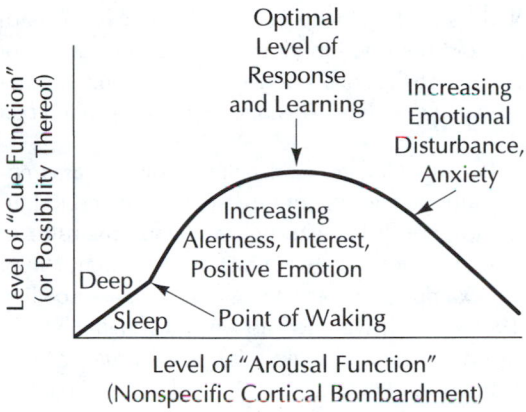

FIGURE 11.9 The relation between arousal and cue functions.

Source: D. O. Hebb (1955). Drive and the C. N. S. (Conceptual Nervous System). *Psychological Review, 62,* 243–254.

Experiments in Sensory Deprivation

The Korean War occurred during the early 1950s, a period when there was an intense interest in the phenomenon of *brainwashing*. The *Oxford English Dictionary* (1989) defines "brainwashing" as "the systematic and often forcible elimination from a person's mind of all established ideas, especially political ones, so that another set of ideas may take their place; this process regarded as the kind of coercive conversion practiced by certain totalitarian states on political dissidents." Some former prisoners of war returned to the United States and Canada apparently having been victims of brainwashing, and its causes were of obvious interest.

One of the conditions of brainwashing appeared to be keeping the person in extreme isolation, without normal stimulation. Hebb and his research group at McGill, funded in part by the Canadian Department of National Defense (Payne, 1986), attempted to mimic such conditions. Paid volunteers were placed in bed in isolation chambers, "wore translucent but not transparent goggles; heard a constant slight buzzing sound from a small speaker in the foam-rubber pillow except when the experimenter was on line with a question; and wore long cardboard cuffs from the middle of the forearm to beyond the fingers. Thus they received much sensory stimulation, but all of it unpatterned, except in the tests or occasional requests for information" (Hebb, 1980a, p. 96). For this reason Hebb preferred the term *perceptual isolation,* rather than "sensory deprivation."

There were four results from experiments like these that were widely reported and believed (Suedfeld & Coren, 1989, p. 18). The first is that after 2 or 3 days subjects began to experience hallucinations. The second is that subjects were more "vulnerable to propaganda than the control subjects who were hired to listen to the same stuff, advocating belief in ghosts and poltergeists as well as clairvoyance and telepathy" (Hebb, 1980, p. 97). The third is that subjects were less able to think about problems, and the fourth is that subjects bailed out of the experiment quickly, terminating the session well before the experimenter had scheduled it to end.

One of the most frequently cited reports of the McGill studies of perceptual isolation was "The Pathology of Boredom," published by *Woodburn Heron* (1954). As Suedfeld & Coren (1989, p. 18) point out, this title has "come to characterize the field in the minds of many nonspecialists." The topic of "sensory deprivation" became a staple of undergraduate education in psychology, and the McGill studies, done in the 1950s, were the standard references in introductory psychology textbooks even in the 1980s. Suedfeld & Coren (1989) observe that the McGill studies continued to be cited even though subsequent research tended to show that their results could not be replicated, and they conclude that "introductory textbook authors have been captured by the dramatic reports of hallucinations, emotional distress and perceptual and cognitive deficits that emanated from the McGill reports. . . . Perhaps textbook authors have ignored the past 25 years of research in order to retain a 'good story'" (pp. 24–25).

The fate of the McGill "sensory deprivation" studies is instructive in several ways. Not the least of these is the fact that once a particular view of a

Box 11.3

The Garcia Effect

John Garcia (1917–) did his graduate training at Berkeley at a time when Tolman's group was active. Garcia was heavily influenced by that milieu, with its emphasis on the importance of central explanatory mechanisms. The line of research that made Garcia famous called into question assumptions that were important to many classical learning theories. One such assumption was that in order for an organism to acquire an association between two events, the events must be contiguous—close together in space and time. For example, it was often argued that for conditioning to occur there must be an optimal, brief interval between the unconditioned and conditioned stimuli, and many theorists have claimed that the most effective reinforcers were those that occurred immediately after a response (Garcia, 1976, p. 79).

In one study, Garcia and Koelling (1966) had rats drink water that had "two sets of salient cues: a light flash activated by a clicking relay and a sweet taste induced by saccharin in the water. . . . For some rats, this bright noisy water was immediately followed by a brief shock to the feet during the session. For other rats, drinking the bright noisy water was punished by an illness induced after the session." After the training, rats that had been shocked would drink the sweet water, but not the "bright noisy" water, while the rats that had become ill, would drink the "bright noisy water," but not the sweet water (Garcia, 1976, pp. 78–79). The animals that had become ill had learned an association between a sweet taste and the fact that they subsequently got sick. "The sick rat acts as if it has formed this hypothesis: 'It must have been something I ate.' Even if it has not eaten for hours, it searches among its food memories for the probable cause of its discomfort" (Garcia, 1976, p. 80). Garcia and his colleagues were able to demonstrate this phenomenon in several other contexts, and it has obvious analogs in the real world. Animals can learn to avoid poisoned food, even though they may not experience the consequences of consuming it immediately after eating. This phenomenon is called *bait shyness*.

Because Garcia's work called traditional assumptions about learning into question, he found it difficult to publish his work in prestigious, mainstream journals (Garcia, 1981; Lubek & Apfelbaum, 1987). For example, the article by Garcia and Koelling (1966), which we cited above, was originally submitted to a very prestigious journal (*Journal of Comparative and Physiological Psychology*), but rejected by the editor and his consultants. The grounds for rejection included the statement that "your results are not particularly surprising but also they are difficult to interpret" (Lubek & Apfelbaum, 1987, p. 73). Garcia then cut the length of the manuscript, and published it in a less prestigious journal, *Psychonomic Science*. This pattern of rejection from prestigious psychological journals and subsequent publication in less mainstream outlets was repeated with other papers written by Garcia.

Of course, the fact that a series of papers by a psychologist is rejected by editors of important psychological journals is not proof that the psychological establishment is resistant to new ideas. However, in this case, Garcia's work was recognized by others (who were not the editors of mainstream psychological journals) as being of major theoretical interest. As a result, Garcia was given the Distinguished Scientific Contribution Award by the American Psychological Association in 1980. The Garcia case suggests that progress in psychology, and perhaps in any science, is not the completely objective process envisioned by Hull, whereby theory is revised in light of new data. Rather, there may be some initial resistance to new data if they are inconsistent with widely held viewpoints. This is a process we will examine further in Chapter 15.

---

phenomenon becomes embedded in introductory courses, it is hard to dislodge it, no matter what subsequent research demonstrates. Certain ways of thinking may attain the status of "what everybody knows," and may be very difficult to modify. Another illustration of the way in which the psychological community may resist change is given in Box 11.3.

Additional Reading on This Topic. Another classic experimental technique used by Hebb's group to investigate cell assemblies involved *stabilized retinal images* (Pritchard, Heron, & Hebb, 1960).

ALBERT BANDURA (1925–)

Bandura was born in Alberta, Canada, and received his undergraduate degree from the University of British Columbia. He then earned his Ph.D. at the State University of Iowa, where he was influenced by Kenneth Spence. Bandura developed "a strong interest in conceptualizing clinical phenomena in ways that would make them amenable to experimental test, with the view that as practitioners, we have a responsibility for assessing the efficacy of our procedures" (Evans, 1976, p. 243). Bandura is generally regarded as having constructed a persuasive synthesis of different approaches to learning as well as providing a framework within which applied psychologists can operate (e.g., Bower & Hilgard, 1981, pp. 461–472).

Social Learning Theory

Bandura has been a leading exponent of *social learning theory,* also known as *social cognitive theory.* A landmark in the development of this approach was *Social Learning and Personality Development,* written by Bandura with his student *Richard Walters* (Bandura & Walters, 1963). In that book, they "outlined a set of social-learning principles that emphasize the role of social variables to a greater extent than existing learning theories and consequently appear more capable of accounting for the development and modification of human behavior" (p. vii). They called their approach *sociobehavioristic.*

Social learning theory stresses the importance of *modeling* in shaping a person's learned behavior. Bandura (e.g., 1986, pp. 46–49) has been careful to differentiate between imitation, identification, and modeling. Imitation refers to occasions when one person mimics another person's specific behaviors, while identification refers to a much vaguer process whereby one person may attempt to take on the entire personality of another person. As a concept, modeling is broader than imitation, and more precise than identification.

Modeling takes place through a process called *observational learning.* Observational learning refers to the fact that a person can acquire novel responses through the observation of another person's actions. The acquisition of new words by children is a small scale example of such a process. Children hear someone else use a word in a particular context, and are then able to use the word appropriately themselves. Bandura and Walters (1963) reported on several experiments attempting to demonstrate that observational learning occurs in a wide range of situations. For example, children who observed a model who behaved aggressively toward a dummy later showed more aggressive behavior themselves than did other children who observed a more inhibited model (Bandura, Ross, & Ross, 1961). Bandura has drawn out the social implications of such modeling, pointing out the potential for both positive and negative influences stemming from the availability of a wide range of models through media such as television. The increase in airplane hijacking after the first occurrence in the United States in 1961 is an example of the negative effects of observational learning (Bandura, 1986, p. 172). However, there are innumerable positive effects. "On the basis of modeled information, people acquire, among other things, judgmental standards, linguistic rules, styles of inquiry, information processing skills, and standards of evaluation" (Bandura, 1986, p. 102).

Behavior Modification

Bandura has become famous partly as a result of his use of modeling techniques to modify behavior in clinical and other applied settings. Of course, *behavior modification* did not originate with Bandura. Everyone acknowledges the pioneering work of *Mary Cover Jones* (1924a, b), who developed the techniques described by Watson and Rayner (1920/1979) that we considered in Chapter 8. In one study, Jones worked with a boy, named Peter, who was afraid of furry objects. She arranged to have a caged rabbit present, but at some distance, while the boy was fed. The distance between the boy and the rabbit was decreased on subsequent occasions. Eventually, the boy was able to tolerate being in close proximity to the rabbit, even when it was uncaged. This technique was subsequently refined and named *systematic desensitization* (e.g., Wolpe, 1958). Bandura and Walters (1963, p. 243) note that Jones (1924a) also "explicitly used the method of social imitation in overcoming children's fears. Fear-reduction was produced by having other children behave in a nonanxious manner in the presence of the avoided object. Jones also demonstrated that a fear could be acquired through social imitation, a finding which suggests that exposure to models who suffer, are punished, or exhibit fear in the course of performing a deviant act may be an effective means of producing conditioned fear reactions, which may be lacking in underinhibited children."

Bandura (1965) compared the relative efficacy of using operant conditioning or modeling to change behavior. He suggested that operant conditioning procedures, which had been advocated by B. F. Skinner, were inefficient because they require the person to emit the desired behavior so that it can be reinforced. "In cases in which a behavioral pattern contains a highly unique combination of elements selected from an almost infinite number of alternatives, the probability of occurrence of the desired response, or even one that has some remote resemblance to it, will be zero" (p. 312). By contrast, Bandura referred to the use of models to provide clients with the opportunity to learn through observation as an example of "*no-trial learning,* a process of response acquisition that is highly prevalent . . . [O]ne does not employ trial-and-error or operant conditioning methods in training children to swim, adolescents to drive an automobile, or in getting adults to acquire vocational skills. Indeed, if training proceeded in this manner, very few persons would ever survive the process of socialization" (p. 312).

In an influential review, Mischel (1968, p. 225) stated the argument from the perspective of social learning theory as follows. "An effective behavior change program . . . must assure that the person learns the necessary response patterns, and that the environment provides the cues necessary to evoke those responses. Exposure to the behavior of appropriate models is one of the most effective ways to enhance the acquisition of new behavior patterns and skills." Mischel (1968) cited a study by Bandura, Grusec, and Menlove (1967) as a particularly powerful demonstration of the efficacy of observational learning. "In one study, groups of preschool children who were intensely afraid of dogs observed a fearless peer model who displayed progressively stronger and more positive approach behavior to a dog. In the course of eight brief sessions the model exhibited increasingly longer and closer interactions with the dog in accord with a prearranged program of graduated steps. The model progressed from briefly petting the dog while the latter was safely confined in a play pen to ultimately joining the dog in the playpen. The results revealed significantly greater approach behavior on the part of children who had watched the non-anxious model when compared to their peers in control groups" (Mischel, 1968, p. 225). It is hard to imagine a more faithful replication and extension of Mary Cover Jones's original findings.

Reciprocal Determinism

A recurrent issue in psychology is whether the person or the situation is more important in determining behavior (Bowers, 1973). Bandura (1978, p. 345) maintained that the social learning perspective provides a resolution to this controversy because it "analyzes behavior in terms of reciprocal determinism," an approach that is different from other forms of explanation in psychology. Reciprocal determinism neither assumes that the environment controls behavior, as did B. F. Skinner, nor that people are free to do as they wish. Rather, the person, the environment, and behavior interact so as to determine each other. "In the social learning view of interaction . . . behavior, interpersonal factors and environmental influences all operate as interlocking determinants of each other" (Bandura, 1978, p. 346). Bandura used television viewing as an example of reciprocal determinism:

> *Personal preferences influence when and which programs, from among the available alternatives, individuals choose to watch on television. Although the potential televised environment is identical for all viewers, the actual televised environment depends on what they select to watch. Through their viewing behavior, they partly shape the nature of the future televised environment. Because production costs and commercial requirements also determine what people are shown, the options provided in the televised environment partly shape the viewers' preferences. Here, all three factors—viewer preferences, viewing behavior, and televised offerings—reciprocally affect each other. (p. 346)*

Additional Reading on This Topic. Another person identified with the social learning theory movement is *Julian Rotter* (1954). Rotter (1966) helped introduce the distinction between *external versus internal locus of control.* This distinction refers to the degree to which people see themselves in control of the conditions influencing their behavior. This construct generated an immense amount of research, as reviewed by Lefcourt (1966, 1992).

Reciprocal determinism was criticized by Philips and Orton (1983), with a reply by Bandura (1983).

KEY NAMES AND CONCEPTS

What follows is an index of some of the most important material in this chapter. The list includes individuals, concepts, and topics you should know. Read through the list, and if anything on it seems unfamiliar, then go back and re-read the appropriate section of the chapter. You should be able to define each concept, briefly discuss each topic, and state the importance of each person on the list. In addition, you should be able to write an account of the work done by each person or topic printed in boldface.

Bandura, Albert, 231
- behavior modification, 231
- modeling, 231
- no-trial learning, 232
- observational learning, 231
- social cognitive theory, 231
- social learning theory, 231
- socio-behavioristic, 231

Berlyne, Daniel, 219
body image and body schema, 228
Bower, Gordon H., 209
Box 11.1—Changing undesirable habits, 213
Box 11.2—Latent learning, 223
Box 11.3—The Garcia effect, 230
- bait shyness, 230
- Garcia, John, 230

Dollard, John, 214
Estes, William K., 211
Guthrie, Edwin R., 211
- breaking undesirable habits, 212
- contiguity, 211

Hebb, Donald O., 211, 226
- *The Organization of Behavior,* 227
- arousal system, 228
- brainwashing, 229
- cell assembly, 227
- cue function, 228
- Hebb rule, 227
- neuropsychology, 227
- neuroscience, 226

perceptual isolation, 229
phase sequences, 227
sensory deprivation, 228
stabilized retinal images, 231
vocal responses, 228
Heron, Woodburn, 229
Hilgard, Ernest R., 209
Conditioning and learning, 209
Theories of learning, 209
Hull, Clark L., 213
conditioned inhibition, 215
drive, 213, 214
habit strength, 215
hypothetico-deductive method, 214
incentive motivation, 215
intervening variables, 214
postulates, 214
primary reinforcer, 214
reaction potential, 215
reactive inhibition, 215
relation to Freudian theory, 214
secondary reinforcer, 214
stimulus intensity dynamism, 215
theorems, 214
Jones, Mary Cover, 231
Krech, David, 222
Miller, Neal, 214
Osgood, Charles E., 217
Evaluation, Potency, Activity, 218
mediating process, 217
semantic differential, 218
sign, 217
Rotter, Julian, 233
locus of control, 233
Simmel, Marianne
phantom limbs, 227
Spence, Kenneth W., 216
explanation of transposition, 216
generalization gradient, 216
systematic desensitization, 232
Tolman, Edward C., 219
cognitive map, 220
expectancies, 220
latent learning, 223
learning versus performance, 224
means-end expectancies, 221
molar versus molecular descriptions of behavior, 220
place versus response controversy, 221
purposive behavior, 220
sign Gestalt, 220
Verbal learning, 222
acquisition, 225
one-trial learning, 225
Robinson, Edward S., 222
Rock, Irvin, 225
serial learning, 226
serial position curves, 226
Underwood, Benton, 226
von Restorff effect, 226
Walters, Richard, 231

CHAPTER 12

THE DEVELOPMENTAL POINT OF VIEW

G. STANLEY HALL (1884–1924)
- *The Theory of Recapitulation*
- *Hall's Life and Career*
- *Hall's Recapitulationism*
- *Questionnaires*
- *"Adolescence"*

JAMES MARK BALDWIN (1861–1934)
- *Psychology of Mental Development*

HEINZ WERNER (1890–1964)
- The Comparative Psychology of Mental Development
- *Uniformity versus Multiformity*
- *Continuity versus Discontinuity*
- *Unilinearity versus Multilinearity*
- *Fixity versus Mobility*
- *Microgenesis*

JEAN PIAGET (1896–1980) AND BÄRBEL INHELDER (1913–)
- *Genetic Epistemology*
- *The Development of Intelligence*
- *Piaget's Clinical Method*
- *Stages in the Development of Intelligence*
- *Piaget as a Structuralist*
- *Wholeness*
- *Systems of Transformations*
- *Self-Regulation*
- *Can Development Ever End?*

LEV S. VYGOTSKY (1896–1934)
- Thought and Language
- *The Zone of Proximal Development*

ERIK H. ERIKSON (1902–)
- *Life-Span Developmental Psychology*
- *Epigenesis*
- *The Eight Stages*

ELEANOR J. GIBSON (1910–)
- *Perceptual Learning*
- *The Visual Cliff*
- *Eleanor Gibson on the Future of Psychology*

Developmental psychology represents not only a specific area of inquiry in psychology, but also a particular approach to the understanding of psychological phenomena. Developmental psychology and child psychology are not the same thing, although, to be sure, the study of children is and always has been a central part of the developmental approach. However, the *concept of development* is complex, and we need to be continuously mindful of the different ways in which this concept has been applied. We can begin to do this by acquainting ourselves with some of the meanings of "development" listed by the *Oxford English Dictionary* (1989). One important meaning is "a gradual unfolding; . . . a fuller disclosure or working out of the details of anything, as a plan, a scheme, the plot of a novel." We shall see that many developmental theorists adopt such a definition of development as a process that unfolds according to a preset plan. However, other theorists regard "development" as synonymous with "evolution," and certainly do not see it as a process that is predetermined, but rather one that is fraught with chance occurrences. Still another variant is the meaning of "development" as a process of "bringing out the latent capabilities" of a person. Certainly many developmentalists were (and are) social reformers who wished to ensure that the developmental process maximized the potential abilities of individuals. Some developmental theorists have regarded development as a process of "advancement through progressive stages," and the question of whether or not there are discernible stages of development has always been a lively issue in this area. As we go along, we will see that there are still more variations on the meaning of "development." With that in mind, let us examine some of the major figures in the history of developmental psychology. In what follows you should bear in mind that in this context the word "genetic," as in "genetic psychology," has the same meaning as "developmental."

G. STANLEY HALL (1884–1924)

The Theory of Recapitulation

One of the recurring themes in developmental theory is the idea of *recapitulation.* This idea is most closely identified with the German biologist and philosopher *Ernst H. Haeckel* (1834–1919). The famous slogan *ontogeny recapitulates phylogeny* captures Haeckel's central idea. "Recapitulation" means "to restate, review or summarize," while "ontogeny" refers to individual development, and "phylogeny" to the evolutionary development of a species. Haeckel's position can be stated as follows:

> *Ontogeny is the short and rapid recapitulation of phylogeny. . . . During its own rapid development . . . an individual repeats the most important changes in form evolved by its ancestors during their long and slow paleological development. (Gould, 1979, pp. 76–77)*

This principle has a long and complex history in biology, and has been the source of a great deal of controversy over the years. One concrete application of the principle was in embryology, where it was sometimes claimed that a human fetus undergoes a condensed form of our evolutionary development. Thus, one nineteenth-century thinker "saw that, at a first stage [of ontogeny], the human brain resembled that of a fish; that at a second stage, it resembled that of reptiles; at a third, that of birds; and at a fourth, that of mammals, in order finally to elevate itself to that sublime organization that dominates all nature" (Gould, 1979, p. 47). The recapitulation principle was extended far beyond the confines of embryology, and was also extensively used in other areas, including psychology. The foremost practitioner of recapitulation theory in developmental psychology was G. Stanley Hall.

Hall's Life and Career

Hall was born in a rural setting in Massachusetts, did his undergraduate work at Williams College, and subsequently went to Union Theological Seminary. He became a minister, but soon went on to pursue further studies. In 1876 he was awarded the first American Ph.D. in psychology, after studying under William James at Harvard. Hall had voracious intellectual interests, and explored a variety of disciplines during visits in Europe between 1870 and 1882 (White, 1992, p. 28). Hall then became professor of psychology at Johns Hopkins University in 1884, but is best known for being the founding president of Clark University in Worcester Massachusetts (Sokal, 1990). Hall was president of Clark for 35 years, from 1888 until 1923. Among his many achievements were his founding of the *American Journal of Psychology* in 1887 and the American Psychological Association in 1892. Among Hall's most famous students was Lewis Terman, the inventor of the Stanford-Binet, whose work we considered in Chapter 7. Hall was also responsible for Freud's visit to Clark in 1909, as we noted in Chapter 6.

As a teacher, Hall believed that the study of the history of philosophy and psychology was particularly important because it "deepens mental perspective . . . and rouses a love of many sides and points of view" (Bringmann, Bringmann, & Early, 1992, p. 287). As a historian of ideas, Hall adopted the personalistic approach, attempting to understand history in terms of the individuals who made it. This approach to the history of psychology was taken up by Edwin G. Boring, whom we have considered earlier (see Chapter 7) as one of the most eminent historians of the discipline. Boring was Hall's colleague at Clark in 1919 (Bringmann, Bringmann, & Early, 1992, p. 287).

Hall's Recapitulationism

Hall's version of the recapitulation principle was informed by a deeply religious sensibility (Vande Kemp, 1992). Not only did he believe that an individual's course of development was a summary of racial history, but he also believed that the historical order in which religions emerged was indicative of their developmental status. Thus, the religious sentiments of a small child are particularly attuned to pagan nature worship, miracles, and myths. However, the developed mind will find itself to be more open to the kind of religious sensibility described by Hall in the following quotation:

> *This whole field of psychology is connected in the most vital way with the future of religious belief in our land . . . The new psychology, which brings simply a new method and a new standpoint to philosophy, is, I believe Christian to its root and center; and its final mission in the world is . . . to flood and transfuse the new and vaster conceptions of the universe and of man's place in it . . . with the Scriptural sense of unity, rationality, and love. . . . The Bible is slowly being re-revealed as man's great text book in psychology—dealing with him as a whole, his body, mind, and will, in all the larger relations to nature, society—which has been misappreciated simply because it is so deeply divine. That something may be done here to aid this development is my strongest hope and belief. (White, 1992, p. 25)*

Recapitulation and religion were linked in Hall's mind because he believed that it was only when people understand themselves as at the pinnacle of a long evolutionary process, which each person undergoes in a condensed form, that they can appreciate their destiny, which is to facilitate further evolutionary progression. Hall believed that the people most fit to lead in this endeavor were research psychologists, because they could provide the means for "self-knowledge and self-control. . . . Psychology was instrumental to the attainment of the perfect social order, and the psychologist occupied a social role consistent with the special obligations of the field" (Morawski, 1982, p. 1084).

As Gould (1977, pp. 139–140) observes, when it came to evidence for recapitulation, Hall pointed to childhood pleasures and fears. A child's love of the beach, for example, could be traced to that time when our evolutionary ancestors had lived in the sea. Similarly, a child's fear of snakes was a relic of ancient times when it was much more realistic to fear snakes and other reptiles. Great emphasis was laid on play as illustrating recapitulationist principles. Children's games were regarded as relics of what once in our history were adaptive activities. "The child revels in savagery," in its "tribal, predatory, hunting, fishing, fighting, roving, playing proclivities" (Hall, 1904/1968, p. 197).

Questionnaires

Hall and his co-workers gathered data on childhood activities through the use of *questionnaires.* Beginning in 1882, Hall (1883/1948) "undertook, soon after the opening of the Boston schools in September, . . . to make out a list of questions suitable for obtaining an inventory of the contents of the mind of children of average intelligence on entering the primary schools of that city. . . . The problem first in mind was strictly practical; viz., what may children be assumed to know and have seen by their teachers when they enter school . . . [K]indergarten teachers were employed by the hour to question three children at a time" (pp. 256–257). This procedure initially produced data on 200 children, which showed that "there is next to nothing of pedagogic value the knowledge of which it is safe to assume at the outset of school life" (p. 275). Because of the highly variable and impoverished nature of many urban children's knowledge, Hall (1904/1968) stressed the importance of acquainting them all with nature and myth, a task which parents should accept.

> *The deep and strong cravings in the individual to revive the ancestral experiences and occupations of the race can and must be met . . . by tales of the heroic virtues the child can appreciate. . . . So, too, in our*

urbanized hothouse life, that tends to ripen everything before its time, we must teach nature, . . . perpetually incite to visit field, forest, hill, shore, the water, flowers, animals, the true homes of childhood in this wild, undomesticated stage from which modern conditions have kidnapped and transported him. Books and reading are distasteful, for the very soul and body cry out for a more active, objective life, and to know nature and man at first hand. These two staples, stories and nature, by these informal methods of the home and environment constitute fundamental education. (p. 197)

Hall's questionnaire approach was extraordinarily influential. The method was taken up by many other students of child development, and a vast amount of data was collected. The *child study movement* was "the most popular educational movement of the 1890s, with followers in two thirds of the states" (Zederland, 1988, p. 155). One of the consequences of this movement was the formation of a bond between psychologists and teachers who worked together in this context. This bond was one of the reasons why psychology became so strongly embedded in the American educational system.

"Adolescence"

Data collected through questionnaires were one of the foundations of Hall's (1904/1967) work on "Adolescence," which was his most ambitious undertaking. Hall is known for drawing attention to adolescence as a period of *storm and stress* in human development (Vande Kemp, 1992, p. 295). The storm and stress of adolescence is caused by the transition from a relatively comfortable relationship with nature to a new, more civilized level of development.

This long pilgrimage of the soul from its old level to a higher maturity which adolescence recapitulates must have taken place in the race in certain of its important lines long before the historic period, because its very nature seems to involve the destruction of all its products and extinction of all records. Just as the well-matured adult . . . has utterly lost all traces and recollection of the perturbations of the storm and stress period, because they are so contradictory and mutually destructive and because feelings themselves cannot be well-remembered, so the race must have gone through a long heat and ferment, of which consciousness, which best develops in stationary periods, was lost . . . (Hall, 1904/1967, p. 219).

Adolescence was a period of "transformation and reconstruction" (Hall, 1904/1967, p. 219). Religious education had a particular importance during adolescence, and religious "conversion was regarded as a normal outcome of the 'storm and stress' of adolescence in individual and species, hastening the transformation from egocentrism to altruism. This theory inspired extensive research on conversion by several generations of psychologists of religion" (Vande Kemp, 1992, p. 295).

Recent evaluations of Hall's contributions to developmental psychology point out that he was much more than just a successful administrator and institutional innovator. As White (1992, pp. 32–33) notes, Hall's questionnaires established the first " 'normal science' of human development." Hall also "elaborated a social-biological conception of childhood" in which the underlying theme is that development involves increasingly elaborate "forms of social participation." Finally, as White (1992, p. 33) sagely observes, Hall's conception of development as a process that unfolds according to its own schedule is a useful corrective to many contemporary attempts to speed up development in the mistaken belief that "the faster the better."

Additional Reading on This Topic. The standard biography of Hall is D. G. Ross (1972). The relation between ontogeny and phylogeny continues to be explored by developmentalists. A good contemporary review of the topic is by Straus (1988).

JAMES MARK BALDWIN (1861–1934)

We have already dealt with a part of Baldwin's life in the section dealing with Watson in Chapter 8 on behaviorism. We noted that Baldwin ran the Johns Hopkins psychology department until he was caught in a police raid on a "colored house" of prostitution, and forced to resign by the Trustees of the university. Following this incident he left the country, and Watson took over at Hopkins. There is, however, much more to Baldwin's career than this unfortunate occurrence might suggest.

Baldwin graduated from Princeton in 1884, and then went to Europe, where, among other things, he studied with Wundt and became a devotee of experimental psychology (Wozniak, 1982, p. 20). He then taught at Princeton and Lake Forest University, and received his Ph.D. from Princeton in 1888. In 1889, Baldwin became a Chair at the University of Toronto, an event that "represents the beginning of modern academic psychology in Canada" (Hoff, 1992, p. 692). Baldwin's interest in development was sparked by the birth of two daughters, and "his intellectual energy . . . shifted away from research . . . in his laboratory at the University College building and toward his 'laboratory of infant psychology' at home" (Hoff, 1992, p. 689).

Baldwin became unhappy with the level of support he received at Toronto, and returned to Princeton in 1893, as professor of psychology. From 1903 until 1912, Baldwin was at Johns Hopkins, where the scandal mentioned earlier took place. "After that incident, he spent little time in the United States, and his name seems to have been virtually blacklisted by the next generation of psychologists" (Cairns, 1992, p. 22). Baldwin then settled in France, and his ideas were taken up in Europe much more so than in America. In fact, he was a major influence on Piaget and Vygotsky (Cairns, 1992, pp. 21–22), whose theories we consider below.

Psychology of Mental Development

As Wosniak (1982, p. 32) observed, Baldwin moved away from experimental, introspective psychology toward developmental psychology partly because he came to believe that mind developed in the individual, and was not always present in the same form.

> *The older idea of the soul was of a fixed substance, with fixed attributes. . . . Under such a conception, the man was father to the child. What the adult consciousness discovers in itself is true, and wherein the child lacks it falls short of the true stature of soul life. . . . The old argument was this, . . . consciousness reveals certain great ideas as simple and original: consequently they must be so. If you do not find them in the child-mind, then you must read them into it.*
>
> *The genetic idea reverses all this. Instead of a fixed substance, we have the conception of a growing, developing activity. . . . Are there principles in the adult consciousness which do not appear in the child consciousness, then the adult consciousness must, if possible, be interpreted by principles present in the child consciousness; and when this is not possible, the conditions under which later principles take their rise and get their development must still be adequately explored. (Baldwin, 1897, pp. 2–3)*

Developmental psychology allowed the psychologist to move beyond mere description of mental events, and to provide an explanation of them, in terms of their genesis. Complicated mental phenomena that appear in the adult may be traced to simpler activities in the child. In this respect, the study of children furnishes us with information that we could never get from animal psychology (Baldwin, 1897, p. 6). Baldwin did not, however, believe in a rigid set of developmental laws. Particular "mental functions" did not emerge like clockwork at specific ages, and only very general norms could be formulated. However, child development normally progressed through invariant *stages,* such that one function emerges before another. For example, "thought develops to a degree independently of spoken language" (Baldwin, 1897, p. 12).

Without committing himself to a strong view of recapitulationism, Baldwin (1897, pp. 15–16) nonetheless believed that there were analogies between phylogenesis and ontogenesis. It was possible to discern four "epochs," or stages, through which both the species and the individual progress. Initially, organisms are concerned with basic sensations and are governed by pleasure and pain. The next stage provides the ability to represent objects and to have memories, but the organism is still quite passive. It is at the third stage that mental life becomes more active, "self-controlled and volitional," while the final stage provides the opportunity for a fully "social and ethical" being (Baldwin,

BOX 12.1

The Baldwin Effect

Recall from our discussion of evolutionary theory in Chapter 2 that Darwin had struggled with the problem of explaining how individual adaptive variations could be transmitted to successive generations. For a while, Darwin had considered Lamarckism, which you should also remember as the hypothesis of the inheritance of acquired characteristics. The classic Lamarckian example is the giraffe's long neck, supposedly acquired as a result of subsequent generations' attempts to reach the tops of trees for food. Lamarckism was discredited in favor of the process of natural selection. Although Baldwin did not favor Lamarckian interpretations, he did believe that "accommodations that occur in the lifetime of the individual could be transmitted to the next by means of the process he labeled *organic selection*" (Cairns, 1992, p. 19). The term *Baldwin effect* refers to processes whereby adaptations that occur ontogenetically can be transmitted to successive generations in a non-Lamarckian way. "No theory of development is complete . . . which does not account for the transmission in some way, from one generation to another, of the gains of the earlier generations, turning individual gains into race gains" (Baldwin, 1897, p. 204). (Baldwin is here using the word "race" in a general way to mean "species.")

As Vonèche (1982, pp. 52–56) points out, the concept of organic selection was intended to explain the way in which small variations, which may not initially make much difference to the organism, nevertheless get selected, and go on to become important adaptive mechanisms in succeeding generations. The best interpretation of organic selection is as a process of coincident variation, in which "a small inborn variation somehow gets amplified by an acquired variation which is grafted onto it, so that the combination of the two sorts of variations gives rise to natural selection . . . [T]he antlers of a stag . . . are not useful unless its neck and shoulder muscles are developed accordingly . . . [T]he development of well-grown antlers in some individuals is the result of an innate variation. Then, because of the extra load of the antlers, the muscles of the neck and shoulders of these animals were developed by adaptive organic variation, which turned the initially innate variation of the size of the antlers into a very useful advantage. Conversely, an innate variation reinforcing the strength of neck and shoulder muscles, would be conserved and transmitted in the presence of antlers, since it would have a determinant role to play in the . . . functioning . . . of the animals concerned. Natural selection protects such a combination of variations, and they keep growing in parallel" (Vonèche, 1982, p. 55).

1897, p. 17). Baldwin presents this complex picture of development as moving along both cognitive and social dimensions (Kohlberg, 1982).

According to Baldwin's theory, development occurs through a series of interactions between the child and the environment (Freeman-Moir, 1982, p. 128). Baldwin (1897) used many concepts that became familiar staples of developmental psychology, such as *assimilation, accommodation,* and *imitation* (Cairns, 1992, p. 19). Assimilation refers to the tendency to respond to the environment in familiar ways. Habits, which involve the tendency to repeat adaptive actions, are the chief process of assimilation. Accommodation, by contrast, is the tendency to respond to the environment in the novel ways that changing circumstances may require (Baldwin, 1897, pp. 478–479). Imitation is the major way in which accommodation takes place. By imitating events in the environment the organism develops new responses. The relation between habit and accommodation is particularly important, because development involves maintaining existing adaptive responses on the one hand (assimilation), while producing novel adaptive responses on the other (accommodation). Over time, the child becomes able to respond to the environment in increasingly complex ways.

One of Baldwin's main claims to fame is his argument for mechanisms that permit acquired characteristics to be passed along to the next generation. This came to be known as the "Baldwin effect," and it is outlined in Box 12.1.

Additional Reading on This Topic. At an early stage of his career, Baldwin (1895/1966; 1896/1966) became involved in a nasty dispute with Titchener (1895/1966; 1896/1966) over the nature of individual differences in reaction time. These lively papers still make good reading.

HEINZ WERNER (1890–1964)

Werner received his Ph.D. in 1914 from the University of Vienna. His original interests were in the psychology of art, and his investigations in that area were typically approached from a genetic point of view (Kaplan & Wapner, 1960). He joined the University of Hamburg in 1917, where he influenced and was influenced by a number of scholars we have considered in previous chapters, including William Stern, Fritz Heider, and particularly the neo-Kantian philosopher, Ernst Cassirer. When the Nazis came to power, Werner left the University of Hamburg in 1933, and held a variety of positions in the United States until he was appointed as G. Stanley Hall Professor of Genetic Psychology at Clark University in 1949 (Franklin, 1990, p. 181). He then proceeded to attract a number of colleagues and students who went on to become prominent developmentalists themselves, including *Seymour Wapner, Bernard Kaplan* and *Edith Kaplan.* "Werner created an atmosphere in which students were treated with unusual respect, and atypically for the times, women were regarded as the intellectual equals of men" (Franklin, 1990, p. 184). Perhaps this atmosphere was responsible for the extraordinary devotion to Werner's ideas still possessed by many of his former students (e.g., Glick, 1992).

The Comparative Psychology of Mental Development

The title of this section is the English title of Werner's best-known work *The Comparative Psychology of Mental Development* (1961), which was originally written in German in 1926. As the title indicates, Werner's approach to development was *comparative,* in the sense of examining the relation between developmental processes in different cultures as well as different species. Moreover, for Werner development is not restricted to the study of the development of individuals. "Each field of psychology—the psychology of the individual and of the human race, animal and child psychology, psychopathology and the psychology of special states of consciousness—all these can be approached from the genetic standpoint" (Werner, 1961, p. 5). In addition to being comparative, Werner's approach was also *organismic,* meaning that "behavior must be considered in relation to the context of total organismic activity" (Wapner, 1964, p. 198).

Precisely what it means to take a developmental point of view was most clearly articulated by Werner (1957) in his paper "The Concept of Development from a Comparative and Organismic Point of View." Development is defined in terms of the *orthogenetic principle,* "which states that wherever development occurs it proceeds from a state of relative globality and lack of differentiation to a state of increasing differentiation, articulation, and hierarchic integration. This principle has the status of a heuristic definition. Though not itself subject to empirical test, it is valuable to developmental psychologists in leading to a determination of the actual range of applicability of developmental concepts to the behavior of organisms" (Werner, 1957, p. 126). This last point is particularly important for understanding Werner's approach. The orthogenetic principle does not purport to be a statement of fact about development. Rather, the orthogenetic principle provides a framework within which development may be studied, and we expand upon it as we go along. "For Werner, development was not a substantive topic area. Rather, it was a way of studying things. Developmental theory was, from his perspective, not an explanation of changes that might be observed with age; it did not really have particularly much to do with age changes at all. It was rather a standpoint for interrogating phenomena. It was a set of questions that investigators posed to themselves about the nature of the phenomena they were studying" (Glick, 1992, p. 560).

The questions that Werner posed when analyzing phenomena developmentally included the following. Is development uniform or multiform? Is development continuous or discontinuous? Is development unilinear or multilinear? Is development fixed or mobile? Let us examine each of these issues in turn.

Uniformity versus Multiformity

Here the issue is whether or not "behavior tends to converge from isolated units toward integrated wholes—i.e., toward uniformity," or whether it becomes increasing differentiated, or "multiform" (Wolff, 1960, p. 33). Examination of behavior reveals that it develops in both ways, a fact that is well-illustrated by a famous study by Werner and E. Kaplan (1952). Participants in this experiment were 8- to 13-year-old children who were given several tasks, of which the following is an example:

A corplum may be used for support.
Corplums may be used to close off an open place.
A corplum may be long or short, thick or thin, strong or weak.
A wet corplum does not burn.
You can make a corplum smooth with sandpaper.
The painter used a corplum to mix his paints.

After being presented with each sentence, the child was asked the meaning of "corplum." The percentage of children at each age who were able to identify "corplum" as "stick" steadily increased. Thus, the ability of children to identify word meanings as a function of the context in which they are used develops *uniformly* with age. However, the methods children use to arrive at a solution are quite varied, and demonstrate that the processes underlying development are *multiform.* Some children generate a unique solution for each sentence and only try to find a general solution at the end, while other children are always looking for a general solution.

The fact that multiple solutions can be generated for the same problem illustrates the importance of the distinction between *process* and *achievement* (Werner, 1937; E. Kaplan, 1983). Werner and his students were less interested in measurements that focused exclusively on achievements, than they were in understanding the processes that enabled such achievements to take place. Thus, an intelligence test score considered by itself is a measure of achievement. Achievement test scores by themselves do not tell the investigator very much about underlying psychological processes. A *process analysis* is one that examines in detail and over time the way in which a person arrives at a particular achievement (E. Kaplan, 1983, p. 155). An example of such an analysis would be to carefully observe a child as he or she attempts to answer each item on an intelligence test, so as to be able to specify the means the person is using to attain particular ends. Such analyses are tailored to specific cases, and rely less on standardized scores than on the analysis of the behavior of individuals.

Continuity versus Discontinuity

The continuity-discontinuity issue has traditionally been a central one in developmental psychology (Lerner, 1986, pp. 183–215). Werner (1957, p. 133) believed that developmental processes had both a continuous and a discontinuous aspect. That is, the child's ability to interact with the world in an increasingly differentiated (precise) and integrated (well-organized) way develops smoothly, but also shows *emergence.* By "emergence" is meant that later forms of behavior have properties not found in earlier forms. Such properties are called *emergent properties.* Wolff (1960, p. 33) gives the development of intentional behavior as an example. Children appear to suddenly develop the ability to set some of their own goals and attempt to achieve them. Thus, intentional behavior is an emergent property, not reducible to previous behaviors, and shows development to be discontinuous as well as continuous.

Unilinearity versus Multilinearity

Although the orthogenetic principle implies that all developmental processes progress in the same way (unilinearity), it nevertheless permits individuals to develop in idiosyncratic ways (multilinearity). Werner (1957, p. 137) recognized the existence of individual differences in development, viewing them as "specializations" or "aberrations." Werner uses the example of physiognomic perception, which we considered in Chapter 9 on Gestalt psychology. You should remember that physiognomic perception involves experiencing the expressive quality of things, such as the friendliness of a face. While Gestalt psychologists believed that physiognomic properties are intrinsic features of percepts, and do not need to be learned, Werner believed that physiognomic perception was a relatively "primitive" form of representation. Children would be expected to "physiognomize" perception, while adults would tend towards a relatively "objective" form of representation (Werner & B. Kaplan, 1963, p. 106). While this is the general rule, there are nevertheless people, such as artists, who specialize in physiognomic perception, and who develop the ability to represent events physiognomically alongside the ability to represent events objectively.

An example of the unilinear aspect of development is the way in which organism-environment interactions progress (Werner & B. Kaplan, 1963, p. 9; Wapner, 1964, p. 196). The most primitive form of interaction involves *tropistic* and/or *reflexive* responses to physical stimuli. These are relatively rigid, biological processes that are early to emerge both phylogenetically and ontogenetically. From a Wernerian standpoint, the studies of behaviorists were preoccupied with this type of process. At the next level of development one finds *sensorimotor* forms of interaction, in which there is "direct, motoric, concrete manipulation of objects" (Wapner, 1964, p. 196). Tool usage by apes would be an example of such a process. This type of interaction differs from the reflexive because the organism can now represent itself as different from the objects with which it deals, and begin to use objects to attain goals. The development of a distinction between subject (self) and object (world) is a central developmental achievement. The third level of organism-environment interaction is *conceptual* or *contemplative*. It is this level that is most characteristic of adult, human thought, and it permits the person to construct tools and symbols "in the service of knowing about and manipulating the environment" (Werner & B. Kaplan, 1963, p. 9).

Fixity versus Mobility

Later developmental levels do not displace earlier ones. Rather, as development proceeds, earlier levels become subordinated to later ones. This is what the orthogenetic principle means by "differentiation and hierarchic integration." The organism attains a greater range of operations, but these are organized hierarchically so that later forms control earlier ones. This implies that earlier ways of behaving tend not to be fixed, but to be mobile enough to change when they become part of a new organization (Wolff, 1960, p. 34). This tendency is well expressed in the Bible (I Corinthians: xiii, 2), "When I was a child I spake as a child, I understood as a child, I thought as a child. But when I became a man, I put away childish things." The adult still speaks and thinks, but usually does so in a way that is different from his or her childish behavior.

Even if an adult has attained a relatively advanced developmental level, adult behavior may still not be fixed at that level. Adults may still sometimes behave in childish ways. Earlier modes of functioning "may come to the fore when the organism is confronted with especially difficult and novel tasks: in such cases, one often finds a partial return to more primitive modes of functioning before progressing towards full-fledged higher operations; we may refer to this tendency as a manifestation of the *genetic principle of spirality*" (Werner & B. Kaplan, 1963, p. 8).

At this point you should be able to appreciate the complexity of Werner's type of developmental analysis. Werner does not provide convenient age norms for the attainment of particular achievements, such as logical thinking. Such norms run counter to the kind of detailed, process analysis that Werner and his students believed was the best way to gain an understanding of development (Glick, 1992, pp. 61–62).

Microgenesis

Werner believed that developmental analysis could be extended to phenomena that develop over relatively brief periods of time, even as short as a few milliseconds (e.g., Werner, 1935). Every psychological process, such as perceiving or speaking, takes time to unfold, and such *microgenetic* (Flavell & Draguns, 1957) processes have the same formal properties as do processes that develop over longer intervals, such as months or even years. This means that the orthogenetic principle can be applied equally to microgenetic and genetic processes. When it is initiated, a psychological process is global and undifferentiated and progresses toward increasing differentiation and articulation.

Werner (1935) pioneered the use of an experimental technique to investigate microgenetic processes in perception. Werner's procedure is best understood by examining Figure 12.1. If you had been a subject in this experiment, you would have been shown a disk, like that labeled "first stimulus" in Figure 12.1, for a brief period. Then you would have been shown a ring, like that labeled "second stimulus" in the figure. The outer contour of the disk was the same as the inner contour of the ring, so that the ring fits exactly over the disk. Werner varied the time between showing the disk and showing the ring. When this interval was relatively long (over 200 milliseconds), the subject saw two stimuli, the first being the disk, followed by the ring. The most interesting cases occurred when the time between the two stimuli was relatively short (between 100 and 200 milliseconds). Under those circumstances subjects reported only seeing the ring, and did not report seeing the disk at all.

Werner explained this result in terms of the time it takes for a perception to be constructed. When

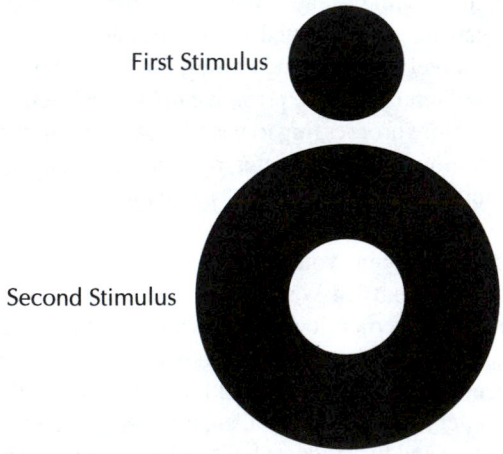

FIGURE 12.1 Werner's backward masking technique (1935).

BOX 12.2

Backward Masking

Werner's experimental procedure (1935) is now called *backward masking,* because one stimulus "masks" a previous stimulus, preventing it from being fully perceived. The interval between the first and second stimulus is called a *stimulus-onset asynchrony* (SOA) (Kahneman, 1968). Werner's technique has been refined and used by numerous experimenters since his initial study. By examining a wide range of SOAs and stimulus materials, psychologists have uncovered an impressive array of findings about microgenetic processes. It now appears that masked stimuli can still influence the subsequent course of perception and cognition (e.g., Marcel, 1983a, 1983b). For example, the meaning of a masked word may alter the course of a person's subsequent experience without their awareness of ever having seen the word. Marcel, Katz, and Smith (1974) showed subjects masked words, such as *orange,* and asked them to report whatever they could. Even though the presented word may not actually be seen, subjects may still report words that have a similar meaning, such as *apple,* the name of another fruit. From a microgenetic viewpoint, under these experimental conditions the word *orange* is only partially constructed. However, the initial stages of the construction of a word include a "global, undifferentiated" sense of its meaning (Werner & B. Kaplan, 1963). From a Wernerian perspective, such a "primitive" stage of perception provides the basis for the subject's subsequent report of words with similar meanings to the one that was shown (e.g., *apple*), but not fully perceived.

the disk is presented, the subject begins to perceive it from the center outward. The last stage in the perception of the disk is the construction of its edge, or contour. Suppose that the ring is presented just as the disk contour is being constructed. Remember that the inner contour of the ring matches the contour of the disk. Consequently, the process of construction of the inner contour of the ring will prevent the completion of the disk. Since the disk is not allowed to be fully constructed, there is no "finished" object to be perceived, and consequently the disk is not seen. Notice how this experiment relies on a detailed "process analysis" of the microgenesis of perception.

Werner's technique (1935) has opened up a very rich area for psychological study, and some of the work that has been spawned as result is reviewed in Box 12.2.

Additional Reading on This Topic. Bernard Kaplan (1992), who was Werner's student and colleague, has written a provocative analysis of the contemporary relation between organismic, developmental, and historical forms of analysis.

Theodore C. Schneirla's (1902–1968) comparative approach (1957; Aronson, Tobach, Lehrman, & Rosenblatt, 1970) is often compared to Werner's, and there are important similarities between the two.

JEAN PIAGET (1896–1980) AND BÄRBEL INHELDER (1913–)

One prominent commentator has observed that Piaget's theory is "the most nearly complete systematization we have of how individuals develop, especially in the cognitive domain" (Sternberg, 1984, p. viii). Piaget's stature in the history of developmental psychology is probably unrivaled by any other theorist, and while he was alive he was perceived even by those outside of psychology as "our leading scholar of child development, one of the most respected intellectuals in the world" (Gould, 1979, p. 144).

Born in Switzerland, Piaget began publishing on biological topics in 1907 when he was 11 years old. His career as a psychologist may be said to have begun in Paris in 1919, where he went to do postdoctoral studies after receiving a Ph.D. in natural science from the University of Neuchâtel. Piaget "was offered the opportunity to work in Binet's laboratory at a Paris grade school. Dr. Simon, who was in charge of the laboratory, suggested that Piaget might try to standardize [Sir Cyril] Burt's reasoning tests on Parisian children. Although Piaget undertook this project without enthusiasm, his interest grew when he began the actual testing. He found himself becoming increasingly fascinated, not with the psychometric and normative aspects of the test data, but with the processes by which the child achieved his [or her] answers—especially his [or her] *incorrect* answers. By adapting psychiatric examining procedures, . . . he was soon using the *clinical method* which was later to become a kind of Piagetian trademark" (Flavell, 1963, p. 3). Piaget returned to Switzerland in 1921, and eventually became Director of the Center for Genetic Epistemology at the University of Geneva.

Although the theory is primarily Piaget's creation, his associate, *Bärbel Inhelder,* helped develop the theory in the period following the Second World War (e.g., Piaget & Inhelder, 1969). In addition to making substantive contributions, "she frequently attended international conferences where American psychologists met her and could converse easily with her, for her English was excellent" (Hilgard, 1993, p. 73). Thus, Inhelder played a crucial role in making Piagetian theory as widespread as it has become.

Genetic Epistemology

Piaget (1968a) called his approach *genetic epistemology,* or the study of the development of knowledge. "Genetic epistemology attempts to explain knowledge, and in particular scientific knowledge, on the basis of its history, its sociogenesis, and especially the psychological origins of the notions and operations upon which it is based" (p. 1). For Piaget, knowledge is not simply the result of the application of innate categories to experience, in the way that Kant proposed. Nor does knowledge simply accumulate as a result of experience in the way that empiricists such as Locke, Berkeley, or Hume suggested. There are "hereditary factors" such as "the constitution of our nervous system and of our sensory organs" that limit the kinds of experiences of which we are capable (Piaget, 1963, p. 2). However, our most important inheritance is the function of intelligence, which enables us to adapt to our environment. Intelligence is not fixed, but develops. The study of the way that intelligence develops is the subject of Piaget's psychology.

The Development of Intelligence

We discuss the development of intelligence in terms presented by Piaget in the introduction to his classic work, *The Origins of Intelligence in Children* (1963). Another very useful translation of the same material, containing extensive explanatory footnotes by David Rapaport, is Piaget (1951).

The study of the development of the ability to think logically owes more to Jean Piaget than to anyone else. Logical thinking is the hallmark of intelligence. Intelligence is rooted in biological processes, which are themselves concerned with furthering the organism's adaptation. Adaptation is an *invariant function* of the organism. Organisms adapt by changing themselves in response to the environment in ways that are not random, but reveal processes that exist at all levels of development. Piaget (1963, p. 6) uses the example of digestion to illustrate the way that the organism changes with changing circumstances. A hungry organism takes in food, and the food is transformed so as to be used by the body. The organism *assimilates* the food by changing it to suit its needs. Eventually the body returns to its original state, and the process begins all over again. Suppose, however, that the organism's diet must change because the food it habitually ingests is no longer available. Now the organism will have to adjust to new foods in order to adapt. Such an adjustment is an *accommodation* of the organism to environmental change.

Assimilation and accommodation exist at all levels of adaptation, including intelligence. Intelligence involves assimilation because we must put things in terms we can understand in order to be able to deal with them. However, we cannot adapt merely by changing everything to fit our own way of doing things. We must also accommodate by changing our way of doing things so as to come to terms with reality.

Piaget (1962) singled out *play* as a relatively pure example of assimilation, and *imitation* as a relatively pure example of accommodation. "Play . . . proceeds by relaxation of the effort at adaptation and by maintenance or exercise of activities for the mere pleasure of mastering them and acquiring a feeling of virtuosity or power" (Piaget, 1962, p. 89). When a child pretends, for example, that a broomstick is a horse, and proceeds to "ride" it all over the house, then the child is disregarding what the broomstick actually is and using it instead for his or her own purposes. By contrast with play, "imitation is a kind of hyperadaptation, through accommodation to models" (Piaget, 1962, p. 89). Imitation plays a central role in the acquisition of language, for example, which begins through the child's attempts to imitate sounds made by others. Neither play by itself, nor imitation by itself is enough to guarantee our well-being. Assimilation and accommodation are opposing tendencies, each one as important as the other. Piaget emphasized the necessity of attempting to achieve a balance between assimilation and accommodation, a process he termed *equilibration.*

Piaget's Clinical Method

As indicated previously, Piaget's studies of the development of intelligence employed a *clinical method.* The method essentially consists of an open-ended series of questions designed to elicit the child's viewpoint on the subject of the investigation. The nature of the method is well-illustrated in Piaget's exploration of the way children understand the rules of the game of marbles (1965/1976):

The experimenter speaks more or less as follows. 'Here are some marbles . . . You must show me how to play. When I was little I used to play a lot, but now I've quite forgotten how to. I'd like to play again. Let's play together. You'll teach me the rules and I'll play with you' . . . It is important to bear in mind all possible contingencies of the game and to ask the child about each. This means that you must avoid making any sort of suggestions. All you need to do is to appear completely ignorant, and even to make intentional mistakes so that the child may each time point out clearly what the rule is. Naturally, you must take the whole thing very seriously, all through the game . . . It is of paramount importance to play your part in a simple spirit and to let the child feel a certain superiority at the game (while not omitting to show by an occasional good shot that you are not a complete duffer). In this way the child is put at ease, and the information he gives as to how he plays is all the more conclusive. (pp. 418–419)

The features of the method Piaget stresses with respect to investigating children's games—such as gaining the child's confidence, not appearing to be superior, asking questions about all aspects of the matter, and avoiding suggestions—are features of the method which are important when one is investigating any aspect of children's activity. The clinical method was criticized by many other developmentalists, especially those trained in America, who preferred more "objective" methods, such as standardized tests. However, Piaget believed that the deficiencies of the clinical method were more than offset by the richness of the information it could provide when used by a skilled and perceptive observer.

Piaget's application of the clinical method to the study of the child's understanding of the rules of the game of marbles showed that these rules went through a sequence of stages. Initially, the child is concerned only with what it is possible to do with the marbles, a stage Piaget (1965/1976, p. 430) calls "simple individual regularity." After the age of 2, a new stage begins to emerge when the child imitates the rules he or she sees others follow. However, the child uses the rules in a personal way, without engaging in any cooperative activity, and Piaget calls this stage "egocentric." Around age 7, children begin a "co-operative" stage by deciding together what the rules will be. However, the rules are formulated neither precisely nor consistently from time to time. The fourth and final stage emerges around age 11 when a consistent and enduring set of rules is subscribed to by all participants. Piaget calls this the stage of "codification." These particular stages are interesting in their own right as illustrating the development of an understanding of the social rules governing an area of interpersonal interaction. However, it was Piaget's contention that the development of rules of the game of marbles was also interesting because it illustrated general stages of intellectual development. For Piaget, there was an invariant sequence of stages that regulated all aspects of intellectual development.

Stages in the Development of Intelligence

Piaget believed that a crucial aspect of intellectual development was a discontinuous series of levels, or *stages*. Stages are qualitatively different modes of psychological organization. Initially, the child responds concretely to particular situations, but by progressing through the developmental stages becomes able to utilize general principles to deal abstractly with the world. Although the sequence of stages through which the child progresses is invariant, there are no firm age norms at which these must occur.

Sensorimotor Period. During the first 2 years of life the child is initially able to interact with objects only in rudimentary ways, but gradually shows a more intelligent approach to these interactions. For example, consider a child who is able to crawl around on the floor, and thus move from one location to another in order to attain a desirable object, such as a favorite toy. Obviously, the child will crawl directly from the first place to the second, provided there are no barriers. This situation is diagrammed in Figure 12.2A on page 248. The situation in Figure 12.2B is more interesting. In this case, there is a barrier, in the form of a round table,

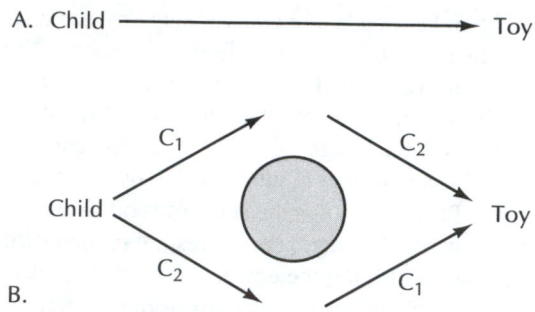

FIGURE 12.2 The attainment of associativity in sensorimotor intelligence.

between the child and the goal. Through active exploration of situations such as this, the child can begin to appreciate that the goal can be attained in different ways (e.g., Berlyne, 1965, p. 205). Two of these alternatives are diagrammed in Figure 12.2B. The child can crawl to its left (C_1) and then to the right after passing the barrier (C_2), or the child can crawl to its right (C_2) and then to the right after passing the barrier (C_1).

Piaget's point (1966, p. 41) in analyzing situations such as this one is that the development of the ability to take detours reveals the beginnings of the development of logic. In this case we can see the roots of the concept of *associativity.* The child begins to realize that actions taken in different orders may lead to the same result. Thus, in our example, $C_1 + C_2 = C_2 + C_1$ since both orders bring the child to the same goal. Moreover, the child may return to its original position after having attained its goal, a sign of the beginnings of *reversibility,* which, as we shall see, is a central concept in Piagetian psychology.

Of course, there is much more going on in the sensorimotor period than the development of the ability to make detours! Another important achievement is the development of *permanent objects.* Initially, the child makes no distinction between itself and objects in the external world. "At about five to seven months, when the child is about to seize an object and you cover it with a cloth or move it behind a screen, the child simply withdraws his already extended hand" and acts as if the object ceased to exist (Piaget & Inhelder, 1969, p. 14). Subsequently, however, the child will look for the hidden object, demonstrating the child's understanding of the fact that the object continues to exist even when it can no longer be seen. This marks the beginnings of the realization that the nature of the external world is not dependent on the child's activities. The emergence and continued refinement of objectivity is one of the hallmarks of the development process.

Preoperational Period. Piaget described this stage as lasting roughly from 2 to 7 years, and having as its major feature the emergence of symbolic activity, including language. As a consequence of the "symbolic function . . . the internalization of actions into thoughts becomes possible" (Piaget, 1957, p. 10). The child is no longer limited to merely doing things, but can now also begin to think about things. Piaget & Inhelder (1969, p. 53) point to *deferred imitation* and *symbolic play* as characteristic of this stage. Deferred imitation refers to the ability to imitate a model in its absence. Such imitation requires that the child be able to internally represent the model so as to be able to mimic it. Symbolic play refers to the ability to pretend that something is the case, as in the broomstick/horse example we considered above.

The preoperational period is also interesting and important for what it shows the child to still be unable to do (Piaget, 1957, p. 11). One of Piaget's most dramatic illustrations (1968b; Piaget & Inhelder, 1973) concerns the preoperational child's memory for ordered events. Piaget (1968b) described one experiment as follows:

> *Children are shown an ordered configuration, that is, 10 sticks, varying in size from about 9 to 15 centimeters, ordered from the biggest to the smallest. . . . The children are asked to have a good look, so that they will be able to draw it later. A week later, without showing them the configuration again, they are asked to draw or to describe verbally . . . what we had shown them before. Six months later, without seeing the configuration they were asked to do the same thing. (p. 3)*

The interesting result of this experiment, and others like it, is that the quality of memory depends on the age of the child. After 1 week, the youngest children in the experiment (3 to 4 years) only remember that they were shown a set of sticks, but do not recall their relative lengths. Only the oldest children (6 to 7 years) remember that the sticks were ordered, or seriated, from small to large. The truly remarkable finding reported by Piaget and Inhelder (1973) is that 6 months later the younger subjects' memory has *improved!* Now children are able to report that the sticks had been in some kind of order, although their recall may not be perfect. Piaget and Inhelder interpreted such findings as meaning that memory changes as the child develops. "Old" memories will be recalled in terms of the child's "new" developmental level. The younger children initially could not represent seriation, and so could not recall it. Later on they have developed the ability to represent an ordered series, and only then are able to reconstruct what they had been shown. Piaget and Inhelder (1973, p. 409) took such findings as showing that individual psychological functions (such as memory) are not determined by the characteristics of particular experiences, but operate in accordance with the general intellectual level of the child.

Concrete Operations. Children in the preoperational period easily confuse the classes to which events belong. Piaget (1957, p. 4) described an experiment in which children who were between 5 and 8 years of age were shown a set of 20 *wooden beads.* The beads were either *brown* or *white,* with the majority being brown. Although you might think that anyone, regardless of age, could say that there were more wooden beads than brown beads, these children are inclined to say that "There are more brown beads than wooden beads, because there are only two or three white ones" (Piaget, 1957, p. 5). The child at this age cannot think in terms of one class (brown beads) being a member of a larger class (wooden beads). Rather, the child believes that if we take the brown beads away from the wooden beads, then the only wooden beads left are the white beads, and there are more brown beads than white beads.

It is during the period of concrete operations (roughly between 7 and 11 years) that children come to understand that something can be placed in one class (e.g., brown beads) and also in another class (e.g., wooden beads) at the same time. To put it more formally, children realize that something can belong to both a subordinate class (e.g., brown beads, white beads) and a superordinate class (e.g., wooden beads). An important next step is the *multiplication of classes.* Multiplication of classes becomes a possibility when the child realizes that something can belong to more than one superordinate class. For example, we can classify people in more than one way simultaneously. People can be classified by such dimensions as *gender* and *income* as well as any number of additional dimensions. An example is shown in Figure 12.3. Suppose we let *A* be one superordinate class (such as gender) and *B* be another superordinate class (such as income). We can further classify people as *men* (A1) or *women* (A2) and as *rich* (B1) or *poor* (B2), resulting in the four classes in Figure 12.3: rich men; rich women; poor men; and poor women.

Multiplication of classes is an example of an *operation,* or internalized action. Instead of actually manipulating objects, such as placing them in boxes, the child can imagine what the results would be of carrying out the action. The stage of concrete operations gives the child much to think about, but

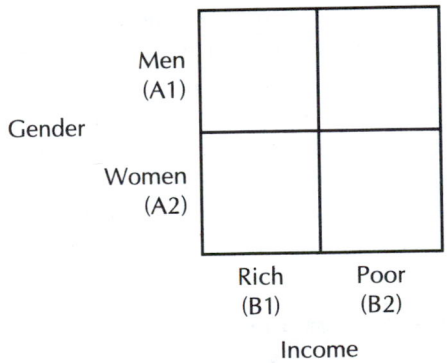

FIGURE 12.3 The multiplication of classes.

all the child is able to think about are specific states of affairs. Operations at this stage are termed "concrete" because they are "not yet completely dissociated from the concrete data to which they apply" (Piaget, 1957, p. 15).

Formal Operations. Sometime around age 12, the child begins to be able to carry out operations on possible as well as actual events. For example, a multiplication of classes may be undertaken in a purely experimental manner. The child can imagine different possible independent variables, such as *income* and *gender,* and formulate hypotheses concerning their possible effects on behaviors of various sorts. These hypotheses can then be tested against observed data. The two-by-two classification in Figure 12.3 is, of course, only one possibility. One could think of any number of alternative classes that could be multiplied, such as *age* (old versus young), or *height* (tall versus short) and so on. Depending on the situation, different classifications would be relevant. Moreover, there is no reason to be limited to multiplying only two dimensions. It is possible to imagine experiments that classify events using three or more variables (e.g., *gender* by *age* by *intelligence*).

Could one imagine multiplying all possible classes? That would result in a "logical space" that contained all possible events. Wittgenstein (1922/1974) put it like this: "Logic deals with every possibility, and all possibilities are its facts. . . . If I know an object, I also know all its possible occurrences in states of affairs. . . . Each thing is, as it were, in a space of possible states of affairs. This space I can imagine empty, but I cannot imagine the thing without the space" (p. 71). It is necessary to have a logical space within which to imagine some of the possibilities, and it is the development of formal operations that makes this logical space possible. However, in any actual experiment, only a part of the logical space can be included.

Piaget as a Structuralist

Piaget was a part of a broad European intellectual movement called *structuralism* (Gardner, 1974; Lane, 1970). Other prominent structuralists include the anthropologist *Claude Levi-Straus* (1967), the linguist *Roman Jacobson* (1967), and the novelist/philosopher *Umberto Eco* (1989). The *Oxford English Dictionary* (1989) defines a *structure* as "an organized body or combination of mutually connected and dependent parts." While there are very great differences between individual structuralists, they all share the assumption that organized systems underlie and control all aspects of human experience from art to politics, and from child development to scientific reasoning (Lane, 1970, p. 13). Contemporary structuralism should not be confused with Titchener's psychology, which is sometimes given the same name.

Piaget (1971, 1973) emphasized that structures must be understood in terms of the way that they develop over time. Developing structures are characterized by three properties: *wholeness; systems of transformations;* and *self-regulation.*

Wholeness

Structures are not merely compounds of elements. Like Gestalten, structures are wholes and, as such, are not reducible to their parts. Unlike the Gestalt psychologists, Piaget did not believe that structures emerged spontaneously in experience. The structure of human experience must be understood in terms of the way it has developed, both historically and in the life of the particular person. Structures develop over historical time as well as within the life of individuals. The structure of the medieval mind was more limited than that of the modern mind in terms of what it was able to conceive. Nevertheless, mentalities at any level of development will be characterized by wholeness.

Systems of Transformations

The wholeness of structures is not static but dynamic. That is, the parts of structures are capable of being transformed into other parts of the same structure according to definite rules. For example, linguistic structures possess grammatical transformations that allow active sentences (e.g., "The cat chased the dog") to be transformed into passive sentences (e.g., "The dog was chased by the cat"). In arithmetic, numbers may be transformed into each other in a variety of ways. For example, 6 may be divided by 2 to get 3, or 1 may be added to 2 to get 3, and so on. These transformations are not arbitrary, but are parts of a self-regulating structure.

Self-Regulation

Self-regulation is the key property of structures. A structure is self-regulating if "transformations inherent in a structure never lead beyond the system but always engender elements that belong to it and preserve its laws" (Piaget, 1971, p. 14). Logical and mathematical structures are good illustrations of self-regulation. In arithmetic, for example, you can transform numbers into each other through unambiguous transformations (addition, subtraction, multiplication, and division). If the transformations are applied properly, then the system always provides the correct answer. Moreover, every transformation has an inverse that enables the transformation to be undone. Thus, by dividing 6 by 2, you get 3, but you can get back to 6 again by multiplying 3 by 2. A perfect structure is reversible if it always allows you to get back to where you started, and such *reversibility* is an extremely important property of high-level structures.

By no means all structures are perfectly self-regulating, although there is a tendency for structures to become self-regulating. It is a large part of Piaget's genius to have described in considerable detail the processes whereby psychological structures develop self-regulation. One of his most famous examples is the achievement of *conservation.* There are many forms of conservation, but perhaps the best known is conservation of quantity, which is illustrated in Figure 12.4.

In a typical conservation task, a child is shown two glasses, each containing the same amount of fluid, as in Figure 12.4A. The fluid from one of the glasses is then poured into another glass of different dimensions, like the one in Figure 12.4B. Although the level of the fluid in the last glass is different from the previous level, adults have no difficulty concluding that the amount of fluid in the glasses is the same. However, as parents know, 5-year-old children may prefer the tall glass because it appears to them to contain more than the short, stubby glass. Such children are termed *preconservative,* because they do not understand that the quantity of liquid is conserved even though its appearance has changed.

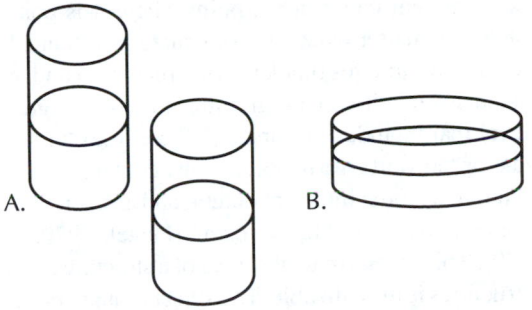

FIGURE 12.4 The conservation of quantity.

The difference between the adult and the child demonstrates the difference between a self-regulating and a non-self-regulating structure. The adult realizes that even though the fluid is transformed when it is poured from one glass to another, these transformations could be reversed, returning everything to its original state. It is precisely this lack of reversibility that makes the child focus on one dimension, such as the height of the fluid, and not take other changes into account, such as the greater width of the fluid. The preconservative child cannot transform one situation into the other, and back again. Rather, the child is *centered* on one aspect of the situation. In order to understand it properly, the child must become *decentered,* which involves allowing each dimension to correct the other one. A decentered view reveals the underlying reality behind changing appearances (Flavell, 1985, p. 96).

Can Development Ever End?

Although structures tend to develop in the direction of self-regulation, it is illusory to imagine that development can reach a point where it is complete. No matter what level of structure is attained, it is impossible for that level of structure to understand itself without progressing to a still higher level that includes the first. "[T]here is no 'terminal' or 'absolute' form because any content is form relative to some inferior content, and any form the content for some higher form" (Piaget, 1970, p. 140). This means that "the ideal of a structure of all structures is unrealizable. The *subject* cannot be . . . a finished . . . structure; rather it is a center of activity. And whether we substitute 'society' or 'mankind' or 'life' or even 'cosmos' for 'subject', the argument remains the same" (Piaget, 1970, p. 142). Thus, living structures are in a continuous, never-ending process of construction.

Additional Reading on This Topic. A very good overview of the area of cognitive development is Siegler (1986).

LEV S. VYGOTSKY (1896–1934)

Although Vygotsky died more than 50 years ago, his ideas are becoming more influential with the passage of time. One reason is that Vygotsky "provides the still needed provocation to find a way of understanding man as a product of culture as well as a product of nature" (Bruner, 1986, p. 78). A noted contemporary Vygotsky scholar (Wertsch, 1985, p. 231) remarked that "it may strike many as ironic that Vygotsky's ideas should appear so fruitful to people removed from him by time and space. . . . Instead of viewing this as paradoxical, however, it should perhaps be seen as a straightforward example of how human genius can transcend historical, social and cultural barriers."

Vygotsky graduated from Moscow University in 1917, and was initially very interested in the relation between art and psychology (Vygotsky, 1971). He gradually began to focus on the psychology of teaching, particularly with respect to physically and mentally challenged children. It was during this period that he wrote what was to become his most influential work, *Thought and Language*. This work was not fully translated into English until many years after its appearance in Russian (Vygotsky, 1934/1962). He died of tuberculosis, bringing to a tragic close a brief but extraordinarily productive life (Luria, 1978).

Because of the time and place in which he worked, we should not be surprised to discover that *Marxist* ideas shaped Vygotsky's thinking. However, it would be a mistake to criticize Vygotsky's theory merely because it has Marxist roots. Many of Vygotsky's ideas have been warmly welcomed in non-Marxist countries, such as the United States, because they can be applied to general developmental issues without raising questions of political ideology.

Thought and Language

An important assumption that Vygotsky borrowed from Marx was that "historical changes in society and material life produce changes in 'human nature' (consciousness and behavior)" (Cole and Scribner, 1978, p. 7). This means that the developmental process is inherently social (Wertsch and Tulviste, 1992, p. 548). Development is not something that is entirely constrained by the nature of the nervous system and it cannot be understood on the level of individual development. Moreover, people cannot be studied in the same way as animals, because this would overlook the essentially social nature of human development.

> *[H]uman behavior differs qualitatively from animal behavior to the same extent that the adaptability and historical development of humans differ from the adaptability and development of animals. The psychological development of humans is part of the general historical development of our species and must be so understood. (Vygotsky, 1978, p. 60)*

A crucial difference between humans and other animals is the way that *tools* are used. A tool is anything that can be used to attain a goal. The distinctively human form of tool use involves language. Initially, language and action proceed independently of each other. "The most significant moment in the course of intellectual development, which gives birth to the purely human forms of practical and abstract intelligence, occurs when speech and practical activity, two previously completely independent lines of development, converge" (Vygotsky, 1978, p. 24). To illustrate this development, Vygotsky uses as an example a 4.5 year old child who is getting candy from a cupboard using a stool and a stick as tools. The child continually describes her action out loud as she carries it out, as if the speech was controlling her action. The development of such linguistic self-regulation was of particular interest to Vygotsky.

Vygotsky began his analysis of the development of language and thought by elaborating on Piaget's (1923/1959) concept of *egocentric speech,* which is speech in which the young child "talks to himself as though he were thinking aloud. He does not address anyone" (Piaget, 1923/1959, p. 9). From Piaget's viewpoint, egocentric speech is replaced around age 7 by socialized speech, in which the child "really exchanges his thoughts with others" (Piaget, 1923/1959, pp. 9–10). Vygotsky (1934/1962, p. 136) studied egocentric speech in various contexts, and concluded that it occurred when other children were around and that the young child did not yet distinguish between private speech and social speech.

Vygotsky believed that what Piaget called egocentric speech did not actually disappear, but become internalized as *inner speech.* Thus, Vygotsky distinguished between inner speech, or "speech for oneself," and external speech, or "speech for others" (Vygotsky, 1934/1962, p. 131). Inner speech comes to control mental life. It is as if we use inner speech to silently give orders, not to other people, but to ourselves. Inner speech is condensed and vivid. Because the speaker and the listener are the same person, a lot can be taken for granted and everything does not need to be spelled out.

The less well you know someone, the more will your speech to that person have all the properties of formal, grammatically correct external speech. However, people who know each other very well may speak in a way that has some of the characteristics of inner speech. Vygotsky (1934/1962) made this point using an example from a story by Dostoyevsky which told of

> *a conversation of drunks that entirely consisted of one unprintable word (*The Diary of a Writer, *for 1873): 'One Sunday night I happened to walk for some fifteen paces next to a group of six drunken young workmen, and I suddenly realized that all thoughts, feelings and even a whole chain of reasoning could be expressed by that one noun, which is moreover extremely short.' (p. 143)*

Vygotsky (1934/1962) gives a beautiful example, taken from Tolstoy's *Anna Karenina,* of the way that two people who share the same intimate context can communicate deeply without saying anything explicitly.

> "I have long wished to ask you something."
> "Please do."
> "This," he said, and wrote the initial letters: *W y a: i c n b, d y m t o n.* These letters meant: "When you answered: it can not be, did you mean then or never?" It seemed impossible that she would understand the complicated sentence.
> "I understand," she said blushing.
> "What word is that?" he asked, pointing to the *n* which stood for never.
> "The word is 'never,' " she said, "but that is not true." He quickly erased what he had written and handed her the chalk, and rose. She wrote: *I c n a o t.*
> His face brightened suddenly: he had understood. It meant: "I could not answer otherwise then."
> She wrote the initial letters: *s t y m f a f w h.* This meant: "So that you might forget and forgive what happened."
> He seized the chalk with tense, trembling fingers, broke it, and wrote the initial letters of the following: "I have nothing to forget and forgive. I never ceased loving you." (p. 140)

The Zone of Proximal Development

One of Vygotsky's (1935/1978) most enduring concepts is the *zone of proximal development,* which he defined as follows: "It is the distance between the actual developmental level as determined by independent problem solving and the level of potential development as determined through problem solving under adult guidance or in collaboration with more capable peers" (p. 86). The actual developmental level may be determined by standardized testing. The potential developmental level requires more sensitive exploration on the part of a teacher to discover what the child is capable of discovering with assistance from an adult. Such a teacher might "offer leading questions or show how the problem is to be solved and the child then solves it, or if the teacher initiates the solution and the child completes it or solves it in collaboration with other children" (Vygotsky, 1978, p. 85).

Vygotsky points out that two children can be at the same actual developmental level, but at different potential developmental levels. It is the potential developmental level that should guide the efforts of educators. Rather than simply teach to the actual developmental level, one should be enabling the child to reach his or her potential developmental level (El'konin, 1969, p. 168). "What is in the zone of proximal development today will be the actual developmental level tomorrow—that is, what a child can do with assistance today she will be able to do herself tomorrow" (Vygotsky, 1978, p. 87).

Additional Reading on This Topic. In addition to the original translation of *Thought and Language* by Hanfmann and Vakar, there is a newer translation by A. Kozulin (Vygotsky, 1934/1986). Applications of Vygotsky's ideas to education and other areas are given in Rogoff and Wertsch (1984).

Goffman (1978) provides interesting and amusing examples of cases in which inner speech, which is normally silent, will become public.

ERIK H. ERIKSON (1902–)

Erikson was born in Germany of Danish parents, who had separated before he was born. When Erikson was 3 years old, his mother married a Dr. Homburger, from whom Erikson gets his middle initial. As a young man, Erikson traveled extensively in Europe, living as an artist. A friend from his schooldays became a teacher in a new school in Vienna that was associated with Anna Freud. In 1927, Erikson became associated with the school, and began to develop his understanding of child development, although at this point he had no formal training in psychology. However, he began an analysis with Anna Freud, and graduated from the Vienna Psychoanalytic Institute in 1933. In 1929, Erikson met and later married a North American, *Joan Serson,* who subsequently played an important role in the development of his theories (Coles, 1970, pp. 13–31).

Partly because of the rise of Nazism in Europe, Erikson moved to Boston in 1933, where he became its first child psychoanalyst. He enrolled in, but never completed, a Ph.D. program at Harvard. Nevertheless, he both taught and did research at Harvard. He also spent time at Yale, where he came into contact with Clark Hull's research group. A fateful period involved a visit to a Sioux Indian reservation in South Dakota. "[H]is work with the Sioux Indians marked the beginning of a life-long effort to demonstrate how the events of childhood are affected by the inevitable encounter with a given society, whose customs affect the way mothers hold and feed infants, and later on bring them up to behave" (Coles, 1970, p. 37).

Erikson was at the University of California at Berkeley from 1939 until 1950, when he resigned over the requirement that all professors take a loyalty oath. (Like Erikson, Edward C. Tolman also refused to sign the oath.) While Erikson declared himself to be a non-Communist, he believed that, as a matter of principle he should make a stand against what he perceived to be an infringement of the right of individuals to think and be judged independently of their political convictions. He eventually ended up back at Harvard, where he became a professor in 1960, and from which he retired in 1970.

Life-Span Developmental Psychology

Erikson created one of the most influential descriptions of the issues and crises that people generally face as their lives unfold. As one might expect, Erikson was heavily influenced by Freudian theories. As did Freud, Erikson emphasized the importance of early childhood experience in shaping the adult personality. However, in his major and most influential work, *Childhood and Society* (1950, 1963), Erikson went well beyond Freud to posit the existence of specific stages of development that occur throughout the entire life cycle, and not just in childhood. Erikson's theory is one of the major reasons why developmental psychology is no longer concerned only with childhood, but with those changes that occur throughout a person's life.

Epigenesis

Erikson (1959) called his theory *epigenetic,* meaning that developmental stages unfold in a necessary sequence.

> *[A]nything that grows has a* ground plan, *and out of this ground plan the* parts *arise, each part having its* time *of special ascendancy, until all parts have arisen to form a* functioning whole . . . *[I]n the sequence of his most personal experiences the healthy child, given a reasonable amount of guidance, can be trusted to obey inner laws of development. . . . Personality can be said to develop according to steps predetermined in the human organism's readiness to be driven toward, to be aware of, and to interact with a widening social radius, beginning with a dim image of his mother, and ending with mankind. (p. 52)*

Thus, the sequence of developmental stages is a "progression through time of a differentiation of parts" (Erikson, 1959, p. 53). However, Erikson was at pains to emphasize that this progression is modulated by the particular society in which the person develops. Moreover, "the theory postulates a *cogwheeling of the life cycles:* the representatives of society, the caretaking persons, are coordinated to the developing individual by their specific inborn responsiveness to his [or her] needs and by phase-specific needs of their own" (Rapaport, 1959b, p. 15). People are inherently social beings, and one of the ways in which this is expressed is in the way that older people feel the need to care for younger ones:

> Care *is a quality essential for psychosocial evolution, for we are the teaching species. Animals, too, instinctively encourage in their young what is ready for release, and, of course, some animals can be taught some tricks and services by man. Only man, however, can and must extend his solicitude over the long, parallel and overlapping childhoods of numerous offspring united in households and communities. . . . Once we have grasped this interlocking of the human life stages, we understand that adult man is so constituted as to* need to be needed *lest he suffer the mental deformation of self-absorption, in which he becomes his own infant and pet. (Erikson, 1964, p. 130)*

While Erikson's developmental stages unfold over time and have an invariant order, it is difficult to be too specific about the times at which the stages emerge, because these will be at least somewhat different for each individual, as a consequence of his or her own unique situation. At best we can make only general estimates for an ideal life cycle, which may only be imperfectly realized in the individual case. Moreover, as Erikson (1959) makes clear, the stages do not proceed like the links in a chain; rather they may overlap. The person may begin working on a new stage before the current one is resolved.

The Eight Stages

Each stage in the life cycle presents the person with a definite task which must be solved at that time. At each stage the person is presented with alternative choices and, through important encounters with the physical and social environment, some resolution of the crisis occurs. There are eight stages in an individual's life (Erikson, 1963, chap. 7), and they are listed below:

1. Basic trust vs. mistrust
2. Autonomy vs. shame and doubt
3. Initiative vs. guilt
4. Industry vs. inferiority
5. Identity vs. identity diffusion
6. Intimacy vs. isolation
7. Generativity vs. stagnation
8. Integrity vs. despair

In Erikson's scheme, each developmental stage involves pairs of opposing tendencies, one with a positive connotation (e.g., "trust") and one with a negative connotation (e.g., "mistrust"). From Erikson's point of view, the successful resolution of each developmental crisis is not seen as meaning that one of the opposites has "won out" over the other. Rather, when a person successfully negotiates a critical period in development, the opposing tendencies are mixed in the right proportion, with an imbalance in favor of the positive (Erikson, 1963, p. 274). Although it is essential, for example, that the child develop a sense of basic trust in the world, "to learn to mistrust is just as important" (Evans, 1976, p. 293). The content of each stage may be described as follows.

Basic Trust versus Mistrust. In the beginning the child is dependent on significant others for his or her well-being and comfort. The child's identity may be captured by the statement "I am what I am given" (Erikson, 1959, p. 82). If the child receives a high enough quality of care during the first year of life, then the child will acquire a sense of confidence, a feeling that he or she can trust the world to be consistent and provident. As with the succeeding stages, too much of the positive quality (trust) can be unhealthy. There are certainly situations in which a skeptical attitude is appropriate, and so the best outcome is a balance between the two, but in favor of basic trust. A positive outcome at this stage gives the child *hope* (Erikson, 1963, p. 274).

Autonomy versus Shame and Doubt. The second and third years of life are associated with the achievement of self-control (e.g., becoming toilet-trained) and the beginnings of mastery of the external world. The child's identity at this stage depends on the emergence of *willpower* (Erikson, 1962, p. 255), and may be characterized as "I am what I will" (Erikson, 1959, p. 82).

Initiative versus Guilt. Now the child is moving around in the environment more freely. He or she begins to use language effectively, and can also start to imagine the sort of person he or she would like to become. Since play and imagination are so salient for the child at this stage (Erikson, 1972), the child's identity is closely tied to what it is possible to imagine becoming, as in "I am what I can imagine I will be" (Erikson, 1959, p. 82). A successful resolution of this stage gives the child a sense of *purpose* (Erikson, 1963, p. 274).

Industry versus Inferiority. Once the child begins school, he or she becomes increasingly reliant on education to master the world. The child's self-definition now becomes "I am what I learn" (Erikson, 1959, p. 82). The desirable outcome of this stage is a feeling of *competence* (Erikson, 1963, p. 274).

Identity versus Identity Diffusion. The problem of establishing a stable personal identity now comes to the fore. The young person has as a central concern the development of a sense of who he or she is, the maintenance of a stable conception of oneself and the way one is seen by others. Of course, this should not be a rigid, inflexible identity determined by peer pressure, but one that expresses and is tolerant of individuality (Erikson, 1959, p. 91). The ideal outcome at this stage is *faithfulness* to oneself and to others (Erikson, 1963, p. 274).

Intimacy versus Isolation. After this sense of identity is established, it is possible to become genuinely intimate with others, as in marriage; and to maintain one's identity without becoming isolated from those around one. Erikson (1950, p. 266) suggested that at this stage an individual should ideally be capable of "mutuality of orgasm . . . with a loved partner . . .with whom one is able and willing to share a mutual trust . . . and with whom one is able and willing to regulate the cycles of . . . work . . . procreation . . . [and] recreation so as to secure to the offspring, too, all the stages of a satisfactory development." Erikson's regarded this kind of *love* as an ideal to aim for rather than a universally achievable goal.

Generativity versus Stagnation. Building on a solid sense of self, and viable interpersonal relationships, the focus turns toward the contribution the person can make to society through creativity in

BOX 12.3

Life Review and Reminiscence in Psychologists

Some support for Erikson's theory comes from a study of autobiographical memories by Mackavey, Malley, and Stewart (1991). They analyzed the autobiographies of 49 well-known psychologists (31 men and 18 women), written when they were an average of 72 years of age, with a range of 54 to 86 years. From Erikson's viewpoint, this group of people should be at the eighth stage (integrity versus despair) and concerned with evaluating their lives, a process called *life review.* The evaluative process should lead them to *reminisce,* which means spending an increased amount of time remembering events from the earlier parts of life. Rubin, Wetzler, and Nebes (1986) reviewed evidence that supports the hypothesis that reminiscence increases after 50 years of age.

When a person reflects on his or her life, it is likely that they will tend to remember episodes from periods in which decisions were made that had consequence for the rest of life (Mackavey, Malley, & Stewart, 1991, p. 52). By counting and dating 250 of these *autobiographically consequential experiences* (ACEs) in the 49 autobiographies, Mackavey, Malley, and Stewart (1991) derived a distribution of ACEs across the typical life span. About 80 percent of the ACEs occurred between the ages of 18 to 35; relatively few were from early childhood or after age 50. Mackavey, Malley, and Stewart (1991) suggested that these results can best be understood in the context of Erikson's theory of the role of identity in the life cycle (1959; Erikson, Erikson & Kivnick, 1986). The most important choices in our lives (e.g., marriage, career) are typically made in late adolescence and young adulthood. These choices have crucial consequences for what happens to us later on. Consequently, it is natural for the process of life review to tend to focus on this period, as the person summarizes and evaluates what has been important and meaningful in their life.

Of course, one cannot be sure that the way that reminiscence seems to work for psychologists will mirror the trends found in other people. However, it demonstrates that Erikson's theory can generate interesting research in contexts beyond that in which the theory was originally created.

a variety of spheres (e.g., as a parent, in a career). *Caring* is the dominant theme of a successful resolution of this period (Erikson, 1963, p. 274).

Integrity versus Despair. As a person's work and family become established, the question of what one's life all adds up to begins to pose itself. "Only he who in some way has taken care of things and people and has adapted himself to the triumphs and disappointments of being, by necessity, the originator of others and the generator of things and ideas—only he may know the fruit of the seven stages. I know of no better word for it than *integrity*" (Erikson, 1959, p. 98). After successfully negotiating the previous crises more or less well, the reward is the achievement of a measure of *wisdom* (Erikson, 1963, p. 274).

Erikson's theory is grounded in clinical observation, particularly of children at play. The theory has been quite fruitful in terms of generating research. An example of such research that is particularly relevant to the history of psychology is given in Box 12.3.

Additional Reading on This Topic. Lerner (1982) contains a useful history of contributors to the life-span approach other than Erikson.

ELEANOR J. GIBSON (1910–)

Eleanor Jack Gibson (1980) did her undergraduate degree at Smith College, graduating in 1931. She met *James J. Gibson,* then teaching psychology at Smith,

> *at a garden party at the end of my junior year. It rained and we were happily stranded in a corner of a quadrangle where he was supposed to be shaking hands with parents of seniors as I offered them punch. He took me back to my dormitory in his ancient Model-T Ford, and the next day I hurried to the class dean's office and changed the following year's schedule to include his class in Advanced Experimental*

Psychology. It was a wonderful course and I fell in love with Experimental Psychology and with the instructor (p. 243).

Eleanor and James subsequently married, and both have had a peerless influence on American psychology. We will consider James J. Gibson's influence in Chapter 14.

Eleanor Gibson also studied with Koffka at Smith, but she "was not attracted by Gestalt psychology and yearned for what I thought of as 'hard' psychology. I didn't like introspective methods. I wanted to be objective, as I thought of it then, and I wanted to work with animals and children" (Gibson, 1980, p. 245). Her interest in "hard" psychology was well served by going on to study at Yale with Clark Hull, who was her Ph.D. dissertation supervisor.

After receiving her Ph.D., Eleanor and James Gibson worked together at Smith, where both were on the faculty. After World War II, they moved to Cornell, where J. J. Gibson was on the faculty, but Eleanor was listed only as a research associate. In those days many universities had nepotism rules that forbade husbands and wives both to be faculty members. Over the years, many women were denied professional opportunities at many universities as a result of such rules. In Eleanor Gibson's case, she did not become a professor of psychology until 1966, when nepotism rules finally began to change (Pick, 1992, p. 789).

Perceptual Learning

One of E. J. Gibson's most enduring contributions has been her research concerning the way children learn to perceive their environment. In a classic paper, J. J. Gibson and E. J. Gibson (1955) argued that learning to perceive has traditionally been conceived of as a process of *enrichment.* For example, associationist theorists such as Locke, Berkeley and Hume, whom we considered in Chapter 2, believed that information that we received through our senses was not intrinsically meaningful. Rather, it was necessary to supplement immediate experience with previous experiences drawn from memory. A similar position was taken by Wundt and Titchener, when they argued that sensations were united by previous experience to form perceptions. Thus, according to these theorists, perceptual learning reflects the extent that immediate experience is enriched by previous experience. We learn what the stimulus is that we are currently experiencing by associating it with other stimuli we have experienced in the past. For example, we are able to recognize the letter "A" because it is similar to, and thus associated with, other stimulus configurations that have the same properties. Perceptual learning is a matter of *generalization.*

By contrast with the enrichment theory, the Gibsons argued that perceptual learning was a matter of *differentiation.* Perceptual learning is not characterized by learning to place stimuli in equivalent classes. Rather, perceptual learning involves becoming increasingly attuned to the specific events that make up the world. Before perceptual learning takes place, we overgeneralize, and see things as similar to each other. Perceptual learning allows us to make distinctions between events that we were not initially able to make. The example of a wine connoisseur is used by the Gibsons to make this point. Someone who is skilled at wine tasting can discriminate between many more different wines than can someone who is just starting out, for whom all wines may taste the same.

In order to illustrate this process of differentiation E. Gibson did an experiment that was reported in the Gibson and Gibson (1955) paper. The experiment made use of a set of "scribbles," as illustrated in Figure 12.5. Casual inspection of the items shows them to all consist of a number of coils. However, these coils differ from each other in three ways. First, the number of coils varies from three to five. Second, the coils are more or less close together. Third, starting from the outermost coil, they spiral in a clockwise or counterclockwise direction. You should inspect the scribbles until you can detect all these differences.

There were three groups of subjects in this experiment. One group consisted of younger children

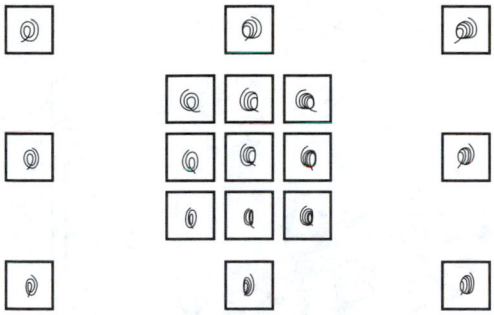

FIGURE 12.5 Nonsense items differing in three dimensions of variation.

Source: J. J. Gibson & E. J. Gibson (1955). Perceptual learning—differentiation or enrichment? *Psychological Review, 62,* 36.

between 6 and 8 years old; another group consisted of older children between 8.5 to 11 years; and a third group consisted of adults. A deck of cards was made up in which each card had one of the scribbles in Figure 12.5 printed on it. In addition, there were also several other nonsense figures printed on cards and interspersed in the deck. One of the scribbles was selected as the target item, and shown to the subjects. Their task was to select those items in the deck that were exactly like the target. After the first trial, the younger children named many more items as the same as the target (13.4) than did the older children (7.9), who in turn named more than the adults (3.0). Moreover the adults took only an average of 3.1 trials to reach a perfect identification of the one coil that corresponded to the target. The older children took 4.7 trials, and many of the younger children failed to identify the target correctly during the course of the experiment.

This experiment demonstrates what the Gibsons' meant by "perceptual learning." Initially, a number of stimuli are easily confused with one another. With repetition, stimuli can be differentiated from one another, although this occurs more quickly with adults than children:

> *Achievement of specificity involves the detection of properties and patterns not previously responded to. Detection of properties was illustrated in the scribble experiment, as the subjects discovered the dimensions of difference. It would be hard to overemphasize the importance for perceptual learning of the discovery of invariant properties which are in correspondence with physical variables. The term 'extraction' will be applied to this process, for the property may be buried, as it were, in a welter of impinging stimulation (E. Gibson, 1969, p. 81).*

E. Gibson (1969) argued that differentiation has characterized the evolutionary and developmental processes. Phylogenetically, different senses have emerged, each attuned to a different kind of stimulus dimension. These senses themselves have become increasingly able to pick up highly specific forms of information. Ontogenetically, perceptual learning enables the person to respond to increasingly differentiated aspects of the environment.

Reading. One of the most important developmental achievements is learning to read. E. Gibson (1965/1991; Gibson & Levin, 1975) explored this process in considerable detail. One question she has explored is "how are words perceived?" This is a complicated question because words have several features that could be perceived by readers. What features allow a successful reader to rapidly differentiate one word from another? While words differ in length and shape, such cues are insufficient to be the entire basis of reading. Gibson, Pick, Osser, & Hammond (1962) suggested that certain strings of letters were more pronounceable than others, and that *pronounceability* was a very important property of words that would-be readers learned to perceive. They observed that particular letters tend to go together in particular positions in words, and that these spelling patterns are always pronounced in the same way. Thus, for example, GLURCK is not an English word, but is pronounceable, while CKURGL is not as pronounceable. This is because a spelling pattern such as GL tends to begin English words, while CK tends to come at the end of English words.

Gibson et al. (1962) showed subjects nonwords (like GLURCK) that are pronounceable and nonwords that are less pronounceable (like

CKURGL). These stimuli were exposed for only very brief durations. Subjects were much more likely to perceive the pronounceable nonwords than the less pronounceable ones. "We conclude from these experiments that skilled readers more easily perceive as a unit pseudo words that follow the rules of English spelling-to-sound correspondence; that spelling patterns which have invariant relations to sound patterns function as a unit" (Gibson, 1965/1991, p. 408). Subsequent research showed that the ability to perceive spelling patterns may already exist in a limited way in first-graders. There is clearly more to reading than simply the ability to pick up spelling patterns, and E. Gibson also investigated many additional aspects of the reading process. Nevertheless, her work on spelling patterns is a good illustration of her careful experimental approach to the discovery of developmentally important processes.

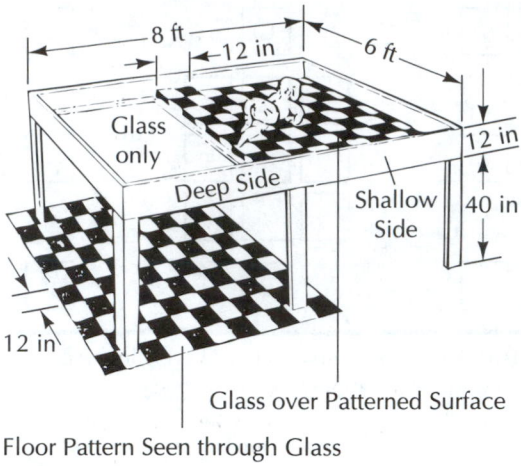

FIGURE 12.6 The visual cliff.

Source: R. D. Walk & E. J. Gibson (1961). A comparative and analytic study of visual depth perception (p. 8). *Psychological Monographs,* Vol. 75 (15, Whole No. 519).

The Visual Cliff

Science often progresses through the invention of a new piece of apparatus that enables the investigation of an important process. Such an invention was the *visual cliff* introduced by Walk and E. Gibson (1961). One version of the visual cliff is shown in Figure 12.6. The visual cliff enabled Gibson and her co-workers to investigate depth perception. You should remember from Chapters 2 and 3 that this is a classic problem in psychology, which has been addressed by a number of the most prominent figures in the history of psychology, from Berkeley to Helmholtz. The usual explanation of our ability to locate objects in space was that we infer, on the basis of previous experience, that particular objects in the external world have given rise to the images on our retinas. The result of this inferential process is the three-dimensional world we experience. Gibson's work with the visual cliff suggested a very different answer to this question.

To begin with, Gibson (1969) pointed out that the ability to see objects in depth is a highly adaptive skill:

> *[O]ne universal requirement holds for all terrestrial animals, the necessity to avoid falling from high places. A long fall means death. Whether the avoidance is learned or innate the animal must be able to respond as soon as he attains free locomotion unguided by a parent. He must be able to see a drop-off, a falling-off place. (p. 267)*

The visual cliff is constructed as follows. There is a center board flanked by a shallow and a deep side. Both the shallow side and the deep side are covered by the same sheet of glass, which is strong enough to carry the weight of an experimental subject. The glass on the shallow side has a patterned surface directly underneath it, while the glass on the deep side has a patterned surface at some distance beneath it. A subject (animal or human) is placed on the center board. The experimenter observes whether the subject has a tendency to move to the shallow side, the deep side, or both sides equally. If the animal is able to perceive depth, one would expect a preference for the shallow over the deep side.

Over the years, a number of infant animals, including rats, chickens, pigs, kittens, puppies, monkeys, turtles, rabbits, ducklings, lions, tigers, leopards, and human infants were tested on the visual cliff by a number of different investigators (E. Gibson, 1969, p. 268). Animals whose natural mountain habitat requires them to avoid sharp drop-offs, such as snow leopards, sheep, and goats, show an avoidance of the deep side of the visual cliff at a very early age. Aquatic animals such as turtles and ducks do not show such a pronounced preference, presumably because their natural habitat enables them to swim over deep places, and so it is less important to avoid them.

Experiments with human infants between 6.5 and 14 months involved placing the infant on the center board and having the baby's mother call to the baby from either side. Almost all those infants able to crawl would do so when the mother called from the shallow side, but were very unlikely to do so to the deep side. It appeared that infants were able to perceive depth by the time they were able to crawl. This calls strongly associationist accounts of the development of space perception into question, since the infants did not appear to have to crawl around in the world in order to develop the ability to perceive depth. Walk and Gibson (1961) took their results to be consistent with the notion that depth perception does not have to be learned, although it is capable of becoming increasingly differentiated with experience.

Eleanor Gibson on the Future of Psychology

One outstanding feature of Gibson's reputation is that of "a consummate experimenter. . . . Throughout her career she has continued to be a model experimenter who has been widely recognized, for example, by her election to the National Academy of Science and the awarding to her of the National Medal of Science (1992)" (Pick, 1992, p. 792). By 1992, the *National Medal of Science* had been awarded since 1962 to a total of 304 recipients. Including Eleanor Gibson, only 10 psychologists had received it (Kent, 1992, p. 15). "She was cited for the National Medal of Science for her 'conceptual insights in developing a theory of perceptual learning and for achieving a deeper understanding of perceptual development in children and basic processes in reading' " (Kent, 1992, p. 14).

E. Gibson (1994) has recently given an overview of the history of psychology over the last few decades. She observed that there was a great deal of general "excitement in the air about the future of psychology in the 1930's," but that "something went wrong with this youthful dream, about halfway into the century" (E. Gibson, 1994, p. 69). She presents a picture of psychology as lacking in coherence, and laments the lack of "a search for encompassing principles, ones that make sense of all the underlying relationships. I think many psychologists have given up on this, a hope we still shared 60 years ago" (E. Gibson, 1994, p. 70). Gibson urges a new agenda, based on a developmental approach, that will restore a unity of purpose to psychology. This question of the perceived fragmentation of psychology, and possible remedies for it, will be taken up in Chapter 15.

Additional Reading on This Topic. A. Pick (1979) contains a number of tributes to Gibson's work and influence. Other important figures in the history of developmental psychology are chronicled in volume 22 of the journal *Developmental Psychology* (1992). These include *Nancy Bayley* (Rosenblith, 1992); *John Bowlby* and *Mary Ainsworth* (Bretherton, 1992); *Arnold L. Gesell* (1880–1961) (Thelen & Adolph, 1992); and *Robert Sears* (Grusec, 1992).

KEY NAMES AND CONCEPTS

What follows is an index of some of the most important material in this chapter. The list includes individuals, concepts, and topics you should know. Read through the list, and if anything on it seems unfamiliar, then go back and re-read the appropriate section of the chapter. You should be able to define each concept, briefly discuss each topic, and state the importance of each person on the list. In addition, you should be able to write an account of the work done by each person or topic printed in boldface.

Ainsworth, Mary, 261
autobiographically consequential experiences, 257
Baldwin, James Mark, 238
accommodation, 240
assimilation, 240
Baldwin effect, 240
imitation, 240
organic selection, 240
psychology of mental development, 239
stages, 239
Bayley, Nancy, 261
Bowlby, John, 261
Box 12.1—The Baldwin effect, 240
Box 12.2—Backward masking, 244
Box 12.3—Life review and reminiscence in psychologists, 257
concept of development, 235
Erikson, Erik H., 254
autonomy versus shame and doubt, 256
basic trust versus mistrust, 256
cogwheeling of life cycles, 255
eight stages of development, 255
epigenesis, 255
generativity versus stagnation, 256
identity versus identity diffusion, 256
industry versus inferiority, 256
integrity versus despair, 256
intimacy versus isolation, 256
initiative versus guilt, 256
life review, 257
life-span developmental psychology, 254
reminiscence, 257
Gesell, Arnold L., 261
Gibson, Eleanor J., 257
differentiation, 258
enrichment, 258
generalization, 258
National Medal of Science, 261
perceptual learning, 258
pronounceability, 259
psychology's future, 261
reading, 259
visual cliff, 260
Gibson, James J., 257
Haeckel, Ernst H., 236
ontogeny recapitulates phylogeny, 236
Hall, G. Stanley, 236
adolescence, 238
child study movement, 238
life and career, 236
questionnaires, 237
recapitulationism, 237
storm and stress in adolescence, 238
Inhelder, Bärbel, 245
Kaplan, Bernard, 241
Kaplan, Edith, 241
Piaget, Jean, 245
accommodation, 246
assimilation, 246
associativity, 248
centered, 251
clinical method, 245, 246
concrete operations, 249
conservation, 251
decentered, 251
deferred imitation, 248
definition of "stage," 247
egocentric speech, 253
equilibration, 246

genetic epistemology, 245
imitation, 246
invariant functions, 246
multiplication of classes, 249
object permanence, 248
operation, 249
play, 246
preconservative, 251
preoperational period, 248
reversibility, 248, 251
self-regulation, 251
sensorimotor period, 247
structuralism, 250
structure, 250
symbolic play, 248
systems of transformations, 250
wholeness, 250
Schneirla, Theodore C., 245
Sears, Robert, 261
Serson, Joan, 254
stimulus-onset asynchrony, 244
Vygotsky, Lev, 252
Marxism, 252
Thought and Language, 252
tools, 252
zone of proximal development, 253
Wapner, Seymour, 241
Werner, Heinz, 241
backward masking, 244
comparative approach, 241
conceptual/contemplative level of development, 243
continuity versus discontinuity, 242
emergence, 242
fixity versus mobility, 243
genetic principle of spirality, 243
microgenesis, 244
organismic approach, 241
orthogenetic principle, 241
process analysis, 242
process and achievement, 242
sensorimotor level of development, 243
tropistic/reflexive level of development, 243
uniformity versus multiformity, 242
unilinearity versus multilinearity, 242

CHAPTER 13

HUMANISTIC PSYCHOLOGY

EXISTENTIALISM
- *Søren Kierkegaard (1813–1855)*
- *Friedrich Nietzsche (1844–1900)*
- *Jean-Paul Sartre (1905–1980)*
- *Ludwig Binswanger (1881–1966)*

THE EMERGENCE OF HUMANISTIC PSYCHOLOGY

ROLLO MAY (1909–1994)

ABRAHAM H. MASLOW (1908–1970)
- *The Hierarchy of Needs*
- *The Self-Actualizing Person*
- *Peak Experiences*
- The Psychology of Science

CARL R. ROGERS (1902–1987)
- Client-Centered Therapy
- *Eugene T. Gendlin*
- *Encounter Groups*
- *What Happened to Humanistic Psychology?*

GEORGE A. KELLY (1905–1967)
- The Psychology of Personal Constructs
- *The Repertory Test*
- *Research in Personal Construct Theory*
- *Qualitative Research Methods*

In 1958, a book called *Existence* was published, edited by Rollo May, Ernest Angel, and Henri F. Ellenberger. This book introduced European *existentialism* to many American psychologists. Existentialism is difficult to define precisely. The *Oxford English Dictionary* (1989) characterizes existentialism as "a doctrine that concentrates on the existence of the individual, who, being free and responsible, is held to be what he makes himself." A particularly clear summary of existentialism is given by Mary Warnock (1970):

> *Broadly speaking, we can say that the common interest which unites Existentialist philosophers is the interest in human freedom. They are all of them interested in the world considered as the environment of [people], who [are] treated as . . . unique object[s] of attention, because of [their] power to choose [their] own course of action . . . [F]or existentialists, uniquely, the problem of freedom is in a sense a practical problem. They aim, above all, to show people* that they are free, *to open their eyes to something which has always been true, but which, for one reason or another may not always have been recognized, namely that [people] are free to choose, not only what to do on a specific occasion, but what to value and how to live. The readers of Existentialist philosophy are being asked, not merely to consider the nature of human freedom, but to* experience *freedom, and to practice it. (pp. 1–2)*

EXISTENTIALISM

Søren Kierkegaard (1813–1855)

Kierkegaard was a Danish philosopher who was preoccupied with the nature of human choice. In a work called *Either/Or,* Kierkegaard (1843/1959) presented the reader with two alternative ways of living one's life: the aesthetic and the ethical. The aesthetic way of life involves the search for sophisticated forms of pleasure. The arbitrariness of the aesthetic approach to living is well captured by the following quotation:

> *If you marry, you will regret it; if you do not marry, you will also regret it . . . Laugh at the world's follies, you will regret it; weep over them, you will also regret that . . . Hang yourself, you will regret it; do not hang yourself, and you will also regret that . . . This . . . is the sum and substance of all philosophy. (p. 37)*

In spite of the melancholy nature of such sentiments, Kierkegaard did not believe that the ethical alternative of living by a rigorous set of idealistic principles was superior to the aesthetic way of life. Both the aesthetic and the ethical are equally justifiable. All choices are arbitrary because no objective rationale exists for one alternative over the other. In the end, one's choices are one's own.

To illustrate the *subjective nature of human choice,* Kierkegaard (1843/1959) considered the case of Abraham. In the Old Testament, Abraham was commanded by God to make a sacrifice of his son, Isaac. Abraham does not have to kill his son simply because God tells him to. God does not *make* Isaac sacrifice his son; it is up to Abraham to choose to do so. Of course, it is *absurd* for Abraham to be presented with such a choice, and Kierkegaard argued that all people are confronted in one way or another with the absurd nature of human existence. Abraham could choose to sacrifice his son because of his *faith* in God. For Kierkegaard, such faith is itself absurd, but possible nonetheless. The *leap of faith* that makes one a religious person is not grounded in any objective fact, but is a purely subjective act.

Friedrich Nietzsche (1844–1900)

Nietzsche's influence on European thought was considerable during his lifetime, and continues to provoke and disturb people until this day. Nietzsche (1967, p. 3) observed the emergence of *nihilism* in Europe, the notion that there are no absolute truths or values. Nietzsche believed that nihilism marked the end of Christianity. "The time has come when we have to pay for having been Christians for two thousand years: we are losing the center of gravity by virtue of which we lived; we are lost for a while" (Nietzsche, 1901/1967, p. 20). In the place of Christianity, Nietzsche saw the emergence of *perspectivism,* the notion that there are any number of interpretations of reality, all of them equally valid (Greer, 1994). Perspectivism rejects the superiority of a scientific understanding of the world, as illustrated in the following quotation (Nietzsche, 1901/1967, p. 267).

> *Against positivism, which halts at phenomena—"There are only* facts*"—I would say: No, facts is precisely what there is not, only interpretations. We cannot establish any fact "in itself": perhaps it is folly to want to do such a thing.*
>
> *"Everything is subjective," you say; but even this is interpretation. The "subject" is not something given, it is something added and invented and projected behind what there is.—Finally, is it necessary to posit an interpreter behind the interpretation? Even this is invention, hypothesis.*
>
> *In so far as the word "knowledge" has any meaning, the world is knowable; but it is* interpretable, *otherwise it has no meaning behind it, but countless meanings.—"Perspectivism."*
>
> *It is our needs that interpret the world; our drives and their For and Against. Every drive is a kind of lust to rule; each one has its perspective that it would like to compel all the other drives to accept as a norm. (p. 267)*

Nietzsche's argument that "it is our needs that interpret the world" leads directly to his concept of the *will to power.* There is no objective description of reality, but all descriptions are intended to accomplish particular ends. "Knowledge works as a tool of power. Hence it is plain that it increases with every exercise of power" (Nietzsche, 1901/1967, p. 266). Something that society as a whole takes to be true is only what powerful people want to be true. However, every individual is free to choose some other interpretation of reality in accordance with his or her own will to power.

If all experience is an interpretation, and all interpretations reflect the will to power, then all experience is "permeated with value judgments" (Nietzsche, 1901/1967, p. 275). No value judgment can be taken to be "better" than any other. They are all "beyond good and evil . . . This world is the will to power—and nothing besides! And you yourselves are also this will to power—and nothing besides!" (Nietzsche, 1901/1967, p. 550).

Jean-Paul Sartre (1905–1980)

Jean-Paul Sartre (1939/1962) is one of the greatest twentieth-century French intellectuals. His companion of many years, *Simone de Beauvoir,* will be discussed in Chapter 15. After teaching in France for a number of years, Sartre lived in Berlin in the early 1930s where he was influenced by Edmund Husserl. You should recall from Chapter 4 that Husserl was a student of Franz Brentano's, and had pioneered the phenomenological method. The phenomenological method is an attempt to describe consciousness as it presents itself to us, without any presuppositions as to its nature or purpose.

Sartre served in the French Army, and was captured by the Germans in World War II. After his release he was active in the French resistance movement. He published his major philosophical work, *Being and Nothingness,* in 1943. Sartre refused to accept the Nobel Prize for Literature that he was awarded in 1964. This refusal was consistent with his general attitude of disdain for established cultural institutions. He was acquainted with, and contemptuous of, the work of academic psychologists who regarded their discipline as an objective, experimental science.

> *[T]he psychologist strictly forbids himself to consider the men around him as men* like himself . . . *[H]is human nature will not be revealed in any special manner under the pretext that he* is *himself that which he is studying. Introspection here, like "objective" experimentation there, will furnish nothing but facts . . . [P]sychology, insofar as it claims to be a science, can furnish no more than a sum of . . . facts, the majority of which have no link between them. What could be more different, for instance, than the study of the stroboscopic illusion and the study of the inferiority complex? This disorder does not arise by chance, but from the very principles of the science of psychology. To wait upon the* fact *is, by definition, to wait upon the isolated; it is to prefer, positively, the accident to the essential, the contingent to the necessary, disorder to order. It is to discard, in principle, the essential as something in the future—"that is for later on, when we have collected enough facts." The psychologists do not notice, indeed, that it is . . . impossible to attain the essence by heaping up the accidents. . . . If their only aim is to accumulate observations of detail there is nothing to be said, except that one can see little interest in the collectors' labours. (pp. 16–18)*

Sartre (1943/1966; 1957) adopted Brentano and Husserl's concept of *intentionality,* meaning that consciousness is always directed at something other than itself. We are always conscious of something, such as the sentence I am now writing and that you are now reading. Our intentions are revealed by our choices. We are always choosing to do one thing as opposed to another. Not only do we choose to do some things and not others, but we also choose to know some things and not others. We are what we have chosen to be, a fact Sartre (1957) sums up in the slogan *existence precedes essence.* By this is meant that people are not predetermined, and cannot claim that they had no choice but to become what they are:

> *Dostoievsky said, "If God didn't exist, everything would be possible." That is the very starting point of existentialism. Indeed, everything is permissible if God does not exist, and as a result man is forlorn, because neither within him nor without does he find anything to cling to. He can't start making excuses for himself.*
>
> *If existence really does precede essence, there is no explaining things away by reference to a fixed and given human nature. In other words, there is no determinism . . . man is condemned to be free. Condemned, because he did not create himself, yet, in other respects is free; because, once thrown into the world, he is responsible for everything he does. (pp. 22–23)*

Sartre placed great importance on honesty, both with oneself and with others. Self-deception arises when we do not take responsibility for our choices. Sartre regarded lying to oneself as a form of *bad faith.* Facing the truth about oneself may be painful, and Sartre acknowledged the fact that existentialism appeared to many to lead to a form of bleak despair, a life without illusions. However, Sartre (1957, p. 51) regarded his approach as a form of *humanism* because it placed the person at the center of the action, the only one responsible for his or her life.

Ludwig Binswanger (1881–1966)

Existentialism provided an alternative to psychoanalytic psychotherapy (May, 1958). This form of psychotherapy not only drew on such people as Kierkegaard and Nietzsche, but also on *Martin Heidegger* (1899–1976). Heidegger was a student of Husserl and had also been an influence on Sartre. Heidegger was Chancellor of the University of Freiburg in the early days of the Nazi regime, and for a few years following the Second World War was forbidden to teach because of pro-Nazi sentiments he had expressed.

Heidegger's (1927/1962) fame rests on his analysis of Being, or *Dasein.* A person is fundamentally concerned with the fact that he or she is a *being-in-the-world.* People want to know what it means to be in the world, and ask fundamental questions about the nature of existence. To be human is to *care* about the nature of existence, and such care is intrinsic to human beings. Heidegger believed that the phenomenological method is the only proper way to investigate the nature of being-in-the-world. A phenomenological description of consciousness reveals that people vary in the way that they are related to the world in which they live. Terms such as "melancholy, boredom, fear, anxiety, and despair" refer to different ways of being-in-the-world (Schrag, 1967). The attempt to understand these moods as different ways of being-in-the-world constitute the starting place for existential psychotherapy.

Binswanger (1975) developed an *existential approach to psychotherapy* by building on Heidegger's basic ideas. Binswanger was originally trained as a psychoanalyst, and then shifted to an existential approach. He recorded a conversation he had with Freud in 1927 in which they discussed a patient who had failed "to take the last decisive step of psychoanalytic insight and to thus continue in his misery in spite of all previous efforts and technical progress. . . . I suggested that such a failure might only be understood as the result of something which could be called a deficiency of spirit, that is, an inability on the part of the patient to raise himself to the level of spiritual communication with the physician" (p. 1). Binswanger then went on to tell Freud that he was "forced to recognize in man something like a religious category" that was fundamental in human beings (p. 2). People must make some spiritual commitment in order to make fundamental changes in themselves.

In his discussion with Binswanger, Freud, of course, did not agree with the notion that people are spiritual as well as biological creatures. However, Binswanger believed that a psychotherapist needs to attend to the spiritual side of the patient, "who is his partner in the community of man and is another 'human soul' " (p. 210). Such an understanding goes beyond mere scientific understanding of the person as a biological object. It "inquires into the being of man as a whole" (p. 210), and requires "a relation rooted equally in 'care' and love. It is of the *essence* of being a psychiatrist, *therefore,* that he reaches beyond . . . *scientific* knowledge found in the fields of psychology, psychopathology, and psychotherapy. . . . The being of a psychiatrist . . . involves, therefore, the insight that . . . no 'whole man' can be 'grasped' with the methods of science" (pp. 219–220).

Binswanger goes on to claim that psychotherapy is not something that one can do with only a part of oneself, like "a hobby or . . . some other scientific activity" (p. 220). Psychotherapy requires a total commitment to "encounter and mutual understanding with [one's] his fellow man and . . . understanding human beings in their totality" (p. 220).

THE EMERGENCE OF HUMANISTIC PSYCHOLOGY

The American psychologists and psychotherapists who imported existentialism from Europe and modified it to suit their own purposes included *Rollo May, Abraham Maslow,* and *Carl Rogers.* We will consider each of them in detail. Now, however, we will outline some features of their common reaction to existentialism. These reactions were expressed at a symposium on existential psychology held at a convention of the American Psychological Association in 1959 (May, 1961).

1. The American psychologists believed that existentialism added important dimensions to psychology. For May (1961, p. 40), this meant a renewed "emphasis on will and decision" as central psychological processes. For Maslow (1961, p. 53), it meant "a radical stress on the concept of identity and the experience of identity." For Rogers (1961a, p. 92), it signaled a concern with an "existing, becoming, emerging, experiencing being."

2. American psychologists disagreed with the antiscientific attitude expressed by many European existentialists. May (1961, p. 37) argued that existentialism was consistent with a broader conception of the nature of science than American academic psychologists usually adopt, and quoted one of the symposium participants as saying that "science offers more leeway than graduate students are permitted to realize." Maslow (1961, p. 58) believed that existentialism would lead to the inclusion of "raw experience" in a psychological science that would have to be radically revised. However, he hoped that existentialism would not "turn into an antipsychology or into an antiscience" (p. 59). Rogers (1961a, p. 92) believed that existentialism could be approached scientifically, and believed that an "empirical research method" properly applied could investigate "subjective qualities."

3. In general, the Americans believed that the Europeans had been too pessimistic. This was especially true of Maslow (1961, p. 60), who called the attitudes of the most pessimistic existentialists "high I.Q. whimpering on a cosmic scale." In place of European pessimism, American psychologists began to see on the horizon an optimistic new science of the experiencing person. "It is possible that existentialism will not only enrich psychology. It may also be an additional push toward the establishment of another *branch* of psychology, the psychology of the fully evolved and authentic self and its ways of being" (Maslow, 1961, p. 59).

Precisely what this new branch of psychology was to be like became clearer when many of the contributors to the 1959 symposium on existential psychology met in November, 1964 at Old Saybrook, Connecticut for the *First Invitational Conference on Humanistic Psychology.* The conference was intended to "launch Humanistic Psychology as an academic and scientific endeavor" (Taylor, 1994, p. 7). Papers presented at the conference by May (1965), Maslow (1965a), and Rogers (1965) were subsequently published in the *Journal of Humanistic Psychology,* which Maslow had helped found in 1961. Another contributor to the conference was *George A. Kelly* (1965), whose work we review later in this chapter.

The papers from the Old Saybrook Conference sounded several themes that were to become characteristic of humanistic psychology. One theme was to be critical of both behaviorist and psychoanalytic approaches to psychology. B. F. Skinner always figured prominently in any critique of behaviorism mounted by humanistic psychologists, who were adamant that human beings could not be regarded as governed entirely by stimulus-response connections (e.g., Rogers, 1964a). Psychoanalysis was criticized for presenting a stunted view of the person as consumed by the necessity of reducing biological drives. Humanistic psychologists were united in believing that there was more to being a person than either of these perspectives admitted. Because they saw themselves as going beyond behaviorism and psychoanalysis, humanistic psychologists often styled themselves as *The Third Force* (e.g., Bugental, 1964). One of the clearest spokespersons for humanistic psychology at this time was *Charlotte Buhler* (1965), who said that the essential difference between humanistic psychology and either behaviorism or psychoanalysis was that

> *It conceives of man as living with intentionality, which means living with purpose. The purpose is to give meaning to life through interpreting it within a bigger context. Within this bigger context, to which*

> *the individual relates, he wants to create values . . . [I]n humanistic psychology, the human being is conceived of as having a primary, or native orientation, in the direction of creating and of values (p. 55)*

Additional Reading on This Topic. Although not to be regarded as a member of the humanistic psychology movement, *Gordon W. Allport* (1897–1967) was very much on the minds of many of those who developed what became humanistic psychology. Allport had earlier considered many of the themes that were to become central to humanistic psychology. In particular, Allport had stressed the importance of the distinction between *idiographic* versus *nomothetic* approaches to the study of the person. On the one hand, psychology was a nomothetic science, meaning that it searched for general laws. On the other hand, psychology had to use idiographic methods, meaning that it was interested in the uniqueness of the individual. Allport's classic book, *Pattern and Growth in Personality* (1964) took the view that we should "not deny the proposition that psychology seeks general laws," but drew "attention to those laws and principles that tell how uniqueness comes about" (p. 572).

Allport also did pioneering research on human values, another area of central concern to humanistic psychologists. The Allport, Vernon, and Lindzey (1960) *scale of values* has proved to be a very useful research tool in a wide variety of areas.

ROLLO MAY (1909–1994)

May was born in Ohio, graduating from Oberlin College in 1930. He studied with Alfred Adler in Vienna before attending Union Theological Seminary in New York, where he received a divinity degree in 1938 (Taylor, 1994). While studying for a doctorate in clinical psychology at Columbia, he came down with tuberculosis, and was required to spend a year and a half convalescing in a tuberculosis sanatorium, during which time he discovered in Kierkegaard's writings a description of "anxiety as the struggle of the living being against non-being—which I could immediately experience there in my struggle with death or the prospect of being a life-long invalid" (May, 1961, p. 19).

May (1950) went on to write *The Meaning of Anxiety.* In that book, and in his other widely read works (e.g., May 1953, 1969b), he elaborated on the nature and importance of *anxiety* as a modern phenomenon. "In anxiety . . . we are threatened without knowing what steps to take to meet the danger . . . [Anxiety is] the human being's basic reaction to a danger to his existence or to some value he identifies with his existence" (1953, pp. 39–40). May distinguished between pathological, *neurotic anxiety* and *normal anxiety.* The former was the kind of anxiety Freud had discussed, and that we considered in Chapter 6. The latter was seen as an inevitable response to the conditions of life in the middle of the twentieth century.

Normal anxiety results in "bewilderment—this confusion as to who we are and what we should do" (May, 1953, p. 44). Modern people are confused and bewildered because the traditional values do not work any longer. Rugged individualism was fine for the nineteenth century, when a new continent needed to be conquered, but it leads to isolation and loneliness in the modern urban context. The glorification of reason, which made sense in the early days of science, has led to a ruinous split between the intellect and other parts of the person, such as the emotions and the will. "The upshot is that the values and goals which provided a unifying center for previous centuries in the modern period no longer are cogent" (May, 1953, p. 55). The task of the modern person is to rediscover a sense of self based on an exploration of one's existence.

The title of one of May's (1969b) books—*Love and Will*—conveys his approach to finding meaning in the modern world. Love and will represent those aspects of ourselves that have been pushed aside as a result of our preoccupation with the intellect. "Apathy is the withdrawal of will and love, a statement that they 'don't matter,' a suspension of commitment" (May, 1969b, p. 33), and apathy is a central part of the modern condition. By apathy, May (1969b, p. 27) meant "a state of feelinglessness, the despairing possibility that nothing matters."

Love is a necessary beginning in the movement away from apathy. May (1969b, p. 306) described the appearance of "a new morality . . . of authenticity in relationship" that he witnessed in the 1960s, and that claimed to be based on love. "[P]eople are not interested in money and success. . . . They seek an honesty, openness, a feeling, a touch, a look in the eyes, a sharing of fantasy." Other people tend to be judged by their "authenticity, doing one's own thing, and giving in the sense of making one's self available for the other." May was not entirely supportive of the morality he saw emerging in the 1960s. He believed that love by itself was not enough. He suggested that the children of the 1960s were emphasizing love at the expense of will precisely because their parents had done the opposite (May, 1969b, p. 278). Although we often think of power and emotion as opposites, they do not need to be. While it is true that the exercise of willpower without love can be very destructive to oneself and to others, this is also true of love that does not discriminate between one person and another.

May argued that love and will both can and should support each other, and suggested that this could come about through *care*. Remember that Heidegger had observed that people *care* about the nature of their existence, and May (1969b, p. 289) argued not only that the loss of such care is what creates apathy but also that the existence of care is what enables love and will to become conjoined. Care begins with love, but goes beyond it. It includes not only the ability to let one's actions be affected by one's immediate feelings, but also to actively "mold and form one's self" over a long period of time (May, 1969b, p. 279). Will is the process whereby the person makes judgments about the value of different alternatives, and actively chooses between them. Without the discrimination that comes from willpower, we treat every experience as equally valuable. We become passive consumers of experience. If all experiences are equally valuable, then they are all equally meaningless. It is only by actively choosing to have some experiences over others that our life becomes meaningful. This should remind you a bit of *William James*'s treatment of the will, and May regarded James as well as the existentialists as providing him with the basis of his approach to psychology.

> *We love and will the world as an immediate, spontaneous totality. We* will *the world, create it by our decision, our fiat, our choice; and we* love *it, give it affect, energy, power to love and change us as we mold and change it. This is what it means to be fully related to one's world. I do not imply that the world does not exist* before *we love or will it. . . . But it has no reality, no relation to me, as I have no effect upon it; I move as in a dream . . . One can choose to shut it out . . . or one can choose to see it, create it. (May, 1969b, p. 324)*

Additional Reading on This Topic. May (1969a) analyzed William James's psychology from the viewpoint of existential and humanistic psychology.

ABRAHAM H. MASLOW (1908–1970)

Born in the Jewish slums in Brooklyn, Maslow overcame numerous obstacles to become one of the most broadly influential American psychologists of the century. After earning an undergraduate degree at City College of New York, he studied with *Harry Harlow* (1905–1981) at the University of Wisconsin. Harlow's (1958) laboratory subsequently became famous for using monkeys to study the nature of attachment in primates. Maslow's doctoral dissertation concerned the relation between dominance and sexual behavior in monkeys. He went on to Columbia Teacher's College, where he was employed by E. L. Thorndike. Thorndike gave Maslow an intelligence test, on which Maslow got the equivalent of an IQ of 195. Suitably impressed, Thorndike gave Maslow full reign to work on whatever topics interested him (Hoffman, 1988, p. 74). Maslow continued his research on dominance and sexuality, only this time by interviewing human subjects.

The period between 1935 and 1940 was extremely important for Maslow. Living in New York City, he "came to know and study with Adler, . . .

and Karen Horney in the field of psychoanalysis, and Kurt Goldstein, Max Wertheimer, and Kurt Koffka in Gestalt psychology" (Hoffman, 1988, p. 87). In some ways, the psychology Maslow went on to create is a blend of neo-Freudianism and Gestalt/organismic psychology. Maslow was also influenced by the anthropologist *Ruth Benedict* (1887–1948). (We mentioned Benedict earlier, in Chapter 2 in our discussion of Mary Wollstonecraft.) Benedict's book, *Patterns of Culture* (1935/1989), has become a classic in cultural anthropology. As a result of Benedict's influence, Maslow spent a summer doing field work on a Northern Blackfoot reservation in Alberta (Hoffman, 1988, p. 116).

Maslow (1964a) later acknowledged Benedict's influence in bringing home to him the importance of *synergy,* or the degree to which the needs of the individual are consistent with the demands of the culture. In a high synergy culture, being selfish also promotes the welfare of others, while in a low synergy culture the needs of the individual conflict with how the culture wants the individual to behave. It became a key assumption of Maslow's psychology that one should attempt to create synergic "social institutions, whether in business, in an army, or in a university, in such a fashion that the people within the organization are co-ordinated with each other and are perforce made into colleagues and teammates rather than into rivals" (Maslow, 1964a, p. 161).

In 1951, Maslow became the founding Chair of the psychology department at Brandeis, a nonsectarian university that had recently been founded by the American Jewish community. He retained his affiliation with Brandeis until 1969, when he became a Resident Fellow at the W. P. Laughlin Charitable Foundation in California. During his time at Brandeis he was responsible for hiring, among others, George Kelly and Ulric Neisser, both of whom made important contributions to psychology quite independently of Maslow's influence.

In many ways, Maslow's career illustrates the fate of humanistic psychology. Although his theory was never regarded as very respectable by academic psychologists, he was nevertheless elected to the presidency of the American Psychological Association in 1967. An index of his widespread popular influence is the fact that Maslow was the only psychologist to be named in a review of the most influential Americans of the previous 50 years conducted by a leading American mass-market magazine (Leonard, 1983). Maslow's influence on psychology as it is taught in psychology departments in universities has been less than his influence on business, education, and the culture as a whole. We return to the general question of the influence of humanistic psychology later in the chapter.

The Hierarchy of Needs

Maslow's book, *Motivation and Personality* (1954) presented the theory of motivation that would eventually penetrate American culture so thoroughly that it would be taught as a part of the curriculum in many high schools. Consequently, most readers are already familiar with Maslow's *hierarchy of needs.* Maslow defined *basic needs* in terms of their importance to the health of the person. Something is a basic need if it is required to preserve health, if its absence causes illness, if its restoration cures illness, and if it is freely chosen by a deprived person. Needs may be organized hierarchically in terms of the order in which they must be satisfied. Thus, the child is first preoccupied with satisfying his or her *physiological needs.* If a child lacks some bodily requirement it will do what it can to remedy that deficiency. For example, the child will strive to maintain the appropriate state of the blood with respect to its water content, salt content, sugar content, protein content and so on (Maslow, 1954, p. 80). The child need not intentionally seek what is needed. Obviously, a child does not say, "Oh, I need more salt," and then add salt to its diet. Rather, the child regulates itself without thinking, naturally and automatically.

Of course, in an environment where these needs are not met it is entirely possible for physiological needs to become a preoccupation. But what happens when these needs *are* met, when there is plenty of bread and the child's belly is usually full? At that point, Maslow (1954, chap. 8) said, a "higher" need emerges. "The higher need is a later . . . evolutionary development. We share the need for food with all living things, the need for love with (perhaps) the higher apes, the need for self-actualization (at least through creativeness) with nobody. The higher the need the more specifically human it is" (Maslow, 1954, p. 147). Next to the physiological needs, come the *safety needs,* which are the requirements we have for shelter, for relative peace and quiet, and for a modicum of comfort and stability. If these needs are met, then we go on to the belongingness or *love needs.* A person requires affectionate relations with other people. Should these needs be satisfied, then the *esteem needs* emerge. These are requirements everyone has "for adequacy, mastery and competence," and they lead to self-esteem. We also need the esteem of others, as manifested by "status, dominance, recognition" (Maslow, 1954, p. 90). If we manage to achieve all this, then the tendency towards *self-actualization* becomes increasingly salient. Maslow (1954, pp. 91–92) attributed the concept of self-actualization to Kurt Goldstein, and meant by it a person's "desire for self-fulfillment," or the tendency "to become everything that one is capable of becoming." The tendency toward self-actualization manifests itself most clearly in what Maslow called the *cognitive-aesthetic needs.* These are "needs to know and understand" things for their own sake, and to be in the presence of and to create beautiful things (Maslow, 1954, pp. 93–98). These needs do not emerge only after the other needs are gratified—after all, preschool children spend a lot of time making art, as any parent should know. However, cognitive-aesthetic needs become increasingly important as the other, more basic needs are gratified.

Maslow argued that his theory of motivation was different from other motivational theories, such as Freud's. In other theories of motivation, needs are regarded as periodic, in the sense that gratifying a need reduces its intensity, which then builds back up, after which the need is gratified again, and so on. You cannot just gratify a need once and then be done with it. (It is nice to imagine the meal to end all meals, but such a meal does not exist. No matter how much you eat on one occasion, you will still have to eat again!) However, Maslow's system emphasizes the degree to which needs are not only periodic. Needs also emerge sequentially, as illustrated in Figure 13.1 on page 274. The intensity with which different basic needs are experienced follows a particular order.

During the initial stage, when physiological needs are the most important, then that need system is at the center of the individual's life, and is experienced the most intensely. Other needs are in the background. All the needs are there all the time, but the person is most concerned with one type of need at any one time. When a person is attending to safety needs, for example, then less attention is paid to esteem needs. When one need is more or less taken care of and one does not have to worry about it, then one of the others emerges to become of central concern. The tendency toward self-actualization is always there in the background, underlying all the other needs, but only comes to the fore after the other needs are gratified. Thus, after a need such as safety is more or less gratified, it is still present, but is no longer a preoccupation. It could become a preoccupation if conditions change. A particular homeowner may not worry about housing needs as long as mortgage rates remain low. However, the same person could become preoccupied with shelter if mortgage rates go up dramatically, and decent housing is no longer affordable. Thus, Maslow's theory regards human development as consisting of a hierarchy of stages but, depending on the circumstances, one can go backward as well as forward.

The Self-Actualizing Person

One of Maslow's (e.g., 1971, chap. 23) most famous concepts is that of the self-actualizing person. Self-actualizing people have managed to

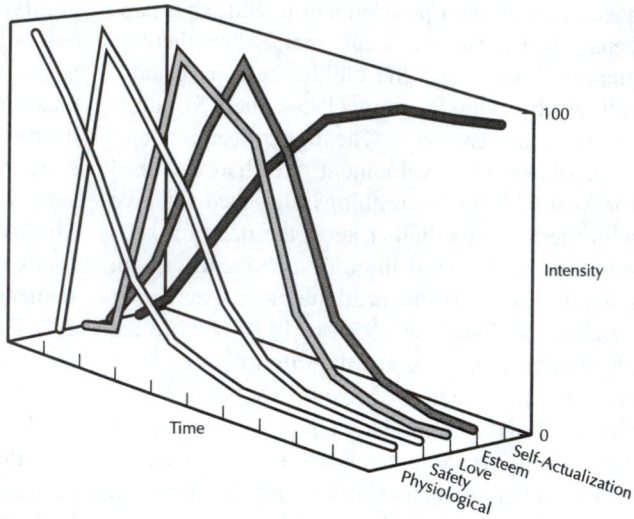

FIGURE 13.1 Maslow's hierarchy of needs.

satisfy their basic needs to a very great extent. To study self-actualizing people, Maslow recorded his observations of individuals such as Max Wertheimer and Ruth Benedict, who seemed to him to have gone beyond satisfying the lower needs. From these records he formulated a theory of the motivations of self-actualizing people. Maslow argued that at this higher level a different set of motives were important, which he called *metamotivations.* "Meta" means beyond, and so metamotivations are motives beyond or above ordinary motives.

Maslow argued that self-actualizing people have different values from those held by ordinary people. The rest of us value that of which we are deprived. For example, people deprived of food value food, while people deprived of shelter value shelter. Maslow (1962) called such motivations *deficiency motives.* The self-actualizing person is not deprived of such things as food, shelter, love, or self-esteem. Self-actualizing persons do not work to gratify deprivation motives. Their work is not something they feel they are being forced to do out of the necessity to satisfy their basic needs. They do not regard their work as drudgery, something from which they escape on the weekends. Self-actualizing persons feel that there is a harmony between themselves and their work, a good match between who they are and what they do for a job. Rather than values based on deprivation, the self-actualizing person has what Maslow (1962) called *Being values,* or *B-values.* B-values are values that follow from the intrinsic worth of an activity.

In his studies of self-actualizing people, Maslow found that they do not rest on their achievements. Maslow (1971, p. 301) used words and phrases such as "devoted," "dedicated," "people who have a calling, or a vocation, or a mission," and "a passionate attachment to their work" to describe self-actualizing people. For Maslow, these are examples of B-values. For metamotivated individuals, their work is something that they feel they *must* do, in the sense that they feel it is their duty, a responsibility that they shoulder voluntarily. For example, a baby requires that someone take care of it, and a self-actualizing caregiver responds without begrudging the attention lavished on the child. To give another example, injustice requires opposition, and a self-actualizing lawyer responds to the challenge willingly, perceiving it as a personal necessity to do so. The self-actualizing person lives synergically, with a correspondence between what he or she wants to do and what the situation demands:

> *At this level the dichotomizing of work and play is transcended. . . . There is certainly no distinction between work and play . . . If a person loves his work and enjoys it more than any other activity in the whole world and is eager to get to it, to get back to it after any interruption, then how can we speak about "labor" in the sense of something one is forced to do against one's wishes? (Maslow, 1971, p. 304)*

For self-actualizing persons, the distinction between work and play *is* irrelevant because their work *is* their play. Imagine that you owned a company. Would you not like to have employees who felt like this about their work? Perhaps this accounts perhaps for the popularity of Maslow among many people in business. Maslow occasionally pointed out that some self-actualizing people will be willing to work for no money at all, preferring not to be bothered with it, just like the members of some religious orders.

Metamotives and their corresponding B-values are the most advanced from an evolutionary or developmental point of view. However, this means that they are also the weakest, in the sense of being the last to emerge and the most easily destroyed. Nevertheless, if they are not gratified, then there will develop a state Maslow called *metapathology.* The metamotives are *instinctoid* in the sense that if they are thwarted, the person becomes sick. The sicknesses that result are the sort of spiritual illnesses that have been described for millennia by religious people and philosophers (Maslow, 1971, p. 316). These illnesses include alienation, boredom, apathy, and despair.

Maslow (1964b, p. 38) argued that "a large proportion of all affluent nations" have spiritual ailments. In spite of having their most basic needs satisfied, many people are not very happy. This is because a life based solely on the gratification of lower needs will strike people as not really worth living (Maslow, 1964b, p. 42). However, many people have become cynical about higher values, believing them to be "a fake and a swindle" (Maslow, 1964b, p. 9). Maslow regarded such attitudes as partly responsible for spiritual illnesses. We should accept higher values as intrinsic parts of our being. B-values are not culturally determined, but are universal values, found in all the great religions.

Peak Experiences

Maslow (1962, chap. 6) is well-known for promoting the concept of *peak experiences,* which have much in common with mystical experiences of a oneness with the world. "The emotional reaction in the peak experience has a special flavor of wonder, of awe, of reverence, of humility and surrender before the experience as before something great" (Maslow, 1962, p. 82). It is from peak experiences that many people become aware of the centrality of B-values in their lives. Peak experiences are intrinsically valuable, and are the experiences that many people regard as the most important experiences they have ever had. While anyone can have a peak experience, they are more common in self-actualizing persons.

Peak experiences are similar to a childlike way of being-in-the-world. Children do not distinguish clearly between themselves and their environment. Similarly, a peak experience reduces feelings of alienation from the world, and enhances the feeling that you are a part of a larger whole. However, peak experiences are more than just a regression to a childish way of experiencing. They represent "a fusion of ego, id, superego, . . . of conscious and unconscious, . . . a synthesizing of pleasure principle and reality principle, a regression without fear in the service of the greatest maturity, a true integration of the person at all levels" (Maslow, 1962, p. 91).

The Psychology of Science

Maslow's investigations of such topics as peak experiences and self-actualization were unorthodox, as he acknowledged himself (e.g., Maslow, 1954, p. 199). He described one of his studies as an

> *impressionistic, ideal, "composite photograph" or organization of personal interviews. . . . I have added together all the partial responses to make a "perfect" composite syndrome. In addition, about fifty people wrote me unsolicited letters after reading my previously published papers, giving me personal reports of peak experiences. Finally, I have tapped the immense literatures of mysticism, religion, art, creativeness, love, etc. (Maslow, 1962, p. 67)*

Not surprisingly, more orthodox academic psychologists took a dim view of what they regarded as a methodology that was too subjective and unreliable to produce any scientifically meaningful results. Maslow's response (1966) was to write a book, called *The Psychology of Science,* which was "a critique of orthodox science . . . [that] rejects the traditional but unexamined conviction that orthodox science is *the* path to knowledge or even that it is the only reliable path" (p. 1). In place of orthodox science, Maslow advocated a science with a number of features not always associated with scientific psychology. For example, he spoke of a *Taoistic science* that would be open and receptive to people, rather than attempting to predict and control them. He also advocated a *problem centered* rather than a *method centered* approach to psychology. Rather than apply the same methodology to all problems, the methods should be tailored to fit the problem. A logical positivist methodology was only suited to the exploration of very limited aspects of behavior. The study of such topics as peak experiences could not be accommodated within traditional methods, but that does not mean that such experiences should be ignored. Rather, more *experiential methods* were required that involved the active participation of the researcher in the phenomenon being investigated. Scientists could not understand all phenomena from the outside, by being a spectator rather than a participant. To truly understand such phenomena as peak experiences one had to experience them firsthand.

Additional Reading on This Topic. Maslow's book, *Eupsychian Management* (1965b) gives an interesting perspective on the way his ideas could be applied in business settings.

CARL R. ROGERS (1902–1987)

Perhaps more than anyone else, Carl Rogers has become synonymous with the practice of clinical psychology. As we shall see, there are good reasons for this, but the fact of the matter is that clinical psychology did not begin with Carl Rogers. Clinical psychology may be defined as "a scientific and professional field that seeks to increase our understanding of human behavior and to promote the effective functioning of individuals" (Reisman, 1991, p. 3). As such, clinical psychology is not defined by any single approach, such as psychoanalysis.

Most people agree that the first person in the United States to define an area called "clinical psychology" was *Lightner Witmer* (1867–1956) of the University of Pennsylvania, although there are those who would credit William James with having taught the first American course in the subject (e.g., Taylor & Butler, 1986). Witmer developed his conception of clinical psychology while working in schools. Clinical psychology was to be used to diagnose and treat deficiencies, practices he carried on at "the first psychological clinic, actually the first child guidance clinic in the world," founded at the University of Pennsylvania in 1896 (Reisman, 1991, p. 38). Witmer went on to develop courses in clinical psychology, which were designed to demonstrate methods useful to would-be practitioners. These courses were the forerunners of the clinical training programs that have subsequently become fixtures in many American graduate programs in psychology.

While mental testing has long been an activity central to the practice of clinical psychology, psychotherapy is perhaps even more closely associated with clinical psychology in the public's mind. Few people are more closely identified with the practice of psychotherapy than Carl Rogers. Rogers (1967) entered the University of Wisconsin in 1919, intending to major in agriculture. An ardent Christian, he was chosen

> *to go to a World Student Christian Federation Conference in Peking, China. . . . Due to this six months' trip I had been able freely, and with no sense of defiance or guilt, to think my own thoughts, come to my own conclusions, and to take the stands I believed in. . . . From the date of this trip, my goals, values, aims, and philosophy have been my own and very divergent from the views which my parents held and which I had held up to this point. (p. 351)*

Rogers subsequently changed his major to history, and graduated in 1924. He then went to Union Theological Seminary in New York, but eventually left the "field of religious work [because], although questions as to the meaning of life and the possibility of the constructive improvement of life for individuals were of deep interest to me, I could not work in a field where I would be required to believe in some specified religious doctrine" (Rogers, 1967, p. 354).

While at Union Theological seminary, Rogers had been taking some courses at Columbia University, one of which was in clinical psychology taught by *Leta Hollingworth* (1886–1939), who is a figure of considerable historical importance in her own right. Hollingworth had been instrumental in the establishment of the American Association of Clinical Psychologists in 1917 (Street, 1994). In addition to being an authority in child clinical psychology, Hollingworth (1914a, b) did foundational work on *gender differences* that "undermined the hypothesis of male superiority . . . and arguments that women were dysfunctional during their menstrual cycle. . . . Work in this tradition died out around 1920 and did not become a focus within academic psychology again until the early 1970s" (Kimball, 1994). Thus, Hollingworth was a pioneer in the *psychology of women,* a topic we consider more fully in Chapter 15. Rogers (1967) described Hollingworth's influence on him as follows. "She was a warm human being, concerned about individuals, as well as a competent research worker. It was under her supervision that I first came in actual *clinical* contact with children—testing them, talking with them, dealing with them as fascinating objects of study, and helping to make plans for their welfare" (p. 355).

After receiving his Ed.D. from Columbia, Rogers went to work at the Rochester Society for the Prevention of Cruelty to Children. Rogers (1967, pp. 358–361) described the 12 years he spent in Rochester as particularly formative ones during which he began to develop the style of psychotherapy which would eventually be called "Rogerian." In 1940, Rogers moved to Ohio State University where he established a "practicum in counseling and psychotherapy," which may have been "the first instance in which supervised therapy was carried on in a university setting" (Rogers, 1967, p. 362). Subsequently, Rogers went on to the University of Chicago, where he established a Counseling Center. In 1947, while at Chicago, Rogers was elected President of the American Psychological Association. After a period at the University of Wisconsin (Madison), Rogers moved to California in 1964, first to the Western Behavioral Sciences Institute and then to the Center for Studies of the Person.

Client-Centered Therapy

In his Presidential address to the American Psychological Association, Rogers (1947/1978) foreshadowed several aspects of what was to become *client-centered* or *non-directive psychotherapy* (Rogers, 1951, 1952). Quoting from a number of taped interviews between therapists and clients, Rogers outlined the ways in which his approach to therapy brought about change. He characterized the nondirective therapist's behavior as expressing an attitude of "warmth and understanding . . . [that] helps maximize the freedom of expression by the individual" (Rogers, 1947, 1978, p. 418). The therapist does not attempt to bias what the client has to say, and attempts to see the client's behavior "through his eyes, and also the psychological meaning it has for him. . . . Only a novelist or a poet could do justice to the deep struggles which we are permitted to observe from within the client's own world of reality" (Rogers, 1947, 1978, p. 419).

Such openness and receptiveness on the part of the therapist came to be called *unconditional positive regard,* which Rogers (1961b) defined as

> *the therapist's genuine willingness for the client to be whatever feeling is going on in him at that moment—fear confusion, pain, pride, anger, hatred, love, courage, or awe. It means that he prizes the client in a total rather than a conditional way. By this I mean that he does not simply accept the client when he is behaving in certain ways, and disapprove of him when he behaves in other ways. It means an outgoing positive feeling without reservations. (p. 62).*

In a nutshell, client-centered therapy provides the therapist with the opportunity to see "the client as the client sees himself, to look at problems through his eyes" in an "atmosphere of complete psychological security" (Rogers, 1952, p. 67). As a result of this *empathic understanding* the client spontaneously begins to "reorganize the structure of self in accordance with reality and his own needs" (Rogers, 1952, p 67). A central notion in Rogers's theory of therapy was the *self-concept,* or the view the person holds of himself or herself. A discrepancy between the person's self-concept and the way the person wished to be (the *ideal self*) was one source of discomfort. Rogers (1961b) believed that nondirective therapy caused the self to become "more positively valued, i.e., . . . more congruent with the ideal, or valued, self" (p. 235).

When humanistic psychology was just beginning, Rogers (e.g., 1964a, p. 5) often spoke of the importance of developing "tough, dedicated, persistent, humanistic scientists," and it was characteristic of Rogers's work that he not only attempted to state his theory in as precise terms as possible (e.g., Rogers, 1959), but also tried to empirically evaluate his therapeutic approach. In his studies, Rogers attempted to test the null hypothesis that clients do not change as a result of nondirective therapy. In the context of Rogerian psychotherapy, the null hypothesis is that the difference between the self-concept and the ideal self-concept is not different at the end of therapy than it was at the beginning of therapy.

In order to measure the self-concept and the ideal self-concept, Rogers and his co-workers used a card sorting technique. This technique uses 100 self-descriptive statements such as "I am a submissive person," "I don't trust my emotions," "I have an attractive personality" (Rogers, 1961b, p. 232). Before therapy (the pretest), clients sorted the cards to represent themselves, and then sorted the cards to represent the person they would like to be (ideal self). They repeated this procedure immediately after therapy (first post-test), and again some time later at a follow-up session (second post-test).

Rogers presented data that allowed him to reject the null hypothesis. The self and ideal self card sorts were typically more similar on both the post-tests than they were before therapy. One difficulty in interpreting data such as these is that we do not know whether or not the outcome is merely due to repeated testing. Perhaps simply retaking the card sorting test results in the observed results, and the findings may not be due to therapy at all. Rogers himself was acutely aware of this problem, and spent a lot of time trying to properly evaluate his psychotherapeutic approach. In the end, he was skeptical of the value of such research programs (Rogers, 1980):

> *Person-centered therapists were under pressure . . . to prove that our approach to therapy was effective. We gradually carried on more and more sophisticated studies to assess the outcomes. But when this was the sole purpose of the research, the results, even though the evidence of effectiveness was positive, were always disappointing. We found, as could have been predicted, that some clients were more successful than others, some therapists more effective than others. But assessment studies are not heuristic, do not lead forward. They offer almost no clues to the elements we need to know to improve therapy or to understand its process. (p. 311)*

In spite of Rogers's skeptical attitude toward evaluative research, his theory has been the focus of many other psychologists' research efforts in a

Box 13.1

Carl Rogers' Theory of Creative Environments

A persistent criticism of humanistic psychology is that there is little empirical support for it. An exception is an article by Harrington, Block, and Block (1987) that provided some support for Carl Rogers' (1954/1970) theory of creative environments. According to Rogers' theory, individuals are able to express themselves most creatively under the following conditions:

1. *Openness to experience,* meaning a "lack of rigidity . . . a tolerance for ambiguity . . . the ability to receive much conflicting information without forcing closure on the situation" (Rogers, 1954/1970, p. 143).
2. *Internal locus of evaluation,* meaning that "the value of his [or her] product is, for the creative person, established not by the praise or criticism of others, but by himself [or herself]" (Rogers, 1954/1970, p. 144).
3. *The ability to toy with elements and concepts,* meaning the "ability to play spontaneously with ideas, colors, shapes, relationships" and so on (Rogers, 1954/1970, p. 144).

In order for the person to develop these characteristics, he or she must be raised in an environment that has the following features:

- *Psychological safety,* meaning that the individual is "understood empathically," accepted as having "unconditional worth," and "external evaluation is absent," (Rogers, 1954/1970, pp. 147–148).
- *Psychological freedom,* meaning the individual is given "complete freedom of symbolic expression" (Rogers, 1954/1970, p. 148).

Harrington, Block, and Block (1987) tried to determine if child-rearing practices such as these consistently lead to more open, creative adults. They studied 106 families over an 11-year period. At the start of the study, when the children in the families were about 3 years of age, the parents filled out a scale describing their child-rearing practices. A little later, parent-child interactions occurring while the parent taught the child a task were videotaped. There was also a set of ratings by trained observers and teachers of how creatively the children behaved at different ages.

Based on these data, it appeared to be the case that the more the child was raised in accordance with Rogerian principles, the more creative the child tended to be rated. These relationships were partly due to the mothers' child-rearing practices, and partly due to the fathers' child-rearing practices. This study is consistent with Rogers' theory that "children raised by parents who provide conditions of psychological safety and freedom will develop their creative potential more fully than will children whose parents do not provide such conditions" (Harrington, Block, & Block, 1987, p. 855).

variety of areas. A typical example is given in Box 13.1.

Rogers remained an active participant in humanistic psychology well after the normal retirement date for most people. For example, in 1986, he visited the then Soviet Union together with his colleague Ruth Sanford, where they came in contact with over 2000 people. "In Moscow and Tbilisi, Rogers and Sanford led day long discussions with large groups and four-day encounter groups with 30–45 members. . . . After the Rogers and Sanford visit, a national Soviet television program carried a one hour special on them" (Hassard, 1990, pp. 27–28). Rogers's visit was part of an exchange program begun in 1983 between the Association of Humanistic Psychologists and Soviet psychologists and educators.

Eugene T. Gendlin

Eugene Gendlin (1962) was a student of Carl Rogers at the University of Chicago who articulated the Rogerian viewpoint and its relation to other forms of psychology in a particularly clear way. Gendlin was also the first editor of the journal *Psychotherapy: Theory, Research and Practice,* which was founded in 1963.

The key concept in Gendlin's exposition (1962, p. 3) is *experiencing,* which is the "flow of feeling, concretely, to which you can every moment attend inwardly, if you wish." Experiencing is a very complex "felt apperceptive mass to which we can inwardly point" (Gendlin, 1962, p. 27). When we attend to our experiencing directly, then we have *felt meanings.*

Gendlin observed that the goal of many personality theories is to be able to tell people who and what they are, as in "You are an introvert," or "You have an Oedipus complex." Gendlin argued that this is the wrong approach. A person *is* "the flow of experiencing. . . . For that is what you are inside, to yourself." Thus, a humanistic approach facilitates the person's discovery of himself or herself through the self experiencing. Gendlin (1962, pp. 30–32) gave an extended example of what he meant by "experiencing." Imagine a situation in which you are trying to impress someone in their home. However, you drop something—a glass of red wine, say—on the brand new white rug. An observer might interpret your behavior as revealing your unconscious hostility toward the other person. Gendlin believed that such interpretations from the outside were meaningless. Rather than accept the "hostile" interpretation, you should attend to the felt meanings you had when you dropped the wine glass.

> *If you refer directly to it . . . you will find much more in this . . . concretely felt experiencing. Perhaps you will now say that you felt apprehensive, lest that other person become impatient with you. His high position made you afraid. His secure ease also made you afraid, for he could afford to lose you, but you had to be glad to receive his time and attention. You would never blame him for your lowly position, of course, but you never do like being put into such a position. Of course, now that we discuss it, who likes to associate with someone on the basis of needing something from him which he may or may not want to give, and that—as you, of course, knew all along—was how it stood. What is more, we have all been in situations of this kind as children, and so you might feel some loss of adulthood when you must plead, appeal, or please. So it may well be as you attend directly to this aspect of experiencing, you find—as you use symbols along with your reference—that all these many meanings can truly be said of how you felt, and were aware of feeling. (Gendlin, 1962, pp. 32–33)*

Experiencing is not limited to simple mental contents, such as sensations or ideas. Felt meanings occur prior to any words or concepts that we may use to interpret them. That is, felt meanings are preverbal and preconceptual. We can try to put these felt meanings into words, but words are often a poor translation of the felt meaning we experience. Consequently, there is a continuous interaction between experiencing and the words and other *symbols* we use to try to represent our experiencing. Our experiencing need not be represented only by words. Music, painting, dancing and other forms of self-expression can also be an appropriate way of representing our experiencing.

In psychotherapy, the client is encouraged, with the support of the therapist, to try to symbolically represent felt meanings. This may involve a change in the way that the client has previously represented his or her experience. The meaning of our experience is something each of us creates through the symbols we use. These symbols should be true to our own experience. We should not try to make our experience fit the symbols we may have been taught by others to use when we describe ourselves. There are many different ways of representing our experience, and there are no fixed patterns to which everyone's experience must conform (Gendlin, 1981). The process of symbolically representing experience need never be complete, and so the process of creating oneself can be a life's work.

Encounter Groups

Recall our discussion of Kurt Lewin in Chapter 9 on Gestalt psychology. We noted then that Lewin had been instrumental in developing *sensitivity training,* or the so-called *T-groups.* We noted that group members often dramatically changed their view of themselves as a result of feedback from other members of the group. T-groups, subsequently renamed *encounter groups* (Rogers, 1970), were taken up with enthusiasm by many humanistic psychologists as vehicles for enabling people to realize their full human potential. Partly as a result of the use of encounter groups and other forms of therapy designed to enhance personal growth, humanistic psychology became virtually synonymous with what came to be called the *human potential movement.*

The "encounter group," was a setting in which people discussed themselves as freely and openly as possible. The original purpose of such groups had been to increase the accuracy of the participants' perceptions of themselves and others. However, it soon became clear that participants did not necessarily change in this manner. For example, Smith (1973) reviewed several studies showing that encounter group experience did not increase *empirical understanding,* which is "the degree to which one person can predict another person's feelings, thoughts and behavior" (p. 32). However, these studies also showed that encounter groups increased "the degree to which a person feels close to, sympathetic with, and understanding of another person" (p. 32). While there was little evidence that encounter group experience increased the extent to which participants saw each other as unique individuals, it did tend to increase the extent to which participants saw themselves as similar to each other (e.g., Benjafield, Pomeroy, & Jordan, 1976). Feelings initially thought to be too private to be expressed may, upon being expressed in the group, turn out to be met with accounts of similar experiences from others. Consequently, encounter group experience seemed to reduce feelings of alienation, and to promote the sense that people are all fundamentally alike. Smith (1973, p. 32) argued that this kind of experience is "more real to us, . . . more deeply desired, and probably more important to our personal survival than is empirical understanding."

What Happened to Humanistic Psychology?

Humanistic psychology fit well with the zeitgeist in American popular culture in the 1960s and 1970s. However, as the 1970s wore on, humanistic psychology began to attract more and more criticism (e.g., Rosen, 1977; Wertheimer, 1978). Much of this criticism came from outside humanistic psychology itself, and focused on the very large number of different "therapies" that had emerged, as well as what appeared to be a general lack of standards for what constituted legitimate forms of therapy. Humanistic psychology seemed to be unable or unwilling to regulate these myriad approaches, and at least some consumers may have been damaged as a result (Wallach & Wallach, 1983). It seemed to many as if "anything goes."

Some of the most trenchant criticisms of the human potential movement came from within humanistic psychology itself. A good example is *Richard Farson's* analysis (1978) of the state of humanistic psychology as the 1970s drew to a close. Farson had been a colleague of Carl Rogers at Chicago, and helped to persuade him to join the Western Behavioral Sciences Institute in La Jolla. In retrospect, Farson lamented the fact that humanistic psychology had done little to build a truly humanistic science. Instead of "systematic research or theory construction," humanistic psychology had witnessed "a massive proliferation of therapies, and other experiential programs generally referred to as the human potential movement" (p. 7). These therapies were the new technology of humanism.

Farson believed that humanistic psychology was no longer a part of the solution to people's problems, so much as it had become itself a part of the problem. Humanistic psychology had become *iatrogenic,* meaning that its treatments now had negative consequences that would not have occurred except for the treatments themselves. The increasing divorce rate, for example, was at least partly the result of rising expectations that had been created by humanistic technology:

> *If we were to ask where married couples got the idea that they should be able to communicate openly, raise their children effectively, and enjoy fulfilled sex lives, the answer would be that, at least to some degree, they have gotten these expectations from us. In our effort to improve those aspects of life we may have so emphasized them that they have now become problems, enormous problems, problems that simply did not exist before our applications of technology provided new definitions of what relationships were supposed to be. (Farson, 1978, p. 11)*

Of course, it is both unfair and unrealistic to lay contemporary social problems at the feet of humanistic psychologists. For one thing, it is impossible to disentangle the extent to which humanistic psychology was simply an expression of the American zeitgeist in the 1960s and 1970s, and the extent to which that zeitgeist was itself shaped by humanistic psychology. Moreover, to some extent humanistic psychology fit in with a rather general, long-standing feature of American culture, which is to be particularly

> *prone to view all human troubles as problems that will yield to technological solutions, rather than as the complicated, paradoxical dilemmas they usually are. Most of the affairs of life, particularly the most intimate and important ones such as marriage, work, and child-rearing, are permanent, inescapable predicaments. We cannot solve them because they are not problems in the first place. (Farson, 1978, p. 14)*

Humanistic psychology is not a major force in academic psychology, partly because, as Farson (1978, p. 29) observed, the leaders of humanistic psychology, such as Rollo May, Abraham Maslow and Carl Rogers, moved away from university settings. This had the consequence that "their theories have not been researched, expanded or revised, and their thinking has not been tested by the critical questioning that would come from students and university colleagues. . . . Moreover, they have not developed students who can extend their work into second and third generations of scholars and scientists."

To a large extent, the enthusiasm that fired humanistic psychology when it was founded has faded away. However, humanistic psychology has had and still continues to have an impact on popular culture. One has only to examine the offerings in the psychology or self-help sections of mass-market bookstores to realize that such topics as interpersonal relationships, marriage, work, and child-rearing are still topics of great concern to many people. Humanistic psychology has shaped the way ordinary people think about these issues even today. Can one say the same about many academic psychologies?

Additional Reading on This Topic. Some humanistic psychologists believed that it did not go far enough. By attending only to individual experience, it paid short shrift to those aspects of human experience that were universal and transcendent. This led to the founding of a *Journal of Transpersonal Psychology* in 1969. Transpersonal psychology tended to be quite respectful of religious and esoteric traditions, no matter where they came from. Tart (1975) contains a collection of basic readings in this area.

GEORGE A. KELLY (1905–1967)

George Kelly attended the Old Saybrook conference that launched humanistic psychology in 1964, and the paper he gave there was later published in the *Journal of Humanistic Psychology* (Kelly, 1965). While Kelly's approach shared some of the characteristics of humanistic psychology, in other ways it was quite distinctive. The following captures one of the essential differences between Kelly and many humanistic psychologists:

> *Because of the present uncertainty of its stand on experimental research, I fear there is a real danger of the recent humanistic psychology movement fizzling out. In their outright opposition to so much that is considered synonymous with "scientific research" and "experimental psychology," humanists may convince themselves and others that they oppose research in general and experimentation in particular. Nothing could be more incongruous than for humanistic psychology to become frozen in this posture. What could be more vital to psychology than to recognize that experimentation is even more charac-*

teristically human than it is scientific? (Kelly, 1969a, p. 144).

Notice that Kelly associates being human with being a scientist. Kelly did not see scientific behavior as something unnatural. Rather, Kelly (1955, p. 569) believed that people naturally wish to "predict and control the course of events with which they are involved," just as scientists do. Kelly's psychology is largely the result of exploring the implications of the notion that *people are scientists.*

The Psychology of Personal Constructs

Kelly first came to widespread attention with the publication in 1955 of his two-volume work, *The Psychology of Personal Constructs.* The *fundamental postulate* of this theory is that "a person's processes are psychologically channelized by the ways in which [that person] anticipates events" (p. 46). By this, Kelly meant that the person "ultimately seeks to anticipate real events. This is where we see psychological processes as tied down to reality. Anticipation is not merely carried on for its own sake; it is carried on so that future reality may be better represented. It is the future which tantalizes [the person], not the past. Always [the person] reaches out to the future through the window of the present" (p. 49).

Kelly believed that the process of anticipation was analogous to the way scientists behave when they are performing experiments to test hypotheses. People attempt to predict, or anticipate, the events they will encounter, just as scientists formulate hypotheses that are then tested against reality. In order to predict events, it is necessary for the person to be able to represent them. From Kelly's viewpoint, we do this by means of *constructs.* In its simplest form, a construct is a way in which two events are alike but different from a third event. "If we choose an aspect in which A and B are similar, but in contrast to C, it is important to note that it is the same aspect of all three, A, B, *and* C, that forms the basis of the construct" (Kelly, 1955, p. 59). For example, if we have three acquaintances—Curly, Moe and Larry—and we see Curly and Moe as similar in that they are *warm,* but different from Larry, who is *cold,* then the aspect underlying the comparison may be said to be *warmth* (cf. Benjafield, 1983).

It is essential to Kelly's psychology (1955) that "people differ from each other in their construction of events" (p. 55). Each person creates *personal constructs,* which are dimensions that may be unique to that individual. Personal constructs are idiosyncratic ways of noting similarities and differences. They are most obvious when people make distinctions using terms that are not opposites in any conventional sense, as in the following illustration. Suppose we ask someone to construe three acquaintances—the ubiquitous Curly, Moe, and Larry. The person replies that Curly and Moe are *intelligent* and Larry is *lazy.* At first this construction may puzzle us. In order to understand it we inquire further, and discover that, according to this person, Curly and Moe are also *rich,* and Larry is *poor.* Now we may be starting to get a better picture of what the construct *intelligent* versus *lazy* means to this person. We need not agree with his construction of Curly, Moe, and Larry in order to be able to understand how he sees them. It is through the pattern of relationships between the person's constructs that the meaning of particular constructs emerges (Kelly, 1955, p. 56).

Once we have a feeling for how some of a person's constructs are related, then we can begin to make hypotheses about how the person might employ other constructs. In the example, since being *intelligent* and *rich* go together, as do being *lazy* and *poor,* then we might infer that this person believes that being intelligent goes with being hard-working. We might turn out to be wrong. Suppose the person says that only Curly *works hard,* and that Moe and Larry *take it easy.* In this case, the person's construct system has turned out to be more complicated than we anticipated. We could continue to probe the other person's constructs by asking for further construals. Kelly's point is that we try to understand someone else's construct system in the same way as we try to understand any other set of events. We try to anticipate the other person's constructions, and modify our understanding of the person in the light of the results of these anticipations (Kelly, 1955, pp. 95–100).

In our running example, we have been considering a hypothetical person for whom the construct *intelligent versus lazy* is related to the construct *rich versus poor.* As a consequence of this linkage between the two constructs, if this person meets someone *rich,* then he or she will anticipate that the new acquaintance will demonstrate *intelligence* as well. Even if the other person's behavior provides no evidence of intelligence, it may still be construed as intelligent in order to validate this prediction. Kelly (1955, p. 510) used the term *hostility* to refer to the process of extorting evidence so as to preserve one's construct system. Kelly (1955, p. 511) likened hostility to the "method of Procrustes, who was always stretching his guests, or cutting them down to a size to fit his bed." A hostile person does not behave as would a good scientist. In fact, poor scientists behave like Procrustes, forcing the facts to fit their theory rather than the other way around. People are better scientists when they are able to revise the linkages between their constructs in the light of new evidence. Thus, in our hypothetical example, finding a *rich* person who was *lazy* should lead to a looser relation between the two constructs.

According to Kelly (1955, pp. 117–119), the pattern of linkages between constructs takes a specific form that may be unique to the individual. It is on the basis of these linkages between our constructs that we are able to explore reality and make predictions about what we will find there. These predictions may be falsified by the events we actually encounter, leading to a revision of the linkages between constructs, and thus a restructured construct system.

The Repertory Test

Personal constructs came to Kelly's attention as a result of his work as a psychotherapist in Kansas in the 1930s. He observed that his clients seldom described themselves in conventional terms. "Each person seeks to communicate his distress in the terms that make sense to [that person], but not necessarily in terms that make sense to others" (Kelly, 1969b, p. 58). Kelly (1955, p. 4) observed that John Locke had begun to write his "Essay Concerning Human Understanding" (which we considered in Chapter 2) on being "struck by the unique imperceptiveness of his friends," just as Kelly was spurred to write the *Psychology of Personal Constructs* because of the uniqueness of the viewpoints his clients had demonstrated. Each person lives in a world that is somewhat unique, as revealed by the uniqueness of their personal constructs. It is vitally important that the psychotherapist somehow be able to construe the idiosyncratic constructions of the client.

One of Kelly's (1955, chap. 5) most influential contributions was to invent a method of eliciting an individual's personal constructs. An example of this instrument is given in Figure 13.2. It is called a *repertory grid,* and allows you to get some idea of how a person applies constructs to a set of *elements.* The elements are usually people, but may be any kind of event. The grid in Figure 13.2 is intended only to give you a general idea of what a grid is like. It is not the same as Kelly's original test (1955). For example, along the top of Figure 13.2 are listed 13 *role titles,* or descriptions of individuals to whom you could give names. For example, the first asks you to name the most successful person known to you personally, and so on. Kelly (1955, p. 274) used a list of 22 role titles, while Figure 13.2 uses only 13 role titles taken from Benjafield & Green (1978).

Each row of the grid gives the person an opportunity to generate his or her own constructs. In each row, there are three role titles circled. For each of these triplets, the person is to think of a way in which two are alike, but different from the third (e.g., two are *authoritarian,* but the third is *democratic*). The way in which two people are similar defines the *construct* pole, and the way in which the third person is different defines the *contrast* pole. After eliciting a construct, the person then goes through the role titles and checks those figures who are best described by the construct pole, and leaves blank those best described by the contrast pole.

Most Successful Person	Most Ethical Person	Happiest Person	Warmest Person	Strongest Person	Most Active Person	Most Unsuccessful Person	Unhappiest Person	Most Unethical Person	Coldest Person	Weakest Person	Most Passive Person	Yourself	Construct	Contrast
○	○	○												
			○	○	○									
						○	○	○						
									○	○	○			
○	○											○		
		○	○									○		
				○	○							○		
						○	○					○		
								○	○			○		
										○	○	○		
		○		○	○									

FIGURE 13.2 A repertory test.

This procedure is repeated for all triplets in the grid. Kelly (1955) provided a rationale for each of the triplets he used, but in Fig. 13.2, the triplets have been assigned arbitrarily. Thus, while Figure 13.2 can give you some idea of what filling out a repertory grid is like, it does not yield any interpretable data.

Research in Personal Construct Theory

It is an interesting quirk of history that Kelly's approach was not taken up by psychologists in the United States to anything like the degree it was adopted in Britain. "By the late 1950s, [personal construct theory] had begun to attract adherents in Great Britain, and by the mid-1960s it was being vigorously debated, and applied by a small but devoted network of psychologists and psychiatrists. Despite its more recent origin, the British theory has grown rapidly, so that by 1980 as many British as American psychologists had published . . . twice in the theory" (Neimeyer, 1985, p. 40). It is generally agreed that the popularity of personal construct theory in Great Britain was largely due to the efforts of *Don Bannister* (e.g., Bannister & Bott, 1973; Bannister & Mair, 1968; Fransella & Bannister, 1977), who brought the theory to the attention of many clinical practitioners (e.g., Ryle, 1975).

Bannister's work drew attention to the many different ways in which a repertory grid can yield information about a person's construct system. For example, repertory grids can be used to measure a person's *cognitive complexity* (Bieri,

1955; Bannister & Mair, 1968, p. 70). "The cognitively complex person is assumed to have a greater number of personal constructs to construe the behavior of others, while the cognitively simple person has available relatively few personal constructs" (Bieri, 1961, p. 359). There are several possible measures of complexity (Adams-Webber, 1970; Fransella & Bannister, 1977, pp. 61–62), but we focus here on only one simple measure, just to get a rough idea of what kinds of measures are possible using the grid. Bieri (1961, p. 361) suggested that a person's construct system, as measured by a grid, may be said to be relatively *simple* if there are a large number of matches between the constructs (rows). It is possible to imagine a grid in which the same pattern of checks and blanks occurred for each construct. For example, suppose the two rows shown below were taken from a repertory grid. In this example, the constructs are perfectly correlated, since every time a role title is judged as *pleasant* it is also judged as *intelligent,* and every time a role title is seen as *unpleasant* it is also seen as *stupid.*

✓			✓	✓		✓	✓	✓	✓			✓	Pleasant	Unpleasant
✓			✓	✓		✓	✓	✓	✓			✓	Intelligent	Stupid

A great many such matches in a grid may indicate that the person is using only one construct, under different names (Bieri, 1961, p. 361). Such a grid may reflect a construct system that is "simple," because there is really only one distinction being made, regardless of what it is called (Ryle, 1975, p. 32). Contrast the situation just described with the one illustrated below. Here the match between constructs is far from perfect.

✓			✓	✓		✓		✓	✓			✓	Pleasant	Unpleasant
✓	✓	✓		✓				✓	✓	✓		✓	Intelligent	Stupid

This sort of relationship between constructs suggests that each construct is being applied in a relatively unique way. Each construct is being used to make a somewhat different distinction, and this is reflected by the different profile of checks and blanks in each row. People who are cognitively complex may be better able to see others as relatively unique individuals, with idiosyncratic combinations of features (Bieri, 1961, p. 360). Particularly during the 1960s and 1970s, an extensive line of research both within personal construct theory and in social psychology generally was concerned with various ways to measure cognitive complexity, and with determining whether or not it was related to the ability to make more precise, differentiated predictions (e.g., Mancuso, 1970; Warr, 1970).

Writing 20 years after Kelly's death, Jankowicz (1987) observed that the flexibility of repertory grid methodology has made it broadly useful in applied settings. "The practice developed of taking as elements any well-defined set of mutually exclusive terms that are exemplars of the particular topic under investigation (Bannister & Fransella, 1971). The technique could then be used in any field of application in which a precise and explicit articulation of a person's construct system is required" (p. 484). Among these fields of application, Jankowicz mentions market research, an area in which it is particularly important to have an understanding of "the idiosyncratic ways in which consumers construe products" (p. 484). In general, the field of industrial-organizational psychology has been particularly receptive to personal construct theory, although, here again, this influence has been most pronounced in Britain. The repertory grid has proven valuable to people who wish to respond to their clients "in the individual's own language . . . rather than in the language of psychological expertise" (Jankowicz, 1987, p. 486).

Qualitative Research Methods

The use of the repertory grid to tap the unique perspectives of individuals has been cited as an example of the kind of *qualitative research methods* that are currently finding favor in some parts of the discipline (e.g., Banister, Burman, Parker, Taylor, & Tindall, 1994). Qualitative research methods are to be distinguished from quantitative research methods, such as those we considered in Chapter 10. Quantitative research methods "aggregate the objects, events or persons under study" in the hope of being able to make general statements about people as a whole (Pyke & Agnew, 1991, p. 134). By contrast, qualitative research methods are not designed to test a particular hypothesis, but rather to develop a description of the way individuals represent the world they inhabit. "Qualitative research methods are based on the assumption that humans do not so much respond to direct stimuli as they do to their interpretations of the information impinging on them. Thus we are constantly involved in an interaction process with environmental elements that we symbolically transform. These symbolic translations or meanings that humans attach to events must be studied if we are to understand the subsequent behavior" (Pyke & Agnew, 1991, p. 136). Since the repertory grid lends itself to the analysis of "symbolic translations or meanings," it can fit quite nicely into the qualitative researcher's toolkit (Banister et al., 1994, chap. 5).

Qualitative research methods are obviously aimed at the same kind of understanding of the person that humanistic psychologists originally sought. They also belong to the same tradition as the case study approach adopted by some clinical psychologists, and the kind of action research that was promulgated by Lewin, and which we considered in Chapter 9. Qualitative research has also been advocated by some feminist scholars, a topic to which we will return in Chapter 15.

Additional Reading on This Topic. The standard review of basic research in personal construct theory is Adams-Webber (1979).

KEY NAMES AND CONCEPTS

What follows is an index of some of the most important material in this chapter. The list includes individuals, concepts, and topics you should know. Read through the list, and if anything on it seems unfamiliar, then go back and re-read the appropriate section of the chapter. You should be able to define each concept, briefly discuss each topic, and state the importance of each person on the list. In addition, you should be able to write an account of the work done by each person or topic printed in boldface.

Allport, Gordon W., 270
- idiographic–nomothetic distinction, 270
- scale of values, 270

Bannister, Don, 285

Beauvoir, Simone de, 267

Benedict, Ruth, 272
- patterns of culture, 272
- synergy, 272

Binswanger, Ludwig, 268
- existential approach to psychotherapy, 268

Box 13.1—Carl Rogers and creative environments, 279

Buhler, Charlotte, 269

emergence of humanistic psychology, 268

Encounter groups, 280
- empirical understanding, 281

existentialism, 265

Farson, Richard, 281
- iatrogenic, 281

First Invitational Conference on Humanistic Psychology, 269

Gendlin, Eugene T., 279
- experiencing, 280
- felt meaning, 280
- symbols, 280

Harlow, Harry, 271

Heidegger, Martin, 268
being-in-the-world, 268
care, 268
Dasein, 268
Hollingworth, Leta, 277
American Association of Clinical Psychologists, 277
gender differences, 277
psychology of women, 277
human potential movement, 281
Journal of Humanistic Psychology, 269
Journal of Transpersonal Psychology, 282
Kelly, George A., 282
constructs, 283
elements, 284
fundamental postulate, 283
hostility, 284
people are scientists, 283
personal constructs, 283
The Psychology of Personal Constructs, 283
repertory grid, 284
repertory test, 284
role titles, 284
Kierkegaard, Søren, 265
absurdity of human existence, 266
leap of faith, 266
subjectivity and human choice, 266
Maslow, Abraham, 271
basic need, 272
Being values, 274
deficiency motives, 274
esteem needs, 273
experiential methods, 276
hierarchy of needs, 272
instinctoid, 275
love needs, 273
metamotivation, 274
metapathology, 275
peak experiences, 275
physiological needs, 272
problem centered versus method centered, 276
The Psychology of Science, 275
safety needs, 273
self-actualization, 273
self-actualizing person, 273
Taoistic science, 276
May, Rollo, 270
anxiety, 270
care, 271
influence of William James, 271
Love and Will, 270
neurotic versus normal anxiety, 270
Nietzsche, Friedrich, 266
nihilism, 266
perspectivism, 266
will to power, 266
Rogers, Carl, 276
client-centered psychotherapy, 277
ideal self, 278
nondirective psychotherapy, 277
self-concept, 278
unconditional positive regard, 278
Sartre, Jean-Paul, 267
bad faith, 267
Being and Nothingness, 267
existence precedes essence, 267
humanism, 268
intentionality, 267
Third Force, 269
Witmer, Lightner, 276

CHAPTER 14

COGNITIVE PSYCHOLOGY

THE CONCEPT OF "INFORMATION"
NOAM CHOMSKY (1928–)
Syntactic Structures
Cartesian Linguistics
GEORGE A. MILLER (1920–)
The Magical Number Seven
Plans and the Structure of Behavior
Subjective Behaviorism
Giving Psychology Away
JEROME S. BRUNER (1915–)
The "New Look" in Perception
A Study of Thinking
SIR FREDERIC BARTLETT (1887–1969)
ULRIC NEISSER (1928–)
Cognitive Psychology
James J. Gibson (1904–1979)
Cognition and Reality
HERBERT A. SIMON (1916–)
Spurious Correlation and the Nature of Causality
Computer Simulation
Criticisms of Computer Simulation

Cognition is a complex area of psychological inquiry that contains a large number of topics. The *Oxford English Dictionary* (1989) defines "cognition" as the *action or faculty of knowing*. Thus, cognitive psychology investigates those processes whereby we understand ourselves and our environment. These processes include attention, memory, concepts, imagery, problem solving, reasoning, judgment, and language (e.g., Benjafield, 1992). These topics have all had a distinguished history in psychology, some of which we have reviewed in previous chapters. By and large, they are topics that were neglected during the behaviorist era in psychology because they appeared to be too "subjective" to admit of scientific investigation. However, this situation began to change after the Second World War. In this chapter we review the work of some of the individuals who made psychology cognitive again.

THE CONCEPT OF "INFORMATION"

One of the most momentous developments in the twentieth century has been the development of computer science and allied disciplines. Over the last five decades, many psychologists have attempted to determine whether concepts derived from computer science can be successfully applied in psychology. Thus, a computing machine can be seen as an *information processing system.* The interesting question is, to what extent can people also be seen as information processing systems? That is one of the central issues we explore in this chapter.

Information is obviously a key concept in any discussion of computers, and a revolutionary change in the way this concept is used was brought about by information theorists such as Shannon and Weaver (1949). Intuitively, "information is something that occurs when some person or machine tells us something we didn't know before" (Garner, 1962, p. 2). Information theorists went beyond this rough definition and proposed to measure the amount of information that is transmitted when an event occurs. The basic idea was that "any communicative act provides information only insofar as it reduces a condition of ignorance or uncertainty about the state of things under consideration" (Garner, 1962, p. 3). Thus, information is the opposite of uncertainty. Consider tossing a coin, for example. Before tossing the coin, we are uncertain about which alternative (heads or tails) will occur. After tossing the coin, our uncertainty is eliminated. Any event that reduces or eliminates uncertainty provides us with information.

Some situations contain more uncertainty than others. In the case of coin tossing, there are only two possible outcomes—heads or tails. In other situations, such as rolling a single die, there are six possible outcomes—the numbers 1 to 6. There is more prior uncertainty in the latter case than in the former, and consequently rolling a die provides more information than does tossing a coin. It is possible to quantify the amount of information provided by the occurrence of an event in terms of *bits*. "Bit" is short for "binary digit." Imagine a situation, such as flipping an unbiased coin, in which we are uncertain about which of two equally likely events will occur. When one of the two events occurs, then we get one bit of information. Every time the number of equally likely alternatives doubles, then the number of bits goes up by one.

The relationship between the number of equally likely alternatives and the amount of information transmitted when one of the events occurs is illustrated in Table 14.1. (The situation becomes more complicated when the alternatives are not equally likely.) A popular illustration of this relationship is a guessing game in which one person thinks of a number and another person tries to guess it (Garner, 1962, p. 5). The number of bits corresponds to the number of questions you would need to ask in order to guess the right answer. For example, if I am thinking of a number between 1 and 8, you need three questions to find it. The correct strategy is to reduce the number of possibilities by one-half with each question. First, ask if the number is above 4. If the answer is "yes," then ask if it is above 6. If the answer is "yes" again, then ask if it is above 7. If the answer is "yes," then the number is 8, if it is "no," then the number is 7. You can work out the scenario for other cases in Table 14.1 at your leisure.

TABLE 14.1 Examples of the Relationship between the Number of Equally Likely Alternatives and the Number of Bits

ALTERNATIVES	BITS
2	1
4	2
8	3
16	4
32	5
64	6
128	7
256	8
512	9
1024	10

Information theory provided a new model for the process of communication (Sperber & Wilson, 1986). This model described the process whereby information was *transmitted* through a *channel of communication.* The first stage in this process is *encoding,* or the transformation of the *input* into a form that can be transmitted. Thus, a telephone encodes the human voice into a set of *signals* that can be transmitted along telephone wires, or some other medium. At the other end of the channel, the message is *decoded* into a form that can be used as *output* by the consumer of the information. This way of representing the flow of information in a system has been enormously influential, as we shall see.

Additional Reading on This Topic. Attneave (1959) is a useful review of early efforts to apply information theory to psychology.

NOAM CHOMSKY (1928–)

Any theory of communication must provide an understanding of the ways in which natural languages function. Understanding the human ability to use language is one of the great challenges that faces psychology. This challenge was taken up by behavioristically oriented psychologists, in particular by B. F. Skinner (1957), who argued that language was governed by the same principles that regulated all other forms of behavior. Words are responses elicited by stimuli, and as such are under the control of environmental reinforcement contingencies. Language is learned behavior. When a child emits a sound, and is reinforced for doing so, then the probability that the child will reproduce this utterance is increased. By reinforcing children for producing the appropriate utterances, parents can shape their children's speech so that it becomes to increasingly approximate their native language.

This behaviorist account of language was attacked by a young linguist from MIT named Noam Chomsky (1959, 1972b). In a review of Skinner's book *Verbal Behavior* (1957), Chomsky argued that behaviorist principles could not explain any significant aspects of language. For example, people are continuously generating sentences that they have never spoken before, and Skinner's approach does not and cannot explain this fact. When people speak a sentence they cannot be doing so in response to a stimulus, since it would be impossible to learn all the stimulus-response connections required to enable people to speak a natural language. Any theory of language worth its salt must explain the fact that language is inherently creative, and no behaviorist theory can do so.

Syntactic Structures

Chomsky's critique of behaviorism attracted a great deal of attention from psychologists who, by the middle of the 1950s, had already begun to doubt the value of the behaviorist program. However, the constituency that was sympathetic to Chomsky's critical analysis was quite different from the constituency that had been attracted to humanistic psychology. Chomsky's ideas appealed to academic psychologists who regarded themselves as scientists first and foremost. Chomsky not only dismissed behaviorism as lacking scientific content, but proposed to replace it with a genuinely scientific theory that could explain the basic facts of language.

The theory Chomsky (1957) proposed had been developed as a part of his doctoral dissertation at MIT. Even within linguistics, Chomsky's approach had been regarded as a radical departure from the prevailing wisdom, and consequently he had difficulty publishing his work. Gradually, however, scholars began to appreciate the originality and power of Chomsky's approach. Chomsky (1957, p. 15) provided an account of aspects of language that were difficult for other theories to explain. For example, he pointed out that native speakers of English have no trouble telling which of the following sentences is grammatical, even though both are meaningless.

Colorless green ideas sleep furiously.
Furiously sleep ideas green colorless.

Chomsky's (1957, pp. 16–17) point was that everyone has the "ability to produce and recognize grammatical utterances" and that "grammar is autonomous and independent of meaning." People have an understanding of grammar that allows them to discern whether or not an utterance is grammatical, even when it is one the like of which they may never have heard before.

Ambiguity is another linguistic fact that Chomsky (1957, chap. 8) believed was particularly revealing. For example, consider the following sentences (Bigelow, 1986, p. 379):

Time flies like an arrow.
Fruit flies like a banana.

Most people interpret the first sentence such that "time" is a noun and "flies" is a verb. However, the second sentence is usually interpreted such that "flies" is a noun. Ambiguity is very common in natural languages. Consider this sentence (Greene, 1972, p. 47):

The shooting of the hunters was awful.

We can interpret this sentence as meaning that the hunters were lousy shots, or that the hunters were shot. How do we arrive at one interpretation or the other? In order to answer questions such as this, Chomsky proposed that language be understood in terms of levels. The particular words that make up a sentence constitute one level, called the *surface structure*. Although surface structures are spoken one word at a time, each successive word does not act as a stimulus for the next word in the sentence. Rather, the surface structure is derived from an underlying *deep structure* by means of *grammatical transformations*. Grammatical transformations are rules that replace one symbol with another. The following are examples of such transformations (Chomsky, 1957, p. 26; Greene, 1972, p. 35):

1. Sentence (S) → Noun Phrase (NP) + Verb Phrase (VP)
2. NP → Article (T) + Noun (N)
3. VP → Verb (V) + NP
4. T → the
5. N → boy, girl, fence, car, etc.
6. V → paints, jumps, etc.

Of course, these are by no means the only rules necessary, and they are only intended to illustrate the general idea. These rules permit the derivation of different surface structures, one of which is given in Figure 14.1.

The important thing to see about Chomsky's approach is that speech is produced by a hierarchical, top-down process that moves from deep to surface structure. When you hear a sentence, then you understand it by simply reversing the process and going from surface to deep structure (Chomsky, 1957, p. 48). Sentences that have similar surface structures, (e.g., "Time flies like an arrow" and "Fruit flies like a banana"), can have different deep structures, and thus be understood in different ways.

You should compare Figure 14.1 with Figure 8.4, which represents Watson's stimulus-response model of serially ordered behavior. In Chomsky's

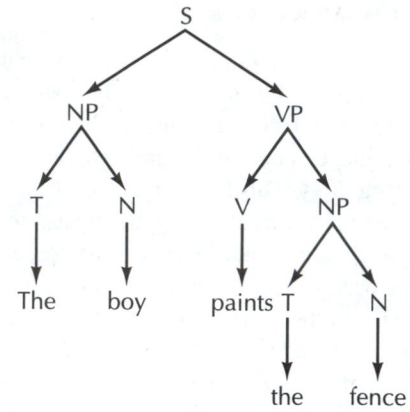

FIGURE 14.1 Derivation of a surface structure from a deep structure.

model, language is not controlled by external stimuli, but by an internally generated system of rules. There is nothing haphazard about the rules that govern language. Grammatical transformations have the same necessity as do mathematical laws (e.g., Chomsky, 1967). However, although there are only a finite number of grammatical rules, they provide the means for generating an infinite number of possible sentences.

Cartesian Linguistics

Chomsky (1966) saw his theory as descended from that of Descartes, whose views we considered in Chapter 2. You should recall that, while Descartes believed that animals were like machines, he did not believe that *human* behavior could be understood in a completely mechanical manner. People differ from both animals and machines by being much more flexible in response to changing circumstances. For example, we are able to speak in ways that are spontaneous and novel, something Descartes believed no animal or machine could be trained or made to do. It is precisely this aspect of Cartesian doctrine with which Chomsky (1966, p. 3) agreed. "[H]uman language is free from stimulus control and does not serve a merely communicative function, but is rather an instrument for the free expression of thought and for appropriate response to new situations" (Chomsky, 1966, p. 13).

You should also recall that Descartes was a nativist, believing that our most human capacities are innate. This is also the position Chomsky took with respect to language:

> *The central doctrine of Cartesian linguistics is that the general features of grammatical structures are common to all languages and reflect certain fundamental properties of the mind. . . . There are, then, certain* language universals *that set limits to the variety of human language. . . . Such universal conditions are not learned; rather they provide the organizing principles that make language learning possible (Chomsky, 1966, p. 60)*

All languages share common principles, and these principles are "known unconsciously" by everyone (Chomsky, 1966, p. 63). When a child is exposed to a natural language, its task is not to learn the language from scratch, but to "discover which of the possible languages he [or she] is being exposed to" (Chomsky, 1972a, p. 259). The child possesses a *language acquisition device* (Chomsky, 1972a, p. 135) that comes equipped with a rich set of hypotheses about the grammatical structure of any possible natural language. Language acquisition occurs quite quickly because each child already has an elaborate theory of language that can be used to make sense of the linguistic data he or she hears. If the child did not innately possess such a language acquisition device, then the rapidity with which a child acquires the ability to generate novel utterances "would be an impenetrable mystery" (Chomsky, 1972a, p. 136).

Over the last 20 years, Chomsky has continued to develop his theory of language. His approach still receives support, although many critics have charged that Chomsky overestimates the role of innate factors in determining the process of language acquisition. However, even those who disagree with Chomsky's theory must still pay attention to it. "The story of psycholinguistics in the second half of the 20th century is to a large extent the story of the evolution of Chomsky's theory of grammar (Chomsky, 1957, 1966, 1980, 1986)" (Rosenberg, 1993, p. 15). Moreover, as we shall see, Chomsky's influence was not restricted to linguistics and the psychology of language. Chomsky's emphasis on the importance of internal processes that operate more or less independently of external stimulus control was one of the factors that facilitated the reemergence of an interest in the scientific study of mental processes. This renewed interest was one of the hallmarks of cognitive psychology.

Additional Reading on This Topic. A very readable account of Chomsky's impact on linguistics (and linguists) is given by Berreby (1994).

GEORGE A. MILLER (1920–)

George Miller was in the right place at the right time. Working at Harvard in the 1950s, Miller (1979) came in contact with many of the central figures in what was to become cognitive psychology. He regarded 1956 as particularly important in the history of cognitive psychology, and singled out a symposium on information theory held at MIT that year as the occasion when the several strands that were to become cognitive psychology came together. In addition to Chomsky, the participants included *Allen Newell* and *Herbert Simon,* whose work in computer simulation we will discuss below. The year 1956 also marked the publication of *A Study of Thinking* by *Jerome Bruner* and his colleagues J. Goodnow and G. Austin. This book reintroduced the study of "higher mental processes" to psychology after decades of neglect. We review Bruner's contributions later on in the chapter, but for now we only note that in 1962 Bruner joined with Miller to open "the Center for Cognitive Studies at Harvard; we spent the next decade simply taking advantage of opportunities that had ripened in the 1950's" (Miller, 1979, p. 10). Over the next several years many such institutes and centers for cognitive studies were created at universities all over the United States and the rest of the world.

Of course, creating new institutions, such as the Center for Cognitive Studies, takes money. As

Miller noted, after 1957 money for such ventures became available because that was the year "when the Russians launched their first manned satellite. Sputnik aroused fears that the United States was falling behind Russia technologically, and Congress opened the purse strings for science, engineering, and education. Enough of this funding spilled over into computers, psychology, and even linguistics that we were able to pursue our ideas as fast as we could think of them—sometimes a little faster, I'm afraid" (Miller, 1979, p. 9).

The Magical Number Seven

Miller (1953) was one of the first psychologists to become aware of and to use information theory in his research. A famous example of his work in this area was his paper "The Magical Number Seven: Plus or Minus Two" (Miller, 1956/1967), in which he considered experiments that regarded the experimental subject as a "communication channel," and the experimenter was interested in how much information can be accurately transmitted through this channel. This amount is called *channel capacity.* For example, a subject might be asked to estimate the magnitude of a stimulus dimension. The dimension might be anything from sounds of different pitch or loudness, to tastes of different saltiness or sweetness.

In experiments like these, subjects could discriminate between about 7 different magnitudes, giving a channel capacity of about 2.5 bits of information. A similar result occurred in investigations of the *span of apprehension.* In Chapter 4, we noted that Wundt (1912/1973, p. 35) had done research on this topic, which refers to how many items we can be aware of at one time. There have been many investigations into the span of apprehension since Wundt's day, and Miller's review of the literature suggests that we can hold about seven items in mind at one time. He called this the *span of immediate memory* (Miller, 1956/1967, p. 34), and observed that the amount of information we can retain in this way is quite limited.

Of course, there is nothing magical about the number 7, although, with tongue-in-cheek Miller (1956/1967, p. 42) drew attention to "the seven wonders of the world, the seven seas, the seven deadly sins, the seven daughters of Atlas in the Pleiades, the seven ages of man, the seven levels of hell, the seven primary colors, the seven notes of the musical scale, and the seven days of the week." In spite of (or perhaps because of) this refreshing willingness to not take oneself or one's research too seriously, Miller's analysis of psychological processes such as judgment and memory tempted many other psychologists to use information theoretical concepts in their own work. In addition, quite independently of Miller's work, there were psychologists in other countries, particularly in Britain, who were also inventing new experimental paradigms to the process of communication. One of these paradigms is discussed in Box 14.1.

Plans and the Structure of Behavior

One of the first attempts to give cognitive psychology a coherent theoretical framework occurred with the publication of *Plans and the Structure of Behavior* by George Miller and his colleagues Eugene Galanter and Karl Pribram (Miller, Galanter, & Pribram, 1960). In addition to information theory and Chomskyian psycholinguistics, Miller, Galanter, and Pribram (1960) drew on *cybernetics* for their core theoretical ideas. "Cybernetics was defined by [the mathematician] *Norbert Wiener* as 'the science of control and communication, in the animal and the machine'—in a word as the art of *steermanship*" (Ashby, 1956, p. 1). Cybernetics was concerned with formulating general principles that control any system, whether organic or inorganic. One of the central concepts of cybernetics was *feedback,* a process in which the output of one part of a system affects another part of the system, which in turn affects the first part. The classic example of a *feedback loop* is a thermostat. Such a device is set to maintain a preset temperature. If the temperature falls below a certain level, then the thermostat sends a signal to the furnace, which turns it on. The furnace then generates heat, which raises the temperature. When the temperature reaches its preset level, the thermostat

Box 14.1

Donald E. Broadbent (1926–1993) and Dichotic Listening

Broadbent (1980) was born in Britain, and served in the Royal Air Force in the Second World War. The RAF trained pilots in the United States, and while there he began to think of becoming a psychologist. Partly this was because, at that time, psychology was a much more common career in the United States than it was in Britain. As a pilot, he also became acutely aware of the way in which "technology . . . was badly matched to human beings." Airplanes and other machines were designed by engineers, and often did not take the psychology of the operator into account. The result was that machines were often difficult and/or dangerous to operate. This early interest in person-machine interactions signaled Broadbent's subsequent involvement in applied psychology. An important component of applied psychology, particularly since the Second World War, has been the study of ways to improve the ease with which people can interact with machines. This area of inquiry is called *ergonomics* in Europe and *human factors* in the United States.

When Broadbent returned to Britain, he took up psychology at Cambridge, studying with, among others, Sir Frederic Bartlett, that giant of British psychology whose work we will review later on in this chapter. Broadbent's early research was driven by practical problems experienced by armed forces personnel. One such problem concerned "those arising in communication centers, where many different streams of speech reached the person at the same time" (Broadbent, 1980, p. 54). This line of research led to one of the most influential papers in the history of experimental psychology. Broadbent (1952/1992, p. 125) created a task in which the subject was required to "answer one of two messages which start at the same point in time, but one of which is irrelevant."

The experimental technique Broadbent used is called *dichotic listening*. Subjects were exposed to two verbal messages presented simultaneously by a tape recorder. The subject was required to answer questions posed in only one of the messages. When subjects knew in advance which of two different voices contained the required message, then performance on this task was very good. Subjects were clearly able to select relevant information, and ignore irrelevant information. Broadbent suggested that this demonstrated the role of *attention* in the selection of information. As Broadbent (1980, p. 55) later noted, the concept of attention "had hardly appeared in respectable circles for forty years," or since the demise of introspectionism.

Partly as a result of Broadbent's experiments and subsequent theoretical work (e.g., Broadbent, 1958), attention is now "a vital component of work in cognitive psychology, cognitive science, and neuroscience. At a more general level, the dichotic listening studies helped fuel the cognitive revolution against behaviorism by pointing to the importance of implicit, unobservable mental representations and processes in understanding behavior. These studies are surely among the most important of the last 100 years" (Egeth, 1992, p. 124).

Broadbent also worked closely with *Colin Cherry* (1914–), who was not a psychologist, but professor of telecommunications at the University of London. Broadbent (1980) described him as "a leading activist in the early days of information theory, and his students were often doing work that might just as well have been done in a psychological laboratory" (p. 59). Cherry (1953) has become famous in psychology for drawing attention to the *cocktail party phenomenon,* a topic that is still mentioned in virtually every introductory text. This phenomenon occurs when you are able to attend to one conversation in a crowded room in which many other conversations are going on. The ability to attend to one message while ignoring another has often been studied using a *shadowing task,* in which an experimental subject wears headphones, and is given two messages, one in each ear. The subject "shadows" one of the two messages by repeating it as it is heard.

---

turns the furnace off. This cycle can go on indefinitely, allowing the maintenance of a more or less *steady state* with respect to temperature.

Miller, Galanter, and Pribram (1960) proposed that the feedback loop be regarded as the basic unit of behavioral control. They called these

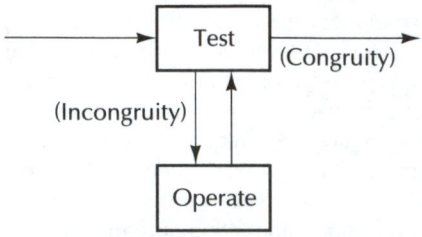

FIGURE 14.2 A TOTE mechanism.

Source: G. A. Miller, E. Galanter, & K. Pribram (1960). Plans and the structure of behavior. New York: Holt, Rinehart & Winston, p. 26. Copyright © 1960 by G. A. Miller. Reprinted by permission.

units *TOTE mechanisms,* short for *T*est-*O*perate-*T*est-*E*xit. A TOTE mechanism is illustrated in Figure 14.2. The mechanism works in the same way as the thermostat did in the example in the previous paragraph. First, the input is *test*ed against a standard. If the input does not match the standard, then the system *operate*s so as to reduce the discrepancy between the two. Once this difference is eliminated, then you *exit* from this routine.

The beauty of TOTE units is that they can be nested within one another to form hierarchies. Figure 14.3 illustrates this kind of structure. Such *hierarchical models* can be used to represent a variety of different activities. Miller, Galanter, and Pribram (1960, p. 36) give the example of hammering a nail, in which the superordinate test is whether or not the nail is flush with board. If not, then proceed to test the hammer. If the hammer is down, then raise it. When the hammer is up, then strike the nail. Then return to the superordinate test, and determine if the nail is flush. If it is not, then go through the subordinate routines again. When the nail is flush, then exit. Another example might have as a superordinate test whether or not you have satisfied your B.A. requirements. The subordinate tests are whether or not you have satisfied your major and minor requirements. If not, then you take courses to pass these tests. When all tests are passed, then you exit college. Yet another example comes from using a recipe to make salad dressing (e.g., Green, 1982). The superordinate test could be whether or not the dressing passes a taste test. The subordinate tests refer to particular ingredients, such as oil and vinegar, which you add until you reach the appropriate amounts.

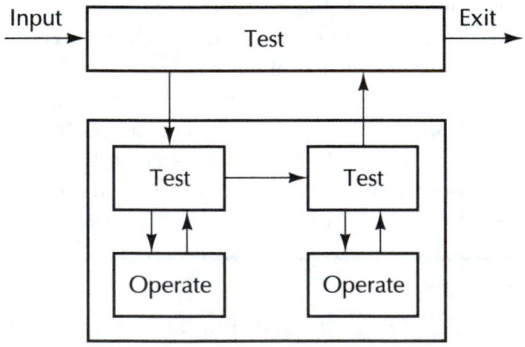

FIGURE 14.3 Hierarchical TOTE mechanisms.

You can see that TOTE mechanisms lend themselves to modeling an enormous range of behaviors. Moreover, they can be much more complex than the simple cases we have considered. For example, when you are making salad dressing, you are likely doing so as a part of making a meal, which would constitute a still more superordinate TOTE mechanism. Making a meal is presumably nested within still more general goals, such as acquiring proper nutrition, and so on. Our more general TOTEs are called *strategies,* while our more concrete activities are called *tactics.* Our strategies tend to be relatively invariant. For example, we always need nutrition. However, our tactics tend to be quite variable depending on the particular context. Thus, we do not always eat the same meal.

Hierarchically organized TOTE mechanisms make up our *plans.* Our plans contain a hierarchically organized set of instructions for conducting all of our actions. Plans are like computer programs, which provide the instructions that tell a computer precisely what operations to perform. For Miller, Galanter, and Pribram (1960) cognitive psychology is the study of plans, which are the programs that regulate all of our behavior. The similarity between people's plans and computer programs is a topic we will return to later in the chapter. However, by now you should be able to see that plans, like computer programs, need not be rigid, inflexible procedures. Rather, plans, like computer programs, are able to adjust their operations as different conditions arise.

Subjective Behaviorism

How do you investigate people's plans? One way is to ask the person what their plans are. Of course, this will not work in every case, because we are simply are not aware of all of our plans. For example, our plans for speaking, in which Chomsky was so interested, are largely unconscious. However, Miller, Galanter, and Pribram (1960) advocated asking people to tell us about their plans as often as was feasible. The procedure they recommended was not introspection as it had been practiced by Wundt and other introspectionists. Rather, they proposed the limited use of *thinking aloud,* a technique that had already been used by many psychologists interested in studying thinking (e.g., Claparède, 1933; Duncker, 1945). What people say when they are asked to think aloud is quite different from what they say when they are asked to introspect (e.g., Benjafield, 1969b), and so the two methods are not the same. Thinking aloud simply involves speaking while you are thinking, and reporting directly on what you are thinking as it occurs.

Miller, Galanter, and Pribram (1960, p. 194) were willing to use methods such as thinking aloud since it "has one great advantage in its favor, because language, with all its notorious shortcomings, is still the least ambiguous of all the channels open from one human being to another." In spite of their willingness to try such apparently "subjective" methods to investigate internal processes, Miller, Galanter, and Pribram (1960) were not even remotely interested in abandoning the objective methods that had characterized behaviorism. Rather, they hoped to have the best of both worlds, and so called their position (only half jokingly) *subjective behaviorism* (Miller, Galanter, & Pribram, 1960, p. 211). This phrase—subjective behaviorism—describes quite nicely the attitudes of most of the founders of cognitive psychology.

Giving Psychology Away

In his Presidential address to the American Psychological Association, Miller (1969/1970) sounded a theme that is still resonating through psychology. He cautioned psychologists against using their expertise to act as agents of social control. Rather, he argued that "understanding and prediction are better goals for psychology than is control—both for psychology and for the promotion of human welfare—because they lead us to think, not in terms of coercion by a powerful elite, but in terms of the diagnosis of problems and the development of programs that can enrich the lives of every citizen" (Miller, 1969/1970, pp. 13–14). In order to accomplish these goals, Miller suggested that psychology be *given away:*

> *Our responsibility is less to assume the role of experts and try to apply psychology ourselves than to give it away to the people who really need it—and that includes everyone. The practice of valid psychology by nonpsychologists will inevitably change people's conception of themselves and what they can do. And when we have accomplished that, we will really have caused a psychological revolution. (Miller, 1969/1970, p. 16)*

The social role of psychology in the United States has been debated throughout the twentieth century. Miller argued that, while psychological science was something of which all citizens can and should become aware, professional organizations such as the American Psychological Association should not become involved in the promotion of social change. As it turned out, the nature and function of the American Psychological Association became an increasingly volatile issue in the 1980s, a matter we will discuss in Chapter 15.

In 1991, George Miller was awarded the National Medal of Science by then President George Bush.

Additional Reading on This Topic. George Miller (1990) is still doing pioneering work in the psychology of language.

JEROME S. BRUNER (1915–)

Reading Jerome Bruner's autobiography (1980) is astonishing, because over the last 50 years he appears to have known virtually every prominent social scientist in America and Europe. The list includes William McDougall, Margaret Mead, Clark Hull, Kurt Goldstein, Gordon Allport, Edwin Boring, Bärbel Inhelder, and Jean Piaget. The range of his acquaintances is matched by the range of his research interests. As we shall see, Bruner has done seminal research on everything from perception and thinking to child development. Bruner (1980) himself believes that there is a consistent functionalist orientation across all these investigations that marks him "as following the tradition of James, Dewey, McDougall, Vygotsky, and Tolman. . . . I am also a mentalist and have always felt that the banning of 'mental' concepts from psychology was a fake seeking after the gods of nineteenth century physical sciences" (p. 146).

The "New Look" in Perception

In the 1940s and 1950s Bruner and his colleagues began a research program in perception that became known as the *New Look.* More traditional approaches to perception had focused primarily on the stimulus, and paid little attention to the role of the perceiver in determining the process of perception. Bruner's group investigated "the effects of need, of interest, of past experience, on the manner of organization of the perceptual field" (Bruner & Klein, 1960, p. 63). The New Look approached perception as a joint function of both the stimulus and the state of the organism.

A good example of the New Look experiments is Bruner and Postman's investigation (1949/1973) of the perception of incongruous events. One of the central axioms of the New Look was called the *minimax axiom:* people "organize the perceptual field in such a way as to maximize percepts relevant to current needs and expectations and to minimize percepts inimical to such needs and expectations" (p. 69). Although people change their expectancies when the evidence requires them to, "for as long as possible and by whatever means available, the organism will ward off the perception of the unexpected, those things which do not fit his [or her] prevailing set" (p. 70).

Events that do not fit our expectancies strike us as incongruous. Bruner and Postman (1949/1973) examined people's reaction to incongruous events by altering a familiar stimulus. They constructed two sets of playing cards, one normal and the other containing trick cards that were printed with the colors reversed. For example, the three of hearts was printed in black, the two of spades in red, and so on. These are the incongruous stimuli. Subjects saw both normal and trick cards presented tachistoscopically. As discussed in Chapter 6, a tachistoscope is a device that allows a visual stimulus to be presented for varying intervals, some so brief (e.g., 1/100 second) that a subject may have difficulty saying what it is that they have been shown. In Bruner and Postman's experiment (1949/1973), each card was initially exposed for 1/100 second, and then exposed at increasingly longer intervals until the subject recognized it.

One result was that subjects required a longer exposure interval to recognize trick cards as opposed to normal cards. This was supportive of the hypothesis that stimuli that conform to people's expectations are more easily seen than those that do not. The responses of individual subjects to particular incongruous stimuli were also informative. Sometimes subjects initially claimed to have seen a normal six of spades. As the exposure duration increased, they came to realize that the card was actually a red six of spades. Sometimes this realization was accomplished all at once, and sometimes it emerged gradually. However, the evidence was consistent with the notion that "perceptual organization is powerfully determined by expectations built upon past commerce with the environment. When such expectations are violated by the environment, the perceiver's behavior can be described as resistance to the recognition of the unexpected or incongruous" (Postman & Bruner, 1949/1973, p. 82).

Bruner (1957/1973) believed this experiment and others like it demonstrated the importance of *perceptual readiness,* or the degree to which one is prepared to perceive what is in the environment. Expectancies consist of categories into which the perceiver attempts to fit the input. One can fail to be ready to perceive what is there, in which case one's experience may not be a very good match for what is actually in the environment. This may be particularly true when we are perceiving other people:

> *If, on the basis of a few cues of personal appearance, for example, one categorizes another person as dishonest, it is extremely difficult in most cases to check for the other cues that one would predict might be associated with instances of this category. . . . Moreover, there is also the likelihood . . . that available equivocal signs will be distorted so as to confirm the first impression. . . . The reticence of the man [or woman] we categorize as dishonest is seen as caginess; the honest man's [or woman's] reticence is seen as integrity and good judgment. (Bruner, 1957/1973, p. 32)*

Bruner was drawing attention to what later came to colloquially be called "putting a spin on events." From this perspective, "putting a spin on events" is a natural process in which everyone engages, not just politicians and their press secretaries. It is not necessary for us to intentionally "put a spin" on events, but it can take place more or less automatically. This general idea has proved to be remarkably durable. As we shall see in Chapter 15, many philosophers of science see "perceptual readiness" or something like it as an important factor in the way scientists are prepared to relate scientific evidence to scientific theories (Anglin, 1973, p. xi).

The New Look was criticized on methodological grounds because the experiments done often lacked appropriate controls. By the end of the 1950s many psychologists believed that the New Look had gone too far in emphasizing the internal, personal determinants of perception. However, while agreeing with many of the criticisms, Bruner and Klein (1960) responded that the New Look had done much to correct an imbalance in the way perception had been studied, and to open up new areas of investigation.

A Study of Thinking

We noted in the previous section that expectancies involve placing events into categories. One of Bruner's contributions was to initiate an experimental study of the formation of categories (Bruner, Goodnow, & Austin, 1956). The process whereby categories develop is called *concept attainment.* The study of concepts had been relatively neglected during the behaviorist period, and Bruner, Goodnow, and Austin's work (1956) did much to make the study of thinking legitimate.

Any time we do not regard an event as unique, but as belonging to a particular category, then we are making use of concepts. For example, whenever something is seen as "red," or as a "musical instrument," or as a "chair," then it is being subsumed by a particular concept. You can see that the range and number of concepts is extremely great. Bruner, Goodnow, and Austin (1956) defined concepts as collections of attributes. Attributes of concepts were properties such as size, shape, or color. Attributes could take on different values. Thus, "size" could be "big" or "small." An event that contained all the attributes necessary for membership in the concept was called a "positive instance," while an event lacking one or more of the required attributes was called a "negative instance." For example, a liquid containing the proper amounts of olive oil, vinegar, and spices could be a positive instance of the concept "salad dressing," but a liquid consisting of just oil would be a negative instance.

Bruner, Goodnow, and Austin (1956) investigated the process of concept attainment using a set of cards similar to those given in Figure 14.4 on page 300. Although the stimuli in Figure 14.4 are simpler than the ones used by Bruner, Goodnow, and Austin (1956), they are fine for our purposes. The cards can be characterized in terms of three attributes: color (gray or white); form (triangle or

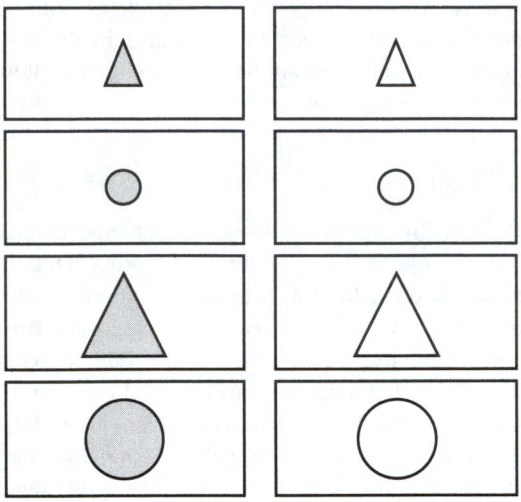

FIGURE 14.4 A set of cards for an experiment in concept attainment.

circle); and size (large or small). In a concept attainment experiment, the experimenter thinks of a concept like "gray triangle" and the subject tries to guess it. (This may remind you of the game of *Mastermind,* which this kind of experiment actually resembles rather closely, as Laughlin, Lange, and Adamopoulos (1982) have noted.) Bruner, Goodnow, and Austin (1956) observed that subjects adopt particular strategies when they try to solve concept attainment problems like these. For example, suppose a subject is told that the card with the large, gray triangle is a positive instance. Then the subject can select another card that differs in one attribute, such as a large, gray circle. On being told that the large, gray circle is a negative instance, the subject can correctly infer that a card must have a triangle on it in order for the card to be a positive instance. By using strategies such as this, the subject can figure out what attributes are in the concept. By examining the choices subjects make as they attempt to discover the concept, the experimenter can learn about the strategies people use as they form concepts.

Bruner, Goodnow, and Austin's work (1956) was subsequently criticized because the concepts they studied, like our example, were somewhat artificial. Subsequent work on concepts tended to focus on concepts that people actually use in everyday life (e.g., Rosch, 1978). Nevertheless, Bruner's work on concepts made it evident that "higher mental processes" could be studied experimentally. Consequently, these experiments were important in setting the stage for subsequent work in cognition.

Additional Reading on This Topic. Bruner has done extremely influential work on education (e.g., Bruner, 1966) as well as cognitive development (Bruner, Olver, & Greenfield, 1966). His more recent work (e.g., Bruner, 1986) draws on a variety of disciplines to "show how human minds and lives are reflections of culture and history as well as of biology and physical resources" (Bruner, 1990, p. 138). Bruner, Jolly, and Sylva (1976) is a delightful collection of articles about play, which is itself a delightful and important topic.

SIR FREDERIC BARTLETT (1887–1969)

Psychology in Britain was for many years more attuned to the study of cognitive processes than was psychology in the United States. To no small extent, this was due to the work of Sir Frederic Bartlett, of Cambridge University. Like many cognitive psychologists, Bartlett's interests were highly interdisciplinary, and he brought neurology, philosophy, and social anthropology to bear on his psychological work. Bartlett's classic study of memory was published in 1932, although the original experiments had been carried out much earlier, between 1914 and 1916 (Zangwill, 1972, p. 124).

One of Bartlett's best known memory experiments utilized the *method of serial reproduction.* This method involves giving an experimental subject something to learn and remember. What the first subject remembers is then given to a second subject to learn and remember. What the second subject remembers is then given to a third subject, and so on. This method allows the experimenter to track the way in which memory changes over time with successive attempts at recall. Bartlett had subjects, who were British, try to recall stories in his experiments. The following is a part of one of the stories, called *The War of the Ghosts,* which was adapted from an Amerindian tale.

> *One night two young men from Egulac went down to the river to hunt seals, and while they were there it became foggy and calm. Then they heard war-cries, and they thought: "Maybe this is a war party." They escaped to the shore, and hid behind a log. Now canoes came up, and they heard the noise of paddles, and saw one canoe coming up to them. There were five men in the canoe, and they said:*
>
> *"What do you think? We wish to take you along. We are going up the river to make war on the people."*
>
> *One of the young men said: "I have no arrows."*
>
> *"Arrows are in the canoe," they said.*
>
> *"I will not go along. I might get killed. My relatives do not know where I have gone. But you," he said, turning to the other, "may go with them."*
>
> *So one of the men went, but the other returned home.*
>
> *And the warriors went on up the river to a town on the other side of Kalama. The people came down to the water, and they began to fight, and many were killed. But presently the young man heard one of the warriors say: "Quick, let us go home: that Indian has been hit." Now he thought: "Oh, they are ghosts." He did not feel sick, but he said he had been shot. (Bartlett, 1932, p. 65)*

You should try yourself to remember this story fragment, now that you have read it. You can imagine that by the time the story has been passed from one subject to another ten times it would have undergone considerable modification. These changes in the story were not random, however, but showed systematic transformations. Over time, the story became increasingly conventional and rational from the point of view of the person trying to remember it. Information that does not fit in with this simplification tended to be omitted. At the same time, the story became more of an "imaginative reconstruction" than a literal rendition (Bartlett, 1932, p. 213).

Bartlett's memory experiments are often contrasted with those of Ebbinghaus, which we reviewed in Chapter 4. Where Ebbinghaus used nonsense syllables, Bartlett used meaningful materials, such as stories. While Ebbinghaus's studies were masterpieces of experimental design and control, Bartlett's work is often thought to be more reflective of real-life memory processes. Although Ebbinghaus studied memory for individual items, Bartlett studied memory for meaningful discourse. Ebbinghaus's experiments lend themselves to a theory in which each item is stored separately in memory. Bartlett's experiments lend themselves to a theory in which individual items are not remembered in isolation, but as part of a larger whole. To explain his results, Bartlett used the *schema* concept, which he borrowed from the neurologist *Henry Head* (1861–1940). By "schema" Bartlett (1932, p. 201) meant an "active organization of past reactions" that provided a setting within which individual events were understood and remembered.

The schema is always actively adjusting to the current situation. Memory of the past is useful only to the extent that it can be adapted to suit the present needs of the organism. Bartlett (1932, pp. 201–202; 1958, p. 11) likened memory and other cognitive processes to *motor skills,* such as those involved in playing a sport. Suppose, for example, that you are at the plate in a baseball game and have two strikes against you. When you try to hit the next pitch, you do not try to simply repeat exactly the same swing that you made on the last pitch. Rather, your next swing attempts to adjust to the characteristics of the next pitch. A skilled hitter is able to make these kinds of adjustments, and not simply do the same thing over and over again. Similarly, when we remember the past we do not simply re-experience it, but we reinvent it so that it fits the requirements of our current situation. Memory is a compromise between what we have actually experienced and what we imagine happened in the past. You should realize how important ideas like this have been in such areas of psychology as eyewitness testimony (e.g., Loftus & Palmer, 1974), because they suggest that we should not be too trusting of our own or other people's memories.

Although read and cited by American psychologists, Bartlett's work did not reach its greatest influence in American psychology until cognitive psychology began to establish itself there. From the new viewpoint that cognitive psychology provided, Bartlett's work not only made sense, but appeared to be foundational. This importance of Bartlett's influence on what was to become cognitive psychology was explicitly recognized by Ulric Neisser, to whose work we next turn.

Additional Reading on This Topic. A useful review of the many studies evaluating Bartlett's memory theory is by Alba and Hasher (1983). The continuing relevance of Bartlett's theory of memory is well illustrated by a study by Vicente and Brewer (1993) of reconstructive remembering by scientists of scientific literature. They found that the details of scientific experiments are often remembered in a more idealized form than was actually the case. Vicente and Brewer (1993) conclude:

> *Our study suggests that scientists also need to be aware of the power of schema-based memory processes so that they will not rely on memory as a replacement for careful re-reading of original sources. In fact, we have recently found an example of a writer attempting to make his readers aware of this problem in an introductory psychology text written in 1939! In that text, Lawrence Cole reviewed Bartlett's (1932) work on reconstructive remembering and then in a prophetic aside to his readers, states that Bartlett's research "might well cause the student of psychology to do some reflecting, since the very textbook which he reads is a reproduction often many times removed from that source (human behavior) to which it professedly refers" (Cole, 1939, p. 516).*

ULRIC NEISSER (1928–)

Neisser got his undergraduate degree at Harvard where he worked with George Miller. He then earned a Master's degree at Swarthmore, which was still home to Gestalt psychologists such as Kohler. After completing a Ph.D. at Harvard, he took a position at Brandeis in 1957, where he was influenced by Abraham Maslow. While Maslow's humanistic orientation was not an explicit part of Neisser's cognitive psychology, it did express itself in Neisser's attitude that cognitive psychology was a more humanistic alternative to behaviorism (Baars, 1986, p. 273).

Although I never knew Neisser very well, I was a first-year graduate student in psychology at Brandeis in 1964, and have a recollection of a meeting where we all heard the faculty introduce themselves and describe their research interests. I recall Neisser saying that he had been doing research in a variety of areas, and up until then had not been able to think of precisely in which area his research interests lay. However, he went on to say, he now believed that all his research interests could be seen as involving cognition, and that he was beginning to think of himself as a cognitive psychologist.

Cognitive Psychology

It was not only Neisser who was beginning to think of himself as a cognitive psychologist. By the middle of the 1960s a great many academic psychologists were thinking of themselves in just that way. What was needed was a text that brought the several strands of research together that were to become cognitive psychology. This is what Neisser (1967) provided in his book *Cognitive Psychology,* which became the bible of the new psychology.

Near the beginning of his book, Neisser spelled out the relationship between cognitive processes and computer programs. Neisser's view of this relationship was to become standard for most cognitive psychologists:

> *The task of a psychologist trying to understand human cognition is analogous to that of a [person] trying to discover how a computer has been programmed; . . . if the program seems to store and reuse information, [we] would like to know by what "routines" or "procedures" this is done . . . [we] will not care much [how] his particular computer stores information . . . [we] want to understand the program, not the "hardware" . . . We must be careful not to confuse the program with the computer that it controls. . . . A program is not a machine; it is a series of instructions for dealing with symbols: "If the input has certain characteristics . . . then carry out certain procedures . . . otherwise other procedures . . . combine the results in various ways . . . store and retrieve various items . . . etc." The cognitive psy-*

chologist would like to give a similar account of the way information is processed by people. (Neisser, 1967, pp. 6–8)

Neisser then proceeded to trace the flow of information through the organism, beginning with the *icon.* The icon is a representation of a stimulus that persists even after the stimulus has ceased. Classic work on the icon had been done by Sperling (1960), who showed subjects three rows of letters like those in Figure 14.5. The letters were exposed tachistoscopically, for 50 milliseconds. After a further 50 milliseconds during which there is no stimulus, the subject was asked to report either the top, or the middle, or the bottom row of letters. Subjects were able to do so, reporting that it was as if the letters were still there to be read. The phrase *iconic storage* was used to refer to a brief period during which information from a stimulus was briefly preserved, and available for further processing.

The next stage of information processing Neisser discussed was *pattern recognition,* or the process whereby a stimulus is recognized as an instance of a particular category. Pattern recognition was difficult to understand from an information processing point of view, because stimuli with very different physical characteristics will often end up being seen as instances of the same category. For example, letters can be presented in different fonts, such as ***b*** and **b,** yet still be properly recognized, as in ***problem*** and **problem.** What kind of program is required to enable these stimuli to be recognized as equivalent? Neisser (1967, p. 84) reviewed research suggesting that pattern recognition relied on the *distinctive features* of stimuli. Distinctive features were those properties, such as the orientation of lines, that served to define a stimulus.

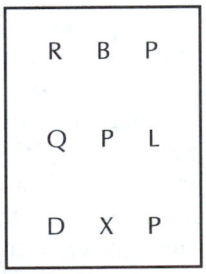

FIGURE 14.5 Stimulus letters similar to those used in Sperling's experiment (1960).

Attention was the next information processing stage to be considered. Neisser distinguished between *preattentive processing* and *focal attention.* Preattentive processing was concerned with constructing "the objects which later mechanisms are to flesh out and interpret" (Neisser, 1967, p. 89). Before you can focally attend to something, it must first be constructed. Preattentive processes are similar to the Gestalt laws of organization (Neisser, 1967, p. 90) and operate automatically to segregate objects in the visual field that can then be attended to. A good demonstration of the automatic nature of preattentive processes is the fact that people can drive a car home along a familiar route without ever paying very much attention to what they are doing (Neisser, 1967, p. 92). The investigation of automatic processing became a focus for many cognitive psychologists, and one of the standard experimental procedures for such investigations is described in Box 14.2 on page 304.

Subsequent chapters in Neisser's book (1967) dealt with what were to become the staples of cognitive psychology: visual and auditory imagery; speech perception; echoic memory (an analog to the visual icon); verbal memory, and psycholinguistics. Finally, Neisser (1967, chap. 11) proposed "a cognitive approach to memory and thought." Here Neisser considered and rejected the *reappearance hypothesis,* which is the notion that information is retrieved from memory in the form in which it is stored. This is a view that Neisser traced back to the British Empiricists, who we considered in Chapter 2. Neisser attributed to them the belief that ideas are copies of previous experiences, and are retained in memory through being associated with other ideas. On the associationist account, when we remember the past, then we are re-experiencing it. Against the reappearance hypothesis, Neisser cited William James (1890, Vol. I, p. 236): "A permanently existing 'idea' . . . which makes its appearance before the footlights of consciousness at

Box 14.2

John R. Stroop (1897–1973) and the Stroop Task

Using the right test, or experimental apparatus, can allow us to explore psychological processes that might otherwise remain unknown to us. A good example is the *Stroop task* (Stroop, 1935/1992), which is one of the most useful research tools ever invented (MacLeod, 1992). The Stroop (1935/1992) task is named after the psychologist who first introduced it. It consists of a list of color names, such as yellow, red, blue, and green. Of course, it is very easy to read color names such as these. However, this task can become quite difficult if the color names are printed in different colors. For example, suppose the word *red* is printed in *blue;* the word *green* is printed in *red;* the word *blue* is printed in *green;* and so on. It turns out to be very difficult to name the colors in which the words are printed.

It would be instructive for you to create your own Stroop task by writing a list of one hundred words in different colors. (You can make up your own list, or see Benjafield, 1994, pp. 194–195 for an example.) First try reading the color names. Then try naming the colors of the words. You will find that the latter task is by far the more difficult of the two. One measure of the relative difficulty of the two tasks is how long it takes you to finish each one. Naming the colors of the words takes longer than reading the color words themselves. As an experience, naming the colors seems to require you to inhibit the tendency to read the names.

Information processing psychologists have typically interpreted the Stroop phenomenon as reflecting the difference between *automatic* and voluntary, or *controlled* processes (MacLeod, 1992). A skill that has been overlearned may tend to run itself off, whether we want it to or not. For example, once reading has become overlearned, then you read without thinking about it, as it were. In the Stroop situation, it is difficult not to read the words. Reading is an example of an *automatic process.* Such a process "takes care of itself." We do not need to pay attention to it in order for it to be done properly. By contrast, *controlled processes* require our attention if they are to be done properly (Shiffrin & Schneider, 1977). Naming the colors in which the words are printed is an example of a controlled process (Shiffrin & Schneider, 1977). The Stroop task has proven to be an invaluable device for investigating the distinction between automatic and controlled processes. As MacLeod (1992) observes, the impact of the Stroop task can be measured by the fact that over 700 studies have employed it since it was introduced in 1935.

Stroop invented his test as a part of his doctoral dissertation at George Peabody College in Nashville. He was by no means the first psychologist to have explored this topic. "In fact, it was imported from philosophy into psychology by James McKeen Cattell (1886) for his own dissertation, which was supervised by Wilhelm Wundt" (MacLeod, 1992, p. 13). Stroop himself took little interest in research after completing his dissertation, but "devoted his attention to religion for the rest of his life," writing seven books on biblical topics (MacLeod, 1992, p. 13).

---

periodical intervals, is as mythological an entity as the Jack of Spades." Neisser (1967) himself agreed with Bartlett's view that "reorganization and change are the rule rather than the exception in memory" (p. 279).

Elaborating on Bartlett's theory, Neisser (1967, p. 284) proposed what he called the *utilization hypothesis.* "There are no stored copies of finished mental events, like images or sentences, but only traces of earlier constructive activity . . . [W]e store traces of earlier cognitive acts, not of the products of those acts. The traces are not simply 'revived' or 'reactivated' in recall; instead the stored fragments are used as information to support a new construction" (Neisser, 1967, pp. 285–286). Neisser drew an analogy between the process of reconstruction and what a paleontologist does when reconstructing an animal. The paleontologist may have only a few bones from which to imaginatively reconstruct the animal. Obviously, the fewer the fragments on which to base the reconstruction, the more possible "memories" we can reconstruct. That is why there is so little difference between memory and imagination.

At the end of his book, Neisser (1967, p. 304) considered the fact that the study of the "higher mental processes," such as thinking and creativity, had thus far in the history of psychology proven to be very difficult to investigate. He suggested that "a really satisfactory theory of the higher mental processes can only come into being when we also have theories of motivation, personality, and social interaction. The study of cognition is only one fraction of psychology, and it cannot stand alone" (Neisser, 1967, p. 305).

The effect of Neisser's book was somewhat ironic. Rather than approach the study of cognition as "only one fraction of psychology," many psychologists enthusiastically seized on the experimental study of cognitive processes, but treated them as if they existed in isolation from other psychological processes. Neisser himself became skeptical of the changes he had been partly responsible for consolidating. By the 1970s, cognitive psychologists began to seem to him to be focusing on details of interest mainly to academics, and not on the importance of cognitive processes as they occurred in the real world (Baars, 1986, p. 282). Moreover, Neisser began to be influenced by the ideas of Cornell's James J. Gibson, who we discussed briefly when we considered Eleanor J. Gibson in Chapter 12. J. J. Gibson's ideas not only influenced Neisser, but are both distinctive and important enough in their own right to merit a consideration of them here.

James J. Gibson (1904–1979)

We considered some of the more important aspects of J. J. Gibson's life when we reviewed E. J. Gibson's work. J. J. Gibson spent several years at Smith College, where Kurt Koffka was an important influence, and he "came to share Koffka's conviction that the problems of perception were the central problems of psychology" (Neisser, 1981, p. 214).

J. J. Gibson's approach to perception was highly distinctive. He did not agree with traditional approaches that treated the stimulus as if it had no intrinsic meaning (J. J. Gibson, 1960). Other theorists treated a visual stimulus, for example, as if it consisted only of wavelengths of light. If that is all there is to a visual stimulus, then the process of perception must enrich that stimulus somehow in order for us to end up perceiving a world of meaningful objects. J. J. Gibson (1966, p. 245) did not believe that stimuli were impoverished sources of information, a point he made by distinguishing between two meanings of the word "information." In the information processing model of communication that we considered above, we receive information about the external world in the form of "signals" that we must "encode" in order to "process" the information contained in them. Thus, in the standard information processing model, there is a lot of "internal processing" required in order to make information meaningful. Information processing psychology, like Gestalt psychology and introspective psychology before it, makes the assumption that what we perceive is the result of adding meaning to a stimulus. By contrast, Gibson believed that information about the world could be directly picked up. The perceiver does not need to add anything to the information available in the world. Rather there is enough information available to enable the person to perceive the world directly.

Gibson (1950, 1966) argued for the creation of an *ecological* approach to perception that would describe environmental stimulation at the appropriate level. Describing stimuli only in the language of physics left out levels of description that were relevant to perception. "The environment consists of *opportunities* for perception, of *available* information, of potential stimuli. Not all opportunities are grasped, not all information is registered, not all stimuli excite receptors. But what the environment *affords* an individual in the way of discrimination is enormous, and this should be our first consideration" (Gibson, 1966, p. 23). Gibson (1950) described a number of *stimulus gradients* that provided information about the environment. A gradient is an "increase or decrease of something along a given dimension" (Gibson, 1950, p. 73). Simple examples of stimulus gradients are given in Figure 14.6 on page 306. It is easy to see the

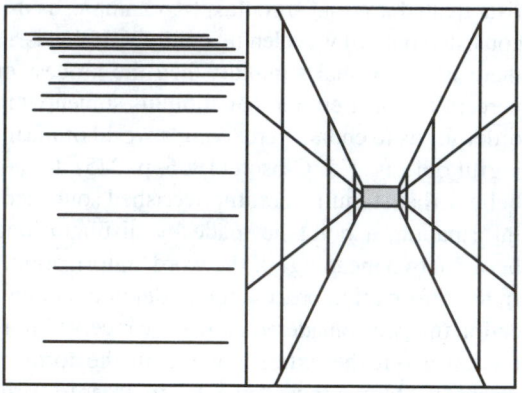

FIGURE 14.6 Stimulus gradients that give rise to the perception of depth.

gradient on the left as a receding pathway, and the converging lines on the right as a hallway. By looking around you, you can probably observe similar gradients, such as the changing distances between floorboards or the changing texture of a rug as it recedes from you (cf. Gibson, 1966, pp. 254–255). Gibson (1950, pp. 88–89) argued that these kinds of information are readily available in the environment, especially as we move around in it.

Gibson also believed that the meaning of objects and events can also be perceived directly through what he called *affordances.* "I have coined this word as a substitute for *values,* a term which carries an old burden of philosophical meaning. I mean simply what things furnish, for good or ill" (Gibson, 1966, p. 285). Thus, stairs afford climbing, food affords eating, ice affords skating, and so on. Of course, one has to learn the affordances of objects, but affordances are still tied to the properties of objects. Thus, Gibson's is a theory of *information pickup,* in which learning means becoming progressively more attuned to what the environment affords us.

Cognition and Reality

As was mentioned previously, Neisser (1976) turned away from information processing psychology because he believed that it had become too narrowly academic in its orientation. He turned toward Gibson's ecological approach, and argued that cognitive psychology needed to become more *ecologically valid.* The concept of ecological validity had originally been introduced by *Egon Brunswik* (1903–1955) (1956) to refer to the extent to which the information available to a perceiver is truly representative of the environment. Neisser used "ecological validity" in a broader sense to mean that a theory should have "something to say about what people do in real, culturally significant situations. What it says must not be trivial, and it must make some kind of sense to the participants themselves" (Neisser, 1976, p. 2). An oft-cited example of an ecologically valid study is Bahrick's (1984) study of long-term retention of Spanish learned as a second language. Instead of studying what subjects learn in a laboratory, Bahrick studied what ordinary people had learned in school. This is the kind of study Neisser (1978) called for when he noted that higher education

> *depends heavily on the assumption that students remember something valuable from their educational experience. One might expect psychologists to leap at the opportunity to study a critical memory problem so close to hand, but they never do. It is difficult to find even a single study, ancient or modern, of what is retained from academic instruction. Given our expertise and the way we earn our livings, this omission can only be described as scandalous. (p. 5)*

By no means all cognitive psychologists appreciated being scolded in this manner, and the issue of ecological validity was and continues to be hotly debated (Loftus, 1991). However, in order to guide those who wished to do ecologically valid research, Neisser (1976, p. 21) proposed a cyclical model of cognition. Rather than completely accept Gibson's view that the perceiver simply picks up information available in the environment, Neisser insisted that the perceiver possesses a schema that represents what the person was likely to find in the environment. This schema directs the person's exploration of the environment. As the environment is explored, the person encounters information that is expected as well as information that is unexpected. The latter kind of information is capable of modifying the schema so as to increase the accuracy with which it represents the environment. Thus, the cycle begins with the schema directing exploration of the environment, which brings the person into contact with information, which in turn corrects the schema, and so on.

Additional Reading on This Topic. Neisser (1964) is an interesting anticipation of many of the themes that were to later be sounded in Neisser (1967). A collection of ecologically valid studies of memory is in Neisser (1982).

HERBERT A. SIMON (1916–)

Herbert Simon (1980, 1991) is one of the most protean intellectuals of the century. He received the Nobel Prize for Economics in 1978, yet his Ph.D. is in political science (from the University of Chicago), and he has also made very important contributions to cognitive psychology. Simon has been a force for change in social science generally. Throughout his career, his work has been characterized by an ability to apply logical and mathematical techniques to complex problems. A good example of the interdisciplinary nature of his approach is a paper he wrote on spurious correlation and the nature of causality (Simon, 1954). This paper not only provides a good introduction to Simon's thought, but also illustrates one of the reasons why computers have become so central to psychology and to social science generally.

Spurious Correlation and the Nature of Causality

The relation between correlation and causality is traditionally one of the most difficult problems in the history of thought. Recall our consideration of this problem in Chapter 2, when we reviewed Hume's argument that there is nothing more to causality than an observed correlation between two events. Simon (1954) notes that nowadays every undergraduate course in statistics teaches students that a correlation between two variables does not mean that the two variables are causally related. Students are taught that correlations can often be spurious. A spurious correlation occurs whenever the correlation between two variables is due to a common cause. Consider the correlation between academic achievement and height in schoolchildren. Such a correlation is spurious because both academic achievement and height increase with age (Pedhazur & Schmelkin, 1991, p. 215).

Simon (1954) pointed out that the concept of a spurious correlation implies the existence of a true correlation, in the sense of a correlation that represents a causal relationship. How can one distinguish between a spurious and a true correlation? He addresses this question by considering some of the possible relationships between three variables. Suppose we calculate the correlation between two variables, X and Y, and find it to be significantly different from zero. We can then speculate that the observed correlation may be due to spurious causes. That is, perhaps there is a third variable, Z, that accounts for the observed correlation between X and Y. In order to investigate this possibility, we can make use of a statistical technique, called partial correlation, that allows us to calculate the correlation between X and Y with the possible effect of Z removed. Suppose that the correlation between X and Y is zero when the effect of Z is removed. There are then two possibilities:

- One possibility is that the correlation between X and Y resulted from the effect of Z on X and on Y, and hence is spurious. This would be the case for our earlier example of the relation between academic achievement (X) and height (Y) being due to the effect of age (Z) on both variables. This case is illustrated in Figure 14.7a on page 308, in which the arrows represent causal relationships.
- However, another possibility is that Z intervenes between X and Y, such that the effect of X on Y is mediated by Z. To illustrate this possibility, we will use a variant of an example Simon (1954) considered. Imagine a hypothetical study of a number of corporations in which three variables were measured. X represents the percentage of employees in

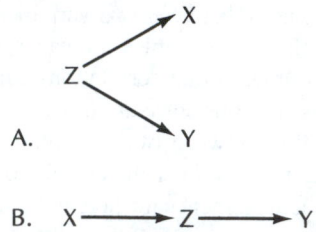

FIGURE 14.7 Possible causal relations between three variables.

each corporation who are married; Y is the average number of absences per week per employee; and Z is the average number of children per employee. Suppose that, when we do the study, we discover a high correlation between X and Y. However, the correlation between X and Y is virtually zero when the effect of Z is taken into account. In this case, we would not want to conclude that the correlation between X and Y is spurious. Rather, we would conclude that there is a causal chain connecting X to Z and then to Y. Z intervenes between X and Y because marriage (X) often results in children (Z) (who make demands of one sort or another on parents' time), which in turn increases absenteeism (Y). This case is represented in Figure 14.7B.

As Simon (1954) pointed out, the same pattern of correlations leads to opposite conclusions in the two cases. It is not the statistical evidence by itself, but the assumptions we make about the situation we are investigating that determines the conclusions we draw from the statistical evidence. There are many possible relations between three variables other than the ones we have considered. Moreover, social scientists often want to investigate systems that contain many more than three variables. Untangling the possible causal relationships in such complex systems is a very difficult matter. The analysis of complex systems would be impossible without the availability of computer programs that perform the appropriate analyses. The advent of the computer after World War II made possible an entire range of statistical analyses that would have earlier been inconceivable.

The ubiquity of computers and the diverse functions they perform belie the prediction made about 40 years ago by the RAND corporation "that because computers were so large and expensive, no more than 12 corporations in the United States would ever need or be able to afford one" (Brzezinski, 1984, p. 7). . . . Within sociobehavioral sciences, the use of computers for data management and analysis comes most readily to mind. As is well known, however, the diverse uses to which computers can be put in research, academic, and clinical endeavors are virtually limitless, including such activities as information retrieval and exchange, presentation of stimuli in research settings, simulations, artificial intelligence, authoring systems, computer aided instruction, computerized testing, and counseling applications. (Pedhazur & Schmelkin, 1991, p. 342).

Computer Simulation

Of all the applications of computers in social science, perhaps none has been more controversial than the computer simulation of psychological processes. Herbert Simon, along with his colleague *Allen Newell* (1927–1992), has been at the forefront of computer simulation for many years. However, the technique of computer simulation had originally been proposed by the British mathematician, *Alan Turing* (1912–1954).

Turing's Test. People often discuss the question, "Can computers really think?' This is a deep question, and possibly undecidable. Turing (1950) proposed that we not try to settle this question through endless discussion, but pay more attention to a concrete situation that illustrates the problem underlying the question. The concrete situation he considered is called the *imitation game* (Gunderson, 1964).

Turing described a game involving three people: A man and a woman, who are in one room, and an interrogator who is in another room. The interrogator is linked to the others by means of a computer terminal. Thus, the interrogator is able to ask questions of the man (let us call him Frank) and/or the woman (let us call her Annette), and they are able to reply using the computer interface. The object of the game is for the interrogator to be able to distinguish between the replies of the man and the replies of the woman.

You might think that this would be a trivial task for the interrogator, because the only question that needs to be asked of either respondent is "Are you Frank or Annette?" However, just like ordinary people, the players of this game can lie. Thus, this game is not as easy as it appears to be at first. Now suppose that we make a change. In place of one of the people, we install a computer. Suppose, for example, we remove the man, and replace him with a computer we also name "Frank." The computer has been programmed to answer questions in the same way that Frank would. The interrogator's job is still to distinguish between Frank and Annette, but now one of the respondents is a computer, while the other is a person. Suppose that the interrogator could not reliably tell which was which. Then, according to Turing, we would have programmed the computer so that it could successfully play the imitation game. The computer would have passed *Turing's test,* and the computer program would be an adequate model of the psychological processes that are involved when one person answers another person's questions.

By no means has everyone been persuaded that Turing's test is the right way to construct a psychological model. Over the years, a lot of ink has been spilled over the question of whether or not a computer program can ever be a realistic model of psychological processes. However, regardless of how we feel about this question, there has still been an enormous amount of work undertaken by psychologists, such as Herbert Simon, who use some version of Turing's test as a methodological tool for evaluating a psychological theory. Notice that it is not the computer itself that constitutes the psychological model, but the computer *program* that actually is the model. Beginning in the 1950s Simon and his colleagues began to put Turing's ideas into practice.

> *Computers, then, could be general symbol systems, capable of processing symbols of any kind—numerical or not. This insight, which dawned on me only gradually, led Al [Newell] and me even more gradually to the idea that the computer could provide the formalism we were seeking—that we could use the computer to simulate all sorts of information processes and use computer languages as formal descriptions of those processes.*
>
> *In the summer of 1954, I taught myself to program the 701, IBM's first stored program computer, and computers were much on my mind. . . . Al and I had a long discussion of the possibility of simulating human thinking by computer. (Simon, 1991, p. 201)*

The fruit of Simon and Newell's discussions was a series of computer simulations of human thinking. The programs they wrote were among the first examples of *artificial intelligence.* A summary of their efforts was published in Newell and Simon (1972). Among the first simulations they produced was a chess playing program (Newell, Shaw, & Simon, 1958). Although such programs are a commonplace now, they were considered to be extremely innovative in the 1950s. The simulation of more mundane forms of human thought was accomplished through the use of *toy problems,* such as the *Tower of Hanoi* problem (e.g., Simon, 1975; Anzai & Simon, 1979). In one form of this problem, there are three pegs on a board, with three disks on the leftmost peg. The person's task is to transfer all three disks to the rightmost peg by moving one disk at a time to one of the other pegs. The person is not allowed to put a larger disk on a smaller disk. Moreover, the subject cannot move a disk that is covered by another disk.

A version of the problem is illustrated in Figure 14.8 on page 310, which gives the moves required for the solution. Although it might seem like a trivial exercise to simulate the solution of such problems on a computer, you should remember that the goal is to program the computer so that its behavior is indistinguishable from that of a person. Thus, the program should not necessarily solve the problem in the best way possible, but in the same way as would a person.

Research using toy problems proceeds by having the person *think aloud* (Newell & Simon, 1972; Anzai & Simon, 1979), the technique we described earlier in this chapter. Ericsson and Simon (1980; 1984) pointed out that thinking aloud involves *concurrent verbalization* and not *retrospective verbalization.* Concurrent verbalization involves saying what you are thinking while you are thinking it.

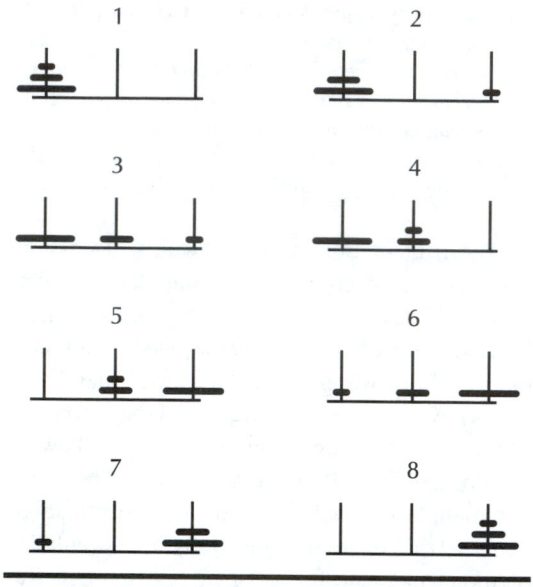

FIGURE 14.8 Solution for the three-disk version of the Tower of Hanoi problem.

This is not as difficult as it seems; you simply "think out loud." By contrast, retrospective verbalization involves trying to recall what you were thinking after it has occurred. This technique is obviously more open to error, and is more like introspection than is concurrent verbalization. Concurrent verbalization can provide a useful description of the process of thinking. A fragment of a thinking aloud protocol is given below, from Anzai and Simon (1979, p. 138). The subject is trying to solve a five-disk version of the Tower of Hanoi puzzle. You might find it instructive to try this yourself.

1. I'm not sure, but first I'll take 1 from A and place it on B.
2. And I'll take 2 from A and place it on C.
3. And then, I take 1 from B and place it on C. (The interrogator asks, "If you can tell me why you placed it there.")
4. Because there was no place else to go, I had to place 1 from B to C.
5. Then, next, I placed 3 from A to B.
6. Well. . . . first I had to place 1 to B, because I had to move all disks to C. I wasn't too sure, though.
7. I thought that it would be a problem if I placed 1 on C rather than B.
8. Now I want to place 2 on top of 3, so I'll place 1 on A.
9. Then I'll take 2 from C, and place it from A to B.
10. And I'll take 1 and . . . place it from A to B.
11. So then, 4 will go from A to C.
12. And then, . . . um, . . . oh, . . . um, . . .

As you can see, there is a lot of information in these protocols. In conjunction with observing the actual behavior of the subject, these protocols can give the experimenter a reasonably complete description of a psychological process. The task of the psychologist is to construct a computer program that will represent the procedures that the subject appears to be using. By studying a number of different problems, the hope is that the computer programs will reveal general principles that regulate human thought.

> *The hypothesis that human thought processes are simple emerged from the information-processing research of the 1950s and 1960s. Most of that research employed puzzlelike tasks, similar to . . . the Tower of Hanoi puzzle, and problems of logical inference, all of which have been studied extensively in the psychological laboratory. . . . It is reasonable that research on human thinking should begin with relatively contentless tasks of these kinds, but not that it should end there. And so in the past decade research in both cognitive psychology and artificial intelligence has been turning more and more to . . . domains that have substantial, meaningful content, where skillful performance depends upon large amounts of specialized knowledge retrieved from memory. (Simon, 1981, p. 102)*

Simon (1981) goes on to review computer simulations of such activities as medical diagnosis and solving physics problems, and concludes that the same simple principles regulate human thinking across a wide range of problems. One finds the same strategies, such as reducing the difference between one's current state and the goal to be achieved, no matter what the domain. This simplicity occurs in part because cognition, like good computer programs, has a *modular* construction. This means that cognitive processes can be decomposed into *modules,* or parts, that can be recombined in different ways to deal with changing circumstances. Each module solves a particular kind of problem, and by combining the appropriate modules, problems of great complexity can be solved using the same kinds of strategies that solve simple problems.

Simon (1981, p. 200) illustrated the importance of modular construction by means of what has now become a famous *parable of the watchmakers,* Hora and Tempus. Tempus constructed watches piece by piece, but once he began to make a watch, he had to finish it, or it would fall apart. Since he was often interrupted, he made few watches. Hora, by contrast, built watches in modules, each one of which could exist on its own. Hora could then combine modules to make a completed watch. The virtue of Hora's procedure is that he could be interrupted and not lose his work.

Simon (1981) goes on to argue that any system that is able to successfully adapt to changing circumstances (such as interruptions) is likely to have a modular structure. Cognitive processes are just one example of an adaptive system. For example, the same modular principles that regulate cognition will be found in successfully adapting social systems as well. Rather than having a single structure in which one part cannot be changed without changing the whole thing, one should design modular systems that allow parts to be changed without disrupting the whole. Simon's concept of modularity has had a very large impact on those who are responsible for designing complex systems (e.g., Green, 1982).

Criticisms of Computer Simulation

It has been a commonplace for computer simulation approaches to psychological processes to be criticized for what they appear to leave out. For example, even some cognitive psychologists (e.g., Neisser, 1964) have suggested that the simulation of emotion by means of a computer program would not be a very meaningful exercise. Although Simon (1967) has attempted to deal with this problem, most work in this area has specialized in cognition (e.g., Simon, 1981, p. 65), and it is perhaps fair to say that the role of emotion in mental life has been neglected.

Another standard criticism is that computer programs do not show the kind of insightful behavior that the Gestalt psychologists such as Kohler believed to be so characteristic of problem solving. Newell and Simon (1972, p. 872) acknowledged that such phenomena were beyond the scope of their approach as it then existed. However, Simon has never acknowledged that phenomena such as insight were beyond computer simulation approaches, and has continued to develop computer simulations of insight problems (e.g., Kaplan & Simon, 1990).

Yet another criticism comes from those who believe that explanations in psychology should come from neurophysiology. Since computer programs tell us little, if anything, about how the nervous system works, they are inadequate explanations of human behavior. H. A. Simon (1992) has refused to accept the validity of this argument, claiming that neurophysiological explanations are an inappropriate level of explanation for cognitive processes. "Explanation of cognitive processes at the information processing (symbolic) level is largely independent of explanation at the physiological (neurological) level that shows how processes are implemented" (Simon, 1992, p. 153). Nevertheless, it is important to "build the bridge theory" between neurophysiology and cognitive psychology "that shows how the symbol structures and symbol-manipulating processes that handle information at a more aggregated level can be implemented by such neuronal structures and organizations" (H. A. Simon, 1992, p. 153).

H. A. Simon (1992, p. 157) maintained that the relationship between cognitive psychology and social psychology was particularly close, since "adaptive behavior is a function of strategies and knowledge, both largely acquired from the social environment." He particularly recommended the study of the history of science as a source of hypotheses concerning the way knowledge is acquired.

Such "histories do not draw a boundary around individual investigators, but encompass the sources of an investigator's knowledge and, more broadly, the social processes that direct the production of scientific knowledge and its communication" (H. A. Simon, 1992, p. 157).

Herbert Simon was awarded the National Medal of Science in 1986, as was Allen Newell in 1992.

Additional Reading on This Topic. Newell (1977) gives several illustrations of the way in which protocols are analyzed, and Newell (1985) is an interesting retrospective account of problem solving research before the advent of the computer.

Boden (1987) is a thorough account of the development of artificial intelligence, while Gardner (1985) is a standard history of the study of cognition.

KEY NAMES AND CONCEPTS

What follows is an index of some of the most important material in this chapter. The list includes individuals, concepts, and topics you should know. Read through the list, and if anything on it seems unfamiliar, then go back and re-read the appropriate section of the chapter. You should be able to define each concept, briefly discuss each topic, and state the importance of each person on the list. In addition, you should be able to write an account of the work done by each person whose name is printed in boldface.

Bartlett, Sir Frederic, 300
- method of serial reproduction, 300
- motor skills, 301
- schema, 301

bit, 290

Box 14.1—Donald E. Broadbent (1926–1993) and dichotic listening, 295
- attention, 295
- Broadbent, Donald E., 295
- Cherry, Colin, 295
- cocktail party phenomenon, 295
- dichotic listening, 295
- ergonomics and human factors, 295
- shadowing task, 295

Box 14.2—John R. Stroop (1897–1973) and the Stroop Task, 304
- automatic versus controlled processes, 304
- John R. Stroop and the Stroop task, 304

Bruner, Jerome S., 293
- concept attainment, 299
- minimax axiom, 298
- New Look, 298
- perceptual readiness, 299

Brunswik, Egon, 306

Chomsky, Noam, 291
- Cartesian linguistics, 292
- critique of Skinner, 291
- deep structure, 292
- grammatical transformations, 292
- language acquisition device, 293
- language universals, 293
- surface structure, 292
- syntactic structures, 291

cybernetics, 294

feedback, 294

feedback loop, 294

Gibson, James J., 305
- affordances, 306
- direct perception, 305
- ecological, 305
- information pickup, 306
- two meanings of "information," 305

Head, Henry, 301
information, 289
information processing system, 289
Miller, George A., 293
Plans and the Structure of Behavior, 294
channel capacity, 294
giving psychology away, 297
hierarchical models, 296
magical number seven, 294
plans, 296
span of immediate memory, 294
strategies versus tactics, 296
subjective behaviorism, 297
TOTE mechanisms, 296
Neisser, Ulric, 302
attention, 303
distinctive features, 303
ecological validity, 306
focal attention, 303
icon, 303
iconic storage, 303
pattern recognition, 303
preattentive processing, 303
reappearance hypothesis, 303
utilization hypothesis, 304
Newell, Allen, 293, 308
Simon, Herbert A., 293, 307
artificial intelligence, 309
computer simulation, 308
modular, 311
parable of the watchmakers, 311
spurious correlation and the nature of causality, 307
thinking aloud, 309
Tower of Hanoi, 309
toy problems, 309
steady state, 294
Turing, Alan, 308
imitation game, 308
Turing's test, 308
Wiener, Norbert, 294

CHAPTER 15

THE FUTURE OF PSYCHOLOGY

THE NEW HISTORY OF SCIENCE
Does Psychology Have Paradigms?
CONTEXTUALISM
FEMINISM AND THE PSYCHOLOGY OF WOMEN
IS PSYCHOLOGY A SOCIAL CONSTRUCTION?
Ludwig Wittgenstein (1889–1951)
Psychological Research as a Social Construction
IS PSYCHOLOGY POSTMODERN?
Modernism
Postmodernism
The American Psychological Society
FUTURE HISTORIES

At the same time as the humanistic and cognitive approaches were changing psychology, there were corresponding changes in the philosophy of science. The logical positivist methodology which we outlined in Chapter 10, and which had been so hospitable to behaviorism, began to be challenged as an adequate description of the way science is actually done. Although logical positivism and operationism are still very strong forces in academic psychology, their influence has been muted somewhat by what *Laurel Furomoto* (1988) has called *the new history of psychology.*

> *Whereas traditional history portrayed the scientist as an objective fact finder and neutral observer, the new history emphasized the notion that scientists often operate in a subjective fashion, under the influence of a variety of extrascientific factors. Also . . . the new history rejected the traditional view of scientific activity as a continuous progression from error to truth, and opted instead for a model that depicts scientific change as a shift from one world view to another—world views that are linked to theoretical commitments involving esthetic as well as metaphysical considerations. (Furomoto, 1988, p. 11)*

Furomoto (1988) drew attention to philosophers and historians of science whose work was responsible for a thoroughgoing reconsideration of the nature of these disciplines. In what follows we will consider the views of some of these "new historians" who have proposed new ways of understanding the nature of psychology.

THE NEW HISTORY OF SCIENCE

Discussions of research methods that have taken place over the last 25 years tend to emphasize the complexity of the research process more than was the case in earlier discussions (e.g., Pedhazur, 1982). We now acknowledge that it is not always easy to specify the relations between independent and dependent variables in an unambiguous manner. The facts may not "speak for themselves," but may need to be understood from within a particular theoretical framework. For example, Pedhazur (1982, p. 575f) points out that it is entirely possible for different theories to all be consistent with the same data. Being consistent with the data is no guarantee of the validity of a theory. In fact, an investigator's theory may, at least partially, determine how the data will be interpreted.

Many contemporary historians and philosophers of science have noted that the process of scientific inquiry inevitably contains a subjective aspect. *Thomas Kuhn* (1970) is among the most influential of these scholars. Kuhn reviewed the historical development of established sciences such as physics. He came to the conclusion that the development of these disciplines had not been smooth. It was *not* the case that they had simply grown and developed by accumulating data that guided the development of an adequate theory. On the contrary, scientific disciplines appeared to develop discontinuously, in that there were long periods during which almost all workers in a discipline had the same beliefs about the methods, data, and theory that were appropriate for their discipline. However, at certain critical junctures, there were radical upheavals, and entire scientific communities changed their minds about what were the proper methods, data, and theory in their discipline. The set of fundamental beliefs that guide workers in a scientific discipline is called a *paradigm.* Revolutionary periods occur in which a new paradigm is emerging and an old paradigm is being overthrown. The controversy surrounding the emergence of Darwin's theory of evolution in the nineteenth century would be an example of such a revolution.

Kuhn argued that paradigms shape the scientist's view of the world. There can be *paradigm clashes* in which fundamentally different ways of interpreting the data exist. Kuhn likened this state of affairs to cases in which we can see different patterns in the same situation. A good example of the sort of thing Kuhn had in mind comes from the work of *Norwood R. Hanson* (1969). Consider Figure 15.1A. What is it—a bird or an antelope? If we view Figure 15.1A in the context of Figure 15.1B, then we are able to see the similarity between it and a bird. As Hanson (1969, p. 13) points out, it is difficult to see it as an antelope when its similarities to all the other "birds" in Figure 15.1B are so evident. However, if we view Figure 15.1A in the context of Figure 15.1C, then its similarity to an antelope becomes clear. Now it looks different. What was formerly the "beak" of a bird is now transformed into the "horns" of an antelope. Hanson's demonstration is intended to make the following point. The two contexts are analogous to two different theories. Each of the "theories" suggests a different interpretation of the same fact. Each "theory" is equally consistent with the datum. In general, the theoretical context within which we interpret data may literally determine how those data are seen. Conflicting interpretations of the same data are entirely possible, perhaps even inevitable.

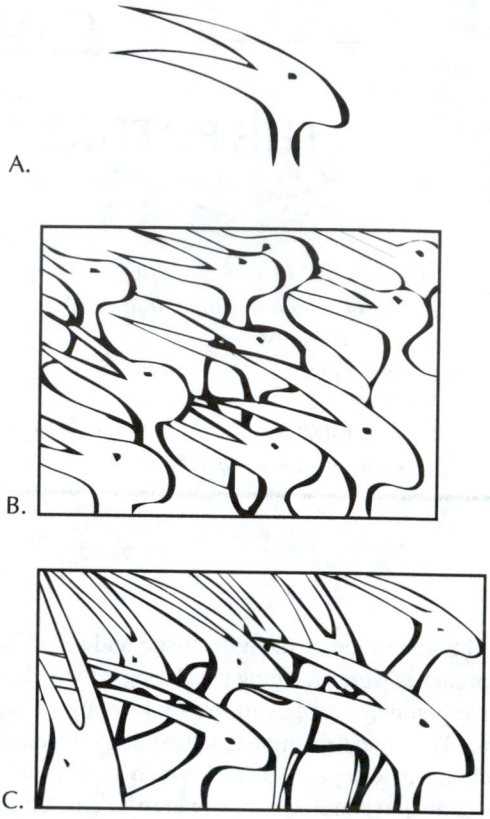

FIGURE 15.1 Is it a bird or an antelope?
Source: N. R. Hanson (1969). *Patterns of discovery* (pp. 13–14). Cambridge, UK: Cambridge University Press. Reprinted by permission of Cambridge University Press.

A related point can be made by adapting an example of *Paul Feyerabend* (1970, p. 220). Consider Figure 15.2. Imagine that the horizontal line represents the range of data that psychologists have considered as relevant or potentially relevant.

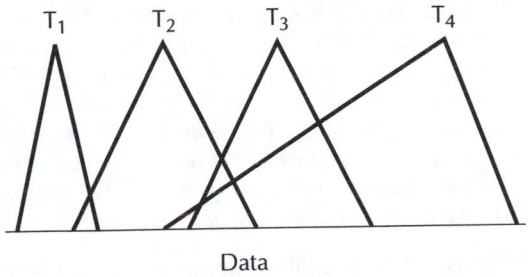

FIGURE 15.2 Different theoretical viewpoints in psychology.

"Data" here means any phenomenon that any psychologist has ever used to support his or her theory. Thus, this range includes introspectionist reports, psychotherapy sessions, case studies, psychophysical judgments, the behavior of animals in mazes, computer simulations, and much else besides. In other words, it includes the entire gamut of phenomena we have considered as we have reviewed the various theoretical viewpoints in psychology. Obviously, what is legitimate data from the viewpoint of one theory is not necessarily legitimate data from the viewpoint of another theory. Thus, the various theories we have reviewed overlap somewhat with respect to the phenomena they attempt to explain, but each theory also tends to specialize in certain phenomena, and to neglect others. This state of affairs is represented in Figure 15.2 by T_1 through T_4, which stand for four different psychological theories. You can see that each theory attempts to explain a different range of data and that no single theory explains all the data. T_1 through T_4 are not intended to represent any particular psychological theories, and we could have made the diagram more complex by adding additional overlapping points of view. The general idea is simply that no theory extends across the entire range, and different theories compete to explain some of the same data.

Another important feature of the history of psychology that is brought out by Figure 15.2 is that some theories (e.g., T_1 and T_4) do not overlap at all, meaning that what one theory explains is not regarded as data by the other theory and vice versa. This state of affairs has often existed in the history of psychology. For example, when behaviorism was taking over from introspectionism, introspectionist experiments were regarded as not yielding "real" data, of which the observation of behavior was seen as the sole source. This example points to what has been a recurrent problem in psychology, which is the specification of the boundaries of the discipline, in terms of what is "in" and what is "out." This was particularly clear during the period when humanistic psychologists were at the height of their influence, and were arguing for the inclusion of a wide range of "subjective" phenomena that had earlier been ruled out of court by the then dominant behaviorist orientation.

It is, of course, not incumbent on psychology to explain everything that anyone who has ever imagined themselves to be a psychologist has wanted explained. From a Kuhnian perspective, the establishment of a single paradigm means that a discipline becomes a *normal science* in which the workers share a united view of what constitutes the proper problems and methods for their discipline. This inevitably means that certain data are regarded as illegitimate. An interesting question concerns whether psychology has ever had a paradigm. Another interesting question concerns whether psychology *should* have a paradigm (cf. Feyerabend, 1970, p. 198).

Additional Reading on This Topic. Marková (1982) provides a scholarly analysis of the historical origins of the paradigm notion and its relation to a variety of psychological viewpoints.

Does Psychology Have Paradigms?

One issue that historians have discussed is whether or not psychology has had paradigms that have unified the discipline at different times, or whether it is still *preparadigmatic* (Farrell, 1978). "Kuhn (1962) himself initially considered psychology (as well as other social sciences to be preparadigmatic, since there was no one single paradigm which was generally accepted within the discipline, and much debate and energy was still being spent on trying to resolve fundamentals" (Buss, 1978, p. 57). However, other historians have argued that psychology has already moved through a succession of paradigms. For example, Kirsch (1977) suggested that Wundtian introspectionism exemplifies the first paradigm in psychology. Kirsch recommended that this paradigm be called *mentalism.* The distinguishing feature of this paradigm was that it defined psychology as "the science of mind" (Kirsch, 1977, p. 322). Up until the behaviorist revolution, the mentalist paradigm united psychologists by providing them with a definition of their subject matter (mental events) and a method (introspection). Although individual groups working within the mentalist paradigm might disagree concerning the precise nature of mental events or the best form of introspection, there was still widespread agreement on these two fundamental points. Thus, as we saw in Chapter 4, Wundt and Külpe could disagree over many particular things, and yet the mentalist paradigm still organized their efforts in a general way.

Those that accept the notion that psychology is a paradigmatic discipline often claim that cognitive psychology has been psychology's emerging paradigm since the 1970s (e.g., Segal & Lachman, 1972). One implication of this view is that the competitors of cognitive psychology, such as psychoanalysis and behaviorism, must be declining in influence. In order to investigate this possibility, Friman, Allen, Kerwin, and Larzelere (1993) counted the frequency with which publications in cognitive psychology, psychoanalysis, and behavioral psychology were cited in journals during the period 1979 to 1988. Such information is available in the *Social Science Citation Index (SSCI) Journal Citation Reports* (Garfield, 1979–1988). It turns out that citations to articles published in cognitive psychology journals did indeed increase during the period studied. Moreover, articles in cognitive psychology had more impact than articles from the other areas as measured by the average number of citations per article. However, the heightened influence of cognitive psychology was not reflected in

> *corresponding decreases in citations to core journals in behavioral psychology. . . . In addition, classic source items in psychoanalysis appear to be cited more than classic source items in behavioral and cognitive psychology. For example, in 1988, Sigmund Freud was cited almost five times as often as B. F. Skinner and four times as often as Herbert Simon. (Friman, Allen, Kerwin, and Larzelere, 1993, p. 661)*

Thus, while cognitive psychology is certainly being supported energetically by its practitioners, it is also true that behavioral psychology and psychoanalysis are still very much going concerns. Cognitive psychology is not forcing other alternative approaches out of the discipline.

Evidence such as that provided by Friman et al. (1993) has led some observers to suggest that psychology is still preparadigmatic, because "various schools compete for dominance but no single paradigm has yet prevailed" (Robins & Craik, 1994, p. 815). Other observers have questioned the usefulness of the paradigm concept itself, and suggested that scientific development in many disciplines does not actually involve "sudden, drastic paradigm shifts" (Mayr, 1994, p. 333). Science may not inevitably lead to a single paradigm within a discipline, and it may not be necessary for different approaches to be mutually exclusive. Rather, it may be possible for different approaches in a discipline such as psychology to coexist, and for "fruitful exchange between rivals" to take place (e.g., Gholson and Barker, 1985, p. 766). Thus, one might expect psychoanalytic, behavioral, and cognitive orientations not only to survive for the foreseeable future, but also to cross-fertilize one another.

Additional Reading on This Topic. An interesting presentation of an increasingly influential approach to the history of science is given by Laudan (1983).

CONTEXTUALISM

We have already seen that while some historians analyze the history of psychology as a succession of paradigms, other historians find the paradigm notion less useful. Nevertheless, few would deny the importance of understanding the ways in which various historical contexts have determined how psychological theories have been both created and consumed by the scientific community. One such approach to the history of ideas has grown out of *Stephen C. Pepper's* (1934, 1970) analysis of *contextualism* as a basic way of interpreting the world. Contextualism was made familiar to many American psychologists by *James J. Jenkins* (1974, p. 786), who pointed out that contextualism has its roots in the work of William James and John Dewey.

"The main categories of contextualism are: (1) *texture,* (2) in an environment of other textures, (3) analyzable into *strands*" (Pepper, 1934, p. 111). While this may sound mysterious, what Pepper means is quite straightforward. The basic point is that events are to be analyzed in terms of textures, rather than in terms of some other units. In order to clarify the meaning of "texture," Pepper contrasted contextualism with *mechanism,* an approach that reduces complex phenomena to elementary units. Pepper (1934, p. 110) regarded both Watson's behaviorism and introspectionism as examples of mechanistic forms of explanation, because "for both, explanation consists in exhibiting the parts out of which a whole is composed." Whether these parts are sensations or conditioned reflexes makes no difference to the style of explanation, which is mechanistic in both cases. Contextualism, by contrast, does not assume that there are constant elementary units into which all phenomena can be decomposed.

> *The most elementary thing, in the sense of that behind or beneath which you cannot go, is a texture. A texture by its very nature is a complex whole. . . . [T]he parts of a whole can be adequately described only as parts of the* whole. *The character of the whole enters into its parts, and unless the function of a part in the whole is exhibited in the description of the part, the part is no longer a part of that whole; it is a part of some other whole. The term "strand" suggests this condition. A strand is relative to a texture. If you follow a strand out of its original texture, thinking thereby to find it isolated from all textures, you deceive yourself; for you will only discover that the strand has entered into a new texture with reference to which it has a new function, and consequently . . . a new quality. (Pepper, 1934, pp. 111–112).*

The preceding may be summarized by the following slogan: "A texture . . . consists of strands lying in a context" (Jenkins, 1974, p. 786). A contextualist does not subscribe to only one analysis of anything. Any theory works only in a particular context. One theory may work well in a particular context, but as the context changes, then the psychologist may find that another theory works better. Whereas the mechanistic psychologist "asserts that there is one correct and final analysis of any psychological event in terms of a set of basic units and their basic relations . . . [t]he contextualist takes the much less comfortable position that a "complete" or "final" analysis is a myth, that analyses mean something only in terms of their utilities for some purposes" (Jenkins, 1974, p. 787).

Good examples of the way a contextual analysis proceeds come from the study of language comprehension (cf. Jenkins, 1974, p. 787). Consider a child listening to a sentence, such as "The dog bit the cat." Any sentence is made up of strands such as "the dog," "the cat," and "bit," and these strands acquire meaning through their relationships to each other in a particular context. The sentence means something different to a child if it is his or her cat rather than his or her dog. Of course, the context within which this utterance is understood could be broadened even further. All attempts to understand events "sheer away" from the immediate context into "more extensive contexts" (Jenkins, 1974, p. 787).

It might be argued against the contextualist position that there really are events that have a fixed meaning, and which don't change as the context changes. For example, take a basic idea such as the concept of a person. Surely, it might be argued, such basic concepts are relatively immune to context. After all, I know a person when I see one. However, as an example of conjoined (Siamese) twins, taken from Gould (1985), demonstrates, even basic concepts such as that of a "person" may be contextually determined. Although many conjoined twins are almost completely separate, some are not. The case Gould considered was that of Ritta and Christina, who had been born in France in 1829. The twins possessed two well-formed heads and separate upper bodies, but shared a lower body and two legs. As Gould (1985, p. 69) reports, a great question at the time was whether they were two persons, or just one.

The answer to the question, "One person or two?" may seem to be obvious to you, but saying just why it is obvious is not as easy as it may seem. Consider another case of conjoined twins that was not taken up by Gould (1985), but that is very instructive nonetheless. These were *Lin* and *Win Htut,* born in Burma in 1982. They were brought to the hospital for Sick Children in Toronto in 1984. They have something in common with Ritta and Christina in that they have two heads, but different in that they have one set of male genitalia. In such a case, how should the line be drawn that separates one child from the other? Here is how the line was determined.

> *How to divide up the twins' body-in-common was a decision to challenge Solomon. "You wonder what happens when they grow up and say, "How come you got that and I didn't?" muses Dr. Robert Filler. After consultation by phone with the parents at . . . home in Burma, the doctors agreed that Lin, the livelier and more aggressive (albeit smaller) of the two, should keep the male genitals. His sexuality is expected to be fully functional. During the surgery the team constructed a vagina for Win from a tubelike section of the colon. Though she will take female hormones when she reaches puberty, she will not be able to have children, or, probably, a full sexual response, says Filler. "In transsexual operations, some penile tissue is left to create a kind of clitoris. In their case, all the genitals went to Lin." (Hollister, 1984)*

While no one would question the sophistication of the medical techniques employed, or the sincerity of the professionals making this separation, it is also true that no one can claim that the line dividing Lin and Win was the only one possible. The decision about where to draw the line between one person and another was at least partly determined by an implicit psychological theory about the nature of the differences between boys and girls. Notice how, in this case, a psychological theory is determining which parts of the conjoined twins are to remain together, and which are to be separated. The physician believes that "boys are livelier and more aggressive." His surgical intervention follows from that within a theoretical context, and not from the physical fact that one child is smaller than the other.

One can easily imagine a different theoretical context that would have produced a different (not necessarily better) intervention. Sometimes it is claimed that science understands nature by carving it at its joints (Ghiselin, 1981), meaning that we should categorize events in terms of the "natural" distinctions between them. From a contextualist viewpoint, nature may not have any necessary divisions. The categories we use to analyze events are not given to us by the events themselves, so much as they flow from within a particular theoretical context. This means that the categories used when someone intervenes in someone else's life are not the only ones that could be used, but inevitably spring from a particular theoretical context. Since placing people in categories such as "intelligent," or "schizophrenic," can have an enormous influence on their lives, it is vital to acknowledge the theoretical context that is guiding the process whereby a decision is made to place someone in one category or another. The theory that we use may end up having a big impact on the people with whom we deal, just as did the line that was drawn to divide one twin from another.

Additional Reading on This Topic. Capaldi and Proctor (1994) are very critical of a contextualist approach to psychology, and provide a thorough bibliography of contextualism.

FEMINISM AND THE PSYCHOLOGY OF WOMEN

Feminism is not a single point of view, but has many different aspects. Beginning with classic texts such as *Simone de Beauvoir's* (1949/1989)

The Second Sex, the perspectives of women have been brought to bear on every aspect of contemporary culture, including psychology. There are several important ways in which feminism and the women's movement have changed psychology. One of the most important contributions of feminist scholarship has been to identify "distortions and biases" in previous research (Banister, Burman, Parker, Taylor, & Tindall, 1994, p. 122). A landmark of this sort was the publication by Bernstein and Russo (1974) of "The History of Psychology Revisited: Or Up with Our Foremothers." In that article, Bernstein and Russo argued that "male bias pervades the very essence of the profession—the historical definition of psychology itself" (p. 130). They went on to demonstrate that the contributions of women to psychology had not been acknowledged, and called for changes to the psychology curriculum so that students not only would be able to "study the psychology of women, [but] also the women of psychology" (p. 133). Furomoto (1988) calls this *compensatory history,* in the sense that it reminds us of the contributions of women that have been neglected by previous historians. For example, the contributions of Christine Ladd Franklin (whom we considered in Chapter 3) and Mary Calkins (whom we considered in Chapter 4) have often been left out of older histories.

Furomoto (1988, p. 24) notes that an extension of such research is the "reconstruction of women's experiences" (e.g., Scarborough & Furomoto, 1987). Describing women's experiences as women has been a central strand of feminist scholarship (Banister et al., 1994, p. 122). A recurrent theme has been that the psychology of women has been presented from a masculine perspective, and not from the perspective of women themselves. One response to this problem has been an increase in the number of discussions of the psychology of women that are written by women (e.g., Dinnerstein, 1977; Matlin, 1987).

Kimball (1994) observes that feminist psychologists have worked within two different traditions. One tradition emphasizes the similarities between the genders, and discounts the importance of differences between them. The work of Leta Hollingworth, which we considered in Chapter 13, belongs to this tradition. The other tradition emphasizes the "positive human characteristics that have been undervalued because they are associated with women and with the symbolic feminine. Central to the concerns of this tradition are the sense of connectedness, concern with human relationships, and caregiving that women, more than men, bring to human culture" (Kimball, 1994, p. 389).

The career of *Evelyn Fox Keller* (1985; Marder, 1993) is a good example of the second tradition in feminist scholarship that has influenced the history of science and of psychology. Keller received her Ph.D. in theoretical physics from Harvard at a time when it was extremely unusual for a woman to do so. She was not only struck by the relative absence of women in the sciences, but also by the fact that the style of thinking practiced by scientists had a masculine origin. Keller (1985) began her analysis of the role of gender in science with the following quote from Simone de Beauvoir:

> *Representation of the world, like the world itself, is the work of men; they describe it from their own point of view, which they confuse with the absolute truth. (p. 3)*

The one-sidedness of masculine-oriented science is reflected in the view that science is an objective set of procedures that has the control of nature as its goal. Keller came to believe that traditional accounts of science tended to ignore the role played by factors such as intuition, empathy, and personal engagement. These qualities are not "actually feminine attributes," but "they have traditionally been seen as such" (Marder, 1993, p. 24). There is no necessity to the traditional view of the nature of science, any more than there is a necessity to traditional views of the differences between genders.

> *Both gender and science are socially constructed categories. Science is the name we give to a set of practices and a body of knowledge delineated by a community, not simply defined by the exigencies of logical proof and experimental verification. Similarly, masculine and feminine are categories defined*

> *by a culture, not by biological necessity. Women, men, and science are created, together, out of a complex dynamic of interwoven cognitive, emotional, and social forces. (Keller, 1985, pp. 3–4)*

Keller (1985, p. 8) argues that we need to become aware of the *science-gender system* whereby our conception of gender and our conception of science mutually determine one another. For example, a feminist analysis of science brings out the extent to which science is a personal as well as a social process, aspects of science that tend not to appear in traditional accounts of the history of science. This does not mean that the successes of "masculine" science should be ignored, but that we need to acknowledge the degree to which the language and practices of science are "fueled and elaborated, and sometimes also subverted, by the more parochial social, political, and emotional commitments (conscious or not) of particular individuals and groups" (Keller, 1985, p. 11). A feminist approach to the history of science insists that these aspects of science be openly discussed, and not dismissed as irrelevant.

IS PSYCHOLOGY A SOCIAL CONSTRUCTION?

The notion that psychology, like other sciences, is a social construction is suggested by the new approaches to history that we have already considered. The paradigm concept, contextualism, and feminism all imply that psychology does not simply involve the objective accumulation of knowledge, but is also driven by social processes (e.g., Gergen, 1985). As a classic text in social constructionism puts it,

> *[People are] biologically predestined to construct and to inhabit a world with others. This world becomes for [them] the dominant and definite reality. Its limits are set by nature, but, once constructed, this world acts back upon nature. In the dialectic between nature and the socially constructed world the human organism is itself transformed. In this same dialectic [people] produce reality and thereby produce [themselves]. (Berger & Luckmann, 1967, p. 204)*

In this context, a *dialectical process* is one in which opposing tendencies shape one another. The opposing tendencies of interest to social constructionists are the *exogenic* and the *endogenic* (Gergen, 1985, p. 269). "Exogenic" means "coming from outside," and many psychologists have stressed the importance of factors external to the person as determinants of human experience. The classic example of the exogenic perspective is British Empiricism, which we considered in Chapter 2. "Endogenic" means "coming from inside," and refers to those psychologists who believe that "humans harbor inherent tendencies . . . to think, categorize, or process information, and it is these tendencies (rather than features of the world in itself) that are of paramount importance in fashioning knowledge" (Gergen, 1985, p. 269). Kant, whom we considered in Chapter 2, is the classic example of a theorist who takes an endogenic perspective.

Social constructionists acknowledge the limitations of both the endogenic and the exogenic perspectives. They attempt to avoid the problems inherent in each by moving to a new level of discourse in which knowledge is no longer seen as "something people possess somewhere in their heads, but rather, something people do together" (Gergen, 1985, p. 270). This means that psychological concepts are understood as the outcome of social processes. In particular, social constructionists focus on the way in which language shapes how we understand ourselves and others. The linguistic philosophy of Ludwig Wittgenstein has been particularly influential in this regard.

Ludwig Wittgenstein (1889–1951)

Born in Austria, Wittgenstein was a charismatic philosopher who deeply influenced many other philosophers, scientists, and social scientists throughout this century. Wittgenstein's work is usually thought of as falling into two distinct periods. It is customary to make a distinction between his early work, such as the *Tractatus Logico-Philosophicus* (1922/1974) and his later work, such as the *Philosophical Investigations* (1953). His early work shaped the logical positivist movement in the 1920s, a movement that we discussed in Chapter 10. However, Wittgenstein subsequently came to believe that approaches such as logical positivism were too simple. He turned to an examination of the way that concepts are used in *ordinary language.* This examination revealed a much more complex array of relationships between concepts than one might have expected. In order to begin to grasp Wittgenstein's method, read the following quotation carefully. Wittgenstein is speaking to the question, "What do all members of a category have in common?" For example, what do all weapons have in common that makes them all weapons? Or what do all vehicles have in common that makes them all vehicles?

> *Consider for example the proceedings we call "games." I mean board-games, card-games, ball-games, Olympic games, and so on. What is common to them all? Don't say: "There must be something common, or they would not be called 'games'"—but look and see whether there is anything common to all.—For if you look at them you will not see something that is common to all, but similarities, relationships, and a whole series of them at that. To repeat: don't think, but look!—Look for example at board-games, with their multifarious relationships. Now pass to card-games; here you find many correspondences with the first group, but many common features drop out, and others appear. When we pass next to ball-games, much that is common is retained, but much is lost.—Are they all "amusing"? Compare chess with noughts and crosses [X's and O's]. Or is there always winning and losing, or competition between players? Think of patience. In ball-games there is winning and losing; but when a child throws his ball at the wall and catches it again, this feature has disappeared. Look at the parts played by skill and luck; and at the difference between skill in chess and skill in tennis. Think now of games like ring-a-ring-a-roses; here is the element of amusement, but how many other characteristic features have disappeared! And we can go through the many, many other groups of games in the same way; can see how similarities crop up and disappear. (Wittgenstein, 1953, pp. 31–32)*

Wittgenstein pointed out that we do not place events together in a category because they all have something in common. Rather, we may give the same name to each member of a very heterogeneous set of events (e.g., "games," "furniture," "weapons"). The concepts we ordinarily use do not admit of a very precise definition. It is impossible to define concepts such as "games," or "furniture," or "weapons," on the basis of what is common to all examples of the category without leaving out some members of the category. Thus, if we define games in terms of winning and losing, then some activities we normally call games will be left out. The same thing happens no matter how we choose to construct the definition. Any definition produces anomalous cases that do not fit the definition.

Psychological concepts can be analyzed in the same way that Wittgenstein analyzed "games." Psychological concepts have their origin in ordinary language. For example, does the concept of "emotion" admit of a precise definition, or will examples of what we ordinarily call emotion always resist a neat, logical classification? Moreover, is not our use of the word "emotion" the result of the socialization practices in our culture? Might not different cultures have very different concepts of emotion, or even none at all?

> *Imagine that the people of a tribe were brought up from early youth to give no expression of feeling* of any kind. *They find it childish, something to be got rid of. Let the training be severe. "Pain" is not spoken of; especially in the form of a conjecture "Perhaps he has got . . .". If anyone complains, he is ridiculed or punished. There is no such thing as the suspicion of shamming. Drilling someone to speak expressionlessly, in a monotone, to move mechanically.*
>
> *I want to say: an education quite different from ours might also be the foundation for quite different concepts. (Wittgenstein, 1980, p. 118)*

If we follow Wittgenstein's analyses, we are led to the conclusion that any theory that is based on precise definitions of concepts will fail to account for all cases. Even though precise definition is the hallmark of science as conceived of by some philosophers of science, such as the logical positivists, it turns out that precise definition leaves out many examples that could be of interest to us. As *David Bloor* (1983, p. 138) has observed, Wittgenstein's analysis implies that everyone, including psychologists, will inevitably encounter events that do not fit nicely into one's favorite theory. Events which do not fit our theories are *anomalies,* and it appears that we have no shortage of them. Drawing on the work of the anthropologist *Mary Douglas* (1978, 1982), Bloor (1983) considers four ways in which we deal with anomalies: *indifference, exclusion, accommodation,* and *opportunism.*

Indifference. One can argue that the anomaly is trivial and not worth bothering with. Thus, events that cannot be accommodated easily within one's favorite theory may be discounted as unimportant. This is the easiest strategy to adopt, and if it works then the theory will be preserved. There is no end to the examples in psychology that illustrate this pattern. Virtually all the major schools, from introspectionism to Gestalt psychology, from psychoanalysis to humanistic psychology, and from behaviorism to cognitive psychology, have argued that the phenomena with which they were dealing were the really important ones, and that the phenomena with which they did not deal were either unimportant, or that a consideration of them could be postponed, perhaps indefinitely.

Exclusion. If an anomaly is acknowledged as important by enough people then it will threaten to force itself to be considered. At that point one may see the occurrence of another strategy that Lakatos (1976) called *monster barring.* Monster barring involves deliberately trying to exclude the anomalous phenomenon. Bloor (1983, p. 143) suggests that the controversy between Wundt and the Würzburg group illustrates this strategy. We considered this controversy in Chapter 4. The Würzburgers had insisted on the legitimacy of experimentally investigating "higher mental processes," which Wundt maintained were outside of the scope of experimental psychology properly so-called. Wundt was not indifferent to the Würzburgers efforts, but actively tried to exclude them. Another example of this strategy that readily comes to mind is Freud's response to anyone who wanted to introduce major changes into psychoanalysis.

Accommodation. If forced to do so, the theorist may accept the importance of the anomaly, and try to restructure the theory so as to accommodate to it. The behavioral theorists' reaction to the phenomenon of transposition, which we considered in Chapter 11, is an example of this possibility.

Opportunism. While accommodation may be the most sociable procedure for dealing with anomalies, it is far from the most common. A very common tactic in psychology is opportunism, which involves regarding anomalies as opportunities for introducing novel theoretical approaches. This leads to the proliferation of theories, a state that the discipline may very well be in now. Every time a new concept is introduced—whether it is the split brain or the inner child—there are many people who rush to generate theories that elaborate on the new idea. This has a positive and a negative aspect. On the one hand, it ensures that the discipline remains active and engaged with contemporary concerns. Thus, psychology is easily the most popular discipline in America among undergraduates. On the other hand, it means that the discipline tends to be faddish, and not to develop in a continuous and consistent way.

Figure 15.3 presents a classification scheme that is derived from the work of Bloor (1983) and Douglas (1978). The two dimensions in that figure have been labeled as *grid* and *group.* By "grid," Douglas (1982) meant the degree to which people occupy specific roles within a group. "High grid" translates into a group with a clear hierarchical arrangement, with individual roles determined by definite rules. "Low grid" means a group lacking these properties. The "group" dimension refers to the degree to which someone belongs to a particular group. "Low group" translates into not belonging to a particular school or faction; "high group" translates into a strong commitment to a particular school or faction. Of course the four quadrants of

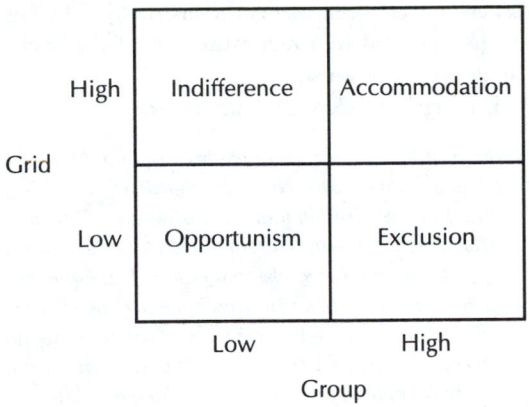

FIGURE 15.3 Responses to anomalies.

Figure 15.3 should not be seen as rigid categories, but only provide a rough guide to the possible social relations between psychologists, and how these social relations influence their theorizing.

According to Bloor (1983, p. 141), the lower right-hand quadrant is characterized by strong feelings of group membership, but low differentiation between group members. The early days of behaviorism must have been like this, and perhaps the early days of most schools are full of enthusiasm, with little internal discord. However, there is a corresponding tendency to exclude anyone who does not share the tenets of the group, again quite characteristic of a school in its early, enthusiastic stages. If there is little feeling of group membership, but a clear pecking order, then the situation is the one described by the top left quadrant. Under such circumstances, everybody looks out for themselves, and is indifferent to the concerns of others. One would not expect to find people becoming outstanding figures in the history of psychology under conditions like these. People who are indifferent to others tend to find that others are indifferent to them. A more interesting case is the lower left quadrant in which one finds the entrepreneurs in psychology. These are people who are not concerned with group membership, or with status, but only with developing whatever new ideas come along. Many of the people we considered in Chapters 13 and 14, such as Maslow and Neisser, might be seen as belonging here. Neither one attempted to recruit followers, yet both were very aware of what were "hot topics." The top right quadrant is probably quite rare in psychology, because few if any approaches have developed to the point where there is not only a clear set of criteria for group membership, but also a clear set of criteria for "progress through the ranks." It will be interesting to see if any current approaches will reach such a state.

Psychological Research as a Social Construction

The idea that psychology is a social construction is disturbing to many people because it suggests that psychological research is not "objective." Although social constructionists vary in the extent to which they believe that psychological research is entirely a social construction, there is no doubt that all of them believe that it is at least to some extent a social construction (Stam, 1990). *Jill Morawski* (1988; Morawski & Steele, 1991) describes the situation as follows:

> *What actually occurs in the design and execution of an experiment includes complex negotiations about what is being observed and what counts as an observation. The written account of a laboratory event is itself the product of rhetorical deftness and artful editing. What kinds of experiments are conducted depends on the research community's customs, ethics, economics, policy interests, and even fads. What goes on in experimental laboratories is not limited solely by explicit methodological rules, but involves practical problem solving by commonsense reasoners. Conventional histories of psychology recount none of these conditions of laboratory work. (Morawski, 1988, p. 73)*

Other scholars point out that scientific research could both be a social construction and still be "true" in some objective sense:

> *The fact that scientific theories are themselves socially constructed is quite neutral with respect to the issue of . . . objectivity. Many theoretical concepts and models are of course socially constructed or created, in the sense that their meaning is not defined . . . by operational definitions in terms of observables. The*

> *concept of the double helical structure of DNA was not introduced by Watson and Crick to conventionally refer to something they could directly observe. This theoretical concept and its meaningful content were social in origin. Yet this does not preclude us from holding the view that Watson and Crick's theoretical account provides a more accurate description of the real dimensions of DNA than alternative theoretical accounts, nor does it oblige us to presuppose that DNA itself (as opposed to our theoretical concept of it) is socially constructed or created. (Greenwood, 1992, p. 139)*

Thus, some social constructionist historians of psychology focus on the social processes that determine the ways in which psychological research is conducted without claiming that the products of this research necessarily have no empirical content. This is the spirit in which *Kurt Danziger* (1987, 1990, 1992, 1994) has contended that the psychological experiment is an elaborate social construction.

From Danziger's perspective (1990), the psychological experiment came about as a part of psychology's overall strategy of claiming to have "expert knowledge or knowledge different from everyday or common knowledge" (Stam, 1992, p. 630). A central feature of this strategy was the creation of a special setting—the psychological experiment—in which "data" could be gathered and analyzed using the kinds of statistical methods we considered in Chapter 10. Thus, a central feature of psychological research in this century was that "researchers moved away from their early emphasis on data ascribed to individual subjects and began to report their results in terms of groups, which were often analyzed statistically" (Capshew, 1992). As Danziger (1990, p. 85) put it, data gathered in the psychological laboratory "points the way to a science that supplies its own categories for classifying people and is not dependent on the unreflected categories of everyday life. . . . [T]here is now the possibility that psychologically constituted collectivities will compete with and even replace some of the more traditional categories of social grouping. Categorizing children or recruits by intelligence quotient was an early example of such a process." Thus, not only has psychological research itself been a social construction, but its results have led to a reconstruction of the social categories we now use.

Danziger (1992, p. 256) argues that

> *the profound relevance of the history of a discipline for understanding the content of that discipline arises out of the recognition that* there is no such thing as a private science. *Any epistemic access to the world afforded by a science like psychology is a collective access, and the objects to which the practices of the science are directed cannot be other than social objects constructed through the interaction of real historical individuals. The norms which regulate psychological research practice are, of course, social norms and as such are the product of specific historical conditions.*

Far from detracting from the scientific content of psychology, "a measure of historical sophistication about their field would work wonders for the ability of psychologists to enrich the cultural life of their own as well as other societies. And because they would be less dependent on current fads the quality of their more technical contributions might be expected to improve as well" (Danziger, 1994, p. 481).

Additional Reading on This Topic. Although we have been focusing on social constructionism as an approach to the history of psychology, Gergen and Gergen (1984) demonstrate how this approach can be applied to the study of psychological processes themselves. Wallach and Wallach (1994) provide an analysis and a critique of the social constructionist approach to social psychology. Mills (1992) and Rogers (1992) offer thoughtful reviews of Danziger's book *Constructing the Subject* (1990). Dorothy Ross (1993) gives an excellent overview of the history of social science from a perspective similar to the one we have been discussing in this section.

IS PSYCHOLOGY POSTMODERN?

Modernism

In many ways, the story of psychology in the twentieth century is the story of a typically modern discipline. That is, psychology has defined itself and been defined in terms that are characteristic of twentieth-century modernism. Although "modernism" is a term that is usually used in connection with the arts, Vitz and Glimcher (1984) have shown that there are numerous parallels between the development of twentieth-century art and the development of twentieth-century psychology. Sometimes the parallels reflect the attempts by a group of artists to apply a particular psychological theory to their work. An example of this kind of parallelism is the use of Gestalt theory by the Bauhaus school of architecture (Vitz & Glimcher, 1984, p. 164). Other times the parallels are less specific, reflecting a mutuality of interest. An example of this kind of parallel is the mutual interest in dreams shared by psychoanalysis and the surrealist movement (Vitz & Glimcher, 1984, p. 257). Although the relations between psychology and art are complex, the parallels between them are sufficient to demonstrate that both psychology and art respond to and illustrate similar cultural trends.

As Janik and Toulmin (1973) have argued, twentieth-century modernism is in part a reaction against what was perceived as the excesses of the late nineteenth century. The nineteenth century, "Victorian" style found expression in the kitsch art we often consider to be representative of the era. For examples of this decorative style, see any Sears catalog from the 1890s. Every object, from stoves to watches, has elaborate ornamentation that is irrelevant to the function of the object. Thus, a pocketwatch has a complex, but merely decorative backing, such as an engraving of a moose emerging from the forest at the edge of a lake. This is quite different from what one would find on the back of a twentieth-century watch, which is likely to be no decoration at all. The same point could be made by comparing objects, such as furniture and buildings, made then and made after a twentieth-century style established itself. Janik and Toulmin (1974, p. 43) describe how a typical parlor looked prior to the emergence of a twentieth-century style:

> *Nowhere was the true nature of the era more apparent than in the lack of style which marked its design. Having no style of their own, they could only imitate the past; so they filled their homes with garish objets d'art in differing styles. Again and again, the complex was preferred to the simple, the decorative to the useful, resulting in rooms that were vulgar to look at and barely habitable.*

Of course, there are still many rooms that fit this description, but it is nonetheless true that many intellectuals in this century have attempted to eliminate anything that might be merely decorative, and have instead insisted that there should be no parts of structures that are merely decorative and serve no function. A pioneer of this way of thinking was the Viennese architect *Adolf Loos* (1870–1933) who said that "cultural evolution is equivalent to the removal of ornament from articles in use," and that "the architect should follow the plumber as his model, not the sculptor" (Janik & Toulmin, 1974, p. 93). Loos was by no means the only person to hold such views. One has only to compare nineteenth-century buildings with the steel and glass slabs that came to dominate the centers of our cities during this century in order to see how widespread has been the attitude expressed by Loos.

Gardner and Stevens (1992) have shown how much of psychology was closely tied to the rich cultural context of Vienna during the first few decades of this century. However, the modern attitude was also present in America, and one does not need to look further than John B. Watson for an example of the way in which early twentieth-century psychologists saw nineteenth-century psychology as "merely decorative." Recall, for example, Watson's claim (1913/1966, p. 74) that "the time seems to have come when psychology must discard all reference to consciousness; when it need no longer delude itself into thinking that it is making mental states the object of observation." The next step in the evolution of psychology, for Watson, entailed the elimination of "philosophical speculation," which "need trouble the student of behavior as little as" it troubles "the student of physics. . . . I can state my position here no better than by saying that I should like to bring my students up in the same ignorance of such hypotheses as one finds among the students of branches of science." Watson should not be singled out, because his writing was only the clearest expression of the modern attitude toward the recent past. Earlier forms of psychology were largely worthless, and could be safely ignored.

However, as the century progressed, the modern attitude toward the past began to wear a bit thin. Some cultural critics even argued that by eliminating so much of the past, we had thrown out the baby with the bathwater. A good example of this development is Wolfe's *From Bauhaus to Our House* (1981), a scathing critique of modern architecture:

> *Every child goes to school in a building that looks like a duplicating-machine replacement parts wholesale distribution warehouse. . . . Every new $900,000 summer house in the north woods or on the shore of Long Island has so many pipe railings, ramps, hob-tread metal spiral stairways, sheets of industrial plate glass, banks of tungsten-halogen lamps, and white cylindrical shapes, it looks like an insecticide refinery. I once saw the owners of such a place driven to the edge of sensory deprivation by the whiteness & lightness & leanness & cleanness & bareness & spareness of it all. They became desperate for an antidote, such as coziness and color.*

Once the products of modernism began to be seen as not satisfying enough, then there was a tendency to turn and look back before modernism to see if there was not something in our earlier history that might improve our current situation. The attempt to recycle the past and use it in a contemporary context is an essential part of the postmodern attitude.

Additional Reading in This Topic. Modernism is nowhere better illustrated than in the writings of the architect Le Corbusier (1954).

Postmodernism

As Kvale (1992, p. 2) observes, "the very term 'postmodern' is controversial and ambiguous." *Christopher Jencks* (1986), a leading postmodern architect, notes that the term was used by *Arnold Toynbee* (1888–1975) in his monumental *A Study of History* (1947/1960) to refer to "a new historical cycle" signifying "pluralism and a world culture" (p. 2). Jencks (1986) goes on to show that postmodernists do not reject the achievements of modernism, but hope to appeal to a broader audience than did modernism. Thus, regardless of the discipline, postmodernists tend to argue for a more democratic and open system than may have existed previously.

As a part of broadening its appeal, postmodernism harks back to earlier forms that had been rejected by modernists. Of course, these earlier forms cannot be used in precisely the same way in which they were originally used. Consequently, a postmodern creation refers to the past ironically. Jencks (1986) uses an example from *Umberto Eco* (1984, pp. 67–68) to illustrate this point:

> *I think of the postmodern attitude as that of a man who loves a very cultivated woman and knows he cannot say to her, "I love you madly," because he knows that she knows (and that she knows that he knows) that these words have already been written by Barbara Cartland. Still, there is a solution. He can say, "As Barbara Cartland would put it, I love you madly." At this point, having avoided false innocence, having said clearly that it is no longer possible to speak innocently, he will nevertheless have said what he wanted to say to the woman: that he loves her, but he loves her in an age of lost innocence. If the woman goes along with this, she will have received a declaration of love all the same. Neither of the two speakers will feel innocent, both will have accepted the challenge of the past, of the already said, which cannot be eliminated, both will consciously and with pleasure play the game of irony . . . But both will have succeeded, once again, in speaking of love.*

One of the signs of postmodernism is the reassertion of values that have previously been rejected. The person confronted with something postmodern "is likely to have a shock of the old" (Jencks, 1986, p. 43). However, these values are not asserted in the same old way, but their historical status is acknowledged. In contemporary psychology, one of the signs of a postmodern attitude is the revival of previously rejected forms of psychology. A good example is the rehabilitation of Wundt's approach to psychology, which we discussed in Chapter 4. It is not that Wundtian psychology is simply being reasserted as the best approach, but rather that its value is being reassessed and used to enrich more modern approaches. One of the prospects of a postmodern psychology is the continuous re-evaluation of the past.

Postmodernism does not only mean an openness to the past. It also means an openness to those whose viewpoints may have been neglected. Postmodernism is pluralistic and multicultural (Gergen, 1991a, 1991b, 1994; Sampson, 1993). A postmodern psychology would be open to the possibility that any approach to psychology might be legitimate. No approach to psychology would necessarily have priority over any other approach. While some lament what they see as the fragmentation of psychology that results from adopting a postmodern attitude (e.g., Smith, 1994), others, such as the postmodernist *Kenneth Gergen* (1994, p. 414) see postmodernism as an opportunity to "live less aggressively, more tolerantly, and even more creatively with others in the world."

The American Psychological Society

One of the consequences of postmodernism is that the previously dominant forms of psychology find themselves competing for attention with any number of alternative approaches to psychology. There can be no doubt that psychology has become more and more differentiated, increasing the number of factions within the discipline. A sense of this differentiation can be gleaned from Table 15.1. Over time, the American Psychological Association has added more and more "special interest groups."

While few would argue with the right to existence of any one of the groups listed in Table 15.1,

TABLE 15.1 Areas of Interest to Psychologists, as Illustrated by the Divisions of the American Psychological Association

DIVISIONS THAT EXISTED IN 1945
Clinical psychology
Consulting psychology
Counseling psychology
Developmental psychology
Educational psychology
Evaluation, measurement and statistics
Experimental psychology
General psychology
Industrial and organizational psychology
Military psychology
Personality and social psychology
Physiological and comparative psychology
Psychologists in public service
Psychology and the arts
School psychology
Psychotherapy
Study of social issues
Teaching of psychology

DIVISIONS ADDED BETWEEN 1945 AND 1979
Adult development and aging
Applied experimental and engineering psychologists
Child, youth and family services
Community psychology
Consumer psychology

DIVISIONS ADDED BETWEEN 1945 AND 1979 (continued)
Experimental analysis of behavior
Health psychology
History of psychology
Humanistic psychology
Mental retardation and developmental disabilities
Population and environmental psychology
Psychological hypnosis
Psychologists interested in religious issues
Psychology of women
Psychopharmacology
Rehabilitation psychology
State psychological association affairs
Theoretical and philosophical psychology

DIVISIONS ADDED IN THE 1980S
American psychology—law society
Clinical neuropsychology
Exercise and sport psychology
Family psychology
Media psychology
Psychoanalysis
Psychological study of ethnic minority issues
Psychological study of lesbian and gay issues
Psychologists in independent practice

those who had hoped for and worked toward a unified discipline may find this state of affairs to be an indication that psychology has become too diversified. "In my worst nightmares I foresee a decimation of institutional psychology as we know it. Human experimental psychologists desert to the emerging discipline of cognitive science; physiological psychologists go happily to departments of biology and neuroscience; industrial/organizational psychologists are snapped up by business schools; and psychopathologists find their home in medical schools" (*Janet T. Spence,* 1987, p. 1053). If there is no unifying paradigm to hold psychology together, what is to keep it from flying apart, with each aspect of psychology being assimilated by more established disciplines, such as biology, medicine, and economics?

Another source of division in psychology over the last few decades has been the growing influence of the nonacademic sector. This is especially clear in the growth in membership of the American Psychological Association (APA) since World War II.

> *The number of health care providers has rapidly expanded to the point of rivaling or outstripping the number of those in academic specialties, and the resulting shift in the balance of power within APA has been well documented. . . . These changes have made it inevitable that attention to professional rather than scientific issues . . . [has] come to dominate APA activities. It was also inevitable that the greatest political and organizational conflicts within the Association would occur along the scientist-practitioner fracture line. (Spence, 1987, p. 1053)*

Thus, by the end of the 1980s many academic psychologists were feeling alienated from the APA. Just as many other groups felt that their voices were not being heard by academic psychology (Sampson, 1993), so also have many academic psychologists felt that their voices were not being heard by the APA. The upshot of this discontent was the formation of the *American Psychological Society* (APS) in 1988, the goal of which was to "advance the discipline of Psychology and preserve its scientific base; to promote public understanding of psychological science and its applications; and to encourage the 'giving away' of psychology in the public interest" (Rodgers, 1990, p. 81).

In 1986, the APA had over 60,000 members. It is possible to gain some insight into the social processes whereby this group of psychologists split into two by examining Figure 15.4. This figure presents a list of the divisions of the APA that were given in Table 15.1. In the figure, however, these divisions are organized in terms of the degree to which they share members. The length of the bar beside each division indicates the degree to which its members are also members of the adjacent division. Thus, working from the top of the figure, the divisions of general psychology and the teaching of psychology share many members. The shortest bars mark discontinuities between divisions. This analysis indicates that there are two basic clusters of psychologists, corresponding to the descriptors "Health Care" and "Academic." Within each of these clusters are smaller groupings, as labeled in the figure. There are two other relevant pieces of information in the figure. One column lists those divisions of APA that voted to become affiliated with APS in 1988: "11 of the 13 active joiners were from the 'Academic Cluster'; 11 of the 13 who had no intention of joining were from 'the Health Care Cluster'" (Rodgers, 1990, p. 84). The other column lists those divisions that sent representatives to an APS-sponsored "Summit Meeting of Scientific Psychological Societies" (Rodgers, 1990, p. 82). It turned out that "15 of the 19 divisions who attended the APS Summit meeting . . . came from the 'Academic Cluster.' Clearly the APS is an outgrowth of substructure already present within the APA at an earlier time" (Rodgers, 1990, p. 84).

Five years after its founding, APS had 15,000 members. Interviews with individuals who had been central figures in the emergence of APS felt that APS met

> *scientific psychologists' need for what many simply called "identification" and "a home." . . . And several added that APS seemed to be reversing a trend that saw researchers casting aside the "psychology" label of their core behavioral discipline and adopting*

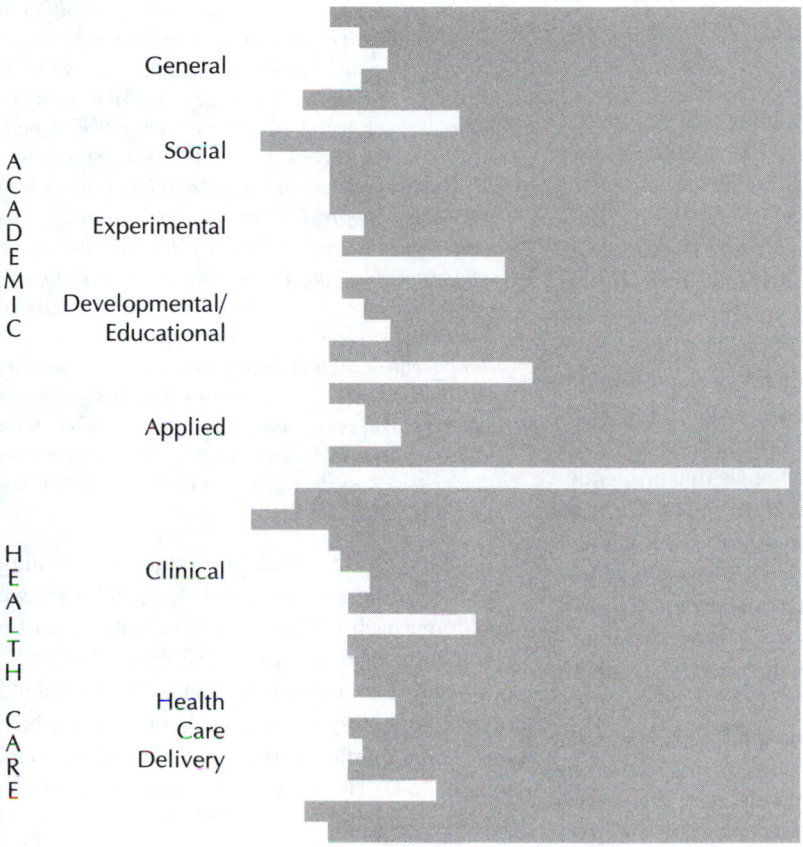

	Division	APS Affiliation?	APS Summit?
1	General	—	No
2	Teaching	Yes	Yes
20	Adult Devel/Aging	—	No
10	Arts	—	Yes
24	Theoretical/Philos	—	No
26	History	—	No
8	Personality/Social	Yes	Yes
9	SPSSI	—	Yes
34	Population/Environ	Yes	Yes
3	Experimental	Yes	Yes
6	Physiol/Compar	Yes	Yes
25	Ex Analysis Behav	—	Yes
28	Psychopharm	Yes	Yes
7	Developmental	Yes	Yes
37	Child/Youth/Family	—	No
33	MR/Devel Disabil	No	No
15	Educational	—	Yes
16	School	—	Yes
5	Eval/Measur/Stat	Yes	Yes
14	Industrial/Organiz	Yes	Yes
23	Consumer	Yes	Yes
19	Military	No	No
21	Engineering	Yes	Yes
12	Clinical	—	No
29	Psychotherapy	No	No
42	Indep Practice	No	No
39	Psychoanalysis	No	No
31	State Assn Affairs	No	No
30	Hypnosis	No	No
43	Family	No	No
13	Consulting	No	No
27	Community	—	No
18	Public Service	—	No
41	Law	—	No
17	Counseling	Yes	Yes
35	Women	Yes	Yes
32	Humanistic	No	No
36	Religious Issues	No	No
22	Rehabilitation	No	No
40	Clin Neuropsych	No	Yes
38	Health	—	Yes

FIGURE 15.4 Cluster analysis of divisional overlap in the APA.

Source: J. L. Rodgers (1990). Structural models of the American Psychological Society at Birth. *Psychological Science, 1,* 83. Reprinted with the permission of Cambridge University Press.

the labels of other fields. Others found that APS was stimulating a deeper awareness of psychology's essentially scientific roots throughout the discipline . . . (Kent, 1993, p. 4).

By stressing the "unity that exists in psychology," APS represented a "trend toward undifferentiation" (Hayes, 1993, p. 16). However, it is important to realize that many of the founders of APS regarded themselves as "scientist-practitioners," and not simply scientists or simply practitioners. By 1993, there was some pressure from within APS to begin to acknowledge the differences that existed even within the APS membership:

APS can be a better umbrella under which all of scientific psychology can reside. But to do so, it must allow for organized diversity in the context of unity and shared values. We need an activist agenda that thoroughly connects with the concerns of scientist-practitioners as well as basic scientists, we need to bridge the applied-basic interface, and we need to find a way to better include the intellectual minorities and their legitimate aspirations. (Hayes, 1993, p. 22)

FUTURE HISTORIES

For decades, academic psychologists subscribed to the version of the history of psychology that had been written by the discipline's best known historian, *Edwin G. Boring* (1929, 1950b). Boring's history was originally written in the 1920s, when psychology in the United States was just as divided between "scientists" and "practitioners" as it appears to be currently (O'Donnell, 1979). Boring realized that a history of psychology was not merely an objective recording of what had happened in the past. Rather, Boring's history was intended to persuade psychologists that academic, experimental psychology was the ideal form of psychology, and should take priority over applied psychology. Although Boring's history was immensely scholarly, it was also intentionally biased toward telling psychology's story from the point of view of an experimental psychologist (O'Donnell, 1979).

Many of the institutional problems that face contemporary psychology are eerily similar to those that faced psychology in Boring's day. As a consequence, it is tempting to conclude that psychology as a discipline has found itself on Ixion's wheel rather than climbing Jacob's ladder, to echo a theme we sounded in Chapter 2. However, the story of psychology does not admit of so simple a conclusion. This is partly true because the nature of storytelling itself has changed since Boring told his story (e.g., O'Hara, 1992).

It was once conventional for stories to be told from a single point of view, with a single protagonist. Thus, Boring's history is from the viewpoint of an experimental psychologist, whose progress is synonymous with the progress of psychology itself. This is analogous to telling the story of evolution from the viewpoint of human beings, whose evolutionary triumph is the point of the story (O'Hara, 1992, p. 144). This way of telling the story of evolution seemed obvious to nineteenth-century thinkers such as Herbert Spencer (whom we discussed in Chapter 3), but it is much less obvious now.

It is instructive to note the emergence of a politics of recognition with the environmental movement as well as with the politics of difference and multiculturalism. The environmentalists demand a respect for animals, trees, rivers, ecosystems. They, like the multiculturalists, are concerned with a new appreciation of diversity and with the moral and legal standing of the rights of oppressed groups. Furthermore, just as multiculturalists might criticize the positing of the achievements of one group, such as white European and American males, as the norm of fully developed humanity, so the environmentalists criticize an anthropocentric outlook that posits human beings as the final end of the creation process and as inherently superior to all other beings. In both cases there is an attack on hierarchical modes of thought that tend to diminish or deny the value of other beings. (Rockefeller, 1994, p. 93)

If "every form of life is unique, warranting respect regardless of its worth to man," then we should approach all forms of life "with at least a presumption of equal value" (Rockefeller, 1994, pp. 93–94). Perhaps the story of evolution should not be told simply as "the story of events which have been important in the history of us" (O'Hara, 1992, p. 154). The history of evolution is not one story, but many:

When we come to realize that even among the vertebrates there are 50,000 different "vertebrate stories," each one with a different ending and each one with a different narrative landscape; when we truly think in terms of the diverging tree, instead of the line; when we understand that it is absurd to talk of one animal being higher than another; only then will we see the full grandeur of the historical view of life. (O'Hara, 1992, p. 157)

The history of psychology is but a tiny part of history as a whole. Nevertheless, within the history of psychology the same principles apply as apply to evolutionary history. There are many more stories that should be told than possibly can be told, and each story deserves as much respect as any other. No matter how inclusive a particular history of psychology may be, there will still be many parts of psychology that will not have been considered as fully as they might be. It is the task of future histories to continue to expand the range of viewpoints included, and to do justice to the variety of psychologies and psychologists.

Additional Reading on This Topic. An excellent review of issues relating to culture, history, and evolution is Harris (1977).

KEY NAMES AND CONCEPTS

What follows is an index of some of the most important material in this chapter. The list includes individuals, concepts, and topics you should know. Read through the list, and if anything on it seems unfamiliar, then go back and re-read the appropriate section of the chapter. You should be able to define each concept, briefly discuss each topic, and state the importance of each person on the list. In addition, you should be able to write an account of the work done by each person whose name is printed in boldface.

American Psychological Society, 329
Boring, Edwin, 332
Contextualism, 318
Htut, Lin and Win, 320
Jenkins, James J., 319
mechanism, 319
Pepper, Stephen C., 319
strands, 319
texture, 319
Feminism, 320
Beauvoir, Simone de, 320
compensatory history, 321
Keller, Evelyn Fox, 321
science-gender system, 322
Feyerabend, Paul, 316
Furomoto, Laurel
the new history of psychology, 315
Hanson, Norwood, 316
Kuhn, Thomas, 316
normal science, 317
paradigm, 316
paradigm clashes, 316
preparadigmatic, 317
mentalism, 318
modernism, 326
Loos, Adolf, 327
postmodernism, 328
Eco, Umberto, 328
Gergen, Kenneth, 329
Jencks, Christopher, 328
Toynbee, Arnold, 328
Social constructionism, 322
anomalies, 324
Bloor, David, 324
Danziger, Kurt, 326
dialectical process, 322
Douglas, Mary, 324
exogenic versus endogenic, 322
grid and group, 324
indifference, exclusion, accommodation, opportunism, 324
monster barring, 324
Morawski, Jill, 325
ordinary language, 323
Wittgenstein, Ludwig, 322
Spence, Janet, 330
The new history of science, 315

BIBLIOGRAPHY

Ach, N. (1951). Determining tendencies and awareness. In D. Rapaport (Ed.), *Organization and pathology of thought* (pp. 15–38). New York: Columbia University Press. (Original work published 1905)

Adams-Webber, J. R. (1970). An analysis of the discriminant validity of several repertory grid indices. *British Journal of Psychology, 61,* 83–90.

Adams-Webber, J. R. (1979). *Personal construct theory: Concepts and research.* New York: Wiley.

Adler, H. E. (1992). William James and Gustav Fechner: From rejection to elective affinity. In M. Donnelly, *Reinterpreting the legacy of William James* (pp. 253–262). Washington, DC: American Psychological Association.

Alba, J. W., & Hasher, L. (1983). Is memory schematic? *Psychological Bulletin. 93,* 203–231.

Alexander, P. (1987). John Locke. In R. L. Gregory (Ed.), *The Oxford companion to the mind* (pp. 438–439). Oxford: Oxford University Press.

Allport, G. (1964). *Pattern and growth in personality.* New York: Holt, Rinehart and Winston.

Allport, G., Vernon, P. E., & Lindzey, G. (1960). *Manual: A study of values.* Boston: Houghton Mifflin.

Amacher, P. (1965). Freud's neurological education and its influence on psychoanalytic theory. *Psychological Issues, 4* (4, Monograph 16).

American Psychological Association. (1953). *Psychoanalysis as seen by analyzed psychologists.* Washington, DC: Author. (Original work published 1940)

Amundson, R. (1985). Psychology and epistemology: The place versus response controversy. *Cognition, 20,* 127–153.

Anastasi, A. (1965). *Individual differences.* NY: Wiley.

Angell, J. R. (1978). The province of a functional psychology. In E. R. Hilgard (Ed.), *American psychology in historical perspective* (pp. 81–104). Washington, DC: American Psychological Association. (Original work published 1907)

Anglin, J. (1973). Editor's preface. In J. Anglin (Ed.), *Beyond the information given* (pp. x–xii). New York: Norton.

Ansbacher, H. L., & Ansbacher, R. R. (1964). *The individual psychology of Alfred Adler.* New York: Harper.

Anscombe, E., & Geach, P. T. (Eds.). (1954). *Descartes: Philosophical writings.* New York: Thomas Nelson.

Anzai, Y., & Simon, H. A. (1979). The theory of learning by doing. *Psychological Review, 86,* 124–140.

Appignanesi, L., & Forrester, J. (1992). *Freud's women.* New York: Basic Books.

Archer, J., & Lloyd, B. (1982). *Sex and gender.* Harmondsworth, UK: Penguin.

Arnheim, R. (1974). *Art and visual perception.* Berkeley, CA: University of California Press.

Arnheim, R. (1986). The other Gustav Theodor Fechner. In R. Arnheim (Ed.), *New essays on the psychology of art* (pp. 39–49). Berkeley, CA: University of California Press.

Aronson, L. R., Tobach, E., Lehrman, D. S., & Rosenblatt, J. S. (1970). *Development and evolution of behavior: Essays in memory of T. C. Schneirla.* San Francisco: Freeman.

Asch, S. E. (1946). Forming impressions of personality. *Journal of Abnormal and Social Psychology, 41,* 258–290.

Asch, S. E. (1952). *Social psychology.* Englewood Cliffs, NJ: Prentice-Hall.

Asch, S. E. (1955). Opinions and social pressure. *Scientific American, 193,* 31–35.

Asch, S. E. (1956). *Studies of independence and conformity: I. A minority of one against a unanimous majority* (pp. 1–70). Psychological Monographs, no. 70.

Asch, S. E. (1968a). Wolfgang Kohler: 1887–1967. *American Journal of Psychology, 81,* 110–119.

Asch, S. E. (1968b). Gestalt theory. In *International Encyclopedia of the Social Sciences* (pp. 158–175). New York: Macmillan.

Asch, S. E., & Witkin, H. A. (1948). Studies in space orientation. I. Perception of the upright with displaced visual fields. *Journal of Experimental Psychology: General, 38,* 325–337.

Asch, S. E., & Witkin, H. A. (1992). Studies in space orientation. II. Perception of the upright with displaced visual fields and with body tilted. *Journal of Experimental Psychology: General, 121,* 407–418. (Original work published 1948)

Asch, S. E., & Zukier, H. (1984). Thinking about persons. *Journal of Personality and Social Psychology, 6,* 1230–1240.

Ashby, W. R. (1956). *Cybernetics.* London: Chapman & Hall.

Attneave, F. (1959). *Applications of information theory to psychology.* New York: Holt, Rinehart & Winston.

Audley, R. J. (1980). Letter. *Bulletin of the British Psychological Society, 33,* 135.

Augarde, T. (Ed.). (1991). *The Oxford dictionary of modern quotations.* Oxford: Oxford University Press.

Ausubel, D. P. (1968). *Educational psychology: A cognitive view.* New York: Holt, Rinehart & Winston.

Ayer, A. J. (1968). *The origins of pragmatism.* London: MacMillan.

Baars, B. J. (1986). *The cognitive revolution in psychology.* New York: Guilford Press.

Bahrick, H. P. (1984). Semantic memory in permastore: Fifty years of memory for Spanish learned in school. *Journal of Experimental Psychology: General, 113,* 1–31.

Bahrick, H. P., & Hall, L. K. (1991). Lifetime maintenance of high school mathematics content. *Journal of Experimental Psychology: General, 120,* 20–33.

Bakan, D. (1966). The test of significance in psychological research. *Psychological Bulletin, 66,* 423–438.

Baldwin, J. M. (1897). *Mental development of the child and the race* (2nd ed.). New York: Macmillan.

Baldwin, J. M. (1966). Types of reaction. In J. M. Vanderplas (Ed.), *Controversial issues in psychology* (pp. 144–155). Boston: Houghton Mifflin. (Original work published 1895)

Baldwin, J. M. (1966). The 'type theory' of reaction. In J. M. Vanderplas (Ed.), *Controversial issues in psychology* (pp. 164–173). Boston: Houghton Mifflin. (Original work published 1896)

Baltes, P. B., & Staudinger, U. M. (1993). The search for a psychology of wisdom. *Current Directions in Psychological Science, 2,* 75–80.

Bandura, A. (1965). Behavioral modifications through modeling procedures. In L. Krasner & L. P. Ullmann (Eds.), *Research in behavior modification* (pp. 310–340). New York: Holt, Rinehart & Winston.

Bandura, A. (1978). The self system in reciprocal determinism. *American Psychologist, 33,* 344–358.

Bandura, A. (1983). Temporal dynamics and decomposition of reciprocal determinism: A reply to Philips and Orton. *Psychological Review, 90,* 166–170.

Bandura, A. (1986). *Social foundations of thought and action: A social cognitive theory.* Englewood Cliffs, NJ: Prentice-Hall.

Bandura, A., Grusec, J. E., & Menlove, F. L. (1967). Vicarious extinction of avoidance behavior. *Journal of Personality and Social Psychology, 5,* 16–23.

Bandura, A., Ross, D., & Ross, S. (1961). Transmission of aggression through imitation of aggressive models. *Journal of Abnormal and Social Psychology, 63,* 575–582.

Bandura, A., & Walters, R. H. (1963). *Social learning and personality development.* New York: Holt, Rinehart & Winston.

Banister, P., Burman, E., Parker, I., Taylor, M., & Tindall, C. (1994). *Qualitative methods in psychology.* Buckingham, UK: Open University Press.

Bannister, D., & Bott, M. (1973). Evaluating the person. In P. Kline (Ed.), *New approaches in psychological measurement* (pp. 157–177). London: Wiley.

Bannister, D., & Fransella, F. (1971). *Inquiring man: The theory of personal constructs.* Harmondsworth, UK: Penguin.

Bannister, D., & Mair, J. M. M. (1968). *The evaluation of personal constructs.* London: Academic Press.

Bantock, G. H. (1984). *Studies in the history of educational theory.* London: George Allen & Unwin.

Barnes, R. M. (1968). *Motion and time study: Design and measurement of work* (6th ed.). New York: Wiley.

Bartlett, F. C. (1932). *Remembering.* Cambridge, UK: Cambridge University Press.

Bartlett, F. C. (1958). *Thinking: An experimental and social study.* New York: Basic Books.

Bauer, R. A. (1952). *The new man in Soviet psychology.* Cambridge, MA: Harvard University Press.

Baumrin, J. (1975). Aristotle's empirical nativism. *American Psychologist, 30,* 486–495.

Beauvoir, S. de (1989). *The second sex.* New York: Vintage. (Original work published 1949)

Beck, J. (Ed). (1982). *Organization and representation in perception.* Hillsdale, NJ: Erlbaum.

Beck, L. W. (Ed.) Introduction. In Kant, I. (1950). *Prolegomena to any future metaphysics* (pp. vii–xx). Indianapolis: Bobbs-Merrill. (Original work published 1783)

Beer, C. G. (1983). Darwin, instinct and ethology. *Journal of the History of the Behavioral Sciences, 19,* 68–80.

Bem, D. J., & Honorton, C. (1994). Does psi exist? Replicable evidence for an anomalous process of information transfer. *Psychological Bulletin, 115,* 4–18.

Benedict, R. (1959). Mary Wollstonecraft. In M. Mead (Ed.), *Anthropologist at work: Writings of Ruth Benedict* (pp. 491–519). Boston: Houghton Mifflin.

Benedict, R. (1989). *Patterns of culture.* Boston: Houghton Mifflin. (Original work published 1935)

Benfari, R. (1991). *Understanding your management style: Beyond the Myers-Briggs type indicators.* Lexington, MA: Lexington Books.

Benjafield, J. (1969a). Logical and empirical thinking in a problem solving task. *Psychonomic Science, 14,* 285–286.

Benjafield, J. (1969b). Evidence that "thinking aloud" constitutes an externalization of inner speech. Psychonomic Science, 15, 83–84.

Benjafield, J. (1983). Some psychological hypotheses concerning the evolution of constructs. *British Journal of Psychology, 74,* 47–59.

Benjafield, J. (1985). A review of recent research on the Golden Section. *Empirical Studies of the Arts, 3,* 117–134.

Benjafield, J. (1992). *Cognition.* Englewood Cliffs, NJ: Prentice-Hall.

Benjafield, J. (1994). *Thinking critically about research methods.* Boston: Allyn & Bacon.

Benjafield, J., & Green, T. R. G. (1978). Golden section relations in interpersonal judgement. *British Journal of Psychology, 69,* 25–35.

Benjafield, J., Pomeroy, E., & Jordan, D. (1976). Encounter groups: A return to the fundamental. *Psychotherapy: Theory, Research and Practice, 13,* 387–389.

Benjamin, L. T. (1988). A history of teaching machines. *American Psychologist, 43,* 703–712.

Benjamin, L. T., Durkin, M., Link, M., Vestal, M., & Acord, J. (1992). Wundt's American doctoral students. *American Psychologist, 47,* 123–131.

Benne, K. D. (1964). History of the T group in the laboratory setting. In L. P. Bradford, J. R. Gibb, & K. D. Benne, (Eds.), *T-group theory and laboratory method* (pp. 80–135). New York: Wiley.

Bennett, J. (1971). *Locke, Berkeley, Hume.* Oxford: Clarendon Press.

Berger, P., & Luckmann, T. (1967). *The social construction of reality.* Harmondsworth, UK: Penguin.

Bergman, G., & Spence, K. W. (1941). Operationism and theory in psychology. *Psychological Review, 48,* 1–14.

Berkeley, G. (1910). *A new theory of vision and other writings.* London: J. M. Dent. (Original work published 1709)

Berlyne, D. E. (1960). *Conflict, arousal, and curiosity.* New York: McGraw-Hill.

Berlyne, D. E. (1965). *Structure and direction in thinking.* New York: Wiley.

Berlyne, D. E. (1975). Behaviourism? Cognitive theory? Humanistic psychology—to Hull with them all! *Canadian Psychological Review, 16,* 69–80.

Bernstein, L. (1976). *The unanswered question.* Cambridge, MA: Harvard University Press.

Bernstein, M. D., & Russo, N. F. (1974). The history of psychology revisited: Or, up with our foremothers. *American Psychologist, 29,* 130–134.

Berreby, D. (1994, January/February). Figures of speech: The rise and fall and rise of Chomsky's linguistics. *The Sciences, 34,* 44–49.

Bieri, J. (1955). Complexity-simplicity and predictive behavior. *Journal of Abnormal and Social Psychology, 51,* 263–268.

Bieri, J. (1961). Complexity-simplicity as a personality variable in cognitive and preferential behavior. In D. W. Fiske & S. R. Maddi (Eds.), *Functions of varied experience* (pp. 355–379). Homewood, IL: Dorsey.

Bigelow, P. (1986). The indeterminability of time in "Sein und Zeit." *Philosophy and Phenomenological Research, 46,* 357–379.

Binet, A. (1969). Imageless thought. In Pollack, R. H., & Brenner, M. J. *The experimental psychology of Alfred Binet* (pp. 207–221). New York: Springer. (Original work published 1903)

Binet, A., & Simon, T. (1915). *A method of measuring the development of the intelligence of young children* (C. H. Town, Trans.). Chicago: Chicago Medical Books. (Original work published 1911)

Binet, A., & Simon, T. (1965). Upon the necessity of establishing a scientific diagnosis of inferior states of intelligence. In A. Anastasi (Ed.), *Individual differences* (pp. 30–34). NY: Wiley. (Original work published 1905a)

Binet, A., & Simon, T. (1965). New methods for the diagnosis of the intellectual level of subnormals. In A. Anastasi (Ed.), *Individual differences* (pp. 35–41). NY: Wiley. (Original work published 1905b)

Binet, A., & Simon, T. (1965). The development of intelligence in the child. In A. Anastasi (Ed.), *Individual differences* (pp. 41–44). NY: Wiley. (Original work published 1908)

Binswanger, L. (1975). *Being-in-the-world.* London: Souvenir Press.

Bitterman, M. E. (1967). Learning in animals. In H. Helson & W. Bevan (Eds.), *Contemporary approaches to psychology* (pp. 139–180). New York: Van Nostrand.

Bjork, D. W. (1993). *B. F. Skinner: A life.* New York: Basic Books.

Bloor, D. (1983). *Wittgenstein: A social theory of knowledge.* New York: Columbia University Press.

Blumenthal, A. L. (1970). *Language and psychology: Historical aspects of psycholinguistics.* New York: Wiley.

Blumenthal, A. L. (1975). A reappraisal of Wilhelm Wundt. *American Psychologist, 30,* 1081–1088.

Blumenthal, A. L. (1977). *The process of cognition.* Englewood Cliffs, NJ: Prentice-Hall.

Blumenthal, A. L. (1979, June). *The Ganzheit psychologists: The second Leipzig school.* Paper presented at the meeting of Cheiron, Akron, OH.

Boden, M. A. (1987). *Artificial intelligence and natural man.* New York: Basic Books.

Bond, M. H., & Hwang, K-H. (1986). The social psychology of the Chinese people. In M. H. Bond (Ed.), *The psychology of the Chinese people* (pp. 213–266). Hong Kong: Oxford University Press.

Boneau, C. A. (1990). Psychological literacy: A first approximation. *American Psychologist, 45,* 891–900.

Boring, E. G. (1929). *A history of experimental psychology.* New York: Century.

Boring, E. G. (1950a). Great men and scientific progress. *Proceedings of the American Philosophical Society, 94,* 339–351.

Boring, E. G. (1950b). *A history of experimental psychology* (2nd ed.). New York: Appleton-Century-Crofts.

Boring, E. G. (1963a). *The physical dimensions of consciousness.* New York: Dover. (Original work published 1933)

Boring, E. G. (1963b). Fechner: Inadvertent founder of psychophysics. In R. I. Watson & D. T. Campbell (Eds.), *History, psychology and science: Selected papers by E. G. Boring* (pp. 126–131). New York: Wiley. (Original work published 1961)

Boring, E. G. (1963c). The use of operational definitions in science. In R. I. Watson & D. T. Campbell (Eds.), *History, psychology and science: Selected papers by E. G. Boring* (pp. 200–209). New York: Wiley. (Original work published 1945)

Boring, E. G. (1963d). The stimulus-error. In R. I. Watson & D. T. Campbell (Eds.), *History, psychology and science: Selected papers by E. G. Boring* (pp. 255–273). New York: Wiley. (Original work published 1921)

Boring, E. G. (1969). Intelligence as the tests test it. In L. Tyler (Ed.), *Intelligence: Some recurring issues* (pp. 25–28). New York: Van Nostrand. (Original work published 1923)

Bornstein, R. F. (1989). Exposure and affect: Overview and meta-analysis of research, 1968–1987. *Psychological Bulletin, 106,* 265–289.

Bower, G. H. (1970). Analysis of a mnemonic device. *American Scientist, 58,* 496–510.

Bower, G. H. (1994). In appreciation of E. R. Hilgard's writings on learning theories. *Psychological Science, 5,* 181–183.

Bower, G. H., & Hilgard, E. R. (1981). *Theories of learning* (5th ed.). New York: Appleton-Century-Crofts.

Bowers, K. S. (1973). Situationism in psychology: An analysis and a critique. *Psychological Review, 80,* 307–336.

Bregman, A. S. (1977). Perception and behavior as compositions of ideals. *Cognitive Psychology, 9,* 250–292.

Brentano, F. (1968). Act psychology. In W. S. Sahakian (Ed.), *History of psychology: A source book in systematic psychology* (pp. 479–486). Itaska, IL: Peacock. (Original work published 1874)

Brentano, F. (1973). *Psychology from an empirical standpoint* (A. Rancurello, Trans.). New York: Humanities Press. (Original work published 1874)

Bretherton, I. (1992). The origins of attachment theory: John Bowlby and Mary Ainsworth. *Developmental Psychology, 28,* 759–775.

Breuer, J., & Freud, S. (1959). On the psychical mechanism of hysterical phenomena. In *Collected Papers* (Vol. 1, pp. 24–41). New York: Basic Books. (Original work published 1893)

Bridgman, P. W. (1927). *The logic of modern physics.* New York: Macmillan.

Bridgman, P. W. (1940). Science: Public or private? *Philosophy of Science, 7,* 36.

Briggs, K. C., & Myers, I. B. (1976). *Myers-Briggs type indicator.* Palo Alto, CA: Consulting Psychologists Press.

Brigham, C. C. (1923). *A study of American intelligence.* Princeton, NJ: Princeton University Press.

Bringmann, W. G., Bringmann, M. W., & Early, C. E. (1992). G. Stanley Hall and the history of psychology. *American Psychologist, 47,* 281–289.

Bringmann, W. G., DePace, A. N., & Balance, W. D. G. (1992, June). *A brief, handwritten autobiography by Fechner.* Paper presented at the meeting of Cheiron, Windsor, ON.

British Psychological Society. (1972). Monthly Report. *Bulletin of the British Psychological Society, 33,* 71–72.

Broadbent, D. E. (1958). *Perception and communication. London: Pergamon.*

Broadbent, D. E. (1980). Donald E. Broadbent. In G. Lindzey (Ed.), *A history of psychology in autobiography* (Vol. 7, pp. 39–73). San Francisco: Freeman.

Broadbent, D. E. (1992). Listening to one of two synchronous messages. *Journal of Experimental Psychology, General, 121,* 125–127. (Original work published 1952)

Brock, A. (1992). Was Wundt a Nazi? *Theory and Psychology, 2,* 205–223.

Brock, A. (1993). Something old, something new: Wilhelm Wundt. *Theory and Psychology, 3,* 235–242.

Brown, J. A. C. (1954). *The social psychology of industry.* Harmondsworth, UK: Penguin.

Brown, R. (1958). *Words and things.* New York: Free Press.

Brown, R., & McNeill, D. (1966). The "tip of the tongue phenomenon." *Journal of Verbal Learning and Verbal Behavior, 8,* 325–337.

Bruce, D. (1986). Lashley's shift from bacteriology to neuropsychology, 1910–1917, and the influence of Jennings, Watson, and Franz. *Journal of the History of the Behavioral Sciences, 22,* 27–43.

Bruce, D. (1991). Integrations of Lashley. In G. A. Kimble, M. Wertheimer & C. L. White (Eds.), *Portraits of pioneers in psychology* (pp. 306–323). Hillsdale, NJ: Erlbaum.

Bruce, D. (1994a). Lashley and the problem of serial order in behavior. *American Psychologist, 49,* 93–103.

Bruce, D. (1994b, June). Criticisms of Lashley. Paper presented at The Jean Pierre Marie Flourens (1794–1867) Bicentennial History Conference, Montreal, PQ.

Brunberg, J. J., & Tomes, N. (1982). Women in the professions: A research agenda for American historians. *Reviews in American History, 10,* 275–288.

Bruner, J. S. (1966). *Toward a theory of instruction.* Cambridge, MA: Harvard University Press.

Bruner, J. S. (1986). *Actual minds, possible worlds.* Cambridge, MA: Harvard University Press.

Bruner, J. S. (1973). On perceptual readiness. In J. Anglin (Ed.), *Beyond the information given* (pp. 7–42). New York: Norton. (Original work published 1957)

Bruner, J. S. (1980). Jerome S. Bruner. In G. Lindzey (Ed.), *A history of psychology in autobiography* (Vol. 7, pp. 75–151). San Francisco: Freeman.

Bruner, J. S. (1990). *Acts of meaning.* Cambridge, MA: Harvard University Press.

Bruner, J. S., Goodnow, J. J., & Austin, G. A. (1956). *A study of thinking.* New York: Wiley.

Bruner, J. S., Jolly, A., & Silva, K. (Eds.) (1976). *Play.* New York: Penguin.

Bruner, J. S., & Klein, G. (1960). The functions of perceiving: New look retrospect. In B. Kaplan & S. Wapner (Eds.), *Perspectives in psychological theory* (pp. 61–77). New York: International Universities Press.

Bruner, J. S., Olver, R. R., & Greenfield, P. M. (1966). *Studies in cognitive growth.* New York: Wiley.

Bruner, J. S., & Postman, L. J. (1973). On the perception of incongruity. In J. Anglin (Ed.), *Beyond the information given* (pp. 68–83). New York: Norton. (Original work published 1949)

Brunswik, E. (1956). *Perception and the representative design of experiments.* Berkeley: University of California Press.

Bryant, D. J., Tversky, B., & Franklin, N. (1992). Internal and external spatial frameworks for representing described scenes. *Journal of Memory and Language, 31,* 74–98.

Brzezinski, E. J. (1984). Microcomputers and testing: Where are we and how did we get there? *Educational Measurement: Issues and Practice, 3,* 7–10.

Buckingham, H. (1984). Early development of associationist theory in psychology as a forerunner to connection theory. *Brain and Cognition, 3,* 19–34.

Buckley, K. W. (1982). The selling of a psychologist: John Broadus Watson and the application of behavioral techniques to advertising. *Journal of the History of the Behavioral Sciences, 18,* 207–221.

Buckley, K. W. (1989). *Mechanical man: John Broadus Watson and the beginnings of behaviorism.* New York: Guilford.

Bugental, J. F. T. (1964). The third force in psychology. *Journal of Humanistic Psychology, 4,* 19–26.

Bühler, C. (1965). Some observations on the psychology of the third force. *Journal of Humanistic Psychology, 5,* 54–55.

Bühler, K. (1951). On thought connections. In D. Rapaport (Ed.), *Organization and pathology of thought* (pp. 39–57). New York: Columbia University Press. (Original work published 1907)

Burnham, J. C. (1972). Thorndike's puzzle boxes. *Journal of the History of the Behavioral Sciences, 8,* 159–167.

Burns, C. (1979, June). *The role of emotion in the development of thought: The psychology of Mary Wollstonecraft.* Paper presented at the meeting of Cheiron (The International Society for the History of the Social and Behavioral Sciences), Akron, OH.

Burt, C. (1972). Inheritance of general intelligence. *American Psychologist, 27,* 175–190.

Buss, A. R. (1978). The structure of psychological revolutions. *Journal of the History of the Behavioral Sciences, 14,* 57–64.

Cairns, R. B. (1992). The making of a developmental science: The contributions and intellectual heritage of James Mark Baldwin. *Developmental Psychology, 28,* 17–24.

Calkins, M. W. (1929). Introduction. In G. Berkeley, *Selections* (pp. ix–li). New York: Scribner's.

Calkins, M. W. (1966). Association. In R. J. Herrnstein & E. Boring (Eds.), *A source book in the history of psychology* (pp. 530–534). Cambridge, MA: Harvard University Press. (Original work published 1896)

Campbell, D. T. (1960). Blind variation and selective retention in creative thought as in other knowledge processes. *Psychological Bulletin, 67,* 380–400.

Campbell, J. (1964). *The masks of God: Occidental mythology.* New York: Viking.

Capaldi, E. J., & Proctor, R. W. (1994). Contextualism: Is the act in context the adequate metaphor for scientific psychology? *Psychonomic Bulletin & Review, 1,* 239–249.

Capshew, J. H. (1992). Constructing subjects, reconstructing psychology. *Theory and Psychology, 2,* 243–247.

Carnap, R. (1959). Psychology in physical language. In A. J. Ayer (Ed.), *Logical Positivism* (pp. 165–198). Glencoe, IL: Free Press.

Carnegie, A. (1979). The gospel of wealth. In P. Appleman (Ed.), *Darwin* (pp. 399–405). New York: Norton. (Original work published 1955)

Carotenuto, A. (1982). *A secret symmetry: Sabina Spielrein between Freud and Jung.* New York: Pantheon Books.

Cartwright, D. (1959). Lewinian theory as a contemporary systematic framework. In S. Koch (Ed.), *Psychology: A study of a science* (Vol. 2, pp. 7–91). New York: McGraw-Hill.

Cassirer, E. (1946). *Language and myth* (S. K. Langer, Trans.). New York: Harper & Brothers.

Cassirer, E. (1963). *Rouseau, Kant and Goethe.* New York: Harper & Row. (Original work published 1945)

Cattell, J. McK. (1903). Statistics of American Psychologists. *American Journal of Psychology, 14,* 297–298.

Cattell, J. McK. (1948). Mental tests and measurements. In W. Dennis (Ed.), *Readings in the history of psychology* (pp. 347–354). New York: Appleton-Century-Crofts. (Original work published 1890)

Cattell, J. M. (1886). The time it takes to see and name objects. *Mind, 11,* 63–65.

Cattell, R. B. (1978) Letter. *Bulletin of the British Psychological Society, 31,* 18–19.

Ceraso, J., Gruber, H., & Rock, I. (1990). On Solomon Asch. In I Rock (Ed.), *The legacy of Solomon Asch* (pp. 3–22). Hillsdale, NJ: Erlbaum.

Chakerian, G. D. (1972). The golden ratio and a Greek crisis. *Fibonacci Quarterly, 11,* 195–200.

Charlesworth, W. R. (1992). Darwin and developmental psychology: Past and present. *Developmental Psychology, 28,* 5–16.

Cherry, E. C. (1953). Some experiments on the recognition of speech with one and with two ears. *Journal of the Acoustical Society of America, 25,* 975–979.

Chomsky, N. (1957). *Syntactic structures.* The Hague: Mouton.

Chomsky, N. (1959). Review of Skinner's verbal behavior. *Language, 35,* 26–58.

Chomsky, N. (1966). *Cartesian linguistics.* New York: Harper & Row.

Chomsky, N. (1967). *The formal nature of language.* In E. Lenneberg, Biological foundations of language (pp. 397–442). New York: Wiley.

Chomsky, N. (1968). *Language and mind.* New York: Harcourt, Brace & World.

Chomsky, N. (1972a). *Language and mind* (Enlarged ed.). New York: Harcourt Brace Jovanovich.

Chomsky, N. (1972b). Psychology and ideology. *Cognition, 1,* 11–46.

Chomsky, N. (1980). *Rules and representations.* New York: Columbia University Press.

Chomsky, N. (1986). *Knowledge of language: Its nature, origin and use.* New York: Praeger.

Ciancia, F. (1988). Tolman and Honzik (1930) revisited or the mazes of psychology (1930–1980). *The Psychological Record, 41,* 461–472.

Claparède, E. (1933). La genèse de l'hypothèse. *Archives de Psychologie, 24,* 1–54.

Clifford, G. J. (1973). E. L. Thorndike: The psychologist as professional man of science. In M. Henle, J. Jaynes & J.J. Sullivan (Eds.), *Historical conceptions of psychology* (pp. 230–245). New York: Springer. (Original work published 1968)

Cockburn, B. (1988). *Big circumstance* (Cassette recording). Hollywood, CA: Gold Castle Records.

Cohen, J. (1968). Multiple regression as a general data-analytic system. *Psychological Bulletin, 70,* 426–443.

Cohen, J., & Cohen, P. (1983). *Applied multiple regression-correlation analysis for the behavioral sciences* (2nd ed.). Hillsdale, NJ: Erlbaum.

Cole, L. E. (1939). *General psychology.* New York: McGraw-Hill.

Cole, M., & Scribner, S. (1978). Introduction. In L. S. Vygotsky, *Mind in society* (pp. 1–16). Cambridge, MA: Harvard.

Coles, R. (1970). *Erik H. Erikson: The growth of his work.* Boston: Little, Brown.

Collingwood, R. G. (1946). *The idea of history.* Oxford: Oxford University Press.

Conway, M. A., Cohen, G., & Stanhope, N. (1991). On the very long-term retention of knowledge acquired through formal education: Twelve years of cognitive psychology. *Journal of Experimental Psychology: General, 120,* 395–412.

Coon, D. J. (1992). Testing the limits of sense and science: American experimental psychologists combat spiritualism, 1880–1920. *American Psychologist, 47,* 143–151.

Coren, S., & Girgus, J. S. (1980). Principles of perceptual organization and spatial distortion: The Gestalt illusions. *Journal of Experimental Psychology: Human Perception and Performance, 6,* 404–412.

Coren, S., Porac, C., & Ward, L. M. (1984). *Sensation and perception* (2nd ed.). New York: Academic Press.

Cornford, F. M. (1939). *Plato and Parmenides.* London: Routledge and Kegan Paul.

Cornford, F. M. (1960). *Plato's theory of knowledge.* London: Routledge & Kegan Paul. (Original work published 1935)

Cornford, F. M. (1967). *The unwritten philosophy and other essays.* Cambridge, UK: Cambridge University Press. (Original work published 1950)

Cornford, F. M. (1974). Mysticism and science in the Pythagorean tradition. In P. D. Mourelatos (Ed.), *The Presocratics* (pp. 135–160). New York: Anchor Press/Doubleday. (Original work published 1922)

Costall, A. (1993). How Lloyd Morgan's Canon backfired. *Journal of the History of the Behavioral Sciences, 29,* 113–122.

Crafts, L. W., Schneirla, T. C., Robinson, E. E., & Gilbert, R. W. (1950). *Recent experiments in psychology.* New York: McGraw-Hill.

Cronbach, L. J. (1960). *Essentials of psychological testing* (2nd ed.). New York: Harper.

Cronbach, L. J. (1978). The two disciplines of scientific psychology. In E. R. Hilgard (Ed.), *American psychology in historical perspective* (pp. 285–308). Washington, DC: American Psychological Association. (Original work published 1957)

Crovitz, H. F. (1970). *Galton's walk.* New York: Harper & Row.

Crovitz, H. F., & Schiffman, H. (1974). Frequency of episodic memories as a function of their age. *Bulletin of the Psychonomic Society, 4,* 517–518.

Crovitz, H. F., Schiffman, H., & Apter, A. (1991). Galton's number. *Bulletin of the Psychonomic Society, 29,* 331–332.

Dallett, J. (1973). Theories of dream function. *Psychological Bulletin, 79,* 408–416.

Danziger, K. (1980). The history of introspection reconsidered. *Journal of the History of the Behavioral Sciences, 16,* 241–262.

Danziger, K. (1983). Origins and basic principles of Wundt's *Volkerpsychologie. British Journal of Social Psychology, 22,* 303–314.

Danziger, K. (1987). Social context and investigative practice in early twentieth-century psychology. In M. G. Ash & W. R. Woodward (Eds.), *Psychology in twentieth-century thought and society* (pp. 13–33). New York: Cambridge University Press.

Danziger, K. (1990). *Constructing the subject.* Cambridge: Cambridge University Press.

Danziger, K. (1992). Ideas and constructions: Reply to reviewers. *Theory and Psychology, 2,* 255–256.

Danziger, K. (1994). Does the history of psychology have a future? *Theory and Psychology, 4,* 467–484.

Darwin, C. (1955). *The expression of the emotions in man and animals.* New York: Philosophical Library. (Original work published 1872)

Darwin, C. (1958). *The autobiography of Charles Darwin and selected letters* (F. Darwin, Ed.). New York: Dover. (Original work published 1892)

Darwin, C. (1964). *The descent of man.* New York: Modern Library. (Original work published 1871)

Darwin, C. (1964). *The origin of species.* New York: Modern Library. (Original work published 1859)

Darwin, F. (1958). Footnote. In C. Darwin, *The autobiography of Charles Darwin and selected letters* (F. Darwin, Ed.) (p. 20). New York: Dover. (Original work published 1892)

Dawkins, R. (1983). The necessity of Darwinism. In Cherfas, J. (Ed.), *Darwin up to date* (pp. 61–63). London: IPC Magazines Ltd.

Dawkins, R. (1988). *The blind watchmaker.* London: Penguin.

Dennis, W. (1948). *Readings in the history of psychology.* New York: Appleton-Century-Crofts.

Dewey, J. (1930). *Individualism old and new.* New York: Minton, Balch.

Dewey, J. (1963). The reflex arc concept in psychology. In J. Ratner (Ed.), *John Dewey: Philosophy, psychology and social practice* (pp. 252–266). New York: Putnam. (Original work published in 1896)

Dewey, J. (1970). Experience and education. In S. M. Cahn (Ed.), *The philosophical foundations of education* (pp. 221–261). New York: Harper & Row. (Original work published 1938)

Dewey, J. (1978). Psychology and social practice. In E. R. Hilgard (Ed.), *American psychology in historical perspective* (pp. 65–79). Washington, DC: American Psychological Association. (Original work published 1900)

Dewsbury, D. A. (1992a). Comparative psychology and ethology. *American Psychologist, 47,* 208–215.

Dewsbury, D. A. (1992b). *The boys of summer at the end of summer: The Watson-Lashley correspondence of the 1950s.* Paper presented to the XXIVth Annual Meeting of Cheiron: International Society of the Behavioral and Social Sciences, Windsor, ON, Canada.

Dinnerstein, D. (1977). *The mermaid and the minotaur.* New York: Harper & Row.

Dixon, T. R., & Horton, D. L. (Eds.). (1968). *Verbal behavior and general behavior theory.* Englewood Cliffs, NJ: Prentice-Hall.

Dollard, J., & Miller, N. E. (1950). *Personality and psychotherapy.* New York: McGraw-Hill.

Douglas, M. (1978). *Natural symbols.* New York: Penguin.

Douglas, M. (1982). Introduction to grid/group analysis. In M. Douglas (Ed.), *Essays in the sociology of perception.* London: Routledge & Kegan Paul.

Dowling, W. J., & Harwood, D. L. (1986). *Music cognition.* Orlando, FL: Academic Press.

Duncker, K. (1945). *On problem solving.* Psychological Monographs, no. 58, (5, Whole No. 270).

Dunkel, H. B. (1969). *Herbart and education.* New York: Random House.

Dunkel, H. B. (1970). *Herbart and Herbartianism: An educational ghost story.* Chicago: University of Chicago Press.

Ebbinghaus, H. (1964). *Memory: A contribution to experimental psychology.* New York: Dover. (Original work published 1885)

Eco, U. (1984). *Postscript to The Name of the Rose.* New York: Harcourt, Brace, Jovanovich.

Eco, U. (1989). *The open work* (A. Cancogni, Trans.). Cambridge, MA: Harvard University Press.

Edgerton, S. (1975). *The Renaissance rediscovery of linear perspective.* New York: Basic.

Egeth, H. (1992). Dichotic listening: Long-lived echoes of Broadbent's early studies. *Journal of Experimental Psychology: General, 121,* 124.

Einstein, A. (1952). Foreword. In I. Newton, *Opticks: Or a treatise of the reflections, refractions, inflections & colours of light* (pp. lix–lx). New York: Dover.

Einstein, G. O., & McDaniel, M. A. (1987). Distinctiveness and the mnemonic benefits of bizarre imagery. In M. A. McDaniel & M. Pressley (Eds.), *Imagery and related mnemonic processes: Theories, individual differences and applications* (pp. 78–102). New York: Springer-Verlag.

Eiseley, L. C. (1987). Charles Darwin. In O. Gingerich (Ed.), *Scientific genius and creativity* (pp. 67–75). New York: Freeman. (Original work published 1956)

El'konin, D. B. (1969). Some results of the study of the psychological development of preschool-age children. In M. Cole & I. Maltzman (Eds.), *A handbook of contemporary Soviet psychology* (pp. 163–208). New York: Basic Books.

Ellenberger, H. F. (1970). *The discovery of the unconscious.* New York: Basic Books.

Ellis, H. C. (1979). Transfer and the educational process. In G. S. Belkin (Ed.), *Perspectives in educa-*

tional psychology (pp. 71–82). Dubuque, Iowa: W.C. Brown. (Original work published 1965)

Ellsworth, P. C. (1994). William James and emotion: Is a century of fame worth a century of misunderstanding? *Psychological Review, 101,* 222–229.

Epstein, R. (1991). Skinner, creativity, and the problem of spontaneous behavior. *Psychological Science, 2,* 362–370.

Ericsson, K. A. & Simon, H. A. (1980). Verbal reports as data. *Psychological Review, 87,* 215–251.

Ericsson, K. A. & Simon, H. A. (1984). *Protocol analysis.* Cambridge, MA: MIT Press.

Erikson, E. H. (1950). *Childhood and society.* New York: Norton.

Erikson, E. H. (1959). Identity and the life cycle. *Psychological Issues, 1* (1, Monograph 1).

Erikson, E. H. (1962). *Young man Luther.* New York: Norton.

Erikson, E. H. (1963). *Childhood and society* (2nd ed.). New York: Norton.

Erikson, E. H. (1964). *Insight and responsibility.* New York: Norton.

Erikson, E. H. (1972). Play and actuality. In M.W. Piers (Ed.), *Play and development* (pp. 127–167). New York: Norton.

Erikson, E. H., Erikson, J., & Kivnick, H. Q. (1986). *Vital involvement in old age.* New York: Norton.

Estes, W. K. (1960). Learning theory and the new mental chemistry. *Psychological Review, 67,* 207–223.

Estes, W. K. (Ed.). (1990). William James symposium. *Psychological Science, 1,* 149–186.

Evans, R. B. (1973). E. B. Titchener and his lost system. In M. Henle, J. Jaynes & J. J. Sullivan (Eds.), *Historical conceptions of psychology* (pp. 83–97). New York: Springer.

Evans, R. I. (1976). *The making of psychology.* New York: Knopf.

Falk, R. (1989). Judgement of coincidences: Mine versus yours. *American Journal of Psychology, 102,* 477–493.

Fancher, R. E. (1983). Biographical origins of Francis Galton's psychology. *Isis, 74,* 227–233.

Fancher, R. E. (1985). *The intelligence men: Makers of the IQ controversy.* New York: Norton.

Fancher, R. E. (1989). Galton on examinations: An unpublished step in his invention of correlation. *Isis, 80,* 446–455.

Farr, R. M. (1983). Wilhelm Wundt (1832–1920) and the origins of psychology as an experimental and social science. *British Journal of Social Psychology, 22,* 289–301.

Farrell, B. A. (1978). The progress of psychology. *British Journal of Psychology, 69,* 1–8.

Farson, R. (1978). The technology of humanism. *Journal of Humanistic Psychology, 18,* 5–35.

Fechner, G. T. (1871). *Zur experimentalen Aesthetik* [Toward an experimental aesthetic]. Leipzig: S. Hirzel.

Fechner, G. T. (1876). *Vorschule der Aesthetik.* Leipzig: Breitkopf & Hartel.

Fechner, G. T. (1966). *Elements of psychophysics* (Vol. 1). New York: Holt Rinehart and Winston. (Original work published 1860)

Ferguson, J. (1970). *Socrates.* London: Macmillan.

Feyerabend, P. K. (1970). Consolations for the specialist. In I. Lakatos & A. Musgrave (Eds.), *Criticism and the growth of knowledge* (pp. 197–230). Cambridge, UK: Cambridge University Press.

Fisher, R. A. (1991). *Statistical methods, experimental design, and scientific inference.* Oxford: Oxford University Press. (Original work published 1925)

Fiske, S. T., & Taylor, S. E. (1991). *Social cognition.* New York: McGraw-Hill.

Fitzpatrick, F. J. (1987). Aquinas. In R. L. Gregory (Ed.). *The Oxford companion to the mind* (pp. 36–38). Oxford: Oxford University Press.

Flavell, J. H. (1963). *The developmental psychology of Jean Piaget.* New York: Van Nostrand.

Flavell, J. H. (1985). *Cognitive development.* Englewood Cliffs, NJ: Prentice-Hall.

Flavell, J. H., & Draguns, J. A. (1957). A microgenetic approach to perception and thought. *Psychological Bulletin, 54,* 197–217.

Fletcher, R. (1991). *Science, ideology, and the media: The Cyril Burt scandal.* New Brunswick, NJ: Transaction Publishers.

Flowers, K. A. (1987). Parkinsonism. In R. L. Gregory (Ed.). *The Oxford companion to the mind* (pp. 587–591). Oxford: Oxford University Press.

Føllesdall, D. (1984). Brentano and Husserl on intentional objects and perception. In H. L. Dreyfus (Ed.), *Husserl, intentionality and cognitive science* (pp. 31–42). Cambridge, MA: MIT Press.

Franklin, M. B. (1990). Reshaping psychology at Clark: The Werner era. *Journal of the History of the Behavioral Sciences, 26,* 176–189.

Fransella, F., & Bannister, D. (1977). *A manual for repertory grid technique.* London: Academic Press.

Franz, M.-L. von (1974). *Number and time.* London: Rider.

Franz, S. I. (1912). New phrenology. *Science, 35,* 321–328.

Fraser, S. (March, 1994). Freud's final seduction. *Saturday Night,* 18–21, 56–59.

Frazer, J. G. (1909). *Psyche's task.* London: MacMillan.

Frazer, J. G. (1959). *The Golden Bough* (abridged). NY: Doubleday (Edited by T. H. Gaster, 1922). (Original work published 1911)

Freeman, L. (1980). Immortal Anna O.: From Freud to feminism. *New York Times Magazine, 30,* pp. 74, 78–83.

Freeman-Moir, D. J. (1982). The origin of intelligence. In J. M. Broughton & D. J. Freeman-Moir (Eds.), *The cognitive-developmental psychology of James Mark Baldwin: Current theory and research in genetic epistemology* (pp. 127–168). Norwood, NJ: Ablex.

Freud, A. (1946). *The ego and the mechanisms of defence.* London: Hogarth. (Original work published 1936)

Freud, A. (1969). *Some difficulties in the path of psychoanalysis.* New York: International Universities Press.

Freud, S. (1946). *Totem and taboo* (A. A. Brill, Trans.). New York: Random House. (Original work published 1913)

Freud, S. (1950). *An autobiographical study* (J. Strachey, Trans.). London: Hogarth Press. (Original work published 1935)

Freud, S. (1953). *The future of an illusion* (W. D. Robson-Scott, Trans.). New York: Doubleday. (Original work published 1927)

Freud, S. (1957). *Beyond the pleasure principle.* New York: Doubleday. (Original work published 1920)

Freud, S. (1959). A note on the unconscious in psychoanalysis. In *Collected Papers: Vol. 4* (pp. 22–29). New York: Basic Books. (Original work published 1912)

Freud, S. (1959). On the history of the psychoanalytic movement. In *Collected Papers: Vol. 1* (pp. 287–359). New York: Basic Books. (Original work published 1914)

Freud, S. (1959). Some points in a comparative study of organic and hysterical paralyses. In *Collected Papers: Vol. 4* (pp. 42–58). New York: Basic Books. (Original work published 1893)

Freud, S. (1959). Why war? In *Collected Papers: Vol. 5* (pp. 273–287). New York: Basic Books. (Original work published 1932)

Freud, S. (1959).The ætiology of hysteria. In *Collected Papers: Vol. 1* (pp. 183–219). New York: Basic Books. (Original work published 1896)

Freud, S. (1961). *Civilization and its discontents* (J. Strachey, Trans.). New York: Norton. (Original work published 1930)

Freud, S. (1964). *New introductory lectures on psychoanalysis.* (J. Strachey, Trans.). New York: Norton. (Original work published 1933)

Freud, S. (1965). *The interpretation of dreams* (J. Strachey, Trans.). New York: Avon. (Original work published 1900)

Freud, S. (1977). *Introductory lectures on psychoanalysis.* New York: Norton. (Original work published 1920)

Friedman, M. (1990). Kant and Newton: Why gravity is essential to matter. In P. Bricker & R. I. G. Hughes (Eds.), *Philosophical perspectives on Newtonian science* (pp. 185–202). Cambridge, MA: MIT Press.

Friman, P. C., Allen, K. D., Kerwin, M. L. E., Larzelere, R. (1993). Changes in modern psychology: A citation analysis of the Kuhnian displacement thesis. *American Psychologist, 48,* 658–664.

Frye, N. (1966). Varieties of literary utopias. In F. Manuel (Ed.), *Utopias and utopian thought* (pp. 25–49). Boston: Houghton Mifflin.

Fryer, D. M., & Marshall, J. C. (1979). The motives of Jacques de Vaucanson, *Technology & Culture, 20,* 257–269.

Furomoto, L. (1987). On the margins: Women and the professionalization of psychology in the United States, 1890–1940. In M. G. Ash & W. R. Woodward (Eds.), *Psychology in twentieth-century thought and society* (pp. 93–114). New York: Cambridge University Press.

Furomoto, L. (1988). The new history of psychology. In I. S. Cohen (Ed.), *The G. Stanley Hall Lecture Series* (Vol. 9) (pp. 9–34). Washington, DC: American Psychological Association.

Furomoto, L. (1991). From "paired associates" to a psychology of self: The intellectual odyssey of Mary Whiton Calkins. In G. A. Kimble, M. Wertheimer & C. L. White, *Portraits of pioneers in psychology* (pp. 57–74). Hillsdale, NJ: Erlbaum.

Furomoto, L. (1992). Joining separate spheres—Christine Ladd-Franklin, woman-scientist (1847–1930). *American Psychologist, 47,* 175–182.

Galton, F. (1965). Hereditary genius: an inquiry into its laws and consequences. In A. Anastasi (Ed.), *Indi-*

vidual differences (pp. 239–248). New York: Wiley. (Original work published 1869)

Galton, F. (1970). Psychometric experiments. In H. Crovitz, *Galton's walk*. New York: Harper & Row. (Original work published 1879)

Galton, F. (1973). *Inquiries into human faculty and its development*. New York: AMS Press. (Original work published 1883)

Gantt, W. H. (1928). Ivan P. Pavlov: A biographical sketch. In I. P. Pavlov, *Lectures on conditioned reflexes* (W. H. Gantt, Trans.) (pp. 11–34). New York: International Universities Press.

Gantt, W. H., Pickenhain, L., & Zwingmann, C. (1970). *Pavlovian approach to psychopathology*. Oxford: Pergamon.

Garcia, J. (1976). I. Krechevsky and I. In L. Petrinovich & J. L. McGaugh (Eds.), *Knowing, thinking, and believing: Festschrift for Professor David Krech* (pp. 71–84). New York: Plenum.

Garcia, J. (1981). Tilting at the papermills of academe. *American Psychologist, 36,* 149–158.

Garcia, J., & Koelling, R. (1966). Relation of cue to consequence in avoidance learning. *Psychonomic Science, 4,* 123–124.

Gardner, H. (1974). *The quest for mind*. New York: Vintage.

Gardner, H. (1982). Ernst Cassirer and the symbolic approach to cognition. In H. Gardner (Ed.), *Art, mind and brain* (pp. 40–47). New York: Basic Books.

Gardner, H. (1983). *Frames of mind*. New York: Basic.

Gardner, H. (1985). *The mind's new science: A history of the cognitive revolution*. New York: Basic Books.

Gardner, S., & Stevens, G. (1992). *Red Vienna and the golden age of psychology, 1918–1938*. New York: Praeger.

Garfield, E. (1979–1988). *The SSCI Journal Citation Reports*. Philadelphia: Institute for Scientific Information.

Garner, W. R. (1962). *Uncertainty and structure as psychological concepts*. New York: Wiley.

Garrett, H. E. (1948). *Great experiments in psychology*. New York: Appleton-Century.

Gauld, A. (1992). *A history of hypnotism*. Cambridge, UK: Cambridge University Press.

Gay, P. (1988). *Freud: A life for our time*. New York: Norton.

Geldard, F. A. (1972). *The human senses* (2nd ed.). New York: Wiley.

Gendlin, E. T. (1962). *Experiencing and the creation of meaning: A philosophical and psychological approach to the subjective*. Glencoe, IL: Free Press.

Gendlin, E. T. (1981). *Focusing*. New York: Bantam Books.

Gentner, D., & Gentner, D. R. (1983). Flowing waters or teeming crowds: Mental models of electricity. In D. Gentner & A. L. Stevens (Eds.), *Mental Models* (pp. 99–129). New York: Erlbaum.

Gentner, D., & Grudin, J. (1985). The evolution of mental metaphors in psychology: A 90-year retrospective. *American Psychologist, 40,* 181–192.

Gentner, D., & Stevens, A. L. (Eds). (1983). *Mental models*. New York: Erlbaum.

Gergen, K. J. (1985). The social constructionist movement in modern psychology. *American Psychologist, 40,* 266–275.

Gergen, K. J. (1991a). Emerging challenges for theory and psychology. *Theory and Psychology, 1,* 13–35.

Gergen, K. J. (1991b). *The saturated self: Dilemmas of identity in contemporary life*. New York: Basic Books.

Gergen, K. J. (1994). Exploring the postmodern: Perils or potentials? *American Psychologist, 49,* 412–416.

Gergen, K. J., & Gergen, M. M. (1984). *Historical social psychology*. Hillsdale, NJ: Erlbaum.

Ghiselin, M. (1966). *The triumph of the Darwinian method*. Berkeley: University of California Press.

Ghiselin, M. (1983). The path to natural selection. In Cherfas, J. (Ed.), *Darwin up to date* (pp. 64–66). London: IPC Magazines Ltd.

Ghiselin, M. (1981). Categories, life and thinking. *Behavioral and Brain Sciences, 4,* 269–313.

Gholson, B. & Barker, P. (1985). Kuhn, Lakatos & Laudan: Applications in the history of physics and psychology. *American Psychologist, 40,* 755–769.

Gibson, E. J. (1941). A critical review of the concept of set in contemporary experimental psychology. *Psychological Bulletin, 38,* 781–817.

Gibson, E. J. (1969). *Principles of perceptual learning and development*. Englewood Cliffs, NJ: Prentice-Hall.

Gibson, E. J. (1980). Eleanor J. Gibson. In G. Lindzey (Ed.), *A history of psychology in autobiography* (Vol. 7, pp. 239–271). San Francisco: Freeman.

Gibson, E. J. (1991). Learning to read. In E. J. Gibson (Ed.), *An odyssey in learning and perception* (pp. 393–412). Cambridge, MA: MIT Press.

Gibson, E. J. (1994). Has psychology a future? *Psychological Science, 5,* 69–76.

Gibson, E. J., & Levin, H. (1975). *The psychology of reading*. Cambridge, MA: MIT Press.

Gibson, E. J., Pick, A., Osser, H., & Hammond, M. (1962). The role of grapheme phoneme correspondence in the perception of words. *American Journal of Psychology, 75,* 554–570.

Gibson, J. J. (1950). *The perception of the visual world.* Boston: Houghton Mifflin.

Gibson, J. J. (1960). The concept of the stimulus in psychology. *American Psychologist, 15,* 694–703.

Gibson, J. J. (1966). *The senses considered as perceptual systems.* Boston: Houghton Mifflin.

Gibson, J. J., & Gibson, E. J. (1955). Perceptual learning—differentiation or enrichment? *Psychological Review, 62,* 32–41.

Gigerenzer, G. (1991). From tools to theories: A heuristic of discovery in cognitive psychology. *Psychological Review, 98,* 254–267.

Gigerenzer, G., & Murray, D. J. (1987). *Cognition as intuitive statistics.* Hillsdale, NJ: Erlbaum.

Gigerenzer, G., Swijtink, Z., Porter, T., Daston, L., Beatty, J., & Kruger, L. (1989). *The empire of chance.* Cambridge, UK: Cambridge University Press.

Gilbert, K. E., & Kuhn, H. (1972). *A history of esthetics.* New York: Dover. (Original work published 1953)

Gillie, O. (1977). Letter. *Bulletin of the British Psychological Society, 30,* 257–258.

Glick, J. (1992). Werner's relevance for contemporary developmental psychology. *Developmental Psychology, 28,* 558–565.

Goethe, J. W. von (1970). *Theory of colors* (C. L. Eastlake, Trans.). Cambridge, MA: MIT Press. (Original work published 1840)

Goffman, E. (1978). Response cries. *Language, 54,* 787–815.

Goldie, P. (1992). *Darwin* [CD-ROM]. San Francisco: Lightbinders, Inc.

Goldstein, H., Krantz, D. L., & Rains, J. D. (1965). *Controversial issues in learning.* New York: Appleton-Century-Crofts.

Goldstein, K. (1963). *Human nature in the light of psychopathology.* New York: Schocken. (Original work published 1940)

Goldstein, K. (1963). *The organism.* Boston: Beacon Press. (Original work published 1939)

Goldstein, K. (1967). Kurt Goldstein. In E. G. Boring & G. Lindzey (Eds.), *A history of psychology in autobiography* (Vol. 5, pp. 147–166). New York: Appleton-Century-Crofts.

Goldstein, K., & Scheerer, M. (1941). *Abstract and concrete behavior: An experimental study with special tests.* Psychological Monographs, no. 53 (Whole no. 2).

Gombrich, E. (1965). The use of art for the study of symbols. *American Psychologist, 20,* 34–50.

Gorfein, D. S., & Hoffman, R. R. (1987) *Memory and learning: The Ebbinghaus centennial conference.* Hillsdale, NJ: Erlbaum.

Gorman, P. (1979). *Pythagoras: A life.* London: Routledge & Kegan Paul.

Gottschaldt, K. (1967). Gestalt factors and repetition. In W. D. Ellis (Ed.), *A source book of Gestalt psychology* (pp. 109–122). New York: Humanities. (Original work published 1926)

Gould, S. J. (1977). *Ontogeny and phyologeny.* Cambridge, MA: Harvard University Press.

Gould, S. J. (1981). *The mismeasure of man.* New York: Norton.

Gould, S. J. (1982, May 6). A nation of morons. *New Scientist,* 349–352.

Gould, S. J. (1985). Living with connections. In S. J. Gould (Ed.), *The Flamingo's Smile* (pp. 64–77). New York: Norton.

Green, B. F. (1992). Exposé or smear? *Psychological Science, 6,* 328–331.

Green, C. D. (1992). Operationism in psychology. *Theory and Psychology, 2,* 291–320.

Green, T. R. G. (1982). Pictures of programs and other processes, or how to do things with lines. *Behaviour and Information Technology, 1,* 3–36.

Greene, J. (1972). *Psycholinguistics: Chomsky and psychology.* Baltimore, MD: Penguin.

Greenglass, E. (1982). *A world of difference: Gender roles in perspective.* Toronto: Wiley.

Greenwald, A. G., Spangenberg, E. R., Pratkanis, A. R., & Eskanazi, J. (1991). Double-blind tests of subliminal self-help audiotapes. *Psychological Science, 2,* 119–122.

Greenwood, J. D. (1992). Realism, empiricism and social construction. *Theory and Psychology, 2,* 131–152.

Greer, S. (1994, June). *Nietzsche and social constructionism.* Paper presented at the meeting of Cheiron, Montreal, 1994.

Gregory, R. L. (1970). *The intelligent eye.* London: Weidenfeld & Nicholson.

Gregory, R. L. (Ed.). (1987). *The Oxford companion to the mind.* Oxford: Oxford University Press.

Grinder, R. E. (1967). *A history of genetic psychology.* New York: Wiley.

Gruber, H. (1981). *Darwin on man: A psychological study of scientific creativity* (2nd ed.). Chicago: University of Chicago Press.

Grusec, J. E. (1992). Social learning theory and developmental psychology: The legacies of Robert Sears and Albert Bandura. *Developmental Psychology, 28,* 776–786.

Gunderson, K. (1964). The imitation game. In A. R. Anderson (Ed.), *Minds and machines* (pp. 60–71). Englewood Cliffs, NJ: Prentice-Hall.

Guthrie, E. R. (1938). *The psychology of human conflict.* New York: Harper & Row.

Guthrie, E. R. (1959). Association by contiguity. In S. Koch (Ed.), *Psychology: A study of a science. Vol. 2. General systematic formulations, learning, and special processes* (pp. 158–195). New York: McGraw-Hill.

Guthrie, E. R. (1960). *The psychology of learning* (Rev. ed.). Gloucester, MA: Peter Smith. (Original work published 1952)

Guthrie, E. R. (1961). Conditioning as a principle of learning. In R. C. Birney & R. C. Teevan (Eds.), *Reinforcement* (pp. 16–32). New York: Van Nostrand. (Original work published 1930)

Guthrie, K. S. (1987). *The Pythagorean sourcebook and library.* Grand Rapids, MI: Phanes Press. (Original work published 1920)

Guthrie, R. V. (1976). *Even the rat was white: A historical view of psychology.* New York: Harper & Row.

Hall, G. S. (1948). The contents of children's minds. In W. Dennis (Ed.), *Readings in the history of psychology* (pp. 255–276). New York: Appleton-Century-Crofts. (Original work published 1883)

Hall, G. S. (1967). The psychology of adolescence. In R. E. Grinder (Ed.), *A history of genetic psychology* (pp. 213–236). New York: Wiley. (Original work published 1904)

Hall, G. S. (1968). Adolescent psychology from a genetic standpoint. In W. S. Sahakian (Ed.), *History of psychology: A source book in systematic psychology* (pp. 195–199). Itaska, IL: Peacock. (Original work published 1904)

Hamilton, E., & Cairns, H. (1961). *Plato: The collected dialogues, including the Letters.* Princeton, NJ: Princeton University Press.

Hamlyn, D. W. (1962). Behavior. In V. C. Chappell (Ed.), *The philosophy of mind* (pp. 60–73). Englewood Cliffs, NJ: Prentice-Hall. (Original work published 1953)

Hannush, M. J. (1987). John B. Watson remembered: An interview with James B. Watson. *Journal of the History of the Behavioral Sciences, 23,* 137–152.

Hanson, N. R. (1969). *Patterns of discovery.* Cambridge, UK: Cambridge University Press.

Hardin, G. (1968). The tragedy of the commons. *Science, 162,* 1243–1248.

Harlow, H. (1958). The nature of love. *American Psychologist, 13,* 673–685.

Harrington, D. M., Block, J. H., & Block, J. (1987). Carl Rogers' theory of creative environments: Child-rearing antecedents of creative potential in young adoloescents. *Journal of Personality and Social Psychology, 52,* 851–856.

Harris, M. (1977). *Cannibals and kings.* New York: Random House.

Harrower, M. (1983). *Kurt Koffka: An unwitting self-portrait.* Gainesville, FL: University of Florida Press.

Hartmann, H. (1976). The historical roots of occupational segregation: Capitalism, patriarchy, and job segregation by sex. *Signs, 1,* 137–169.

Hassard, J. (1990). The AHP Soviet exchange project: 1983–1990. *Journal of Humanistic Psychology, 30,* 5–51.

Hatfield, G., & Epstein, W. (1987). The status of the minimum principle in the theoretical analysis of visual perception. *Psychological Bulletin, 97,* 155–186.

Hayes, S. C. (1993). Balancing unity and diversity: Reflections on the five year history of APS. *APS Observer, 6,* pp. 2, 16, 22.

Hearnshaw, L. S. (1979). *Cyril Burt, psychologist.* Ithaca, NY: Cornell University Press.

Hebb, D. O. (1949). *The organization of behavior.* New York: Wiley.

Hebb, D. O. (1955). Drives and the C.N.S. (Conceptual Nervous System). *Psychological Review, 62,* 243–354.

Hebb, D. O. (1958). *A textbook of psychology.* Philadelphia: Saunders.

Hebb, D. O. (1959). A neuropsychological theory. In S. Koch (Ed.), *Psychology: A study of a science. Vol. 1. Sensory, perceptual and physiological formulations* (pp. 622–643). New York: McGraw-Hill.

Hebb, D. O. (1960). The American revolution. *American Psychologist, 15,* 735–745.

Hebb, D. O. (1968). Concerning imagery. *Psychological Review, 75,* 466–478.

Hebb, D. O. (1980a). *An essay on mind.* Hillsdale, NJ: Erlbaum.

Hebb, D. O. (1980b). D. O. Hebb. In G. Lindzey (Ed.), *A history of psychology in autobiography* (Vol. 7, pp. 275–303). San Francisco: Freeman.

Heidbreder, E. (1933). *Seven psychologies.* New York: Appleton-Century-Crofts.

Heidbreder, E. (1969). Functionalism. In D. L. Krantz (Ed.), *Schools of psychology* (pp. 35–50). New York: Appleton-Century-Crofts.

Heidegger, M. (1962). *Being and time.* London: SCM. (Original work published 1927)

Heider, F. (1958). *The psychology of interpersonal relations.* New York: Wiley.

Heider, F. (1983). *The life of a psychologist: An autobiography.* Lawrence: University of Kansas Press.

Helmholtz, H. von (1954). *On the sensations of tone.* New York: Dover. (Original work published 1885)

Helmholtz, H. von (1961). The sensations of vision. In Teevan, R. C., & Birney, R. C. (Eds.), *Color vision* (pp. 10–27). New York: Van Nostrand. (Original work published 1909)

Helmholtz, H. von. (1962). *Popular scientific lectures.* New York: Dover. (Original work published 1881)

Henle, M. (1968). Deductive reasoning. In P. C. Wason & P. N. Johnson-Laird (Eds.). *Deductive reasoning* (pp. 93–107). Baltimore: Penguin. (Original work published 1962)

Henle, M. (1978). Gestalt psychology and Gestalt therapy. *Journal of the History of the Behavioral Sciences, 14,* 23–32.

Henle, M. (1986). One man against the Nazis—Wolfgang Kohler. In M. Henle (Ed.), *1879 and all that: Essays in the theory and history of psychology* (pp. 225–237). New York: Columbia University Press. (Original work published 1978)

Henle, M. (1986). Some problems of eclecticism. In M. Henle (Ed.), *1879 and all that: Essays in the theory and history of psychology* (pp. 81–92). New York: Columbia University Press. (Original work published 1957)

Henle, M. (1986). The influence of Gestalt psychology in America. In M. Henle (Ed.), *1879 and all that: Essays in the theory and history of psychology* (pp. 118–132). New York: Columbia University Press. (Original work published 1977)

Henle, M. (1987). Koffka's "*Principles*" after fifty years. *Journal of the History of the Behavioral Sciences, 23,* 14–21.

Herbart, J. F. (1966). A text book in psychology (M. K. Smith, Trans.) In B. Rand (Ed.), *The classical psychologists* (pp. 395–415). Gloucester, MA: Peter Smith. (Original work published 1891)

Hering, E. (1961). Principles of a new theory of the color sense. In R. C. Teevan & R. C. Birney (Eds.), *Color vision* (pp. 28–31). New York: Van Nostrand. (Original work published 1878)

Heron, W. (1957). The pathology of boredom. *Scientific American, 196,* 52–56.

Herrnstein, R. J. (1967). Introduction. In J. B. Watson, *Behavior: An introduction to comparative psychology* (pp. xi–xxi). New York: Holt, Rinehart & Winston.

Herrnstein, R. J. (1977). The evolution of behaviorism. *American Psychologist, 32,* 593–603.

Herrnstein, R. J., & Boring, E. G. (1966). *A source book in the history of psychology.* Cambridge, MA: Harvard University Press.

Hilgard, E. R. (1948). *Theories of learning.* New York: Appleton-Century-Crofts.

Hilgard, E. R. (1953). *Introduction to psychology* (1st ed.). New York: Harcourt, Brace, and Co.

Hilgard, E. R. (1956). *Theories of learning* (2nd ed.). New York: Appleton-Century-Crofts.

Hilgard, E. R. (1964). Introduction. In H. Ebbinghaus, *Memory: A contribution to experimental psychology* (pp. vii–x). New York: Dover.

Hilgard, E. R. (1969). Levels of awareness: Second thoughts on some of William James's ideas. In R. B. MacLeod (Ed.), *William James: Unfinished business* (pp. 45–58). Washington, DC: American Psychological Association.

Hilgard, E. R. (1980). The trilogy of mind: Cognition, affection and conation. *Journal of the History of the Behavioral Sciences, 16,* 107–117.

Hilgard, E. R. (1987). *Psychology in America: An historical survey.* New York: Harcourt Brace Jovanovich.

Hilgard, E. R. (1993). Which psychologists prominent in the second half of this century made lasting contributions to psychological theory? *Psychological Science, 4,* 70–80.

Hilgard, E. R., & Bower, G. H. (1966). *Theories of learning* (3rd ed.). New York: Appleton-Century-Crofts.

Hilgard, E. R., & Bower, G. H. (1975). *Theories of learning* (4th ed.). New York: Appleton-Century-Crofts.

Hilgard, E. R., & Marquis, D. (1948). *Conditioning and learning.* New York: Appleton-Century.

Hillman, J. (1972). *The myth of analysis.* Evanston, IL: Northwestern University Press.

Hindle, E. (1983). Darwin's greatest work. In Cherfas, J. (Ed.), *Darwin up to date* (pp. 67–68). London: IPC Magazines Ltd.

Hirst, W., Neisser, U., & Spelke, E. (1978). Divided attention. *Human Nature, 1,* 54–61.

Hirst, W., Spelke, E. S., Reaves, C. C., Caharack, G., & Neisser, U. (1980). Dividing attention without alternation or automaticity. *Journal of Experimental Psychology: General, 109,* 98–117.

Hochberg, J. (1988). Perception in space. In E. R. Hilgard (Ed.), *Fifty years of psychology: Essays in honor of Floyd Ruch* (pp. 57–73). Glenview, IL: Scott, Foresman.

Hodos, W., & Campbell, C. B. G. (1969). *Scala naturae:* Why there is no theory in comparative psychology. *Psychological Review, 76,* 337–350.

Hoff, E. T. (1992). Psychology in Canada one hundred years ago: James Mark Baldwin at the University of Toronto. *Canadian Psychology, 33,* 683–694.

Hoffding, H. (1955). *A history of modern philosophy* (Vol. 2). New York: Dover. (Original work published 1900)

Hoffman, E. (1988). *The right to be human: A biography of Abraham Maslow.* Los Angeles: Tarcher.

Hofstadter, T. (1979). The vogue of Spencer. In P. Appleman (Ed.), *Darwin* (pp. 389–399). New York: Norton. (Original work published 1955)

Holland, J. G. (1962). Teaching machines: An application of principles from the laboratory. In W. I. Smith & J. W. Moore (Eds.), *Programmed learning: Theory and research* (pp. 34–48). New York: Van Nostrand.

Hollingworth, L. S. (1914a). Variability as related to sex differences in achievement. *American Journal of Sociology, 19,* 510–530.

Hollingworth, L. S. (1914b). *Functional periodicity: An experimental study of the mental and motor abilities of women during menstruation.* New York: Teachers College, Columbia University.

Hollister, A. (1984, October). From one life to two (Htut twins separation surgery). *Life, 7,* 48–52.

Holzman, P. S. (1994). Hilgard on psychoanalysis as science. *Psychological Science, 5,* 190–191.

Horney, K. (1950). *Neurosis and human growth.* New York: Norton.

Hornstein, G. A. (1985, June). *The "quantity objection" in psychophysics: A neglected chapter in the institutionalization of a quantitative perspective in psychology.* Paper presented at the meeting of Cheiron, Philadelphia.

Hornstein, G. A. (1992). The return of the repressed: Psychology's problematic relations with psychoanalysis, 1909–1960. *American Psychologist, 47,* 254–263.

Horton, D. L., & Dixon, T. R. (1968). Traditions, trends, and innovations. In T. R. Dixon & D. L. Horton (Eds.), *Verbal behavior and general behavior theory* (pp. 572–580). Englewood Cliffs, NJ: Prentice-Hall.

Hull, C. L. (1943). *Principles of behavior.* New York: Appleton-Century.

Hull, C. L. (1952). *A behavior system.* Yale: Yale University Press.

Hume, D. (1927). The natural history of religion. In C. W. Hendel (Ed.), *Hume selections* (pp. 253–282). New York: Scribner's. (Original work published 1757)

Hume, D. (1951). An enquiry concerning human understanding. In D. C. Yalden-Thomson (Ed.), *Hume: Theory of knowledge* (pp. 2–176). Edinburgh: Thomas Nelson. (Original work published 1748)

Humphrey, G. (1951). *Thinking: An introduction to its experimental psychology.* London: Methuen.

Hunt, E. (1992). Editor's statement. *Journal of Experimental Psychology, 121,* 403.

Hunt, R. R. (1995). The subtlety of distinctiveness: What von Restorff really did. *Psychonomic Bulletin and Review, 2,* 105–112.

Huntley, H. E. (1970). *The divine proportion.* New York: Dover.

Hurvich. L., & Jameson, D. (1957). An opponent-process theory of color vision. *Psychological Review, 64,* 384–390.

Husserl, E. (1965). *Phenomenology and the crisis of philosophy.* New York: Harper. (Original work published 1910)

I ching, or Book of changes (1967). (Cary F. Baynes, Trans. from the German version of R. Wilhelm). Princeton, NJ: Princeton University Press.

Izard, C. E. (1977). *Human emotions.* New York: Plenum.

Jacobi, J. (1968). *The psychology of C. G. Jung.* London: Routledge & Kegan Paul.

Jacobi, J. (1971). *Complex/Archetype/Symbol.* Princeton: Princeton University Press.

Jacobson, E. (1925). Progressive relaxation. *American Journal of Psychology, 36,* 73–87.

Jacobson, E. (1938). *Progressive relaxation* (2nd ed.). Chicago: University of Chicago Press.

Jacobson, E. (1977). *You must relax* (5th ed.). London: Unwin.

Jacobson, R. (1967). *Selected writings.* The Hague: Mouton.

James, W. (1890). *The principles of psychology* (2 vols.). New York: Holt.

James, W. (1950). *The principles of psychology* (2 vols.). New York: Dover. (Original work published 1890)

James, W. (1958). *The varieties of religious experience.* New York: New American Library. (Original work published 1902)

James, W. (1962). *Psychology: Briefer course.* New York: Collier. (Original work published 1892)

James, W. (1968). Psychological types. In W. S. Sahakian (Ed.), *History of psychology: A source book in systematic psychology* (pp. 216–217). Itaska, IL: Peacock. (Original work published 1908)

Janik, A., & Toulmin, S. (1973). *Wittgenstein's Vienna.* New York: Simon & Schuster.

Jankowicz, A. D. (1987). Whatever became of George Kelly? *American Psychologist, 42,* 481–487.

Jaynes, J. (1973). Animate motion in the 17th century. In M. Henle, J. Jaynes & J. J. Sullivan (Eds.), *Historical conceptions of psychology* (pp. 166–179). New York: Springer.

Jencks, C. (1986). *What is postmodernism?* New York: St. Martin's Press.

Jenkins, J. J. (1974). Remember that old theory of memory? Well, forget it. *American Psychologist, 29,* 785–795.

Jensen, A. R. (1972). *Genetics and education.* New York: Harper & Row.

Johnson, D. (1990). Animal rights and human lives: Time for scientists to right the balance. *Psychological Science, 1,* 213–214.

Johnson, R. C., MacClearn, G. E., Yuen, S., Nagoshi, C. T., Ahern, F. M., & Cole, R. E. (1985). Galton's data a century later. *American Psychologist, 40,* 875–892.

Jones, E. (1963). *The life and work of Sigmund Freud.* New York: Anchor.

Jones, M. C. (1924a). The elimination of children's fears. *Journal of Experimental Psychology, 7,* 383–390.

Jones, M. C. (1924b). A laboratory study of fear: The case of Peter. *Journal of Genetic Psychology, 31,* 308–315.

Joynson, R. B. (1989). *The Burt affair.* London: Routledge.

Judd, D. B. (1970). Introduction. In J. W. von Goethe, *Theory of colors* (C. L. Eastlake, Trans.). Cambridge, MA: MIT Press.

Jung, C. G. (1933). *Modern man in search of a soul.* New York: Harcourt Brace.

Jung, C. G. (1950). Foreword. In *the I ching, or Book of changes* (pp. xxi–xxxix). Princeton, NJ: Princeton University Press.

Jung, C. G. (1956). *Two essays on analytical psychology.* New York: World Publishing. (Original work published 1943)

Jung, C. G. (1965). *Memories, dreams and reflections.* New York: Vintage.

Jung, C. G. (1969). *Analytical psychology: Its theory and practice.* New York: Pantheon.

Jung, C. G. (1973). *Synchronicity: An acausal connecting principle.* Princeton, NJ: Princeton University Press. (Original work published 1960)

Jung, C. G. (1974). Psychoanalysis and association experiments. In C. G. Jung, *The psychoanalytic years* (pp. 3–32). Princeton: Princeton University Press. (Original work published 1904)

Jung, C. G. (1976). *Psychological types* (A revision by R. F. C. Hull of the translation by H. G. Baynes). Princeton, NJ: Princeton University Press. (Original work published 1921)

Kahneman, D. (1968). Method, findings, and theory in studies of visual masking. *Psychological Bulletin, 69,* 404–425.

Kaltenmark, M. (1969). *Lao Tzu and Taoism.* Stanford, CA: Stanford University Press

Kamin, L. J. (1974). *The science and politics of IQ.* New York: Wiley.

Kamin, L. J. (1977). Letter. *Bulletin of the British Psychological Society, 30,* 259.

Kant, I. (1950). *Prolegomena to any future metaphysics.* Indianapolis: Bobbs-Merrill. (Original work published 1783)

Kant, I. (1960). *Observations on the beautiful and sublime.* (J. T. Goldthwait, Trans.). Berkeley: University of California Press. (Original work published 1763)

Kant, I. (1965). *Critique of pure reason* (N. K. Smith, Trans.). New York: St. Martin's Press. (Original work published 1787)

Kant, I. (1968). *Selective pre-critical writings and correspondence with Beck* (G. B. Kerferd and D. E. Walford, Trans.). Manchester, UK: Manchester University Press. (Original work published 1768)

Kaplan, B. (1992). Strife of systems: Tension between organismic and developmental points of view. *Theory and Psychology, 2,* 431–443.

Kaplan, B., & Wapner, S. (1960). Introductory remarks. In B. Kaplan & S. Wapner (Eds.), *Perspectives in psychological theory* (pp. 13–19). New York: International Universities Press.

Kaplan, C. A., & Simon, H. A. (1990). In search of insight. *Cognitive Psychology, 22,* 374–419.

Kaplan, E. (1983). Process and achievement revisited. In S. Wapner & B. Kaplan (Eds.), *Toward a holistic developmental psychology.* Hillsdale, NJ: Erlbaum.

Katona, G. (1967). *Organizing and memorizing.* New York: Hafner. (Original work published 1940)

Keegan, R. T., & Gruber, H. E. (1983). Love, death, and continuity in Darwin's thinking. *Journal of the History of the Behavioral Sciences, 19,* 15–30.

Keller, E. F. (1985). *Reflections on gender and science.* New Haven: Yale University Press.

Keller, F. S. (1991). Burrhus Frederic Skinner (1904–1990). *Journal of the History of the Behavioral Sciences, 27,* 3–6.

Kellman, P., & Spelke, E. S. (1983). Perception of partly occluded objects in infancy. *Cognitive Psychology, 15,* 483–524.

Kelly, G. A. (1955). *The psychology of personal constructs.* New York: Norton.

Kelly, G. A. (1965). The threat of aggression. *Journal of Humanistic Psychology, 5,* 195–201.

Kelly, G. A. (1969a). Humanistic methodology in psychological research. In B. Maher (Ed.), *Clinical psychology and personality: The selected papers of George Kelly* (pp. 133–146). New York: Wiley.

Kelly, G. A. (1969b). The autobiography of a theory. In B. Maher (Ed.), *Clinical psychology and personality: The selected papers of George Kelly* (pp. 46–65). New York: Wiley.

Kent, D. (1992, September). E. Gibson, A. Newell receive National Medal of Science. *APS Observer, 5,* pp. 1, 14–15.

Kent, D. (1993). Accomplished at 5, APS remains on track. *APS Observer, 6,* 1, 4, 14, pp. 28–31.

Kepler, J. (1966). *The six-cornered snowflake.* Oxford: Oxford University Press. (Original work published 1611)

Kevles, D. J. (1985). *In the name of eugenics.* New York: Knopf.

Keynes, J. M. (1956). Newton, the man. In J. R. Newman (Ed.), *The world of mathematics* (pp. 277–285). New York: Simon & Schuster.

Kierkegaard, S. (1959). *Either/Or.* New York: Anchor Books.

Kierkegaard, S. (1959). *Fear and trembling* and *The sickness unto death.* New York: Anchor Books. (Original works published 1843 and 1849)

Kiesler, D. J. (1983). The 1982 interpersonal circle: A taxonomy for complementarity in human transactions. *Psychological Review, 90,* 185–214.

Kihlstrom, J. F. (1987). The cognitive unconscious. *Science, 237,* 1445–1452.

Kihlstrom, J. F. (1994). Ernest R. Hilgard: A life in psychology. *Psychological Science, 5,* 179–180.

Kihlstrom, J. F., & McConkey, K. M. (1990). William James and hypnosis: A centennial reflection. *Psychological Science, 1,* 174–178.

Kimball, M. M. (1994). The worlds we live in: Gender similarities and differences. *Canadian Psychology, 35,* 388–404.

Kimble, G. A. (1961). *Hilgard and Marquis' conditioning and learning* (2nd ed.). New York: Appleton-Century-Crofts.

Kimble, G. A. (1990). Mother Nature's bag of tricks is small. *Psychological Science, 1,* 36–41.

Kimble, G. A. (1993). A modest proposal for a minor revolution in the language of psychology. *Psychological Science, 4,* 253–255.

Kirk, G. S., & Raven, J. E. (1957). *The Presocratic philosophers.* London: Cambridge University Press.

Kirsch, I. (1977). Psychology's first paradigm. *Journal of the History of the Behavioral Sciences, 13,* 317–325.

Klein, P., & Westcott, M. R. (1994). The changing character of phenomenological psychology. *Canadian Psychology, 35,* 133–156.

Kline, M. (1962). Introduction. In Helmholtz, H. von, *Popular scientific lectures* (pp. vii–xii). New York: Dover.

Kline, M. (1985). *Mathematics and the search for knowledge.* New York: Oxford University Press.

Knight, I. F. (1984). Freud's "Project": A theory for *Studies on hysteria. Journal of the History of the Behavioural Sciences, 20,* 340–358.

Knox, B. (1993). *The oldest dead white European males.* New York: Norton.

Koch, S. (1992). Psychology's Bridgman vs Bridgman's Bridgman. *Theory and Psychology, 2,* 261–290.

Koestler, A. (1974). *The roots of coincidence.* Bungay, UK: Picador.

Koffka, K. (1935). *Principles of Gestalt psychology.* New York: Harcourt, Brace & World.

Koffka, K. (1959). *The growth of the mind.* Paterson, NJ: Littlefield Adams. (Original work published 1928)

Kohlberg, L. (1982). Moral development. In J. M. Broughton & D. J. Freeman-Moir (Eds.), *The cognitive-developmental psychology of James Mark Baldwin: Current theory and research in genetic epistemology* (pp. 277–325). Norwood, NJ: Ablex.

Kohler, W. (1956). *The mentality of apes.* New York: Vintage. (Original work published 1925)

Kohler, W. (1959). *Gestalt psychology.* New York: Mentor. (Original work published 1947)

Kohler, W. (1960). *Dynamics in psychology.* New York: Grove. (Original work published 1940)

Kohler, W. (1967). Physical gestalten. In W. D. Ellis, (Ed.), *A source book of Gestalt psychology* (pp. 17–53). New York: Humanities. (Original work published 1920)

Kohler, W. (1967). Simple structural functions in the chimpanzee and the chicken. In W. D. Ellis (Ed.), *A source book of Gestalt psychology* (pp. 217–227). New York: Humanities. (Original work published 1918)

Kohler, W. (1969). Gestalt psychology. In D. L. Krantz (Ed.), *Schools of psychology: A symposium.* New York: Appleton-Century-Crofts. (Original work published 1967)

Kohler, W. (1969). *The task of Gestalt psychology.* Princeton: Princeton University Press.

Kohler, W. (1971). Unsolved problems in the field of figural aftereffects. In M. Henle (Ed.), *The selected papers of Wolfgang Kohler* (pp. 274–302). New York: Liveright. (Original work published 1965)

Kohler, W., & Wallach, H. (1944). Figural after-effects: An investigation of visual processes. *Proceedings of the American Philosophical Society, 88,* 269–357.

Korn, J. H., Davis, R., & Davis, S. F. (1991). Historians' and Chairpersons' judgments of eminence among psychologists. *American Psychologist, 46,* 789–792.

Koutstaal, W. (1992). Skirting the abyss: A history of experimental explorations of automatic writing in psychology. *Journal of the History of the Behavioral Sciences, 28,* 5–27.

Koyré, A. (1954). Introduction. In E. Anscombe & P. T. Geach (Eds.), *Descartes: Philosophical writings* (pp. vii–xliv). New York: Thomas Nelson.

Krantz, D. L. (1969). The Baldwin-Titchener controversy: A case study in the functioning and malfunctioning of schools. In D. L. Krantz (Ed.), *Schools of psychology* (pp. 1–19). New York: Appleton-Century-Crofts.

Krasnick, C. L. (1982). "In charge of the loons": A portrait of the London, Ontario Asylum for the Insane in the Nineteenth Century. *Ontario History, 74,* 138–184.

Kraus, O. (1976). Biographical sketch of Franz Brentano. In L. L. McAlister (Ed.), *The philosophy of Brentano* (pp. 1–9). Atlantic Highlands, NJ: Humanities Press. (Original work published 1926)

Krech, D. (1962). Cortical localization of function. In L. Postman (Ed.), *Psychology in the making* (pp. 31–72). New York: Knopf.

Krecz, C. A. (1986). Parts and pieces. *Philosophy and Phenomenological Research, 46,* 381–400.

Kreitler, H., & Kreitler, S. (1972). *The psychology of the arts.* Durham, NC: Duke University Press.

Kubie, L. (1961). *Neurotic distortion of the creative process.* New York: Noonday Press.

Kubovy, M. (1986). *The psychology of perspective and Renaissance art.* New York: Cambridge University Press.

Kuhn, T. S. (1962). *The structure of scientific revolutions.* Chicago: University of Chicago Press.

Kuhn, T. S. (1970). *The structure of scientific revolutions* (2nd ed.). Chicago: University of Chicago Press.

Külpe, O. (1964). The modern psychology of thinking. In Mandler, J. M., & Mandler, G. (Eds.), *Thinking: From association to gestalt* (pp. 208–216). New York: Wiley. (Original work published 1912)

Kvale, S. (Ed.) (1992). *Psychology and postmodernism.* London: Sage.

Laberge, D. L. (1990). Attention. *Psychological Science, 1,* 156–162.

Laberge, D. L. (1994). Hilgard's *Introduction to psychology. Psychological Science, 5,* 184–185.

Ladd-Franklin, C. (1929). *Color and color theories.* New York: Harcourt, Brace.

Lagerwey, J. (1987). *Taoist ritual in Chinese society and history.* New York: Macmillan.

Lakatos, I. (1976). Proofs and refutations. In J. Worral & E. Zahar (Eds.), *Proofs and refutations: The logic of mathematical discovery* (pp. 6–105). Cambridge, UK: Cambridge University Press.

Lamarck, J. B. (1914). *Zoological philosophy* (H. Elliot, Trans.). London: Macmillan. (Original work published 1809)

Landsberger, H. A. (1958). *Hawthorne revisited: Management and worker, its critics and developments in human relations in industry.* Ithaca, NY: Cornell University Press.

Lane, M. (1970). *Introduction to structuralism.* New York: Basic.

Lashley, K. S. (1929). *Brain mechanisms and intelligence.* Chicago: University of Chicago Press.

Lashley, K. S. (1951). The problem of serial order in behavior. In L. A. Jeffress (Ed.), *Cerebral mechanisms in behavior: The Hixon symposium* (pp. 112–146). New York: Wiley.

Lashley, K. S. (1978). Basic neural mechanisms in behavior. In E. R. Hilgard (Ed.), *American psychology in historical perspective* (pp. 265–283). Washington, DC: American Psychological Association. (Original work published 1930)

Lashley, K. S., Chow, K. L., & Semmes, J. (1951). An examination of electrical field theory of cerebral integration. *Psychological Review, 58,* 123–136.

Lau, D. C. (Ed. & Trans.).(1963). *Lao Tsu/Tao te ching.* Baltimore: Penguin Books.

Laudan, L. (1983). The demise of the demarcation problem. In R. S. Cohen & L. Laudan (Eds.), *Physics, philosophy and psychoanalysis* (pp. 111–128). Dordrecht: D. Reidel.

Laughlin, P., Lange, R., & Adamopoulos, J. (1982). Selection strategies for "Master-mind" problems. *Journal of Experimental Psychology: Learning, Memory and Cognition, 8,* 475–483.

Lavie, P., & Hobson, J. A. (1986). Origin of dreams: Anticipation of modern theories in the philosophy and physiology of the eighteenth and nineteenth centuries. *Psychological Bulletin, 100,* 229–240.

Lazarus, R. S. (1984). On the primacy of cognition. *American Psychologist, 39,* 124–129.

Le Corbusier. (1954). *The modulor.* Cambridge, MA: Faber.

Le Ny, J. F. (1964). Conditioned reactions. In P. Fraisse & J. Piaget (Eds.), *Experimental psychology: Its scope and method* (Vol. IV). London: Routledge & Kegan Paul.

Leary, D. (1980). The historical foundation of Herbart's mathematicization of psychology. *Journal of the History of the Behavioral Sciences, 16,* 150–163.

Lederer, S. E. (1985). Hideo Noguchi's luetin experiment and the antivivisectionists. *Isis, 76,* 31–48.

Leeuwenberg, E., & Boselie, F. (1988). Against the likelihood principle in visual form perception. *Psychological Review, 95,* 485–491.

Lefcourt, H. M. (1966). Internal versus external control of reinforcement: A review. *Psychological Bulletin, 65,* 206–220.

Lefcourt, H. M. (1992). Durability and impact of the locus of control construct. *Psychological Bulletin, 112,* 411–414.

Legeza, L. (1973). Introduction to Taoist art. In *Art and Tao: An exhibition of Taoist symbolism in Chinese art.* Durham, UK: University of Durham.

Leonard, G. (1983, December). Abraham Maslow and the new self. *Esquire,* pp. 326–328, 331–332, 335–336.

Lerner, R. M. (1986). *Concepts and theories of human development.* New York: Random House.

Lerner, R. M. (Ed.). (1982). *Developmental psychology: Historical and philosophical perspectives.* Hillsdale, NJ: Erlbaum.

Levi-Straus, C. (1967). *The savage mind.* London: Weidenfeld & Nicholson.

Lewin, K. (1936). *Principles of topological psychology* (F. Heider & G. M. Heider, Trans.). New York: McGraw-Hill.

Lewin, K. (1946). Action research and minority problems. *Journal of Social Issues, 2,* 34–46.

Lewin, K. (1951). *Field theory in social science* (D. Cartwright, Ed.). New York: Harper & Row.

Lewin, K., & Grabbe, P. (1945). Conduct, knowledge and the acceptance of new values. *Journal of Social Issues, 1,* 53–63.

Lindsley, O. (1969). The secret life of William James. In R. B. MacLeod (Ed.), *William James: Unfinished business* (pp. 35–43). Washington, DC: American Psychological Association.

Livingstone, M. S. (1988). Art, illusion and the visual system. *Scientific American, 258,* 78–85.

Locke, J. (1964). *An essay concerning human understanding.* London: Fontana/Collins. (Original work published 1690)

Loehlin, J. C. (1989). Partitioning environmental and genetic contributions to behavioral development. *American Psychologist, 44,* 1285–1292.

Loehlin, J. C. (1992). *Latent variable models* (2nd ed.). Hillsdale, NJ: Lawrence Erlbaum.

Loftus, E. F. (1991). The glitter of everyday memory . . . and the gold. *American Psychologist, 46,* 16–18.

Loftus, E. F., & Loftus, G. R. (1980). On the permanence of stored information in the human brain. *American Psychologist, 35,* 409–420.

Loftus, E. F., & Palmer, J. C. (1974). Reconstruction of automobile destruction: An example of the interaction between language and memory. *Journal of Verbal Learning and Verbal Behavior, 13,* 585–589.

Logan, F. A. (1959). The Hull-Spence approach. In S. Koch (Ed.), *Psychology: A study of a science. Vol. 2. General systematic formulations, learning, and special processes* (pp. 293–358). New York: McGraw-Hill.

Lovejoy, A. O. (1971). *The great chain of being.* Cambridge, MA: Harvard University Press. (Original work published 1936)

Lovelock, J. E. (1987). *Gaia: A new look at life on earth.* New York: Oxford University Press.

Lovie, A. D., & Lovie, P. (1993). Charles Spearman, Cyril Burt, and the origins of factor analysis. *Journal of the History of the Behavioral Sciences, 29,* 308–321.

Lubek, I., & Apfelbaum, E. (1987). Neo-behaviorism and the Garcia effect: A social psychological approach to the history of a paradigm clash. In M. G. Ash & W. R. Woodward (Eds.), *Psychology in twentieth-century thought and society* (pp. 59–91). New York: Cambridge University Press.

Luria, A. R. (1978). Biographical note on L. S. Vygotsky. In L. S. Vygotsky, *Mind in society* (pp. 15–16). Cambridge, MA: Harvard.

Lyell, C. (1969). *Principles of geology* (Vols. 1–3). New York: Johnson Reprint Corp. (Original work published 1830–1833)

Lyell, C. (1979). Principles of geology. In P. Appleman (Ed.), *Darwin: A Norton critical edition* (pp. 10–15). New York: Norton. (Original work published 1853)

Lyons, W. (1983). The transformation of introspection. *British Journal of Social Psychology, 22,* 327–342.

Lyons, W. (1986). *The disappearance of introspection.* Cambridge, MA: MIT Press.

MacIntyre, A. C. (1958). *The unconscious.* London: Routledge & Kegan Paul.

Mackavey, W. R., Malley, J. E., & Stewart, A. J. (1991). Remembering autobiographically consequential experiences: Content analysis of psychologists' accounts of their lives. *Psychology and Aging, 6,* 50–59.

MacLennan, J. H. (1945). *Two solitudes.* New York: Duell, Sloan & Pearce.

MacLeod, C. M. (1992). The Stroop task: The "Gold Standard" of attentional measures. *Journal of Experimental Psychology: General, 121,* 12–15.

MacLeod, R. B. (1969). James as a phenomenologist. In R. B. MacLeod (Ed.), *William James: Unfinished business* (pp. v–ix). Washington, DC: American Psychological Association.

MacLeod, R. B. (1975). *The persistent problems of psychology.* Pittsburgh: Duquesne University Press.

Madigan, S., & O'Hara, R. (1992). Short-term memory at the turn of the century: Mary Whiton Calkins's memory research. *American Psychologist, 47,* 170–174.

Maier, N. R. F., & Schneirla, T. C. (1964). *Principles of animal psychology.* New York: Dover. (Original work published 1935)

Malthus, T. R. (1956). Mathematics of population and food. In J. R. Newman (Ed.), *The world of mathematics* (pp. 1192–1202). New York: Simon & Schuster. (Original work published 1798)

Mancuso, J. C. (1970). *Readings for a cognitive theory of personality.* New York: Holt, Rinehart & Winston.

Mandler, G. (1962). From association to structure. *Psychological Review, 69,* 415–427.

Mandler, G. (1975). *Mind and emotion.* New York: Wiley.

Mandler, G. (1990). William James and the construction of the emotions. *Psychological Science, 1,* 179–180.

Mandler, J. M., & Mandler, G. (Eds.) (1964). *Thinking: From association to gestalt.* New York: Wiley.

Manuel, F. E. (1965). *Shapes of philosophical history.* Stanford: Stanford University Press.

Manuel, F. E. (1966). Toward a psychological history of Utopias. In F. E. Manuel (Ed.), *Utopias and utopian thought* (pp. 69–98). Boston: Houghton Mifflin.

Manuel, F. E. (1968). *A portrait of Isaac Newton.* Cambridge, MA: Harvard University Press.

Manuel, F. E. (1974). *The religion of Isaac Newton.* Oxford: Oxford University Press.

Marcel, A. J. (1983a). Conscious and unconscious perception: Experiments on visual masking and word recognition. *Cognitive Psychology, 15,* 197–237.

Marcel, A. J. (1983b). Conscious and unconscious perception: An approach to the relations between phenomenal experience and perceptual processes. *Cognitive Psychology, 15,* 238–300.

Marcel, A. J., Katz, L., & Smith, M. (1974). Laterality and reading proficiency. *Neuropsychologia, 12,* 131–139.

Marder, B. (1993). Evelyn Fox Keller '57 reflects on gender and science. *Brandeis Review, 12,* 22–25.

Margenau, H. (1954). Introduction. In H. von Helmholtz, *On the sensations of tone* (pp. i–xi). New York: Dover. (Original work published 1885)

Marková, I. (1982). *Paradigms, thought, and language.* Chichester, UK: Wiley.

Marks, L. E. (1984). Psychology and physics: An historical perspective. In M. H. Bornstein (Ed.), *Psychology and its allied disciplines: Vol. 3: The natural sciences* (pp. 229–264). Hillsdale, NJ: Erlbaum.

Markus, H. (1990). On splitting the universe. *Psychological Science, 1,* 181–184.

Marrow, A. J. (1969). *The practical theorist: The life and work of Kurt Lewin.* New York: Basic Books.

Marshall, M. (1990). The theme of quantification and the hidden Weber in the early work of Gustav Theodor Fechner. *Canadian Psychology, 31,* 45–53.

Martindale, A. E., & Martindale, C. (1988). Metaphorical equivalence of elements and temperaments: Empirical studies of Bachelard's theory of imagination. *Journal of Personality and Social Psychology, 55,* 836–848.

Martindale, C. (1984). The pleasures of thought: A theory of cognitive hedonics. *Journal of Mind and Behavior, 5,* 49–80.

Martindale, C., & Moore, K. (1988). Priming, prototypicality, and preference. *Journal of Experimental Psychology: Human Perception and Performance, 14,* 661–670.

Maslow, A. H. (1954). *Motivation and personality.* New York: Harper & Row.

Maslow, A. H. (1961). Existential psychology: What's in it for us? In R. May (Ed.), *Existential Psychology* (pp. 52–60). New York: Random House.

Maslow, A. H. (1962). *Toward a psychology of being.* New York: Van Nostrand.

Maslow, A. H. (1964a). Synergy in the society and in the individual. *Journal of Individual Psychology, 20,* 153–164.

Maslow, A. H. (1964b). *Religions, values and peak-experiences.* Columbus, OH: Ohio State University Press.

Maslow, A. H. (1965a). Humanistic psychology and transcendent experiences. *Journal of Humanistic Psychology, 5,* 219–228.

Maslow, A. H. (1965b). *Eupsychian management.* Homewood, IL: Dorsey.

Maslow, A. H. (1966). *The psychology of science: A reconnaissance.* New York: Harper & Row.

Maslow, A. H. (1971). *The farther reaches of human nature.* New York: Viking.

Masson, J. M. (February, 1984). Freud and the seduction theory. *The Atlantic Monthly,* 33–60.

Matlin, M. W. (1987). *The psychology of women.* New York: Holt, Rinehart & Winston.

May, R. (1950). *The meaning of anxiety.* New York: Ronald Press.

May, R. (1953). *Man's search for himself.* New York: Norton.

May, R. (1958). Existential psychotherapy. In R. May, E. Angel, & H. F. Ellenberger, *Existence: A new dimension in psychiatry and psychology* (pp. 37–91). New York: Basic Books.

May, R. (1965). Intentionality, the heart of human will. *Journal of Humanistic Psychology, 5,* 202–209.

May, R. (1969a). William James's humanism and the problem of the will. In R. B. MacLeod (Ed.), *William James: Unfinished business* (pp. 73–92). Washington, DC: American Psychological Association.

May, R. (1969b). *Love and will.* New York: Norton.

May, R. (Ed.). (1961). *Existential psychology.* New York: Random House.

May, R., Angel, E., & Ellenberger, H. F. (1958). *Existence: A new dimension in psychiatry and psychology.* New York: Basic Books.

Mayer, R. E. (1983). *Thinking, problem solving, cognition.* New York: Freeman.

Mayo, E. B. (1960). *The human problems of an industrial civilization.* New York: Viking Press. (Original work published 1933)

Mayr, E. (1991). The ideological resistance to Darwin's theory of natural selection. *Proceedings of the American Philosophical Society, 135,* 123–139.

Mayr, E. (1994). The advance of science and scientific revolutions. *Journal of the History of the Behavioral Sciences, 30,* 328–334.

Mazur, J. E. (1990). *Learning and behavior* (2nd ed.). Englewood Cliffs, NJ: Prentice-Hall.

McCarley, R. W., & Hobson, J. A. (1977). The neurobiological origins of psychoanalytic dream theory. *American Journal of Psychiatry, 134,* 1211–1221.

McClearn, G. E. (1991). A trans-time visit with Francis Galton. In G. A. Kimble, M. Wertheimer, & C. L. White, *Portraits of pioneers in psychology* (pp. 1–11). Hillsdale, NJ: Erlbaum.

McClelland, J. L., Rumelhart, D. E., & Hinton, G. E. (1986). The appeal of parallel distributed processing. In D. E. Rumelhart & J. L. McClelland (Eds.), *Parallel distributed processing: Explorations in the microstructure of cognition.* (Vol. 1: Foundations) (pp. 3–44). Cambridge, MA: MIT Press.

McCrae, R. R., Costa, P. T., & Piedmont, R. L. (1993). Folk concepts, natural language, and psychological constructs: The California Psychological Inventory and the five-factor model. *Journal of Personality, 61,* 1–26.

McCrary, J. W., & Hunter, W. S. (1953). Serial position curves in verbal learning. *Science, 117,* 131–134.

McGuire, W. (Ed.). (1974). *The Freud/Jung letters.* Princeton, NJ: Princeton University Press.

McKeon, R. (Ed.). (1941). *The basic works of Aristotle.* Oxford: Oxford University Press.

McLaren, A. (1990). *Our own master race.* Toronto: McClelland & Stewart.

Mednick, S. A. (1962). The associative basis of the creative process. *Psychological Review, 69,* 220–227.

Metcalfe, J., & Wiebe, D. (1987). Intuition in insight and non-insight problem solving. *Memory and Cognition, 15,* 238–246.

Meyer, A. E. (1975). *Grandmasters of educational thought.* New York: McGraw-Hill.

Meyer, A., & Orth, J. (1964). The qualitative investigation of associations. In Mandler, J. M., & Mandler, G. (Eds.), *Thinking: From association to gestalt* (pp. 135–143). (Original work published 1901)

Meyer, G. E., & Hilterbrand, K. (1984). Does it pay to be "Bashful"? The seven dwarfs and long term memory. *American Journal of Psychology, 97,* 47–55.

Michotte, A. (1963). *The perception of causality* (T. R. Miles and E. Miles, Trans.). New York: Basic Books.

Mill, J. S. (1986). *The subjection of women.* Buffalo, NY: Prometheus Books. (Original work published 1861)

Miller, A. (1988). Toward a typology of personality styles. *Canadian Psychology, 29,* 263–283.

Miller, G. A. (1953). What is information measurement? *American Psychologist, 8,* 3–11.

Miller, G. A. (1967). The magical number seven, plus or minus two. In G. A. Miller (Ed.), *The psychology of communication: Seven essays* (pp. 14–44). New York: Basic Books. (Original work published 1956)

Miller, G. A. (1956). The magical number seven plus or minus two: Some limits on our capacity for processing information. *Psychological Review, 63,* 81–97.

Miller, G. A. (1964). *Mathematics and psychology.* New York: Wiley.

Miller, G. A. (1970). Psychology as a means of promoting human welfare. In F. F. Korten, S. W. Wood, & J. I. Lacey (Eds.), *Psychology and the problems of society* (pp. 5–21). Washington, DC: American Psychological Association. (Original work published 1969)

Miller, G. A. (1979, June). *A very personal history.* Talk given to Cognitive Science Workshop, MIT, Boston, MA.

Miller, G. A. (1990). The place of language in a scientific psychology. *Psychological Science, 1,* 7–14.

Miller, G. A., Galanter, E. & Pribram, K. (1960). *Plans and the structure of behavior.* New York: Holt, Rinehart & Winston.

Mills, J.A. (1988). The genesis of Hull's *Principles of behavior. Journal of the History of the Behavioral Sciences, 24,* 392–401.

Mills, J. A. (1992). Deconstructing *Constructing the subject. Theory and Psychology, 2,* 248–250.

Milner, P. M. (1993, January). The mind and Donald O. Hebb. *Scientific American, 268,* 124–129.

Mischel, T. (1967). Kant and the possibility of a science of psychology. *The Monist, 51,* 599–622.

Mischel, T. (1969). Scientific and philosophical psychology: An historical introduction. In T. Mischel (Ed.). *Human action* (pp. 1–40). New York: Academic Press.

Mischel, W. (1968). *Personality and assessment.* New York: Wiley.

Morawski, J. G. (1982). Assessing psychology's moral heritage through our neglected Utopias. *American Psychologist, 37,* 1082–1095.

Morawski, J. G. (1988). Impossible experiments and practical constructions: The social bases of psychologists' work. In J. G. Morawski (Ed.), *The rise of experimentation in American psychology* (pp. 72–93). New Haven: Yale University Press.

Morawski, J. G. (1992). There is more to our history of giving: The place of introductory textbooks in American psychology. *American Psychologist, 47,* 161–169.

Morawski, J. G., & Steele, R. S. (1991). The one or the other? Textual analysis of masculine power and feminist empowerment. *Theory and Psychology, 1,* 107–131.

Morgan, C. L. (1968). Lloyd Morgan's canon. In R. J. Herrnstein & E. Boring (Eds.), *A source book in the history of psychology* (pp. 462–468). Cambridge, MA: Harvard University Press. (Original work published 1894)

Morgan, C. L. (1979). The canon of interpretation of animal activity. In R. I. Watson (Ed.), *Basic writings in the history of psychology* (pp. 184–186). New York: Oxford. (Original work published 1894)

Morris, P. E., Jones, S., & Hampson, P. (1978). An imagery mnemonic for the learning of people's names. *British Journal of Psychology, 69,* 335–336.

Moruzzi, G., & Magoun, H. W. (1949). Brain stem reticular formation and activation of the EEG. *EEG Clinical Neurophysiology, 1,* 455–473.

Müller, J. (1964). Of the senses. In W. Dember (Ed.), *Visual perception: The nineteenth century* (pp. 35–70). New York: Wiley. (Original work published 1838)

Mumford, L. (1966). Utopia, the city and the machine. In F. Manuel (Ed.), *Utopias and utopian thought* (pp. 3–24). Boston: Houghton Mifflin.

Mungello, D. E. (1977). *Leibniz and Confucianism, the search for an accord.* Honolulu: University of Hawaii Press.

Murphy, G., & Murphy, L. B. (1968). *Asian psychology.* New York: Basic Books.

Murray, D. J. (1993). A perspective for viewing the history of psychophysics. *Behavioral and Brain Sciences, 16,* 115–186.

Nagel, E. (1960). Methodological issues in psychoanalytic theory. In S. Hook (Ed.), *Psychoanalysis: Scientific method and philosophy* (pp. 38–56). New York: Grove.

Natsoulas, T. (1978). Consciousness. *American Psychologist, 33,* 906–914.

Necker, L. A. (1964). On an apparent change of position in a drawing or engraved figure of a crystal. In W. Dember (Ed.), *Visual perception: The nineteenth century* (pp. 78–83). New York: Wiley. (Original work published 1832)

Needham, J. (1962). *Science and civilization in China* (Vol. 2). Cambridge (UK): Cambridge University Press.

Neimeyer, R. A. (1985). *The development of personal construct psychology.* Lincoln: University of Nebraska Press.

Neisser, U. (1964). The multiplicity of thought. *British Journal of Psychology, 54,* 1–14.

Neisser, U. (1967). *Cognitive psychology.* New York: Appleton-Century-Crofts.

Neisser, U. (1976). *Cognition and reality.* San Francisco: Freeman.

Neisser, U. (1978). Memory: What are the important questions? In M. M. Gruneberg, P. M. Morris & R. N. Sykes (Eds.), *Practical aspects of memory* (pp. 3–24). London: Academic Press.

Neisser, U. (1981). Obituary: James J. Gibson (1904–1979). *American Psychologist, 36,* 214–215.

Neisser, U. (Ed.). (1982). *Memory observed: Remembering in natural contexts.* San Francisco: Freeman.

Newell, A. (1977). On the analysis of human problem solving protocols. In P. N. Johnson-Laird & P. Wason (Eds.), *Thinking: Readings in cognitive science.* Cambridge: Cambridge University Press.

Newell, A. (1985). Duncker on thinking: An inquiry into progress in cognition. In S. Koch & D. Leary (Eds.), *A century of psychology as science: Retrospections and assessments* (pp. 392–419). New York: McGraw-Hill.

Newell, A., & Simon, H. A. (1972). *Human problem solving.* Englewood Cliffs, NJ: Prentice-Hall.

Newell, A., Shaw, J. C., & Simon, H. A. (1958). Chess-playing programs and the problem of complexity. *IBM Journal of Research and Development, 2,* 320–335.

Newton, I. (1952). *Opticks: Or a treatise of the reflections, refractions, inflections & colours of light.* New York: Dover. (Original work published 1730)

Nietzsche, F. (1967). *The will to power* (W. Kaufmann & R. J. Hollingdale, Trans.). New York: Random House.

O'Donnell, J. M. (1979). The crisis of experimentalism in the 1920s: E. G. Boring and his uses of history. *American Psychologist, 34,* 289–295.

O'Hara, R. J. (1992). Telling the tree: Narrative representation and the study of evolutionary history. *Biology and Philosophy, 7,* 135–160.

O'Meara, D. J. (1987). *Pythagoras revived: Mathematics and philosophy in late antiquity.* Oxford: Clarendon Press.

Olton, D. S. (1992). Tolman's cognitive analyses: Predecessors of current approaches in psychology. *Journal of Experimental Psychology: General, 121,* 427–428.

Osgood, C. E. (1952). The nature and measurement of meaning. *Psychological Bulletin, 49,* 197–237.

Osgood, C. E. (1980). Charles E. Osgood. In G. Lindzey (Ed.), *A history of psychology in autobiography* (Vol. 7, pp. 335–393). San Franciso: Freeman.

Osgood, C. E., May, W. H., & Miron, M. S. (1975). *Cross-cultural Universals of Affective Meaning.* Urbana, IL: University of Illinois Press.

Osgood, C. E., & Richards, M. M. (1973). From Yang and Yin to "and" or "but." *Language, 49,* 380–412.

Osgood, C. E., Suci, G. J., & Tannenbaum, P. (1957). *The Measurement of meaning.* Urbana, IL: University of Illinois Press.

Oxford English Dictionary. (1989). (2nd ed.). Oxford, UK: Oxford University Press.

Oxford English Dictionary [Compact Disk] (1992). Oxford: Oxford University Press.

Paivio, A. (1971). *Imagery and verbal processes.* New York: Holt, Rinehart & Winston.

Paivio, A. (1986). *Mental representations.* Oxford: Oxford University Press.

Palmer, S. E. (1990). Modern theories of Gestalt perception. *Mind & Language, 5,* 290–323.

Palmer, S. E. (1992). Common region: A new principle of perceptual grouping. *Cognitive Psychology, 24,* 436–447.

Pastore, N. (1971). *Selective history of visual perception.* New York: Oxford University Press.

Pauli, W. (1955). *The influence of archetypal ideas on the scientific theories of Kepler.* New York: Pantheon.

Pauly, P. J. (1979, December). Psychology at Hopkins: Its rise and fall and rise and fall and . . . *Johns Hopkins Magazine,* pp. 36–41.

Pavlov, I. P. (1928). *Lectures on conditioned reflexes* (W. H. Gantt, Trans.). New York: International Publishers.

Pavlov, I. P. (1960). *Conditioned reflexes* (G. V. Anrep, Ed. and Trans.) New York: Dover. (Original work published 1927)

Payne, D. (1986, November 6). The dirty legacy of brainwashing. *New Scientist,* 28–29.

Pears, D. (1990). *Hume's system: An examination of the first book of the treatise.* Oxford: Oxford University Press.

Pedhazur, E. J. (1982). *Multiple regression in behavioral research.* New York: Holt, Rinehart & Winston.

Pedhazur, E. J., & Schmelkin, L. P. (1991). *Measurement, design and analysis: An integrated approach.* Hillsdale, NJ: Erlbaum.

Pegis, A. C. (Ed.). (1948). *Introduction to Saint Thomas Aquinas.* New York: Modern Library.

Pepper, S. C. (1934). The conceptual framework of Tolman's purposive behaviorism. *Psychological Review, 4,* 108–133.

Pepper, S. C. (1970). *World hypotheses.* Berkeley, CA: University of California Press.

Petrinovich, L., & McGaugh, J. L. (Eds.). (1976). *Knowing, thinking, and believing: Festschrift for Professor David Krech.* New York: Plenum.

Pfungst, O. (1911). *Clever Hans (the horse of Mr. von Osten): A contribution to experimental animal, and human psychology.* New York: Holt.

Philip, J. A. (1966). *Pythagoras and early pythagoreanism.* Toronto: University of Toronto Press.

Philips, D. C., & Orton, R. (1983). The new causal principle of cognitive learning theory: Perspectives on Bandura's "reciprocal determinism." *Psychological Review, 90,* 158–165.

Piaget, J. (1951). The biological problem of intelligence. In D. Rapaport (Ed.), *Organization and pathology of thought* (pp. 176–192). New York: Columbia University Press. (Original work published 1936)

Piaget, J. (1957). *Logic and psychology.* New York: Basic Books.

Piaget, J. (1959). *The language and thought of the child.* London: Routledge and Kegan Paul. (Original work published 1923)

Piaget, J. (1962). *Play, dreams and imitation in childhood* (G. Gattegno & F. M. Hodgson, Trans.). London: Routledge & Kegan Paul.

Piaget, J. (1963). *The origins of intelligence in children* (M. Cook, Trans.). New York: W.W. Norton.

Piaget, J. (1966). *Psychology of intelligence.* Totawa, NJ: Littlefield, Adams.

Piaget, J. (1968a). *Genetic epistemology* (E. Duckworth, Trans.). New York: Columbia University Press.

Piaget, J. (1968b). *On the development of memory and identity* (E. Duckworth, Trans.). Worcester, MA: Clark University Press.

Piaget, J. (1971). *Structuralism.* New York: Harper.

Piaget, J. (1973). *Main trends in psychology.* New York: Harper.

Piaget, J. (1976). The rules of the game of marbles. In J. S. Bruner, A. Jolly, & K. Sylva (Eds.), *Play* (pp. 413–441). New York: Penguin. (Original work published 1965)

Piaget, J., & Inhelder, B. (1969). *The psychology of the child.* New York: Basic Books.

Piaget, J., & Inhelder, B. (1973). *Memory and intelligence* (A. J. Pomerans, Trans.). New York: Basic Books.

Pick, A. (Ed.). (1979). *Perception and its development: A tribute to Eleanor J. Gibson.* Hillsdale, NJ: Erlbaum.

Pick, H.L. (1992). Eleanor J. Gibson: Learning to perceive and perceiving to learn. *Developmental Psychology, 28,* 787–794.

Platt, J. (1973) Social traps. *American Psychologist, 28,* 641–651.

Popper, K. R. (1965). *The logic of scientific discovery.* New York: Harper.

Postman, L. (1962). Repetition and paired-associate learning. *American Journal of Psychology, 75,* 372–389.

Postman, L., & Keppel, G. (Eds.) (1969). *Verbal learning and memory.* Baltimore, MD: Penguin.

Pötzl, O. (1960). The relationship between experimentally induced dream images and indirect vision. *Psychological Issues, 2,* 41–120. (Original work published 1917)

Pressey, S. L. (1926). Simple apparatus which gives test and scores and teaches. *School and Society, 23,* 373–376.

Pressey, S. L. (1962). Development and appraisal of devices providing immediate automatic scoring of objective tests and concomitant self-instruction. In W. I. Smith & J. W. Moore (Eds.), *Programmed learning: Theory and research* (pp. 111–149). New York: Van Nostrand.

Pribram, K. (1981). The brain, the telephone, the thermostat, the computer, and the hologram. *Cognition and Brain Theory, 4,* 105–122.

Pribram, K., & Gill, M. (1976). *Freud's project re-assessed.* London: Hutchinson.

Pritchard, R. M., Heron, W., & Hebb, D. O. (1960). Visual perception approached by the method of stabilized images. *Canadian Journal of Psychology, 14,* 67–77.

Pyke, S., & Agnew, N. M. (1991). *The science game* (5th ed.). Englewood Cliffs, NJ: Prentice-Hall.

Quinn, S. (1987). *A mind of her own: The life of Karen Horney.* New York: Summit Books.

Rancurello, A. C. (1968). *A study of Franz Brentano.* New York: Academic Press.

Randall, J. H. (1953). Introduction. In H. S. Thayer (Ed.), *Newton's philosophy of nature: Selections from his writings* (pp. ix–xvi). New York: Hafner Press.

Rao, C. R. (1992). R. A. Fisher: The founder of modern statistics. *Statistical Science, 7,* 34–48.

Rapaport, D. (1959a). The structure of psychoanalytic theory. In S. Koch (Ed.), *Psychology: A study of a science* (Vol. 3) (pp. 55–183). New York: McGraw-Hill.

Rapaport, D. (1959b). Introduction. *Psychological Issues, 1* (1, Monograph 1), 5–17.

Raphelson, A. C. (1982). The history course as the capstone of the psychology curriculum. *Journal of the History of the Behavioral Sciences, 18,* 279–285.

Rawson, P., & Legeza, L. (1973). *Tao: The Chinese philosophy of time and change.* London: Thames & Hudson.

Reber, A. S. (1985). *Dictionary of psychology.* New York: Penguin.

Reichenbach, H. (1938). *Experience and prediction.* Chicago: University of Chicago Press.

Reisman, J. M. (1991). *A history of clinical psychology.* New York: Hemisphere.

Richards, R. J. (1983). Why Darwin delayed, or interesting problems and models in the history of science. *Journal of the History of the Behavioral Sciences, 19,* 45–53.

Robins, R. W., & Craik, K. H. (1994). A more appropriate test of the Kuhnian displacement thesis. *American Psychologist, 49,* 815–916.

Robinson, D. N. (1977). Preface. In G. J. Romanes, *Animal intelligence* (pp. xxi–xxxv). New York: University Publications.

Robinson, D. N. (1989). *Aristotle's psychology.* New York: Columbia University Press.

Robinson, E. S. (1964). *Association theory today.* New York: Hafner. (Original work published 1932)

Rock, I. (1957). The role of repetition in associative learning. *American Journal of Psychology, 70,* 186–193.

Rock, I. (1983). *The logic of perception.* Cambridge, MA: MIT Press.

Rock, I. (1992). Comment on Asch & Witkin's *Studies in space orientation II. Journal of Experimental Psychology: General, 121,* 404–406.

Rock, I., & Heimer, W. (1959). Further evidence of one-trial associative learning. *American Journal of Psychology, 72,* 1–16.

Rock, I., & Palmer, S. E. (1990, December). The legacy of Gestalt psychology. *Scientific American, 236,* pp. 84–90.

Rockefeller, S. C. (1994). Comment. In A. Gutman (Ed.), *Multiculturalism: Examining the politics of recognition* (pp. 87–103). Princeton: Princeton University Press.

Rodgers, J. L. (1990). About APS: Structural models of the American Psychological Society at birth. *Psychological Science, 1,* 85–96.

Roediger, H. L. (Ed.). (1985). Ebbinghaus centennial. *Journal of Experimental Psychology: Learning, Memory and Cognition, 11,* 414–435.

Roediger, H. L., & Crowder, R. G. (1982). A serial position effect in recall of United States Presidents. In U. Neisser (Ed.), *Memory observed* (pp. 230–237). San Francisco: Freeman.

Rogers, C. R. (1951). *Client-centered therapy.* Boston: Houghton Mifflin.

Rogers, C. R. (1952). "Client-centered" psychotherapy. *Scientific American, 187,* 66–74.

Rogers, C. R. (1959). A theory of therapy, personality, and interpersonal relationships, as developed in the client-centered framework. In S. Koch (Ed.), *Psychology: A study of a science* (Vol. 3) (pp. 184–256). New York: McGraw-Hill.

Rogers, C. R. (1961a). Two divergent trends. In R. May (Ed.), *Existential Psychology* (pp. 85–93). New York: Random House.

Rogers, C. R. (1961b). *On becoming a person.* Boston: Houghton Mifflin.

Rogers, C. R. (1964a). Some questions and challenges facing a humanistic psychology. *Journal of Humanistic Psychology, 5,* 1–5.

Rogers, C. R. (1964b). Toward a science of the person. In T. W. Wann (Ed.), *Behaviorism and phenomenology: Contrasting bases for modern psychology* (pp. 109–140). Chicago: University of Chicago Press.

Rogers, C. R. (1965). Some thoughts regarding the current philosophy of the behavioral sciences. *Journal of Humanistic Psychology, 5,* 182–194.

Rogers, C. R. (1967). Carl R. Rogers. In E. G. Boring & G. Lindzey (Eds.), *A history of psychology in autobiography* (Vol. 5, pp. 343–384). New York: Appleton-Century-Crofts.

Rogers, C. R. (1970). *On encounter groups.* New York: Harper & Row.

Rogers, C. R. (1970). Towards a theory of creativity. In P. E. Vernon (Ed.), *Creativity* (pp. 137–151). Harmondsworth, UK: Penguin. (Original work published 1954)

Rogers, C. R. (1978). Some observations on the organization of personality. In E. R. Hilgard (Ed.), *American psychology in historical perspective* (pp. 417–434). Washington, DC: American Psychological Association. (Original work published 1947)

Rogers, C. R. (1980). *A way of being.* Boston: Houghton Mifflin.

Rogers, T. B. (1989). Operationism in psychology: A discussion of contextual antecedents and an historical interpretation of its longevity. *Journal of the History of the Behavioral Sciences, 25,* 139–153.

Rogers, T. B. (1992). Danziger and psychological testing. *Theory and Psychology, 2,* 251–254.

Rogoff, B., & Wertsch, J. (1984). *Children's learning in the zone of proximal development.* San Francisco: Jossey-Bass.

Romanes, G. J. (1977). *Animal intelligence.* New York: University Publications. (Original work published 1883)

Ronan, C. A., & Needham, J. (1978). *The shorter science and civilization in China.* New York: Cambridge University Press.

Rosch, E. H. (1978). Principles of categorization. In E. Rosch & B. Lloyd (Eds.), *Cognition and categorization* (pp. 27–48). Hillsdale, NJ: Erlbaum.

Rosen, R. D. (1977). *Psychobabble: Fast talk and quick cure in the era of feeling.* New York: Atheneum.

Rosenberg, S. (1993). Chomsky's theory of language: Some recent observations. *Psychological Science, 4,* 15–19.

Rosenblith, J. F. (1992). A singular career: Nancy Bayley. *Developmental Psychology, 28,* 747–758.

Rosenthal, R. (1966). *Experimenter effects in behavioral research.* New York: Appleton-Century Crofts.

Rosenthal, R. (1967). Covert communication in the psychological experiment. *Psychological Bulletin, 67,* 356–367.

Rosnow, R. L., & Rosenthal, R. (1989). Statistical procedures and the justification of knowledge in psychological science. *American Psychologist, 44,* 1276–1284.

Ross, B. (1992). William James: Spoiled child of American psychology. In Kimble, G. A., Wertheimer, M., & White, C. L., *Portraits of pioneers in psychology* (pp. 13–26). Hillsdale, NJ: Erlbaum.

Ross, D. (1993). An historian's view of American Social Science. *Journal of the History of the Behavioral Sciences, 29,* 99–111.

Ross, D. G. (1972). *Stanley Hall: The psychologist as prophet.* Chicago: University of Chicago Press.

Rossotti, H. (1983). *Colour.* Harmondsworth, UK: Penguin.

Roth, N. (1962). Freud and Galton. *Comprehensive Psychiatry, 3,* 77–83.

Rotter, J. (1954). *Social learning and clinical psychology.* Englewood Cliffs, NJ: Prentice-Hall.

Rotter, J. (1966). *Generalized expectancies for internal versus external control of reinforcement.* Psychological Monographs, no. 80 (1, Whole No. 609).

Rozin, P. (1990). Social and moral aspects of food and eating. In I. Rock (Ed.), *Legacy of Solomon Asch: Essays in cognition and social psychology* (pp. 97–110). Hillsdale, NJ: Erlbaum.

Rozin, P., & Fallon, A. E. (1987). A perspective on disgust. *Psychological Review, 94,* 23–41.

Rozin, P., Fallon, A. E., & Augostoni-Ziskind, M. (1985). The child's conception of food: The development of contamination sensitivity to "disgusting" substances. *Developmental Psychology, 21,* 1075–1079.

Rozin, P., Millman, L., & Nemeroff, C. (1986). Operation of the laws of sympathetic magic in disgust and other domains. *Journal of Personality and Social Psychology, 50,* 703–712.

Rubin, D. C., Wetzler, S. E., & Nebes, R. D. (1986). Autobiographical memory across the lifespan. In D. C. Rubin (Ed.), *Autobiographical memory* (pp. 202–221). Cambridge, UK: Cambridge University Press.

Rubin, E. (1958). Figure and ground. In D. C. Beardslee & M. Wertheimer (Eds.), *Readings in perception* (pp. 194–203). Princeton, NJ: Van Nostrand. (Original work published 1915)

Russell, B. (1945). *A history of Western philosophy.* New York: Simon & Schuster.

Russell, J. A. (1980). A circumplex model of affect. *Journal of Personality and Social Psychology, 39,* 1161–1178.

Rycroft, C. (1969, January 16). All in the mind. *New York Review of Books,* p. 4.

Ryle, A. (1975). *Frames and cages.* Sussex: Sussex University Press.

Ryle, G. (1949). *The concept of mind.* New York: Barnes & Noble.

Sacks, O. (1974). *Awakenings.* Garden City, NY: Doubleday.

Saltz, E. (1971). *The cognitive bases of human learning.* Homewood IL: Dorsey.

Sambursky, S. (1956). *The physical world of the Greeks.* London: Routledge & Kegan Paul.

Samelson, F. (1992, June). *On resurrecting the reputation of Sir Cyril [Burt].* Paper presented at the meeting of Cheiron. Windsor, ON.

Samelson, F. (1993, June). *Grappling with fraud charges in science, or: Will the Burt Affair ever end?* Paper presented at the meeting of Cheiron. Durham, NH.

Sampson, E. E. (1993). Identity politics. *American Psychologist, 48,* 1219–1230.

Sapiro, V. (1992). *A vindication of political virtue: The political theory of Mary Wollstonecraft.* Chicago: University of Chicago Press.

Sappington, A. A. (1990). Recent psychological approaches to the free will versus determinism issue. *Psychological Bulletin, 108,* 19–29.

Sartre, J.-P. (1957). *Existentialism and human emotions.* New York: Philosophical Library.

Sartre, J.-P. (1962). *Sketch for a theory of the emotions.* London: Methuen. (Original work published 1939)

Sartre, J.-P. (1966). *Being and nothingness.* New York: Washington Square Press. (Original work published 1943)

Sayers, J. (1991). *Mothers of psychoanalysis.* New York: Norton.

Scarborough, E., & Furomoto, L. (1987). *Untold lives: The first generation of American women psychologists.* New York: Columbia University Press.

Schachter, S. (1959). *The psychology of affiliation.* Stanford, CA: Stanford University Press.

Schlick, M. (1962). Meaning and verification. In W. Barrett & H. D. Aiken (Eds.), *Philosophy in the twentieth century* (Vol. 3) (pp. 28–51). New York: Random House. (Original work published 1938)

Schlosberg, H. (1952). The description of facial expressions in terms of two dimensions. *Journal of Experimental Psychology, 44,* 229–237.

Schmeidler, G. (1992). William James: Pioneering ancestor of modern parapsychology. In M. Donnelly, *Reinterpreting the legacy of William James* (pp. 339–352). Washington, DC: American Psychological Association.

Schneirla, T. C. (1957). The concept of development in comparative psychology. In D. B. Harris (Ed.), *The concept of development* (pp. 78–108). Minneapolis: University of Minnesota Press.

Schrag, C. O. (1967). Phenomenology, ontology, and history in the philosophy of Heidegger. In J. J. Kockelmans (Ed.), *Phenomenology* (pp. 277–293). New York: Anchor.

Schull, J. (1992). Selection—James's principal principle. In M. Donnelly, *Reinterpreting the legacy of William James* (pp. 139–152). Washington, DC: American Psychological Association.

Seaman, J. D. (1984). On phi-phenomena. *Journal of the History of the Behavioral Sciences, 20,* 3–8.

Sears, F. W., & Zemansky, M. W. (1970). *University physics.* Reading, MA: Addison-Wesley.

Sedgwick, H. A. (1980). The geometry of spatial layout in pictorial representation. In M. A. Hagen (Ed.), *The perception of pictures* (pp. 33–90). New York: Academic Press.

Segal, I., & Lachman, R. (1972). Complex behavior or higher mental process: Is there a paradigm shift. *American Psychologist, 27,* 46–55.

Senders, V. L. (1958). *Measurement and statistics.* New York: Oxford.

Shakow, D. (1969). Psychoanalysis. In D. L. Krantz (Ed.), *Schools of psychology* (pp. 87–122). New York: Appleton-Century-Crofts.

Shakow, D., & Rapaport, D. (1964). The influence of Freud on American psychology. *Psychological Issues, 4* (1, Monograph 13).

Shannon, C., & Weaver, W. (1949). *The mathematical theory of communication.* Urbana, IL: University of Illinois Press.

Shapiro, K. J., & Alexander, I. E. (1975). *The experience of introversion.* Durham, NC: Duke University Press.

Shelley, M. (1963). *Frankenstein.* New York: NAL Penguin. (Original work published 1818)

Shepard, R. (1978). The mental image. *American Psychologist, 33,* 125–137.

Shiffrin, R. M. & Schneider, W. (1977). Controlled and automatic human information processing: II. Perceptual learning, automatic attending, and a general theory. *Psychological Review, 84,* 155–171.

Shortt, S. E. D. (1986). *Victorian lunacy: Richard M. Bucke and the practice of late nineteenth-century psychiatry.* Cambridge, UK: Cambridge University Press

Siegler, R. S. (1986). *Children's thinking.* Englewood Cliffs, NJ: Prentice-Hall.

Simmel, M. L. (1956). Phantoms in patients with leprosy and in elderly digital amputees. *American Journal of Psychology, 69,* 529–545.

Simmel, M. L. (1968). Kurt Goldstein 1878–1965. In M. L. Simmel (Ed.), *The reach of mind* (pp. 3–12). New York: Springer.

Simon, H. A. (1954). Spurious correlation: A causal interpretation. *Journal of the American Statistical Association, 49,* 467–479.

Simon, H. A. (1967). Motivational and emotional controls of cognition. *Psychological Review, 74,* 29–39.

Simon, H. A. (1975). The functional equivalence of problem solving skills. *Cognitive Psychology, 7,* 268–288.

Simon, H. A. (1980). Herbert A. Simon. In G. Lindzey (Ed.), *A history of psychology in autobiography* (Vol. 7, pp. 435–472). San Francisco: Freeman.

Simon, H. A. (1981). *The sciences of the artificial* (2nd ed.). Cambridge, MA: MIT Press.

Simon, H. A. (1991). *Models of my life.* New York: Basic Books.

Simon, H. A. (1992). What is an "explanation" of behavior? *Psychological Science, 1992,* 150–161.

Simon, L. (1992). Reform starts at the dinner table. *Brandeis Review, 11,* 34–39.

Simonton, D. K. (1984). *Genius, creativity and leadership.* Cambridge, MA: Harvard University Press.

Simonton, D. K. (1988). *Scientific genius.* New York: Cambridge University Press.

Skinner, B. F. (1938). *The behavior of organisms.* New York: Appleton-Century-Crofts.

Skinner, B. F. (1945a). The operational analysis of psychological terms. *Psychological Review, 52,* 270–277.

Skinner, B. F. (1945b, October). Baby in a box. *Ladies Home Journal, 62,* 30–31; 135–136; 138.

Skinner, B. F. (1948). *Walden Two.* New York: Macmillan

Skinner, B. F. (1954). Behaviorism at fifty. In T. W. Wann (Ed.), *Behaviorism and phenomenology: Contrasting bases for modern psychology* (pp. 79–97). Chicago: University of Chicago Press.

Skinner, B. F. (1956). A case history in scientific method. *American Psychologist, 11,* 221–233.

Skinner, B. F. (1957). *Verbal behavior.* New York: Appleton-Century.

Skinner, B. F. (1961). Freud's psychoanalytic theory. In P. K. Frank (Ed.), *The validation of psychoanalytic theory* (pp. 110–121). New York: Collier. (Original work published 1953)

Skinner, B. F. (1962). The science of learning and the art of teaching. In W. I. Smith & J. W. Moore (Eds.), *Programmed learning: Theory and research* (pp. 19–33). New York: Van Nostrand.

Skinner, B. F. (1979). *The shaping of a behaviorist.* New York: Knopf.

Skinner, B. F. (1980). *Notebooks.* Englewood Cliffs, NJ: Prentice-Hall.

Skinner, B. F. (1984). Selection by consequences. *Behavioral and Brain Sciences, 7,* 477–481.

Skinner, B. F. (1986). What is wrong with daily life in the Western world? *American Psychologist, 41,* 568–574.

Skinner, B. F. (1987). *Upon further reflection.* Englewood Cliffs, NJ: Prentice-Hall.

Slamecka, N. J. (Ed.). (1967). *Human learning and memory.* Oxford: Oxford University Press.

Slamecka, N. J. (1985). Ebbinghaus: Some associations. *Journal of Experimental Psychology, 11,* 414–435.

Smith, C. U. M. (1987). David Hartley's Newtonian neuropsychology. *Journal of the History of the Behavioral Sciences, 23,* 123–138.

Smith, H. C. (1973). *Sensitivity training: The scientific understanding of individuals.* New York: McGraw-Hill.

Smith, M. B. (1994). Selfhood at risk: Postmodern perils and the perils of postmodernism. *American Psychologist, 49,* 405–411.

Snyderman, M., & Herrnstein, R. J. (1983). Intelligence tests and the immigration act of 1924. *American Psychologist, 38,* 986–995.

Sokal, M. M. (1984). The Gestalt psychologists in behaviorist America. *American Historical Review, 89,* 1240–1263.

Sokal, M. M. (1990). G. Stanley Hall and the institutional character of Clark University. *Journal of the History of the Behavioral Sciences, 26,* 114–124.

Sokolov, A. N. (1969). Studies of the speech mechanisms of thinking. In M. Cole & I. Maltzman, *A handbook of contemporary Soviet psychology* (pp. 531–573). New York: Basic Books.

Soyland, A. J. (1994). After Lashley: Neuropsychology, metaphors, promissory notes. *Theory and Psychology, 4,* 227–244.

Spearman, C. (1904). "General intelligence" objectively determined and measured. *American Journal of Psychology, 15,* 201–292.

Spearman, C. (1970). *The abilities of man: Their nature and measurement.* New York: AMS Press. (Original work published 1932)

Spelke, E., Hirst, W., & Neisser, U. (1976). Skills of divided attention. *Cognition, 4,* 215–230.

Spence, J. T. (1987). Centrifugal versus centripetal tendencies in psychology: Will the center hold? *American Psychologist, 42,* 1052–1054.

Spence, K. W. (1937). The differential response in animals to stimuli varying within a single dimension. *Psychological Review, 44,* 430–444.

Spence, K. W. (1944). The nature of theory construction in contemporary psychology. *Psychological Review, 51,* 47–68.

Spence, K. W. (1956). *Behavior theory and conditioning.* New Haven: Yale.

Spence, K. W. (1960). *Behavior theory and learning: Selected papers.* Englewood Cliffs, NJ: Prentice-Hall.

Spencer, H. (1880). *First principles* (5th ed.). New York: A. L. Burt. (Original work published 1862)

Spencer, H. (1897). *Principles of psychology.* New York: Appleton.

Spencer, H. (1968). Life as a continuous adjustment. In W. S. Sahakian (Ed.), *History of psychology* (pp. 181–182). Itasca, IL: Peacock. (Original work published 1855)

Sperber, D., & Wilson, D. (1986). *Relevance: Communication and cognition.* Cambridge, MA: Harvard University Press.

Sperling, G. (1960). *The information available in brief visual presentations.* Psychological Monographs, Vol. 74, No. 11.

Sperry, R. W., & Milner, N. (1955). Pattern perception following the insertion of mica plates into visual cortex. *Journal of Comparative and Physiological Psychology, 48,* 463–469.

Staeuble, I. (1983, June). *William Stern's research program of differential psychology: Why did psychotechnics outstrip psychodiagnostics?* Paper presented at the annual meeting of Cheiron. Toronto, ON.

Stam, H. J. (1990). Rebuilding the ship at sea: The historical and theoretical problems of constructionist epistemologies in psychology. *Canadian Psychology, 31,* 239–261.

Stam, H. J. (1992). Deconstructing the subject: Banishing the ghost of Boring. *Contemporary Psychology, 37,* 629–632.

Steinem, G. (1994). What if Freud were Phyllis? or, The Watergate of the Western World. In *Moving beyond words* (pp. 32–92). New York: Knopf.

Steinfeld, G. J., & Rock, I. (1968). Control for item selection and familiarization in the formation of associations. *American Journal of Psychology, 61,* 42–46.

Stern, W. (1967). On the mental quotient. In R. J. Herrnstein & E. Boring (Eds.), *A source book in the history of psychology* (pp. 450–453). Cambridge, MA: Harvard University Press. (Original work published 1912)

Sternberg, R. J. (1984). Preface. In R. J. Sternberg (Ed.), *Mechanisms of cognitive development* (pp. vii–ix). New York: Freeman.

Sternberg, R. J. (1992). Ability tests, measurements, and markets. *Journal of Educational Psychology, 84,* 134–140.

Stevens, G., & Gardner, S. (1982). *The women of psychology* (Vol. I). Cambridge, MA: Schenkman.

Stevens, P. S. (1974). *Patterns in nature.* Boston: Little, Brown.

Stevenson, L. (1974). *Seven theories of human nature.* New York: Oxford University Press.

Stigler, S. M. (1986). *The history of statistics: The measurement of uncertainty before 1900.* Cambridge, MA: Harvard University Press.

Stillings, N. A., Feinstein, M. H., Garfield, J. L., Rissland, E. L., Rosenbaum, D. A., Weisler, S. E., and Baker-Ward, L. (1987). *Cognitive science: An introduction.* Cambridge, MA: MIT Press.

Stone, I. (1983). The death of Darwin. In Cherfas, J. (Ed.), *Darwin up to date* (pp. 68–69). London: IPC Magazines Ltd.

Stratton, G. M. (1964). Vision without inversion of the retinal image. In W. Dember (Ed.), *Visual perception: The nineteenth century* (pp. 143–154). New York: Wiley. (Original work published 1897)

Strauss, S. (Ed.). (1988). *Ontogeny, phylogeny and historical development.* Norwood, NJ: Ablex.

Street, W. R. (1994). *A chonology of noteworthy events in American psychology.* Washington, DC: American Psychological Association.

Stricker, L. J., & Ross, J. (1964). An assessment of some structural properties of the Jungian personality typology. *Journal of Abnormal and Social Psychology, 68,* 62–71.

Stroop, J. R. (1992). Studies of interference in serial verbal reactions. *Journal of Experimental Psychology: General, 121,* 15–23. (Original work published 1935)

Suedfeld, P., & Coren, S. (1989). Perceptual isolation, sensory deprivation, and rest: Moving introductory psychology texts out of the 1950s. *Canadian Psychology, 30,* 17–29.

Sulloway, F. J. (1979). *Freud: Biologist of the mind.* New York: Basic Books.

Suls, J. M., & Rosnow, R. L. (1988). Concerns about artifacts in psychological experiments. In J. Morawski (Ed.), *The rise of experimentation in American psychology* (pp. 163–187). New Haven: Yale University Press.

Suzuki, D. T. (1956). *Zen Buddhism: Selected writings of D. T. Suzuki* (W. Barrett, Ed.). Garden City, NY: Doubleday.

Tanner, N. M. (1983). Hunters, gatherers and sex roles in space and time. *American Anthropologist, 85,* 335–341.

Tart, C. T. (1975). *Transpersonal psychologies.* New York: Harper & Row.

Tavolga, W. N. (1969). *Principles of animal behavior.* New York: Harper & Row.

Taylor, E. (1994, Fall/Winter). Rollo May (1909–1994). *The Cheiron Newsletter, 22,* pp. 6–7.

Taylor, E., & Butler, R. A. (1986, June). *Was Lightner Witmer the "founder" of modern clinical psychology?* Paper presented at the meeting of Cheiron, Guelph, ON.

Taylor, F. W. (1967). *The principles of scientific management.* New York: Norton. (Original work published 1911)

Terman, L. M. (1948).The measurement of intelligence. In W. Dennis (Ed.), *Readings in the history of psychology* (pp. 485–496). New York: Appleton-Century-Crofts. (Original work published 1916)

Thelen, E., & Adolph, K. E. (1992). Arnold L. Gesell: The paradox of Nature and nurture. *Developmental Psychology, 28,* 368–380.

Thompson, D. W. (1929). Excess and defect: or the little more and the little less. *Mind, 38,* 43–55.

Thompson, D. W. (1942). *On growth and form.* Cambridge, UK: Cambridge University Press.

Thorndike, E. L. (1917). Individual differences in judgements of the beauty of simple forms. *Psychological Review, 24,* 147–153.

Thorndike, E. L. (1948). Animal intelligence. In W. Dennis (Ed.), *Readings in the history of psychology* (pp. 377–387). New York: Appleton-Century-Crofts. (Original work published 1898)

Thorndike, E. L. (1949) *Selected writings from a connectionist's psychology.* New York: Appleton-Century-Crofts.

Thorndike, E. L. (1949). Edward Lee Thorndike. In E. L. Thorndike, *Selected writings from a connectionist's psychology* (pp. 1–11). New York: Appleton-Century-Crofts. (Original work published 1936)

Thorndike, E. L. (1949). The constitution of arithmetic abilities. In E. L. Thorndike, *Selected writings from a connectionist's psychology* (pp. 165–175). New York: Appleton-Century-Crofts. (Original work published 1922)

Thorndike, E. L. (1949). The law of effect. In E. L. Thorndike, *Selected writings from a connectionist's psychology* (pp. 13–26). New York: Appleton-Century-Crofts. (Original work published 1933)

Thorndike, E. L. (1966). *Human learning.* Cambridge, MA: MIT Press. (Original work published 1931)

Thorndike, E. L. (1979). Animal and human learning by trial and error. In R. I. Watson (Ed.), *Basic writings in the history of psychology* (pp. 255–262). New York: Oxford. (Original work published 1898)

Thorndike, E. L., & Lorge, I. (1944). *The teacher's word book of 30,000 words.* New York: Columbia University Press.

Thorndike, E. L., & Woodworth, R. S. (1948). The influence of improvement in one mental function upon the efficiency of other functions. In W. Dennis (Ed.), *Readings in the history of psychology* (pp. 388–398). New York: Appleton-Century-Crofts. (Original work published 1901)

Thorndike, R. L. (1954). The psychological value system of psychologists. *American Psychologist, 9,* 787–790.

Thurstone, L. L. (1938). *Primary mental abilities. Chicago: University of Chicago Press.*

Thurstone, L. L. (1944). *A factorial study of perception.* Chicago: University of Chicago Press.

Thurstone, L. L. (1965). Psychological implications of factor analysis. In A. Anastasi (Ed.), *Individual differences* (pp. 58–64). New York: Wiley. (Original work published 1948)

Thurstone, L. L. (1978). The vectors of mind. In E. R. Hilgard (Ed.), *American psychology in historical perspective* (pp. 285–308). Washington, DC: American Psychological Association. (Original work published 1934)

Titchener, E. B. (1966). From *A text-book of psychology.* In R. J. Herrnstein & E. Boring (Eds.), *A source book in the history of psychology* (pp. 599–605). Cambridge, MA: Harvard University Press. (Original work published 1910)

Titchener, E. B. (1966). The "type theory" of the simple reaction. In J. M. Vanderplas (Ed.), *Controversial issues in psychology* (pp. 173–179). Boston: Houghton Mifflin. (Original work published 1896)

Titchener, E. B. (1966). The postulates of a structural psychology. In J. M. Vanderplas (Ed.), *Controversial issues in psychology* (pp. 35–47). Boston: Houghton Mifflin. (Original work published 1898)

Titchener, E. B. (1966). The type theory of the simple reaction. In J. M. Vanderplas (Ed.), *Controversial issues in psychology* (pp. 155–164). Boston: Houghton Mifflin. (Original work published 1895)

Titchener, E. B. (1968). Brentano and Wundt: Empirical and experimental psychology. In L. L. McAlister (Ed.), *The philosophy of Brentano* (pp. 80–90). Atlantic Highlands, NJ: Humanities Press. (Original work published 1921)

Titchener, E. B. (1971). *Experimental psychology: A manual of laboaratory practice* (Vol. I). New York: Johnson Reprint Corporation. (Original work published 1902)

Titchener, E. B. (1971). *Experimental psychology: A manual of laboaratory practice* (Vol. II, Parts I & II). New York: Johnson Reprint Corporation. (Original work published 1905)

Titchener, E. B. (1972). *Systematic psychology: Prolegomena.* Ithaca, NY: Cornell University Press. (Original work published 1929)

Tolman, E. C. (1951). *Behavior and psychological man.* Berkeley, CA: University of California Press.

Tolman, E. C. (1959). Principles of purposive behavior. In S. Koch (Ed.), *Psychology: A study of a science* (Vol. 2) (pp. 92–157). New York: McGraw-Hill.

Tolman, E. C. (1967). *Purposive behavior in animals and men.* New York: Appleton-Century-Crofts. (Original work published 1932)

Tolman, E. C., & Honzik, C. H. (1930). Degrees of hunger, reward and non-reward, and maze learning in rats. *University of California Publications in Psychology, 4,* 241–256.

Tolman, E. C., Ritchie, B. F., & Kalish, D. (1992). Studies in spatial learning: I. Orientation and the short cut. *Journal of Experimental Psychology: General, 121,* 429–434. (Original work published 1946)

Toman, W. (1960). *An introduction to the psychoanalytic theory of motivation.* New York: Pergamon.

Toman, W. (1971). The duplication theorem of social relationships as tested in the general population. *Psychological Review, 78,* 380–390.

Toulmin, S. (1972). *Human understanding: The collective use and evolution of concepts.* Princeton: Princeton University Press.

Toynbee, A.J. (1960). *A study of history.* Oxford: Oxford University Press. (Original work published 1947)

Tracy, T. J. (1969). *Physiological theory and the doctrine of the mean in Plato and Aristotle.* The Hague: Mouton.

Trilling, L. (1972). *Sincerity and authenticity.* Cambridge, MA: Harvard University Press.

Turing, A. (1950). Computing machinery and intelligence. *Mind, 59,* 433–450.

Tweney, R. D. (1987). Programmatic research in experimental psychology: E. B. Titchener's laboratory investigations, 1891–1927. In M. G. Ash & W. R. Woodward (Eds.), *Psychology in twentieth-century thought and society* (pp. 35–58). New York: Cambridge University Press.

Underwood, B. J. (1964). The representativeness of rote verbal learning. In A. W. Melton (Ed.), *Categories of verbal learning* (pp. 48–78). New York: Academic.

Underwood, B. J., Rehula, R., & Keppel, G. (1962). Item-selection on paired associate learning. *American Journal of Psychology, 75,* 353–371.

Urban, W. J. (1989). The Black scholar and intelligence testing: The case of Horace Mann Bond. *Journal of the History of the Behavioral Sciences, 25,* 323–334.

van Elteren, M. (1992). Kurt Lewin as filmmaker and methodologist. *Canadian Psychologist, 33,* 599–608.

Vande Kemp, H. (1992). G. Stanley Hall and the Clark school of religious psychology. *American Psychologist, 47,* 290–298.

Varela, F. J., Thompson, E., & Rosch, E. (1991). *The embodied mind.* Cambridge, MA: MIT.

Vicente, K. J., & Brewer, W. F. (1993). Reconstructive remembering of the scientific literature. *Cognition, 46,* 101–128.

Vickery, J. B. (1973). *The literary impact of the Golden Bough.* Princeton, NJ: Princeton University Press.

Vidal, F., Buscaglia, M., & Voneche, J. J. (1983). Darwinism and developmental psychology. *Journal of the History of the Behavioral Sciences, 19,* 81–94.

Vitz, P. C., & Glimcher, A. B. (1984). *Modern art and modern science.* New York: Praeger.

Von Mayrhauser, R. T. (1989). Making intelligence functional: Walter Dill Scott and applied psychological testing in World War I. *Journal of the History of the Behavioral Sciences, 25,* 60–72.

Von Mayrhauser, R. T. (1992). The mental testing community and validity. *American Psychologist, 47,* 244–253.

von Restorff, H. (1933). Über die Wirkung von Bereichsbildungen im Spurenfeld. *Psychologische Forschung, 18,* 299–342.

Vonèche, J. J. (1982). Evolution, development, and knowledge. In J. M. Broughton & D. J. Freeman-Moir (Eds.), *The cognitive-developmental psychology of James Mark Baldwin: Current theory and research in genetic epistemology* (pp. 51–79). Norwood, NJ: Ablex.

Vygotsky, L. S. (1962). *Thought and language.* (E. Hanfmann & G. Vakar, Trans.). Cambridge, MA: MIT Press. (Original work published 1934)

Vygotsky, L. S. (1971). *The psychology of art.* Cambridge, MA: MIT Press.

Vygotsky, L. S. (1978). *Mind in society.* Cambridge, MA: Harvard. (Original work published 1935)

Vygostky, L. S. (1986). *Thought and language* (A. Kozulin, Trans.). Cambridge, MA: MIT. (Original work published 1934)

Walk, R. D., & Gibson, E. J. (1961). *A comparative and analytic study of visual depth perception.* Psychological Monographs, no. 75, (15, Whole No. 519).

Wallach, L., & Wallach, M. A. (1994). Gergen versus the mainstream. *Journal of Personality and Social Psychology, 67,* 233–242.

Wallach, M. A., & Wallach, L. (1983). *Psychology's sanction for selfishness: The error of egoism in theory and therapy.* San Francisco: Freeman.

Wallas, G. (1926). *The art of thought.* London: Cape.

Wapner, S. (1964). Some aspects of a research program based on an organismic-developmental approach to cognition: Experiments and theory. *Journal of the American Academy of Child Psychiatry, 3,* 193–230.

Ward, J. (1910). Herbart, Johann Friedrich. In *Encyclopedia Britannica* (11th ed., Vol 13, pp. 335–338). New York: Encyclopedia Britannica Company.

Warden, C. J., Jenkins, T. N., & Warner, L. H. (1934). *Introduction to comparative psychology.* New York: Ronald.

Warnock, G. J. (1987). George Berkeley. In R. L. Gregory (Ed.), *The Oxford Companion to the Mind* (pp. 82–83). Oxford: Oxford University Press.

Warnock, M. (1970). *Existentialism.* London: Oxford University Press.

Warr, P. B. (1970). *Thought and personality.* Harmondsworth, UK: Penguin.

Watson, J. B. (1962). *Behaviorism* (Rev. ed.). Chicago: University of Chicago Press. (Original work published 1930)

Watson, J. B. (1966). Psychology as the behaviorist views it. In J. M. Vanderplas (Ed.), *Controversial issues in psychology* (pp. 70–84). Boston: Houghton Mifflin. (Original work published 1913)

Watson, J. B. (1970). The place of the conditioned reflex in psychology. In W. H. Gantt, L. Pickenhain & C. Zwingmann (Eds.), *Pavlovian approach to psychopathology* (pp. 35–46). Oxford: Pergamon. (Original work published 1916)

Watson, J. B., & Rayner, R. (1979). Conditioned emotional reactions. In R. I. Watson (Ed.), *Basic writings in the history of psychology* (pp. 280–283). New York: Oxford. (Original work published 1920)

Watson, R. I. (1979). *Basic writings in the history of psychology.* New York: Oxford.

Weidman, N. (1994a). Mental testing and machine intelligence: The Lashley-Hull debate. *Journal of the History of the Behavioral Sciences, 30,* 162–180.

Weidman, N. (1994b, June). *Lashley, race, and the writing of history.* Paper presented to the XXVIth Annual Meeting of Cheiron: International Society of the Behavioral and Social Sciences, Montreal, Canada.

Weimer, W. B. (1973). Psycholinguistics and Plato's paradoxes of the *Meno. American Psychologist, 28,* 15–32.

Weisberg, R. W., & Alba, J. W. A. (1981). An examination of the role of fixation in the solution of several insight problems. *Journal of Experimental Psychology: General, 110,* 169–192.

Werner, H. (1935). Studies on contour: I. Qualitative analyses. *American Journal of Psychology, 47,* 40–64.

Werner, H. (1937). Process and achievement: A basic problem of education and developmental psychology. *Harvard Educational Review, 7,* 353–368.

Werner, H. (1957). The concept of development from a comparative and organismic point of view. In D. B. Harris (Ed.), *The concept of development* (pp. 125–148). Minneapolis: University of Minnesota Press.

Werner, H. (1961). *The comparative psychology of mental development.* New York: Science Editions.

Werner, H., & Kaplan, B. (1963). *Symbol formation.* New York: Wiley.

Werner, H., & Kaplan, E. (1952). The acquisition of word meanings: A developmental study. *Monographs of the Society for Research in Child Development, 15* (1, Serial No. 51).

Wertheimer, Max (1912). Experimentelle Studien über das Sehen von Bewegung. *Psychologische Forschung, 61,* 161–265.

Wertheimer, Max (1958). Principles of perceptual organization. In D. C. Beardslee & Michael Wertheimer (Eds.), *Readings in perception* (pp. 115–135). Princeton, NJ: Van Nostrand.

Wertheimer, Max (1959). *Productive thinking.* New York: Harper.

Wertheimer, Max (1961). On truth. In M. Henle (Ed.), *Documents of Gestalt psychology* (pp. 19–28). Berkeley, CA: University of California Press. (Original work published 1934)

Wertheimer, Max (1961). Some problems in the theory of ethics. In M. Henle (Ed.), *Documents of Gestalt psychology* (pp. 29–41). Berkeley, CA: University of California Press. (Original work published 1935)

Wertheimer, Max (1967). Gestalt theory. In W. D. Ellis (Ed.), *A source book of Gestalt psychology* (pp. 1–16). New York: Humanities. (Original work published 1925)

Wertheimer, Max (1967). Laws of organization in perceptual forms. In W. D. Ellis (Ed.), *A source book of Gestalt psychology* (pp. 71–88). New York: Humanities Press. (Original work published 1923)

Wertheimer, Michael, King, D. B., Peckler, M. A., Raney, S., & Schaef, R. W. (1992). Carl Jung and Max Wertheimer on a priority issue. *Journal of the History of the Behavioral Sciences, 28,* 45–56.

Wertheimer, Michael. (1978). Humanistic psychology and the humane but tough-minded psychologist. *American Psychologist, 33,* 739–745.

Wertsch, J. V. (Ed.). (1985). *Vygotsky and the social function of mind.* Cambridge, MA: Harvard University Press.

Wertsch, J. V., & Tulviste, P. (1992). L. S. Vygotsky and contemporary developmental psychology. *Developmental Psychology, 28,* 548–557.

Wertz, F. J. (1994). Of rats and psychologists: A study of the history and meaning of science. *Theory and Psychology, 4,* 165–197.

Westkott, M. (1986). *The feminist legacy of Karen Horney.* New Haven: Yale University Press.

Wheelwright, P. (1966). *The Presocratics.* New York: Odyssey Press.

White, G. S. (1992). G. Stanley Hall: From philosophy to developmental psychology. *Developmental Psychology, 28,* 25–34.

Whorf, B. L. (1956). *Language, thought and reality.* Cambridge, MA: MIT.

Wilhelm, H. (1975). *Change* (Cary F. Baynes, Trans.). London: Routledge & Kegan Paul.

Wilhelm, R. (1967). Introduction. In *The I ching, or Book of changes* (Cary F. Baynes, Trans. from the German version of R. Wilhelm) (pps. xii–lxii). Princeton, NJ: Princeton University Press.

Windholz, G. (1990). Pavlov and the Pavlovians in the laboratory. *Journal of the History of the Behavioral Sciences, 26,* 64–74.

Winner, E. (1982). *Invented worlds.* Cambridge, MA: Harvard University Press.

Winston, A. S. (1989). Robert S. Woodworth's "Experimental Psychology": The "Columbia Bible." *Proceedings of the XXIst Annual Meeting of Cheiron: International Society of the Behavioral and Social Sciences* (pp. 97–108). Kingston, ON, Canada: Queen's University.

Wisdom, J. (1957). *Philosophy and psychoanalysis.* Cambridge: Basil Blackwell.

Witkin, H. A., Lewis, H. B., Hertzman, M., Machover, K., Meissner, P. B., & Wapner, S. (1954). *Personality through perception.* New York: Harper.

Witmer, L. (1894). Zur experimentellen Aesthetik einfacher räumlicher Formverhältnisse [Toward an experimental aesthetic of simple spatial proportions]. *Philosophische Studien, 9,* 96–144, 209–263.

Wittgenstein, L. (1953). *Philosophical investigations.* Oxford: Blackwell.

Wittgenstein, L. (1974). *Tractatus Logico-philosophicus.* London: Routledge & Kegan Paul. (Original work published 1922)

Wittgenstein, L. (1980). *Remarks on the philosophy of psychology* (Vol. II). Chicago: University of Chicago Press.

Wolfe, T. (1982). *From Bauhaus to our house.* New York: Pocket Books.

Wolff, P. (1960). The developmental psychologies of Jean Piaget and psychoanalysis. *Psychological Issues, 2* (1, Monograph 5).

Wollstonecraft, M. (1988). A vindication of the rights of woman. In C. H. Poston (Ed.), *A vindication of the rights of woman, an authoritative text, backgrounds, the Wollstonecraft debate, criticism* (pp. 1–194). New York: Norton. (Original work published 1792)

Wolman, B. B. (1968). Immanuel Kant and his impact on psychology. In B. B. Wolman (Ed.), *Historical roots of contemporary psychology* (pp. 229–247). New York: Harper and Row.

Wolpe, J. (1958). *Psychotherapy by reciprocal inhibition.* Stanford: Stanford University Press.

Woodworth, R. S. (1931). *Schools of psychology.* New York: Ronald.

Woodworth, R. S. (1938). *Experimental psychology.* New York: Holt.

Woodworth, R. S. (1940). *Psychology* (4th ed.). New York: Holt.

Woodworth, R. S., & Schlosberg, H. (1954). *Experimental Psychology* (2nd ed.). New York: Holt.

Wosniak, R. (1982). Metaphysics and science, reason and reality: The intellectual origins of genetic epistemology. In J. M. Broughton & D. J. Freeman-Moir (Eds.), *The cognitive-developmental psychology of James Mark Baldwin: Current theory and research in genetic epistemology* (pp. 13–45). Norwood, NJ: Ablex.

Wulf, M. D. (1959). *The system of Thomas Aquinas.* New York: Dover. (Original work published 1922)

Wulff, D. M. (1985). Experimental introspection and religious experience. *Journal of the History of the Behavioral Sciences, 21,* 131–150.

Wundt, W. (1970). The psychology of the sentence. In A. L. Blumenthal (Ed.), *Language and psychology: Historical aspects of psycholinguistics* (pp. 20–31). New York: Wiley. (Original work published 1912)

Wundt, W. (1973). *An introduction to psychology.* New York: Arno Press. (Original work published 1912)

Yates, F. A. (1966). *The art of memory.* Chicago: University of Chicago Press.

Yerkes, R. M. (1948). Psychological examining in the United States Army. In W. Dennis (Ed.), *Readings in the history of psychology* (pp. 528–540). New York: Appleton-Century-Crofts. (Original work published 1921)

Zangwill, O. L. (1972). *Remembering* revisited. *Quarterly Journal of Experimental Psychology, 24,* 123–138.

Zaretsky, E. (1994). The attack on Freud. *Tikkun, 9,* 65–70.

Zederland, L. (1988). The child-study legacy. *Journal of the History of the Behavioral Sciences, 24,* 152–165.

Zeigarnik, B. (1967). On finished and unfinished tasks. In W. D. Ellis, (Ed.), *A source book of Gestalt psychology* (pp. 300–314). New York: Humanities. (Original work published 1927)

INDEX

Ablation, 159–160
Abnormal psychology, 122
Absolute threshold, Fechner's concept of, 55
Abstract attitude, Goldstein's concept of, 191–192
Acceleration, 28
Accommodation
  of anomalies, 324
  Baldwin's concept of, 240
  Piaget's concept of, 246
Ach, Narciss, 79–80
Acquisition, and learning, Rock's experiments and, 225–226
Act(s)
  automatic (habitual), 89
  impulsive, Wundt's concept of, 73
  mental, Brentano's concept of, 78
  voluntary, Wundt's concept of, 73
Action, human, versus motion, 17–18, 212, 220
Action research, Lewin's advocacy of, 187
Activity (A) set of dimensions, 218–219
Act psychology, Brentano and, 78
Ad Herennium, 19
Adler, Alfred, 108
Adolescence
  Hall's work on, 238
  storm and stress of, Hall's concept of, 238
Advertising, Watson's thinking about, 158
Aesthetics from above, versus aesthetics from below, 56
Affection, Titchener's concept of, 124
Affordances, J. J. Gibson's concept of, 306
Afterimages, 30
  negative, 60
Ainsworth, Mary, 261
Aircrib, Skinner's, 165
Albert B., 156
Alchemy, 27, 115
  Jung and, 115
Allport, Gordon W., 270
  idiographic–nomothetic distinction, 270
  Pattern and Growth in Personality, 270
  scale of values of, 270
American Association of Clinical Psychologists, establishment of, 277
American Institute for Psychoanalysis, 110
American Journal of Psychology, 236
American Psychological Association, 133, 297, 329–332
  membership of, 330
  special interest groups, 329–330
    overlap of, 330–331
American Psychological Society, 330–332
Anal stage, Freud's concept of, 102
Analytical psychology, Jung and, 112
Anamnesis, doctrine of, 10
Anecdotal psychology, 139
Angell, James R., 129–130
  on unconscious, 97
Anima, Jungian, 114
Animal intelligence, Thorndike's work on, 140–141, 148–149
Animal magnetism, 97
Animal rights, 152
Animals. *See also* Cats; Chickens; Chimpanzees; Rats
  Cartesian concept of, 26
  experimentation on, Pavlov's, 147–150, 151–152
  psychology of, 122
  Romanes' study of, 139–140
Animal welfare, 152
Animism, 163
Animus, Jungian, 114
Anna O., 99
Anomalies, 324–325
  accommodation of, 324
  exclusion of, 324
  indifference to, 324
  opportunism and, 324
  responses to, 324–325
Anthropomorphic psychology, 139–140
Anti-vivisectionism, 151–152
Anxiety
  absence of abstract attitude and, 192
  basic, Horney's theory of, 110
  Freud's concept of, 104
  May's views on, 270
  moral, Freud's concept of, 104
  neurotic
    Freud's concept of, 104
    versus normal, May's views on, 270
  realistic, Freud's concept of, 104
Apparent motion, Wertheimer's study of, 172–173
Apperception
  Herbart's concept of, 51
  Leibniz's concept of, 51
  Wundt's concept of, 71
Apperceptive mass, Herbart's concept of, 50–51
Application, in education, 52
Applied psychology, 131
  Cronbach on, 206

Apprehension, Wundt's concept of, 72
Aptitude treatment interaction, 206–207
Archetypal psychology, Jung and, 112
Archetypes
  definition of, 114
  Jung's theory of, 114
Architecture, and modernism, 327–328
Aristotle, 15–21, 130
  Plato and, comparison of, 15–17
  Scala naturae of, 20–21
Army Alpha, 134
Army Beta, 134
Army intelligence testing, 134–135
Arousal system, Hebb's concept of, 228–229
Art
  psychology and, 327
  psychology of, 192
Artificial intelligence, 309, 312
Artificial memory, 19–20
Asch, Solomon, 187, 188–190
Assimilation
  Baldwin's concept of, 240
  Piaget's concept of, 246
Associated motor reflexes, Bekhterev's study of, 152–153
Association(s)
  by contiguity, 18
  by contrast, 18
  in education, 52
  laws of, 18
  memory and, 18
  remote, Ebbinghaus's concept of, 76
  by similarity, 18
Association of ideas, Titchener's concept of, 125
Association reflex, Bekhterev's concept of, 152–153
Associative chain theory, 161
  Lashley's criticism of, 161–162
Associativity, Piaget's concept of, 248
Atheoretical observation versus theory-driven observation, 14
Attachment, Freud's concept of, 102–103
Attention
  Broadbent's work on, 295
  divided, 90
  James on, 89
  Neisser's concept of, 303
  Titchener's concept of, 124–125
Austin, G., 291, 299–300
Autobiographically consequential experiences, Erikson's concept of, 257
Autobiographical memories, Galton's concept of, 64
Automatic acts, 89
Automatic writing, 89, 90

Baby tender, Skinner's, 165
Backward masking, 244
Bad faith, Sartre's concept of, 267–268
Bait shyness, 230
Balanced states, Heider's concept of, 187–188
Baldwin, James Mark, 70, 153–154, 238–241
  accommodation concept, 240
  assimilation concept, 240
  career of, 238–239
  imitation concept, 240
  organic selection concept, 240
  psychology of mental development, 239–240
Baldwin effect, 240
Bandura, Albert, 231–233
  behavior modification and, 231–232
  no-trial learning concept, 232
  observational learning concept, 231
  social cognitive theory, 231
  social learning theory, 231
Bannister, Don, 285–286
Bartlett, Frederic, 295, 300–302
  memory theory, 300–302, 304
  motor skills concept, 301
  research on memory, compared with Ebbinghaus's studies, 301
  schema concept, 301
Basic anxiety, Horney's theory of, 110
Bayley, Nancy, 261
Beagle, voyage of, 41–42
Beauvoir, Simone de, 267, 320–321
  The Second Sex, 320–321
Behavior
  Aristotle's view of, 17–18
  definition, 18
  Gestalt theory of, 182–183
  interpretation of, 109
    psychoanalytic, 109
  molar description of, Tolman's concept of, 220
  molecular description of, Tolman's concept of, 220
  purposive, Tolman's work on, 220
  as subject matter of psychology, 28
Behavioral environment, Gestalt theory of, 182–183
Behavioral psychology, current status of, 318
Behavioral trap(s), 167
Behaviorism, 147–169, 171. *See also* Lashley, Karl S.; Pavlov, Ivan P.; Skinner, B. F.; Watson, John B.
  characteristics of, 162
  Chomsky's views on, 291
  criticism of, 269–270
  methodological, 198
  purposive, 220
  subjective, 297
  Watson on, 154–155
Behaviorism (Watson), 155–156
Behavior modification, 231–232
The Behavior of Organisms (Skinner), 163–164

Being and Nothingness (Sartre), 267
Being-in-the-world, Heidegger's concept of, 268
Being values (B-values), Maslow's concept of, 274
Bekhterev, Vladimir M., 152–153
Benedict, Ruth, 36, 272
  Maslow's observations on, 273
  Patterns of Culture, 272
Berkeley, George, 32–33
  A New Theory of Vision, 32
  theory of existence, 33
Berlyne, Daniel E., *Structure and Direction in Thinking,* 219
Bernays, Martha, 98
Bernstein, Leonard, 2
Bias, experimenter, 200
Binary number system, 12–13
Binet, Alfred, 70, 79, 133–134
Binswanger, Ludwig, 268
  existential approach to psychotherapy, 268
Birth order, Adler's theory of, 108
Bits, 290
Blacks
  intelligence test scores, 135
  in science, 70
Bleuler, Eugen, 111
Blind variation and selective retention, 43–44
Bloor, David, 324–325
Body, as machine, Cartesian concept of, 25–27
Body image, Hebb's concept of, 228
Body schema, Hebb's concept of, 228
Bond, Horace Mann, 135
Bonnet, Charles, 41
Book of Changes (I Ching), 12–15
Boring, Edwin G., 125, 135, 236–237, 332
Bower, Gordon H., 209
Bowlby, John, 261
Brain damage, Goldstein's work on, 191
Brain Mechanisms and Intelligence (Lashley), 160
Brain theory, Kohler's, 180–182
Brainwashing, definition of, 229
Brentano, Franz, 77–80, 267
  act psychology and, 78
Breuer, Joseph, studies of hysteria, 98, 99
Bridgman, Percy, 197, 198
British empiricists, 30–35
Broadbent, Donald E., 295
Brücke, Ernst, 98
Bruner, Jerome, 298–300
  and New Look in perception, 298–299
  perceptual readiness concept, 299
  study of concept attainment, 299–300
  A Study of Thinking, 291, 299–300
Brunswik, Egon, 306
Buddha, 15
Buhler, Charlotte, 269
Bühler, Karl, 79
Burt, Cyril, 132, 201, 202–204
Burt scandal, 202–204
Business, psychology in, 136–139

Calkins, Mary Whiton, 76–77, 222
  paired associates method and, 76–77, 222
Cannon, Walter B., 91
Canon
  definition of, 140
  Morgan's, 140
Care
  Heidegger's concept of, 268
  May's views on, 271
Caring, Erikson's concept of, 257
Carnap, Rudolph, 195–196
Carnegie, Andrew, 66
Carr, Harvey, 126
Cartesian doubt, 24
Cartesian linguistics, Chomsky's theory of, 292–293
Cassirer, Ernst, 184–185, 241
Catharsis, 99
Cathartic method, of Freud and Breuer, 99
Cathexis, Freud's concept of, 100
Cats, Thorndike's work with, 141–142, 179, 212
Cattell, James McKeen, 70, 132–133, 304
Cattell, Raymond B., 203
Causality
  Hume's concept of, 33–34
  Kant's view of, 37–38, 174
  spurious correlation and, Simon's work on, 307–308
Cause(s), final, Aristotle's concept of, 17
CD-ROM, 8
Cell assembly(ies), Hebb's concept of, 227–228
Censor, Freud's concept of, 101
Channel capacity, 294
Channel of communication, 290
Charcot, Jean-Martin, 98
Cherry, Colin, 295
Chickens, Kohler's work with, 180
Childhood and Society (Erikson), 255
Child psychology, Darwin's ideas and, 44
Child-rearing practices, Rogers' views on, 279
Children. *See also* Developmental psychology
  and recapitulationism, Hall's theory of, 237
Child study movement, 238
Chimpanzees, Kohler's work with, 179–180
Choice, subjective nature of, Kierkegaard's view of, 266

Choleric temperament, 15
Chomsky, Noam, 291–293
  Cartesian linguistics and, 292–293
  critique of Skinner, 291
  deep structure concept, 292
  grammatical transformations concept, 292
  language acquisition device concept, 293
  language theory, 291–293
  surface structure concept, 292
  on syntactic structures, 291–292
Circular model(s). *See also* Circumplexes
  of *I Ching,* 13
Circumplexes, 14–15
Clark, Kenneth B., 70
Clark, Mamie Phipps, 70
Clever Hans, 200
Client-centered therapy, 277–279
Clinical psychology
  historical perspective on, 276
  Rogers and, 276–277
  Witmer and, 276
Closure, Gestalt principle of, 175
Cocktail party phenomenon, 295
Cogito, ergo sum, 24
Cognition, definition of, 289
Cognitive complexity, 285–286
Cognitive development, Bruner's work on, 300
Cognitive maps, Tolman's concept of, 220–221
Cognitive psychology, 224, 289–313. *See also* Bartlett, Frederic; Bruner, Jerome; Chomsky, Noam; Miller, George A.; Neisser, Ulric; Simon, Herbert
  current status of, 318
  historical perspective on, 302–306
  neurophysiology and, 311
Cogwheeling of life cycles, 255
Coincidence, meaningful, in Jungian thought, 117
Collective unconscious
  and external world, 116–117
  Jung's concept of, 113
Color
  achromatic versus chromatic, 60
  nature of, Newton's work on, 28–30
  as subjective experience, 30
Color blindness, 60–61
Color perception
  Helmholtz's trichromatic theory of, 58
  Ladd-Franklin's theory of, 60–61
  Young-Helmholtz theory of, 58
Color vision, opponent process theory of, 60
Common-sense psychology, 187
Comparative approach, to development, Werner's, 241–245
Comparative method, James on, 85
Comparative psychology, 44, 139–143, 147. *See also* Thorndike, Edward L.
The Comparative Psychology of Mental Development (Werner), 241–245
Compensatory history, 321
Competence, Erikson's concept of, 256
Computer(s)
  applications in social science, 308
  simulations of psychological processes, 308–311
    criticisms of cognitive processes, 311–312
  statistical analysis by, 308
Concept attainment, 299–300
Concepts, Wittgenstein's analysis of, 323–324
Conceptual/contemplative level of development, 243
Concrete operations, Piaget's concept of, 249–250
Concrete performance, Goldstein's concept of, 191
Conditioned inhibition, Hull's concept of, 215
Conditioned reflexes
  as conditional, 149
  Pavlov's work on, 147–150
  versus unconditioned reflexes, 149–150
Conditioned response, 149–150
Conditioned stimulus, 149–150
  inhibition of, 150
  as signal, 150
  temporary nature of, 150
Conditioning. *See also* Operant conditioning
  characteristics of, 149–150
  higher order, 150–151
  respondent, Skinner's view of, 164
  Watson's use of, 155
Conditioning and Learning (Hilgard), 209–210
Conformity, Asch's research in, 189–190
Confucianism, Taoism and, comparison of, 11–12
Confucius, 11–12
Conjoined twins, personhood of, 319–320
Connectionism, Thorndike's theory of, 142–143
Conscious, Freud's concept of, 101
Consciousness. *See also* Mind
  as accommodatory process, 130
  as changing, James on, 86
  as continuous, James on, 86–87
  dimensions of, Titchener's concept of, 125–126
  fringe of, 86
  objects in, James on, 87
  as personal, James on, 85–86
  as selective, James on, 87–88
  Skinner's view of, 162–163

stream of, James's concept of, 85–88
substantive versus transitive parts, James on, 86
unity of, James on, 87
Watson on, 154
Consensus, Asch on, 190
Conservation, Piaget's concept of, 251
Constructs, Kelly's concept of, 283
Context of discovery, context of justification versus, 198, 220
Context of justification versus context of discovery, 198, 220
operationism and, 198
Contextualism, 318–320
versus mechanism, 319
strands in, 319
texture in, 319
Contiguity, Guthrie's principle of, 211–212
Continuity, Romanes' hypothesis of, 139
Controlled (conscious) versus automatic (unconscious) processes, Angell's concept of, 97–98
Conversion hysteria, 98–99
Copernicus, 37
Correlational methods, 200–201
Correlational psychology, 205–206
Correspondence theory of truth, 177–178
Cortical localization of function, 158–161
Countercathexis, Freud's concept of, 100
Creationism, Darwinism and, 44
Creative environments, Rogers' theory of, 279
Creative people, characteristics of, 40–41
Cronbach, Lee J., 204–207
Cross-cultural research, Osgood's, 219
Cue function, of stimuli, Hebb's concept of, 228–229
Cues, Guthrie's concept of, 212, 213
Cultural bias, in mental tests, 134
Cultural psychology, Wundt and, 73–75
Culture, Freud on, 104–106
Cybernetics, 294
Cyclical change
history and, 45
in *I Ching*, 13

Danziger, Kurt, 326
on investigative practices, 207
Darwin, Charles, 40–45, 130, 240
Malthus's influence on, 42–43
theory of evolution
development of, 42–44
psychology and, 44–45
traditional theology and, 44
Darwin, Erasmus, 41
Dasein, 268
da Vinci, Leonardo, 59
Death instinct, Freud on, 105–106
Decoding, 290
Defense mechanisms, Anna Freud's concept of, 108–109
Deferred imitation, Piaget's concept of, 248–249
Deficiency motives, Maslow's concept of, 274
Demonstrations, Wertheimer's use of, 172
Descartes, René, 23–27
Chomsky and, 292–293
Determining tendencies, 79–80
de Vaucanson, Jacques, 25–26
Development
comparative approach to, Werner's, 241–245
conceptual/contemplative level of, 243
continuity of, Piaget's concept of, 251
continuity versus discontinuity, Werner's concept of, 242
meanings of, 235–236
orthogenetic principle of, Werner's, 241
sensorimotor level of, 243
tropistic/reflexive level of, 243
uniformity versus multiformity, Werner's concept of, 242
unilinearity versus multilinearity, Werner's concept of, 242–243
Developmental psychology, 235–263. *See also* Baldwin, James Mark; Erikson, Erik H.; Gibson, Eleanor J.; Hall, G. Stanley; Inhelder, Bärbel; Piaget, Jean; Vygotsky, Lev S.; Werner, Heinz
life-span, Erikson's, 254–255
Dewey, John, 70, 127–131
attitude toward formal disciplines, 129
critique of reflex arc concept, 127–128
influence on educational practice, 128–129
Dialectical process, 322
Dichotic listening, 295
Difference threshold, Fechner's concept of, 55
Differentiation
in development, Lewin's theory of, 186
in perceptual learning, Gibsons' concept of, 258–259
Displacement, as defense, 108
Dispositional concepts
Carnap's theory of, 196
falsifiability, 196–197
Dissociated streams of consciousness, 97
Distributed practice, 156
Divided attention, 90
Dollard, John, 214

Double blind procedures, 200
Douglas, Mary, 324
Dream(s)
day residue in, Freud's concept of, 102
Freud's theory of, 100–102
interpretation of, Freud on, 100–102
latent content, Freud's concept of, 101
manifest content, Freud's concept of, 101
preconscious material in, 101–102
Drive(s), Hull's concept of, 213–216
Dualism, Cartesian, 24
Dynamic model, Freud's, 100–101
Dystopia, Skinner's, 167–168

Ebbinghaus, Hermann, 70, 75–77, 222
research on memory, 75, 222
compared with Bartlett's studies, 301
use of nonsense syllables, 75, 222
Eclecticism, 127
Eco, Umberto, 250, 328
Ecological validity, 306
Education
Bruner's work on, 300
Dewey's influence on, 128–129
progressive, Dewey and, 129
Wollstonecraft's views on, 35–36
Educational psychology, Herbart's influence on, 51–52
Ego. *See also* Pure ego
Freud's concept of, 103–104
Egocentric speech, 253
Einstein, Albert, Freud's letter to, 105–106
Either/Or (Kierkegaard), 265–266
Elements, Kelly's concept of, 284
Emergence, Werner's concept of, 242
Emergent properties, Werner's concept of, 242
Emotion(s)
Darwinian concept of, 44
Herbart's concept of, 50
James's theory of, 89–91
Wollstonecraft's views on, 36
Wundt's concept of, 72
Emotional (visceral) habits, Watson's concept of, 156
Empirical self, James on, 88
Empirical understanding, 281
Empiricism, 30
Encoding, 290
Encounter groups, 280–281
Endogenic, definition of, 322
Enrichment, Gibsons' concept of, 258
Environment, geographical versus behavioral, 182
Environmentalism, Watson's, 155
Epigenetic theory, Erikson's, 255
Equilibration
Piaget's concept of, 246
Spencer's concept of, 65–66
Equilibrium, of ideas, Herbart's concept of, 50
Ergonomics, 295
Erikson, Erik H., 254–257
Childhood and Society, 255
cogwheeling of life cycles, 255
epigenetic theory, 255
life cycle theory, eight stages of, 255–257
life-span developmental psychology of, 254–255
Erogenous zones, Freud's concept of, 102
Eros, Freud on, 105–106
Estes, William K., in Hilgard's textbook, 211
Ethnocentric, definition, 8
Eugenics
Galton's concept of, 62
Thorndike and, 142
Eupsychian Management (Maslow), 276
Evaluation (E) set of dimensions, 218–219
Evolution
etymology of, 41
theory of, 41, 240
Darwin's
development of, 42–44
psychology and, 44–45
traditional theology and, 44
development of, 42–44
Spencer's, 65
Excitation, Pavlov's concept of, 151
Exclusion, of anomalies, 324
Existence (May, Angel, Ellenberger), 265
Existence, Berkeley's theory of, 33
Existence precedes essence, Sartre's concept of, 267
Existentialism, 265–268. *See also* Binswanger, Ludwig; Kierkegaard, Søren; Nietzsche, Friedrich; Sartre, Jean-Paul
American psychologists and, 268–270
Exogenic
definition of, 322
versus endogenic, 322
Expectancies, in cognitive maps, 220–221
Experience
Fechner's concept of, 54–55
Kant's view of, 37–38
simplicity in, in Gestalt psychology, 173
Experiencing, Gendlin's concept of, 280
Experiential methods, Maslow's concept of, 276
Experimental aesthetics, Fechner and, 56
Experimental psychology, 205–206
first laboratory in, 69

Experimental Psychology (Titchener), 124–125
Experimental Psychology (Woodworth), 130
Experimenter bias, 200
Experiment(s)/experimentation
laboratory-based, 69–73
methods, 198
Fisher's, 198–199
James on, 85
repeatability, 199–200
results
replication, 200
statistical significance of, 200
Titchener's advocacy of, 122–123
Extensity of experience, Titchener's concept of, 125
External sense, for Kant, 38–40
Extinction, of conditioned response, 150
Extraversion, Jung's concept of, 112–114, 115

Factor analysis, 201, 202, 218
Thurstone's work in, 204
Faith. *See also* Bad faith
Kierkegaard's view of, 266
Faithfulness, Erikson's concept of, 256
Falsifiability, of scientific concepts, 196–197
Farson, Richard, 281–282
Fear(s), conditioned, 156
Fechner, Gustav Theodor, 52–56, 70
experimental aesthetics and, 56
just noticeable difference (jnd) concept, 54
method of average error, 55
method of just noticeable differences (method of limits), 55
method of right and wrong cases, 55
and psychophysics, 53–56
Feedback, 294
Feedback loop, 294–296
Felt meanings, Gendlin's concept of, 280
Feminism, 320–322
Feyerabend, Paul, 316–317
Fibonacci numbers, 6–7
Field dependent versus field independent individuals, 190
Field theory
in Hilgard's textbook, 210–211
Lewin's definition of, 185
and psychology, 180–182
Figure/ground discrimination, Gestalt principle of, 175–176
Final cause, Aristotle's concept of, 17
First Invitational Conference on Humanistic Psychology, 269
Fisher, Ronald A., 198–200
Five ways of instruction, Herbart's, 51–52
Fixation, Freud's concept of, 102–103
Fixity versus mobility, Werner's concept of, 243
Fletcher, Horace, 91–92
Fletcher, Ronald, 203
Fletcherizing, 91
Focal attention, Neisser's concept of, 303
Forgetting, Ebbinghaus's study of, 75–76
Forgetting curve, Ebbinghaus's, 75–76
Form(s)
versus appearances, 7–11
platonic, 7–11, 15
and substance, Aristotle's concept of, 15–16
Formal operations, Piaget's concept of, 250
Four functions, in Jungian theory, 115–116
Frame of reference, Asch's research in, 190
Franz, Marie-Louise von, 117
Franz, Shepherd Ivery, 159–160
Frazer, James, 104, 105
Free association, 101
Freud, Anna, 106, 108–109, 254
Freud, Sigmund, 70, 98–110
Binswanger's discussion with, 268
cathexis and countercathexis concepts, 100
censor concept, 101
conscious, preconscious, and unconscious concepts, 101
critics of, 108
on culture, 104–106
death of, 106
dynamic model, 100–101
free association technique, 101
in Hilgard's textbook, 211
hysteria concept, 99
id, ego, and superego concepts, 103–104
on incest taboo, 104
The Interpretation of Dreams, 100–102
Jung and, 110–112
meeting with James, 92
Project for a Scientific Psychology, 100
psychoanalysis and, 107–108
on religion, 104–106
structural model, 103–104
theory
of dreams, 100–102
of infantile sexuality, 99
of libido, 102, 112
of life and death instincts, 105–106
of Oedipus complex, 99
of personality, 102–103
psychoanalytic, 106–107
of psychosexual development, 102
of reality and pleasure principles, 100
of sexual instincts, 102
on unconscious, 96–97
and women, 108
From Bauhaus to our House (Wolfe), 328

Functionalism, 66, 127, 210
and verbal learning, 222–225
Functional psychology. *See also* Angell, James R.; Dewey, John; Woodworth, Robert S.
Watson on, 154
Furomoto, Laurel, on new history of psychology, 315

g
Spearman's concept of, 201–202
Thurstone's work and, 204
Galanter, Eugene, 294
Galapagos Islands, Darwin's visit to, 42
Galen, typology of temperaments, 15
Gall, Franz Joseph, 159
Galton, Francis, 61–64, 132, 200
autobiographical memories concept, 64
eugenics concept, 62
hereditary genius and, 61–62
statistical principles and analyses employed by, 62–64
Galton's law, 61
Games, children's. *See also* Play
Piaget's study of, 246–247
Garcia, John, 230
Garcia effect, 230
Gender differences, Hollingworth's work on, 277
Gendlin, Eugene T., 279–280
Generalization
in education, 52
in perceptual learning, 258
Generalization gradient, Spence's concept of, 216–217
Generativity, 164–165
Genetic epistemology, Piaget's, 245–246
Genetic principle of spirality, 243
Genetic psychology, 236
Genital phase, Freud's concept of, 102
Genius, hereditary, Galton's concept of, 61–62
Gergen, Kenneth, 329
Gesell, Arnold L., 261
Gestalt, definition of, 10, 171
Gestalt laws of organization, 174–176, 183–184
Gestalt psychology, 10, 171–193. *See also* Koffka, Kurt; Kohler, Wolfgang; Lewin, Kurt; Wertheimer, Max
criticisms of, 197
founder of, 172
historical perspective on, 178
minimum principle in, 173, 183
phenomenology and, 174
as philosophy, 177–178
precursors of, 172, 173–174
simplicity in experience and, 173
Gestalt therapy, 192
Gibson, Eleanor J., 257–261
on future of psychology, 261
National Medal of Science won by, 261
perceptual learning concept, 258–260
visual cliff experiments, 260–261
work on reading, 259–260
Gibson, James J., 257–258, 305–306
affordances concept, 306
direct perception concept, 306
ecological approach to perception, 305, 306
information pickup theory, 306
stimulus gradient concept, 305–306
Gilbreth, Frank and Lillian, 137–138
Gillie, Oliver, 203
Glove anesthesia, 98
Gnomon, 4–5
Goethe, Johann Wolfgang von, 30
Golden Section, 6–7
Fechner's work on, 56
Goldstein, Kurt, 190–192, 272, 273
anxiety theory, 192
concept of abstract attitude, 191–192
organismic theory, 191
self-actualization concept, 191
self-realization concept, 191
Good continuation, Gestalt principle of, 175. *See also* Pragnanz
Goodnow, J., 291, 299–300
Gospel of wealth, Carnegie's, 66
Grammatical transformations, Chomsky's concept of, 292
Great chain of being, 21
Grid and group, for social relations between psychologists, 324–325
Group dynamics, Lewin's interest in, 187
The Growth of the Mind (Koffka), 183–184
Guthrie, Edwin R., 210, 211–213, 225
contiguity principle, 211–212
method for breaking undesirable habits, 212–213

Habit(s)
emotional (visceral), Watson's concept of, 156
Guthrie's concept of, 212
James on, 84
manual, Watson's concept of, 156
undesirable, Guthrie's method for breaking, 212–213
verbal, Watson's concept of, 157
Watson's concept of, 155–157
Habit strength, 223
Hull's concept of, 215
Haeckel, Ernst H., 236

Hall, G. Stanley, 70, 236–238
and child study movement, 238
life and career of, 236–237
recapitulation theory, 236, 237
use of questionnaires, 237–238
work on adolescence, 238
Hanson, Norwood R., 316
Harlow, Harry, 271
Harmony
in cosmology, 3
in Pythagorean thought, 2, 3
Hawthorne effect, 138
Head, Henry, 301
Hearnshaw, Leslie, 203
Hebb, Donald O., 162, 226–231
arousal system concept, 228–229
body image concept, 228
cell assembly concept, 227–228
cue function concept, 228–229
in Hilgard's textbook, 211
neuropsychology and, 227–228
The Organization of Behavior, 227–228
perceptual isolation concept, 229
phase sequences concept, 227–228
research on sensory deprivation, 228–230
vocal responses to sensation concept, 228
Hebb rule, 227
Heidegger, Martin, 268
being-in-the-world concept, 268
Heider, Fritz, 187–188, 241
Helmholtz, Hermann von, 56–61
and nature of perception, 57–59
place theory of pitch perception, 58–59
trichromatic theory of color perception, 58
unconscious inference theory, 59
Heraclitus, 12
Herbart, Johann Friedrich, 49–52
influence on educational psychology, 51–52
Hereditary genius, Galton's concept of, 61–62
Hering, Ewald, 59–60
opponent process theory of color vision, 60
Heron, Woodburn, 229
Hierarchy of needs, Maslow's, 272–273
Hilgard, Ernest R., 209–211
Conditioning and Learning, 209–210
Theories of Learning, 209–210
Hippocrates, 151
History. *See also* Psychology, history of
concepts of, 45–46
Hobbes, Thomas, 25
Holland, J. G., 166
Hollingworth, Leta, 277, 321
Homunculus, 163
Hooker, Joseph, 41
Hope, Erikson's concept of, 256
Horney, Karen, 109–110, 272
Hostility, Kelly's concept of, 284
Htut, Lin and Win, 320
Hull, Clark L., 210, 213–219
conditioned inhibition concept, 215
description of intervening variables, 214
drive concept, 213–216
Eleanor Gibson and, 258
habit strength concept, 215
hypothetico-deductive method, 214
incentive motivation concept, 215
and latent learning controversy, 223–224
mathematical learning theory, 214–216
postulates of, 214–216
and psychoanalytic theory, 214
reaction inhibition concept, 215
reaction potential concept, 215
reinforcement theory, 214
stimulus-intensity dynamism concept, 215
Human factors, 295
Humanism, Sartre's concept of, 267–268
Humanistic psychology, 265–288. *See also* Existentialism; Kelly, George A.; Maslow, Abraham H.; May, Rollo; Rogers, Carl R.
emergence of, 268–270
historical perspective on, 281–282
Human potential movement, 281
Hume, David, 33–35
Husserl, Edmund, 78, 174
and Sartre, 267
Hypnosis, 96–97
early use of, 99
Freud's use of, 99
Hypothesis/hypotheses. *See also* Null hypothesis
Hull's, 214
research, 199–200
Hypothetico-deductive method, Hull's, 214
Hysteria, 98–100
Freud's concept of, 99
theories of, 98

Iatrogenic, definition of, 281
I Ching, 12–15
hexagrams of, 13–14
trigrams of, 13
Ickes, Mary, 153
Icon, Neisser's concept of, 303
Iconic storage, Neisser's concept of, 303
Id, Freud's concept of, 103–104
Ideal self, Rogers' concept of, 278
Ideas
association of, for Locke, 31
clear and distinct, Cartesian concept of, 24
elementary, Herbart's concept of, 49
equilibrium of, Herbart's concept of, 50

Ideas (*cont.*)
Hume's concept of, 34
inhibition of, Herbart's concept of, 49–50
innate, 10–11, 24
intensity of, Herbart's concept of, 49–50
latent, 97
Locke's definition of, 31
simple and complex, for Locke, 31
Identification, Bandura's concept of, 231
Idiographic–nomothetic distinction, Allport's, 270
Imageless thought, 79
Titchener and, 125
Images
Aristotle's concept of, 20
in artificial memory, 19
Titchener's concept of, 124
Imagination, in memory, 18–20
Imitation
Baldwin's concept of, 240
Bandura's concept of, 231
Piaget's concept of, 246
Imitation game, Turing's concept of, 308
Immigration Act of 1924, 135
Impassible, Aristotle's concept of, 17
Impression(s), Hume's concept of, 34
Impulsive act, Wundt's concept of, 73
Incentive motivation, Hull's concept of, 215
Incest taboo, Freud's concept of, 104
Indifference, to anomalies, 324
Individual case versus general law, 14
Individual differences, Darwinian concept of, 44
Industrial psychology, 138–139
Inertia, 28
Infantile sexuality, Freud's concept of, 99
Inferiority feelings, Adler's concept of, 108
Information
concept of, 289–290
J. J. Gibson's two meanings of, 305
Information pickup theory, J. J. Gibson's, 306
Information processing
automatic versus controlled processes in, 304
in Hilgard's textbook, 211
Neisser's concept of, 302–306
Stroop task and, 304
Information processing system, 289
Information theory, 289–290
Inhelder, Bärbel, 245–252
Inheritance of acquired characteristics, Lamarckian principle of, 42, 43
Inhibition
of conditioned stimulus, 150
Pavlov's concept of, 151
Innate ideas, 24
Innate knowledge, 10–11
Inner perception, Wundt's concept of, 70
Inner psychophysics, Fechner's concept of, 53
Inner speech, 253
Innovative people, characteristics of, 40
Input, 290
Insight, Kohler's concept of, 179
Instinct(s)
Darwinian concept of, 44
death, Freud on, 105–106
life, Freud on, 105–106
sexual, Freud's concept of, 102
Instinctoid, Maslow's concept of, 274
Instruction
five ways of, Herbart's, 51–52
interest in, Herbart's concept of, 52
Intelligence
Binet and Simon's definition of, 133
development of
Piaget's theory of, 246
stages in, Piaget's concept of, 247–250
education and, 201–202
functional definition of, 133
Galton's concept of, 62
heredity and, 134–135, 201–202
meaning of, 135–136
measurement of, issues in, 134–136
national differences in, 134
Thorndike's concept of, 142
Thorndike's work on, 140–141
two-factor theory of, 201
Intelligence testing, 131–136. *See also* Binet, Alfred; Cattell, James McKeen
market forces and, 135–136
in United States Army, 134–135
Intensity of experience, Titchener's concept of, 125
Intentionality, 267
Brentano's concept of, 78
Husserl's concept of, 78
Interactionism, Cartesian, 25
Interest in instruction, Herbart's concept of, 52
Internal sense, for Kant, 38–40
Intervening variables, Hull's description of, 214
Introjection, Freud's concept of, 104
Introspection
Cartesian concept of, 25
James on, 84
systematic experimental, 79
Titchener's concept of, 122, 123
Wundt's use of, 69–73
Introspectionism, 171
language of, 124
Titchener's, 124–125
Introversion, Jung's concept of, 112–114, 115
Invariant functions, 246
Investigative practices, 195
IQ, 133–134

Irrational, problem of, for Greek mathematicians, 6–7
Irrational number(s), 6–7
Isomorphism, Kohler's concept of, 181–182
Ixion's wheel, as metaphor for history, 45

Jacob's ladder, as metaphor for history, 45
Jacobson, Edmund, 125, 126
Jacobson, Roman, 250
James, Henry, 83
James, William, 56, 70, 83–93, 276, 303–304
  approach to psychology, 84–85
  on attention, 89
  on consciousness of self, 88–89
  on habit, 84
  influence on Rollo May, 271
  meeting with Freud, 92
  metaphors employed by, 85
  as phenomenologist, 84–85
  Principles of Psychology, 83–92
  on pure ego, 88–89
  stream of thought (consciousness) concept, 85–88
  theory of emotions, 89–91
  on tip-of-the-tongue phenomenon, 87
  on unconscious, 96
  on will, 91–92
James-Lange theory, 89–91
Jastrow, Joseph, 70
Jencks, Christopher, 328
Jenkins, James J., 319
Jennings, Herbert S., 158
Jensen, Arthur, 203
Job satisfaction, Lewin's theory of, 185
Jones, Mary Cover, 231–232
Journal Citation Reports, 318
Journal of Humanistic Psychology, 269, 282
Journal of Transpersonal Psychology, 282
Joynson, Robert B., 203
Jung, Carl G., 12, 108, 110–117
  archetypal psychology and, 112
  collective unconscious and, 113
    and external world, 116–117
  four functions and, 115–116
  introvert–extravert distinction, 112–114, 115
  objective unconscious and, 116
  Psychological Types, 112
  relationship with Freud, 110–112
  on synchronicity, 117
  theory of archetypes, 113
  on unconscious, 97
  on union of opposites, 115
  and Wertheimer, 172
  Word association technique, 111
Just noticeable difference (jnd), Fechner's concept of, 54

Kamin, Leon, 203
Kant, Immanuel, 37–40, 174, 322
  second Copernican revolution, 37–38
Kaplan, Bernard, 241, 245
Kaplan, Edith, 241
Katona, George, 176
Kekulé, Friedrich, 116
Keller, Evelyn Fox, 321–322
Kelly, George A., 269, 272, 282–287
  concept of people as scientists, 283
  constructs concept, 283
  Elements concept, 284
  fundamental postulate of, 283
  hostility concept, 284
  personal construct theory, 283–284
    research in, 285–286
  The Psychology of Personal Constructs, 283–284
  repertory grid, 284–285
  repertory test, 284–285
  role titles concept, 284–285
Kepler, Johann, 3
Kierkegaard, Søren, 265–266
  on absurdity of human existence, 266
  Either/Or, 265–266
  on leap of faith, 266
  on subjectivity of human choice, 266
Koch, Sigmund, 198
Koffka, Kurt, 178, 182–184, 272
  and J. J. Gibson, 305
  The Growth of the Mind, 183–184
  Principles of Gestalt Psychology, 182–183
  theory of infant perception, 183–184
Kohler, Wolfgang, 178, 179–182
  insight concept, 179
  isomorphism concept, 181–182
  The Mentality of Apes, 179
  satiation theory of, 181–182
  on Tolman, 219
  transposition experiments, 180
    Spence's analysis of, 216–217
Krech, David, 222
Krechevsky, Isidore. *See* Krech, David
Krueger, Felix, 75
Kuhn, Thomas, 315–316
  paradigm concept, 316
Külpe, Oswald, 79, 318

Ladd, George T., 70
Ladd-Franklin, Christine, 60–61
Lamarck, Jean Baptiste, 42, 43
Lamarckism, 240
Lange, Carl G., 89
Language
  Chomsky's theory of, 291–293
  ordinary, Wittgenstein's analysis of, 323–324
  Skinner's views on, 291
  Wundt's theory of, 74
Language acquisition device, Chomsky's concept of, 293
Lao-Tsu, 11–15

Lashley, Karl S., 158–162, 181–182, 191, 227
Brain Mechanisms and Intelligence, 160
correspondence with Watson, 159
studies of cortical localization of function, 158–161
Latent ideas, 97
Latent learning, controversy about, 222, 223–224
Law of contagion, 105
Law of effect, Thorndike's, 142
Law of equipotentiality, 161
Law of mass action, 161
Law of progressions and pathologies, 60–61
Law of similarity, 105
Laws of motion, 27–28
Leap of faith, Kierkegaard's view of, 266
Learning. *See also* Verbal learning
associative, Calkins' concept of, 76–77
Calkins' study of, 76–77
Ebbinghaus's study of, 75–76
as formation of connections, Thorndike's concept of, 141–143
frequency in, Calkins' study of, 77
in Gestalt psychology, 176–177
latent, controversy about, 222, 223–224
no-trial, Bandura's concept of, 232
observational, 231
one-trial, 212–213, 225–226
perceptual, E. J. Gibson's concept of, 258–260
programmed, 166
as remembering, 10
Skinner's view of, 164
theories of, 209–234. *See also* Bandura, Albert; Guthrie, Edwin R.; Hebb, Donald O.; Hilgard, Ernest R.; Hull, Clark L.; Tolman, Edward C.
Learning curve, Thorndike's use of, 141–142
Le Corbusier, 328
Leibniz, Gottfried Wilhelm
apperception and, 51
and *I Ching,* 12, 14
Levi-Strauss, Claude, 250
Lewin, Kurt, 178, 184–190, 280–281
in Hilgard's textbook, 210–211
interest in group dynamics, 187
Libido
Freud's concept of, 102, 112
Jung's concept of, 112
Life cycle theory, Erikson's
autonomy versus shame and doubt, 256
basic trust versus mistrust, 256
eight stages of, 255–257
generativity versus stagnation, 256–257
identity versus identity diffusion, 256
industry versus inferiority, 256
initiative versus guilt, 256
integrity versus despair, 257
intimacy versus isolation, 256
Life instinct, Freud on, 105–106
Life review, 257
Life space
barriers in, 185–186
equilibrium in, 186
foreign hull of, 186
Lewin's concept of, 185–186
permeable membrane of, 186
regions of, 185–186
valences in, 186
Life-span developmental psychology, Erikson's, 254–255
Linguistics, Chomsky's effect on, 291–293
Little Albert, 156
Loci, in artificial memory, 19
Locke, John, 30–32
Locus of control, external versus internal, 233
Loeb, Jacques, 153
Logical positivism, 195–198, 315
Loos, Adolf, 327
Lorge, Irving, 143
Love
Erikson's concept of, 256
May's views on, 270–271
Love and Will (May), 270–271
Luria, Alexander R., 111
Lyell, Charles, 41–42, 43

"The Magical Number Seven: Plus or Minus Two" (Miller), 294
Magical thinking, 105
Malthus, Thomas, 42–43
Mandalas, 115
Manual habits, Watson's concept of, 156
Marxism, Vygotsky and, 252
Maslow, Abraham H., 268–269, 271–276
Being values (B-values) concept, 274
deficiency motives concept, 274
Eupsychian Management, 276
experiential methods, 276
hierarchy of needs, 272–273
instinctoid concept, 275
metamotivations concept, 274
metapathology concept, 275
Motivation and Personality, 272
and Neisser, 302
peak experiences concept, 275–276
on problem-centered versus method-centered approach, 276
The Psychology of Science, 276
self-actualization theory, 273
self-actualizing person concept, 273–275
on Taoistic science, 276
Massed practice, 156
Materialism
definition of, 148

Pavlov's work and, 148
Material self, James on, 88
Mathematical learning theory
in Hilgard's textbook, 211
Hull's, 214–216
Mathematical psychologist(s), 49
Mathematics
Fechner's use of, 53–54
Kant's view of, 39
and music, 2
in psychology, 5–6, 117
Pythagorean, 4–6
Maxwell, Clerk, 181
May, Rollo, 268–269, 270–271
on care, 271
influence of William James on, 271
Love and Will, 270–271
The Meaning of Anxiety, 270
Mayo, Elton, 137, 138–139
Mean
definition of, 64
regression toward, 63–64
The Meaning of Anxiety (May), 270
Means-end expectations, 221
Mechanical models, of body, 25–27
Mechanism, versus contextualism, 319
Mediational processes, Osgood's concept of, 217–218
Medieval period, theology in, 21
Melancholic temperament, 15
Memory
Aristotle's concept of, 18–20
artificial, 19–20
Bartlett's theory of, 300–302, 304
Ebbinghaus's study of, 75–76
Galton's concept of, 64
Zeigarnik effect in, 186–187
Meno (Plato), 9–10, 11
Mental abilities
primary, 204
profile of, Thurstone's work on, 204
Mental act, Brentano's concept of, 78
Mental age, 133–134
Mental development
comparative psychology of, Werner's work on, 241–245
psychology of, Baldwin's, 239–240
stages, Baldwin's concept of, 239
Mental energy, Spearman's concept of, 201
Mentalism, 318
The Mentality of Apes (Kohler), 179
Mental test(s). *See also* intelligence testing
Cattell's, 132
validity of, 132
Mesmer, Anton, 97
Metamotivations, Maslow's concept of, 274
Metapathology, Maslow's concept of, 274
Metaphor, James's use of, 85
Method of average error, Fechner's, 55
Method of constant stimuli, Fechner's concept of, 55
Method of just noticeable differences (method of limits), Fechner's, 55
Method of right and wrong cases, Fechner's, 55
Method of serial reproduction, Bartlett's work on, 300–301
Metronome, Wundt's use of, 70–71, 196
Meyer, A., 79
Microgenesis, Werner's concept of, 244–245
Mill, John Stuart, 37
Miller, George A., 293–298
channel capacity concept, 294
and giving psychology away, 297
"The Magical Number Seven: Plus or Minus Two," 294
National Medal of Science won by, 297
Plans and the Structure of Behavior, 294–297
span of apprehension and, 294
span of immediate memory and, 294
strategies versus tactics concept, 296
TOTE mechanism concept, 296–297
Miller, Neal, 214
Mind. *See also* Consciousness
Aristotle's concept of, 17
Cartesian concept of, 24–25
evolution of, Spencer's theory of, 65
Freud's model of. *See* Structural model, Freud's
as ghost in the machine, 25
Herbart's concept of, 50
impassible, Aristotle's concept of, 17
James on, 85
Jung's model of, 113–114
Titchener's concept of, 122
Minimax axiom, 298
Minimum principle, in Gestalt psychology, 173, 183
Mnemonics, 18–20
ancient, and contemporary psychology, 20
Modeling
versus operant conditioning, Bandura's research on, 232
in social learning theory, 231
Modernism, 326–328
architecture and, 327–328
Modules, in cognitive processes, 311
Monster barring, 324
Moral anxiety, Freud's concept of, 104
Morawski, Jill, 325

Morgan, C. Lloyd, 139
canon of, 140
observations of Tony (his dog), 139–140
Motion
action versus, 17–18, 212, 220
apparent, Wertheimer's study of, 172–173
Newton's laws of, 27–28
Motivation
Hebb's concept of, 228
Lewin's theory of, 185
Maslow's theory of, 273
Motivation and Personality (Maslow), 272
Motor skills, and memory, Bartlett's concept of, 301
Müller, Johannes, 57, 98
Muller-Lyer illusion, 121–122
Multiplication of classes, Piaget's concept of, 249–250
Münsterberg, Hugo, 70, 136
Music, mathematics and, 2
Music of the spheres, 3

National Medal of Science
to E. J. Gibson, 261
to G. A. Miller, 297
National Training Laboratories, 187
Nativism-empiricism dichotomy, 183
Natural selection, 43
Nature
versus culture, 14
Helmholtz's understanding of, 57
Necker, Louis Albert, 181
Necker cube, 181
Needs, Maslow's concept of
basic, 272
cognitive-aesthetic, 273
esteem, 273
hierarchy of, 272–273
love, 273
physiological, 272
safety, 273
Negative afterimages, 60
Negative reinforcement, Skinner's concept of, 163
Neisser, Ulric, 272, 302–307
attention concept, 303
Cognitive Psychology, 302–306
cyclical model of cognition, 306–307
distinctive features of stimuli concept, 303
ecological validity concept and, 306
focal attention concept, 303
and Gibson's ecological approach to perception, 306
icon concept, 303
iconic storage concept, 303
information processing theory, 302–306
pattern recognition concept, 303
preattentive processing concept, 303
reappearance hypothesis and, 303–304
utilization hypothesis, 304
Neobehaviorists, 197
Nepotism rules, in academia, 258
Neural networks, 182
Neurophysiology
and cognitive psychology, 311
in Hilgard's textbook, 211
Neuropsychology, Hebb's theory and, 227–228
Neuroscience, emergence of, 226–228
Neurosis, Horney's theory of, 110
Neurotic anxiety
Freud's concept of, 104
versus normal anxiety, May's views on, 270
Newell, Allen, 291, 308, 309, 311, 312
New history of psychology, 315
New history of science, 315–318
New Look, in perception, 298–299
A New Theory of Vision (Berkeley), 32
Newton, Isaac, 26–30
laws of motion, 26–28
Principia, 26
work on color, 28–30
Nietzsche, Friedrich, 266–267
nihilism and, 266
perspectivism and, 266
will to power concept, 266–267
Nihilism, 266
Non-directive psychotherapy, 277–279
Nonsense syllables, Ebbinghaus's use of, 75, 222
Normal distribution, 62–64
Normal science, 317
No-trial learning, Bandura's concept of, 232
Null hypothesis, 199–200
Number(s), rational versus irrational, 6–7

Objective unconscious, 116
Object permanence, Piaget's concept of, 248
Observation, naturalistic, 69
Observational learning, 231
Ockham, William of, 140
Oedipus complex, Freud's concept of, 99
One-trial learning, 212–213, 225–226
Ontogeny, 3
recapitulation of phylogeny, 236, 239
Operant behavior, Skinner's concept of, 163
Operant conditioning
efficacy of, 232
versus modeling, Bandura's research on, 232
Skinner's view of, 164
Operational definitions, 197
Operationism, 197–198, 315
and context of justification, 198
criticisms of, 198

Opportunism, and anomalies, 324
Oral stage, Freud's concept of, 102
Organic selection, Baldwin's concept of, 240
Organismic approach, Werner's, 241
Organismic theory
  Goldstein's, 191
  in Hilgard's textbook, 210–211
The Organization of Behavior (Hebb), 227–228
The Origins of Intelligence in Children (Piaget), 246
Orth, J., 79
Orthogenetic principle of development, Werner's, 241
Osgood, Charles E., 217–218
  semantic differential technique, 218–219
Outer psychophysics, Fechner's concept of, 53
Output, 290
Oxford English Dictionary, 8

Paired associates method, 76–77, 222
Panpsychism, Fechner's doctrine of, 53
Pappenheim, Bertha, 99
Parable of the watchmakers, 311
Paradigm(s)
  clashes, 316
  definition of, 316
  in psychology, 316–318
Parapsychology, James on, 92
Parts versus pieces, Gestalt theory of truth and, 177
Pattern and Growth in Personality (Allport), 270
Pattern recognition, Neisser's concept of, 303
Patterns of Culture (Benedict), 272
Pauli, Wolfgang, 116–117
Pavlov, Ivan P., 70, 147–153
  in Hilgard's textbook, 211
  Institute of Experimental Medicine, 148
  on Lashley, 161
  work on conditioned reflexes, 147–150
Peak experiences, Maslow's concept of, 275–276
Penis envy, 108
Pepper, Stephen C., 319
Perception
  ecological approach to, 305
  Gestalt theory of, 183
  J. J. Gibson's ecological approach to, 305
  Helmholtz's theory of, 57–59
  infant, Koffka's theory of, 183–184
  James's concept of, 91
  minimum principle in, 173, 183
  New Look in, 298–299
  physiognomic, 243
  subliminal, 102
  Titchener's concept of, 125
  visual, 26, 27
Perceptual constancies, 183
Perceptual isolation
  Hebb's concept of, 229
  McGill studies on, 229–230
Perceptual learning, E. J. Gibson's concept of, 258–260
Perceptual readiness, 299
Persona, Jungian, 114
Personal constructs, Kelly's theory of, 283–284
  research in, 285–286
Personality
  characterization of, factor analytic study of, 204
  forming impressions in, Asch's research in, 189–190
  structure of, Freud's concept of, 103–104
Personality and Psychotherapy (Dollard and Miller), 214
Personality theory, Freud's, 102–103
Personal unconscious, Jung's concept of, 113
Perspective, concept of, 26–27
Perspectivism, 266
Pfungst, Oscar, 200
Phallic stage, Freud's concept of, 102
Phantom limbs, Hebb's theory and, 227–228
Phase sequences in experience, Hebb's concept of, 227–228
Phenomenal world, of lived experience, 182
Phenomenological psychology, Brentano and, 78
Phenomenology, 219
  and Gestalt psychology, 174
  James and, 84–85
  Titchener and, 125–126
Phi phenomenon, 172–173
Phlegmatic temperament, 15
Phrenology, 159, 160
Physics and psychology. *See also* Psychophysics
  Kohler's ideas about, 180–182
Physiognomic perception, 243
Physiognomic properties, of percepts, 184
Piaget, Jean, 70, 111, 123, 138, 239, 245–252
  accommodation concept, 246
  assimilation concept, 246
  associativity concept, 248
  centered versus decentered concept, 251
  clinical method, 245, 246–247
  concrete operations concept, 249–250
  conservation concept, 251
  deferred imitation concept, 248–249
  equilibration concept, 246
  formal operations concept, 250
  genetic epistemology, 245–246
  in Hilgard's textbook, 211
  imitation concept, 246
  invariant functions concept, 246

Piaget, Jean (*cont.*)
multiplication of classes concept, 249–250
object permanence concept, 248
The Origins of Intelligence in Children, 246
preoperational period concept, 248–249
reversibility concept, 248
self-regulation concept, 251
sensorimotor period concept, 247–248
as structuralist, 250
symbolic play concept, 248–249
systems of transformation concept, 250–251
theory of development of intelligence, 246
stages in, 247–250
view of play, 246
wholeness concept, 250
Pineal gland, Descartes' hypothesis about, 24–25
Pinel, Philippe, 98
Place theory, 59
Place versus response controversy, 221–222
Planck, Max, 181
Plans
computer programs and, comparison of, 296–297
Miller's concept of, 296–297
Plans and the Structure of Behavior (Miller, Galanter, and Pribram), 294–297
Plasticity, James's concept of, 84
Plato, 6–11, 12
Aristotle and, comparison of, 15–17
dialogues of, 9–10
importance in Western thought, 7–9
Meno, 9–10, 11
Play
Bruner's work on, 300
Piaget's concept of, 246
Pleasant/unpleasant distinction, Titchener's, 124
Pleasure principle, Freud's concept of, 100
Point of subjective equality, Fechner's concept of, 55
Point of view
in art, 26–27
Titchener's concept of, 121–122
Popper, Karl, 196
Positive reinforcement, Skinner's concept of, 163
Posthypnotic suggestion
Ach's experiment on, 80
Freud on, 96
Postmodernism, 328–329
Postulates, Hull's, 214–216
Potency (P) set of dimensions, 218–219
Potentiality versus actuality, Aristotle's concept of, 16
Pötzl, Otto, 101–102
Practice, distributed versus massed, 156
Pragnanz, 183, 188
Preattentive processing, Neisser's concept of, 303
Preconscious, 97
Freud's concept of, 101
Preconservative children, Piaget's concept of, 251
Preformation, theory of, 41
Preoperational period, Piaget's concept of, 248–249
Preparation
in education, 51
importance of, 51
Presentation, in education, 51–52
Pressey, Sidney, 166
Pribram, Karl, 294
Primal horde, Freud's concept of, 104
Primary process, Freud's concept of, 100
Primary signaling system, 150–151
Priming, of responses, 161
Principles of Gestalt Psychology (Koffka), 182–183
Principles of Psychology (James), 83–92
Prism, dispersal of white light through, 29, 30
Prismatic lenses, 33
Problem-centered versus method-centered approach, Maslow's concept of, 276
Process
versus achievement, Werner's concept of, 242
versus structure, 14
Process analysis, 242
Productive Thinking (Wertheimer), 176–177
Programmed learning, 166
Progressive change, history and, 45
Progressive education, Dewey and, 129
Progressive relaxation, 125, 126
Projection
in art, 27
as defense, 109
Promissory notes
definition of, 155
Watson's, 155
Pronounceability, and reading, E. J. Gibson's work on, 259
Proportion, in Pythagorean thought, 3
Protensity of experience, Titchener's concept of, 125
Protocol sentences, Carnap's concept of, 196
Proximity, Gestalt law of, 175
Psyche, in Pythagorean thought, 3–4
Psychic energy, Jung's concept of, 112
Psychoanalysis
criticisms of, 197, 269–270

current status of, 318
Freud's proprietary attitude toward, 107–108
in Hilgard's textbook, 211
Psychoanalytic theory
academic psychologists and, 106–107
in America, 106–107
Freud and, 106–107
Hull and, 214
influence on 20th-c. culture, 109
Psychoanalytic therapy, 107
Psychoid, Jung's concept of, 116
Psychological community, resistance to change, 230
Psychological research, as social construction, 325–326
Psychological Types (Jung), 112
Psychologische Forschung, 190–191
Psychologist(s)
eminent, ranking of, 70
methodological preferences of, Cronbach's analysis of, 205–206
social relations between, grid and group for, 324–325
Psychologist's fallacy, James on, 84–85
Psychology
abnormal, 122
act, Brentano and, 78
analytical, Jung and, 112
anecdotal, 139
anthropomorphic, 139–140
applied, 131
Cronbach on, 206
archetypal, Jung and, 112
and art, 327
behavioral, current status of, 318
child, Darwin's ideas and, 44
cognitive. *See* Cognitive psychology
common-sense, 187
comparative. *See* Comparative psychology
correlational, 205–206
cultural, Wundt and, 73–75
cyclical nature of, 45
developmental. *See* Developmental psychology
educational, Herbart's influence on, 51–52
evolutionary theory and, 44–45
future of, 315–333
E. J. Gibson on, 261
genetic, 236
Gestalt. *See* Gestalt psychology
history of, 236–237
future, 332–333
studying, 45–46
humanistic. *See* Humanistic psychology
industrial. *See* Industrial psychology
nature of, for Kant, 38–40
Newtonian physics and, 28
as paradigmatic discipline, 317–318
phenomenological, Brentano and, 78
physics and. *See also* Psychophysics
Kohler's ideas about, 180–182
as postmodern, 326–328
as preparadigmatic discipline, 317–318
progress in, 45
scientific, two disciplines of, 204–207
scope of, Titchener's concept of, 122
social. *See* Social psychology
as social construction, 322–326
social role of, Miller's views on, 297
subject matter of, 28
theoretical viewpoints in, 316–317
Transpersonal, 282
Watson's, 155
Psychology (Woodworth), 130
The Psychology of Personal Constructs (Kelly), 283–284
The Psychology of Science (Maslow), 275
Psychology of women, 320–322
Hollingworth's work on, 277, 321
Psychometric information, 206–207
Psychophysical parallelism
Fechner's concept of, 53
Titchener's concept of, 122
Wundt's concept of, 73
Psychophysics, 29
Fechner and, 53–56
inner versus outer, Fechner's concept of, 53
quantity objection to, 56
Psychosexual development, Freud's concept of, 102
Psychotherapy, existential approach to, Binswanger's, 268
Psychotherapy: Theory, Research and Practice (journal), 280
Punishment(s)
versus negative reinforcement, 163
Skinner's concept of, 163
Pure ego, James on, 88, 89
Purpose, Erikson's concept of, 256
Purposive behavior, Tolman's work on, 220
Purposive behaviorism, 220
Puzzle boxes, 141–142, 212
Pythagoras, 1–6
Pythagorean cosmology, 3
Pythagorean mathematics, 4–6
Pythagorean opposites, 3–4, 5
Pythagorean theorem, 5, 6

Qualitative research methods, 286–287
Qualities, primary and secondary, for Locke, 32

Quality of experience, Titchener's concept of, 125
Quantitative research methods, 287
Questionnaires, Hall's use of, 237–238

Rationalism, 24, 30
Rationalization, as defense, 109
Rational number(s), 6
Rats
  Garcia's learning experiments with, 230
  latent learning experiments with, 223–224
  Tolman's work with, 221–222
  white, Watson's use of, 153
Rayner, Rosalie, 156, 157–158
Reaction formation, as defense, 109
Reaction inhibition, Hull's concept of, 215
Reaction potential, Hull's concept of, 215
Reaction time, individual differences in, Baldwin–Titchener dispute over, 241
Reading, E. J. Gibson's work on, 259–260
Realistic anxiety, Freud's concept of, 104
Reality principle, Freud's concept of, 100
Reappearance hypothesis, Neisser and, 303–304
Reason
  Aristotle's concept of, 16–17
  Wollstonecraft's views on, 36
Recapitulation, theory of, 236, 237
Recapitulationism, Baldwin and, 239
Reciprocal determinism, Bandura's concept of, 232–233
Rectangle, area of, 39
Reflection, as source of ideas, for Locke, 31
Reflex(es). *See also* Conditioned reflexes
  association, Bekhterev's concept of, 152–153
  conceptions of, 128
  Goldstein on, 191
Reflex arc concept, Dewey's critique of, 127–128
Reflexology, Bekhterev's, 152–153
Regression, Freud's concept of, 101, 103
Regression toward the mean, 63–64
Reinforcement
  Hull's theory of, 214
  negative, versus punishment, 163
  pleasing effects of versus strengthening effects of, 167–168
  positive and negative, Skinner's concept of, 163
  schedules of
    fixed ratio, 164
    Skinner's concept of, 164
    variable ratio, 164
  Skinner's concept of, 163–164
Reinforcer(s), primary and secondary, Hull's concepts of, 214
Reinforcing stimulus, 163
Relaxation, progressive, 125, 126
Religion
  Freud on, 104–106
  and recapitulationism, for Hall, 237
Religious experiences, James on, 92
Remembering, Ebbinghaus's study of, 75–76
Reminiscence, Erikson's concept of, 257
Remote associations, Ebbinghaus's concept of, 76
Renaissance, definition, 23
Repertory grid, Kelly's concept of, 284–285, 285–286
Repertory test, Kelly's concept of, 284–285
Repetition and learning
  Guthrie's concept of, 212, 225
  Rock's experiments and, 225–226
Repetition compulsion, Freud's concept of, 103
Replication, of experimental results, 200
Repression, Freud's concept of, 99
Reputation
  judgments about, 203–204
  and natural ability, Galton's concept of, 61–62
Research
  action, Lewin's advocacy of, 187
  cross-cultural, Osgood's, 219
  methods, 195–208
    qualitative, 286–287
    quantitative, 287
  psychological, as social construction, 325–326
Research hypothesis, 199–200
Resistance, Freud's concept of, 100
Respondent behavior, Skinner's concept of, 163
Respondent conditioning, Skinner's view of, 164
Response(s)
  conditioned, 149–150
  priming of, 161
  Skinner's concept of, 163
  unconditioned, 149–150
  vocal, to sensation, Hebb's theory and, 228
Retrospection, 79
Reversibility, Piaget's concept of, 248
Reward(s)
  Guthrie's concept of, 212
  Skinner's concept of, 163
Robinson, Edward S., 222–225
Rock, Irvin, 225–226
Rockefeller, John D., 66

Rogers, Carl R., 268–269, 276–282
client-centered therapy, 277–279
clinical psychology and, 276–277
self-concept theory, 278
theory of creative environments, 279
unconditional positive regard concept, 278
Role titles, Kelly's concept of, 284–285
Romanes, George John, 139
Rosenthal, Robert, 200
Rotter, Julian, 233
Royce, Josiah, 70
Rozin, Paul, 105
Rubin, Edgar, 175–176

s, Spearman's concept of, 201
Sacks, Oliver, *Awakenings,* 17
Sagacity, definition of, 165
Sage, definition, 11
St. Thomas Aquinas, 21
Salpêtriére, 98
Samelson, Franz, 203–204
Sanford, Ruth, 279
Sanguine temperament, 15
Sartre, Jean-Paul, 267–268
Being and Nothingness, 267
existence precedes essence concept, 267
humanism and, 267–268
intentionality concept, 267
Satiation theory, Kohler's, 181–182
Scala naturae, 20–21
Scale of values, Allport, Vernon, and Lindzey's, 270
Schema, Bartlett's concept of, 301
Schizophrenia, 111
Schmidt, Taylor's use of, 137
Schneirla, Theodore C., 245
Scholastic Aptitude Test, 135
Schools of psychology, 127
Schur, Max, 106
Science
masculine-oriented, feminist views on, 321
normal, 317
philosophy of, 195–198
Science-gender system, 322
Scientific inquiry, subjective aspects of, 315–316
Scientific management, Taylor's use of, 137–138
Scientific psychology, two disciplines of, 204–207
Scott, Walter Dill, 136–137
Scott Corporation, 137
Sears, Robert, 261
Sechenov, Ivan M., 148
Secondary process, Freud's concept of, 100
Secondary signaling system, 150–151
The Second Sex (Beauvoir), 320–321
Selectivity of consciousness, James on, 87–88
Self
Calkins' concept of, 77
Hume's concept of, 34
James on, 88–89
Jungian concept of, 115
Self-actualization
Goldstein's concept of, 191, 273
Maslow's concept of, 273
Self-actualizing person, Maslow's concept of, 273–275
Self-concept, Rogers' theory of, 278
Self-observation, Wundt's concept of, 70
Self-realization, Goldstein's concept of, 191
Self-regulation, Piaget's concept of, 251
Semantic differential technique, Osgood's, 218–219
Sensation, Wertheimer's concept of, 174
Sensations, Titchener's concept of, 124
Sensibility, Wollstonecraft's views on, 36
Sensitivity training, 187, 280–281
Sensorimotor level of development, 243
Sensorimotor period, Piaget's concept of, 247–248
Sensory deprivation, Hebb's research on, 228–230
Sensory experience, as source of ideas, for Locke, 31
Sentence(s)
deep structure of, Chomsky's concept of, 292
surface structure of, Chomsky's concept of, 292
Serendipity
definition of, 165
Skinner and, 165
Serial learning, 226
Serially ordered behavior, Watson's model of, 157
Lashley's criticism of, 161–162
Serial position curves, 226
Serson, Joan, 254
Set, Woodworth's concept of, 131
Sexual abuse, Freud's attitude toward, 99–100
Sexual instincts, Freud's concept of, 102
Sexuality, Darwinian concept of, 44
Shadowing task, 295
Shadow world, Jungian, 114
Shape constancy, 183
Signals
in communication, 290
Guthrie's concept of, 212, 213
Sign Gestalts, 220–221
Signs, Osgood's concept of, 217–218
Similarity, Gestalt law of, 175
Simmel, Marianne L., 228
Simon, Herbert A., 33, 291, 307–312
career of, 307

Simon, Herbert A. (*cont.*)
modular construction of cognition concept, 311
parable of the watchmakers, 311
on spurious correlation and the nature of causality, 307–308
work on computer simulation of psychological processes, 308–312
Simon, Theophile, 133
Simonton, D. K., 40–41
Simplicity in experience, in Gestalt psychology, 173
Size constancy, 32–33, 183
Skeptic(s)
definition of, 34
Hume as, 34
Skinner, B. F., 70, 162–168, 232
baby tender, 165
The Behavior of Organisms, 163–164
criticism of, 269
operationism and, 197
programmed learning and, 166
radical behaviorism of, 162–163
sagacity and, 165
serendipity and, 165
teaching machines, 165–166
unformalized principles of scientific practice, 164–165
utopian and dystopian views of, 166–168
Verbal Behavior, 291
views on language, 291
Walden Two, 166–168
on Watson, 162
Skinner, Deborah, 165
Skinner box, 162, 163
Social anthropology, Frazer's, 104, 105
Social cognition, Asch's study of, 189
Social construction
psychological research as, 325–326
psychology as, 322–326
Social constructionism, 322
Social Darwinism, 65
Social Learning and Personality Development (Bandura and Walters), 231
Social learning theory, Bandura's, 231
Social psychology. *See also* Asch, Solomon; Heider, Fritz; Lewin, Kurt
Asch's research in, 189–190
emergence of, 184–190
Social Science Citation Index, 318
Social self, James on, 88
Socio-behavioristic approach, 231
Socrates, 9–10
Solomons, L. M., 90
S-O-R framework, 131
Soul
Aristotle's concept of, 17
in Pythagorean thought, 3–4
Skinner's views on, 163
Span of apprehension
Miller's work on, 294
Wundt's concept of, 72
Spearman, Charles, 132, 201–202
g concept, 201–202
mental energy concept, 201
s concept, 201
two-factor theory of intelligence, 201
Specific energy of nerves, Müller's theory of, 57
Speech
egocentric, 253
in higher order conditioning, 150–151
inner, 253
Watson's concept of, 157
Spence, Janet T., 330
Spence, Kenneth W., 216–217
Spencer, Herbert, 41, 64–66, 130, 332
theory of evolution, 65
Sperry, Roger, 181–182
Spielrein, Sabina, 111
Spiritualism, James on, 92
Spiritual self, James on, 88
Spontaneous recovery, of conditioned response, 150
Spoonerisms, 161–162
Spurzheim, J. G., 159
Stabilized retinal images, 231
Stanford-Binet test, 133
Station point, 27
Statistical inference, 198
Statistical significance, 199–200
Statistics, 62–64
Steady state, 295
Steermanship, 294
Stein, Gertrude, 90
Stereoscope, 59
Stern, William, 133–134, 241
Sternberg, Robert J., 135–136
Stimulus/stimuli
conditioned, 149–150
inhibition of, 150
as signal, 150
temporary nature of, 150
cue function of, Hebb's concept of, 228–229
distal versus proximal, 183
distinctive features of, Neisser's concept of, 303
reinforcing, 163
Skinner's concept of, 163
unconditioned, 149–150
Stimulus error, 124, 126
Stimulus gradients, J. J. Gibson's, 305–306
Stimulus-intensity dynamism, Hull's concept of, 215
Stimulus-onset asynchrony, 244
Stimulus-response relationships. *See also* Behaviorism
conceptions of, 128
Watson on, 154
Strands, in contextualism, 319
Strategies, versus tactics, 296
Stratton, George, 33
Stream of consciousness, James's concept of, 85–88
Stream of thought, James's concept of, 85–88

Stroop, John R., 304
Stroop task, 304
Structuralism, 250. *See also* Titchener, Edward B.
  Piaget and, 123
  Titchener and, 123–124
Structural model, Freud's, 103–104
Structure, definition of, 250
Structure and Direction in Thinking (Berlyne), 219
Structure/function distinction, Titchener's, 123
A Study of Thinking (Bruner, Goodnow, and Austin), 291, 299–300
Stumpf, Carl, 77, 78, 184
Subjective behaviorism, 297
Subjective experience, Kant's view of, 38–40
Subliminal perception, 102
Sumner, Cecil, 70
Superego, Freud's concept of, 103–104
Surplus meaning, Carnap's concept of, 196
Survival of the fittest, 43, 65
Syllogism
  Aristotle's interest in, 16
  practical, 16
Symbolic forms, Cassirer's concept of, 184–185
Symbolic play, Piaget's concept of, 248–249
Symbols, Gendlin's concept of, 280
Synchronicity, Jung's concept of, 117
Synergy, Maslow's views on, 272
Syntactic structures, Chomsky's views on, 291–292
Systematic desensitization, 232
Systematic experimental introspection, 79
Systems of transformation, Piaget's concept of, 250–251

Tachistoscope, 102, 298
Tao, 12
Taoism
  Confucianism and, comparison of, 11–12
  definition, 11
Taoistic science, Maslow's concept of, 276
Tao-Te Ching, 12
Taylor, Frederick W., 137–138, 138–139
Teaching, structurally blind methods, 176–177
Teaching machines, Skinner's, 165–166
Teleology, definition, 18
Temperament(s)
  choleric, 15, 151
  Galen's typology of, 15
  melancholic, 15, 151
  Pavlov's concept of, 151
  phlegmatic, 15, 151
  and psychopathology, 151
  sanguine, 15, 151
Terman, Lewis M., 133, 236
Textbook writers, importance of, 209
Texture, in contextualism, 319
T-groups, 187, 280–281
Thanatos, Freud on, 105–106
Theorems, Hull's, 214
Theories of Learning (Hilgard), 209–210
Thinking aloud, 297, 309–310
Third Force, humanistic psychologists as, 269–270
Thorndike, Edward L., 132, 140–141, 147, 271
  connectionism theory, 142–143
  law of effect, 142
  puzzle boxes, 141–142, 212
  work on animal intelligence, 140–141, 148–149
Thought
  chain of, 86
  imageless, 79
    Titchener and, 125
  internal speech and, 157
  stream of, James's concept of, 85–88
  train of, 86
  Würzburgers' concept of, 79
Thought and Language (Vygotsky), 252–253, 254
Three-term contingencies, Skinner's concept of, 163
Threshold
  absolute, Fechner's concept of, 55
  difference, Fechner's concept of, 55
Threshold concept, 29, 49
Thurstone, Louis Leon, 204
Time and motion study, 138
Tip-of-the-tongue phenomenon, 87
Titchener, Edward B., 70, 121–127, 130
  approach to psychology, 121–122
  career of
    first phase, 123
    fourth phase, 123, 125–126
    second phase, 123–125
    third phase, 123, 125
  concept of mind, 122
  concept of point of view, 121–122
  concept of sensations, 124
  dimensions of consciousness and, 125–126
  Experimental Psychology, 124–125
  imageless thought controversy and, 125
  influence on psychology, 126–127
  introspectionism and, 122–125
  perceptual learning concept, 258
  phenomenology and, 125–126
  psychophysical parallelism concept, 122
  qualitative and quantitative methods, 124–125
  structuralism and, 123–124

Titchener, Edward B. (*cont.*)
structure/function distinction, 123
To be is to be perceived, Berkeley's theory of, 33
Tolman, Edward C., 210, 219–222, 254
cognitive map concept, 220–221
and latent learning controversy, 223–224
molar versus molecular description of behavior, 220
place versus response controversy and, 221–222
sign Gestalts and, 220–221
work on purposive behavior, 220
Tools, Vygotsky's view on, 252–253
Topology, Lewin's use of, 185–186
TOTE mechanisms, 296
hierarchical models of, 296–297
Touchstone, definition of, 1
Tough-mindedness versus tender-mindedness, James on, 92
Tower of Hanoi problem, 309, 310
Toynbee, Arnold, 328
Toy problems, 309
Trained subjects, Wundt's use of, 71
Transfer of training, 143
Transpersonal Psychology, 282
Transposition
definition of, 180
Gestalt principle of, 180
Spence's analysis of, 216–217
Triads, in balanced and unbalanced states, Heider's concept of, 188
Tridimensional theory of feeling, Wundt's, 72–73, 219
Trigrams, of *I Ching,* 13
Tropisms, 153
Tropistic/reflexive level of development, 243
Truth
correspondence theory of, 177–178
Gestalt theory of, 177–178
Turing, Alan, 308–309
Turing's test, 308–309
Twins, conjoined, personhood of, 319–320
Twin studies, Burt's, 202
Two-factor theory of intelligence, 201

Unconditional positive regard, 278
Unconditioned reflexes, 149–150
Unconditioned response, 149–150
Unconditioned stimulus, 149–150
Unconscious, 95–98
Angell's concept of, 97
collective
and external world, 116–117
Jung's concept of, 113
definition of, 95–96
Freud's concept of, 96–97, 101
Herbart's concept of, 49
James on, 96
Jung's concept of, 97
objective, 116
personal, Jung's concept of, 113
Unconscious inference, Helmholtz's theory of, 59
Unconscious mind, 97
Underwood, Benton J., 226
Union of opposites, Jung's concept of, 115
Unity, in Pythagorean thought, 2
Unverbalized, Watson's concept of, 157
Uroboros, 116
Utilization hypothesis, Neisser's, 304
Utopia, Skinner's, 166–168
Utopian tradition, in psychology, 36

Valences, in life space, 186
Validity, of test, 132
Variation, Darwinian concept of, 43–44
Verbal Behavior (Skinner), 291
Verbal habits, Watson's concept of, 157
Verbalization, concurrent versus retrospective, 309–310
Verbal learning
fate of, 226
functionalism and, 222–225
Verbal reports, 196
Verification principle, 196
Vienna Circle, 195
Vision, projective model of, 27, 59
Visual cliff, 260–261
Visual pyramid, 26
Visual spectrum, Helmholtz's theory and, 57–58
Vivisection, 151–152
Vocal responses to sensation, Hebb's theory and, 228
Volition. *See also* Will
Wundt's concept of, 73
Voluntary act, Wundt's concept of, 73
von Ehrenfels, Christian, 173–174
von Restorff effect, 226
Vygotsky, Lev S., 111, 239, 252–254
on egocentric speech, 253
on inner speech, 253
Marxism and, 252
Thought and Language, 252–253, 254
zone of proximal development concept, 253–254

Walden Two (Skinner), 166–168
Wallace, Alfred Russel, 43
Walpole, Horace, 165
Walters, Richard, 231
Wapner, Seymour, 241

Washburn, Margaret Floy, 70, 122
Watson, John B., 70, 153–158, 162, 327–328
Behaviorism, 155–156
on behaviorist view of psychology, 154–155
career in advertising, 158
correspondence with Lashley, 159
psychology of, 155
and Rosalie Rayner, 157–158
serially ordered behavior model, 157
Lashley's criticism of, 161–162
Weber, Ernst H., 54
Weber's law, 54
Werner, Heinz, 241–245
backward masking technique, 244
The Comparative Psychology of Mental Development, 241–245
conceptual/contemplative level of development concept, 243
continuity versus discontinuity concept, 242
emergence concept, 242
fixity versus mobility concept, 243
microgenesis concept, 244–245
organismic approach, 241
orthogenetic principle of development, 241
process versus achievement concept, 242
sensorimotor level of development concept, 243
tropistic/reflexive level of development concept, 243
uniformity versus multiformity concept, 242
unilinearity versus multilinearity concept, 242–243
Wertheimer, Max, 10, 172–178, 272
demonstrations used by, 172
Maslow's observations on, 273
phi phenomenon and, 172–173
Productive Thinking, 176–177
sensation concept, 174
Wheatstone, Charles, 59
White rats, Watson's use of, 153
Wholeness, Piaget's concept of, 250
Whorf, Benjamin Lee, 15–16
Wiener, Norbert, 294
Will. *See also* Volition
James on, 91–92
Willpower, 92
Erikson's concept of, 256
Will to power
Adler's concept of, 108
Nietzsche's concept of, 266–267
Witkin, H. A., 190
Witmer, Lightner, 276
Wittgenstein, Ludwig, 322–324
Wolfe, T., *From Bauhaus to our House,* 328
Wollstonecraft, Mary, 35–37
Womb envy, 110
Women
Freudian psychology and, 108
J. S. Mill's view of, 37
nepotism rules and, 258
professional advancement in psychology, 258
and psychology, 35
psychology of, 320–322
Hollingworth's work on, 277, 321
Horney and, 109–110
roles of, Wollstonecraft's views on, 35–36
in science, 60, 70, 77. *See also* Spielrein, Sabina
Woodworth, Robert S., 130–131, 132, 143
Experimental Psychology, 130
Psychology, 130
S-O-R framework, 131
W-O-W formula, 131
Wooley, Helen Thompson, 153
Word association technique
Jung and, 111
Wertheimer's use of, 172
Word count, Thorndike and Lorge, 143
Words, in higher order conditioning, 150–151
Work, as social activity, 138
W-O-W formula, 131
Wundt, Wilhelm, 69–75, 121, 136, 304, 318, 324
cultural psychology and, 73–75
eminence of, 69, 70, 74–75
experimental method of, 69–73
first laboratory in experimental psychology, 69
metronome experiment, 70–71, 196
perceptual learning concept, 258
postmodernism and, 328–329
tridimensional theory of feeling, 72–73, 219
Würzburg school, 78–80, 324

Yang and Yin, 13
Yates, Frances, 19–20
Yerkes, Robert M., 134
Young, Thomas, 58
Young-Helmholtz theory of color perception, 58

Zeigarnik, Bluma, 186
Zeigarnik effect, 186–187
Zeitgeist, 45–46
Zone of proximal development, Vygotsky's concept of, 253–254

WARNER MEMORIAL LIBRARY
EASTERN UNIVERSITY
ST. DAVIDS, PA 19087-3696